IFIP – The International Federation for Information Processing

IFIP was founded in 1960 under the auspices of UNESCO, following the first World Computer Congress held in Paris the previous year. A federation for societies working in information processing, IFIP's aim is two-fold: to support information processing in the countries of its members and to encourage technology transfer to developing nations. As its mission statement clearly states:

IFIP is the global non-profit federation of societies of ICT professionals that aims at achieving a worldwide professional and socially responsible development and application of information and communication technologies.

IFIP is a non-profit-making organization, run almost solely by 2500 volunteers. It operates through a number of technical committees and working groups, which organize events and publications. IFIP's events range from large international open conferences to working conferences and local seminars.

The flagship event is the IFIP World Computer Congress, at which both invited and contributed papers are presented. Contributed papers are rigorously refereed and the rejection rate is high.

As with the Congress, participation in the open conferences is open to all and papers may be invited or submitted. Again, submitted papers are stringently refereed.

The working conferences are structured differently. They are usually run by a working group and attendance is generally smaller and occasionally by invitation only. Their purpose is to create an atmosphere conducive to innovation and development. Refereeing is also rigorous and papers are subjected to extensive group discussion.

Publications arising from IFIP events vary. The papers presented at the IFIP World Computer Congress and at open conferences are published as conference proceedings, while the results of the working conferences are often published as collections of selected and edited papers.

IFIP distinguishes three types of institutional membership: Country Representative Members, Members at Large, and Associate Members. The type of organization that can apply for membership is a wide variety and includes national or international societies of individual computer scientists/ICT professionals, associations or federations of such societies, government institutions/government related organizations, national or international research institutes or consortia, universities, academies of sciences, companies, national or international associations or federations of companies.

More information about this series at http://www.springer.com/series/6102

Sujeet K. Sharma · Yogesh K. Dwivedi ·
Bhimaraya Metri · Nripendra P. Rana (Eds.)

Re-imagining Diffusion and Adoption of Information Technology and Systems: A Continuing Conversation

IFIP WG 8.6 International Conference
on Transfer and Diffusion of IT, TDIT 2020
Tiruchirappalli, India, December 18–19, 2020
Proceedings, Part I

 Springer

Editors
Sujeet K. Sharma
Indian Institute of Management
Tiruchirappalli
Tiruchirappalli, India

Bhimaraya Metri
Indian Institute of Management Nagpur
Nagpur, India

Yogesh K. Dwivedi
Swansea University
Swansea, UK

Nripendra P. Rana
University of Bradford
Bradford, UK

ISSN 1868-4238   ISSN 1868-422X (electronic)
IFIP Advances in Information and Communication Technology
ISBN 978-3-030-64851-0   ISBN 978-3-030-64849-7 (eBook)
https://doi.org/10.1007/978-3-030-64849-7

This Springer imprint is published by the registered company Springer Nature Switzerland AG
The registered company address is: Gewerbestrasse 11, 6330 Cham, Switzerland

Preface

The IFIP Working Group (WG 8.6) was established in the early '90s "to foster understanding and improve research in practice, methods, and techniques in the transfer and diffusion of information technology within systems that are developed, and in the development process[1]." The 2020 IFIP WG 8.6 conference on the theme "Re-Imagining Diffusion of Information Technology and Systems: A Continuing Conversation" was held at Tiruchirappalli, India, and was hosted by the Indian Institute of Management (IIM) Tiruchirappalli during December 18–19, 2020. We are grateful to IIM Tiruchirappalli for providing all required facilities and the IFIP WG 8.6 for mentoring the successful organization of the conference. The proceedings volumes of this conference focus on the re-imagination of diffusion and adoption of emerging technologies.

Developments in blockchain, artificial intelligence, Internet of Things, social media, mobile computing and applications, agile systems development techniques, cloud computing, and business analytics have become central to the business and the cycle of innovation has sped up, platforms provide quick access to infrastructure, and information spreads on a 24-h cycle. These developments, in turn, have impacted the way both organizations and societies, engage with transfer and diffusion of information technology (IT) systems within and between organizations, in interactions with customers, and society in general. The question is no longer how to adopt and diffuse IT systems, but how to quickly assess and manage those that best serve the broader purposes of businesses and societies. In addition to the idea of adoption and diffusion of IT systems, IT teams in organizations and individuals are also working on how IT systems are contributing to the value creation in both organizations and society.

There is an innate need for understanding the diffusion and adoption of emerging information technologies and systems (i.e., artificial intelligence, blockchain, Fin-Tech applications, Internet of Things, social media), which are expected to have a substantial impact on future economic development of society, organizations, and individuals (Borus et al. 2020; Dwivedi et al. 2019ab; Hughes et al. 2019; Ismagilova et al. 2019; Janssen et al. 2019). A review of the role of information technologies, particularly over the past two decades, clearly shows the vital link between technology adoption and socio-economic development in many economies (Venkatesh et al. 2016; Williams et al. 2015). The Gartner report on "Top Strategic Technology" in 2019[2] lists trends including blockchain, artificial intelligence, autonomous things (robots, vehicles, drones, etc.) among others as the game changers that could revolutionize industries and their strategic models through 2023. These emerging technologies have great potential to contribute to organizational and societal reforms. Thus, in the recent past, the

---

[1] http://ifipwg86.wikidot.com/about-us.

[2] https://www.forbes.com/sites/peterhigh/2019/10/21/breaking-gartner-announces-top-10-strategic-technology-trends-for-2020/#47dbbb940744.

scholarly body is showing an increased interest in the understanding of adoption, usage, impact, and potential of aforementioned technologies mentioned on individuals, societies, and organizations.

This conference brought together scholars and practitioners from interdisciplinary areas for the enrichment of scholarly deliberations on the adoption, usage, impact, and potential of emerging technologies. The conference mainly focused on the papers that addressed questions related to the diffusion and adoption of emerging technologies. Besides, we were also open and committed to the broader theme of the IFIP WG 8.6. We created 15 tracks with 2 or 3 track chairs. We received 247 papers, including 214 through EasyChair account and 33 direct submissions through conference email. All submissions were double-blind reviewed by at least two knowledgeable reviewers. This process resulted in 122 full and short papers. The acceptance rate of the papers in the conference proceedings is about 49.4%. We are grateful to all track chairs who selected reviewers and provided constructive and timely comments to authors to revise and resubmit their manuscripts.

Due to a large number of submissions, the conference proceedings of IFIP WG 8.6 are divided into two volumes. There are seven sections in Volume I and eight sections in Volume II.

Volume one includes sections namely:

- Artificial Intelligence and Autonomous Systems
- Big Data and Analytics
- Blockchain
- Diffusion and Adoption Technology
- Emerging Technologies in e-Governance
- Emerging Technologies in Consumer Decision Making and Choice
- Fin-Tech Applications
- Healthcare Information Technology
- Internet of Things

Volume two includes:

- Information Technology and Disaster Management
- Adoption of Mobile and Platform-Based Applications
- Smart Cities and Digital Government
- Social Media
- Diffusion of Information Technology and Systems (Conference Theme)

We sincerely thank all authors, reviewers, participants, Program Committee members, track chairs, advisory board, IFIP WG 8.6 officials, and IIM Tiruchirappalli staff who helped in making this conference a grand success.

October 2020

Sujeet K. Sharma
Yogesh K. Dwivedi
Bhimaraya Metri
Nripendra P. Rana

References

Brous, P., Janssen, M., and Herder, P., 2020. The dual effects of the Internet of Things (IoT): A systematic review of the benefits and risks of IoT adoption by organizations. *International Journal of Information Management*, 51, p.101952.

Dwivedi, Y. K., Rana, N. P., Jeyaraj, A., Clement, M., and Williams, M. D. 2019a. "Re-Examining the Unified Theory of Acceptance and Use of Technology (UTAUT): Towards a Revised Theoretical Model," *Information Systems Frontiers* (21:3), Springer New York LLC, pp. 719–734. (https://doi.org/10.1007/s10796-017-9774-y).

Dwivedi, Y.K., Hughes, L., Ismagilova, E., Aarts, G., Coombs, C., Crick, T., Duan, Y., Dwivedi, R., Edwards, J., Eirug, A., and Galanos, V., 2019b. Artificial Intelligence (AI): Multidisciplinary perspectives on emerging challenges, opportunities, and agenda for research, practice and policy. *International Journal of Information Management*, p.101994. DOI: https://doi.org/10.1016/j.ijinfomgt.2019.08.002

Hughes, L., Dwivedi, Y. K., Misra, S. K., Rana, N. P., Raghavan, V., and Akella, V. (2019). Blockchain research, practice and policy: Applications, benefits, limitations, emerging research themes and research agenda. *International Journal of Information Management*, 49, 114-129.

Ismagilova, E., Hughes, L., Dwivedi, Y. K., and Raman, K. R. (2019). Smart cities: Advances in research—An information systems perspective. *International Journal of Information Management*, 47, 88-100.

Janssen, M., Luthra, S., Mangla, S., Rana, N. P., and Dwivedi, Y. K. 2019. "Challenges for Adopting and Implementing IoT in Smart Cities: An Integrated MICMAC-ISM Approach," *Internet Research* (29:6), Emerald Group Publishing Ltd., pp. 1589–1616. (https://doi.org/10.1108/INTR-06-2018-0252).

Venkatesh, V., Thong, J. Y. L., and Xu, X. 2016. "Unified Theory of Acceptance and Use of Technology: A Synthesis and the Road Ahead," *Journal of the Association for Information Systems* (17:5), pp. 328–376. (https://doi.org/10.17705/1jais.00428).

Williams, M. D., Rana, N. P., and Dwivedi, Y. K. 2015. "The Unified Theory of Acceptance and Use of Technology (UTAUT): A Literature Review," *Journal of Enterprise Information Management*, Emerald Group Publishing Ltd., pp. 443–448. (https://doi.org/10.1108/JEIM-09-2014-0088).

Organization

Conference Committee

General Chairs

Viswanath Venkatesh	University of Arkansas, USA
Yogesh K. Dwivedi	Swansea University, UK
Deborah Bunker	The University of Sydney, Australia
Dave Wastell	University of Nottingham, UK

Conference Chairs

Sujeet K. Sharma	IIM Tiruchirappalli, India
Satish S. Maheswarappa	IIM Tiruchirappalli, India
Helle Zinner Henriksen	Copenhagen Business School, Denmark
Santosh K. Misra	CEO and Commissioner of e-Governance, Government of Tamil Nadu, India

Program Chairs

Sujeet K. Sharma	IIM Tiruchirappalli, India
Banita Lal	University of Bedfordshire, UK
Amany Elbanna	Royal Holloway, University of London, UK
Nripendra P. Rana	University of Bradford, UK
Moutusy Maity	IIM Lucknow, India
Jang Bahadur Singh	IIM Tiruchirappalli, India
Saji Mathew	IIT Madras, India

Organizing Chairs

Rajesh Chandwani	IIM Ahmedabad, India
Prashant Gupta	IIM Tiruchirappalli, India
Arpan Kar	DSM, IIT Delhi, India
Sankalp Pratap	IIM Tiruchirappalli, India
Sumeet Gupta	IIM Raipur, India
Sirish Kumar Gouda	IIM Tiruchirappalli, India
Satish Krishnan	IIM Kozhikode, India
G. P. Sahu	MNNIT Allahabad, India

Uthayasankar (Sankar) Sivarajah	University of Bradford, UK
Rajan Yadav	Delhi Technological University, India
Shalini Srivastava	Jaipuria Institute of Management Noida, India
Zahran Al-Salti	Sultan Qaboos University, Oman

Track Chairs

Artificial Intelligence and Autonomous Systems;

Ilias Pappas	University of Agder (UiA), Norway
Amany Elbanna	Royal Holloway, University of London, UK
Kshitij Sharma	Norwegian University of Science & Technology, Norway

Big Data and Analytics;

| Patrick Mikalef | NTNU, Norway |
| Anastasia Griva | National University of Ireland Galway |

Blockchain;

Samuel Fosso Wamba	Head of Artificial Intelligence and Business Analytics Cluster, Toulouse Business School, France
Santosh K. Misra	IAS, CEO & Commissioner of e-Governance, Govt of TN, India
Maciel M. Queiroz	Universidade Paulista, Brasil

Diffusion and Adoption of Technology;

Jyoti Choudrie	University of Hertfordshire, Hatfield, UK
Anand Jeyaraj	Wright State University, USA
Harminder Singh	AUT Business School, Auckland University of Technology, New Zealand

Emerging Technologies in e-Governance;

| Satish Krishnan | IIM Kozhikode, India |
| G. P. Sahu | MNNIT, Allahabad, India |

Emerging Technologies in Consumer Decision Making and Choice;

| Moutusy Maity | IIM Lucknow (IIM-L), India |
| Sathish S. Maheshwarappa | IIM Tiruchirappalli, India |

Fin-Tech Applications;

| M. N. Ravishankar | Director of Internationalisation, Loughborough University, UK |
| Barney Tan | The University of Sydney Business School, Australia |

Healthcare Information Technology;

Rajesh Chandwani	IIM Ahmedabad, India
Jang Bahadur Singh	IIM Tiruchirappalli, India

Internet of Things;

Denis Dennehy	National University of Ireland, Galway
Samuel Fosso Wamba	Head of Artificial Intelligence and Business Analytics Cluster, Toulouse Business School, France
Samrat Gupta	IIM Ahmedabad, India

Information Technology and Disaster Management;

Rameshwar Dubey	Montpellier Business School, France
Sirish Kumar Gouda	IIM Tiruchirappalli, India

Adoption of Mobile and Platform-Based Applications;

Parijat Upadhyay	Institute of Management Technology (IMT), Nagpur
R. Raman	Symbiosis Institute of Business Management, Pune
Arpan Kumar Kar	IIT Delhi, New Delhi

Smart Cities and Digital Government;

Vigneswara Ilavarasan	DMS, IIT Delhi, New Delhi
Endrit Kromidha	University of Birmingham, UK

Social Media.

Nripendra P. Rana	University of Bradford, UK
Kuttimani Tamilmani	University of Bradford, UK

Diffusion of Information Technology and Systems (Conference Theme);

Yogesh Dwivedi	Swansea University, UK
Deborah Bunker	University of Sydney, Australia
Sujeet K. Sharma	IIM Tiruchirappalli, India

Contents – Part I

Big Data and Analytics

Blockchain

Diffusion and Adoption Technology

Emerging Technologies in e-Governance

Emerging Technologies in Consumer Decision Making and Choice

Fin-Tech Applications

Healthcare Information Technology

Internet of Things

Contents – Part II

Smart Cities and Digital Government

Social Media

Diffusion of Information Technology and Systems (Conference Theme)

Artificial Intelligence and Autonomous Systems

Analysis of Factors Influencing the Adoption of Artificial Intelligence for Crime Management

Praveen R.S. Gummadidala[1]([✉]), Nanda Kumar Karippur[2],
and Maddulety Koilakuntla[1]

[1] S P Jain School of Global Management, Mumbai, India
{pravin.dbaon03004,k.maddulety}@spjain.org
[2] S P Jain School of Global Management, Singapore, Singapore
kumar.karippurnanda@spjain.org

Abstract. Despite the benefits of Artificial Intelligence (AI) and its potential to produce deep insights and predictions, its adoption and usage are still limited in the area of crime management. Over the years, crime rates have been increasing in India, and law enforcement agencies face enormous challenges given the increasing population, urbanization, limited resources, and ineffective conventional models of reactive and investigative policing. There is an unprecedented opportunity for AI to be leveraged together with new policing models such as intelligence-led policing and predictive policing for effective crime management. In this research-in-progress paper, we offer a deeper understanding of factors significant for the adoption intention of AI for crime management in India. Further, on the practical front, the study will help law enforcement agencies to effectively leverage AI and implement innovative policing models for crime management.

Keywords: Artificial Intelligence · Crime management · AI adoption

1 Introduction

Law enforcement agencies (LEA) in India are facing tremendous challenges in crime management due to several factors such as increasing crime rates, low police per person ratio, increasing population, and ineffective models of policing. The nature and methods of committing crimes are also changing rapidly, posing serious challenges to law enforcement agencies and other stakeholders of the criminal justice system in India.

The models of reactive, investigative policing are not enough to contain the increase in crimes. There is a compelling opportunity for implementing new policing models such as Intelligence-led policing (ILP) and Predictive policing to be more effective with limited resources. For example, there are vast volumes of data that are being collected internally that could be used for crime analysis and to influence police decision making. Predictive policing aims to rely on computer algorithms to see patterns, predict the occurrence of future events based on large quantities of data and aims

S. K. Sharma et al. (Eds.): TDIT 2020, IFIP AICT 617, pp. 3–9, 2020.
https://doi.org/10.1007/978-3-030-64849-7_1

to carefully target police presence to the necessary minimum to achieve desired results (Sanders and Sheptycki 2017). The main objective of Intelligence-led policing is to apply crime data analysis to objectively inform policy, policing strategies, and tactical operations to reduce and prevent crime emphasizing the proactive use of police resources (Ratcliffe 2016). However, such approaches are not easy to implement using manual processes and existing infrastructure.

There is growing interest in using digital technologies to address the challenges faced by law enforcement agencies in India. The use of data to detect crimes has long been a central feature in the security policies' decision-making process (Peeters and Schuilenburg 2018). The fast availability of data has brought AI closer to commercial use (Kruse et al. 2019). AI integrated with other technologies such as Machine learning, Big data, Geospatial technologies could bring out innovativeness to the approach of solving problems in crime management and contribute to a safer environment. While there is growing interest in exploiting the potential of AI, several challenges in adoption have been reported, such as unclear relative advantage, issues in technology readiness, disconnect between strategies and automation, and regulatory support.

To the best of our knowledge, there is no empirical study done to understand the factors critical for the adoption intention of AI for crime management. To fill this research gap, we intend to use Technology-Organization-Environment (TOE) framework (Tornatzky and Fleischer 1990) as the comprehensive theoretical lens along with other relevant theories such as Diffusion of Innovation (Rogers 2003), Routine Activity Theory (Fernando 2014) and Near repeat phenomenon (Bowers and Johnson 2004). We seek to explore the key factors that influence the adoption intention of AI in crime management. Our primary research question is:

RQ: What are the key factors that influence AI adoption intention by Law enforcement agencies for effective Crime management in India.

2 Theoretical Background

2.1 Adoption Theories

TOE framework has emerged as a valuable theoretical lens for understanding technology adoption. Diffusion of Innovation theory can explain intra-firm innovation diffusion (Hsu et al. 2006). TOE is also not limited by industry and company size (Wen and Chen 2010). TOE has been applied successfully as key contextual elements that determine new IT adoption at the Organization level (Baker 2012). Moreover, the TOE framework has been used for the adoption of technologies such as Customer-based IOS, Open Systems, EDI, RFID, Enterprise systems, and E-Business (Chandra and Kumar 2018). We apply the TOE framework for understanding the facilitators of AI adoption in Crime management. On the other hand, Diffusion of Innovation theory (DOI) seeks to explain 'how, why, and at what rate new ideas and technology spread'. Both of these theories are applied to understand the adoption intention of AI for Law enforcement agencies in India.

2.2   Crime Management Theories

The potential to predict crime follows from the empirical observation that most crimes do not happen randomly, and often tend to be concentrated in time and space in socalled crime hotspots. Routine activity theory is, in short, an attempt to identify, at the macro-level, criminal activities and their patterns through explanation of changes in crime rate trends (Fernando 2014). Routine activity theory argues that three fundamental "almost-always" elements define criminal acts: a likely offender, a suitable target, and the absence of a capable guardian (Felson 2002). So, to prevent crime – reduce the suitability of the victim, demotivate offenders, and improve guardianship. The nearrepeat phenomenon states that if a location is the target of a crime such as a burglary, the homes within a relatively short distance have an increased chance of being burgled for a limited number of weeks (Ratcliffe and Rengert 2008). This pattern of space-time clustering has been referred to as the 'near repeat' phenomenon to reflect the association with repeat victimization. Policing strategies and models such as predictive policing and intelligence-led policing are based on these theories and are factored in building the research framework discussed.

3   Research Framework and Hypotheses

In our study, the framework was operationalized using TOE framework, as depicted in Fig. 1 below. The rationale for the selection of the factors under each context for AI adoption is specified below.

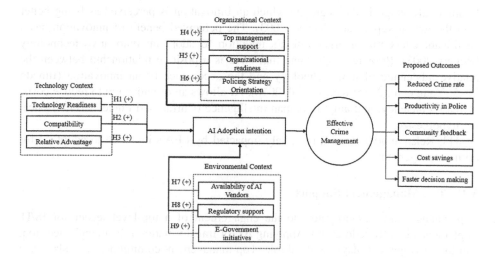

Fig. 1. Adoption of artificial intelligence for crime management

3.1 Technology Readiness

Technology readiness is an important factor for adoption intention. In the context of AI, technology readiness is tightly coupled with the availability of quality data, availability of AI-enhanced products and services for crime management, and readiness of infrastructure (Kruse et al. 2019). AI systems require a tremendous amount of quality data for training the algorithms and for better predictability that needs to be deployed across the law enforcement agencies. Hence, we hypothesize,

H1: Technology readiness is positively impacted by LEA's intention to adopt AI for crime management

3.2 Compatibility

Compatibility is the degree to which an innovation is perceived as consistent with the existing values, past experiences, and needs of potential adopters (Rogers 2003). Compatibility is an important determinant of innovation adoption (Oliveira et al. 2014). In the Indian crime management context, compatibility of AI applications with data sources, IT Infrastructure, and systems such as Crime and Criminal Tracking Network System (CCTNS) and National Intelligence Grid (NATGRID) is essential. Hence, we hypothesize,

H2: Compatibility is positively impacted by LEA's intention to adopt AI for crime management

3.3 Relative Advantage

Relative advantage is the degree to which an innovation is perceived as being better than the idea it supersedes (Rogers 2003). The perceived benefit of innovation has a significant effect on an organization's intention to adopt an innovative technology (Rogers 2003). Prior research found that there is a positive relationship between the relative advantage of new technology and the acceptance of an innovation (Ifinedo 2005; Yang et al. 2015; Kumar et al. 2016). AI allows an organization to reduce costs, increase efficiency, and amplify human intelligence (Curran and Purcel 2017). Hence, we hypothesize,

H3: Relative advantage is positively impacted by LEA's intention to adopt AI for crime management

3.4 Top Management Support

Top management support refers to the engagement of a top-level leader for IS/IT implementations (Ifinedo 2005). Applying AI for transformation is a strategic decision, and top management plays a critical role. Top management commitment can also have a significant positive influence on new technology adoption in terms of articulating a vision (Yang et al. 2015), providing capital funds (Hung et al. 2016) and allocating resources. Hence, we hypothesize,

H4: Top management support is positively impacted by LEA's intention to adopt AI for crime management.

3.5   Organizational Readiness

Organizational readiness refers to the extent to which organizational divisions are prepared to adopt new technology and implement organizational change. The barriers to AI adoption are not limited to the technical context, but also relate to the skills, organizational resources, processes, structures, and agility of the organization (Alsheibani et al. 2018). Hence, we hypothesize,

H5: Organizational readiness is positively impacted by LEA's intention to adopt AI for crime management

3.6   Policing Strategy Orientation

Policing strategies extend beyond conventional models of responding to calls for service and seek to increase crime prevention, intervention, and response effectiveness. The ability to forecast where and when the next crime or series of crimes take place (Uchida 2014) has become of utmost importance to prevent crime from happening by effectively using new strategies such as Intelligence-led policing and Predictive policing. Greater emphasis on tackling criminals would be more effective than focusing on Crime. Hence, we hypothesize,

H6: Policing strategy orientation is positively impacted by LEA's intention to adopt AI for crime management

3.7   Availability of AI Vendors

AI vendors refer to the companies that possess the necessary knowledge, skills, and experience in AI technologies that offer products or solutions for the organizations seeking an opportunity to transform their business. Vendor partnership has been empirically supported as one of the critical determinants for innovation adoption (Ahmadi et al. 2015). If agencies know they can collaborate effectively with vendors, they are more likely to adopt the new technology (Huang and Palvia 2001). Hence, we hypothesize,

H7: Availability of AI vendors positively impacts the adoption intention of AI by LEA for crime management

3.8   Regulatory Support

Regulatory support refers to the policies and regulations that encourage and accelerate the adoption of innovative systems at the organizational and community levels. Government regulatory issues are the main environmental factors that can affect new innovation adoption (Ifinedo 2005; Yang et al. 2015). Governments need to put in place necessary data protection, ethical and legal frameworks to ensure that AI systems are developed and applied based on the values and citizen's fundamental rights. This leads to the following hypothesis:

H8: Supportive regulatory environment is positively impacted by LEA's intention to adopt AI for crime management

3.9   E-Government Initiatives

E-Government initiatives target increasing accessibility to the needed information, enhancing the efficiency of operations, facilitating collaboration, lowering maintenance and operating costs, and improving organizational (and inter-organizational) performance and productivity (Moore 2009). Many governments across the world have since developed or in the process of developing National AI strategy and action plans, such as access to data through open platforms that will help drive the adoption of AI systems. This leads to the following hypothesis:

H9: Supportive e-Government initiatives are positively impacted with LEA's intention to adopt AI for crime management.

4   Proposed Methodology and Future Work

We will be using a survey methodology for testing the proposed hypotheses. Validated scales from existing literature will be adapted to the research context to formulate the questionnaire. To measure the items, we would use a 5-point Likert scale. Questionnaires so formulated would be distributed to middle and senior-level members of law enforcement agencies and relevant AI technology providers.

5   Expected Contribution

This Research-in-progress paper is expected to make three significant contributions. First, the validated model will help provide insights into how the adoption theories such as TOE and DOI could be extended in the context of AI adoption and crime management and set the direction for future research in this area. Second, this would help in formulating and updating AI policies and regulations. Third, on the practical front, the results of the study will be useful for law enforcement agencies to strategize and focus on factors and capabilities which will drive AI adoption, contributing to significant crime reduction and management.

References

Ahmadi, H., Nilashi, M., Ibrahim, O., Ramayah, T., Wong, M.W., Alizadeh, M., et al.: Exploring potential factors in total hospital information system adoption. J. Soft Comput. Decis. Support Syst. **2**(1), 52–59 (2015)

Alsheibani, S., Cheung, Y., Messom, C.: Artificial intelligence adoption: AI-readiness at firm-level. In: Tanabu, M., Senoo, D., (eds.) Proceedings of PACIS2018, IL, USA, vol. 37 (2018)

Baker, J.: The technology–organization–environment framework. In: Dwivedi, Y., Wade, M., Schneberger, S. (eds.) Information Systems Theory. Integrated Series in Information Systems, vol. 28, pp. 231–245. Springer, New York, NY (2012). https://doi.org/10.1007/978-1-4419-6108-2_12

Bowers, K.J., Johnson, S.D.: Who commits near repeats? a test of the boost explanation. Western Criminol. Rev. **5**(3), 12–24 (2004)

Chandra, S., Kumar, K.N.: Exploring factors influencing organizational adoption of augmented reality in E-Commerce: empirical analysis using technology-organization-environment model. J. Electron. Commer. Res. **19**(3), 237–265 (2018)

Curran, R., Purcell, B.: The Forrester Wave: Artificial Intelligence Technologies. Q1 2017, Japan (2017)

Huang, Z., Palvia, P.: ERP implementation issues in advanced and developing countries. Bus. Process Manag. J. **7**(3), 276–284 (2001). https://doi.org/10.1108/14637150110392773

Hsu, P.F., Kraemer, K.L., Dunkle, D.: Determinants of e-business use in US firms. Int. J. Electron. Commer. **10**(4), 9–45 (2006). https://doi.org/10.2753/JEC10864415100401

Felson, M.: Crime and Everyday Life: Insight and Implications for Society, 3rd edn. SAGE, CA (2002)

Hung, S.-Y., Huang, Y.-W., Lin, C.-C., Chen, K., Tarn, J.M.: Factors influencing business intelligence systems implementation success in the enterprises. In: PACIS (2016)

Ifinedo, P.: Measuring Africa's E-readiness in the global networked economy: a nine country data analysis. Int. J. Educ. Dev. ICT **1**(1), 53–71 (2005)

Ratcliffe, J.H., Rengert, G.F.: Near-repeat patterns in Philadelphia shootings. SECURITY J. **21**, 58–76 (2008)

Kruse, L., Wunderlich, N., Beck, R.: Artificial intelligence for financial services industry: what challenges organizations to succeed. In: Proceedings of the 52nd Hawaii International Conference on System Sciences, pp. 6408–6417 (2019)

Kumar, K.N., Chandra, S., Bharati, S., Manava, S.: Factors influencing adoption of augmented reality technology for E-Commerce. In: PACIS (2016)

Miró-Llinares, F.: Routine Activity Theory (2014). https://doi.org/10.1002/9781118517390/wbetc198

Moore, B.: Emotional intelligence for school administrators: a priority for school reform? Am. Second. Educ. **37**(3), 20–28 (2009)

Oliveira, T., Thomas, M., Espadanal, M.: Assessing the determinants of cloud computing adoption: an analysis of the manufacturing and services sectors. Inf. Manag. **51**(5), 497–510 (2014). https://doi.org/10.1016/j.im.2014.03.006

Peeters, R., Schuilenburg, R.: Machine justice: governing security through the bureaucracy of algorithms. Inf. Polity **23**(3), 267–280 (2018)

Ratcliffe, J.: Intelligence-Led Policing, 2nd edn. Routledge, London (2016)

Rogers, E.M.: The Diffusion of Innovation, 5th edn. Free Press, New York (2003)

Sanders, C.B., Sheptycki, J.: Policing, crime and 'big data'; towards a critique of the moral economy of stochastic governance. Crime Law Soc. Change **68**, 1–15 (2017)

Tornatzky, L.G., Fleischer, M., Chakrabarti, A.K.: Processes of Technological Innovation. Issues in Organization and Management Series. Lexington Books, Michigan (1990)

Uchida, C.D.: Predictive policing. In: Bruinsma, G., Weisburd, D. (eds.) Encyclopedia of Criminology and Criminal Justice, pp. 3871–3880. Springer, New York (2014)

Wen, K.W., Chen, Y.: E-business value creation in Small and Medium Enterprises: a US study using the TOE framework. Int. J. Electron. Bus. **8**(1), 80100 (2010)

Yang, Z., Sun, J., Zhang, Y., Wang, Y.: Understanding SaaS adoption from the perspective of organizational users: a tripod readiness model. Comput. Hum. Behav. **45**, 254–264 (2015)

Organizational Adoption of Artificial Intelligence in Supply Chain Risk Management

Souma Kanti Paul[1($\boxtimes$)], Sadia Riaz[2], and Suchismita Das[1]

[1] S P Jain School of Global Management, Mumbai, India
souma.djl19dba001@spjain.org
[2] S P Jain School of Global Management, Dubai, UAE

Abstract. With the growing complexity of global supply chains, geopolitical events, pandemics, and just-in-time processes, organizations can benefit immensely in managing supply chain risks by adopting artificial intelligence (AI). Building upon past research in technology adoption, we study factors influencing the adoption intention of AI in SCRM across organizations in India. Based on a qualitative study, we discuss the applications and uniqueness of AI adoption in the field of supply chain risk management (SCRM) and propose a research model on the adoption, implementation, and routinization intention of AI in SCRM at an organizational level. Secondly, we discuss the implications of the study and the benefits to decision-makers and supply chain planners in devising effective strategies when adopting AI in SCRM.

Keywords: Adoption · Artificial intelligence · Supply Chain Risk Management

1 Introduction

Growing incidences of events like natural disasters, pandemics, just-in-time processes, and global supply chain networks have resulted in increased vulnerability of supply chains to disruptions [1]. A report [2] on the impact of Covid-19 on global Gross Domestic Product (GDP) cites that more than five million companies, including greater than 90% Fortune 1000 companies, had one or multiple tier-2 suppliers in the impacted region in China during the initial months of the pandemic. There has been a growing interest in the application of Artificial Intelligence (AI) in Supply Chain Risk Management (SCRM). However, there has been limited research on the adoption of AI in SCRM at an organizational level across industry verticals in India. The objective of this research is to identify factors that influence the adoption intention, implementation intention, and routinization intention of AI in SCRM at an organizational level in India. The industries considered for this study cover consumer-packaged-goods (CPG), consumer durables, wholesale, logistics, and retail.

© IFIP International Federation for Information Processing 2020
Published by Springer Nature Switzerland AG 2020
S. K. Sharma et al. (Eds.): TDIT 2020, IFIP AICT 617, pp. 10–15, 2020.
https://doi.org/10.1007/978-3-030-64849-7_2

2   Literature Review

2.1   Definition of AI

The field of AI has evolved over the past few decades and accordingly, the definition and scope of AI have been continually evolving. Today, Artificial Neural Networks (ANN) and Deep Learning (DL), form the core of applications classified under AI [3]. Accordingly, for this study we consider deep learning techniques that use artificial neural networks as the definition of AI.

2.2   Definition of SCRM

Based on past research, SCRM is defined as the management of supply chain risks through active coordination between all supply chain partners to identify, assess, and respond to risks ensuring disruptions are mitigated leading to business continuity and profitability [4]. It should also be noted that SCRM is a part of Enterprise Risk Management (ERM) [5].

2.3   Application of AI in SCRM

Recent studies have argued that AI will fundamentally change the way organizations make decisions and interact with their external stakeholders [6]. Due to the rise of big data and advances in computing, it is today possible to analyze billions of real-time transactions, process a wide range of unstructured data like pictures, videos, and natural language, and generate predictive and prescriptive insights for decision making. These advances in the field of AI stand to benefit SCRM immensely and hence the growing interest in the application of AI in SCRM. Recent studies cite the use of AI to predict the probability of occurrence of risks and costs of risks [7], reduce risk of churn in distribution management [8], predict damage parameters in logistics [9], and forecasting the level of integration of supply chain to minimize risks [10].

2.4   The Uniqueness of AI Adoption

Organizational agility, in terms of rapidly responding to external shocks like pandemics or geopolitical situations, adapting to market changes, or responding to customer demands plays a critical role in AI adoption. It is also important to note that the implementation of AI solutions, often in conjunction with other advanced digital technologies [11], involves an entire ecosystem of technologies right from high-end computing hardware, big data platforms, data processing tools, analytical tools, and open source technologies. Moreover, AI adoption, implementation, and routinization intentions in SCRM greatly depend on the integration and compliance of AI solutions to ERM policies and processes.

2.5   Applicability of Technology Adoption Theories to AI Adoption in SCRM

The Technology-Organisation-Environment (TOE) framework [12] identifies three independent contexts that influence the adoption, implementation, and routinization intention of technologies at an organizational level. Based on the TOE framework, past researchers have studied the adoption intention of technologies like Big Data Analytics [13] and Predictive Analytics [14]. But there is clearly a need to study the applicability of the TOE framework for AI adoption in the field of SCRM. A recent study cites that managers of global organizations have limited empirical advice on how to implement AI in the companies' operations [11]. It also calls for a study on the current prevalence of AI in business and the exploration of key dimensions of AI implementations. Hence, it is important to study the implementation intention and routinization intention of AI and not just the intent to adopt AI. Given the earlier cited uniqueness of AI adoption in SCRM, the authors suggest using the three contexts of the TOE framework, namely technological context, organizational context, and environmental context but include factors that are newly added and defined by the authors in the context of AI.

3   Research Model and Hypothesis

The authors have used keyword-based search of past technology adoption studies indexed in ProQuest, EBSCO, and Google Scholar, coupled with interviews of nine industry subject matter experts (SMEs) in India to identify and validate independent factors as part of the technological, organizational, and environmental contexts of TOE framework. The adoption intention, implementation intention, and routinization intention of AI in SCRM have been identified as dependent variables (Fig. 1).

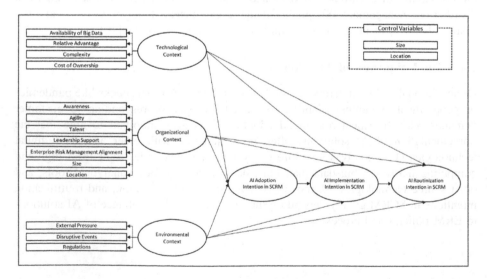

Fig. 1. Research model

3.1   Technological Context

The authors argue that organizations that have large and diverse datasets available across supply chain systems [13] like transactional data, pictures, videos, texts, and real-time data are in a better position to initiate AI projects. Past studies have shown relative advantage and complexity as oft used factors to study technology adoption [15] and is applicable to AI as well. Also, the cost of ownership is a critical determinant [13] of AI adoption in a market like India. Taking these factors into consideration, the following hypotheses have been proposed: (H1) Availability of big data is positively related to AI adoption intention, AI implementation intention, and AI routinization intention in SCRM, (H2) Relative advantage is positively related to AI adoption intention, AI implementation intention, and AI routinization intention in SCRM, (H3) Complexity is negatively related to AI adoption intention, AI implementation intention, and AI routinization intention in SCRM, and (H4) Cost of ownership is negatively related to AI adoption intention, AI implementation intention, and AI routinization intention in SCRM

3.2   Organizational Context

Apart from organizational characteristics like location and size, organizational awareness of AI's possibilities and understanding of how to best utilize the capabilities of AI in SCRM is an important determinant [11]. Organizational agility has been cited as a key determinant of AI success [11]. The availability of talent has been cited as an important indicator of the adoption of innovation [16]. As cited by past research, one of the best predictors is leadership support by influencing the organization's intention to adopt innovative technologies [14]. Given that SCRM is a part of ERM, it is essential that any AI-based decision making complies to ERM policies and is integrated into ERM systems and processes. Based on the above factors, following hypotheses have been proposed: (H5) Awareness of AI is positively related to AI adoption intention, AI implementation intention, and AI routinization intention in SCRM, (H6) Organizational agility is positively related to AI adoption intention, AI implementation intention, and AI routinization intention in SCRM, (H7) Talent is positively related to AI adoption intention, AI implementation intention, and AI routinization intention in SCRM, (H8) Leadership support for AI is positively related to AI adoption intention, AI implementation intention, and AI routinization intention in SCRM, (H9) ERM alignment is positively related to AI adoption intention, AI implementation intention, and AI routinization intention in SCRM, (H10) Organizational size is positively related to AI adoption intention, AI implementation intention, and AI routinization intention in SCRM, and (H11) Organizational location is positively related to AI adoption intention, AI implementation intention, and AI routinization intention in SCRM.

3.3   Environmental Context

External pressure has been cited to be a significant factor in adoption research [17] for innovative technologies. Also, past negative effects of disruptive events on the supply chain are a strong predictor of AI adoption given its potential to predict such events and its impact. Recent reports indicate a growing involvement of governments in prioritizing AI and taking proactive steps to fund AI research [18]. On the other hand, government regulations on data privacy and data security could be limiting AI adoption. The following hypotheses have been proposed: (H12) External pressure is positively related to AI adoption intention, AI implementation intention, and AI routinization intention in SCRM, (H13) Disruptive event is positively related to AI adoption intention, AI implementation intention, and AI routinization intention in SCRM, and (H14) Regulation is negatively related to AI adoption intention, AI implementation intention, and AI routinization intention in SCRM.

3.4 Dependent Variables

The authors propose the following hypothesis based on the adoption stages for the dependent variables namely, the AI adoption intention, AI implementation intention, and AI routinization intention in SCRM: (H14) AI adoption intention is positively related to AI implementation intention in SCRM, and (H15) AI implementation intention is positively related to AI routinization intention in SCRM.

4 Implications

From a short to mid-term perspective, as businesses in India gradually emerge from a global pandemic that has devasted operations and supply chains globally, the need to adopt, implement and routinize AI in the field of SCRM is rapidly becoming a business priority. Also, the value of AI as applied to the larger supply chain risk domain will attract a lot of attention and research in the coming years. To do so, it is imperative to first understand the factors influencing the adoption, implementation, and routinization intention. The authors argue that the proposed research model based on the TOE framework with newly added factors will enable further studies and empirical research. Furthermore, this study will greatly benefit business leaders, supply chain planners, and risk professionals to devise strategies in their respective organizations to adopt, implement, and routinize AI in the field of SCRM.

5 Conclusion

This study provides an in-depth analysis of factors influencing AI adoption, implementation, and routinization intention. It proposes a research model that can be used for further empirical research across industries in India.

References

1. Snyder, L.V., Atan, Z., Peng, P., Rong, Y., Schmitt, A.J., Sinsoysal, B.: OR/MS models for supply chain disruptions: a review. IIE Trans. **48**(2), 89–109 (2016)

2. Dun and Bradstreet. https://www.dnb.com/content/dam/english/economic-and-industry-insight/DNB_Business_Impact_of_the_Coronavirus_US.pdf. Accessed 05 Aug 2020
3. Haenlein, M., Kaplan, A.: A brief history of artificial intelligence: on the past, present, and future of artificial intelligence. Calif. Manag. Rev. **61**(4), 5–14 (2019)
4. Colicchia, C., Strozzi, F.: Supply chain risk management: a new methodology for a systematic literature review. Supply Chain Manag. **17**(4), 403–418 (2012)
5. Curkovic, S., Scannell, T., Wagner, B., Vitek, M.: Supply chain risk management within the context of COSO's enterprise risk management framework. J. Bus. Adm. Res. **2**(1), 15 (2013)
6. Haenlein, M., Kaplan, A.: A Brief History of Artificial Intelligence: On the Past, Present, and Future of Artificial Intelligence. Calif. Manag. Rev. **61**(4), 5–14 (2019)
7. Ojha, R., Ghadge, A., Tiwari, M.K., Bititci, U.S.: Bayesian network modelling for supply chain risk propagation. Int. J. Prod. Res. **56**(17), 5795–5819 (2018)
8. Necula, S.-C.: Deep learning for distribution channels' management. Inf. Econ. Bucharest **21**(4), 73–85 (2017)
9. Gürbüz, F., Eski, İ., Denizhan, B., Dağlı, C.: Prediction of damage parameters of a 3PL company via data mining and neural networks. J. Intell. Manuf. **30**(3), 1437–1449 (2017). https://doi.org/10.1007/s10845-017-1337-z
10. Muñoz, E.G., Cossío, N.S., del Monserrate Ruiz Cedeño, S., Ricardo, S.E.L., Hernández, Y. C., Crespo, E.O.: Application of neural networks in predicting the level of integration in supply chains. J. Ind. Eng. Manag. Barcelona **13**(1), 120–132 (2020)
11. Brock, J.K.-U., Wangenheim, F.V.: Calif. Manag. Rev. **61**(4), 26 (2019)
12. Tornatzky, L., Fleischer, M.: The Process of Technology Innovation. Lexington Books, Lexington (1990)
13. Chen, D.Q., Preston, D.S., Swink, M.: How the use of big data analytics affects value creation in supply chain management. J. Manag. Inf. Syst. **32**(4), 4–39 (2019)
14. Banerjee, A., Banerjee, T.: Determinants of analytics process adoption in emerging economies: perspectives from the marketing domain in India. Vikalpa: J. Decis. Makers **42**(2), 95–110 (2017)
15. Awa, H.O., Ojiabo, O.U., Orokor, L.E.: Integrated technology-organization-environment (T-O-E) taxonomies for technology adoption. J. Enterp. Inf. Manag. Bradford **30**(6), 893–921 (2017)
16. Queiroz, M.M., Telles, R.: Big data analytics in supply chain and logistics: an empirical approach. Int. J. Logistics Manag. **29**(2), 767–783 (2018)
17. Hossain, M.A., Quaddus, M., Islam, N.: Developing and validating a model explaining the assimilation process of RFID: an empirical study. Inf. Syst. Front. **18**(4), 645–663 (2014). https://doi.org/10.1007/s10796-014-9537-y
18. Bughin, J., Seong, J., Manyika, J., Chui, M., Joshi, R.: Notes from the AI frontier: modeling the impact of AI on the world economy. McKinsey Global Institute (2018)

Language Model-Driven Chatbot for Business to Address Marketing and Selection of Products

Amit Kumar Kushwaha$^{(\boxtimes)}$ and Arpan Kumar Kar

Department of Management Studies, Indian Institute of Technology Delhi,
New Delhi 110016, India
kushwaha.amitkumar@gmail.com, arpan_kar@yahoo.co.in

Abstract. Artificial Intelligence has been increasingly gaining acceptance across advanced functions in numerous fields and industries. This includes marketing, customer support, and leads generation in healthcare, transportation, education, and off late in e-commerce. Machine learning as a subset of artificial intelligence techniques provides various algorithms that enable machines to learn from historical data and make realtime predictions on numbers and texts. Most of the businesses nowadays are trying to increase their reach and making sure that they are available to cater to the customers when they need help. This also enables the companies to market and respond to the queries of potential customers on a realtime basis. Chatter robots or chatbot is one such application of machine learning which allows the business to provide round the clock support to customers and potential leads for marketing questions. Most of the business fail to venture in the domain of hosting chatbot on the website as they do not have enough conversational data with them to train the machine learning algorithm and wait for years to collect enough sample. With the proposed language model-driven chatbots, businesses starting fresh in the domain of the hosting this application can use the user-generated content on social media to fuel the backend framework for the chatbots and start hosting the application.

Keywords: Artificial intelligence · Chatbots · Language modeling · NLP · Deep learning · Reinforcement learning · Marketing

1 Introduction

The emergence of web 2.0 as a communication channel has opened up enormous opportunities for organizations to increase digital footprints. These digital footprints are primarily used for a range of online organization-customer interactions in marketing and customer support. One of the use cases of these interactions consists of information search for company/product details as an outcome of marketing promotions done by the organizations. The advent of e-commerce has shortened the lifecycle of potential lead identification to actual customer conversion. The e-commerce has been defined where 'transaction can happen at any-time and any-place' [1]. To enable these transactions by supporting marketing queries or even lead generation, followed by actual marketing, requires more one-to-one communications enabling live customer

© IFIP International Federation for Information Processing 2020
Published by Springer Nature Switzerland AG 2020
S. K. Sharma et al. (Eds.): TDIT 2020, IFIP AICT 617, pp. 16–28, 2020.
https://doi.org/10.1007/978-3-030-64849-7_3

interactions [2]. To compete against the e-commerce companies, even the general business and retail houses have started hosting websites to support the marketing needs.

A website can act as an online shopping catalog or a virtual store over the internet [3, 4]. Marketing promotions that act as a pull strategy will attract customers to browse these online catalogs and choose the merchandize which interests them before paying for the actual transaction. Prior work [5] suggests that responding without any latency has become an integral part of marketing management, which needs to be supported by operational tactics. Maintaining live channels for $24 \times 7 \times 365$ days is not operationally efficient and is neither a cost-effective way of catering customers for whom most of the interaction is through web 2.0 technologies.

A chatbot also referred to as a software program that can simulate the intelligent exchange of conversations with humans (customers) on the other end, driven and trained by machine learning algorithms. Users can interact with the chatbots using conversational interface through text as an input. If thoroughly trained, a chatbot can welcome a potential customer to the website, guide through the catalog or product and finally help to complete the transaction, which would make the outcome of a marketing promotion successful.

The fuel for training and designing the chatbot is data. An actual conversation with live representatives responding to customer queries through customer support chat is the ideal data. The more the historical data, the better the chatbot is trained and able to provide a better experience to customers. Studies [6, 7, 8] suggest that with this online presence, business organizations try to not only improve the customer experience [9], but it also increases the chances of purchase. The primary hindrance in the adoption of a chatbot by the native e-commerce companies or the conventional business organizations having a presence in the brick and mortar space using websites as a catalog is: the availability of sizeable historical chat manuscripts for training the chatbot. This means that the companies must wait for years to first record the data before being able to adapt and host a well-trained chatbot.

Hence, there exists a gap in terms of time to collect the data (which can be years ranging from 2–5 years) before a business organization can start building a chatbot. We consider the following research questions:

RQ1: Is there a corresponding unsupervised task and the corresponding machine learning framework that can allow a model to learn specific information from very generic conversations on social media platforms like Twitter as a language model saving the time to collect the conversations chat manuscripts?

RQ2: Can this unsupervised language model fuel the chatbots?

RQ2: Can we incorporate the same unsupervised language model to validate the responses to questions?

The central thesis of the current paper is to present a framework [10] that can shorten the lead time to adapt to the chatbot. We propose a language model-driven chatbot that is fueled by marketing promotions, interactions, queries on a [11] social media platform (SMP) like Twitter, which can be used to train a chatbot.

We borrow the design theory nexus [12, 13] to idealize the framework designing with goals of improvement based of theory and design solutions. We are rooting the proposed framework on the websites and the theoretical blocks of interaction, search, and inquiry, which act as links between customer's online access (OA) and business' intent of improving the customer experience (CE) on one end. The user and company fuel the other end of the framework generated tweets on Twitter. These tweets could be in the form of marketing, product and feature promotions, responses to queries by customers. Websites have been proven successful and eventually has become a commodity for improving the CE. The proposed framework would further improve the CE on top of websites. We define the proposed framework as a language model-driven bot customer experience: the building and theoretical blocks of this framework is represented in Fig. 1.

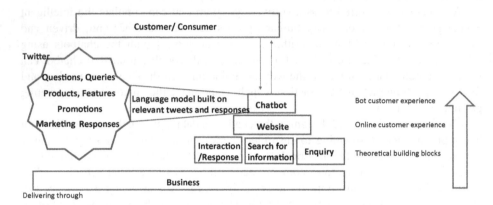

Fig. 1. Various theoretical and building blocks of the framework

2 Prior Literature

Several studies [14] have explored the role of the internet in enriching the marketing and buying experience of the consumers by taking advantage of their OA. Especially the work is done by researchers [3], suggests critical elements that can enhance the CE for a marketing campaign to be successful. These include: communication, connectivity, and content, aspects that can be seen relevant within the guide rails OA. Several studies further connect the link between OA and CE, which can be pivoted to three main areas. The first set of studies have explored the "quality" of the various elements of a website that can help e-marketer [15, 16, 17]. These elements could be general "flow" on a website, or a "response" in any manner.

The second set of studies done to further link OA to CE focus upon "search" and purchases are done online. Summarizing the works of [18, 19, 20, 21] identify the antecedents of consumer purchase behavior as search for information related to a product and the company (in the sense of frequency). Risks associated with online transactions through e-commerce have been proven to be reduced by a presence of search and interaction by these works. This establishes search and presence as the second connecting link after interaction between OA and CE.

The third set of studies pivot around the response to inquiry done by the consumers [15, 22, 3]. While the internet opens opportunities for the full delivery of customer services, it also opens the gates of inquiries done by consumers. These prior researches are done, establishes "inquiry" as to the third link between OA and CE. In most of the business organization setup, websites are filling the gap between OA and CE. With the literature review done, and with more and more penetration of the SMP we feel that the user-generated content (UGC) in response to the specific or generic marketing campaigns done by a business can be utilized to improve the efficiency of the frameworks that bridge the gap between OA and CE which can be placed on top of a website that has been proven as a strong element filling the gap between OA and CE.

Researchers [23] have proposed software programs that can be hosted on a website accessed through a desktop machine, laptop, tablet, or even a mobile device, enabling a virtual conversational partner (VCP). This VCP can respond to queries and questions of a customer who is already accessing the website through OA. In the current capacity, most of these VCPs hosted are driven by simple linear programming, by a matching logic of queries from the relational database stored. Scholars [24] have also proposed a pre-logic before a VCP that can decide if the query from the customer can be answered by the VCP or not on a software as a service (SaaS) architecture.

Chatterbot, or more commonly chatbot as a term for VCP, was first proposed in 1994 [25] and is now widely used to refer to a VCP. Researchers [26] have further established the link of natural language processing (NLP) to fine-tune the results of a chatbot to make it more conversationally intuitive. However, the flexibility of the chatbot in responding to customers with intuitive answers depends on the training done on vast historical information stored on the dialogue exchanges between either a live representative and customer and a massive amount of historical data [27, 28].

Distributed language modeling has been a long-standing open problem at the intersection of machine learning and language understanding. Several works in recent years have tried to fill this gap [29, 30] using algorithms like recursive networks [31], recurrent and convolutional networks [32] RNN and CNN [33]. However, all these methods pass sentences to a supervised setup and need a large set of data and labels in order to back-propagate and learn the sentence representations [34, 35]. Consequently, being dependent on volume and supervised labels, these techniques are fine-tuned for specific tasks and are not scalable.

With the proposed framework well-motivated by theoretical frameworks of marketing, customer experience, we abstract away from the supervised sentence summarization and try to fill the gap of distributed unsupervised language modeling, which can fuel the chatbots hosted on websites. This language model first trains on the vast UGC created through interactions between business organizations to promote their products and features queries posted by customers, and their inline responses on SMPs. By reducing the lead time of the conversational data collection, the proposed framework built on the theoretical frameworks of interaction, search, and inquiry further enhances the OCE with the help of BCE, which further closes the gap between OA and CE and is an essential contribution to information systems (IS) literature.

3 Proposed Framework

With advances and penetration in online media marketing and technologies, business organizations widely share product features and promotions and encourage users to write, interact, and further share on various SMPs like Twitter. Within a few months, this can generate a vast volume of UGC. Numerous studies [36] show that this conversational UGC is highly abundant, and often at times has been used to extract independent topics [37]. This UGC is widely available, low cost, disaggregate (days, hours, minutes), and is easy for business organizations to monitor and administer. We extend the approach taken by the marketers to mine the UGC in the research [37] to build a theme silo.

The current study proposes a unified framework as represented in Fig. 2 which: (1) uses the UGC through preprocessing and feeding few words ascertaining the valence, validity, product name, organization name to filter out the specific conversation of own organization, product, and sentiment, (2) uses proposed topic vectors to generate three silos of the dimensions of information, and (3) use these dimensions to respond to chatbots which act as an interface between users and these silos.

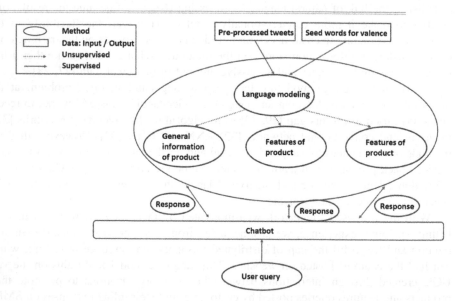

Fig. 2. Framework for unsupervised language modeling and fueling chatbot

3.1 The Text Mining Apparatus

Our objective is to mine promotion and discussions on products from UGC. For this, we chose SMP Twitter, which is an excellent place for relatively newer originations to not only brand, market, promote the products but also get the UGC generated quickly.

Step1: We downloaded over 15 lakh tweets from the domain of artificial intelligence (AI) as several start-ups are launching the products as elements of AI.

Step2: We thoroughly cleaned for the noise in tweets like HTML tags and non-textual information like images, commercials.

Step3: Specific terms related to organization and products are extracted, which are used for moderating the further preprocessing.

Step4: The entire set of tweets is further chunked into information units like threads, messages, and original tweets, of which only original tweets and responses are considered for analysis.

We have collected tweets around trending hashtags like #ArtificialIntelligence, #AI, #Chatbots, #Virtualreality, #Augmentedreality, #bots, #roboadvisor, #AIproducts, #AIsolutions, #mlsolution, ##mlproducts. The associated hashtags of #ArtificialIntelligence were determined based on the collection of the first 1000 tweets and mining it for hashtag association rules. The resulting dataset consisted of 15,54,782 tweets posted by 100,142 users. We have further deployed control mechanisms to make sure that the tweets are posted by actual users and not bots by pulling few historical tweets of these users and looking at the trend of posting these tweets in terms of the hour of the day, day of the week and average tweets in a time-period. A summarization of the tweet corpus is represented in Table 1 below.

Table 1. Summary statistics of the training corpus

# of tweets	# of processed tweets	# of words	mean # of words per sentence
15,54,782	10,12,276	22,270,072	22

3.2 Language Model

We design the language model by inducing a topic vector built on the encoder-decoder setup. That is, an encoder will be trained to learn and map words to a sentence vector. A decoder will follow to generate the surrounding sentences that will go as a response from the silo to a chatbot. Assuming we have a sequence of sentences (s_{i-1}, s_i, s_{i+1}), and a word w_i^n denotes the nth word and let X_n represent the embedding, we can describe the model in three parts: encoder, decoder, and the topics expansion function.

Encoder: Assuming there are 'N' number of words in the ith sentence (tweet) represented as $w_i^1 \ldots w_i^N$. At each sequence step, the encoder produces a hidden state h_i^t, which is a learned representation of the sequence $w_i^1 \ldots w_i^n$. The hidden state h_i^N would then learn and store the entire sequence. This loop runs over the entire set of sentences using the following sequence of equations.

$$r^t = \sigma\left(W_r x^t + U_r h^{t-1}\right) \tag{1}$$

$$z^t = \sigma\left(W_z x^t + U_z h^{t-1}\right) \tag{2}$$

$$h^t = tanh\left(Wx^t + U\left(r^t.h^{t-1}\right)\right) \tag{3}$$

$$h^t = (1 - z^t).h^{t-1} + z^t.h^t \tag{4}$$

Where z^t is the update gate, r^t is the reset gate, '.' Represents a dot product, and h^t is the proposes state update at the state t.

Decoder: A decoder is a neural network model which decodes the encoder output h_i^t. The computational iteration is like in the above section of an encoder, except for the fact that we now introduce bias matrices that are used at every gate (update, reset, and hidden). Every sentence will have its decoder. For instance, sentence s_{i+1} will have the first decoder, while S_{i-1} will have the second decoder used for the previous sentence.

Topics Expansion Function: Given a sequence of sentences (s_{i-1}, s_i, s_{i+1}), the job of the objective function will be to maximize the log-probabilities of word prediction through forward and backward learning and representation through encoder and decoder. The log-probabilities equation can be represented as below:

$$\sum log P\left(w_{i+1}^t \mid w_{i+1}^{<t}, h_i\right) + \sum log P\left(w_{i-1}^t \mid w_{i-1}^{<t}, h_i\right)$$

We further try to expand the topics or vocabulary list of the encode-decoder to words that have not been seen during the time of training. Assuming a model trained on word representation like word2vec [38] using RNN. Let E_{w2v} is the embedding space of all the words in the training sample, and E_{rnn} is the learned embedding space by the RNN model. We assume that E_{w2v} is much larger than E_{rnn} in the actual population. Hence we should be able to construct and map E_{w2v} to a much larger space, using a function mapping f: $E_{w2v} \rightarrow E_{rnn}$ parameterized by a matrix **W**. Inspired by the proven works [39] of similarity measures to find similar words, we solve for an un-regularized L2 regression for matrix **W**. This produces a table of similar words as represented in Table 2 below using neighbor of words that were not part of the training set.

Table 2. The nearest neighbor of words after vocabulary expansion

Neuronal	Undermine	Amplitude	Rehearse
neural	exculpate	modulation	choreograph
neuron	absolve	harmonics	trial

There can be alternate strategies for solving this problem like replace the RNN embedding space with a pre-trained embedding like global vector space (GloVe) or use of a more sophisticated cost function followed by clipping the word space by a decoder. This process is computationally costly. For the scope of the current paper, we are restricting ourselves to only RNN embedding space for experimentation.

4   Experimentation

With the experimental setup, we intend to evaluate the capability of our encoderde-coder as a general topic extractor after training on the preprocessed tweet corpus we have collected. Experimentation setup consists of below tasks:

- Train an encoder that acts as a topic feature extractor from all the sentences
- Compute topic wise features between the sentence pairs
- Train a neural network model on the extracted features, back-propagating the encoded features

4.1   Details of Experimentation

The model consists of two encoders with different parameters, one for learning the words from the sentence in the correct order and second in the reverse order. The outputs are then used to construct a 2400 dimension vector. We define this as a bi-encoder model. Minibatches of 64 were used while training, and the gradient values are clipped to avoid any loss while the model learns. Adam [40] optimizer is used for fine-tuning the model parameters.

Post-training the encoder-decoder models, we now proceed to expand the topic to map embeddings into RNN encoder space. Openly available continuous bag of words (CBOW) [41] model was used for this step. The models were initially trained on 100,000 words. Expanded topic vector space was of size 10,930,112 words. Since our goal is to test the intuitiveness of the language model, hence the tweet preprocessing plays a very critical role here.

4.2   Semantic Similarity

Because the entire setup of our model is through unsupervised learning, in order to evaluate the model, we test for the semantic similarity of the generated words from the model and an annotated output on a humanly pre-annotated dataset SICK [42]. The sentences in the dataset are already scored by human annotators between 1 to 5. The dataset has a pre-split of 4500 training sentence pairs, and 4927 test pairs. The evaluation metrics is Pearson's r, Spearman's ρ, and mean squared error (MSE). We test how well our learned representation on an already annotated dataset.

To represent a sentence pair, we deploy two features: given two topic vectors: u and v we compute their component-wise product $u.v$ and the difference between their scales $| u - v |$. These features have already been used in prior researches [43] and accepted well. To predict the similarity score, we use the same setup as used by the researchers in [43]. Table 3 presents our results through the trained model on the SICK dataset. The bi-encoder model with 2400 dimensions seems to have outperformed all.

Table 3. The model results on SICK dataset

		SICK Dataset		
Models and embeddings tested		r	ρ	MSE
Uni-encoder	Word2Vec	0.7008	0.6794	0.3019
Bi-encoder 1200 dimension		0.8349	0. 6297	0.3084
Bi-encoder 2400 dimension		**0.8256**	**0.7953**	**0.2652**
Uni-encoder	GloVe	0.8028	0.6258	0.1058
Bi-encoder 1200 dimension		0.8220	0.7638	0.2983
Bi-encoder 2400 dimension		0.8085	0.7036	0.2056

5 Discussion

5.1 Summary of Findings

The main findings of the proposed study are as follows:

- Organizations doing campaigning on SMP and interaction on SMPs can use the UGC to fuel the chatbot on the website to provide BCE to customers.
- UGC is rich in capturing conversational chatter, and with a structured preprocessing can be used to train a model fueling the chatbot responses.
- UGC, with the help of unsupervised distributed language modeling, can be scaled to multidimensional language silos.
- These multidimensional silos can capture the organization's or product's position, features, and availability.
- These chatbots hosted on websites fueled can be further improved as more conversational data gets recorded by responding to customers through these hosted chatbots.

5.2 Theoretical Contribution

To enhance the experience [3, 44, 45] between customers and machines on an ecommerce website, the concepts of AI, such as artificial neural networks and natural language processing, can be used in the proposed system. The proposed framework further bridges the gap between OA and CE [18, 20, 21], and rests on a proven link between OA and CE, which is a website. The framework is an essential addition to the IS literature to the lists of frameworks improving the customer experiences, which increases the chances of customer purchasing by engaging in interaction.

This study has proposed a unified framework that uses NLP to create various dimensions from UGC while simultaneously extracting topic vectors from the text using encoder-decoder algorithms. The framework not only captures the heterogeneity but also captures the time-varying discussions from the UGC that changes over the course and will reflect in responses on a chatbot to customers. The framework has been tested on various exiting semantic systems and various annotated datasets, making it generalizable and a contribution to the literature.

5.3 Practice Implications

The study has many valuable practice implications for marketing, customer support, and social media managers. First, the framework enables these managers to ascertain the valence of the responses of customers through UGC. If the initials signals are not good as expected, then a quick course correction can help to get the right message floated on SMPs. Second, it helps these managers to make sure that the right latent dimensions related to features and quality of products are known by the users and potential consumers on the SMP.

If initial modeling results do not generate specific silos, then a course correction of campaigning on SMPs can be done to make sure that the right message is conveyed to the potential consumers. Third, it enables a customer support manager to further enhance the customer experience by using this chatbot as a live response to customer's queries and questions. It also enables the managers to track how competition varies over time while mining and perform the language modeling on UGC in generic. Finally, it allows the business organizations to start immediately hosting a chatbot and not wait for years to have the conversational data accumulated and train an ML model to fuel a chatbot.

6 Limitations and Future Research

This research has few limitations which have been made as assumptions. First, the business organizations should be active on any of the SMPs and have been using the same for doing digital marketing and campaigns. Second, the business has a working website available online, having the technical ability to host a microservice like a chatbot. Third, the initial few iterations of the language model are computationally extensive. Forth, the current research has been restricted to one SMP like Twitter only. As part of the future research, we plan to extend the language modeling to the UGC from other SMPs like LinkedIn and Facebook advertisement posts.

References

1. Balasubraman, S., Peterson, R.A., Jarvenpaa, S.L.: Exploring the implications of m-commerce for markets and marketing. J. Acad. Mark. Sci. **30**(4), 348–361 (2002). https://doi.org/10.1177/009207002236910
2. (Ivy) Yuan, L., Dennis, A.R.: Acting like humans? anthropomorphism and consumer's willingness to pay in electronic commerce. J. Manage. Inf. Syst. **36**(2), 450–477 (2019). https://doi.org/10.1080/07421222.2019.1598691
3. Lee, G., Lin, H.: Customer perceptions of e-service quality in online shopping. Int. J. Retail Distrib. Manage. **33**(2), 161–176 (2005). https://doi.org/10.1108/09590550510581485
4. Kar, A.K.: Integrating websites with social media – an approach for group decision support. J. Decis. Syst. **24**(3), 339–353 (2015). https://doi.org/10.1080/12460125.2015.969585
5. Pachamanova, D., Lo, V.S.Y., Gülpınar, N.: Uncertainty representation and risk management for direct segmented marketing. J. Mark. Manage. **36**(1–2), 149–175 (2020). https://doi.org/10.1080/0267257X.2019.1707265

6. Koponen, J.P., Rytsy, S.: Social presence and e-commerce B2B chat functions. Eur. J. Mark. **54**(6), 1205–1224 (2020). https://doi.org/10.1108/EJM-01-2019-0061
7. How Industry Will be Affected by Tech in the Future: Business Fundas. https://www.business-fundas.com/2019/how-industry-will-be-affected-by-techin-the-future/
8. 5 Great Ways Big Data can Help Small Businesses Thrive: Tech Talk 29 October 2019. https://tech-talk.org/2019/10/29/5-great-ways-big-data-can-help-smallbusinesses-thrive/
9. Alba, J.W., Hutchinson, J.W.: Dimensions of consumer expertise. J. Consum. Res. **13**(4), 411–454 (1987). https://doi.org/10.1086/209080
10. Applications of Machine Learning in Business – Business Frontiers: https://business-frontiers.org/2020/07/24/applications-of-machine-learning-in-business/
11. Rathore, A.K., Kar, A.K., Ilavarasan, P.V.: Social media analytics: literature review and directions for future research. Decis. Anal. **14**(4), 229–249 (2017). https://doi.org/10.1287/deca.2017.0355
12. Rai, A.: Editor's comments: diversity of design science research. MIS Q. **41**(1), iii–xviii (2017)
13. Pries-Heje, J., Baskerville, R.: The design theory nexus. MIS Q. **32**(4), 731–755 (2008). https://doi.org/10.2307/25148870
14. Khalifa, M., Liu, V.: Satisfaction with internet-based services: the role of expectations and desires. Int. J. Electron. Commer. **7**(2), 31–49 (2002). https://doi.org/10.1080/10864415.2002.11044267
15. Kaynama, S.A., Christine, I.: A proposal to assess the service quality of online travel agencies: an exploratory study. J. Prof. Serv. Mark. **21**(1), 63–88 (2000). https://doi.org/10.1300/j090v21n01_05
16. Loiacono, E.T., Watson, R.T., Goodhue, D.L.: WEBQUAL: a measure of website quality. In: American Marketing Association. Conference Proceedings, 13, pp. 432–438, p. 71 (2002)
17. Shchiglik, C., Barnes, S.J.: Evaluating website quality in the airline industry. J. Comput. Inf. Syst. **44**(3), 17–25 (2004). https://doi.org/10.1080/08874417.2004.11647578
18. Cases, A.-S.: Perceived risk and risk-reduction strategies in Internet shopping. Int. Rev. Retail Distrib. Consum. Res. **12**(4), 375–394 (2002). https://doi.org/10.1080/09593960210151162
19. Cheung, C.M.K., Chan, G.W.W., Limayem, M.: A critical review of online consumer behaviour: empirical research. J. Electron. Commer. Organ. **3**, 1–19 (2005)
20. Childers, T.L., Carr, C.L., Peck, J., Carson, S.: Hedonic and utilitarian motivations for online retail shopping behavior. J. Retail. **77**(4), 511–535 (2001). https://doi.org/10.1016/S0022-4359(01)00056-2
21. Johnson, E.J., Moe, W.W., Fader, P.S., Bellman, S., Lohse, G.L.: On the depth and dynamics of online search behavior. Manage. Sci. **50**(3), 299–308 (2004). https://doi.org/10.1287/mnsc.1040.0194
22. Khalifa, M., Liu, V.: Online consumer retention: contingent effects of online shopping habit and online shopping experience. Eur. J. Inf. Syst. **16**(6), 780–792 (2007). https://doi.org/10.1057/palgrave.ejis.3000711
23. Jeong, S.-S., Seo, Y.-S.: Improving response capability of chatbot using twitter. J. Ambient Intell. Hum. Comput. (2019). https://doi.org/10.1007/s12652-019-01347-6
24. D'silva, G.M., Thakare, S., More, S., Kuriakose, J.: Real world smart chatbot for customer care using a software as a service (SaaS) architecture. In: 2017 International Conference on I-SMAC (IoT in Social, Mobile, Analytics and Cloud) (I-SMAC), pp. 658–664 Febraury 2017. https://doi.org/10.1109/i-smac.2017.8058261

25. Mauldin,M.L.: Chatterbots, tinymuds, and the turing test entering the loebner prize competition. In: Proceedings of the Twelfth AAAI National Conference on Artificial Intelligence, Seattle, Washington, pp. 16–21 August 1994
26. Baby, C.J., Khan, F.A., Swathi, J.N.: Home automation using IoT and a chatbot using natural language processing. In: 2017 Innovations in Power and Advanced Computing Technologies (i-PACT), pp. 1–6 April 2017. https://doi.org/10.1109/ipact.2017.8245185
27. Rajkumar, R., Ganapathy, V.: Bio-inspiring learning style chatbot inventory using brain computing interface to increase the efficiency of E-learning. IEEE Access **8**, 67377–67395 (2020). https://doi.org/10.1109/ACCESS.2020.2984591
28. Cerezo, J., Kubelka, J., Robbes, R., Bergel, A.: Building an Expert Recommender Chatbot. In: 2019 IEEE/ACM 1st International Workshop on Bots in Software Engineering (BotSE), pp. 59–63 May 2019. https://doi.org/10.1109/botse.2019.00022
29. Le, Q., Mikolov, T.: Distributed Representations of Sentences and Documents. pp. 9. ICML (2014)
30. Chakraborty, A., Kar, A.K.: Swarm intelligence: a review of algorithms. In: Patnaik, S., Yang, X.-S., Nakamatsu, K. (eds.) Nature-Inspired Computing and Optimization. MOST, vol. 10, pp. 475–494. Springer, Cham (2017). https://doi.org/10.1007/978-3-319-50920-4_19
31. Socher, R., et al.: Recursive deep models for semantic compositionality over a sentiment treebank. In: Proceedings of the 2013 Conference on Empirical Methods in Natural Language Processing, Seattle, Washington, USA, pp. 1631–1642 October 2013
32. Zhao, H., Lu, Z., Poupart, P.: Self-adaptive hierarchical sentence model. In: Presented at the Twenty-Fourth International Joint Conference on Artificial Intelligence Jun 2015
33. Kushwaha, A.K., Kar, A.K., Vigneswara Ilavarasan, P.: Predicting information diffusion on twitter a deep learning neural network model using custom weighted word features. In: Hattingh, M., Matthee, M., Smuts, H., Pappas, I., Dwivedi, Y.K., Mäntymäki, M. (eds.) I3E 2020. LNCS, vol. 12066, pp. 456–468. Springer, Cham (2020). https://doi.org/10.1007/978-3-030-44999-5_38
34. Hassanpour, S., Tomita, N., DeLise, T., Crosier, B., Marsch, L.A.: Identifying substance use risk based on deep neural networks and Instagram social media data. Nature **44**(3), 487–494 (2019). https://doi.org/10.1038/s41386-018-0247x. Art. no. 3
35. Quiroz, J.C., Laranjo, L., Kocaballi, A.B., Berkovsky, S., Rezazadegan, D., Coiera, E.: Challenges of developing a digital scribe to reduce clinical documentation burden. Nature **2**(1), 114 (2019). https://doi.org/10.1038/s41746019-0190-1. Art. no. 1
36. Reich, T., Maglio, S.J.: Featuring mistakes: the persuasive impact of purchase mistakes in online reviews. J. Mark. **84**(1), 52–65 (2020). https://doi.org/10.1177/0022242919882428
37. Netzer, O., Feldman, R., Goldenberg, J., Fresko, M.: Mine your own business: market-structure surveillance through text mining. Mark. Sci. **31**(3), 521–543 (2012). https://doi.org/10.1287/mksc.1120.0713
38. Mikolov, T., Chen, K., Corrado, G., Dean, J.: Distributed representations of words and phrases and their compositionality. In: Advances in Neural Information Processing Systems 26: 27th Annual Conference on Neural Information Processing Systems 2013. Proceedings of a meeting held December 5–8, 2013, Lake Tahoe, Nevada, United States, pp 3111–3119 (2013). arXiv:1301.3781 [cs], September 2013
39. Mikolov, T., Le, Q.V., Sutskever, I.: Exploiting similarities among languages for machine translation. arXiv preprint arXiv:1309.4168 (2013). arXiv:1309.4168 [cs] September 2013
40. Kingma, D.P., Ba, J.: Adam: a method for stochastic optimization. ICLR (2015). arXiv: 1412.6980 [cs] January 2017

41. Mikolov, T., Chen, K., Corrado, G., Dean, J.: Efficient Estimation of Word Representations in Vector Space. arXiv:1301.3781 [cs], September 2013, Accessed: 26 Jul. 2020. [Online]. Available: http://arxiv.org/abs/1301.3781

42. Marelli, M., Menini, S., Baroni, M., Bentivogli, L., Bernardi, R., Zamparelli, R.: A SICK cure for the evaluation of compositional distributional semantic models. pp. 9. ICML

43. Tai, K.S., Socher, R., Manning, C.D.: Improved semantic representations from tree-structured long short-term memory networks. ACL (2015). arXiv:1503.00075 [cs]

44. Kar, A.K., Rakshit, A.: Flexible pricing models for cloud computing based on group decision making under consensus. Global J. Flex. Syst. Manage. **16**(2), 191–204 (2015). https://doi.org/10.1007/s40171-015-0093-1

45. Aswani, R., Ghrera, S.P., Kar, A.K., Chandra, S.: Identifying buzz in social media: a hybrid approach using artificial bee colony and k-nearest neighbors for outlier detection. Soc. Netw. Anal. Min. **7**(1), 1–10 (2017). https://doi.org/10.1007/s13278-017-0461-2

Using Work System Theory, Facets of Work, and Dimensions of Smartness to Characterize Applications and Impacts of Artificial Intelligence

Steven Alter(✉)

University of San Francisco, San Francisco, CA 94117, USA
alter@usfca.edu

Abstract. This paper presents an approach for describing and characterizing algorithms that are discussed as though they embody artificial intelligence. After identifying key assumptions related to algorithms and summarizing work system theory (WST), this paper uses a hypothetical example to introduce aspects of WST and two additional ideas, facets of work and dimensions of smartness in devices and systems. Next, it applies those ideas to aspects of five AI-related examples presented by entrepreneurs and researchers at an MIT AI conference in July 2020. Those examples were selected because they illustrated many AI-related issues. This paper's contribution is a new approach for characterizing real world applications and impacts of almost any system that uses algorithms or is associated with artificial intelligence.

Keywords: Artificial Intelligence · Algorithm · Work system theory · Facets of work · Dimensions of smartness

1 Moving Beyond the Multiple Meanings of AI

Many discussions of AI in academia and in public venues revolve around vague definitions, cherry-picked examples, and a mélange of diverse opinions and observations from pundits and researchers whose comments are often taken out of context. Examples often fall into categories that are only tangentially related to each other: intelligent machines, neural networks, machine learning, expert systems, smart systems, cognitive computing, natural language processing, pattern recognition, image recognition, statistical algorithms, automated decision-making, and so on. Beyond various historical and technical commonalities, those topics seem less like instances of a coherent and well-defined phenomenon and more like assorted topics huddled under an umbrella called AI. The lack of clarity about what AI means makes it difficult to discuss whether the benefits, risks, and ethics of using AI differ in any significant way from the benefits, risks, and ethics of automation or computerization in general.

Goal and Assumptions. This paper explains how to use work system theory, facets of work, and dimensions of smartness for characterizing applications and impacts of AI. Those ideas are introduced through an illustrative hypothetical example. This paper

Published by Springer Nature Switzerland AG 2020
S. K. Sharma et al. (Eds.): TDIT 2020, IFIP AICT 617, pp. 29–42, 2020.
https://doi.org/10.1007/978-3-030-64849-7_4

assumes that understanding affordances, benefits, and risks of AI applications in sociotechnical contexts can be viewed as a special case of concerns about algorithms, which was the central topic of the IFIP 8.2 working conference "Living with Monsters? Social Implications of Algorithmic Phenomena, Hybrid Agency, and the Performativity of Technology" [1]. Also, instead of speaking about algorithms in general, we look at algorithms (and hence AI) in the context of sociotechnical or totally automated work systems in which they are used.

Organization. After identifying key assumptions related to algorithms and summarizing work system theory (WST), this paper uses a hypothetical example to introduce aspects of WST and two additional ideas, facets of work and dimensions of smartness in devices and systems. Next, it applies those ideas to aspects of five AI-related examples presented by entrepreneurs and researchers at an MIT AI conference in July 2020. Those examples were selected because they illustrate many AI-related issues. This paper's contribution is a new approach for characterizing applications and impacts of almost any system that uses algorithms, including systems whose algorithms are associated with AI, big data, block chain, Internet of things, social media, and other current areas of interest associated with emerging technologies.

2   Assumptions Related to Algorithms

The examples in Table 1 use algorithms that may or may not be associated with AI. Some of those algorithms might be simple decision rules such as allowing no more than 30% of applicants to be classified in category X. Even a simple algorithm like that one can have other important and far reaching effects such as favoring one group of people over other groups, as when category X is acceptance into college. Examples in Table 1 illustrate the difficulty of generalizing about benefits, risks, and ethics of AI without specifying the area of application and the specific problem addressed.

Table 1. Potential application situations for algorithms that might or might not use AI

• using facial images to identify people • converting spoken words into equivalent text • deciding which applicants should be hired or accepted by a university • deciding whether to alert medical staff about a change in a patient's condition • deciding which is the best target for a missile • deciding a person's salary or bonus • deciding whether an autonomous (selfdriving) vehicle needs to stop or swerve • controlling the aerodynamics of a rocket	• deciding whether to turn off a machine likely to have a mechanical failure soon • deciding where police should be deployed over the next eight hours • selecting defective items that are being moved on a conveyor belt • combining multiple items in a customer order to minimize mailing cost • translating a text between languages • finding the laws that are most relevant to a specific lawsuit

3   Assumptions Related to Algorithms

A series of assumptions are a starting point for visualizing and evaluating algorithms.

Algorithms as Specifications for Transforming Inputs into Outputs. An algorithm specifies exactly how human and/or nonhuman actors can convert specific inputs into specifics outputs. Algorithms are abstractions that cannot do anything on their own. Human and/or nonhuman actors perform the transformations.

Goals, Constraints, Other Parameters. Algorithms pursue goals, operate within constraints, and may be guided by other situation-specific parameters or inputs.

Omissions. Most algorithms that are not derived directly from mathematics have omissions, i.e., potentially important topics or issues that the algorithm ignores.

Biases. Most algorithms not derived directly from mathematics or theory bring purposeful or accidental biases. Those biases may be based on viewpoints of the algorithm's creators or on unintended results of omissions, biased training data, other shortcomings of the algorithm, or unanticipated interactions with the environment.

Areas of Greater and Lesser Acuity: Algorithms apply to specific domains, i.e., defined sets of things or conditions. Often they have areas of maximum relevance and acuity and other areas of limited relevance and acuity. Applying an algorithm near or just beyond the boundaries of its domain of maximum acuity may generate answers that seem sensible, but that often need to be examined and questioned carefully.

Stakeholders: Algorithms affect stakeholders directly or indirectly. Often different stakeholders have different or even conflicting interests.

Embedding. Algorithms may be embedded within other algorithms. For example, a decades-old optimization algorithm might be embedded within a situation-specific algorithm for assigning shipment orders to available trucks in a specific setting.

Fitness for Purpose. An algorithm's fitness for purpose is determined by 1) the form, operation, and goals of work systems within which it operates, 2) its impact on human and nonhuman actors within the work system, and 3) its impact on other stakeholders such as recipients or users of whatever the work system produces.

4   The Work System Perspective and Work System Theory

The work system perspective (WSP) is a general approach to understanding systems in organizations based on viewing those systems as work systems. The core of WSP is work system theory (WST), which consists of three components: the definition of WS plus two frameworks (Fig. 1) for understanding a work system: the work system framework (a static view for summarizing how a work system operates) and the work system life cycle model (WSLC - how a work system evolves through planned and unplanned change). [2]. The discussion of WST had to be abbreviated due to changes in the paper's max length just before publication. The originally cited papers include [3–6], which can be found on Google Scholar. [3, 4] explain how the work system method (WSM) based on WST was used in various courses, mostly were directed at employed MBA and EMBA students. Individual students or teams of students used WSM templates to produce over 700 management briefings recommending improvements to IT-reliant WS during 2003-2017, mostly in their own organizations.

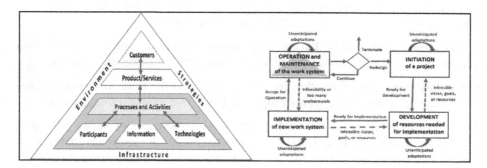

Fig. 1. Work system framework and work system life cycle model

Definition of WS. A work system is a system in which human participants *and/or* machines perform work (processes and activities) using information, technology, and other resources to produce specific product/services for internal and/or external customers. [2]. The first *and/or* addresses trends toward service-orientation and automation of work by saying that work systems may be sociotechnical (where human participants do some or all of the work) or totally automated (where all of the work is done by machines). A WS usually is identified based on what it is designed to accomplish and not based on software that it uses.

ISs and projects as special cases of WS. [5, 6]. An IS may be sociotechnical (e.g., financial analysts creating economic projections with the help of modeling software) or totally automated (e.g., computers generating economic projections automatically). A project is a WS designed to produce specific product/services and then go out of existence, e.g., software development, which can be executed in many ways.

5 Example Illustrating the Work System Perspective on AI

To illustrate a WSP for a situation that might involve AI, Table 2 provides a WS snapshot (a tool from WSM) of a hypothetical hiring system that PQR Corp implemented two years ago. The goal was to improve a previous hiring WS that absorbed too much effort inside PQR Corp and was so slow that candidates sometimes went elsewhere before receiving offers. Also, it hired too many unsuitable candidates.

The new hiring work system used AlgoComm and AlgoRank from a suite of software tools provided by AlgoCorp. AlgoComm provided capabilities for posting job ads, receiving applications, setting up appointments, and performing other communication with candidates. AlgoRank ranked candidates based on job criteria and a neural network application driven by AlgoCorp's database of job qualifications, salaries, and other information. Both AlgoComm and AlgoRank are algorithms that perform specified processing. AlgoRank can be seen as an AI application, whereas AlgoComm is more like typical information processing even though certain parts of it apply AI technologies such as natural language processing (NLP). After two years of use, management is once again dissatisfied. Excessive effort and delays have been reduced, but interviewers and applicants find the interface mechanical and lacking a human feel. Also, three hires proved disastrous despite use of AlgoRank capabilities. Management wants to launch a new project to upgrade the hiring work system once again.

Interpretation Based on WST. The WS snapshot in Table 2 summarizes the WS, which involves much more than AlgoComm and AlgoRank. The hiring WS uses AI, but should not be viewed as an AI system. The transition from the previous WS to the current WS started with an *initiation phase* in the WSLC (Fig. 1) in which management decided to develop a new hiring system using vendor software. The *development phase* acquired resources needed for implementation. Developers selected AlgoCorp as a vendor, installed AlgoCorp's software, set a group of parameters to fit it to PQR Corp's needs, and adapted AlgoCorp's training material for PQR Corp's users. The *implementation phase* was quick because of the nature of the hiring process. The subsequent *operation and maintenance phase* continued for two years during which AlgoCorp updated the neural network component of AlgoRank automatically to reflect job market changes. Several incidents occurred where managers worked around the standard

Table 2. Work System Snapshot of the Current Hiring System

Customers		Product/services	
• Hiring manager • Larger organization (which will have the applicant as a colleague • HR manager (who will use the applications to analyze the nature of applicants)		• Applications (which may be used for subsequent analysis) • Job offers • Rejection letters • Hiring of the applicant	
Major activities and processes			
• **AlgoComm** publicizes the position. • **Applicants** submit resumes to **AlgoComm**. • **AlgoRank** selects shortlisted applicants and sends the list to the hiring manager. • **Hiring manager** decides who to interview. • **AlgoComm** sets up interviews.		• **Interviewers** perform interviews and provide comments about applicants. • **AlgoRank** evaluates candidates. • **Hiring manager** makes hiring decision. • **AlgoComm** notifies applicants. • **Applicant** accepts or rejects job offer.	
Participants	Information		Technology
• Hiring manager • Applicants • Other employees who perform interviews	• Job requisition • Job description • Advertisements • Job applications • Cover letters • Applicant resumes	• Applicant short list • Information and impressions from the interviews • Job offers • Rejection letters	• AlgoComm • AlgoRank • Office software • Internet

process (enacting what the WSLC calls *unanticipated adaptations*) when talented individuals became available and might have been hired by a competitor. A division VP was consulted in one case but learned about the other workaround months later. Management is looking now at a new *initiation phase* to launch a project aimed at improving the hiring system further.

Using Facets of Work to Look More Deeply. The situation can be observed more deeply by using an extension of WST called *facets of work*. Two recent conference papers (blinded) explain that *facets of work* grew out of research attempting to bring richer and more evocative concepts to systems analysis and design (SA&D). The notion of facet is analogous to how a cut diamond is a single thing that has multiple facets. Table 3 identifies 18 facets of work, all of which describe a unique aspect of the activities that occur. Table 3 briefly mentions issues that the first 7 facets of work highlight related to how algorithms associated with AI might help in generating better results. Similar issues for the other 11 are not included due to length limitations but are easy to imagine. All 18 facets satisfy a series of criteria related to usefulness related to most systems in organizations: They apply to both sociotechnical and totally automated systems; they bring many concepts for analyzing system-related situations; they are associated with evaluation criteria and typical trade-offs; they have sub-facets that can be discussed; they bring open-ended questions that can help in starting conversations. Other researchers might have used a different set of facets that satisfy those criteria. Also, facets do not have to be independent, e.g. how decision-making often involves communication. The main point for current purposes is that each facet provides a lens for thinking about a work system that uses algorithms (or AI).

Table 3. Issues related to potential use of algorithms (specifically AI) in the hiring system

Facet	Issues related to potential use of AI in the hiring system
Making decisions	How could AI support decisions more fully in this system? Should AI suggest decisions or make decisions?
Communicating	How can AI explain how it makes or suggests decisions? How can AI help work system participants communicate more effectively?
Processing information	Can AI play any special role in capturing, transmitting, storing, retrieving, deleting, manipulating, or displaying information?
Thinking	Are there any areas in which it would be beneficial for AI to replace or augment thinking done by work system participants?
Representing reality	Does AI represent reality in a biased way? For example, what about possible bias or omissions in the dataset used to train the neural network?
Providing information	Could AI provide more meaningful information to work system participants than would otherwise be available?
Applying knowledge	Could AI identify and provide specific knowledge that would help in evaluating applicants?
.... Similar questions for 11 other facets of work	Length limitations prevent listing similar questions for Planning, Controlling execution, Improvising, Coordinating, Performing physical work, Performing support work, Interacting socially, Providing service, Creating value, Co-creating value, and Maintaining security

Using Dimensions of Smartness to Look More Deeply at AI Applications. Existing AI applications can be viewed as "weak AI" because they address highly constrained problems such as those in Table 1 and in the hiring example. That approach to AI has led to important breakthroughs and efficiencies in many situations, but is nothing like science fiction dreams of "strong AI" exhibited by humanoid robots that can reason and interact at a human or superhuman level [7]. This paper describes current AI capabilities using a set of dimensions of smartness in devices and systems that diverges from views of smartness in most current papers related to smartness involving things, devices, systems, cities, and so on (e.g., [8–14]).

This paper's classification matrix for smart capabilities is organized around four categories: information processing, internal regulation, action in the world, and knowledge acquisition [8]. Each category identifies separate capabilities, in essence separate dimensions on a continuum from not smart to somewhat smart to extremely smart based on a complex definition of smart: "Purposefully designed entity X is smart to the extent to which it performs and controls functions that attempt to produce useful results by applying automated capabilities and other physical, informational, technical, and intellectual resources for processing information, interpreting information, and/or learning from information that may or may not be specified by its designers." Table 4 identifies 23 dimensions of smartness, each associated with one of four categories. Every dimension in Table 4 is a continuous variable extending from not smart at all to increasing levels of smartness including scripted execution, formulaic adaptation, creative adaptation, and unscripted or partially scripted invention. [8]. Very few existing systems are even close to the higher levels of smartness.

Categories and dimensions in Table 4 can be used to see that the hypothetical hiring example is not very smart even though it uses AI. AlgoComm processes information by using mechanical, pre-specified capabilities when it captures, transmits, stores, retrieves, deletes, manipulates, and displays information. The neural network that provides AlgoRank's parameters for ranking candidates performs a type of knowledge acquisition (classifying and compiling) using techniques that are best described as scripted execution. Neither AlgoComm nor AlgoRank demonstrate internal regulation or action in the world.

Table 4. Dimensions of smartness related to four categories of smartness [8]

Category of smartness	Dimensions of smartness
Information processing	capture, transmit, store, retrieve, delete, manipulate, display information
Internal regulation	self-detection, self-monitoring, self-diagnosis, self-correction, self-organization
Action in the world	sensing, actuation, coordination, communication, control, physical action
Knowledge acquisition	sensing or discovering, classifying, compiling, inferring or extrapolating from example, inferring or extrapolating from abstractions, testing and evaluating

The hypothetical hiring system example was designed to illustrate the relevance of WST, facets of work, and dimensions of smartness in describing AI applications. The next section applies those ideas to five real world AI applications mentioned at the "MIT AI Conference 2020: AI for a Better World" presented as a series of webinars by the MIT Club of Northern California during July 14-18, 2020.

6   Application of WST, Facets of Work and Dimensions of Smartness to Real Examples

The five real world AI applications discussed here were chosen because they illustrate current or potential integration into operational work systems. They are identified as A1, A2, etc., and will be named based on their purpose: (A1) performing fetal screening for heart defects, (A2) finding defects in electronics manufacturing, (A3) supporting personalized learning in coursework, (A4) receiving and responding to IT help desk requests, (A5) producing useful notes from meetings. Three were discussed in 25-minute presentations that covered a variety of business, personal, and AI topics; one was presented in a research slam; one was discussed in an interview covering many topics. All involved digitalization applications including at least one algorithm associated with AI. Since the presenters were not available for in-depth interviews, this paper's descriptions are interpretations of webinars viewed on youtube.com. That suffices for the current goal of demonstrating the relevance of WST, facets of work, and dimensions of smartness for characterizing real world AI applications.

Each of the following discussions touches on the nature of the WS (Fig. 1, Table 2) that is being supported, the goal of the AI application within that WS, an overview of how the AI application was developed (WSLC in Fig. 1) how it was or can be implemented as part of a WS, the main facets of work (Table 3) that are supported or automated, and aspects of relevant dimensions of smartness (Table 4).

(A1) Performing Fetal Screening for Heart Defects.   [15] Congenital heart disease (CHD) occurs in 1% of live births. Fetal ultrasound screening at 20 weeks of gestation should detect over 90% of CHD but is often less than 50% accurate because it is difficult to build and maintain skills for a rare condition and because of difficulties of ultrasound imaging. Researchers created A1 as an ensemble of neural networks to detect CHD. They used clinical guidelines (medical knowledge) to identify five key screening views of the heart instead of looking at thousands of images for each ultrasound. This allowed them to perform an analysis based on a training dataset of 100,000 images from 1,300 ultrasounds. Later, they achieved 95% sensitivity and 96% specificity, far better than levels in current practice, in a test on a much large dataset. Their first step was training a convolutional neural network to distinguish the five screening views. Diagnostic classifiers determined whether a heart was normal for each view. Combining those classifiers gave a composite indicator of whether a heart was normal. Thus, deep learning combined with clinical knowledge and expert annotation of cases resulted in a possibly important way to improve practice.

A1 might be used in future practice during exams as a physician tries to decide whether a 20-week fetus has CHD. In terms of facets of work, A1 will perform extensive *processing of information* to *represent reality* with a diagnostic score that *provides information* to physicians that will help them in *making decisions* about leading to treatments. In terms of dimensions of smartness, A1 *processes information* in a prescripted manner to create useful diagnostic scores. A1 does not exercise *internal regulation* or *take action* in the world. A1 does not *create knowledge*, which was created previously by the researchers using their neural network approach.

(A2) Finding Defects In Electronics Manufacturing. [16] Inefficiencies in electronics manufacturing waste 20%–30% of expenses through scrap and rework, product returns, mistakes and experiments, and underutilized human resources. Methods for monitoring problems include automated optical inspection, functional testing, daily build reports, failure analysis reports, and analysis of customer returns. Underlying issues often are dark yield problems, i.e., defects that cannot be found through a test of function but that may cause a unit to fail later – incorrect cable routing, cold solder failures, glue overflow, connectors not fully mated, and misassembled parts such as a screw that is not fully inserted. With the COVID pandemic, engineers are prevented from going to remote factories. Merely taking pictures of work in progress or completed units in the factory is insufficient because solving problems requires tracking specific units back to specific production steps where their problems occurred. Trying to record a complete history of production units including photos during production generates a great deal of data that might have to be transmitted to the cloud from factories in remote locations where data transmission capabilities are limited. A2 compares production units to other production units at a specific point in assembly. It can start with as few as 30 initial units before production stabilizes. It identifies anomalies such as tape and label defects, missing foams that keep components in place, missing functional parts, incorrect cable routing, and glue issues. A2 reduces the amount of labeling of defects that people need to do by sorting the images in order from totally conforming to highly nonconforming, thereby helping with decisions on cutoffs for labeling defects as consequential or not. Users can identify areas where problems are likely to occur, but that is not necessary. Thus, A2's algorithms can be trained without examples that are labeled in advance as defects. All of the training is done using software in the cloud, not on premises.

A2's work system is manufacturing of electronic items such as phones. Its algorithms are used for quick identification of defective units, even with dark yield problems, before additional defective units are manufactured. The training uses images of important parts (e.g., the front of a phone) and identifying anomalies that differentiate one unit from others. A person decides whether a unit's anomaly is serious enough to declare the unit defective. After training, algorithms can be used to monitor production to find defective units. The relevant facets of work touched directly by A2 are *processing information* (capturing images and identifying anomalies between units), *providing information* about anomalies, and *making decisions* by identifying defective units after A2 has been trained. In terms of smartness, A2 *processes information* using pre-defined scripts. It does not *perform self-regulation* or *take action in the world*. It acquires knowledge through the training process. The presentation implied that training on specific problem areas can be repeated if the product design changes.

(A3) Supporting Personalized Learning in Coursework. [17, 18] This research involved working with students using coursework available through the Khan Academy, which provided an anonymized dataset of 50 K elementary through high school students solving 1.4 million math problems. The dataset included a history of every problem that each student tried to solve, whether the answer was correct, and how long the student worked on the problem. The researchers trained a neural network to take as input the complete history of a student's (correct and incorrect) answers and to try to predict their answer to the next question. This created a complex vector for any student that predicts whether that student would solve any math problem that might appear next. In aggregate across all students, the neural network learned which skills are needed to answer any question. It represented the pedagogical structure of the mathematics students were trying to learn. That knowledge provides hints about what other problems students will be able to solve after they acquire a specific skill. In effect this knowledge graph describes in a data-driven way the prerequisite structure in learning mathematics and therefore provides a data-driven window into the learning process. A3 was developed in research reported in [18]. Real world applications are easy to imagine although the closest the webinar discussion [17] came to discussing actual applications was a few comments about a MOOC that taught coding. The very large set of student exercises and related comments by teaching assistants might be a step toward automation of some aspects of grading of coding exercises.

In a real-world application of something like A3, the work system would be students trying to learn specific coursework. A3 or something like it would hasten learning by predicting immediate difficulties students might experience and by looking ahead to provide an optimal learning sequence. In terms of facets of work, the learning management system would *process information* by storing and retrieving the student's history. It would use a student's history and a course-related neural network to *decide* what problems the student should see next. It would *represent reality* as the student's progress to date. A learning management system would *communicate* with the student through online interactions. A3 would *control* the learning process to maximize learning. In terms of smartness, all of the *information processing* would be done based on scripts that use the current state of the recurrent neural network. A3 would perform *internal regulation* and *action in the world* in the sense of using each student's history and the structure of the subject matter to decide what the student should see next. It would *acquire knowledge* by applying pre-specified neural network techniques to deepen its own knowledge as students answers problems.

(A4) Receiving and Responding to IT Help Desk Requests. [19] The firm Moveworks provides a chatbot for handling IT help requests for firms. The average time before an agent looks at an IT help request averages 5 h and a response often takes 3 days. This problem cannot be solved with big data approaches that work in the consumer space (e.g. billions of items from webpages, documents, etc.) because the IT help desk of a firm with 1000 employees might have 100 laptop requests and 10 VPN connection requests every year, not enough to serve as a training dataset for deep learning related to IT requests in that firm. As a result, chatbots often rely on hard coded logic that leads to frustrating endless loops for users. One of the problems with IT requests is that the requests are often ambiguous, e.g., "how do I get my laptop running?" The A4 approach was to build a conversational AI system that uses machine learning with "small data." The trick in teaching the neural network was to abstract from sentence data by labeling recurrent elements, i.e., using labels that describe categories rather than instances (e.g., PC rather than Dell vs. HP vs. Lenovo). Converting sentences such as "I need Trello capability" or "Joe needs a Windows password" into a more general form like "$PERSON wants $SOFTWARE access" was a starting point for generating a large number of possible sentences that can be linked to actual help desk requests. A4 uses "collective learning" by applying the same learning approach across many firms that have IT help desks. It also used "transfer learning" by extracting universal language patterns (e.g., that good answers often have instructions in the form of lists) that can be applied across domains. Initially they used stackoverflow.com, a website for software developers that contains millions of help requests and related answers. The ultimate result is a chatbot that can completely answer around 40% of help requests and can escalate the others to human operators. As a result, the human operators handle many fewer IT tickets, a great saving in the use of a scarce resource.

A4 is part of a WS that answers IT help requests. Facets of work include *making decisions, communicating, processing information, providing information,* and *representing reality.* In terms of smartness, every type of *information processing* is present in a scripted form. A4 performs *internal regulation* by recognizing the current state of its dialogue with a user and trying to respond appropriately. It *takes action in the world* by engaging in a dialogue with users. It *acquires knowledge* from its usage.

(A5) Producing Useful Notes From Meetings.   [20] Fireflies.ai is a commercial product that records meetings and generates transcripts automatically. A5 is the basis of "Fred," an automated voice assistant that records meetings, produces transcripts, and performs other tasks to make meetings and their aftermath more efficient. A user invites fred@fireflies.ai to an online meeting on Zoom, WebEx, or other platforms. Fred captures and transcribes voice conversations, indexes the notes to make them useful, and routes the notes to anyone who should receive them. Action items can be transferred automatically to project management systems such as Trello or to customer relationship management systems such as Salesforce without doing a lot of manual work. Maintaining a complete history of meetings makes it possible to find details of meetings that may have happened months ago.

In effect, A5 is the technical basis of an automated work system that is created through three main steps, two of which are in the WSLC *development phase.* The first step is collecting relevant language data (sentences, keywords, etc.) from users and public sources, storing the data, and labeling the data to make it useful. For example, the founders of Fireflies.ai developed some of their ideas by labeling 20 K data points (basically sentences) from their own meeting notes and recordings by using a yes/no binary classification model (important or unimportant). The initial trial use of the resulting model led to more language data that could be incorporated. The second main step was to get the model running using available software that fit the model and making sure that errors and duplicates in the data (terms and sample sentences) were eliminated. The third step was benchmarking and performance improvement (e.g., minimizing false positives and false negatives) as part of an *operation and maintenance phase.* Subsequent use in different industries is accommodated by having users pick a domain such as health care or sales when they sign up. Each industry has keywords that appear on user dashboards. Users add other keywords. Meeting agendas and user edits to transcripts provide more industry-specific jargon.

The relevant facets of work *processing information* (recording and transcribing meetings), *providing information* in the form of transcripts. In terms of smartness, A2 *processes information* using pre-defined scripts. It does not *perform self-regulation*. It *takes action in the world* by producing and distributing transcripts. It *acquires knowledge* by improving its language models every time it is used.

7 Conclusion

This paper's contribution is way to describe and characterize AI applications and their impacts instead of just talking about AI in general, often based on cherry-picked examples. This paper used a hypothetical hiring example to illustrate the ideas and then applied those ideas to five real examples. The five examples illustrate a number of points that are not evident from many attempts to talk about AI in general.

Integration With Work Systems. (Figure 1, Table 2). In all five cases, the AI algorithm was part of an actual work system (A2, A4, A5) or was developed as research with a high potential for application in work systems (A1, A3).

Facets of Work. (Table 3) All of the examples *process information, provide information,* and *represent reality.* All *create value.* Algorithms in A1, A2, and A3 contribute to *making decisions* that matter. A4 and A5 *perform support work.* A2 helps in *controlling execution* by identifying anomalies. The chatbot in A4 *communicates* with customers of the help desk. A1 and A2 *communicate* in a more structured way.

Smartness. (Table 4) All five examples *process information* in a scripted way. A4 exhibits a form of *internal regulation*. A1 and A2 identify problems but do not *take action in the world*. A4, and A5 *take action in the world*, and A3 has a potential to do so. All use knowledge built into neural networks. A3, A4, and A5 *acquire knowledge*. Relevant dimensions of smartness in all cases are handled through scripted execution of algorithms rather than by autonomous modification of algorithms.

Importance of Domain Knowledge. The neural networks in A1, A2, A4, and A5 all depend on domain knowledge built into their design. A3 is more like unsupervised learning based on histories of students answering problems. Unsupervised learning seems most relevant where situational knowledge is not necessary, such in Open AI's GPT-3 system, whose 1.5 billion "parameters" describe the likelihood that specific words occur next to other words in a vast training dataset of texts [21].

Big Data or Little Data. Some AI algorithms such as GPT-3 are built on huge data bases, but A2 could start being useful after training with only 30 examples. A1, A4, and A5 also used knowledge as a way to reduce the size of training datasets.

Visibility to Users. General discussions of AI often mention the lack of visibility to users. A1 is based on ultrasound data that is understood by highly skilled users. A2 finds anomalies that are visible. A3 is hidden within a learning management system. A4 and A5 perform support work where most errors are easily identified.

Is AI Inherently Ethically Suspect? General discussions of AI frequently focus on harm that may occur when algorithms are used to identify people or suggest important decisions related to specific individuals. Biased decisions may result from biased training datasets and/or biased logic of the work system. On the other hand, it is also obvious that almost any technology can contribute to work systems that harm people. The issue is not with AI as a category, but rather with work systems and/or algorithms that fail to provide equitable treatment for all customers and other stakeholders.

References

1. Schultze, U., et al.: Living with monsters? social implications of algorithmic phenomena, hybrid agency, and the performativity of technology. In: Proceedings of IFIP WG 8.2 Working Conference on the Interaction of Information Systems and the Organization. December 11–12. San Francisco, CA, USA. (2018)
2. Alter, S.: Work system theory: overview of core concepts, extensions, and challenges for the future. J. Assoc. Inf. Syst. **14**(2), 72–121 (2013)
3. Truex, D., Alter, S., Long, C.: Systems analysis for everyone else: empowering business professionals through a systems analysis method that fits their needs. In: ECIS (2010)
4. Truex, D., Lakew, N., Alter, S., Sarkar, S.: Extending a systems analysis method for business professionals. In: Helfert, M., Donnellan, B. (eds.) EDSS 2011. CCIS, vol. 286, pp. 15–26. Springer, Heidelberg (2012). https://doi.org/10.1007/978-3-642-33681-2_2
5. Alter, S.: The Work System Method: Connecting People, Processes, and IT for Business Results. Work System Press, Larkspur, USA (2006)
6. Alter, S.: Defining information systems as work systems: implications for the IS field. Eur. J. Inf. Syst. **17**, 448–469 (2008)
7. Iansiti, M., Lakhani, K.R.: Competing in the Age of AI: Strategy and Leadership When Algorithms and Networks Run the World. HBS Press, Cambridge, USA (2020)
8. Alter, S.: Making sense of smartness in the context of smart devices and smart systems. Inf. Syst. Frontiers **22**(2), 381–393 (2020). https://doi.org/10.1007/s10796-019-09919-9
9. Strozzi, F., et al.: Literature review on the 'Smart Factory'concept using bibliometric tools. Int. J. Prod. Res. **55**(22), 6572–6591 (2017)
10. Romero, M., et al.: Towards a characterisation of smart systems: a systematic literature review. Comput. Ind. **120**, 103224 (2020). in press
11. Elbanna, A.R., et al.: The Search for Smartness in Working, Living and Organising: Beyond the 'Technomagic'. Inf. Syst. Frontiers **22**(2), 275–280 (2020)
12. Langley, D.J., et al.: The internet of everything: smart things and their impact on business models. J. Bus. Res. **122**, 853–863, January 2021
13. Wolf, V., et al.: Establishing smart service systems is a challenge: a case study on pitfalls and implications. In: Wirtschaftsinformatik 2020 Zentrale Tracks (2020)
14. Anke, J., et al.: Joining forces: understanding organizational roles in inter-organizational smart service systems engineering. In: Wirtschaftsinformatik 2020 Zentrale Tracks (2020)
15. Arnaout, R.: Improving fetal heart screening with deep learning (2020). https://www.youtube.com/watch?v=76WvsHhCyko
16. Shedietsky, A-K.: How COVID-19 is driving adoption of AI in electronics manufacturing (2020). https://www.youtube.com/watch?v=DIuuVTJKoLs

17. Ganguli, S.: Learning in Humans and Machines: From Optimizing Our Biology to Colluding With AI's (2020). https://www.youtube.com/watch?v=OL89f0mnJ00
18. Piech, C., et al.: Deep knowledge tracing. In: Advances in Neural Information Processing Systems, pp. 505–513 (2015)
19. Shah, B.: How Conversational AI Will Empower One Billion Knowledge Workers (2020). https://www.youtube.com/watch?v=bzBZA_2kkNE
20. Udotong, S.: Practical Deep Learning: How It Is Used in Production and Already Revolutionizing Enterprise Work (2020). https://www.youtube.com/watch?v=ywhY2DCIZqU
21. Manjoo, F.: How Do You Know a Human Wrote This? New York Times, Editorial 29 July 2020. https://www.nytimes.com/2020/07/29/opinion/gpt-3-ai-automation.html

Visualising the Knowledge Domain of Artificial Intelligence in Marketing: A Bibliometric Analysis

Elvira Ismagiloiva[1]([⊠]), Yogesh Dwivedi[2], and Nripendra Rana[1]

[1] Faculty of Management, Law and Social Sciences, University of Bradford, Bradford, UK
{e.ismagilova, n.p.rana}@bradford.ac.uk
[2] Emerging Markets Research Centre, School of Management, Swansea University, Swansea, UK
y.k.dwivedi@swansea.ac.uk

Abstract. As the number of research outputs in the field of AI in Marketing increased greatly in the past 20 years, a systematic review of the literature and its developmental process is essential to provide a consolidated view of this area. This study conducted a bibliometric analysis for the knowledge domain of AI in Marketing by using 617 research outputs from the Web of Science database from 1992 to 2020. Knowledge maps of AI in marketing research were visualised by employing CiteSpace software.

Keywords: Artificial intelligence · Marketing · Bibliometric analysis

1 Introduction

With the rapid development of technologies, it is predicted that Artificial intelligence (AI) will significantly change traditional marketing including marketing strategies, business models, sales processes, and customer service options [1]. AI is defined as "the ability of a machine to learn from experience, adjust to new inputs and perform human-like tasks" [2]. Due to the relevance of the application of AI in marketing for a broad group of stakeholders and the benefits and challenges connected with its implementation, adoption, and use, the field has been attracting high attention from researchers and practitioners. The previous studies investigated the application of AI in the context of sales forecasting [3], recommendation systems [4], customer classification [5], profit maximization [6], retail store scheme [7, 8], and design of the marketing campaign [9], to name a few.

A number of studies conducted a review of the literature in the field of AI [1, 10, 11]. However, limited research has been done using bibliometric analysis. It is argued that a thorough analysis and review of the key topics can offer researchers a consolidated view on this area [12, 13]. Thus, the current study aims to provide in-depth analysis with a bibliometric method of accumulated studies on AI and Marketing. To conduct the bibliometric analysis, the CiteSpace software was used to visualize and analyse trends and patterns in the scientific literature.

© IFIP International Federation for Information Processing 2020
Published by Springer Nature Switzerland AG 2020
S. K. Sharma et al. (Eds.): TDIT 2020, IFIP AICT 617, pp. 43–53, 2020.
https://doi.org/10.1007/978-3-030-64849-7_5

The rest of the paper is organised as follows. First, the research design section provides the details of the data collected and software used. Next, a statistical analysis of data is presented, followed by hotspot analysis. Finally, the paper is concluded in Sect. 5.

2   Methodology

2.1   Source of Data

This study used data from the Web of Science databases. Web of science was chosen because of its wide coverage of publications on overall academic fields and includes all bibliographic information (e.g. authors, citations, journals) for analysis. The following search terms were used TOPIC: ("Artificial intelligence" OR "artificial-intelligence" OR "machine learning" OR "neural network" OR "neural-network" OR "machine-learning") AND TOPIC: ("marketing"). Only scientific articles written in English were used for this research. As a result, a dataset of 617 articles with a period of 1992 to 2020 were collected for this analysis.

2.2   Data Analysis Tool

This study employed CiteSpace to analyses the data. CiteSpace is the analytical tool that uses Java for visualizing and analysing patterns and trends in the scientific literature [14]. This tool was applied by a number of studies from various fields [12, 13].

3   Research Overview

3.1   Number of Publications by Year

In order to provide a picture of a development trend of the academic field, the number of publications over ears in AI in the marketing domain is presented in Fig. 1. As can be seen, the first article in this field was published in 1992. 56% of the articles were published in the last three years. The rapid increase from 2017 could be connected to the next-generation computing architecture, access to historical datasets, and advances in deep neural networks [15].

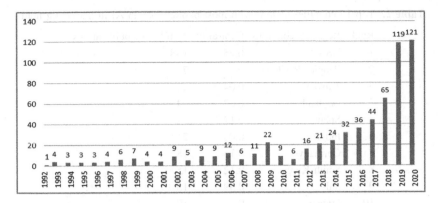

Fig. 1. Number of publications of AI in Marketing articles-1992–2020

3.2 Source of Publications

Table 1 presents the top 10 journals which published articles in the field of AI in Marketing. It was found that 617 articles were published in 353 journals. The most productive journal is found to be Expert systems with applications (45 articles), IEEE Access (14 articles), and European Journal of Operational Research (13 articles).

Table 1. Top 10 journals of AI in marketing research

Journal name	Number of articles	%
Expert systems with applications	45	7.293
IEEE Access	14	2.269
European Journal of Operational Research	13	2.107
Industrial Marketing Management	9	1.459
European Journal of Marketing	8	1.297
Marketing Science	8	1.297
Decision Support Systems	7	1.135
International Journal of Advanced Computer Science and Applications	7	1.135
Sustainability	7	1.135
Journal of Business Research	6	0.972

3.3 Major Publication Countries and Institutions Analysis

The top 15 countries of publications in the field of AI in Marketing are presented in Table 2. The USA, China, Taiwan, England, and Spain rank the top five and cover 48% of total publications in the dataset. It is observed that most of the countries on the list are highly economically developed countries.

Table 2. Top 15 countries/regions with most publications in AI in marketing field

Rank	Research countries	Centrality	Number of publications
1	USA	0.45	148
2	Peoples R China	0	71
3	Taiwan	0.04	31
4	England	0.67	24
5	Spain	0.12	24
6	India	0.08	21
7	Germany	0.16	18
8	South Korea	0.12	15
9	Italy	0.39	15
10	France	0	10
11	Australia	0.09	10
12	Turkey	0.01	9
13	Poland	0.02	7
14	Netherlands	0.06	6
15	Canada	0.12	5

To examine the collaboration between countries, node types "Country" was used in CiteSpce. Figure 2 shows the collaborated network between the countries. This network has 33 nodes, 46 links, and a density of 0.0871. The results show that strong cooperation exists in groups.

Fig. 2. Country collaboration network analysis

3.4   Author Analysis

The frequency of citations on a specific author can be applied to measure the level of influence in the field. In order to do it, node type "Author" in CiteSpace was used. Figure 3 provides a knowledge map of the highly cited authors and their collaboration network; and Table 3 shows the list of highly cited authors in the field.

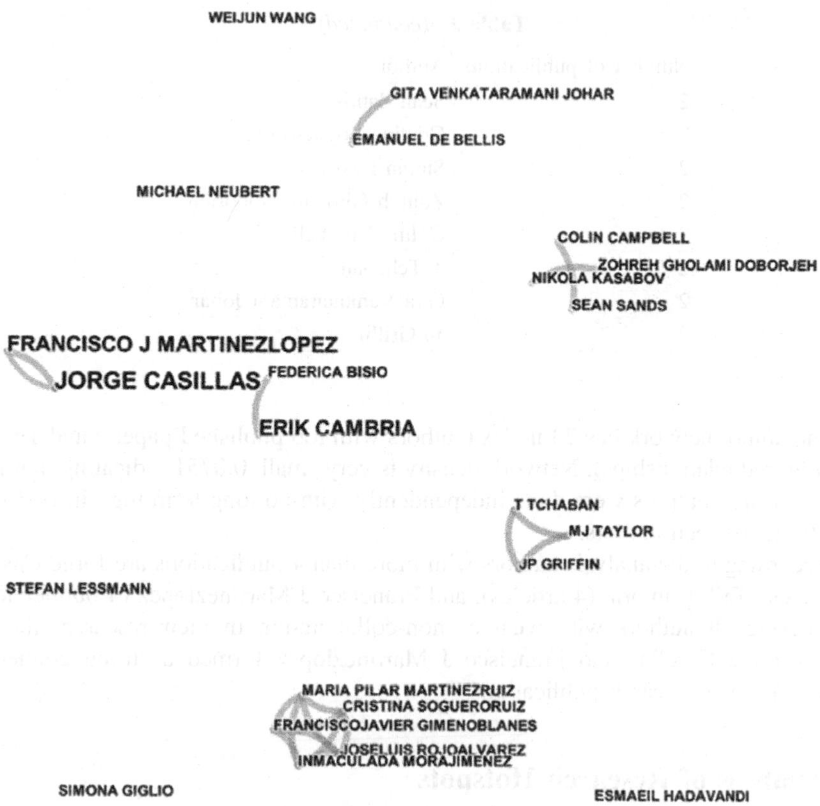

WEIJUN WANG

GITA VENKATARAMANI JOHAR

EMANUEL DE BELLIS

MICHAEL NEUBERT

COLIN CAMPBELL
ZOHREH GHOLAMI DOBORJEH
NIKOLA KASABOV

SEAN SANDS

FRANCISCO J MARTINEZLOPEZ

JORGE CASILLAS FEDERICA BISIO

ERIK CAMBRIA

T TCHABAN
MJ TAYLOR
JP GRIFFIN

STEFAN LESSMANN

MARIA PILAR MARTINEZRUIZ
CRISTINA SOGUERORUIZ
FRANCISCOJAVIER GIMENOBLANES
JOSELUIS ROJOALVAREZ
INMACULADA MORAJIMENEZ

SIMONA GIGLIO

ESMAEIL HADAVANDI

Fig. 3. Author collaboration network

Table 3. Most highly cited authors

Number of publications	Author
5	Jorge Casillas
4	Erik Cambria
4	Francisco J Martinezlopez
2	Maria Pilar Martinezruiz
2	Inmaculada Morajimenez
2	Michael Neubert
2	Nikola Kasabov
2	Franciscojavier Gimenoblanes
2	Weijun Wang
2	Mj Taylor
2	Joseluis Rojoalvarez
2	Emanuel De Bellis
2	Esmaeil Hadavandi
2	Federica Bisio
2	Simona Giglio

(*continued*)

Table 3. (*continued*)

Number of publications	Author
2	Sean Sands
2	Cristina Sogueroruiz
2	Stefan Lessmann
2	Zohreh Gholami Doborjeh
2	Colin Campbell
2	T Tchaban
2	Gita Venkataramani Johar
2	Jp Griffin

The author network has 23 nodes (authors with top published papers) and 19 links (co-authored relationships). Network density is very small, 0.0751 indicating that most of the research outputs were done independently with no long term high-intensity co-operations between authors.

According to the analysis authors with more than 4 publications are Jorge Casellas (5 articles), Erik Cambria (4 articles), and Francisco J Martinezlopez (4 publications). Considering all authors with weal or non-collaboration in their research, the two authors Jorge Casellas and Francisco J Martinezlopez formed a strong connection network in their research publications

4   Analysis of Research Hotspots

Hotspots in the research field can be identified by the analysis of keywords [12]. A knowledge map of keywords in AI in the marketing field is presented in Fig. 4. The keywords network has 141 nodes and 459 links.

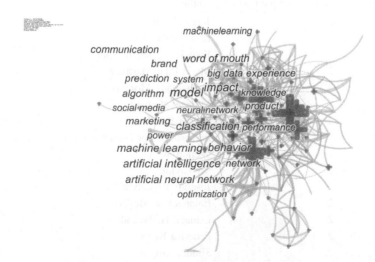

Fig. 4. Co-occurrence analysis of keywords

Table 4 presents the top 10 keywords according to frequency and centrality.

Table 4. Top 10 keywords according to frequency and centrality

Keyword	Frequency	Keyword	Centrality
Neural network	81	Model	0.21
Machine learning	74	Behaviour	0.19
Model	58	Classification	0.15
Classification	50	Artificial intelligence	0.15
Artificial intelligence	46	Algorithm	0.14
Marketing	35	Neural network	0.13
Social media	29	Machine learning	0.13
Impact	27	Framework	0.12
Algorithm	26	Experience	0.10
Artificial neural network	26	Choice	0.09

Log-likelihood Ratio (LLR) was used to cluster the keywords. The network was divided into 8 co-citation cluster. Four major clusters will be discussed in more details below.

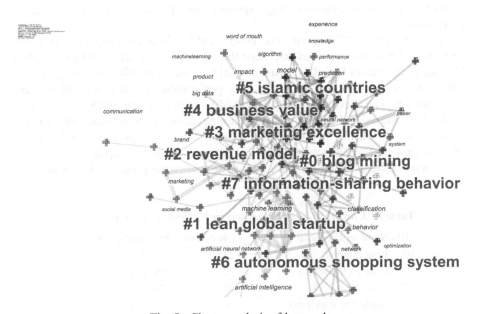

Fig. 5. Cluster analysis of keywords

The largest cluster (#0) which is label "Blog mining" has 23 members. Studies in this cluster investigate how online data collected from the internet (blogs, website, social media, e-commerce sites) can facilitate companies' decision-making process. For example, [16] focused on the use of blogs for gaining insights for companies about customer segmentation and classification. The study proposed a blog mining model that extracts knowledge from blogs. The experimental results demonstrated successful segmentation of customers and building classifier to predict characteristics of unknown customers. Another study by [17] showed how data such as movie viewing, basket addition, and purchase in e-commerce can be used for the development of deep learning-based prediction model of the next purchase in e-commerce. The experimental results showed that the proposed model based on time series analysis is more successful in comparison with other models (random forest, Autoregressive Integrated Moving Average, Convolutional Neural Network, Multilayer Perceptron). It is argued that it is important for companies to consider ethical concerns when applying AI in social media environment as it can result in consumers' distrust [18].

The second-largest cluster (#1) called "Lean global startup" has 22 members. This cluster is focusing on the use of AI to make strategic decisions. [19] argue that the application of AI in strategic marketing decisions has a number of benefits such as identification of missing data, increased rationality, incorporation of learning from experience, and creation of a common basis for decision-making.

Cluster #2 is named as "Revenue model" and has 20 members. The studies in this cluster are focusing on ways to maximise companies' revenues. For example, [20] built and tested a simulation model using large-scale eye-tracking data to train an artificial neural network. It was found that the model helps to forecast gaze hits for various types of marketing communications (e.g. sponsorship, product placement, in-game advertising).

Cluster #3 is named "Marketing excellence" and has 20 active members. Marketing excellence refers to the activities that shape the organisation, market, and environment [21]. One of the studies from this cluster by [22] focused on the effect of user-generated content from social media platforms on stock performance in the context of b2b and b2c companies. The study collected a dataset of 84 million tweets and 8 years of stock data for 407 companies. By using machine learning methods it was found that UGC has a positive impact on the company's stock performance. It was also found that this impact is stronger for b2c companies in comparison with b2b companies.

All eight clusters, their size, and example of studies are presented in Table 5.

Table 5. Clusters of research hotspots in the field of AI in marketing.

ID	Name of cluster label	Cluster size	Example of studies
0	Blog mining	23	[16, 17]
1	Lean global startup	22	[19, 23]
2	Revenue model	20	[20, 24]
3	Marketing excellence	20	[21, 22]
4	Business value	18	[25, 26]
5	Islamic countries	17	[27, 28]
6	Autonomous shopping system	10	[29, 30]
7	Information-sharing behaviour	9	[31, 32]

5 Conclusion

The current study identified the knowledge domain in the field of AI in Marketing by using the analysis of temporal distribution, cited countries, cited journals, cited authors, and hotspots from 1992 to 2020. The CiteSpace software was used for this quantitative analysis and visualizing the knowledge gap in AI in Marketing research. As a result, a holistic picture of this domain is provided which can help researchers to get an overview of this developing field.

Use of AI by companies can lead to new business models and create business value, as it has been proposed for big data analytics and ML techniques [18, 33–35]. Additionally, AI could be used beyond marketing in other fields such as healthcare, manufacturing, operations management, and transportation to name a few [36–38].

This study has some limitations. All the retrieved research articles were English-based, which could result in neglecting publications written in other languages. Future studies could conduct a study using multilanguage publications. Additionally, future research could use other databases such as Scopus and Google scholar to conduct the analysis.

References

1. Davenport, T., Guha, A., Grewal, D., Bressgott, T.: How artificial intelligence will change the future of marketing. J. Acad. Mark. Sci. **48**(1), 24–42 (2019). https://doi.org/10.1007/s11747-019-00696-0
2. Duan, Y., Edwards, J.S., Dwivedi, Y.K.: Artificial intelligence for decision making in the era of Big Data–evolution, challenges and research agenda. Int. J. Inf. Manage. **48**, 63–71 (2019)
3. Kuo, R.: A sales forecasting system based on fuzzy neural network with initial weights generated by genetic algorithm. Eur. J. Oper. Res. **129**, 496–517 (2001)
4. Hung, L.-P.: A personalized recommendation system based on product taxonomy for one-to-one marketing online. Expert Syst. Appl. **29**, 383–392 (2005)
5. Kaefer, F., Heilman, C.M., Ramenofsky, S.D.: A neural network application to consumer classification to improve the timing of direct marketing activities. Comput. Oper. Res. **32**, 2595–2615 (2005)
6. Zakaryazad, A., Duman, E.: A profit-driven Artificial Neural Network (ANN) with applications to fraud detection and direct marketing. Neurocomputing **175**, 121–131 (2016)
7. Liu, L., Zhou, B., Zou, Z., Yeh, S.-C., Zheng, L.: A smart unstaffed retail shop based on artificial intelligence and IoT. In: 2018 IEEE 23rd International Workshop on Computer Aided Modeling and Design of Communication Links and Networks (CAMAD), pp. 1–4. IEEE (2018)
8. Pillai, R., Sivathanu, B., Dwivedi, Y.K.: Shopping intention at AI-powered automated retail stores (AIPARS). J. Retail. Consum. Serv. **57**, 102207 (2020)
9. Gómez-Pérez, G., Martín-Guerrero, J.D., Soria-Olivas, E., Balaguer-Ballester, E., Palomares, A., Casariego, N.: Assigning discounts in a marketing campaign by using reinforcement learning and neural networks. Expert Syst. Appl. **36**, 8022–8031 (2009)
10. Dwivedi, Y.K., et al.: Artificial Intelligence (AI): multidisciplinary perspectives on emerging challenges, opportunities, and agenda for research, practice and policy. Int. J. Inf. Manage. (2019). https://doi.org/10.1016/j.ijinfomgt.2019.08.002

11. Martínez-López, F.J., Casillas, J.: Artificial intelligence-based systems applied in industrial marketing: an historical overview, current and future insights. Ind. Mark. Manage. **42**, 489–495 (2013)
12. Peng, R.-Z., Zhu, C., Wu, W.-P.: Visualizing the knowledge domain of intercultural competence research: a bibliometric analysis. Int. J. Intercult. Relat. **74**, 58–68 (2020)
13. Ye, N., Kueh, T.-B., Hou, L., Liu, Y., Yu, H.: A bibliometric analysis of corporate social responsibility in sustainable development. J. Clean. Prod. **272**, 122679 (2020). https://doi.org/10.1016/j.jclepro.2020.122679
14. Chen, C., Ibekwe-SanJuan, F., Hou, J.: The structure and dynamics of cocitation clusters: A multiple-perspective cocitation analysis. J. Am. Soc. Inform. Sci. Technol. **61**, 1386–1409 (2010)
15. MSV, J.: Here Are Three Factors That Accelerate The Rise Of Artificial Intelligence (2018). https://www.forbes.com/sites/janakirammsv/2018/05/27/here-are-three-factors-that-accelerate-the-rise-of-artificial-intelligence
16. Chen, L.-S., Hsu, C.-C., Chen, M.-C.: Customer segmentation and classification from blogs by using data mining: an example of VOIP phone. Cybern. Syst. Int. J. **40**, 608–632 (2009)
17. Utku, A., Akcayol, M.A.: Deep learning based prediction model for the next purchase. Adv. Electr. Comput. Eng. **20**, 35–44 (2020)
18. Dwivedi, Y.K., et al.: Setting the future of digital and social media marketing research: perspectives and research propositions. Int. J. Inf. Manage. 102168 (2020). https://doi.org/10.1016/j.ijinfomgt.2020.102168
19. Stone, M., et al.: Artificial intelligence (AI) in strategic marketing decision-making: a research agenda. The Bottom Line (2020). https://doi.org/10.1108/BL-03-2020-0022
20. Rumpf, C., Boronczyk, F., Breuer, C.: Predicting consumer gaze hits: a simulation model of visual attention to dynamic marketing stimuli. J. Bus. Res. **111**, 208–217 (2020)
21. Homburg, C., Theel, M., Hohenberg, S.: Marketing excellence: nature, measurement, and investor valuations. J. Mark. **84**(4), 1–22 (2020). https://doi.org/10.1177/0022242920925517
22. Liu, X.: Analyzing the impact of user-generated content on B2B firms' stock performance: big data analysis with machine learning methods. Ind. Mark. Manage. **86**, 30–39 (2020)
23. Neubert, M.: The impact of digitalization on the speed of internationalization of lean global startups. Technol. Innov. Manage. Rev. **8**(5), 44–54 (2018)
24. Tidhar, R., Eisenhardt, K.M.: Get rich or die trying… finding revenue model fit using machine learning and multiple cases. Strateg. Manage. J. **41**, 1245–1273 (2020)
25. Baray, J., Pelé, M.: A new geographical pricing model within the principle of geomarketing-mix. Recherche et Applications en Marketing (Engl. Ed.) **35**(3), 29–51 (2020). https://doi.org/10.1177/2051570720906077
26. Wamba-Taguimdje, S.-L., Wamba, S.F., Kamdjoug, J.R.K., Wanko, C.E.T.: Influence of artificial intelligence (AI) on firm performance: the business value of AI-based transformation projects. Bus. Process Manage. J. (2020). https://doi.org/10.1108/BPMJ-10-2019-0411
27. Kirilenko, A.P., Stepchenkova, S.O., Kim, H., Li, X.: Automated sentiment analysis in tourism: comparison of approaches. J. Travel Res. **57**, 1012–1025 (2018)
28. Sobhanifard, Y.: Hybrid modelling of the consumption of organic foods in Iran using exploratory factor analysis and an artificial neural network. Br. Food J. (2018). https://doi.org/10.1108/BFJ-12-2016-0604
29. De Bellis, E., Johar, G.V.: Autonomous shopping systems: identifying and overcoming barriers to consumer adoption. J. Retail. (2020). https://doi.org/10.1016/j.jretai.2019.12.004

30. Tsafarakis, S., Saridakis, C., Baltas, G., Matsatsinis, N.: Hybrid particle swarm optimization with mutation for optimizing industrial product lines: an application to a mixed solution space considering both discrete and continuous design variables. Ind. Mark. Manage. **42**, 496–506 (2013)

31. Kumar, S., Gahalawat, M., Roy, P.P., Dogra, D.P., Kim, B.-G.: Exploring impact of age and gender on sentiment analysis using machine learning. Electronics **9**, 374 (2020)

32. Wang, C.-Y., Lin, Y.-C., Chang, H.-C., Chou, S.-C.T.: Consumer sentiment in tweets and coupon information-sharing behavior: an initial exploration. In: Information Diffusion Management and Knowledge Sharing: Breakthroughs in Research and Practice, pp. 823–842. IGI Global (2020)

33. Mikalef, P., Pappas, I.O., Krogstie, J., Pavlou, P.A.: Big data and business analytics: a research agenda for realizing business value. Inf. Manage. **57**, 103237 (2020)

34. Pappas, I.O., Mikalef, P., Giannakos, M.N., Krogstie, J., Lekakos, G.: Big data and business analytics ecosystems: paving the way towards digital transformation and sustainable societies. IseB **16**(3), 479–491 (2018). https://doi.org/10.1007/s10257-018-0377-z

35. Kar, A.K., Dwivedi, Y.K.: Theory building with big data-driven research–Moving away from the "What" towards the "Why". Int. J. Inf. Manage. **54**, 102205 (2020). https://doi.org/10.1016/j.ijinfomgt.2020.102205

36. Mikalef, P., Fjørtoft, S.O., Torvatn, H.Y.: Artificial Intelligence in the public sector: a study of challenges and opportunities for Norwegian municipalities. In: Pappas, I., Mikalef, P., Dwivedi, Y., Jaccheri, L., Krogstie, J., Mäntymäki, M. (eds.) Digital Transformation for a Sustainable Society in the 21st Century. I3E 2019. Lecture Notes in Computer Science, vol. 11701, pp. 267–277. Springer, Cham (2019). https://doi.org/10.1007/978-3-030-29374-1_22

37. Sun, T.Q., Medaglia, R.: Mapping the challenges of Artificial Intelligence in the public sector: Evidence from public healthcare. Gov. Inf. Quart. **36**, 368–383 (2019)

38. Grover, P., Kar, A.K., Dwivedi, Y.K.: Understanding artificial intelligence adoption in operations management: insights from the review of academic literature and social media discussions. Ann. Oper. Res. 1–37 (2020). https://doi.org/10.1007/s10479-020-03683-9

Emerging Technologies and Emergent Workplaces: Findings from an Ethnographic Study at an Indian IT Organization

Vinay Reddy Venumuddala[✉] and Rajalaxmi Kamath

Indian Institute of Management Bangalore, Bengaluru, Karnataka, India
vinay.venumuddala17@iimb.ac.in

Abstract. Over the past four decades, Indian Information Technology (IT) industry has been delivering traditional software and BPM (Business Process Management) services to its clients across the globe. Providing cost-optimized, yet high-quality services following standard process methodologies has made it an attractive destination to clients across industry verticals. Today, the challenge before this industry is to provide emerging technology solutions to clients in their digital transformation drive. Situated at this pivotal juncture in its journey, the 'work from home' (WFH) norm during to the recent COVID-19 pandemic posits challenges of a new kind for this sector. We explore these challenges based on our four-month ethnographic study (Jan-May, 2020) in a service-based IT organization situated in Bengaluru, which over the past five years has been developing Artificial Intelligence (AI) based solutions to its clients.

Keywords: Work from home · Artificial Intelligence · Indian IT industry

1 Introduction

Indian Information Technology (IT) Industry has now had over a four-decade history of providing software and business process outsourcing/management (BPO/M) services to its clients across the globe. It has moved from providing labour arbitrage driven simple software coding and BPO services, to providing high-end custom software and BPM services [1–3]. Providing cost optimized, yet high quality software and BPM services, following standard process methodologies has made Indian IT an attractive destination to clients across industry verticals [3]. The challenge before this industry today is to provide emerging technology solutions around Artificial Intelligence (AI), Big Data, Cloud and IoT, to clients in their digital transformation drive. While developing new technology solutions that build on existing standard process workflows may be smooth, the challenge is to integrate solutions around technologies such as AI which require an overhaul of process workflows [4, 5].

Situated at this pivotal juncture in its journey, the 'work from home' (WFH) norm during to the recent COVID-19 pandemic posits challenges of a new kind for this sector. Though the usual software services and emerging technology projects continued to be served with employees working from home [6], visible concerns around security and infrastructure limitations made it harder for Indian IT/BPM firms to facilitate their

© IFIP International Federation for Information Processing 2020
Published by Springer Nature Switzerland AG 2020
S. K. Sharma et al. (Eds.): TDIT 2020, IFIP AICT 617, pp. 54–66, 2020.
https://doi.org/10.1007/978-3-030-64849-7_6

employees working from home [7]. In our study we attempt to understand the impact of WFH as it was unfolding in an AI based project in an Indian IT organisation. We were involved in an ethnographic study in a service-based IT organization situated in Bengaluru, which has been developing and delivering customized software solutions over the past 25 years and for the past 5 years has started delivering AI based projects to its long-standing clients. As a part of this ethnographic study, during the months Jan-May, 2020, one of us worked as an intern in this organization and was a member of a running AI project team. Because of the nation-wide lock-down due to pandemic in March 2020, the researcher worked for about 3 months in office and slightly over a month at home. Serendipitously, we were thus able to observe the nature of work interactions between employees both in office and while working on the project from home. Our research method, which is to carry out ethnographies at workplaces, is motivated by the works of Barley and Kunda [8, 9]. Our findings suggested that while the organization's efforts in streamlining workflows for AI project are still a work in progress and fraught with challenges, these challenges have further deepened because of a transition to WFH during this pandemic. We illustrate this gap by deep diving into the nature of interaction between work roles in a typical AI project carried out in office and how it changed during work from home.

2   Emerging Technologies Indian IT and WFH

2.1   Emerging Technologies and Indian IT Sector

A major portion of Indian IT industry is constituted by organizations that cater to custom software and BPO/M services. As of the year 2016, these services together contributed to around 49% of the total service exports from the country, to over 7% of the country's GDP, and constituted over 70% of the offerings from this industry in total [10]. Prior to the year 2000, Indian IT was mainly known for providing simple software programming services relying on its vast pool of engineers, with limited scope for technical innovation or managerial contributions [1]. The key driver during this time was the reengineering movement of the 90 s which necessitated a standardization of work processes and practices around software development and business process outsourcing so that the work can be distributed across the globe [2]. This service globalization facilitated Indian IT companies to provide customized software and BPO services that were mainly driven by labour or cost arbitrage deals [1–3]. Further global standard software platforms reduced the reliance on firm-specific investments, as individuals anywhere from the globe could now cater to the business requirements provided they have the necessary skills to work on such platforms [2]. This implied a vast manpower availability, in the form of engineering workforce, enabled the Indian IT industry to quickly reap the benefits from this global changes in service industry [1, 2]. Not only did Indian IT helped global enterprises with skilled manpower at low cost, but they also ensured quality of software and service delivery. Majority of the global IT companies that registered highest levels in their maturity of software development processes were from India [3, 11].

Today, both the IT and BPM segments of the industry have to gear up to provide emerging technology solutions to its clients around Artificial Intelligence (AI) and Cloud. Immense amount of data is being generated within organizations across industry verticals, and the social world, at an unprecedented rate in terms of its volume, variety, velocity and veracity constituting what is often termed as the 'Big Data' [12]. Analysing such Big Data will rely on cloud services to manage the data storage and service requirements [13], and AI based solutions can generate actionable insights from such data for organizational decision makers [12, 14]. Adoption of these new technologies enhance the competitive advantage of firms [15], through improvements in their supply chains [16], by enabling swift responses to prospective business opportunities [17], enhancing the likelihood to produce new products and services in comparison to their peers [18], and therefore improve their overall performance [17]. Driven by these factors clients are driven to adopt emerging technology solutions and for which they are again looking towards their long-standing service providers – the Indian IT [19]. While Indian IT traditionally catered to a majority of clients from industry verticals like manufacturing, telecom, banking and finance, driven by digital transformation goals around emerging technologies new verticals like retail and healthcare are getting added to this list [10]. The need for delivering emerging technology solutions to clients is necessitating organizations within Indian IT to incorporate new work roles, and form new teams to develop in-house capabilities around such technologies. These teams are now comprised of diverse work roles spanning both traditional and emerging technologies such as data scientists, data/cloud/software engineers, cloud/software architects, and also including traditional project management roles such as business analysts, and project managers [10, 20]. It is now imperative for Indian IT organizations working on integrated software and emerging technology projects, to facilitate a seamless collaboration across such a diversity of work roles.

2.2   Work from Home

With the COVID-19 pandemic shifting the office work to home, a slew of changes are expected in the manner in which work might be carried out in future if the situation persists over a longer period of time. It is expected that the usage of digital platforms and the demand for expert workforce in technologies such as Cloud might increase, while the need for commute and office space may come down. Further, in the long term, working from home may also lead to detrimental effects on work-life balance of employees, when the convenience of working from home gives rise to some sort of 'permanently-at-work' culture [21]. In addition to these expected changes, literature also discusses about the ways in which digital work can alter the forms of leadership and work autonomy [22], how they can blur the boundaries between public and private spheres of life [23]. Increased digital work can also result in 'techno stress' [24], reduce employee autonomy [25] and therefore it is important that organizations carefully balance all these positives and negatives of WFH [26].

While these impacts of WFH are discussed in the context of organizations in general, we intend to understand the concrete implications of WFH in Indian IT service-based organizations that are currently transitioning towards providing emerging technology solutions, in particular around AI. It is widely acknowledged that a move towards providing AI solutions, that require building machine learning (ML) models, requires a rather revolutionary adjustment of existing traditional software work processes [4, 27]. The absence of strict abstraction boundaries between different ML work components [4, 27], forecloses the possibility of modular development [4], warranting a constant iterative interactions between work-roles handing different stages of the ML workflow [4, 5, 27]. In contrast to AI solution development, the key tenets of traditional software development are that it is modular, and allows for customizability and reuse of software programs or modules [4, 28]. These tenets enable clear division of tasks between various work roles in different stages of an SDLC, i.e., software development life cycle [29–31]. Our ethnography provided us an opportunity to observe the WFH related challenges facing an AI team within this service-based IT organization, who have been attempting to work around the traditional standardized software development processes while working for an AI project.

3   Research Context and Methodology

3.1   Empirical Context

Our empirical context is a service-based organization based in Bengaluru, India, providing IT-BPM services to its clients across the globe for over 25 years. In addition to traditional software and BPM services, this organization in the past few years has been actively responding to the emerging technology needs of its clients. By gathering members from traditional software teams and recruiting employees for new roles, this organization has formed an in-house team specifically for this purpose. This team, which we call AI team, has been developing customized AI solutions for clients seeking business process automation, and in the process accumulated several proprietary AI solutions (IPs) over the past 5 years. Solution stack constituted by such IPs has enabled this organization to not only offer turnkey services around AI for its future clients, but also to deploy them over cloud platforms such as AWS (Amazon Web Services), Azure and GCP (Google Cloud Platform) allowing their generic usage in the online marketplace. While client centric projects formed the major source of building IPs (for eventual customization and reuse), research projects related to AI utilizing off-the-shelf data is another source. Since our research objective was to understand the changing nature of work and mobility in the Indian IT industry, working as a resource in a project was beneficial over formal interviews or questionnaires, because it allowed us to understand the situated work-practices as they unfolded. Taking into account our research objectives, and the researcher's prior qualifications (industry experience, and knowledge of machine learning from doctoral coursework) the head of the team assigned three tasks to the intern while he/she worked in this team. (1) to work as a full-time resource in a running Natural Language Processing (NLP) based project, (2) to understand, identify and document a common workflow based on the team members' experience of working across multiple projects over the past 5 years, and (3) to periodically report our research findings to members from the team. The first two tasks were considered as a value-addition that the researcher would bring to the team, and the last task was to help researcher triangulate and validate his/her findings. These assigned tasks allowed researcher to become a usual member of the team.

3.2 Ethnography at Workplace

According to Barley [9], study of work in organizational theory has gone into the background, and many studies either simply acknowledge the complexity of work or just gloss over the 'issue of how work might be changing'. However, according to him, pushing the complexities of work into the background while studying organization is not of much help in understanding organizational change. Because, "when nature of work in an organisation changes because of new technologies, or markets - organisational structures have to adapt or risk becoming misaligned with the activities they organise" [8]. It is therefore argued that bringing work back into organizational studies is imperative especially in today's context where technologies are rapidly evolving and markets are constantly expanding, affecting organizations both from within and from outside. Our method of research was ethnography at a workplace motivated by these works of Barley and Kunda [8, 9]. According to them, ethnographic research that engages closely with work practices, allows researchers to provide 'in-situ' explanations about the complexities of work and how they impact organizational responses to changes happening in the environment around. While providing a rich 'emic' perspective or the 'native point of view' about the day-to-day work and work interactions, it also motivates the researcher to simultaneously relate it with the 'etic' concepts which are the 'analytic constructs removed from the native point of view' [8]. It also provides a possibility to understand the deeper causes of organizational change with changing nature of work [8, 9]. Further in the context of work roles within organizations, by studying situated and actual roles rather than ideal-typical ones, researchers can have a more nuanced understanding of these roles, both in their relational and nonrelational aspects.

3.3 Data

Working with team members in a project, joining them for breakfast, lunch, and coffee, engaging in impromptu conversations near cubicles, attending team meetings, knowledge transfer sessions, birthday celebrations, employee farewells, and many more events laid the basis for the researcher building a strong rapport with the team members. Further, the assigned task of conducting unstructured interviews with some of the team members to understand the project work flows, allowed the researchers to get a concrete sense of the overarching work processes within the organizational structure. Since the researcher had also worked from home for over a month, he/she was able to document the nature of interactions between different work roles that happened in the context of an AI project. The contrasting observations between work interactions at office and from home, in the context of this project was the prime motivation to carry out this particular study. Observations during interactions at work (either in office or from home), unstructured interviews, and impromptu conversations, allowed the researcher to not only internalize his experiences from the field, but also document them in rich detail on a daily basis in the field notes. This field notes were constantly shared between the two researchers, which motivated numerous discussions and reflections which guided our overall research. Our ethnographic field notes ran into over 100 single-spaced pages that amounted to over 75000 words. In total the ethnographer closely interacted with around 24 team members with their experience in this industry ranging from 6 months to over 15 years. These members occupy work roles such as data engineers, business analysts, managers, data scientists, software engineers, technical architects, and team lead.

4 Findings – AI Projects and Work Interactions

A majority of the AI projects taken up by this team were for the long-standing clients of this organization. Having established itself as a major service provider of IT-BPM services to its clients over two decades, it has recently ventured into providing emerging technology solutions. Standard work processes around custom software maintenance and BPM services ensured this organization to maintain quality while delivering cost optimized solutions. As a continuation of this client-service provider relationship, most of the long-standing clients of this organization now expect it to also provide AI based solutions. However, given the organizational structure built around traditional software and BPM, a majority of the projects were of an integrated nature, predominantly AI integrated on top of traditional BPO or custom software services. Nevertheless, in the process of working on AI projects for clients over the past 5 years, the AI team within this organization also managed to develop standalone IP cores related to AI, with the intention of enabling reuse for future projects.

4.1   Typical Project Workflow

One of the researcher's assigned task of documenting project workflows, enabled us to observe an important aspect of AI projects within this organization – the continued dominance of traditional software work processes. The project proposal meetings often revealed that there were inherent assumptions about customizability and reuse of AI project components previously developed. During the team meetings, those in project management roles like the business analysts, and managers, usually presented high-level architectural diagrams that assumed some sort of modularity in AI project components. During their initial stages, many of these projects involved constant back and forth interaction between clients, and project managers and data scientists from this organization to enable AI use-case identification. However, after these initial rounds, when data engineers take up the execution tasks, status of work was often evaluated through agile status meetings. An experienced senior manager in this regard said that, 'in service-based companies where research wings on AI are setup, they often tend to follow traditional software kind of methodologies.' Since the organization has to make trade-offs between accuracy and resource usage in these projects, we find the Team Lead and Project Managers pushing for maximum reuse of existing project components. Data-scientists are typically considered costly resources, and as a result they are often engaged only during the initial stages of the project or while eventual signing-off of the work done by data engineers. In an ideal scenario, the two major work components, i.e., data pre-processing and model development need to be worked out in tandem for a given use case [4, 27]. But what we noticed in typical AI projects here, was a clear separation of tasks between data engineers who work predominantly on the pre-processing components, and data scientists who work independently on the model development tasks. Data scientists are more involved in the work of IP development from the client's business use-cases. As a result, they pick up off-the-shelf data sets relevant to similar use-cases and build standalone machine learning (ML) models as IPs to be reused in future projects. Data engineers on the other hand, encountering a changing volume and variety of data from the clients during the time of project execution, are constantly involved in sharpening the pre-processing programs for feature data-extraction. Insofar as model development is concerned, they often end up feeding their extracted data to the standalone IPs that have already been developed by the data scientists, which would now be a part of the solution stack of this team. While this strategy could result in an accuracy drop [4, 27], the 'project managers' (business analysts and managers) find it a better option because given the manual validation by BPO workforce to fill the gaps, it saves costs.

4.2   Project Execution and Work Interactions in Office

The ethnographer worked with two data engineers, business analyst, and a senior manager, during the project execution phase, where he/she worked closely with the two data engineers and their work together was periodically overseen by a senior manager and a business analyst. Weekly status meetings were therefore organized between the data engineers and the business analyst and/or project manager in order to evaluate the progress. Since the project was ultimately headed by the team lead, a monthly status meeting used to be conducted where the team lead evaluated the overall progress of the project and the work done by each of the data engineers. This project like standard AI projects involve pre-processing data, model-building, training, and deployment which ideally needs constant collaborative efforts across different work roles [4]. However, we observe a separation of tasks and very little formal collaboration between work roles in this team. At the start of the project, the data engineers' task was to build on existing pre-processing programs taken from previous projects and try to see if they can be reused for the given client use-case. It was too early in the project execution phase and the volume and variety of client data was so low that it was hard for the data engineers to even think of model building. Model building needs data that is representative of the observations related to client's business use-case – and therefore it calls for ample volume/sample size, and enough variety. Despite not having a chance to build models, the data engineers used to have informal discussions with the data scientists about the appropriate model building strategy and the fit of the existing IPs to be used in the future, for this project.

In office, such discussions happened at the convenience of the data-scientists who sat very close to our cubicles. Data-scientists, involved with IP development for the organisation, often are part of the proposal/project initiation phases of upcoming projects, and work towards streamlining AI workflows. It is not easy to get their time. Their skype (formal chat platform for employees) status used to be one of 'do-not-disturb', 'busy' or, 'in-a-meeting' all the time. To give an instance, for the very first meeting around a better way to start executing the current AI project, the researcher and the two data engineers caught the data scientist during lunch and talked to him about the project. We also asked him for his free time when we could have a discussion about this. Since he was busy, he called sometime later in the evening and explained on a white-board in a discussion room about how he developed ML models around similar use-case for a previous project that is now an IP. After an hour, he quickly realized that there is another meeting that he was required to attend, and left abruptly. But over the next couple of days, the data engineers were still able to ask him their doubts and get clarifications, whenever they found him free in his office.

However, the interaction between data engineers and business analysts/senior managers was slightly different. Their task was to oversee the data engineers' utilization and project status and these meetings were more formal and happened on a weekly basis. During these meetings each of the data engineers present the status of their work, and what they intend to do in future. A formal meeting with team lead that happened on a monthly basis also proceeded along similar lines, only that the team lead interacted mostly with the project managers, who in turn questioned the data engineers about the progress. Following quotes from our field notes summarize the kind of interactions that happened during these meetings.

> Data Engineers (DE) reporting status to Business Analyst (BA)/Project Manager (PM): *"We tried this out, we worked on this with the help of another person [software engineer] in the team. There are some problems that we are facing. We will ask any data scientist in the team and finalize the way to go for this problem."*
> BA reply to the DEs: *"BA seems to be guiding the implementation based on his experience from previous project. He is directing the Data Engineers for building plans for themselves and work. During the meeting he made statements like we need to identify, we need to do this, don't do everything at once, take up one task after the other, try a script or hand-based rules for this problem, you guys refer to what we did in our previous project, look at the files that were prepared."*
> PM reply to the DEs: *"If you are finding that this problem is taking too long time and needs extra hands, you can take help from any data engineer or check with any data scientist whenever he/she is free. In the previous project we did it like this. In your whiteboard discussion with data scientist he would have explained you some 3–4 approaches. Take 1 or 2 and try them out and see if they work."*

Not only with respect to their own projects, but the overall work in office allowed these data engineers to gain knowledge from their team mates about other projects and also about other kind of work beyond AI, such as integrating AI modules into existing softwares and their deployment in the cloud. The researcher was part of many such informal discussions these data engineers had with their lunch mates who were also their college friends. Conversations between them always started with a common question, 'what are you currently working on?', that is posed on a daily basis. Unknowingly, in these conversations, a good amount of talk about happenings in their organization, knowledge of the projects they are working on, and the projects others were working on, got passed around. From the field notes, we were thus able to intuit these informal channels through which 'tacit' knowledge got accumulated within an organization.

Lastly, the researcher noticed that the data engineers usually worked together to complement each other's work when in office. We noticed that one of them was good at programming, while the other was reluctant to spend time on programming and instead was more interested in the model building component of their project. Anything related to the project they used to engage in it together. The one who was less interested in programming used to consciously find ways to engage with data scientists. He used to take his fellow mate and approach data scientists whenever he found them free and used to engage in informal discussions about existing ML strategies for different projects. He also used to ask business analysts to involve him in the meetings with clients so that he could understand the business use case better. The other person who was good at programming used to similarly approach software/cloud engineers and architects for getting clarifications about best ways to build their pre-processing programs, to gain a general understanding of how the software/cloud engineers usually integrate AI modules on custom software and how they deploy it in the cloud, and so on. Since both of them mostly worked together, despite one person's initiative, both the team members used to benefit from such interactions.

To summarise, we noticed that, the overarching work processes in this organisation, which are heavily oriented towards traditional software development have provided very few formal avenues for data engineers to gain understanding beyond their data pre-processing work. However, we observe that in the office spaces, informal interactions with their seniors afforded them a possibility for gaining such understanding. For example, they were able to approach data scientists about ML model building, cloud architects about model deployment in cloud and business analysts about the nature of client interactions, informally. This was less likely within the formal project setup that was largely dominated by the regular project meetings between data engineers and those executing the project in the organisation.

4.3 Project Meetings During WFH

"Less or no scope for informal knowledge sharing like in office. Every call becomes a client call where one reports status and other evaluates status. Persuading supervisors through effective communications becomes most important." – Reflections from attending project status meetings online, Field Notes

During the lock down period when employees of this team were asked to work from home, the dynamics of interaction between team members working on this AI project had changed. The formal status meetings with project managers and the team happened online, but still followed a similar style of interactions. But the data engineers now lost all those informal pathways to gain situated knowledge from experienced technical experts and business analysts which used to be possible while in office.

"WFH demands that individuals spend a lot more time before having to present anything in a meeting. A lot more work needs to be done in preparing the presentation so that it can be shared, read out and articulated properly so that the others could understand. Further it happened that the two data engineers were asked to present their respective works, and it became difficult for them to segregate and present. While in the meeting room last time they were able to take turns and jointly present, here it was a bit difficult for them to do that, so they divided the same presentation between the two and presented." - Reflections from attending project status meetings online, Field Notes

Another conspicuous observation we could identify based on the online project status meetings was the mode of communication. We noticed that the two data engineers who used to work together while preparing their status presentations in office, failed to do that when the meetings shifted online. Each one of them independently prepared very detailed presentations indicating their share of work done in the project. Hitherto in office, especially during the status meetings with the business analysts and managers, we noticed that the two data engineers used to go onto the board intermittently while presenting their progress of work in the project. Sometimes when their presentations weren't ready, they used to present their status on the board, extempore. However, with work from home, we noticed that in every weekly status meeting and the monthly meeting, they came with detailed presentations describing what they have done over that particular week or month and what will they do in future.

We also noticed that clarity of presentation is very important during these online meetings. For example, the two data engineers during their presentations in office were able to complement each other while presenting, since they worked on it or at least discussed with each other in office. However, during online meeting we noticed that this did not happen. Since each of them prepared their presentations independently and didn't get a chance to informally discuss, like they would have done in office, we noticed that while one of them was presenting the other was silent.

5 Discussion and Conclusion

Our situated description of project work flows at the organizational level indicate that there is a clear separation of tasks between data scientists and the data engineers, which is not ideal while developing an AI project [4, 27]. Further, based on the interaction between work roles during the regular project status meetings, we observe that the traditional project managers continue to push for customization and reuse of prior project components. As a result, in this organisation, AI projects are still being carried through the traditional software workflows and processes. Building workflows suiting AI projects, which allow for constant back and forth collaboration between work roles, is still a work in progress. We observed that data scientists who are engaged in developing standalone AI related IPs, were also actively trying to promote workflow changes suiting the requirements of AI projects. Data Engineers on the other hand are making efforts to go beyond the task separation envisaged within traditional software methodologies, and collaborate with other work roles. Office spaces provided them avenues for having informal interactions with data scientists which enabled them to reflect about ML model building while working on their usual pre-processing tasks. However, during WFH, data engineers were unable to gain this situated understanding of ML model development. On the other hand, the influence of traditional software project management continued undeterred even when project meetings shifted online. Figure 1 illustrates the interaction between work roles and changes during WFH diagrammatically.

From our ethnographic findings and discussion, it is clear that this IT based organization, is largely embedded in traditional software work processes, despite its avowed move towards delivering AI based projects. However, we surmise that the lack

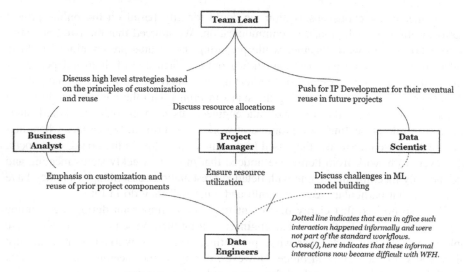

Fig. 1. Work interactions during AI project

of formal AI workflows was actually being made good, tacitly, through informal interactions among its employees. In the absence of a well laid out AI structure, the beginning of what goes in the name of 'tacit' AI structure was being actualized in this organization. To that end, the Organization had done the right thing in having a nascent 'AI team', irrespective of work domains, where all employees working on such AI projects sat and worked together. This is bound to change with the shift towards WFH, as replicating such tacit structures online is a challenge facing this organization. While for established MNCs, that specialize in emerging technologies, and provide plat-formised AI products to the industry, transition to WFH might not be that difficult. However, for Indian IT industry which is newly venturing into these emerging technologies, we find that the extant organizational workflows and processes are posing unique challenges that needs attention.

References

1. Arora, A., Arunachalam, V.S., Asundi, J., Fernandes, R.: The Indian software services industry. Res. Policy **30**(8), 1267–1287 (2001)
2. Dossani, R., Kenney, M.: The next wave of globalization: relocating service provision to India. World Dev. **35**(5), 772–791 (2007)
3. Jalote, P., Natarajan, P.: The growth and evolution of India's software industry. Commun. ACM **62**(11), 64–69 (2019)
4. Amershi, S., et al.: Software engineering for machine learning: a case study. In: 2019 IEEE/ACM 41st International Conference on Software Engineering: Software Engineering in Practice (ICSE-SEIP), pp. 291–300 (2019)
5. Zaharia, M., et al.: Accelerating the machine learning lifecycle with MLflow. IEEE Data Eng. Bull. **41**(4), 39–45 (2018)

6. News18: Work from home: if the experiment works, it can continue when the world is better again, 09 Apr 2020
7. Economic Times: Covid-19 impact: IT firms seek client waivers so staff can work from home, 16 Mar 2020
8. Barley, S.R., Kunda, G.: Bringing work back in. Organ. Sci. **12**(1), 76–95 (2001)
9. Barley, S.R.: Technicians in the workplace: ethnographic evidence for bringing work into organizational studies. Adm. Sci. Quart. **41**(3), 404–441 (1996)
10. NASSCOM: IT-BPM strategic review. Nat. Assoc. Softw. Serv. Comp. (2017)
11. Naidu, B.V.: India: emerging knowledge base of the 21st century. STPI: Delhi, vol. 72 (2006)
12. Abbasi, A., Sarker, S., Chiang, R.H.: Big data research in information systems: toward an inclusive research agenda. J. Assoc. Inf. Syst. **17**(2), 3 (2016)
13. Buytendijk, F.: Hype cycle for big data. Gartner (2014)
14. Constantiou, I.D., Kallinikos, J.: New games, new rules: big data and the changing context of strategy. J. Inf. Technol. **30**(1), 44–57 (2015)
15. Chen, H., Chiang, R.H., Storey, V.C.: Business intelligence and analytics: from big data to big impact. MIS Quart. **36**(4), 1165–1188 (2012)
16. Wang, G., Gunasekaran, A., Ngai, E.W., Papadopoulos, T.: Big data analytics in logistics and supply chain management: certain investigations for research and applications. Int. J. Prod. Econ. **176**, 98–110 (2016)
17. Liu, Y.: Big data and predictive business analytics. J. Bus. Forecast. **33**(4), 40 (2014)
18. Ransbotham, S., Kiron, D.: Analytics as a source of business innovation. MIT Sloan Manage. Rev. **58**(3) (2017)
19. Fersht, P., Snowdon, J.: Making the leap from strategic to effective BPM. Nat. Assoc. Softw. Serv. Comp. (2016). Accessed 16 Apr 2020. https://www.nasscom.in/knowledge-center/publications/making-leap-effective-strategic-bpm
20. NASSCOM: Uncovering the True value of AI, executive AI playbook for enterprises. Nat. Assoc. Softw. Serv. Comp. (2019)
21. De, R., Pandey, N., Pal, A.: The tech effects of Covid-19, and offices of the future, 02 Aug 2020
22. Dittes, S., Richter, S., Richter, A., Smolnik, S.: Toward the workplace of the future: how organizations can facilitate digital work. Bus. Horiz. **62**(5), 649–661 (2019)
23. Jarrahi, M.H., Crowston, K., Bondar, K., Katzy, B.: A pragmatic approach to managing enterprise IT infrastructures in the era of consumerization and individualization of IT. Int. J. Inf. Manage. **37**(6), 566–575 (2017)
24. Ayyagari, R., Grover, V., Purvis, R.: Technostress: technological antecedents and implications. MIS Quart. **35**(4), 831–858 (2011)
25. Mazmanian, M., Orlikowski, W.J., Yates, J.: The autonomy paradox: the implications of mobile email devices for knowledge professionals. Organ. Sci. **24**(5), 1337–1357 (2013)
26. Richter, A.: Locked-down digital work. Int. J. Inf. Manage. **55**, 102157 (2020)
27. Sculley, D., et al.: Hidden technical debt in machine learning systems. In: Advances in Neural Information Processing Systems, pp. 2503–2511 (2015)
28. de Souza, C.R., Redmiles, D., Cheng, L.-T., Millen, D., Patterson, J.: Sometimes you need to see through walls: a field study of application programming interfaces. In: Proceedings of the 2004 ACM Conference on Computer Supported Cooperative Work, pp. 63–71 (2004)
29. Dennis, A., Wixom, B.H., Roth, R.M.: Systems Analysis and Design. Wiley (2018)

30. Esbensen, M., Bjørn, P.: Routine and standardization in global software development. In: Proceedings of the 18th International Conference on Supporting Group Work, pp. 12–23 (2014)
31. Yilmaz, M., O'Connor, R.V., Clarke, P.: A systematic approach to the comparison of roles in the software development processes. In: International Conference on Software Process Improvement and Capability Determination, pp. 198–209 (2012)

Learning Environments in the 21st Century: A Mapping of the Literature

Tumaini Kabudi$^{(\boxtimes)}$, Ilias Pappas, and Dag Håkon Oslen

University of Agder, Kristiansand, Norway
tumaini.kabudi@uia.no

Abstract. Education has been transformed by significant breakthroughs in AI, mobile internet, cloud computing and Big Data technologies. More personalized educational settings are developed by increasingly integrating contemporary learning environments with new technologies. However, few examples of executed AI enabled learning interventions have been identified. Therefore, a mapping of literature on AI enabled learning systems was done. 121 studies published in the last five years were analyzed. This paper presents a discussion regarding on what mainly AI enabled contemporary learning environments are designed to achieve. The major contribution of the study is bringing awareness to researchers and system developers on the purposes of AI enabled contemporary learning environments. This review will act as a guide for future studies on how to better design AI enabled learning environments.

Keywords: Contemporary learning environments · AI · Systematic literature mapping · Adaptive learning systems

1 Introduction

AI enabled learning environments are gaining traction as they can deliver learning content and adapt to individual student needs. [1]. These contemporary learning systems are characterized by students thriving in a digital environment, where current technologies shape expectations of students and *"their abilities to access, acquire, manipulate, construct, create and communicate information"* [2]. The resources in AI enabled learning environments (both physical and virtual) are developed to deliver effective learning, by helping students construct their knowledge. Adaptive learning systems, Intelligent tutoring Systems and Recommender systems are good examples of recent AI enabled learning environments. Research on intelligent tutors, Big Data analytics, learning analytics and educational data mining techniques developed these AI enabled learning systems. Recommender systems are *"software tools based on machine learning and information retrieval techniques that provide suggestions for potential useful items to someone's interest"* [3]. On the other hand, Adaptive learning systems are platforms for personalized learning that adapt to students' learning strategies, the sequence and difficulty of the task, learning styles, abilities, time of feedback and preferences [4]. The advantages of using adaptive learning systems include efficiency, interaction, support and effectiveness [5]. These systems encourage

S. K. Sharma et al. (Eds.): TDIT 2020, IFIP AICT 617, pp. 67–76, 2020.
https://doi.org/10.1007/978-3-030-64849-7_7

students to own their learning journey via automated feedback cycles that allow the students to progress independently from the course instructor.

Advancement in new data analytical techniques has brought more successful learning systems in the education sector. Furthermore, several studies have discussed on how AI techniques can be applied to learning systems. Nevertheless, few examples of executed AI enabled learning interventions have been identified [6]. Consequently, implementation of these systems in education settings seems to be at its early stage. It is stated, *"Many of these learning systems as well as Intelligent Tutoring Systems (ITS) are described in the literature, and their effectiveness has been proved. However, these systems are rarely used in real educational settings practices in ordinary courses."* [7]. ITS are basically designed to enable tutoring and personalized support. In Addition, another significant challenge is bridging the gap between pedagogy and emerging AI techniques.

The main aim of this study was to map latest literature and present the summarized findings related to contemporary learning systems. The main research question of this study is: "What are the AI enabled learning environments designed to do?" The topic discussed in this paper is AI-enabled learning systems, which deliver solutions for overcoming challenges students face. These challenges include inefficiently capturing student proficiency, lacking metacognition to self-assess students' knowledge decay, lack of accommodation of practical skills in the systems, facing student disengagement and poor student motivation and utilizing outdated adaptation technologies [8, 9]. The next section introduces the systematic literature mapping (SLM) process, search protocol and results from the execution of the SLM. Results and Analysis are presented in Sect. 3. Section 4 concludes the paper with summarized discussions of findings from retrieved literature and recommendations.

2   Research Methodology

This study was conducted using the systematic literature review methodology guidelines proposed by [10]. The researchers utilized EndNote X9, NVivo 11 and Excel spreadsheets to extract publication outlets, find duplicates and organize the information. A review protocol was used to guide the whole research method. This study selected previous works published in the past five years to avoid outdated research.

The first step in conducting the systematic review is to formulate the search strategy. This strategy is formulated based on review protocol to reduce research bias. The search strategy was formulated by following and expanding the research question. Then search keywords were identified and search strings generated to minimize the number of articles. Synonyms and substitute spellings were identified too. Focus was placed on two main terms of interest to perform database searches. These two main terms of interest included "adaptive learning system" and "artificial intelligence". Two parallel searches were conducted as the two main terms of interest are sometimes used interchangeably. "Adaptive learning ecosystem," "adaptive learning environment," "adaptive learning platform," "adaptive learning setting" and "adaptive learning technology" were used as synonyms for adaptive learning system. The Boolean operators *OR* and *AND* were used.

The search was conducted between November and December 2019. The search was done on eight databases i.e. ACM, Web of Science, EBSCO Host, Wiley, SAGE Journals, IEEE Xplore, Scopus, and Taylor and Francis. These eight databases were chosen as they have wide selection of relevant and recent articles in this SLM/SLR. The databases include numerous AI-related academic journals such as Journal of Artificial Intelligence and Soft Computing Research, IEEE Transactions on Pattern Analysis and Machine Intelligence, British Journal of Educational Technology, and International Journal of Intelligent Systems. 1699 articles were retrieved using the above-mentioned search strategies. These number of articles were retrieved also by choosing the publication years between 2014 and 2019. To reduce the number of retrieved articles, the study went under further refinement. Several articles were selected by considering certain criteria. This was done to ensure that the selected articles are relevant and answer the RQ. Consequent to the search, all documents retrieved went through duplicate removal using EndNote software. Figure 1 shows steps of the study selection criteria, which comprises inclusion and exclusion criteria.

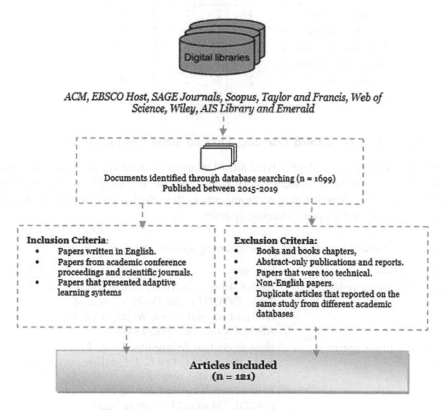

Fig. 1. The systematic literature mapping process

3   Results and Analysis

The 121 selected papers were published between 2014 and 2019. In terms of publication channels, 63 of the papers were academic journals, 55 were conference papers, and 3 were published in conference proceedings. The selected papers were categorized based on the type of research approach used. This categorization is based on an existing research approach classification by Wieringa et al. (2006). Evaluation research was the most utilized research approach (35 articles), followed by validation research (30 articles). The third and fourth used research approach were the philosophical approach and literature review approach, with 24 and 22 papers, respectively. The distribution of documents per year is shown in Table 1. A note to the reader: The complete database that include all the 121 references in RIS format can be downloaded

Table 1. The distribution of papers per year

	2014	2015	2016	2017	2018	2019
Evaluation research	4	4	7	7	4	9
Literature review	0	3	4	9	2	4
Validation research	2	0	7	6	8	7
Philosophical paper	2	3	3	6	5	5
Solution proposal	0	2	0	2	2	3
Opinion paper	0	0	0	0	0	1

3.1   RQ: What AI Enabled Learning Environments Designed to Do

The study's RQ aimed to identify what are AI enabled learning environments designed to do. As shown in Table 1, there are different types of AI enabled learning environments. Majority of these learning environments in the selected papers were intelligent tutoring systems and adaptive learning systems.

Table 2. Kinds of AI-enabled learning systems and their examples

Kind of system	Examples	References
Intelligent tutoring system	English Tutor, AutoTutor, Passive Voice Tutor, INTUITEL, the DARPA Tutor, Ms. Lindquist, Crystal Island, Wayang Outpost, ANDES, Guru, ACTIVEMATH	[7, 11–17]
Adaptive learning system	Fishtree, System designed by Tseng, S., Su J., Hwang, G.J. Tsai C. J, QuizBot, Adaptive Mobile Learning System (AMLS), Personalized Adaptive Learning Dashboard (PALD), "MostSaRT" system, Smart Sparrow, System developed by Realizeit, OPERA, LearnSmart, Personal Assistant for Life-Long Learning (PAL3), INSPIREus, ProSys INSPIRE	[13, [8, 18–26]

(*continued*)

Table 2. (*continued*)

Kind of system	Examples	References
Adaptive system	Student Diagnosis, Assistance, Evaluation System based on Artificial Intelligence (StuDiAsE), The LeaPTM system, ADAPTIVE INSTRUCTOR OPERATING SYSTEMS	[22, 27, 29]
AI enabled system (machine learning)	The Early Recognition System, MeuTutor	[29]
A knowledge grid based intelligent system personalized E-learning system	KGTutor	[30]
Adaptive digital teaching and learning environment	Connect ™	[31]
Intelligent and adaptive learning environment	FIT Java Tutor	[15]
Web-based intelligent computer-assisted language learning (iCALL) system	E-Tutor	[15]
Adaptive and intelligent web based educational systems (AIWBES)	SQL-Tutor, ALEA, Quiz Guide and Flip	[32]
Adaptive learning environment	ACTIVEMATH	[15]
Context-aware adaptive mobile learning system	Units of Learning mobile (UoLmP)	[21]
Intelligent learning system	Yixue	[33]
Intelligent system	BOXFiSH	[34]
Recommendation system	NetCoach	[22]

Table 2 highlights the various categories and themes of the designed aims of these AI enabled learning environments. Many of the published papers identified that the AI enabled learning environments were designed to assist with teaching several courses. These courses included mathematics, physics, psychology, nursing, computer literacy and biology. It was also identified that these systems were designed as platforms to teach and learn languages. The identified languages that were taught in these systems include English, German, and Greek. Another category of what AI enabled learning environments were designed to do is improve students' performance through Personalization of Learning. These systems were designed to act as platforms to provide personalized content based on their level. Also, the AI enabled learning environments are designed to teach and learn programming languages such as SQL and Java. The rest remaining identified themes are shown in the table below (Table 3).

Table 3. Categories of what AI enabled learning environments designed to do

Category	Examples of the mentioned systems	References
Teach courses (17)	System developed by Realizeit, OPERA, ACTIVEMATH, AutoTutor, Ms. Lindquist, UZWEBMAT, AutoTutor, Crystal Island, Oscar Wayang Outpost, ANDES, Guru, ACTIVEMATH, English Tutor, Student Diagnosis, Assistance, Evaluation System based on Artificial Intelligence (StuDiAsE), Yixue, Lumilo	[13, 14, 17, 23, 33, 35–37]
Platforms for teaching and learning languages (6)	QuizBot, AutoTutor, Passive Voice Tutor, BOXFiSH, E-Tutor	[11–13, 15, 34]
Improve students' performance through personalization of learning (8)	Adaptive Mobile Learning System (AMLS), INSPIREus MeuTutor Knewton, INSPIRE, Units of Learning mobile (UoLmP), An Online Webbased Adaptive Tutoring System, Connect™	[18, 21, 26, 38–40]
Platform for quizz, exercises, training (6)	Smart Sparrow, Tamaxtil, affective tutoring system (ATS), QuestionIT	[16, 18, 19, 41–43]
Teach and help with programming language (5)	SQL-Tutor, The intelligent Teaching Assistant for programming (ITAP), ALEA, QuizGuide and Flip, FIT Java Tutor, Gerdes' tutor	[15, 32]
Evaluate and improve students' knowledge (4)	LearnSmart, Personal Assistant for LifeLong Learning (PAL3), DeepTutor, Protus	[8, 15, 25, 36]
Consider and examine learners requirements (4)	Personalized Adaptive Learning Dashboard (PALD) "MostSaRT" system, INTUITEL, KGTutor	[7, 21, 22, 30]
Identify and inform students (2)	The LeaPTM system, The Early Recognition System	[22, 29]

4 Discussion and Conclusion

There were some interesting insights revealed in the conducted SLM. Regarding types of AI enabled learning environments, intelligent tutoring systems and adaptive learning systems were the most utilized. Our mapping of the literature revealed that the use of both these types of systems play an important role to improve performance of students through personalization of their learning, and mitigating poor levels of motivation [15, 41, 44, 45]. A possible reason of adaptive learning systems and intelligent tutoring systems to be mostly used is the recent acknowledgement of AI enabled learning environments in assisting teaching languages, several courses and programming languages. The increasing usage of these systems is in agreement with [8] and [9] on using AI enabled learning environments to improve students' performance, improve students' knowledge, and examine learners requirements such as previous knowledge and the learners' targets. Our review indicated that however there is low number of implemented interventions designed to address major concerns and problems identified in the papers. Difficulty in attaining learners' skills, background and profile of student issues are some of the overlooked concerns. This observation is in agreement with [46] who identified that designers of adaptive learning systems give little attention to courses that have practical skills as a prerequisite. This research gap should be addressed.

Designing and assessing adaptive courses issues, in our review, are problems that are not highly considered. The low usage of adaptive learning systems concern is noted by [7]. The authors stated, *"Many of these learning systems as well as Intelligent Tutoring Systems (ITS) are described in the literature, and their effectiveness has been proved. However, these systems are rarely used in real educational settings practices in ordinary courses."* This concern needs to be addressed in the research of AI enabled learning environments in the future. The issue of better designing adaptive learning systems and adaptive courses should be given attention to increase the usage of these systems in real educational settings. Only three papers out of 121 papers identified this concern to be addressed [15, 47, 48].

The contribution of this study is the identification of AI enabled learning systems and what they are designed to do. It is to be noted that the AI enabled learning environments are still underresearched. The other contribution of this study is to bringing awareness to researchers and system developers on contemporary learning systems. Hopefully, the study will provide important insights for practitioners in education settings who are interested in adaptive learning systems. The authors recommend for future research, more adaptive learning systems, frameworks and models should be developed. More systems should be developed in order to provide solutions for overcoming the overlooked problems that students face, especially attaining skills [49]. The existing systems lack novel AI techniques or tools for students to practice and master their learning skills. This lack is because of complex measurement models for skills and limited learning support. Nevertheless, this challenge can be addressed by boosting the learning content in the adaptive learning system using AI techniques [50]. A system that accommodates the required skills and requirements for students is also needed. Similarly, to address the issue of complexity, current adaptive learning models should be enhanced by AI techniques building on learning analytics [49].

Due to the nature of research, this study was related with several limitations. The search words, strings and databases may have limited the review, despite the recommendations by [10] were followed. The key strings were limited to adaptive learning systems only. The key strings may be extended to other types of contemporary learning environments, such as recommender systems. Also, the selected databases, inclusion criteria and exclusion criteria may have excluded some studies. In addition, research questions like what problems and concerns did the AI enabled contemporary learning environments address and types of interventions that utilized AI in addressing the problems were not reviewed. These research questions can be reviewed in future research.

References

1. Mousavinasab, E., Zarifsanaiey, N., Niakan Kalhori, S.R., Rakhshan, M., Keikha, L., Ghazi Saeedi, M.: Intelligent tutoring systems: a systematic review of characteristics, applications, and evaluation methods. Interact. Learn. Environ. 1–22 (2018)
2. Green, T.D., Donovan, L.C.: Learning anytime, anywhere through technology. In: The Wiley Handbook of Teaching and Learning, pp. 225–256 (2018)
3. Syed, T.A., Palade, V., Iqbal, R., Nair, S.S.K.: A personalized learning recommendation system architecture for learning management system. In: IC3K 2017 – Proceedings of 9th International Joint Conference on Knowledge Discovery, Knowledge Engineering and Knowledge Management, vol. 1, pp. 275–282 (2017)
4. Johnson, D., Samora, D.: The potential transformation of higher education through computer-based adaptive learning systems. Glob. Educ. J. 2016(1), 1–17 (2016)
5. Hasanov, A., Laine, T.H., Chung, T.S.: A survey of adaptive context-aware learning environments. J. Ambient Intell. Smart Environ. 11(5), 403–428 (2019)
6. Wakelam, E., Jefferies, A., Davey, N., Sun, Y.: The potential for using artificial intelligence techniques to improve e-learning systems, pp. 762–770 (2015)
7. Verdú, E., et al.: Intelligent tutoring interface for technology enhanced learning in a course of computer network design. In: Proceedings - Frontiers in Education Conference, FIE, vol. 2015, February 2015
8. Hampton, A.J., Nye, B.D., Pavlik, P.I., Swartout, W.R., Graesser, A.C., Gunderson, J.: Mitigating knowledge decay from instruction with voluntary use of an adaptive learning system. In: Penstein Rosé, C., et al. (eds.) AIED 2018. LNCS (LNAI), vol. 10948, pp. 119–133. Springer, Cham (2018). https://doi.org/10.1007/978-3-319-93846-2_23
9. Tommy, R., Amala, N., Ram, S., Kumar, B., Jose, H.: Intelligent and Adaptive Test System. Information Science and Applications (ICISA) 2016. LNEE, vol. 376, pp. 895–902. Springer, Singapore (2016). https://doi.org/10.1007/978-981-10-0557-2_85
10. Kitchenham, B., Charters, S.: Guidelines for performing systematic literature reviews in software engineering. Technical report, Ver. 2.3 EBSE Technical Report. EBSE (2007)
11. Bradáč, V., Kostolányová, K.: Intelligent tutoring systems. J. Intell. Syst. 26(4), 717–727 (2017)
12. Lippert, A., Gatewood, J., Cai, Z., Graesser, A.C.: Using an adaptive intelligent tutoring system to promote learning affordances for adults with low literacy skills. In: Sottilare, R.A., Schwarz, J. (eds.) HCII 2019. LNCS, vol. 11597, pp. 327–339. Springer, Cham (2019). https://doi.org/10.1007/978-3-030-22341-0_26
13. Ruan, S., et al.: QuizBot: a dialogue-based adaptive learning system for factual knowledge. In: Conference on Human Factors in Computing Systems – Proceedings (2019)
14. Brawner, K.W., Gonzalez, A.J.: Modelling a learner's affective state in real time to improve intelligent tutoring effectiveness. Theor. Issues Ergon. Sci. 17(2), 183–210 (2016)
15. Bimba, A.T., Idris, N., Al-Hunaiyyan, A., Mahmud, R.B., Shuib, N.L.B.M.: Adaptive feedback in computer-based learning environments: a review. Adapt. Behav. 25(5), 217–234 (2017)
16. Fletcher, J.D.: Adaptive instructional systems and digital tutoring. In: Sottilare, R.A., Schwarz, J. (eds.) HCII 2019. LNCS, vol. 11597, pp. 615–633. Springer, Cham (2019). https://doi.org/10.1007/978-3-030-22341-0_48
17. Almohammadi, K., Hagras, H., Alghazzawi, D., Aldabbagh, G.: A survey of artificial intelligence techniques employed for adaptive educational systems within e-learning platforms. J. Artif. Intell. Soft Comput. Res. 7(1), 47–64 (2017)

18. Kasinathan, V., Mustapha, A., Medi, I.: Adaptive learning system for higher learning. In: ICIT 2017 - 8th International Conference on Information Technology, Proceedings, pp. 960–970 (2017)

19. Natriello, G.: The adaptive learning landscape. Teach. Coll. Rec. **119**(3) (2017)

20. Pandey, B., Mishra, R.B., Khamparia, A.: CBR based approach for adaptive learning in e-learning system (2014)

21. Louhab, F.E., Bahnasse, A., Bensalah, F., Khiat, A., Khiat, Y., Talea, M.: Novel approach for adaptive flipped classroom based on learning management system. Educ. Inf. Technol. **25**(2), 755–773 (2019)

22. Liu, M., McKelroy, E., Corliss, S.B., Carrigan, J.: Investigating the effect of an adaptive learning intervention on students' learning. Educ. Tech. Res. Dev. **65**(6), 1605–1625 (2017)

23. Johanes, P., Lagerstrom, L.: Adaptive learning: the premise, promise, and pitfalls, vol. June 2017 (2017)

24. Oliveira, M., Barreiras, A., Marcos, G., Ferreira, H., Azevedo, A., De Carvalho, C.V.: Collecting and analysing learners data to support the adaptive engine of OPERA, a learning system for mathematics. In: CSEDU 2017 - Proceedings of the 9th International Conference on Computer Supported Education, vol. 1, pp. 631–638 (2017)

25. Sun, Q., Abdourazakou, Y., Norman, T.J.: LearnSmart, adaptive teaching, and student learning effectiveness: an empirical investigation. J. Educ. Bus. **92**(1), 36–43 (2017)

26. Dounas, L., Salinesi, C., El Beqqali, O.: Requirements monitoring and diagnosis for improving adaptive e-learning systems design (2019)

27. Samarakou, M., et al.: Evaluation of an intelligent open learning system for engineering education. Knowl. Manag. E-Learn. **8**(3), 496–513 (2016)

28. Milham, L.M., Pharmer, J.A., Fok, A.W.: Adaptive instructor operating systems: design to support instructor assessment of team performance. In: Proceedings of the Human Factors and Ergonomics Society, vol. 2015-January, pp. 1801–1805 (2015)

29. Ciolacu, M., Tehrani, A.F., Binder, L., Svasta, P.M.: Education 4.0 - artificial intelligence assisted higher education: early recognition system with machine learning to support students' success. In: 2018 IEEE 24th International Symposium for Design and Technology in Electronic Packaging, SIITME 2018 - Proceedings, pp. 23–30 (2019)

30. Mudrak, M.: Analysis and implementation of adaptive course in Moodle. IN: ICETA 2017 - 15th IEEE International Conference on Emerging eLearning Technology and Applications Proceedings (2017)

31. Kakish, K., Pollacia, L.: Adaptive learning to improve student success and instructor efficiency in introductory computing course, pp. 72–78 (2018)

32. Jonsdottir, A.H., Jakobsdottir, A., Stefansson, G.: Development and use of an adaptive learning environment to research online study behaviour (2015)

33. Wang, S., Feng, M., Bienkowski, M., Christensen, C., Cui, W.: Learning from an adaptive learning system: Student profiling among middle school students. In: CSEDU 2019 - Proceedings of the 11th International Conference on Computer Supported Education, vol. 1, pp. 78–84 (2019)

34. Cui, W., Xue, Z., Thai, K.P.: Performance comparison of an AI-based adaptive learning system in China. In: Proceedings 2018 Chinese Automation Congress, CAC 2018, pp. 3170–3175 (2019)

35. Sosnovsky, S., Chacon, I.A.: Semantic gap detection in metadata of adaptive learning environments. In: Proceedings - IEEE 14th International Conference on Advanced Learning Technologies, ICALT 2014, pp. 548–552 (2014)

36. Gallego-Durán, F.J., Molina-Carmona, R., Llorens-Largo, F.: Measuring the difficulty of activities for adaptive learning. Univers. Access Inf. Soc. **17**(2), 335–348 (2017)

37. du Boulay, B.: Escape from the skinner box: the case for contemporary intelligent learning environments. Br. J. Educ. Technol. **50**(6), 2902–2919 (2019)
38. De Santana, S.J., Paiva, R., Bittencourt, I.I., Ospina, P.E., De Amorim Silva, R., Isotani, S.: Evaluating the impact of mars and venus effect on the use of an adaptive learning technology for Portuguese and mathematics. In: Proceedings - IEEE 16th International Conference on Advanced Learning Technologies, ICALT 2016, pp. 31–35 (2016)
39. Wongwatkit, C.: An online web-based adaptive tutoring system for university exit exam on IT literacy. In: International Conference on Advanced Communication Technology, ICACT, 2019, vol. 2019-February, pp. 563–568 (2019)
40. Kakish, K., Pollacia, L.: Adaptive learning to improve student success and instructor efficiency in introductory computing course. In: Proceedings of the 34th Information Systems Education Conference, ISECON 2018, pp. 72–78 (2018)
41. Padron-Rivera, G., Joaquin-Salas, C., Patoni-Nieves, J.-L., Bravo-Perez, J.-C.: Patterns in poor learning engagement in students while they are solving mathematics exercises in an affective tutoring system related to frustration. In: Martínez-Trinidad, J.F., Carrasco-Ochoa, J.A., Olvera-López, J.A., Sarkar, S. (eds.) MCPR 2018. LNCS, vol. 10880, pp. 169–177. Springer, Cham (2018). https://doi.org/10.1007/978-3-319-92198-3_17
42. Houa, M., Fidopiastis, C.: A generic framework of intelligent adaptive learning systems: from learning effectiveness to training transfer. Theor. Issues Ergon. Sci. **18**(2), 167–183 (2017)
43. Milham, L.M., Pharmer, J.A., Fok, A.W.: Adaptive instructor operating systems: design to support instructor assessment of team performance. In: Proceedings of the Human Factors and Ergonomics Society, vol. 2015-January, no. 1, pp. 1801–1805 (2015)
44. El Janati, S., Maach, A.: Towards a new adaptive e-learning framework for adapting content to presentation. In: 2017 Intelligent Systems and Computer Vision, ISCV 2017 (2017)
45. Maravanyika, M., Dlodlo, N., Jere, N.: An adaptive recommender-system based framework for personalised teaching and learning on e-learning platforms. In: 2017 IST-Africa Week Conference, IST-Africa 2017 (2017)
46. Xie, H., Chu, H.C., Hwang, G.J., Wang, C.C.: Trends and development in technology-enhanced adaptive/personalized learning: a systematic review of journal publications from 2007 to 2017. Comput. Educ. **140** (2019)
47. Chen, W., Joe-Wong, C., Brinton, C.G., Zheng, L., Cao, D.: Principles for assessing adaptive online courses (2018)
48. Tsarev, R.Yu.: An approach to developing adaptive electronic educational course. In: Silhavy, R. (ed.) CSOC 2019. AISC, vol. 986, pp. 332–341. Springer, Cham (2019). https://doi.org/10.1007/978-3-030-19813-8_34
49. Papamitsiou, Z., Economides, A.A., Pappas, I.O., Giannakos, M.N.: Explaining learning performance using response-time, self-regulation and satisfaction from content: an fsQCA approach. In: ACM International Conference Proceeding Series, pp. 181–190 (2018)
50. Giannakos, M.N., Sharma, K., Pappas, I.O., Kostakos, V., Velloso, E.: Multimodal data as a means to understand the learning experience. Int. J. Inf. Manag. **48**, 108–119 (2019)

Artificial Intelligence in Practice – Real-World Examples and Emerging Business Models

Jayanthi Radhakrishnan[(⊠)] and Sumeet Gupta

Indian Institute of Management Raipur, Atal Nagar, P. O. – Abhanpur, Raipur
493 661, (C.G.), India
{19efpm001, sumeetgupta}@iimraipur.ac.in

Abstract. There are everyday examples of Artificial Intelligence (AI) in different areas. Some of the prominent AI applications are virtual assistants, robots, AI applications related to computer vision and those used in medicine. This paper attempts to examine the recent trend of the real-world applications of AI and also identify the business models for these. The business models are then examined to see if these are existing business models that are used to enhance businesses using AI or if new AI-driven business models have emerged. The emerging AIdriven business models are Federated learning, the triangular partnership model and the use of Emotion AI to come up with new business models. The existing ones enhanced by AI are the freemium model, Rent to Buy model, leverage customer data and the land and expand model.

Keywords: Artificial Intelligence · AI in practice · AI real-world examples · AIdriven business models

1 Introduction

Artificial Intelligence (AI) – machine intelligence that enables machines to perform cognitive functions that are mostly associated with human minds is revolutionizing businesses around the world. There are several everyday examples of how AI applications are impacting our lives. The collection and availability of huge amounts of data coupled with improvements in computer technology have made it possible to use AI for various functions. Research shows that AI has applications in numerous areas such as agriculture [18], in autonomous vehicles [1], computer vision [12], in virtual assistants [13], chatbots both in the private firms and in Government [3], in robots [17] and medicine [21]. Research papers present advances made in the medical field using AI in areas such as cardiology [11], drug discovery [6] and ophthalmology [20].

According to the McKinsey Report[1], there has been a substantial increase in the number of companies that use AI in multiple areas of their business with an almost 25% increase in the use of AI as compared to the previous year in standard business processes. The report also talks about an increase in revenue in the business areas

---

[1] https://www.mckinsey.com/featured-insights/artificial-intelligence/global-ai-survey-aiproves-its-worth-but-few-scale-impact.

S. K. Sharma et al. (Eds.): TDIT 2020, IFIP AICT 617, pp. 77–88, 2020.
https://doi.org/10.1007/978-3-030-64849-7_8

where AI was used and also a reduction in costs. Uses of AI are spread across a wide range of industries and business functions. AI is being used for business process automation, to create intelligent robots, chatbots for customer service, customer segmentation, agricultural process automation, educational learning platforms, virtual assistants, to build medical tools, surgical robots and as radiology assistants.

Considering that AI is still in evolving stage and business models using AI are yet to emerge clearly, in this study we wish to delineate a possible evolution of AI-driven business models. This aspect of AI has remained relatively unexplored in the research papers.

AI is driven by vast data, raw computing power, and complex algorithms. Are organizations using AI to enable and enhance the businesses using existing business models or are they using AI to create new business models? The aim of this paper is to understand the current status of AI in practice and summarize the most recent AI implementations by different organizations as well as to delineate business models emerging in the field of AI. This has been done by analyzing company reports, website articles, and research papers. To the best of our knowledge, there is a lack of systematic study in this area. The specific research questions addressed in this study are: (i) What are the real-world implementations of AI and the business models used? (ii) Is AI being used to enhance businesses by using an existing business model or are there new AIdriven emerging business models?

2 Literature Review

To understand the state of research on AI, we searched for keywords 'AI in Practice' in ScienceDirect, Google Scholar, and the Internet. We looked for research articles, review articles and real-world examples of applications of AI. Research papers have been published on AI implementations for use in robots, agriculture, computer vision, cognitive engagement, and in medicine in areas such as cardiology and drug discovery. The real-world examples of AI applications were categorized into different areas, namely, medicine, robotics, agriculture, computer vision, and cognitive engagement. The AI-driven business models were also identified for these areas. Here we present a review of studies on AI applications in various areas as well as the AI business models emerging in these areas.

2.1 Medicine: Cardiology

Echocardiography. AI can be used for automated interpretation of echocardiograms with accurate and consistent results. They will help, especially those with less experience, to treat and diagnose more accurately [2].

Heart Murmur Detection. Astudy was done to classify heart sounds into normal and murmur types [8].

Ejection Fraction Calculation. In a research study, ejection fraction (EF) was calculated using ECG image analysis and AI trained pattern recognition. Auto EF could calculate EF in 15 s. The results showed less variability when compared to the manual process [5].

Table 1. Real-world AI applications in medicine

Application	Description	Business/Revenue model
Apple Watch ECG https://www.apple.com/in/applewatch-series-5/	It captures heart rhythm irregularities. Users take own ECG and data is passed on to the doctors	Integrator Business Model - Apple owns it completely with a vertically integrated model integrating operating systems, hardware, application software, and services. On-device Edge AI - Training and Inference done on the device keeping personal data under control ensuring customer privacy
AI-ECG Platform, Lepu Medical http://www.carewellhealth.com/products_aiecg.html	A diagnostic program that can detect various heart conditions	Open Business Model/Partnership: Has a strategic agreement with Intel. The goal is to diversify their respective services and capabilities in the medical AI fields thus strengthening both companies
Cloud-based eMurmur ID Platform. https://emurmur.com	Cloud-based eMurmur ID Platform	Freemium Business Model– eMurmur Primer - free. Core - In-App Purchases, subscription-based. eMurmur University offers comprehensive heart murmur training & testing modules free for instructors and students
Artery's Cardio AI https://www.acrdsi.org/DSIServices/FDA-Cleared-AI-Algorithms	For viewing and quantifying cardiovascular MR images. To visualize and quantify MRI data	Open Business Model/Partnership – Arterys and GE Healthcare have collaborated to combine Arterys's medical imaging technology with GE's magnetic resonance cardiac solutions. The result is a diagnosis that is comprehensive

The most predominant AI-driven business model in Cardiology is the Open Business Model/Partnership model showing the trend of medical firms and AI startups/technological companies teaming up to innovate and provide end to end solutions. Apple follows the Integrator Business Model and on-device Edge AI to address privacy concerns and network latencies for individual users. The Freemium model and Community edition vs paid enterprise edition Model are also used where the basic version is offered free and the customers are charged for the premium version which in turn finances the free version.

2.2 Robotics

Humanoid Robots. Several studies have examined the application of AI in the area of humanoid robots. A good example of this would be Sophia – a humanoid robot – which expresses and interacts the way a real human does. Another humanoid robot called the NAO robot was explored in a study where the robot plays the role of an artist. Different techniques were studied to overcome calibration issues [19]. In another study, the walking behaviour of a humanoid robot was studied where the robot walks faster than usual and safe reinforcement learning was proposed [9].

Robotics in Surgery. The application of robotics in surgery has been on the rise. The da Vinci robot was one of the first to be used for minimally invasive surgeries. The da Vinci robot is currently being used in various fields such as urology, general surgery, gynaecology, cardiothoracic, paediatric and ENT surgery" [15]. A study was done to understand how good the robot manoeuvres were when used in laparoscopic surgeries. "A hierarchical intelligent expert system was proposed. The method was constructed based on the integration of a swarm-based clustering approach, modular extreme learning machine (M-ELM) identifier, and Mamdani fuzzy system" [14].

Home Robotics. The robot-integrated smart home (RiSH) with capabilities to monitor and assist elderly residents integrates a home service robot that recognizes "37 human activities with an average accuracy of 88% and detects falling sounds with an accuracy of 80%", a home sensor and body sensor networks, a mobile device, cloud servers along with remote caregivers [7].

Table 2. Real-world AI applications in robotics

Application	Description	Business/Revenue model
Medical Robots - AIassisted surgery robot. http://microsure.nl/ microsurefor-surgeons	It can suture tiny blood vessels that are as small as 0.03 mm and up to 0.08 mm across	Rent or Buy Business Model Medical Robots – Revenue model includes "leasing, pay-peruse, bundled payments, rental agreements, and expanded payment terms, among others."
Sophia by Hanson Robotics https://www. hansonrobotics.com/ sophia/	Humanoid robot able to display over 50 facial expressions. Little Sophia is 14" tall and is just like big sister Sophia	Rent or Buy Business Model - The price of Little Sophia is somewhere between $99 and $149. Sophia is available for participation in public events and takes part in topics related to AI and robotics
Connie, the Hilton Robot Concierge	The robot uses IBM WATSON. It has speech recognition, interacts with guests, learns and adapts over time	Open Business Model/Partnership - The robot is based on a humanoid Nao robot made by French robotics company Aldebaran. Software is Watson from IBM, which mostly helps with natural language processing. Travel information is from WayBlazer, an IBM partner that uses Watson for personalized recommendations.[a]
1A-TA, Amadeus's travel assistant using Pepper Robot	Pepper cognitive development kit integrated with some complex deep learning AI algorithms	Rent or Buy Revenue Model – SoftBank's Pepper and Nao Robots available for rent or purchase.[b]

[a]https://www.theverge.com/2016/3/9/11180418/hilton-ibm-connie-robot-watson-hotel-concierge
[b]https://www.robot-rentals.com/

The predominant business model in this area is the Rent or Buy Revenue Model/Rent to Own business model. The robots are available for rent, on lease and for purchase. The other model followed is the Open Business Model. Connie, the Hilton Concierge uses a NAO humanoid robot, IBM Watson for natural language processing and WayBlazer for the travel Information.

2.3 Agriculture

In the field of agriculture, AI has been used for crop protection and weed control. AI is used in precision agriculture to detect and remove weeds by using computer vision to identify potato plants and 3 different kinds of weeds. Image processing was used to train and test the neural network classifiers which were optimized by two meta-heuristics algorithms [18]. An AI-based smart sprayer with a machine vision software using deep learning to detect specific weeds was developed and evaluated [16].

Table 3. Real-world AI applications in agriculture

Application	Description	Business/Revenue model
Blue river, weed control – "See and Spray". www.bluerivertechnology.com	It uses computer vision to monitor and spray weedicide precisely	Open Business Model/Partnership-John Deere & Company, which designs, manufactures, and distributes innovative agricultural products, acquired Blue River. Together, there are many opportunities in agriculture beyond spraying.[a]
Harvest CROO Robotics strawberry harvester https://harvestcroo.com	Helps strawberry farmers in picking and packing their crops	Rent to Own Business Model- The business model is to "lease machines from HCR on a per box basis. This emulates how they do business now, which is to pay humans a piece-rate." The objective is to make it easier for the grower and to create a continuous revenue stream for the company.[b]

[a]https://www.deere.com/en/our-company/news-and-announcements/news-releases/2017/corporate/2017sep06-blue-river-technology
[b]https://www.roboticsbusinessreview.com/rbr/harvest_croo_robotics_strawberry_picker/

2.4   Computer Vision

There has been an enormous growth in computer vision applications. There is a vast amount of data that is generated today and which is used as training data to make computer vision better. The research papers in this area talk about using AI Deep learning algorithms in classifying images for detecting various illnesses. It is also used for face recognition and facial emotion recognition.

Table 4. Real-world AI applications in facial and emotion recognition

Application	Description	Business/Revenue model
Facebook - DeepFace	It can determine whether two photographed faces belong to the same person	Leverage Customer Data - Customer data is collected and value created by using data both internally and externally by third parties. Revenue is generated by leveraging it for own purpose by increasing the effectiveness of advertising or selling it to others [10]
Google - FaceNet	It can link a face to its owner with almost perfect results	Leverage Customer Data -The primary revenue stream for Google is the search engine which is powered by ads. Google offers this free to online users. Marketers target online users with its ad products.[a]
Hirevue - Unilever using facial emotion recognition technology HireVue	An AI algorithm measures the facial expressions, emotions and other personality traits making interviews bias-free	Land and Expand Strategy - As per gowtheverywhere.com, HireVue employs a 'land and expand model' by getting a foot in a business and then works to build credibility and trust to expand and increase their offerings. Tiered Pricing Model– They use a very simple metrics around the scope of usage, whether it is a single site, a single country, or globally, as they work inside of hiring programs, and then scale of hires
Affectiva Software motion as a Service - Kellogg's is using emotion recognition	Multiple versions of ads are shown to the viewers and emotions captured using facial recognition	Emotion as a Service Business Model- Affectiva is now offering the product through its partner iMotions and not directly.[b]

[a]https://www.cleverism.com/google-business-model/
[b]https://www.affectiva.com/what/products/

The predominant business model used is Leverage Customer Data. The other Business Models are Land and Expand Strategy, Tiered Pricing Model and Emotion as a Service Business Model.

2.5   Cognitive Engagement

There are several user-friendly digital assistants such as Alexa, Siri, Google Assistant, and chatbots which use AI and which interact with users in a conversational manner (bi-directional). A study was done to understand the adoption determinants of AI inhome Voice Assistants like Alexa. Results showed that the users are motivated by "utilitarian benefits, symbolic benefits and social benefits" that voice assistants provide.

Only in smaller households, hedonic benefits were one of the motivating factors. Perceived privacy risks played a moderating role in negatively influencing its use [13]. It is not only the private firms that are implementing and using AI applications, but the Government has also started adopting these by use of AI chatbots that use "natural language processing, machine learning, and data mining technologies" [3]. In the United Kingdom, National Health Service is conducting a non-randomized trial comparing the Babylon chatbot to get advice and information based on the symptoms and the non-emergency telephone number. There is another study that evaluates an ECA Oncology trial advisor on chemotherapy regimens for cancer trials [4].

Table 5. Real-world AI applications in cognitive engagement

Application	Description	Business/Revenue model
Sam, intelligent travel chatbot that uses AI – FCM Travel Solution.	Smart Assistant for Mobile is a pocket travel assistant. It is simple and intuitive due to the chatbot-based interface	Freemium – The basic version, which offers a comprehensive overview of the travel itineraries, is free for download. However, if corporate travellers want to access the full capability, it needs to be integrated with the FCM Connect technology suite
Jill Watson, a virtual teaching assistant chatbot	It can reply to questions regarding assignments. Trained on data based on previous questions & answers	Freemium and Subscription Model – Digital Lite version is free which is capped at 10,000 free API calls. Paid Standard, Plus, Premium and Deploy Anywhere versions available. https://www.ibm.com/cloud/watson-assistant/pricing/
Drift – Conversational Marketing https://www.drift.com/marketing/	AI-enabled chatbot made for some compelling marketing strategies for connecting businesses to only the best leads in real-time	Freemium and Subscriptions Models- Free: For sites that want basic chat capability. Standard: Enterprise Partnership ModelCustomers can be a strategic partner and Drift can help with its martech experience

The predominant Business model used in this area is Freemium and Subscription models. The other models used are the Crowd Sourcing Model and the partnership model.

3 Findings

From the data shown above in Tables 1, 2, 3, 4 and 5, we can summarize business models as follows (Table 6).

Table 6. AI business models summary

Business Models	Description Models	Emerging AI	Remarks
Vertical Integration and On-device Edge AI – Apple	Apple owns it all starting from the chip to run deep learning algorithms on the Edge, to the App store	Federated Learning: A New AI Business Model[a]	Vertical Integration and On-device Edge AI - Apple
Open Business Model/Partnership – Lepu Medicals, Artery Cardio, Zebra Medicals, Hilton Robot, Blue River weed control	Partnership between companies providing infrastructure and computational services, AI dev companies and companies providing the business knowledge and domain expertise	Triangular Partner ship model	Partnership between 1) Companies that provide infrastructure, computational services and pre-trained models 2) AI development companies, mostly startups. 3) Businesses with domain expertise that can provide the data
Freemium and subscription Model – eMurmur Id, Buoy Health, Sam Intelligent Chatbot, Jill Watson teaching assistant, Drift and Duolingo	Subscription model has been the most common for chatbots	The freemium model is an existing one. In this study, we find it is mainly used for medical tools, chatbots and virtual assistants	
Rent or Buy/Rent to own Business Model	Revenue model mainly used for robots – lease, pay per use, rental agreements etc.	The Rent or Buy model is an existing one. In this study, they have been used mainly for Robots	Emulates how the companies do business traditionally by paying humans and now Robots

(continued)

Table 6. (*continued*)

Business Models	Description Models	Emerging AI	Remarks
Leverage Customer Data	Data is central to AI. Customer data is collected and value created for internal and external use	Leverage Customer Data is an existing one but enhanced by AI	AI has enhanced this by the use of Big Data Analytics and Deep learning algorithms
Land and expand model	Getting a foot in a business and then working to build credibility and trust to expand and increase their offerings and revenue		Land and expand model
Emotion as a service - Affectiva	Emotions captured using AI can be used for marketing dynamically	Create new Business Models using Emotion AI Straker et al. 2015	Emotion as a service - Affectiva

[a]https://towardsdatascience.com/federated-learning-a-new-ai-business-model-ec6b4141b1bf

The emerging AI-driven business models are Federated learning, the triangular partnership model, using Emotion AI to come up with new business models. The existing ones enhanced by AI are the freemium model, Rent to Buy model, leverage customer data and the land and expand model.

4   Implications for Managers and Researchers and Future Work

This paper has made a systematic study of the real-world applications of AI and has summarized the emerging AI-driven business models. It is important for managers who want to implement AI in their organizations to have a facilitating AI strategy that supports and enables AI. This paper will serve as a knowledge base and a quick guide for the managers to help them come up with the AI strategy using the emerging AI business models that have emerged from the literature review. It will also help the researchers to gain an understanding of the latest AI research trends and how AI has been operationalized from the research labs into the real-world.

The emerging AI-driven business models are Federated learning, the triangular partnership model, and using Emotion AI to come up with new business models. The existing ones enhanced by AI are the freemium model, Rent to Buy model, leverage customer data and the land and expand model.

The most common one is the Open Business Model/Partnership model. Companies that adopt an open business model find innovative ways of working together with partners to diversify their business [10]. Pursuing an open business model strengthens both companies by diversifying their respective capabilities and programs. Managers can use this business model to implement AI in their companies if they are not able to own it completely and they are dependent on partners willing to collaborate and help with technical skills, infrastructure needs, machine learning algorithms, etc. They can team up with companies in the AI space, partner with key players and have a strategic agreement with companies to diversify their capabilities.

The other most common business models are the *Rent or Buy/Rent to Own Business Models* and the Freemium models. If the customer rents the product, he saves on the capital and the company benefits from higher profit. Product is effectively utilized as the period of non-usage is reduced [10].

In the Freemium business model, there is a basic free version that attracts a high volume of customers and a premium version with additional features/services. The hope is that those customers who start with the free version will, later on, pay for the premium version. Revenue is obtained from the premium customers who cross-finance the free version [10].

An analysis of the research papers and real-world applications were mainly done in the five areas, namely, medicine, robotics, agriculture, computer vision, and cognitive engagement. This can also be extended to other areas. In medicine, most of the examples pertained to cardiology and robotic surgery. Future work can look at other domains in medicine. The paper does not look into the challenges of AI implementations in the different areas and determinants of its adoption. This can also be taken up in the future.

5   Conclusions

The paper gives an insight into the emerging AI-driven business models.

Apple puts AI/machine intelligence at the edge with on-device Edge AI where devices are smart enough to function when they are offline and secure enough to take care of the privacy of the customers. This follows the federated learning business model.

Many companies are using a partnership model to reduce costs and to also help with training the machine learning model on a diverse set of data. Tech giants have been using the strategy of acquiring startups working in AI. Some companies use the Rent or Buy Revenue Model/Rent to Own business Model. Renting a product helps save on the capital for the customers and the company benefits due to higher profits.

Some of the other interesting business models that have emerged are the Emotion as a service model which is used for emotion-based innovation, the 'land and expand model' wherein the organization first gets a foot in a business and then works to build credibility and trust to expand and increase its offerings and revenue.

The findings from this study will provide a road map and serve as a guide for other organizations that are keen on creating value through AI adoption.

References

1. Adnan, N., Nordin, S.M., bin Bahruddin, M.A., Ali, M.: How trust can drive forward the user acceptance to the technology? In-vehicle technology for autonomous vehicle. Transp. Res. Part A: Policy Pract. **118**, 819–836 (2018)
2. Alsharqi, M., Woodward, W.J., Mumith, J.A., Markham, D.C., Upton, R., Leeson, P.: Artificial intelligence and echocardiography. Echo Res. Pract. **5**(4), R115–R125 (2018)
3. Androutsopoulou, A., Karacapilidis, N., Loukis, E., Charalabidis, Y.: Transforming the communication between citizens and government through AI-guided chatbots. Gov. Inf. Q. **36**(2), 358–367 (2019)
4. Bibault, J.E., Chaix, B., Nectoux, P., Brouard, B.: Healthcare ex machina: are conversational agents ready for prime time in oncology? Clin. Translat. Radiat. Oncol. (2019)
5. Cannesson, M., et al.: A novel two-dimensional echocardiographic image analysis system using artificial intelligence-learned pattern recognition for rapid automated ejection fraction. J. Am. Coll. Cardiol. **49**(2), 217–226 (2007)
6. Chen, H., Engkvist, O., Wang, Y., Olivecrona, M., Blaschke, T.: The rise of deep learning in drug discovery. Drug Discov. Today **23**(6), 1241–1250 (2018)
7. Do, H.M., Pham, M., Sheng, W., Yang, D., Liu, M.: RiSH: a robot-integrated smart home for elderly care. Robot. Auton. Syst. **101**, 74–92 (2018)
8. Eslamizadeh, G., Barati, R.: Heart murmur detection based on wavelet transformation and a synergy between artificial neural network and modified neighbor annealing methods. Artif. Intell. Med. **78**, 23–40 (2017)
9. García, J., Shafie, D.: Teaching a humanoid robot to walk faster through safe reinforcement learning. Eng. Appl. Artif. Intell. **88**, 103360 (2020)
10. Gassmann, O., Frankenberger, K., Csik, M.: The St. Gallen business model navigator (2013)
11. Johnson, K.W., et al.: Artificial intelligence in cardiology. J. Am. Coll. Cardiol. **71**(23), 2668–2679 (2018)
12. Kurup, A.R., Ajith, M., Ramón, M.M.: Semi-supervised facial expression recognition using reduced spatial features and deep belief networks. Neurocomputing **367**, 188–197 (2019)
13. McLean, G., Osei-Frimpong, K.: Hey Alexa… examine the variables influencing the use of artificial intelligent in-home voice assistants. Comput. Hum. Behav. **99**, 28–37 (2019)
14. Mozaffari, A., Behzadipour, S.: A modular extreme learning machine with linguistic interpreter and accelerated chaotic distributor for evaluating the safety of robot maneuvers in laparoscopic surgery. Neurocomputing **151**, 913–932 (2015)
15. Palep, J.H.: Robotic assisted minimally invasive surgery. J. Min. Access Surg.ry **5**(1), 1 (2009)
16. Partel, V., Kakarla, S.C., Ampatzidis, Y.: Development and evaluation of a lowcost and smart technology for precision weed management utilizing artificial intelligence. Comput. Electron. Agric. **157**, 339–350 (2019)
17. Rajan, K., Saffiotti, A.: Towards a science of integrated AI and robotics (2017)
18. Sabzi, S., Abbaspour-Gilandeh, Y., García-Mateos, G.: A fast and accurate expert system for weed identification in potato crops using metaheuristic algorithms. Comput. Ind. **98**, 80–89 (2018)
19. Singh, A.K., Nandi, G.C.: NAO humanoid robot: analysis of calibration techniques for robot sketch drawing. Robot. Auton. Syst. **79**, 108–121 (2016)
20. Tan, J.H., et al.: Age-related macular degeneration detection using deep convolutional neural network. Future Gener. Comput. Syst. **87**, 127–135 (2018)
21. Toh, T.S., Dondelinger, F., Wang, D.: Looking beyond the hype: applied AI and machine learning in translational medicine. EBioMedicine (2019)

Determinants and Barriers of Artificial Intelligence Adoption – A Literature Review

Jayanthi Radhakrishnan[(✉)] and Manojit Chattopadhyay

Indian Institute of Management Raipur, Atal Nagar, P. O. - Abhanpur,
Raipur 493 661, C.G., India
{19efpm001, mchattopadhyay}@iimraipur.ac.in

Abstract. Different theories, models and frameworks have been used to study technology adoption, some explaining the determinants of adoption at the individual level, some at the organizational level and some at both. As Artificial Intelligence (AI) is gaining traction in many sectors, it will be beneficial to understand the determinants and barriers to AI adoption. In this paper, an attempt has been made to review journal articles and other reports pertaining to AI adoption and understand the adoption theories used and the factors that facilitate and those that hinder AI adoption. Articles on adoption studies of autonomous vehicles, big data analytics, robots and cognitive engagement applications dominated the list of journal articles. Diffusion of Innovation, Technology, Organization and Environment Framework and the unified theory of acceptance and use of technology (UTAUT) were some of the dominant theories/frameworks used. Factors influencing adoption at the individual level were related to trust, security, purchase price, intrinsic motivation, social influence, utilitarian benefit whereas at the organizational level, it was related to the technical competencies, strategic road mapping for AI, top management support and the digital maturity of the organization.

Keywords: Artificial Intelligence adoption · AI adoption · Technology adoption · Adoption theories

1 Introduction

Artificial Intelligence (AI) which is machine intelligence that enables them to perform cognitive human like functions is one of the hot topics of discussion these days. Adoption is the process of implementing a technology new to the organization and the acceptance and use by the users in the society. But there are many challenges faced by organizations in their adoption journeys. It will be beneficial to know the extent to which AI has been adopted by organizations in their various functions and to also know the determinants and barriers of AI adoption. According to the McKinsey Report (Nov 2019)[1], adoption of AI continues to increase and there has been significant increase in revenue and reduction in costs especially among the AI users who have adopted AI in

---

[1] https://www.mckinsey.com/featured-insights/artificial-intelligence/global-ai-survey-ai-provesits-worth-but-few-scale-impact.

S. K. Sharma et al. (Eds.): TDIT 2020, IFIP AICT 617, pp. 89–99, 2020.
https://doi.org/10.1007/978-3-030-64849-7_9

multiple business activities. 58% of the survey respondents had used at least one AI capability in at least one business unit. But there are other companies who have been lagging behind in AI adoption.

Against this backdrop of the results of the survey with respect to real life AI adoption, it will be useful to get an understanding of the factors that facilitate AI adoption, the factors that hinder adoption and the factors that determine the rate of diffusion of AI in the organization. It will also be beneficial to understand the interactions of the users with the AI systems in order to understand the factors influencing the AI adoption at the individual consumer levels. The adoption process may be a complex phenomenon being influenced by various factors.

In order to have a comprehensive understanding of the adoption behavior of the users and organizations, it is necessary to understand the different theories and frameworks used in studying AI adoption. These theories may be further extended to suit new adoption cases.

There have been many articles published on technology adoption and more recently on AI adoption in specific areas such as smart manufacturing [13], medicine [41], robotics [19], smart homes [33], virtual assistants [27], autonomous vehicles [1] and Big Data Analytics [3]. It will be beneficial to both the researchers and the practitioners to know the factors that facilitate AI adoption in the different areas. The managers can use this as a guide in implementing AI in their organizations. It will also help them in understanding how to increase the adoption rate amongst the individual users. The researchers will also be able to use this information in their future research initiatives on AI.

A comprehensive and systematic review of the articles on AI adoption has been done in this paper. Articles were taken from Science Direct and Google scholar using the descriptors "Artificial Intelligence adoption"/"AI adoption"/"AI adoption theories"/ "AI determinants and challenges". Only recent articles published in reputed journals were included. A total list of 45 articles on AI adoption in different areas were selected.

The research questions addressed in this study are: What are the dominant theories/frameworks that are used to understand AI adoption at the organization and individual level? What are the determinants and barriers to adoption at the organization and individual level?

1.1 Theories/Frameworks Used to Study AI Adoption

Technology-Organization-Environment Framework. The Technology-organization environment (TOE) framework describes factors in the context of technological, organizational and environmental elements that influence adoption and implementation of technological innovations. The TOE framework has been used to study CRM adoption stages [9], SaaS adoption [30], adoption of mobile reservation systems in hotels [39].

Diffusion of Innovations. The Diffusion of innovations (DOI) explains the rate at which new technology and ideas diffuse in organizations and how and why they spread. DOI can be used to study adoption of technological innovations at both the organization and individual levels. DOI has been used in mobile cloud computing adoption [6], in financial markets [7], autonomous vehicles [35], and Big Data Analytics [17].

Unified Theory of Acceptance and Use of Technology (UTAUT). UTAUT is a technology acceptance model that uses the three constructs, performance expectancy, effort expectancy and social influence to explain user intentions to use an information system. Another construct, facilitating conditions is used to explain user behavior. UTAUT has been used to study the clinician adoption of health information systems in developing countries [4], adoption of mHealth by the elderly [15], in predicting multigenerational tablet adoption practices [25] and in autonomous vehicle adoption.

Technology Acceptance Model. TAM, introduced by Davis (1986) was used for modelling user acceptance of information systems, with two primary factors viz perceived ease of use and perceived usefulness. Tam has been used in the extended form in investigating acceptance of telemedicine services adoption [16], in implementing citizen centric technology in developing smart cities [31], in studying the antecedents to virtual reality hardware acceptance [26] etc.

2 Research Methodology

The literature review was done by doing a search in science direct and Google scholar for research and review articles. The keywords used were Artificial Intelligence adoption, AI adoption, AI adoption theories and AI determinants & challenges.

All the papers mentioned above were reviewed and analyzed in detail. The journal name, the year of publication, AI adoption topic and application, the domain, the theory used to study the adoption process, the determinants of adoption and the barriers to adoption mentioned in the papers were noted down. The articles covered AI applications in many areas such as cognitive engagement (CE), cognitive process automation (CPA), big data analytics (BDA), computer vision (CV), in autonomous vehicles (AV), robots and in medicine.

2.1 Theories, Frameworks, Models and Methods Used in the Papers

Apart from the dominant theories/frameworks mentioned above, the following were also used in the papers to understand the AI adoption process (Table 1).

Dynamic Stackelberg Games (DSG). Stackelberg game has been used to show how asymmetric information influences strategic decisions of new technology adoption and how better information is not always a good thing [44]. This game theory was used to find an optimal subsidy policy considering the asymmetry of information between the government agency and the subsidized entities and market forecast uncertainties [24].

Best Worst Modeling and Binary Choice Model. Best-worst scaling is a survey method that can be used for examining individuals' attitude towards technological innovation. It uses the extremes, best and worst items, most and least appealing factors that influence attitude towards adoption. The Binary Choice model is further used to

Table 1. Details of theories/frameworks/techniques used

Name	#	Level	Application
Technology, Organization and Environment	6	Organization	CPA, BDA
Diffusion of Innovation	6	Both	AV, BDA
Unified Theory of Acceptance and Use of Technology	4	Individual	AV, Robots, Medicine
Technology Acceptance Model	3	Individual	AV, CE, BDA
Dynamic Stackelberg Games	1	Individual	AV
Best Worst Modeling and Binary Choice Model	1	Individual	AV
Uncertainty Reduction Theory	1	Individual	AV
Agent Based Modeling	1	Individual	AV
Theories of Risk Perception and Trust	1	Individual	AV
Cognitive Appraisal theory, Cognitive Dissonance Theory	1	Individual	Robots
Technology, Organization and Environment	6	Organization	CPA, BDA
Watching Eyes Effect	1	Organization	Robots
Bandura's theory of Self-efficacy	1	Individual	Robots
The 'Media Richness Theory'	1	Individual	CE
Multivariate Probit Model	1	Individual	CE
Uses and Gratification theory	1	Individual	CE

understand how these attitudes influence the purchase decision [32]. This can be used to study AI adoption at an individual level.

Uncertainty Reduction Theory (URT). According to URT, individuals try to reduce uncertainty by seeking information. Uncertainty arises when one is unable to determine the actions of another. Uncertainty is inversely proportional to trust. According to URT, uncertainty is decreased by acquiring information about the other person [11]. This has been used to study whether explanations promote acceptance of innovations.

Agent Based Simulation Modeling. It is used to model heterogeneous individuals who behave differently and are linked together. It is used for simulating the actions and interactions of autonomous agents to assess effects on the system as a whole. Combination of DOI and Agent Based Modelling can be used to model adoptions [35].

Theories of Risk Perception and Trust. These theories may include factors such as perceived benefit and risk, anticipated perceived and trust while studying adoption [21].

Cognitive Appraisal Theory, Cognitive Dissonance Theory. Cognitive appraisal consists of the primary appraisal process where a person examines a situation and finds out how that event will affect him and the secondary appraisal process where a response is arrived at. The outcome stage will determine how willing or reluctant they are, to accept the use of AI devices [14]. According to cognitive dissonance theory, individuals like to have consistency in their beliefs, opinions and behaviour. When there is lack of agreement, the attitude will change to resolve the dissonance.

Multivariate Probit Model. The multivariate probit model, a generalization of the probit model can been used to describe technological innovation diffusion. It is used to examine decisions with choices that are interdependent by estimating several correlated binary outcomes together. It was used in a study to describe the diffusion of smart homes [33].

Watching Eyes Effect. People behave altruistically in front of watching eyes to maintain a positive social reputation. This has been used to study robotic adoption [23].

Bandura's Theory of Self-efficacy. Self-efficacy is the confidence in oneself to be able to influence events. A study was done to show how self-efficacy with regard to robot use is associated with its acceptance [19].

The 'Media Richness Theory' (MRT). This shows the relationship between the qualities and features of the communication task and the communication channel used for it. The theory has been used a lot in research related to e-government to examine why citizens continue to use the traditional methods [2].

Uses and Gratification Theory. Uses and gratification theory is used to explain why people prefer to adopt certain media or innovation. The assumption is that the consumers are not passive. A study was done to understand the adoption of Alexa and other technological innovations [27].

3 Determinants and Barriers to AI Adoption

3.1 Autonomous Vehicles

Adoption of Autonomous Vehicles topped the list of topic wise articles with 13 articles under this category (Table 2).

Table 2. Autonomous vehicles adoption

Facilitating factors
Purchase subsidies, AV related infrastructure [8]
Individual's need, cost, overall impression, word of mouth [35]
Rate at which autonomous technology improves over time, status and environment consciousness, disability, age, gender, income, education [10]
Perceived safety, perceived usefulness [42]
Household composition [5], Parking cost [32]
Self-fulfilment including quality of life, security, responsibility [28]
Being technologically savvy, perceived benefits [20]
Coefficient of imitation such as observability, coefficient of innovation such as compatibility, relative advantage [34]
Barriers
Changes to established routines, perceived risk, perceived concerns, lack of accountability, lack of trust, system failure, privacy concerns, deprivation from the joy of driving, overreliance on AV, loss of driving skill, perceived dread [1]

3.2 Big Data Analytics

See Table 3.

Table 3. Big data analytics adoption

Facilitating factors
Top management support, organizational data environment [38]
Cloud provision and platforms, stronger and clearer privacy and governance, innovativeness approach, competitiveness and resources [40]
Barriers
Adapting the organizational processes to the new technology, managers feeling threatened due to fear of losing their jobs to the new technology

3.3 Cognitive Engagement

See Table 4.

Table 4. Cognitive engagement

Facilitating factors
Social influence, hedonic motivation, performance expectancy [14] Utilitarian hedonic and symbolic benefits, social attractiveness [27] Novelty of AI activity, attitude towards the organization [37]
Barriers
Adaptation challenges and use for elderly people, interaction with other technologies [29]. Lower communication richness and expressiveness [2], more complexity and ambiguity

3.4 Robots

See Table 5.

Table 5. Robots

Facilitating factors
Performance efficacy, intrinsic motivation, facilitating conditions [23]
Competitive market environment and customer needs [18]
Robot use self-efficacy [19], social influence, trust, culture, prior experience
Barriers
Anthropomorphism [23], low levels of acceptance toward an intervention, privacy and ethical concerns, job insecurity

3.5   Medicine

See Table 6.

Table 6. Medicine

Facilitating factors
Efforts required to install and use the tool [43]
Reproducibility [41]
Accuracy, trust [12]
Ability to explain and easily interpret predictions, robust regulatory framework for managing changes to algorithms, time to delivery, cost [22]
Initial trust has four determinants - propensity to trust, social influence, performance expectancy and effort expectancy [12]
Barriers
Algorithmic transparency and reproducibility [41]
Variations between experimental and clinical data, the need for regulators approve the computational methods [36], Error rates, potential risks on lives [12]

4   Results

4.1   AI Adoption Theories

Referring to Table 1 above, we see that the most dominant theories used to study AI adoption are Technology, Organization and Environment (TOE) and Diffusion of Innovation (DOI). TOE and DOI have been used in six articles each. TOE has been used to study adoption at the organization level where as DOI has been used both at the organization and at the individual levels.

TOE and DOI have been followed closely by UTAUT and its extension followed by TAM and its extension. Both UTAUT and TAM have been used at the individual adoption levels. We also observe that the topic of AV adoptions dominates the list of articles. AV was followed by Big Data Analytics, Robots and AI uses in Cognitive Engagement in the count of number of articles (Tables 7 and 8).

Table 7. Dominant theories

Level	Theories
Organization	TOE, DOI
individual	UTAUT, DOI, TAM

Table 8. Application wise details

Application	Theories
AV	DOI, UTAUT, TAM, DSG, Best Worst Modeling and Binary Choice Model, Uncertainty Reduction theory, Agent Based Modeling and Theories of Risk Perception and Trust
BDA	TOE, DOI and TAM
Robots	UTAUT, Cognitive Appraisal Theory & Cognitive Dissonance Theory, Watching Eyes Effect and Bandura's theory of self-efficacy
CE	TAM, the Media Rich Theory, Multivariate Probit Model and Uses and Gratification theory

4.2   Determinants and Barriers

Aggregating the determinants and barriers from the different papers, there was a huge number of factors that facilitated and hindered AI adoption for the different applications.

At the organization level, the key determinants were found to be Organizational strategy and roadmap for AI, top management support, existing infrastructure, digital maturity, trust, skill base, competitive market environment, compatibility, relative Advantage, observability, cost of adoption, external pressure, Government support, privacy laws, organizational innovativeness etc. In the area of medicine, the key determinants were establishment of an eco-system of key players, regulatory approvals, anonymization of data and accuracy.

At the individual level, it was trust, cost, social influence, hedonic motivation, performance expectancy, utilitarian benefits, safety, intrinsic motivation, prior experience with AI tools.

5   Discussion and Implications for Managers and Researchers

This paper has done a systematic review of journal articles in the area of AI adoption and has summarized the dominant adoption theories used along with the determinants and barriers to adoption for the different AI applications at the organization and individual levels. It has helped in creating a knowledge base which can be used by the future researchers while studying adoption of AI and other technological innovations.

The paper will also help the managers by providing an insight into the factors that facilitate and those that hinder AI adoption and the factors that determine the rate of diffusion of AI in the organization in the different application areas. It will be useful to study AI adoption at the individual consumer levels by understanding the interactions of the users with the AI systems. This information can be used while implementing AI in their organizations by knowing the customer needs and by addressing the apprehensions the users might have towards AI.

All the papers were selected from reputed Journals adding to the usefulness of the study. The paper can serve as a quick guide for both the researchers and the managers to know about the latest research details in AI adoption and know which theories to use and hence, what parameters to look for while studying adoption. The study was based on the study of 45 research papers comprising of the 7 application areas of AV, Big Data Analytics, Robots, Cognitive Engagement, Medicine, Computer Vision and Cognitive automation. Future research can be done in more detail in each of the above areas.

References

1. Adnan, N., Nordin, S.M., bin Bahruddin, M.A., Ali, M.: How trust can drive forward the user acceptance to the technology? In-vehicle technology for autonomous vehicle. Transp. Res. Part A: Policy Pract. **118**, 819–836 (2018)
2. Androutsopoulou, A., Karacapilidis, N., Loukis, E., Charalabidis, Y.: Transforming the communication between citizens and government through AI-guided chatbots. Gov. Inf. Q. **36**(2), 358–367 (2019)
3. Baig, M.I., Shuib, L., Yadegaridehkordi, E.: Big data adoption: state of the art and research challenges. Inf. Process. Manag. **56**(6), 102095 (2019)
4. Bawack, R.E., Kamdjoug, J.R.K.: Adequacy of UTAUT in clinician adoption of health information systems in developing countries: the case of Cameroon. Int. J. Med. Inform. **109**, 15–22 (2018)
5. Berliner, R.M., Hardman, S., Tal, G.: Uncovering early adopter's perceptions and purchase intentions of automated vehicles: insights from early adopters of electric vehicles in California. Transp. Res. Part F: Traffic Psychol. Behav. **60**, 712–722 (2019)
6. Carreiro, H., Oliveira, T.: Impact of transformational leadership on the diffusion of innovation in firms: application to mobile cloud computing. Comput. Ind. **107**, 104–113 (2019)
7. Chakravarty, S., Dubinsky, A.: Individual investors' reactions to decimalization: innovation diffusion in financial markets. J. Econ. Psychol. **26**(1), 89–103 (2005)
8. Chen, S., Wang, H., Meng, Q.: Designing autonomous vehicle incentive program with uncertain vehicle purchase price. Transp. Res. Part C: Emerg. Technol. **103**, 226–245 (2019)
9. Cruz-Jesus, F., Pinheiro, A., Oliveira, T.: Understanding CRM adoption stages: empirical analysis building on the TOE framework. Comput. Ind. **109**, 1–13 (2019)
10. Cunningham, M.L., Regan, M.A., Horberry, T., Weeratunga, K., Dixit, V.: Public opinion about automated vehicles in Australia: results from a large-scale national survey. Transp. Res. Part A: Policy Pract. **129**, 1–18 (2019)
11. Du, N., et al.: Look who's talking now: implications of AV's explanations on driver's trust, AV preference, anxiety and mental workload. Transp. Res. Part C: Emerg. Technol. **104**, 428–442 (2019)
12. Fan, W., Liu, J., Zhu, S., Pardalos, P.M.: Investigating the impacting factors for the healthcare professionals to adopt artificial intelligence-based medical diagnosis support system (AIMDSS). Ann. Oper. Res. 1–26 (2018)
13. Ghobakhloo, M., Ching, N.T.: Adoption of digital technologies of smart manufacturing in SMEs. J. Ind. Inf. Integr. **16**, 100107 (2019)
14. Gursoy, D., Chi, O.H., Lu, L., Nunkoo, R.: Consumers acceptance of artificially intelligent (AI) device use in service delivery. Int. J. Inf. Manag. **49**, 157–169 (2019)
15. Hoque, R., Sorwar, G.: Understanding factors influencing the adoption of mHealth by the elderly: an extension of the UTAUT model. Int. J. Med. Inform. **101**, 75–84 (2017)

16. Kamal, S.A., Shafiq, M., Kakria, P.: Investigating acceptance of telemedicine services through an extended technology acceptance model (TAM). Technol. Soc. **60**, 101212 (2020)
17. Lai, Y., Sun, H., Ren, J.: Understanding the determinants of big data analytics (BDA) adoption in logistics and supply chain management. Int. J. Logist. Manag. (2018)
18. Lakshmi, V., Bahli, B.: Understanding the robotization landscape transformation: a centering resonance analysis. J. Innov. Knowl. **5**(1), 59–67 (2020)
19. Latikka, R., Turja, T., Oksanen, A.: Self-efficacy and acceptance of robots. Comput. Hum. Behav. **93**, 157–163 (2019)
20. Lee, Y.C., Mirman, J.H.: Parents' perspectives on using autonomous vehicles to enhance children's mobility. Transp. Res. Part C: Emerg. Technol. **96**, 415–431 (2018)
21. Liu, P., Guo, Q., Ren, F., Wang, L., Xu, Z.: Willingness to pay for self-driving vehicles: influences of demographic and psychological factors. Transp. Res. Part C: Emerg. Technol. **100**, 306–317 (2019)
22. Liu, Z., Zhu, L., Roberts, R., Tong, W.: Toward clinical implementation of next generation sequencing-based genetic testing in rare diseases: where are we?. Trends Genet. (2019)
23. Lu, L., Cai, R., Gursoy, D.: Developing and validating a service robot integration willingness scale. Int. J. Hospital. Manag. **80**, 36–51 (2019)
24. Luo, Q., Saigal, R., Chen, Z., Yin, Y.: Accelerating the adoption of automated vehicles by subsidies: a dynamic games approach. Transp. Res. Part B: Methodol. **129**, 226–243 (2019)
25. Magsamen-Conrad, K., Upadhyaya, S., Joa, C.Y., Dowd, J.: Bridging the divide: using UTAUT to predict multigenerational tablet adoption practices. Comput. Hum. Behav. **50**, 186–196 (2015)
26. Manis, K.T., Choi, D.: The virtual reality hardware acceptance model (VR-HAM): extending and individuating the technology acceptance model (TAM) for virtual reality hardware. J. Bus. Res. **100**, 503–513 (2019)
27. McLean, G., Osei-Frimpong, K.: Hey Alexa… examine the variables influencing the use of artificial intelligent in-home voice assistants. Comput. Hum. Behav. **99**, 28–37 (2019)
28. Merfeld, K., Wilhelms, M.P., Henkel, S.: Being driven autonomously–a qualitative study to elicit consumers' overarching motivational structures. Transp. Res. Part C: Emerg. Technol. **107**, 229–247 (2019)
29. Montenegro, J.L.Z., da Costa, C.A., da Rosa Righi, R.: Survey of conversational agents in health. Expert Syst. Appl. (2019)
30. Oliveira, T., Martins, R., Sarker, S., Thomas, M., Popovič, A.: Understanding SaaS adoption: the moderating impact of the environment context. Int. J. Inf. Manag. **49**, 1–12 (2019)
31. Sepasgozar, S.M., Hawken, S., Sargolzaei, S., Foroozanfa, M.: Implementing citizen centric technology in developing smart cities: a model for predicting the acceptance of urban technologies. Technol. Forecast. Soc. Chang. **142**, 105–116 (2019)
32. Shabanpour, R., Golshani, N., Shamshiripour, A., Mohammadian, A.K.: Eliciting preferences for adoption of fully automated vehicles using best-worst analysis. Transp. Res. Part C: Emerg. Technol. **93**, 463–478 (2018)
33. Shin, J., Park, Y., Lee, D.: Who will be smart home users? An analysis of adoption and diffusion of smart homes. Technol. Forecast. Soc. Chang. **134**, 246–253 (2018)
34. Simpson, J.R., Mishra, S., Talebian, A., Golias, M.M.: An estimation of the future adoption rate of autonomous trucks by freight organizations. Res. Transp. Econ. **76**, 100737 (2019)
35. Talebian, A., Mishra, S.: Predicting the adoption of connected autonomous vehicles: a new approach based on the theory of diffusion of innovations. Transp. Res. Part C: Emerg. Technol. **95**, 363–380 (2018)
36. Toh, T.S., Dondelinger, F., Wang, D.: Looking beyond the hype: applied AI and machine learning in translational medicine. EBioMedicine (2019)

37. Van Esch, P., Black, J.S., Ferolie, J.: Marketing AI recruitment: the next phase in job application and selection. Comput. Hum. Behav. **90**, 215–222 (2019)
38. Verma, S., Bhattacharyya, S.S.: Perceived strategic value-based adoption of big data analytics in emerging economy. J. Enterp. Inf. Manag. (2017)
39. Wang, Y.S., Li, H.T., Li, C.R., Zhang, D.Z.: Factors affecting hotels' adoption of mobile reservation systems: a technology-organization-environment framework. Tour. Manag. **53**, 163–172 (2016)
40. Wright, L.T., Robin, R., Stone, M., Aravopoulou, D.E.: Adoption of big data technology for innovation in B2B marketing. J. Bus. Bus. Mark. **26**(3–4), 281–293 (2019)
41. Xu, J., et al.: Translating cancer genomics into precision medicine with artificial intelligence: applications, challenges and future perspectives. Hum. Genet. **138**(2), 109–124 (2019)
42. Zhang, T., Tao, D., Qu, X., Zhang, X., Lin, R., Zhang, W.: The roles of initial trust and perceived risk in public's acceptance of automated vehicles. Transp. Res. Part C: Emerg. Technol. **98**, 207–220 (2019)
43. Zheng, K., et al.: Ease of adoption of clinical natural language processing software: an evaluation of five systems. J. Biomed. Inform. **58**, S189–S196 (2015)
44. Zhu, K., Weyant, J.P.: Strategic decisions of new technology adoption under asymmetric information: a game-theoretic model. Decis. Sci. **34**(4), 643–675 (2003)

Public Policy and Regulatory Challenges of Artificial Intelligence (AI)

Santosh K. Misra[1(✉)], Satyasiba Das[2], Sumeet Gupta[2],
and Sujeet K. Sharma[3]

[1] CEO, Tamil Nadu e-Governance Agency, Chennai, India
santoshmisraias@gmail.com
[2] Indian Institute of Management, Raipur, India
[3] Indian Institute of Management, Tiruchirappalli, India

Abstract. Artificial Intelligence (AI) usage is rapidly expanding in our society. Private sector has already taken the leap of faith in using AI for efficiency and for generating better value for the customers and shareholders. The promise of AI is quite alluring for the governments as well. It promises to be the break-through technology which can catapult public sector to hitherto unseen efficiency and productivity. It has the potential to truly transform the public service delivery and the way government interfaces with citizens – from a demand driven model to a predictive model of public service delivery. However, there are a large number of pitfalls and blind-spots associated with AI, which make its adoption in government particularly challenging. For successful adoption of AI in public sector, governments must understand these challenges clearly and lay down regulatory public policies to ensure that the possible adverse impacts (such as exclusion, bias etc.) of AI are mitigated. This paper attempts to systematically explore these challenges with a view to enable public policy makers to respond to them.

Keywords: Public policy · Artificial intelligence · Regulation of AI ·
Challenges of AI · IoT · Machine learning · ANN · Regulatory challenges of
AI · Autonomous systems · Ethics · Safety · Privacy · Equity · Fairness · Bias

1 Introduction

Quest for knowledge and using the acquired knowledge creatively has been the defining feature of human race. Human curiosity, what Berlyne calls the 'epistemic curiosity' [1], has resulted in some of the greatest inventions on earth. Humans have always been trying to create new knowledge and applying it to build machines to make life easier and more comfortable. Even though the field of Artificial Intelligence (AI) formally came into existence in late 50s, it is argued that designing machines was in some way a precursor to the formal AI [2]. Spector argues that creating intelligence (i.e. building machines) can be thought of as designing intelligence, and that in his opinion is the beginning point of human quest for AI. While one may or may not agree with this argument, the fact remains that humans have always been fascinated with designing autonomous intelligence – machines which could perform without

S. K. Sharma et al. (Eds.): TDIT 2020, IFIP AICT 617, pp. 100–111, 2020.
https://doi.org/10.1007/978-3-030-64849-7_10

supervision or at least with least amount of human supervision. In this sense we can treat a range of machines- from ordinary bread toasters to missile equipped drones – as examples of machines which have built in logic (or intelligence) and are substantially free from active human supervision.

Of course, the definition of AI is continuously evolving as the technology keeps rapidly changing, and there has been an unprecedented growth and maturity in the area of AI in last one decade. We already have autonomous driverless cars, delivery drones, voice based personal assistants like Alexa, Siri etc., dexterous and intelligent humanoid Robots like those from Boston Dynamics, AI based machine diagnostics of medical images, among numerous other AI based machines and applications.

A PWC report [3] estimates AI contribution to the global economy at US $15.7 trillion by 2030. Companies like Amazon, Google, Baidu, Alibaba, Netflix, Facebook, Apple, Microsoft, IBM are all using AI for delivering better value to their customers. From recommending products or movies to voice assistants (like alexa or siri) they are using AI. There is a slew of start-ups offering personalised online education, investment advisories, and healthcare diagnostics using AI. Oncora medical, Babylon Health, Butterfly network Atomwise and Enlitic are healthcare AI companies working in areas of cancer research, medical imaging, drug discovery etc. [4]. While private sector has been leading the AI adoption, Governments around the world have begun experimenting with use of AI in public space. They have started exploring ways of using AI for better public service delivery to their citizens.

While the usage of AI might be similar for the public and the private sector, there are significant differences in their approach and consequences. While a poor recommendation by an AI system for a product or a movie would only mean one less customer for the company and the damages, if any, are reversible, an error by AI system in public service delivery may lead to an irreversible damage. A person may be unfairly denied a job, credit or bail. S/He can be wrongly classified as a delinquent or a trouble maker and can be wrongly convicted just because the AI system has been trained incorrectly. The consequences of these mistakes can be devastating for individuals, families and societies. Government initiated AI systems, if not carefully calibrated, can lead to systematic exclusion of marginalised and vulnerable sections of society. People may get shut out of the government support system based on their colour, race, gender, looks or simply because of their geographical location, which the AI system 'learns' to associate with say crime or delinquency. Poorly designed AI systems can exacerbate the inequality in the society and can potentially damage the social equilibrium.

Rolling out AI programs for public without understanding its challenges clearly, would be the surest path to failure. For example, a biased decision making or privacy intrusion into citizen's lives, would quickly lead to erosion of public trust and the system would have to be abandoned. For the governments its critical to understand these challenges and respond to them by appropriate public policy measures to mitigate their possible adverse impacts. This leads us to the research question-

RQ: What are the key public policy challenges of AI?

2 Literature Review

2.1 Definition of AI

One of the earliest scientists to talk about AI was Alan Turing, the famous British mathematician credited with having cracked the codes of dreaded German Enigma machines during second world war. He wrote, in 1950, what can be termed as possibly the first paper on artificial intelligence, 'Computing machinery and intelligence' [5]. Even though he did not explicitly define machine intelligence or AI, he devised the famous 'Turing Test' of machine intelligence, which says that if a machine can remain indistinguishable from a human while in conversation with another human being then it is an 'intelligent' machine.

Professor John McCarthy of Dartmouth College, New Hampshire, USA, is credited with introducing the term 'artificial intelligence'. He defines it as "the science and engineering of making intelligent machines."

UK Parliament Committee on Science and Technology has used the following definition of AI in its report on AI and Robotics [6]:

"…a set of statistical tools and algorithms that combine to form, in part, intelligent software that specializes in a single area or task. This type of software is an evolving assemblage of technologies that enable computers to simulate elements of human behaviour such as learning, reasoning and classification."

ASSOCHAM (Association of Chambers of Industries) India and PWC in their joint report on AI titled 'Artificial Intelligence and Robotics – 2017' define AI as [7]-

"Artificial intelligence refers to the ability of a computer or a computer-enabled robotic system to process information and produce outcomes in a manner similar to the thought process of humans in learning, decision making and solving problems."

Another definition of AI given in Stanford's 2016 report - Artificial Intelligence and Life in 2030 – is by Nils J. Nilsson:

"Artificial intelligence is that activity devoted to making machines intelligent, and intelligence is that quality that enables an entity to function appropriately and with foresight in its environment" [8].

The Stanford's 2016 report quoted above has also used another definition of AI, which states, "AI can also be defined by what AI researchers do. This report views AI primarily as a branch of computer science that studies the properties of intelligence by synthesizing intelligence" [8].

2.2 Evolution of AI

Subsequent decades, after Turing, were somewhat disappointing for the AI progress. The initial euphoria subsided as no 'intelligent' machine could be built successfully and most of the public funding for AI dried up. In 1965 Lofti Zadeh of University of Berkeley published his paper on Fuzzy Logic. This reignited the interest of scientific community in intelligent machines. However it was another two decades before Zadeh's idea could be fully tapped into.

One of the reasons for these early failures of AI research was their focus on overambitious general purpose intelligence building. The available computing system of that time were too limited to try this. This barrier was successfully overcome by DENDRAL expert-system commissioned by NASA in 1971, for its mission to mars. The key was to take a very narrow and specific problem, in this case that of mass spectrometry, and build a rule-based intelligent system for it which would match the ability of a human expert.

This expert-system approach to AI started yielding handsome results. Expert systems like DENDRAL, MYCIN (a medical diagnostic expert system) and PROSPECTOR (a mining exploration expert system developed in Stanford in 1979) successfully took shape with this approach.

AI got a major boost in 1980s with the arrival of relatively powerful desktop computers. Artificial Neural Network (ANN), mimicking human brain's interconnection of neurons, became a popular choice for building AI systems. New algorithms and techniques were developed.

Today with heavy duty computational power available even in the hand held mobiles, and of-course the 'cloud-computing' has opened up new avenues of AI application and system design. Now speed of computation is not so relevant anymore in development of AI, instead the focus has shifted to writing cleverer software and designing of efficient algorithms.

AI can be said to have arrived on the world stage, when in March 2016, the Google's AI program Alpha Go defeated the world champion of Go – an ancient Chinese game which managed to elude the reach of AI for so long. This was possibly the watershed moment in AI development.

While discussing AI, it is appropriate to talk of Machine learning and IoT (Internet of Things) and their relation with each other. AI is essentially the outcome of Machine Learning. Machines (Software Models of ANN etc.) are fed with huge amount of training data. This data is labeled (the actual output which should be generated by the machine given the input is told to the machine- this is also known as supervised learning system as opposed to unsupervised learning or reinforced learning) and the machine tries to identify a pattern in the data input and tries to predict the outcome. This process is called Machine Learning.

IoT or Internet of Things refers to a vast number of small (and some not so small) devices and sensors connected to the internet and transmitting and receiving relevant data. These devices can be cell phones, CCTVs, temperature or pressure sensors, pollution sensors, electricity consumption meters, refrigerators or even cars. IoT is an essential part of generating training data for machine learning for many AI applications. IoTs and Big-Data analytics are quietly transforming the entire human ecosystem in ways never imagined before. To safely harness this transformative power, Public Policy is one of the key tool [9].

2.3   AI in Governance

The increasing role of autonomous machines in human life is posing unique challenges to Public Policy. World Bank has estimated that two-thirds of all jobs in developing countries are susceptible to automation (World Bank 2016). For Ethiopia this number goes to an astronomical 85%. The proliferation of machines in critical areas of human life such as health care, education, geriatric care and transportation necessitates updating of extant Public Policies. In the chapter titled "Reclaiming Public Space: Drawing Lessons from the Past as We Confront the Future", Chester Newland and Demetrios Argyriades write about the challenges ahead for public service professionals - "A new profile is needed for civil service professionals; a profile that combines deep knowledge and high-level skills with fortitude, forbearance, integrity, capacity to offer sound evidence-based advice but, more than anything else, steadfast adherence to constitutionally democratic principles and values in search for reasonableness and shared human dignity" [10].

It is not that the machines were absent from the picture earlier, but what makes the situation very different now that the new machines are autonomous, each equipped with necessary computational power to take unguided independent decisions. What makes the situation even more complicated is the fact that the decision making process of the AI driven machines tends to be opaque and sometimes the decision making process may not be understood even by the creators of the algorithm. To make matters worse, is a set of people and media who drive the fear that AI would dominate and rule the world [11].

These autonomous machines bring some very different dimensions to Public Policy and throw up new challenges. There are issues of ethics, responsibility, decision audit, and legality in AI enabled machines. Policy experts have opined that State must 'filter-out' such innovations that conflict with fundamental rights and public [12].

This is what makes AI and Public Policy a fascinating area to research in. Realizing the strategic importance of AI, Governments around the world have declared AI development as their national priority and have committed huge amount of resources with a stated aim of becoming the world leader in AI [13, 14].

China has started deploying SmartHS for public service delivery improvement [15]. Spain has created an Urban Platform for their smart-city project [16]. Dubai government has 'Smart Dubai' project which uses AI for citizen service [16]. UK National Health Service has adopted an AI chatbot- based triage system in 2019 [17]. US Food and Drug Administration (FDA) has categorised AI algorithms in health sector as medical devices - AI/ML SaMD (Software as a Medical Device) and a regulatory framework for them is proposed [18]. EU has built a Consumer ODR (Online Dispute Resolution) platform [16] which could harness AI driven dispute resolution. NITI Aayog in India in its National Strategy for AI has identified health, education and agriculture as priority areas for using AI [19].

This, of course, is apart from the phenomenal development in AI taking place in the private sector. Interaction of autonomous machines with humans at the levels we are likely to witness is un-precedented. With the computational power readily available and smart algorithms possibilities of 'malicious usage' of AI is not at all remote. A systematic policy response to malicious usage is required which can tackle its multiple dimensions namely – expansion of existing threats, new threats, and mutating threats on digital, physical and political security [20].

3 Method

3.1 Literature Selection

We conducted the literature search using Google scholar. We limited ourselves to the published literature in English language alone. We ran searches using a combination of key words "Artificial Intelligence", "AI Challenges", "AI Public Policy", " AI Public Administration", " AI Public sector", "AI principles", " AI Ethics" and "AI Governance". We limited our search to 2017 to 2020 to keep the most recent research in focus. A total of 193 research papers, books and reports were found. We further filtered the results by three step filtering –

De-duplication of papers and elimination of books and reports
Title based shortlisting
Abstract based shortlisting

We first removed all the entries which were appearing more than once. Then we removed the books and reports from the search results. Next we filtered the search result by relevance of the title. Since our purpose is to bring out the challenges of AI from public policy perspective, we first shortlisted only those articles which were about AI challenges. Thus article like "Trade secrets, big data and artificial intelligence innovation: a legal oxymoron?" which figured in the search result were dropped and entries like "Artificial intelligence and the public sector—applications and challenges" were retained. It is important to note that a large number of articles thrown up by the search were irrelevant. We had a large number of articles like -"Tstarbots: Defeating the cheating level builtin AI in starcraft ii in the full game", "Cybersecurity and its discontents: Artificial intelligence, the Internet of Things, and digital misinformation", "AI for medical imaging goes deep" - all these had to be discarded.

This reduced our shortlist to 72 articles. To narrow down our search further the articles were further shortlisted based on their abstract. Only the papers which focussed on either public policy issues or regulatory issues or social issues of AI were shortlisted. This reduced the total count to 48. The literature selection process is described in Fig. 1 below.

Key word Search

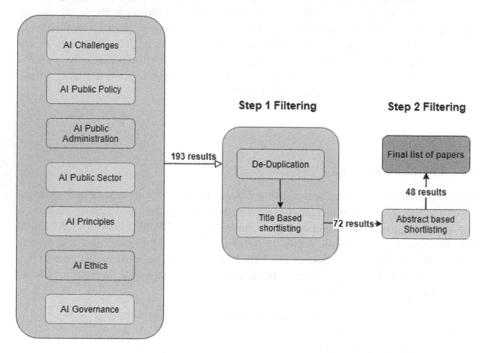

Fig. 1. Literature selection process.

3.2 Challenges Identified

There has been a lot of research towards identifying challenges posed by AI systems (we use AI as an inclusive term which covers autonomous systems as well). However, every researcher has used her/his own terminology to describe them. For example 'equity' [21, 22] has been described using terms like 'economic inequality' [23], 'shared benefit' and 'shared prosperity' [24]. To be able to design a public policy response for tackling the challenges of AI is impossible unless there is an agreed set of challenges and terminology used in describing them is uniform.

A review of the literature selected above reveals a big list of challenges of AI systems.

Asilomar principles list Liberty and Privacy, Transparency, Responsibility, Shared Prosperity, Value Alignment, Human Values, Safety, Shared Benefit, Human Control, Arms Race, control of Recursive self improvement and Non-Subversion - as key challenges of AI implementation [24]. British Standards Institute has identified explainability, transparency, safety, verifiability, security and privacy, controllability, resiliency, reliability, robustness, accuracy, as important challenges of AI [25].

Several national governments have also worked towards identifying the key challenges of AI. For example, Germany has identified transparency, privacy and ethics as key challenges for AI adoption [26], India has prioritized Fairness, Transparency, Privacy and Security as the key challenges of AI [19], Japan has listed Database

Protection, Employment, Skilling, changes in Laws and Global collaboration as main policy challenges [27], Canada's researchers are focussing on transparency, trust and accountability as prime AI policy challenges [28]. IEEE has undertaken to develop standards for safe and ethical AI, in form of IEEE standards 7000 through 7012 [29].

After the full text review of the shortlisted papers we have arrived at the following list of public policy challenges of AI.

Ethics	Equity	Accuracy	Personal liberty and autonomy
Bias	Explainability	Stability	Transparency and trust
Privacy	Rights and liberties	Shared benefit	Responsibility
Fairness	Labour and automation	Shared prosperity	Value alignment
Accountability	Use of force	Societal stability	
Human Control	Misuse protection	Human values (dignity, rights, freedom, cultural diversity)	

4 Result

Full text review of the shortlisted papers gave us an exhaustive list of pubic policy challenges of AI. We have listed these in Sect. 3.2 above. If we carefully examine them we can see that these 22 challenges are not fully independent of each other. Many of them, even though worded differently, describe the same essential idea. If we club similar ideas into one broad category, we can identify a set of core challenges of AI. Since our focus in this article is to identify public policy related challenges of AI, we would examine each of the challenge from public policy lens and categorise them accordingly.

Our findings are best summarised in the table below. Even though, each paper cited has identified between 3 to 10 challenges, in the interest of listing as many different papers as possible, we have tried to limit listing of each paper to two or three themes only (Table 1).

There is a strong need for laying of ground rules in form of Public Policy to keep the AI proliferation beneficial to the society. As of now there hasn't been much research on the intersection of AI and Public Policy, whereas individually they both have been studied well. Therefore it is an opportune time to work in this area and to help find insights which would keep the power of AI safe for serving humanity.

Table 1. AI challenges for public policy

S No	Type of challenge	Alternate terminology used	Papers
1	Ethics	–	[30–38]
2	Bias	Diversity, Data parity, Data asymmetry	[29, 39–43]
3	Privacy	Personal privacy	[44–48]
4	Fairness	No discrimination	[19, 49–51]
5	Accountability	Responsibility	[52–55]
6	Equity	Societal stability, Economic Inequality, Labour and automation, Shared benefit, Shared prosperity	[13, 24, 42, 45, 56–60]
7	Rights and liberties	Personal Liberty and autonomy, Fundamental Rights	[38, 61, 62]
8	Transparency and trust	Auditability, Explainability	[7, 46, 63, 64]
9	Value alignment	Human values (dignity, rights, freedom, cultural diversity)	[26, 32, 65]
10	Human Control	Use of force under human supervision	[41, 66]
11	Misuse protection	Safety and certification, Hacking, Cyberattack, non-manipulation	[20, 24, 41, 53, 67–70]

5 Discussion and Future Research

As we saw in earlier sections, AI and autonomous systems pose a number of serious public policy challenges. A wide scale public roll out of AI (and autonomous systems) can not be done without addressing these challenges. So severe are some of these issues that few researchers have advocated completely avoiding AI in Government decision making [71]. It has been pointed out that it is the Government which is tasked with mitigating any adverse impact of AI on society [72]. To be able to lay down public policies which make AI ethical and safe to use in public domain, governments need to understand each of these challenges very well and accordingly create a robust regulatory framework.

Our literature search indicates that there has been very little research, towards comprehensively identifying challenges (or inhibitors) of AI adoption in the public services. There is a strong need to explore the following research questions:

1. To identify the contextual and hierarchical relationships among identified challenges (inhibitors) of adopting AI in public services
2. To group these challenges based on their dependence and driving power
3. To develop an integrated model to understand the dynamics of challenges for minimizing their impact and for encouraging greater AI adoption in public service.

References

1. Berlyne, B.: A theory of human curiosity. Br. J. Psychol. **45**, 180–191 (1954)
2. Spector, L.: Evolution of artificial intelligence. Artif. Intell. **170**, 1251 (2006)
3. PWC: Sizing the prize - what's the real value of AI for your business and how can you capitalise ? (2017)
4. A Guide to Artificial Intelligence in Healthcare (2020). Retrieved from The Medical Futurist website: https://medicalfuturist.com/top-artificial-intelligence-companies-in-healthcare/#
5. Turing, A.M.: Computing machinery and intelligence. Mind **59**, 433 (1950)
6. UK Parliament: UK House of Commons - Science and Technology Committee report on AI and Robotics (2016). Accessed 12 May 2018
7. Indranil, M.,et al.: AI and robotics, leveraging artificial intelligence and robotics for sustainable growth. PWC ASSOCHAM Report (2017)
8. Stone, P.: Artificial Intelligence and Life in 2030. Stanford 52 (2016)
9. Jesse, N.: Internet of Things and Big Data: the disruption of the value chain and the rise of new software ecosystems. AI Soc. **33**(2), 229–239 (2018)
10. Newland, C., Argyriades, D.: Reclaiming Public Space: Drawing Lessons from the Past as We Confront the Future Sustainable Development Goal
11. Anderson, M.L.: Why is AI so scary? Artif. Intell. **169**, 201–208 (2005)
12. Butenko, A., Larouche, P.: Regulation for innovativeness or regulation of innovation? Law, Innov. Technol. **7**, 1–31 (2017)
13. European Parliament: Civil Law Rules on Robotics - European Parliament Resolution of 16 February 2017
14. Metz, C.: As China marches forward on AI, the White House is silent. New York Times 2–7 (2018)
15. Zheng, Y., et al.: SmartHS: an AI platform for improving govt service provision. In: 32nd AAAI Conference 7704 (2018)
16. Engin, Z., Treleaven, P.: Algorithmic government: automating public services and supporting civil servants in using data science technologies. Comput. J. **62**, 448–460 (2019)
17. Verma, A., Rao, K., Eluri, V., Sharma, Y.: Regulating AI in Public Health : Systems Challenges and Perspectives (2020)
18. USFDA: Proposed Regulatory Framework for Modifications to Artificial Intelligence/Machine Learning (AI/ML)-Based Software as a Medical Device (SaMD)-Discussion Paper and Request for Feedback (2019)
19. NITI Aayog: National Strategy for Artificial Intelligence. Discussion Paper (2018)
20. Vanderelst, D., Winfield, A.: The dark side of ethical robots. In: 2018 AAAI/ACM Conference on AI, Ethics, and Society, New Orleans, pp. 317–322 (2018)
21. Sobel, B.L.W.: Artificial intelligence's fair use crisis. Columbia J. Law Arts. **41**(1), 45–97 (2017)
22. UNESCO: Artificial intelligence in education: challenges and opportunities for sustainable development. Working Papers on Educational Policy, 7, 46 p. (2019)
23. Lee, K.-F.: The Four Waves of AI - A White Paper Adapted from AI Superpowers- China, Silicon Valley, and the New World Order (2018)
24. Future of Life Institute: Asilomar AI Principles. Future of Life Institute (2017)
25. BSI: Information Technology - Artificial Intelligence - Risk Management - Standard - Proposed (2019)
26. Harhoff, D., Heumann, S., Jentzsch, N., Lorenz, P.: Outline for a German Strategy for Artificial Intelligence. (2018)

27. METI - Ministry of Economy, Trade and Industry: Vision of New Industrial Structure - Japan's strategies for taking the lead in the Fourth Industrial Revolution - Interim Report by New Industrial Structure Committee. METI, Japan (2016)
28. Gaon, A., Stedman, I.: A Call to action : moving forward with the governance of artificial intelligence in Canada. Alta. Law Rev. **56** (2019)
29. Koene, A., Smith, A.L., Egawa, T., Mandalh, S., Hatada, Y.: IEEE P70xx, Establishing Standards for Ethical Technology. In: KDD 2018, London, UK (2018)
30. IEEE: The IEEE Global Initiative on Ethics of Autonomous and Intelligent Systems. Ethically Aligned Design: A Vision for Prioritizing Human Well-being with Autonomous and Intelligent Systems, Version 2. IEEE (2017)
31. Kankanhalli, A., Charalabidis, Y., Mellouli, S.: IoT and AI for smart government: a research agenda. Gov. Inf. Q. **36**, 304–309 (2019)
32. Cave, S., Nyrup, R., Vold, K., Weller, A.: Motivations and risks of machine ethics. Proc. IEEE **107**, 562–574 (2019)
33. Floridi, L., et al.: AI4People—an ethical framework for a good AI society: opportunities, risks, principles, and recommendations. Minds Mach. **28**(4), 689–707 (2018)
34. Hutchins, N., et al.: Social impacts of ethical artificial intelligence and autonomous system design. In: 2017 IEEE International Systems Engineering Symposium (2017)
35. Leikas, J., et al.: Ethical framework for designing autonomous intelligent systems. J. Open Innov. Technol. Mark. Complex. **5**, 18 (2019)
36. Weng, Y.H., Hirata, Y.: Ethically Aligned Design for Assistive Robotics. In: 2018 International Conference on Intelligence and Safety for Robotics, ISR 2018, pp. 286–290 (2018)
37. Ema, A., et al.: Clarifying privacy, property, and power: case study on value conflict between communities. Proc. IEEE **107**, 575–581 (2019)
38. Tamburrini, G.: On the ethical framing of research programs in robotics. AI Soc. **31**(4), 463–471 (2015)
39. Olhede, S.C., Wolfe, P.J.: The growing ubiquity of algorithms in society: implications, impacts and innovations. Phil. Trans. R. Soc. **A376**, 20170 (2018)
40. Caliskan, A., Bryson, J.J., Narayanan, A.: Semantics derived automatically from language corpora contain human-like biases. Science **356**, 183–186 (2017). COGNITIVE SCIENCE
41. Calo, R.: Artificial intelligence policy: a roadmap. SSRN Electron. J. 1–28 (2017)
42. Adam, T., O'Sullivan, A.C., Russell, R.: Artificial Intelligence and Public Policy. Mercatus Center at George Mason University (2017)
43. Intel: Artificial Intelligence - The Public Policy Opportunity (2017). https://doi.org/10.1007/978-1-4471-2359-0_15
44. Mergel, I., Rethemeyer, R.K., Isett, K.: Big data in public affairs education. J. Public Aff. Educ. **22**, 231–248 (2016)
45. Dwivedi, Y.K., et al.: Artificial Intelligence (AI): multidisciplinary perspectives on emerging challenges, opportunities, and agenda for research, practice and policy. IJIM (2019). https://doi.org/10.1016/j.ijinfomgt.2019.08.002
46. Bleicher, A.: Demystifying the black box that is AI. Sci. Am. (2017)
47. Bughin, J., et al.: Notes from the AI frontier: modeling the global economic impact of AI. McKinsey Global Institute, September, pp. 1–64 (2018)
48. Boden, M., et al.: Principles of robotics: regulating robots in the real world. Connect. Sci. **29**, 124–129 (2017)
49. Wirtz, B.W., Weyerer, J.C., Geyer, C.: Artificial intelligence and the public sector—applications and challenges. Int. J. Public Adm. **00**, 1–20 (2018)
50. Microsoft: The Future Computed (2018)

51. Dhasarathy, A., Jain, S., Khan, N.: When governments turn to AI: algorithms, trade-offs, and trust. McKinsey&Company (2019)
52. Schwab, K.: The Fourth Industrial Revolution (2016)
53. How, J.: Ethically Aligned Design (2018)
54. Adamson, G., et al.: Designing a value-driven future for ethical autonomous and intelligent systems. Proc. IEEE **107**, 518–525 (2019)
55. Lenk, H.: Ethics of responsibilities distributions in a technological culture. AI Soc. **32**(2), 219–231 (2016). https://doi.org/10.1007/s00146-015-0642-3
56. Bryson, J., Winfield, A.: Standardizing ethical design for artificial intelligence and autonomous systems. Computer **50**, 116–119 (2017)
57. Furman, J., Seamans, R.: AI and the economy. Innov. Policy Econ. **19**, 161–191 (2018). https://doi.org/10.1086/699936
58. Shava, E., Hofisi, C.: Challenges and opportunities for public administration in the fourth industrial revolution. Afr. J. Public Aff. **9**, 203–215 (2017)
59. Frey, C.B., Osborne, M.: The Future of Employment: How Susceptible are Jobs to Computerisation? (2013)
60. Arnaldi, S.: Responsible governance in science and technology policy: reflections from Europe, China and India. Technol. Soc. **42**, 81–92 (2015)
61. Ponce, A.: A Law on Robotics and Artificial Intelligence in the EU? SSRN (2018)
62. European Parliament 2014–2019: Civil Law Rules on Robotics. European Parliament resolution of 16 February 2017 with recommendations to the Commission on Civil Law Rules on Robotics 2103, 22 (2016)
63. Miller, T.: Explanation in artificial intelligence: insights from the social sciences (2019). https://doi.org/10.1016/j.artint.2018.07.007
64. Craglia, M., Hradec, J., Troussard, X.: The Big Data and Artificial Intelligence: Opportunities and Challenges to Modernise the Policy Cycle. Elsevier (2020)
65. Gill, K.S.: Uncommon voices of AI. AI Soc. **32**(4), 475–482 (2017)
66. Russell, S., Hauert, S., Altman, R., Veloso, M.: Ethics of artificial intelligence. Nature **521** (2015)
67. Berkeley, U.C., Song, D., Digital, E., Autopilot, T.: How we might protect ourselves from malicious (2019)
68. Mika, N., et al.: Ethical AI for the governance of the society: challenges and opportunities. CEUR Workshop Proc. **2505**, 20–26 (2019)
69. Taeihagh, A., Lim, H.S.M.: Governing autonomous vehicles: emerging responses for safety, liability, privacy, cybersecurity, and industry risks. Transp. Rev. **39**, 103–128 (2019)
70. Truong, T.C., Zelinka, I., Plucar, J., Čandík, M., Šulc, V.: Artificial intelligence and cybersecurity: past, presence, and future. In: Dash, S.S., Lakshmi, C., Das, S., Panigrahi, B. K. (eds.) Artificial Intelligence and Evolutionary Computations in Engineering Systems. AISC, vol. 1056, pp. 351–363. Springer, Singapore (2020). https://doi.org/10.1007/978-981-15-0199-9_30
71. Mehr, H.: Artificial Intelligence for Citizen Services and Government. Harvard Kennedy School, Ash Center for Democratic Governance and Innovation 19 (2017)
72. Duan, Y., Edwards, J.S., Dwivedi, Y.K.: Artificial intelligence for decision making in the era of Big Data – evolution, challenges and research agenda. IJIM (2019). https://doi.org/10.1016/j.ijinfomgt.2019.01.021

Big Data and Analytics

Value Creation from the Impact of Business Analytics

Hari Saravanabhavan[1(✉)], Seetha Raman[2], and K. Maddulety[1]

[1] SP Jain School of Global Management, Mumbai, India
{hari.ds19dba005,k.maddulety}@spjain.org
[2] SP Jain School of Global Management, Singapore, Singapore
seetha.raman@spjain.org

Abstract. Digital transformation is a key imperative across multiple industries globally. One of the main tenets of digital transformation is improving the intelligence quotient in an organization in order to enable accurate decision-making. Intelligence in the digital era is fueled by data and by the ability to analyze data in a way that generates meaningful insights, thereby making an organization competitive. Literature shows that the benefits of being analytically competitive are widespread and impactful across many organization functions like strategy, finance, marketing and operations; but this can be accomplished only if an organization has the right level of capability for adopting and executing analytics initiatives. Data, leadership, people skills, culture and governance are capabilities that are essential for successful analytics endeavors in an organization. This study is focused on building an end-to-end perspective comprising input factors and outcomes of being analytically competitive.

Keywords: Big data · Business analytics · Culture · Governance · Strategy · Technology · Talent · Business value · Leadership

1 Introduction

In coming years, the most intelligent organizations will need to blend technology-enabled insights with a sophisticated understanding of human judgment, reasoning, and choice. Those that do this successfully will have an advantage over their rivals (Schoemaker and Tetlock 2017). The Authors further state, a relatively new phenomenon, the Global intelligent enterprise is shaped by the growing power of computers and big data, which provide the foundation for operations research, forecasting models, and artificial intelligence (AI). An analogy to this, is Sam Palmisano, IBM CEO's, coining of the term "Globally Integrated Enterprise" (GIE) in his 2006 article where he terms it as this emerging business model that is built completely on the base of data and analytics. Prominent researchers within the field use the following definition of Business Analytics (BA): a combination of data, tools and technology, analysis and quantitative and qualitative methods used to build statistical, mathematical or computer-based models that can provide organizations with better insights to drive

© IFIP International Federation for Information Processing 2020
Published by Springer Nature Switzerland AG 2020
S. K. Sharma et al. (Eds.): TDIT 2020, IFIP AICT 617, pp. 115–125, 2020.
https://doi.org/10.1007/978-3-030-64849-7_11

intelligent fact-based decisions (Davenport 2005). Thomas Davenport introduces his latest publication Analytics 4.0 by stating that artificial intelligence (AI) is intrinsic to analytics; This statement emphasizes the significance of business analytics in an organization (Davenport and Ronanki 2018) culminating to AI.

A review of the literature indicates that the value of BA is in its strategic competitive advantage (Sprongl 2013) and that business analytics is also a means for improved performance (Whitelock 2018). Various studies expand the value of BA to include the supply chain, research and development, pricing and human capital interventions (Davenport 2005). Multiple articles also refer to the causal relationship between BA and organization performance, including an improvement in financial outcomes (Jamshi and Ganeshkumar 2017; Rouhani et al. 2016). However, in order to realize the impact of BA, organizations need to have the right capabilities for gaining these benefits. The studies point towards analytics capabilities being adapted from the capability maturity model for software (Paulk 2009). Research reveals that more than 150 versions are being studied in order to try and establish a BA maturity framework (Chuah and Wong 2011).

1.1 Research Objective

The Capability Maturity Model (CMM) was first introduced by Watts Humphrey in 1988 at the Software Engineering Institute which then empowered organizations to gain an understanding of software process development and were able to improve their capabilities (Paulk et al. 2018). The CMM allowed organizations to measure their software process development and enable them to improve their capabilities. Since its introduction, there has been a steady growth of maturity models applicable to various domains. The objective of this paper is to build a preliminary understanding of a standardized global BA capability framework from existing literature that can create value for organizations. Thus, the Research questions (RQ) being addressed herein are:

RQ1: What are the significant variables contributing towards the BA framework?
RQ2: What are the potential outcomes from deploying a BA capabilities framework in an organization?

1.2 Scope of the Study

Maturity models have been developed for both BA and BI separately (Ariyarathna and Peter 2019) An exhaustive study of maturity models brings out two distinct concepts, namely, Business Analytics and Business Intelligence maturity models. What distinguishes the two concepts is that BI builds analysis based on past data as support for decision-making, while analytics also have predictive capabilities that can analyze and suggest future changes ahead of time (Davenport 2005). BI and BA have emerged as strategic differentiators for organizations globally. Cloud, AI and other advancements such as Internet of Things (IOT) are also quickly converging to the larger analytics canvas; however, this qualitative research is focused on studying business intelligence and business analytics capabilities and their impact on a firm.

2 Research Methodology

Research methodology helps to bridge the gap of understanding in a structured and systematic manner (Saunders and Townsend 2016). Research methodology is the science of studying techniques, based on which, the researcher can decide what study is to be conducted. Additionally, it includes logical, productive and planned steps that help lead to a better understanding of a phenomenon (Zikmund et al. 2013). The research methodology in this study details the existing core variables identified through an exhaustive literature survey.

Searching and reviewing of literature for BA and BI maturity models laid the foundation of this study. Over twenty related models or studies were found from Google Scholar, Emerald Insight, Research Gate and IEEE Xplore Digital Library and after an initial screening nine were selected for further assessment. Finally, variables were identified. The researchers do not claim this to be entirely exhaustive; however, the papers selected and reviewed considerably represent the wide-ranging body of the research work accomplished in this area. The review focuses on research institutes' papers and conference papers within the period of 2009–2020.

3 Background

BA has been an evolving science and has manifested into a critical component in the world of business. There are multiple capability models that have been studied in the past that take their inspiration from the Capability Maturity Model for software (Paulk 2009). The models from the literature have been segmented into four types, as represented below.

Real-World Models (Case-Study Based)
Davenport (2005) recommended a framework for analytics maturity based on extensive real experiences of an organization in their journey of building analytics capabilities. They advocated the concept of analytics competitor, the highest level of utilising analytics within an organization to drive strategic value from business analytics investments. The framework emphasises five dimensions for analytics capability building: data and technology, enterprise, leadership, targets and techniques, Analysts (DELTA) based on various case studies. Although empirical evidence shows that BA systems bring benefits to organizations (Kohavi and Quinlan 2002) , few studies provide a sound theoretical basis for understanding how and why these benefits are achieved. The resource-based view theory discussed in the next section provides this theoretical base.

Theoretical Resource-Based Models
Studies indicate multiple theoretical models that have been researched to build analytics capability within firms. One of the widely cited models is the Business Analytics Capability Framework (BACF) developed by Cosic et al. (2015) that helps organizations to evaluate their current Business Analytics initiatives. BACF arrived after an in-depth study of more than 50 publications. The framework refers to 16 variables that are clustered into four major capability areas, namely people, culture, technology & governance.

Another framework that builds an interesting perspective in BA capability is the Analytics Processes Maturity Model commonly referred to as APMM (Grossman 2018). The APMM identifies analytics intervention within the firm processes into six key areas: Building analytic models, Deploying analytics models, Managing and operating analytics infrastructure, Protecting analytics assets through policies and procedures, Operating an analytics governance structure and Driving analytics strategy within the organization.

Based upon the maturity of these processes, the APMM divides organizations into five maturity levels and the framework contributes very significantly in differentiating Analytics Maturity Level (AML) between organizations.

Business-Intelligence Models

BI has existed for a long time, and there have been multiple studies that have worked to establish the maturity factors for Business Intelligence. An exhaustive paper (Chuah and Wong 2011) indicates that there are over 150 versions of BI models that have been studied in the past. From the vast number of models, the dominant variables that emerge are culture, strategy, business understanding and enablement along with data and skills.

Consulting-Led Models

Given the importance of BI and BA in the digital era, there have been significant studies done by Tier 1 consulting firms to understand the analytics maturity factors and the value of analytics initiatives for an organization. Studies by McKinsey (McKinsey, The Age of Analytics) (McKinsey, Building an Advanced Analytics Organization) point towards similar factors, as described earlier in the theoretical models, such as data, process management and culture as well as to more practical variables such as picking the right use cases that were not referred to in the previous frameworks. Additional interesting studies on analytics by AT Kearney (a study referred to as The Analytics Impact Index) and by Deloitte (a study referred to as The Analytics Advantage) point to organization structure (Analytics Centre of Excellence) as being a key component in driving analytics capability beyond the other factors described in the studies that were mentioned earlier. In summary, the emerging pattern of variables from various models is mentioned below:

1. DELTA model (Davenport and Ronanki 2018): Data, Enterprise Leadership, Targets, Analysts, Technology, Techniques
2. BACF (Cosic et al. 2015), APMM (Grossman 2018): People, Process, Culture, Technology, Infrastructure, Governance
3. Gartner maturity model, TDWI maturity model, Hewlett Package business intelligence model (Chuah and Wong 2011): People, Process, Technology, Culture, Strategy, Business enablement
4. McKinsey Model (2016), AT Kearney Maturity Assessment framework (2020), Deloitte Analytics Advantage (Davenport 2013): Data, Process, Culture, Use Cases, Leadership, Strategy, Management, Information Technology, People, Governance

Observations from the literature review of multiple capability models highlight four recurrent independent variables that can drive the dependent variable 'BA capabilities' in an enterprise. These four variables are:

- Leadership (Management, vision and strategy)
- Information technology (data, tools and systems)
- Human capital (talent, skills and competency)
- Organization (structure, process, culture and governance).

3.1 Leadership (Management Vision and Strategy)

The analytics maturity of an organization depends on the outlined strategy (Raber et al. 2012) as well as the level of executive leadership and support (Cosic et al. 2015). In his book competing on Analytics, Thomas Davenport characterizes an analytics competitor as an organization that champions analytics from the top. The literature reveals the following critical success factors:

- Top-down support–the top-down leadership and executive support needed to drive an analytics agenda within an organization (Davenport 2005).
- The type of industry and size of the firm–the nature of industry is a strong determinant in the BA capability of a firm. Digital natives such as Google and Amazon have a higher disposition towards analytics initiatives compared to the traditional firms (Sharon and Aggarwal 2019). Studies also indicate that within an industry, the larger a firm, higher is the analytics maturity level. Therefore, industry and size are important to be considered from a competitive perspective (Müller et al. 2018).
- Analytics strategy – firms that have a clear and well-defined analytics strategy and road map have higher business analytics capability levels compared to organizations that have a tactical approach to the competency (AT Kearney).

3.2 IT (Data, Tools and Systems)

The digital world throws up various types of unstructured data (beyond the well-known structured data component) such as image data, speech data and text data (Verhoef and Lemon 2015) that needs to be managed well prior to analysis. There are multiple interesting views or categorization on the dynamic state of data; a common one is referred to as the seven 'V' by Whitelock (2018) and it classifies data under one of seven 'V' dimensions. In analytics terms, the key imperatives on the data front need to be: (1) Is the data relevant? (2) Do we have enough volume of data? (3) How accessible is the data? (4) Does the data reflect all types of sources? (5) Can the data be trusted? Enabling technology is defined as an ecosystem that allows for the storage and processing of data inputs using multiple hardware and software processes, such as ETL and governance capabilities, either internally or through partner systems (Seddon et al. 2017). Tools are the functionality provided by the technology ecosystem that allow the organization to access, manage and analyze data effectively and efficiently (Seddon et al. 2017).

3.3 Human Capital (Talent, Skills and Competency)

As data becomes more available, the ability to analyze and drive insights from data is becoming more critical (McAfee et al. 2012). This requires human skills and expertise that are extremely dynamic and ever-increasing. Human skills in the business analytics domain include technological skills, business skills and management skills. These skills also emphasise the importance of being able to translate and communicate insights and values to the executives in an organization (Cosic et al. 2015). Davenport emphasises the need to not only recruit people with analytics skills but to also recruit people who have the ability to explain complex outcomes to decision makers in simple business terms (Davenport 2005). A common term used to address the combined skill set is data sciences; according to a survey by McKinsey (2016), data sciences is one of the most coveted professional jobs of the digital era. Being a data scientist entails having a broad perspective, from data to analysis to outcomes, which combines quantitative numbers analysis with qualitative insights and focuses on delivering business results within the organization.

3.4   Organization (Structure, Process, Culture and Governance)

A well-reputed study by AT Kearney, a leading consulting firm, assigns the highest weights to the factor of organization that is composed of cross-functional data-driven decision-making, embedding analytics within the processes, tightly articulated roles and responsibilities and key constructs around building internally vs. outsource/partner (AT Kearney, The Value of Analytics 2019). In a study of 25 business intelligence and analytics models (Foshay et al. 2015), 65% of the models emphasised the need for robust processes, 40% of the models reinforced the need for a formal organizational structure to enable business analytics, 60% of the models highlighted governance as a key aspect and 40% of the models valued the concept of cost-benefit analysis, thereby pointing towards the overall significance of the organization factor in business analytics capabilities. Another framework that focuses on the process aspect of BA capability is the Analytics Processes Maturity Model (APMM) (Grossman 2018). The APMM identifies analytics intervention within the firm processes into six key areas building analytic models, deploying analytics models, managing and operating analytics infrastructure, protecting analytics assets through policies and procedures, operating an analytics governance structure and driving analytics strategy within the organization.

3.5   Findings

The literature review thus validates that these four variables indeed enhance the impact on BA capabilities of an organization. It is now important to analyze these variables from the value creation standpoint.

4   Analysis

Big data and BA can lead to more informed insight, that in turn can result in better decisions and hence, greater performance gains (Sharma et al. 2014), A large proportion of empirical studies assume a direct relationship between big data and business analytics capabilities and performance outcomes, or through mediating organizational capabilities (Wamba et al. 2017). A combination of the four variables' (Leadership, IT, Human Capital and Organization) drives BA capabilities that creates value.

4.1   Leadership

In an issue on leadership development, Harvard Business Review (Ashkenas and Manville 2018) aptly describes leadership as uniting people around an exciting, aspirational vision and as building a strategy for achieving the vision by attracting and developing the best possible talent to implement the strategy and relentlessly focusing on results in the context of the strategy. Studies indicate that the importance of leadership for BA is the same as any other function (Grossman 2018). Successful analytics endeavours depend on multiple factors, including strategy and leadership. Successful companies have built a role around Data and analytics commonly referred to as the Chief Data Officer or Chief Analytics Officer thereby placing critical importance on the strategic leadership aspect for the competency. Another research study on five diverse reputed global brands, Ebay, Cancer LinQ, Walmart, Deutsche Bank and UPS (Grover et al. 2018), demonstrated that, with strong leadership as a moderating/driving factor, these organizations achieved:

- Functional benefits – financial performance, growth, revenue, cost reduction and customer retention
- Strategic benefits – reputation, satisfaction and market leadership

4.2   IT

Business analytics or Big Data Analytics (BDA) is often referred to as a 'new paradigm of knowledge assets' (Hagstrom 2012), or 'the next frontier for innovation, competition, and productivity' (Manyika et al. 2011, p. 1). This is possible due to the adoption and use of data, tools, technologies, infrastructure and platforms for a firm's operations to achieve and sustain competitive advantage.

Another key component of the IT solution is to have a clear information agenda that can enable BA initiatives to drive the necessary outcomes. A well-acknowledged and comprehensive study by MIT Sloan (LaValle et al. 2011) on big data and analytics charted information agendas as visions and road maps that can align IT with analytics and business needs. The IT agenda spans information governance policies and tools and data architecture, including structured and unstructured data, data relevance and currency, master data management and analytics tool kits that support reporting and visualization in advanced analytics.

4.3   Human Capital

Talent is a critical driver in building a competitive advantage and helping organizations innovate with analytics (Ransbotham et al. 2015). Talent capability refers to the competence to deliver BA in a big data environment. Talent capability for BA is a combination of technical skills, technology understanding, business knowledge and domain. An interesting quantitative study of service analytics which is categorized as a dynamic capability shows how talent capability mediates the relationship between technology, information and firm performance (Akter et al. 2019). Another study's findings indicate that the outcomes of BA are significantly driven by talent capability, which can be achieved by maintaining a balance of hiring external people with sound analytical skills and of upskilling the existing team through customized training programs (Ransbotham et al. 2015).

4.4   Organization

In a study entitled 'Building an Analytics Organization', McKinsey describes an analytics organization (department) as an ecosystem that is enabled by deep functional expertise and that provides access to data, tools and technology and fosters talent development to deliver business outcomes. It has the responsibility to govern and encourage an analytics culture across the company. Similarly, a study (Krishnamoorthi and Mathew 2018) using a case study methodology proved that Organization variables contribute positively to BA capabilities that in turn deliver positive business performance.

Another study (Espinosa and Armour 2016) provides a valuable framework that serves as an ecosystem for capturing the essential elements of an organization that enable big data/business analytics outcomes.

4.5   Results

The effective outcome of BA capability driven by the four variables impacts four key areas:

- Financials, which includes profitability, cash flow management and risk mitigation.
- Operations/shared services, which includes optimization, human-resource effectiveness, improving IT effectiveness and mitigating cyber-security challenges.
- Sales marketing and customer management focused on acquiring and retaining customers, improving customer experience, marketing Return on Investment optimisation and product-portfolio management.
- Strategic imperatives around increasing market share, market growth and competitive advantage.

5   Conclusions

Globally, firms are investing in business intelligence and business analytics with the objective of gaining a competitive advantage in an intensifying market. However, to gain this advantage, firms need to focus on building the right maturity levels and stay invested in the journey of analytics. Higher the maturity of the capabilities, better is the quality of analytics and broader are the impacts for the organization.

5.1   Discussions

This research paper is based on qualitative research from relevant papers and is validated using secondary data. A conceptual framework identifying relevant factors contributing towards BA capability within an organization has been outlined and the study also provides a preliminary view on the value creation by implementing the framework. This research contributes to the global BA and BI practice and helps organizations in their path of becoming Globally Integrated Enterprises.

5.2   Recommended Contribution of Theory (Integrated Model)

Previous papers have successfully drawn out the contribution of BA to individual theories - TOE framework (Nam et al. 2019) and the TAM framework (Brock and Khan 2017). However, given the wholistic nature of the analytics function there is a potential opportunity to validate the framework towards an integrated model (Wilber 1997) The Integral model emphasises that in the new world, the sum total of multiple theories is successfully applied to achieve a superior outcome.

5.3   Limitations and Scope for Future Research

BA is an extremely dynamic subject, and it covers a wide variety of competencies under its span. In addition, analytics maturity is a concept that is derived from the capability model, and there is no standard industry level framework to assess maturity. Given this background, the interpretation of BA factors and related variables on maturity may tend to be subjective, depending on the user approach. The preliminary impact of BA is clearly tangible and needs to be further studied by industry, geography and functions using primary data in order to harness the optimal value from the competency.

References

Akter, S., Fosso Wamba, S., Barrett, M., Biswas, K.: How talent capability can shape service analytics capability in the big data environment. J. Strat. Mark. 27(6), 521–539 (2019)

Mckinsey Analytics: The age of analytics: competing in a data-driven world (2016)

Ariyarathna, K., Peter, S.: Business analytics maturity models: a systematic review of literature. Focus 3(10), 4 (2019)

Ashkenas, R., Manville, B.: The Harvard Business Review Leader's Handbook: Make an Impact, Inspire Your Organization, and Get to the Next Level. Harvard Business Press, Boston (2018)

Brock, V.F., Khan, H.U.: Are enterprises ready for big data analytics? A survey based approach. Int. J. Bus. Inf. Syst. 25(2), 256277 (2017)

Chuah, M.H., Wong, K.L.: A review of business intelligence and its maturity models. Afr. J. Bus. Manag. 5(9), 3424–3428 (2011)

Cosic, R., Shanks, G., Maynard, S.B.: A business analytics capability framework. Australas. J. Inf. Syst. 19 (2015)

Davenport, T.H.: Thinking for a Living: How To Get Better Performances and Results From Knowledge Workers. Harvard Business Press, Boston (2005)

Davenport, T.H.: The analytics advantage: we're just getting started. Deloitte Analytics (2013)

Davenport, T.H., Ronanki, R.: Artificial intelligence for the real world. Harv. Bus. Rev. 96(1), 108–116 (2018)

Espinosa, J.A., Armour, F.: The big data analytics gold rush: a research framework for coordination and governance. In: 2016 49th Hawaii International Conference on System Sciences (HICSS), pp. 1112–1121. IEEE (2016)

Foshay, N., Yeoh, W., Boo, Y.L., Ong, K.L., Mattie, D.: A comprehensive diagnostic framework for evaluating business intelligence and analytics effectiveness. Australas. J. Inf. Syst. 19 (2015)

Grossman, R.L.: A framework for evaluating the analytic maturity of an organization. Int. J. Inf. Manag. **38**(1), 45–51 (2018)

Grover, V., Chiang, R.H., Liang, T.P., Zhang, D.: Creating strategic business value from big data analytics: a research framework. J. Manag. Inf. Syst. **35**(2), 388–423 (2018)

Hagstrom, M.: High-performance analytics fuels innovation and inclusive growth: use big data, hyperconnectivity and speed to intelligence to get true value in the digital economy. J. Adv. Anal. **2**, 3–4 (2012)

https://industrytoday.com/wp-content/uploads/2019/09/A.T.-Kearney-Melbourne-Business-School_The-Value-of-Analytics-in-2019.pdf. Accessed 01 Mar 2020

https://www2.deloitte.com/.../dttl-analytics-analytics-advantage-report-061913.pdf. Accessed 19 Feb 2020

Jamshi, J., Ganeshkumar, C.: Causal linkage among business analytics, supply chain performance, firm performance and competitive advantage. Parikalpana: KIIT J. Manag. **13** (2), 29–36 (2017)

Kohavi, R., Quinlan, J.R.: Data mining tasks and methods: classification: decision tree discovery. In: Handbook of Data Mining and Knowledge Discovery, pp. 267–276 (2002)

Krishnamoorthi, S., Mathew, S.K.: Business analytics and business value: a comparative case study. Inf. Manag. **55**(5), 643–666 (2018)

LaValle, S., Lesser, E., Shockley, R., Hopkins, M.S., Kruschwitz, N.: Big data, analytics and the path from insights to value. MIT Sloan Manag. Rev. **52**(2), 21–32 (2011)

Verhoef, P.C., Lemon, K.N.: Advances in customer value management. In: Handbook on Research in Relationship Marketing. Edward Elgar Publishing (2015)

Manyika, J., et al.: Big Data: The Next Frontier for Innovation, Competition, and Productivity. McKinsey Global Institute (2011)

McAfee, A., Brynjolfsson, E., Davenport, T.H., Patil, D.J., Barton, D.: Big data: the management revolution. Harv. Bus. Rev. **90**(10), 60–68 (2012)

Müller, O., Fay, M., VomBrocke, J.: The effect of big data and analytics on firm performance: an econometric analysis considering industry characteristics. J. Manag. Inf. Syst. **35**(2), 488–509 (2018)

Nam, D., Lee, J., Lee, H.: Business analytics adoption process: an innovation diffusion perspective. Int. J. Inf. Manag. **49**, 411–423 (2019)

Palmisano, S.: Re-Think: A Path to the Future. Center for Global Enterprise, New York (2014)

Paulk, M.C.: A history of the capability maturity model for software. ASQ Softw. Qual. Prof. **12** (1), 5–19 (2009)

http://sunnyday.mit.edu/16.355/cmm.pdf. Accessed 15 Feb 2020

http://www.un.org/millenniumgoals/pdf/GP%20Baclqgrotmder–General2013_Sept2013.Pdf. Accessed 05 Feb 2020

Raber, D., Winter, R., Wortmann, F.: Using quantitative analyzes to construct a capability maturity model for business intelligence. Paper Presented at the System Science (HICSS), 2012 45th Hawaii International Conference on System Sciences, 4–7 January 2012 (2012)

Ransbotham, S., Kiron, D., Prentice, P.K.: Minding the analytics gap. MIT Sloan Manag. Rev. **56**(3), 63 (2015)

Rouhani, S., Ashrafi, A., Ravasan, A.Z., Afshari, S.: The impact model of business intelligence on decision support and organizational benefits. J. Enterp. Inf. Manag. **29**, 19–50 (2016)

Saunders, M.N., Townsend, K.: Reporting and justifying the number of interview participants in organization and workplace research. Br. J. Manag. **27**(4), 836–852 (2016)

Schoemaker, P.J., Tetlock, P.E.: Building a more intelligent enterprise. MIT Sloan Manag. Rev. **58**(3), 28 (2017)

Seddon, P.B., Constantinidis, D., Tamm, T., Dod, H.: How does business analytics contribute to business value? Inf. Syst. J. **27**(3), 237–269 (2017)

Sharon, M.S.D., Aggarwal, V.: Implementation of Industry 4.0: influence of digital natives and agility of employees (2019)

Sharma, R., Mithas, S., Kankanhalli, A.: Transforming decision-making processes: a research agenda for understanding the impact of business analytics on organisations (2014)

Sprongl, P.: Gaining competitive advantage through business analytics. Acta Universitatis Agriculturae et Silviculturae Mendelianae Brunensis **61**(7), 2779–2785 (2013)

Wamba, S.F., Gunasekaran, A., Akter, S., Ren, S.J.F., Dubey, R., Childe, S.J.: Big data analytics and firm performance: effects of dynamic capabilities. J. Bus. Res. **70**, 356–365 (2017)

Whitelock, V.: Business analytics and firm performance: Role of structured financial statement data. J. Bus. Anal. **1**(2), 81–92 (2018)

Wilber, K.: An integral theory of consciousness. J. Conscious. Stud. **4**(1), 71–92 (1997)

Zikmund, W.G., Carr, J.C., Griffin, M.: Business Research Methods. Cengage Learning, Boston (2013)

Exploring Associations Between Participant Online Content Engagement and Outcomes in an Online Professional Development Programme

Ketan S. Deshmukh$^{(\boxtimes)}$ ⓘ, Vijaya Sherry Chand, Kathan D. Shukla, and Arnab K. Laha

Indian Institute of Management Ahmedabad, Ahmedabad 380015, Gujarat, India
ketand@iima.ac.in

Abstract. Online Professional Development (PD) programmes for government school teachers provide benefits of low costs to the administration and flexible schedules for the participants. However, research on the use of technology in PD programmes has reported mixed results, thus warranting further investigation. Exploring the associations between the variation in engagement of and outcomes among the participants may provide insights for future research. The paper presents analysis of pageview logs and survey responses of 6933 participants of an online PD programme. First, four latent online engagement profiles were extracted using mixture modelling. Then, associations between participants' latent profiles and reported change in self-efficacy beliefs were analyzed. Finally, limitations and implications of the work are presented.

Keywords: Online professional development · Mixture modelling · Latent profile analysis · Self-efficacy beliefs

1 Introduction

The benefits of low cost and flexible schedules made it attractive and viable to adopt information technology to facilitate professional development (PD) programmes [1, 2]. The advances in data gathering and analysis, in recent times, provided precise tools to answer the "what works?" question for in-service teacher's online PD. We present the results of an exploratory study of online learner's engagement patterns and their association with outcomes within the context of an online professional development programme for teachers.

The next section (Sect. 2) provides the background of study viz. teacher professional development programme. Next, we present the method in Sect. 3 and present the findings in Sect. 4. Subsequently, we proceed to discuss these findings in Sect. 5 and highlight the limitations of the work in Sect. 6. Finally, we mention the implications of the study in Sect. 7, followed by the acknowledgment section.

© IFIP International Federation for Information Processing 2020
Published by Springer Nature Switzerland AG 2020
S. K. Sharma et al. (Eds.): TDIT 2020, IFIP AICT 617, pp. 126–136, 2020.
https://doi.org/10.1007/978-3-030-64849-7_12

2 Background

Teacher's PD programmes improve implementation of education policy and student outcomes [3, 4]. Many studies have indicated that improving teacher's self-efficacy beliefs is a desirable objective for PD programmes [5–8]. Teaching self-efficacy belief is defined as " the judgement of one's capabilities to influence student engagement and learning" [9]. Improving teacher's self-efficacy beliefs is associated with higher student achievement [9–11] and effective classroom practice [12–16].

Facilitating a PD programme for teachers involves huge costs, which can be reduced by adoption of technology. Evaluation studies of technology-based PD have reported mixed results [17–19], warranting additional research on outcomes of technologybased PD. Studies have not only found that participants in the same PD vary in their preference for and access to the different components of the programme [20, 21], but also found variation in outcomes for participants attending the same programme [22]. One of the affordances of technology-based PD is the ability to track and analyze participants engagement with the PD content. Tracking learners enables identification of specific content or activities which improve participant outcomes.

The prominent field that deals with studying a learner's engagement/participation in a programme is Educational Data Science (EDS). EDS grew due to Massive Open Online Courses (MOOCs) which generated huge amounts of data on participant's interaction with educational content [23, 24]. EDS is constituted of various sub-fields like Learning Analytics, Educational Data Mining, Institutional/ Academic Analytics, etc. [23]. Researchers who studied the patterns of participant engagement in MOOCs have classified them into either four [25] or seven [26] groups. Analyzing patterns of participant engagement one could identify areas of improvement in courses [27], design courses that accommodate different learning styles [28] and understand how to retain learners till the end of the course [29]. Kalakoski, Ratilainen, and Drupsteen [30] proposed the use of EDS methods to improve job training for professionals. Our study intends to identify groups of learners with similar engagement patterns and determine if the change in participant's self-efficacy is associated with their engagement pattern.

3 Method

3.1 Context

An online PD programme was offered to all teachers (19,267) in the state teaching science and mathematics at upper primary level in state-run primary schools. The training was offered in two batches and teachers were randomly assigned to one of the two batches. This article deals with the outcomes and engagement profiles of the participants in the first batch. In the first batch, a total of 10535 had registered and filled the pre-training survey of which 7935 participants completed the full programme and then completed the post-training survey. The course content consisted of Subject specific content (Science & Mathematics) and Managerial content (Classroom Management, School Comprehensive Evaluation (SCE) and Use of ICT). Content for the PD was from two sources, subject matter expert and authentic case studies. The teachers were required to execute a real-world project in classroom, which was peer evaluated by other participants on the platform.

3.2 Self-efficacy Belief

Participant's self-efficacy beliefs were measured via online surveys when they registered for the programme in May – June 2018 and later once they completed it. As selfefficacy beliefs are subject specific, teachers' self-efficacy beliefs about teaching Science and Mathematics were captured using instruments Science Teaching Efficacy Belief Instrument (STEBI) [31] and Mathematics Teaching Efficacy Belief Instrument (MTEBI) [32]. The subject specific self-efficacy scales each consist of two sub-constructs the personal subject teaching efficacy belief and the subject teaching outcome expectancy beliefs. In this article, we will be analyzing participant responses to only the personal science teaching efficacy belief. The personal science teaching efficacy belief subscales measure the teacher's own efficacy belief about teaching science using items like "I generally teach science effectively" and "I find it easy to explain to students why science experiments work". The scales were translated to local language by experts and validated by back translation. The responses to the survey were recorded on a 5-point Likert scale.

3.3 Online Content Engagement

Online activities of the participants on the platform were captured by logging pageviews on an external server. This provided pageview logs of the participants as they engaged with content on the PD website. Activity logs of participants were downloaded from the server in the form of json files. Data from the downloaded files was extracted using R [33] with R-Studio [34]. The difference between timestamps was used to calculate the time spent on the content. Additionally, time spent on pages at the end of the session was estimated using the user level average time spent on the page when the pageview was not at end of session.

3.4 Analysis

We analyzed the survey responses using Mplus 8.4 [35]. We conducted a confirmatory factor analysis. The responses to survey items were treated as categorical and the weighted least square (WLSMV) estimator [36] was used in the analysis. Measurement model consisting of both Pre-test and Post-Test responses was evaluated. Model Fit was evaluated based on criteria provided by Hu and Bentler [37] & Marsh, Hau and Wen [38] i.e. CFI > = .95, TLI > = .95, RMSEA <= .06, & SRMR <= .08. Items with standardized loadings less than 0.5 and with correlation with other items were dropped. The different patterns of engagement with online content were determined using mixture modelling [35, 39]. Percentage of total time calculated from pageview logs was used to determine latent profiles among the participants. Nylund, Asparouhov and Muthén [40] recommended the use of Bayesian Information Criteria (BIC) or Bootstrapped Likelihood Ratio tests (BLRT) to determine the appropriate number of homogenous classes/profiles. They also note that at a higher number of observations (n > 1000) the performance of Likelihood Ratio tests (LRT), viz. VLMR LRT & ALMR LRT, is reliable. Also, they mention that the LRTs are robust and valid even if the distribution of data within classes/profile is non-normal. The steps outlined in the software user guide were followed to determine the final number of latent groups among the learners.

4 Findings

Complete pageview log and survey responses to both Pre and Post training were available for 6933 participants. Majority of the participants, 81%, had qualified the State's Teacher Eligibility Test (TET) and 44.9% of the total participants were females. Among the participants, 51.8% had a graduation degree and 44.5% of the teachers had earned a post-graduate degree while the rest had either a diploma or professional teachers' certification. The average work experience was 75.20 months and the average age was 32.14 years.

4.1 Self-efficacy Beliefs

The analysis of survey responses resulted in a good model fit for measuring the latent constructs. The item-wise descriptive of survey responses is provided in the following table. The self-efficacy constructs at both time points demonstrated composite reliability of above 0.7 and had average variance explained more than 0.5 (Table 1).

Table 1. Responses to Personal Science Teaching Efficacy Scale

	Range	Pre	Post	Pre	Post
		M (SD)	M (SD)	Std. loadings	Std. loadings
				CR = .93 AVE = .57	CR = .94 AVE = .58
I am continually finding better ways to teach science	1–5	4.469 (.58)	4.578 (.70)	0.657	0.588
I know how to teach science concepts effectively	1–5	4.071 (.64)	4.478 (.60)	0.776	0.794
I am very effective in monitoring science experiments	1–5	4.241 (.62)	4.492 (.61)	0.819	0.816
I generally teach science effectively	1–5	4.332 (.58)	4.576 (.57)	0.823	0.822
I understand science concepts well enough to be effective in teaching elementary science	1–5	4.318 (.59)	4.552 (.56)	0.839	0.846
I find it easy to explain to students why science experiments work	1–5	4.284 (.61)	4.543 (.57)	0.841	0.850

(continued)

Table 1. (*continued*)

	Range	Pre	Post	Pre	Post
		M (SD)	M (SD)	Std. loadings	Std. loadings
I am always able to answer students' science questions	1–5	4.086 (.73)	4.346 (.68)	0.754	0.753
Given a choice, I would invite the principal to evaluate my science teaching	1–5	4.128 (.73)	4.404 (.74)	0.577	0.611
When a student has difficulty understanding a science concept, I am usually not at a loss about how to help the student understand it better	1–5	4.028 (.77)	4.347 (.79)	0.621	0.652
When teaching science, I usually welcome student questions	1-5	4.555 (.53)	4.715 (.49)	0.712	0.741
I know how to motivate students to study science	1–5	4.323 (.58)	4.603 (.54)	0.802	0.821
Correlation Pre vs Post				0.569	

4.2   Latent Profiles of Online Engagement

Pageview logs of 8,131 participants were downloaded from the external server. The timestamped entry of page URL was used to determine the time spent on the page content. As the logging of pageviews was being maintained on an external server, entries for some participants were incomplete. We analyzed pageview logs of 7037 participants to identify the different online engagement profiles. The percentage of time spent on content was used for analyses. This enabled comparisons between time spent in one content with another while accounting for variations due to internet speeds, reading proficiency and module content. Also, the values were median centered to enable easy identification of the latent profiles in the output. The summary of the time spent on the content by the participants is tabulated as the percentage of total time logged online in Table 2. The range, mean and median values indicate that the time spent on each content is a long-tailed distribution.

As the distribution of time spent is long-tailed, LRT tests are more valid than BLRT to determine the correct number of latent profiles. The latent profile analysis shows LRTs favor a four-profile solution. Thus, we accept the four-profile solution of the analysis. The extracted profiles of the participants can be interpreted based on the content they spent most of their time Project Feedback (5.0%), Subject Modules (57.9%), Case-Study Content (30.0%) and Expert Content (7.1%) (Fig. 1).

Table 2. Percentage of time spent by participants in the online programme

Content	Time (as a percentage of total time)			
	Range	Mean	Std. Dev.	Median
Science expert content	0.77–38.95	11.795	4.44	11.526
Science case study	0.43–23.41	7.163	2.84	6.86
Math expert content	0.37–24.11	7.39	3.34	6.932
Math case study	0–21.71	6.115	2.31	5.888
Classroom management expert content	0–18.49	4.459	2.19	4.073
Classroom management case study	2.14–43.49	17.011	4.98	16.957
SCE expert content	0–10.08	1.239	1.07	0.914
SCE case study	0–15.39	2.418	1.22	2.18
ICT use expert content	0–13.01	1.618	1.25	1.253
ICT use case study	0.15–17.83	4.337	1.9	4.104
Grade peer projects	0–17.80	1.787	1.35	1.413
View peer feedback on project	0–13.52	0.951	1.15	0.589

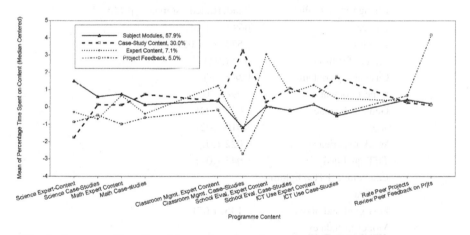

Fig. 1. Latent profiles of participants based on the percentage of time spent on content

4.3 Association of Online Content Engagement and Change in Self-efficacy Belief

Alessandri, Zuffiano, and Perinelli's [41] method of setting up of the second-order latent variables which measure baseline and change in the latent constructs was implemented to analyze the association of the engagement patterns with the change in selfefficacy. The article's example was adapted for categorical responses using the Mplus user guide and reference materials available on their website. The model regressed the change in self-efficacy upon the profile membership indicators (here, the Most likely profile membership) and participant covariates (Fig. 2). The relevant results of the analysis have been tabulated in the following table (Table 3).

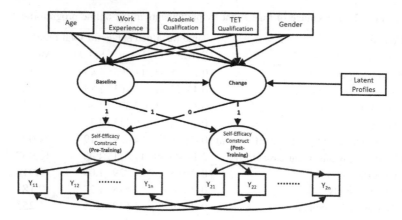

Fig. 2. Structural Model to evaluate association of latent online profiles to change in self-efficacy

Table 3. Association of most likely Online Latent profile with change in self-efficacy beliefs

Change in self-efficacy	Standardized estimates [β (S.E.)]
Intercept	.668*** (.14)
Baseline	−.573*** (.02)
Project feedback	.059 (.06)
Case study content	.028 (.03)
Expert content	−.098. (.05)
Gender: Female	−.021 (.02)
Age	−.010 (.02)
Work experience	−.022 (.02)
TET qualified	−.043 (.04)
Education: (PTC/Diploma)	
Graduate	−.087 (.07)
Post grad and above	−.135. (.07)
Model fit indices	
χ2	1486.185
df	413
CFI	0.993
TLI	0.993
SRMR	0.031
RMSEA	0.019
RMSEA 90% CI	[.018 .020]

Note: "." $p < 0.1$ "*" $p < .05$, "**" $p < .01$, "***" $p < .001$

The findings show that the participants reported a large and significant positive change in their personal science teaching efficacy beliefs. Additionally, participants who reported low teaching efficacy beliefs benefitted significantly more from the programme. Participant's age, gender and work experience did not have a significant effect on the change in self-efficacy. We do notice a slight negative association with change in self-efficacy, at the 90% significance level, among participants who engaged more with expert content. Similarly, participants with post graduate degrees seemed to have an adverse association with change in self-efficacy (at 90% significance level).

5 Discussions

The different online engagement profile of the participants clearly shows 1. Variations in needs of teachers from a professional development course and 2. Need for an online PD programme which can offer the flexibility of indulging in desired content. The large, significant and positive change among the participants validate the design and content of the programme. Further, the effect size of the negative association of participants who indulged in expert content is very small and failed to be rejected at 95% significance. We could ignore the negative effects for practical reasons, but it satisfies the objective of the article by demonstrating the benefit of extracting latent engagement profiles of participants to evaluate the content of an online course.

6 Limitations

The external server used for tracking pageview activity provided log entries with time precision in minutes. Thus, page views which occurred within than a minute were not captured, thus time on content may have been underestimated. Further, for this article, we have used "most likely profile membership" to analyze the relationship between engagement profile and change in self-efficacy. Latent profile memberships in probabilities, with suitable transformations, could be used in the analysis to provide a more accurate estimate of the association.

7 Implications

The first implication of our findings is that the contents of this particular online PD programme for teachers were sufficiently varied to cater to all participants. Irrespective of whether the teachers engaged more with the subject specific content, case-studies, expert content or project feedback there was no variation (at 95% significance) in the reported positive change in science teaching self-efficacy. Thus, the online programme offered a sufficient balance of content from both experts and peers that the participants needed. Secondly, our study shows one way of evaluating the contents of online programmes. Extracting latent profiles based on navigation logs enables further investigation on the effects of the programme on subgroups of participants. This would facilitate continuous improvement of content and design of the online course or programme. Future research could attempt at exploring these latent profiles with qualitative methods. Researchers could also investigate activities participants undertake outside the learning platform and the effect of these off-platform activities on outcomes.

Acknowledgements. The online professional development programme was developed as a collaboration between the Government of Gujarat and Ravi J Matthai Center for Educational Innovation, IIM Ahmedabad. We are thankful for the time and support provided by various professionals working at both these institutions. We also like to thank Mr. Avinash Bhandari, Ms. Megha Gajjar, Mr. Sanket Savaliya, Mr. Lekh Nakrani & Ms. Nishanshi Shukla in coordinating the development and implementation of the programme.

References

1. Terwiesch, C., Ulrich, K.: Will Video Kill the Classroom Star? the Threat and Opportunity of Massively Open Online Courses for Full-Time Mba Programs (2014)
2. Dede, C., Jass Ketelhut, D., Whitehouse, P., Breit, L., McCloskey, E.M.: A research agenda for online teacher professional development. J. Teach. Educ. **60**(1), 8–19 (2009)
3. Borko, H.: Professional development and teacher learning: mapping the terrain. Educ. Res. **33**(8), 3–15 (2004)
4. Desimone, L.M.: Improving impact studies of teachers' professional development: toward better conceptualizations and measures. Educ. Res. **38**(3), 181–199 (2009)
5. Desouza, J.M.S., Boone, W.J., Yilmaz, O.: A study of science teaching self-efficacy and outcome expectancy beliefs of teachers in India. Sci. Educ. **88**(6), 837–854 (2004)
6. Dyer, C., et al.: Knowledge for teacher development in India: the importance of 'local knowledge' for in-service education. Int. J. Educ. Dev. **24**(1), 39–52 (2004)
7. Singh, R., Sarkar, S.: Does teaching quality matter? Students learning outcome related to teaching quality in public and private primary schools in India. Int. J. Educ. Dev. **41**, 153–163 (2015)
8. Sehgal, P., Nambudiri, R., Mishra, S.K.: Teacher effectiveness through self-efficacy, collaboration and principal leadership. Int. J. Educ. Manage. **31**(4), 505–517 (2017)
9. Tschannen-Moran, M., Hoy, A.W.: Teacher efficacy: capturing an elusive construct. Teach. Teach. Educ. **17**(7), 783–805 (2001)
10. Goddard, R.D., Hoy, W.K., Hoy, A.W.: Collective teacher efficacy : its meaning, measure, and impact on student achievement. Am. Educ. Res. J. **37**(2), 479–507 (2010)
11. Lumpe, A., Czerniak, C., Haney, J., Beltyukova, S.: Beliefs about teaching science: the relationship between elementary teachers' participation in professional development and student achievement. Int. J. Sci. Educ. **34**(2), 153–166 (2012)
12. Gabriele, A.J., Joram, E.: Teachers' reflections on their reform-based teaching in mathematics: implications for the development of teacher selfefficacy. Action Teach. Educ. **29**, 60–74 (2007)
13. Gibson, S., Dembo, M.H.: Teacher efficacy: a construct validation. J. Educ. Psychol. **76**(4), 569–582 (1984)
14. Gregoire, M.: Is it a challenge or a threat? a dual-process model of teachers' cognition and appraisal processes during conceptual change. Educ. Psychol. Rev. **15**(2), 147–179 (2003)
15. Levenson, E., Gal, H.: Insights from a teacher professional development course: Rona's changing perspectives regarding mathematicaly-talented students. Int. J. Sci. Math. Educ. Dordrecht **11**(5), 1087–1114 (2013)
16. Summers, J.J., Davis, H.A., Hoy, A.W.: The effects of teachers' efficacy beliefs on students' perceptions of teacher relationship quality. Learn. Individ. Differ. **53**, 17–25 (2017)
17. Hill, H.C., Beisiegel, M., Jacob, R.: Professional development research: consensus, crossroads, and challenges. Educ. Res. **42**(9), 476–487 (2013)

18. Pehmer, A.K., Gröschner, A., Seidel, T.: How teacher professional development regarding classroom dialogue affects students' higher-order learning. Teach. Teach. Educ. **47**, 108–119 (2015)
19. Kennedy, M.J., Rodgers, W.J., Romig, J.E., Lloyd, J.W., Brownell, M.T.: Effects of a multimedia professional development package on inclusive science teachers' vocabulary instruction. J. Teach. Educ. **68**(2), 213–230 (2017)
20. Qian, Y., Hambrusch, S., Yadav, A., Gretter, S.: Who needs what: recommendations for designing effective online professional development for computer science teachers. J. Res. Technol. Educ. **50**(2), 164–181 (2018)
21. Rosaen, C.L., Carlisle, J.F., Mihocko, E., Melnick, A., Johnson, J.: Teachers learning from analysis of other teachers' reading lessons. Teach. Teach. Educ. **35**, 170–184 (2013)
22. Minor, E.C., Desimone, L.M., Lee, J.C., Hochberg, E.D.: Insights on how to shape teacher learning policy : the role of teacher content knowledge in explaining differential effects of professional development. Educ. Policy Anal. Arch. **24**(61), 1–34 (2016)
23. Romero, C., Ventura, S.: Educational data science in massive open online courses. Wiley Interdisc. Rev. Data Min. Knowl. Discovery **7**(1), 1–12 (2017)
24. Tseng, S.-F., Tsao, Y.-W., Yu, L.-C., Chan, C.-L., Lai, K.R.: Who will pass? Analyzing learner behaviors in MOOCs. Res. Pract. Technol. Enhanced Learn. **11**(1), 1–11 (2016). https://doi.org/10.1186/s41039-016-0033-5
25. Kizilcec, R.F., Piech, C., Schneider, E.: Deconstructing disengagement: analyzing learner subpopulations in massive open online courses. In: Proceedings of the Third International Conference on Learning Analytics and Knowledge - LAK 2013, p. 170 (2013)
26. Ferguson, R., Clow, D.: Examining engagement: analysing learner subpopulations in massive open online courses (MOOCs). In: Proceedings of the Fifth International Conference on Learning Analytics and Knowledge - LAK 2015, pp. 51–58 (2015)
27. Coffrin, C., Corrin, L., de Barba, P., Kennedy, G.: Visualizing patterns of student engagement and performance in MOOCs. In: Proceedings of the Fourth International Conference on Learning Analytics and Knowledge - LAK 2014, pp. 83–92, March 2014
28. Milligan, C., Littlejohn, A., Margaryan, A.: Patterns of engagement in connectivist MOOCs. MERLOT J. Online Learn. Teach. **9**(2), 149–159 (2013)
29. Ramesh, A., Goldwasser, D., Huang, B., Daum, H., Getoor, L.: Modeling learner engagement in MOOCs using probabilistic soft logic. In: NIPS Workshop on Data Driven Education, pp. 1–7 (2013)
30. Kalakoski, V., Ratilainen, H., Drupsteen, L.: Enhancing learning at work . How to combine theoretical and data-driven approaches, and multiple levels of data ? In: Esann 2015, pp. 22–24, April 2015
31. Riggs, I.M., Enochs, L.G.: Toward the development of an elementary teacher' s science teaching efficacy belief instrument. Sci. Educ. **74**(6), 625–637 (1990)
32. Enochs, L.G., Smith, P.L., Huinker, D.: Establishing factorial validity of the mathematics teaching efficacy beliefs instrument. Sch. Sci. Math. **100**(4), 194–202 (2000)
33. R-Core Team, R: A language and environment for statistical computing. R Foundation for Statistical Computing, Vienna, Austria (2016)
34. RStudio-Team, RStudio: Integrated Development for R. RStudio, Inc., Boston, MA (2016)
35. Muthén, L.K., Muthén, B.O.: MPlus User's Guide, 8th edn. Muthén & Muthén, Los Angeles (2017)
36. Muthén, B.O., Du Toit, S.H.C., Spisic, D.: Robust inference using weighted least squares and quadratic estimating equations in latent variable modeling with categorical and continuous outcomes. Psychometrika, p. 49 (1997)
37. Hu, L.T., Bentler, P.M.: Cutoff criteria for fit indexes in covariance structure analysis: conventional criteria versus new alternatives. Struct. Equ. Model. **6**(1), 1–55 (1999)

38. Marsh, H.W., Hau, K.T., Wen, Z.: In search of golden rules: comment on hypothesis-testing approaches to setting cutoff values for fit indexes and dangers in overgeneralizing Hu and Bentler's (1999) findings. Struct. Equ. Model. **11**(3), 320–341 (2004)
39. Magidson, J., Vermunt, J.K.: Latent class models for clustering: a comparison with K-means. Can. J. Market. Res. **20**(1), 36–43 (2002)
40. Nylund, K.L., Asparouhov, T., Muthén, B.O.: Deciding on the number of classes in latent class analysis and growth mixture modeling: a Monte Carlo simulation study. Struct. Equ. Model. **14**(4), 535–569 (2007)
41. Alessandri, G., Zuffianò, A., Perinelli, E.: Evaluating intervention programs with a pretest-posttest design: a structural equation modeling approach. Front. Psychol. **8**, 223 (2017). https://doi.org/10.3389/fpsyg.2017.00223

Exploring the Students Feelings and Emotion Towards Online Teaching: Sentimental Analysis Approach

T. PraveenKumar[1]([✉]) [iD], A. Manorselvi[2], and K. Soundarapandiyan[3]

[1] Ramaiah Institute of Management, Bangalore, India
praveen@msrim.org
[2] St. Peters Institute of Higher Education and Research, Chennai, India
[3] Sri Sai Ram Engineering College, Chennai, India

Abstract. Data mining is a method to refine raw data to useful information. In education, data mining is a significant research part used to progress the value of education by observing students' performance and understanding their learning patterns. Real-time student feedback would empower faculty and students to comprehend the teaching and learning problems in the most user-friendly way for the students. This paper uses a Lexicon based sentimental analysis technique to analyze students' feelings and emotions through their feedback by correlating learning analytics to grounded theory. The sentiment analysis technique is a computational process to identify and classify subjective information such as positive, negative, and neutral from the source material. It can extract feelings and emotions from a piece of a sentence. Hence this paper aims to recognize the students' positive or negative feelings and distinguished emotions, towards online teaching. The methodology undertakes four processes. The first process is data extraction from the feedback collected from the students through open-ended questions (Text) and is used as source material and imported to R studio. The second process is data cleaning /data preprocessing, removal of annoying data, and separation of data. The third process is sentimental analysis, which divides the data into positive, negative, and neutral categories/groups. This lexicon-based method of sentimental analysis is used to classify the sentiments. The results were estimated using sentiment scores and emotional variance. The sentiment scores result found that students have positive sentiments/emotions towards online teaching and emotions vary concerning the online class timing.

Keywords: Learning analytics · Sentimental analysis · Text mining · Students emotion and learning

1 Introduction

Students Feedback is an essential component in the global education system, especially more so for the Indian higher education system. The apex accreditation agencies of the country like NBA, NAAC, etc. have included the students' feedback as one of the measuring criteria for assessing the quality of the teaching-learning process, students' feedback supports progresses in teaching (Poulos et al. 2008). Students may have

S. K. Sharma et al. (Eds.): TDIT 2020, IFIP AICT 617, pp. 137–146, 2020.
https://doi.org/10.1007/978-3-030-64849-7_13

different issues concerning their class lectures (Cummins et al. 2012). Evidence of this is once a student does not know the content of the lecture or an exact case, the Students' feedback can explore what students understand and what they do not understand; what they like and dislike about the class. Moreover, students' feedback can support the faculty to realize the students' learning behavior (Calders et al. 2012). Collecting the feedback is usually taken after a semester or course (Cain et al. 2007, Toon Calders et al. 2012). Students are requested to express various problems that they may have encountered in the course (Baradwaj et al. 2011). But, students' feedback is highly helpful when it is taken in real-time, as it permits them to report problems promptly (Rogers et al. 2013). Students' feedback is very significant as it can help the faculty to realize the students learning behavior. Now and then students do not understand what the faculty is tiresome to describe, students can indicate this to the faculty through their feedback. Student's feedback is mostly measured on Likert-scale through a closed-ended question. However, there are some open-ended questions where the responses cannot be analyzed structurally. Therefore, these descriptive answers are analyzed thoroughly. This analysis will become a tedious task when numbers are huge. In a higher education institution in India where the students mostly come from different states, there are differences in languages used when the students expressing their feelings for the semester that recently passed. So structural analysis is needed for open-ended answers, by adopting a sentiment analysis technique this study to detect the students' positive or negative feelings and distinguished emotions, texted feedback. The question posed in the present study is: How the student's real-time feedback helps in identifying the student's sentiments and emotion towards online teaching? we ask two research questions

RQ1. Would student's sentiments and emotions vary in online teaching?
RQ2. Would students' sentiments and emotions indicate their satisfaction and engaged level in online teaching?

To answer these questions, we conducted a literature review, from which three objectives were formulated. The data used for the user is the student's feedback (text form) collected through google forms. Lexicon-based Sentimental analysis was used to obtain the result. R Studio was used in this study to do the analysis.

This paper is categorized as follows: first, based on the research question the literature is reviewed and discussed, second, the objectives identified, Then, the study methodology and analysis are described. Finally, results are obtained and discussed.

2   Related Work and Research Gap

2.1   Sentimental Analysis in Education

Ortigosa et al. (2014). studied the Facebook data collected from Spanish students, the sentiments in expressions of polarity (positive, negative, and neutral) was detected by using the two methods in sentimental analysis, lexicon approach and combine approach, noticed the polarity in terms of in the perspective of e-learning and pointy out that noticing polarity could be used in adaptive e-learning systems to support personalized learning. Troussas et al. (2016). Used a machine learning approach like Naive Bayes, Rocchio, and Perceptron classifiers to discovered students' divergence through Facebook in the circumstance of a language learning application. Troussas et al. (2020) say that students who are functioning to manage with sentiments may not have appropriate resources accessible to engage in learning. Besides, emotions such as anger, anxiety, and sadness harm students' learning and can disturb students. Further happy students typically perform better. So noticing these feelings can help teachers to take action by concentrating on particular students. Song et al. (2018). also reconnoitered sentiment analysis on online learning systems to discover students 'opinions about courses, lecturers, and online learning systems, this study was conducted using Chinese language data to segregate polarity (i.e. positive and negative) from the sentiments through the SVM classifier machine-learning approach. Tian et al. (2017). spotted e-learners' emotions (i.e. Love, Joy, Anger, Frustration) from their texts in a chat system using POS-tags features and C4.5 decision tree as a classifier this study emphasized the benefits of identifying emotions through text, which is a less expensive method compared to others. Munezero et al. (2014). discovered students' emotions from their learning diaries using lexicon-based sentimental analysis and identified the eight emotions are joy, sadness, fear, anger, anticipation, surprise, disgust, and trust. Utmost all the research on sentiment analysis in the educational area has been focused on the e-learning area. Though, there are differences between e-learning and classroom-based sentiment analysis given the words used differently in each area. Only one study was related to classroom-based sentiment analysis where the authors applied sentiment analysis to students' diaries Munezero et al. (2013), Francis et al. (2016) developed a Sentimental analysis system to appraise English and Filipino course teacher performance. They estimated sentiment scores from student's ratings both in terms of qualitative and quantitative using a Naïve Bayes algorithm and vividly represented the percentage of positive and negative sentiments of students to help university administrators be aware of students' concerns. The literature exposes that there is limited research on sentiment analysis for students' real-time classroom feedback that uses machine learning techniques. But the student's feedback will have varied in the online mode of teaching so based on this the objectives of the study were formulated.

3   Objectives of the Study

- To recognize the students' positive or negative feelings, distinguished emotions, towards online teaching.
- To measure the sentimental word association
- To express the results and generate sentiment visualization.

4 Methodology

4.1 Data Selection and Extraction

The data used for the study was mined from student's feedback for online courses conducted in selected Top B Schools in Bangalore. The nonprobability sampling method of purposive sampling was used in this study. Purposive sampling technique is an approach where members conform to certain criteria. The main criteria for collecting students' feedback is the student must have attended at least 20 h of online classes in a particular course handled by the concerned faculty. About 350 written feedbacks were taken for the study to do the sentimental analysis. Feedback from the students collected through Google forms.

5 Data Analysis and Discussion

The machine learning technique of Lexicon based sentimental analysis was used to do the sentimental analysis. The analysis of this study is separated into three-steps, the first is text mining, the next step is estimating sentiment score and the third step is the classification of student sentiment. R Studio was used in this study to do the analysis. R contains a huge set of Natural Language Processing (NLP) packages. The initial stages contain stacking the feedback (text file) into an R, then data preprocessing was done beforehand executing the sentimental analysis. This analysis demonstrates the following phases and analyses like Data preprocessing, Word Frequency, Word Cloud generation, Word Association, Sentiment Scores, and Emotion Classification.

5.1 Text Mining

Data Reading
The input case for this analysis has "Raw text" of replies (student's feedback), and is a text file. so here we used to read Lines function to read the data. The read Lines function merely abstracts the text from the Text document and consider each line as a character string. To read a subset of lines from the text document the n = argument logic was used

Data Preprocessing
Data preprocessing is starts from cleaning the text data, which means removing distinct characters from the text. By using the tm_map function, the distinct characters like @, /, and | converted into space. The succeeding process is to eliminate the excessive space and convert the full-text data into lower case. Then the stop words are eliminated. The stop words are the most frequently occurring words in any language, example in English "the", "is", "are" have very minute value for NLP and it should remove for further processing. Then SnowballC package was used to do the stemming process. The stemming procedure shortens the word to its common source. The previous studies related to sentimental analysis in the educational domain were used this all mentioned preprocessing technique (J.M. Martin, A. et al. 2013 & Erik Tromp, 2014).

Word Frequency

After data preprocessing, the following phase is to build the document matrix, this table contains the frequency of words detected form the input text document, this frequency of words used to detect general or trending words in the feedback. By using the TermDocumentMatrix () function from the text mining package, the below Document Matrix – a table was built. The resulting Table 1 shows the word frequency of input text document (students feedback).

Table 1. Word frequency

S. no	Words	Frequency
1	Good	265
2	Pattern	40
3	Lecturer	39
4	Student	38
5	Interaction	38
6	Paper	35
7	Teacher	34
8	Exam	34
9	University	32
10	Check	32

The maximum frequently occurring word is "good". Also noticed in the table there are no negative words like "not", which shows there are no negative prefixes to change the context or meaning of the word "good" (In short, this shows most replies don't comment negative phrases like "not good"). Pattern, Lecture, student, interact are the subsequent repeatedly occurring words, which direct that utmost the students feel good about their lecture and pattern. Finally, the root "interact" and "lectur" for words like "interaction" and "lecturer", etc. is also on the chart, and further analysis is needed to identify whether the perspective is positive or negative.

Word Association

Word association means to find the relationship between the pairs of words, Correlation is a statistical technique used to find out the magnitude of the relationship between two variables. This tool was used to examine the association between the most recurrently occurring words in the student's feedback and is used to view the student's perspective about these words.

Table 2. Word association

Words	Good lecture	Lecture	Student	Style	Understand		
teach	0.35	0.3	0.25	0.29	0.28		
Words	Interact	Teacher	Lecture	Delivery	Knowledge	Proper	Staff
punctual	0.54	0.52	0.48	0.44	0.3	0.25	0.25

The above Table 2 shows the words which are most often associated with the selected three terms (The Lower corlimit = 0.25 is set). The output specifies that "teach" (which is the root for the word "teacher "or "teaching") has the highest of 35% association with good lecture and the lowest of 25% association with the student. So the most frequently occurring word ("teach") is positive. Similarly, another important word "Punctual" is extremely associated with the word "interact". These results show that most feedback of students is mentioning the faculty "Punctual and interaction" and can be taken from a positive perspective.

Sentiment Scores
Student sentiment towards online teaching was measured through sentiment scores. Here the sentiments are categorized as positive, negative, and neutral. And its denoted by a numeric scale. The numeric scale provides better details in identifying the unit of positive or negative strength of the sentiment enclosed in a student's feedback. In this, we used the Syuzhet package for generating sentiment scores, which has four sentiment dictionaries and offers a technique for retrieving the sentiment. This sentiment extraction tool (NLP) was developed at Stanford University. The get sentiment function takes two arguments: a character vector (of sentences or words) and a method. The designated technique decides which of the four available sentiment extraction methods will be used. The four techniques are syuzhet bing, afinn, and nrc. Each technique uses a diverse scale and hence results are marginally different.

Syuzhet Vector Results From the above Table 3, summary results of the Syuzhet vector show the first component has a value of 2.35. It means the sum of the sentiment scores of all important words in the first response(line) in the text file, adds up to 2.35. The scale used for measuring sentiment scores ranges from -1(indicating most negative) to +1(indicating most positive). The summary statistics table showed that the median value is 0.7500 and the mean value is 0.8665, which is above zero and inferred as the overall average sentiment across all the responses (student's feedback) is positive. It means students' sentiment towards online teaching is positive.

Table 3. Summary Results of Syuzhet Vector

S.No	1	2	3	4	5
1	2.35	0.75	1.50	0.75	1.5
S.No	Min	1st Qu	Median	Mean	3rd Qu	Max
1	-1.3000	0.5000	0.7500	0.8665	1.0000	5.35

Bing and Affin Vector Results

The Sentiment scores scale for bing is a binary scale with −1 representing negative and +1 representing positive sentiment and afinn is an integer scale ranging from -5 to +5. From the above Table 4. summary results of bing and afinn vectors also show that the Median value of Sentiment scores is above 0 and inferred as the overall average sentiment across all the student's responses (feedback) is positive.

Table 4. Summary Results of Bing and Affin Vector

S.No	Vector	1	2	3	4	5	
1	Bing	1	1	2	1	1	
2	Affin	3	3	3	2	2	
S.No	Vector	Min	1st Qu	Median	Mean	3rd Qu	Max
1	Bing	−2	0	1.00	0.87	1.00	5.00
2	Affin	−5	1	3.00	2.52	3.00	10.00

Comparison of Three Vectors

Meanwhile, the study used three different methods and three diverse scales, it's well to change their output to a common scale before relating them. By using sign function in R, the basic scales were converted, the sign function converts all positive numbers to 1 and all negative numbers to −1, and all zeros remain 0.

Form the above Table 5 it's Noted the first element of the first two rows (vector) is 1, indicating that all three methods have calculated a positive sentiment score, for the first response (line) in the text.

Table 5. Normalize scale and compare three vectors

	1	2	3	4	5	6
1	1	1	1	1	1	1
2	1	1	1	1	1	1
3	0	1	1	1	1	1

Emotion Classification

This study used the NRC Word-Emotion Association Lexicon to classify the emotion of students towards online teaching. The NRC Emotion Lexicon is a list of English words and their associations with eight basic emotions (anger, fear, anticipation, trust, surprise, sadness, joy, and disgust) and two sentiments (negative and positive). get_nrc_sentiments function was used in this study. This function, which returns a data frame with each row representing a sentence from the original text. The data frame has ten columns (one column for each of the eight emotions, one column for positive sentiment valence, and one for negative sentiment valence). The data in the columns (anger, anticipation, disgust, fear, joy, sadness, surprise, trust, negative, positive) can be accessed individually or in sets. The following table shows the Data frame returned by the get_nrc_sentiment function

From the above Table 6, it inferred that Zero existences of words related to emotions of disgust, anger, sadness. and fear. 1 incidence each of the words linked with emotions of anticipation, joy, and surprise. And 2 incidences of words linked with emotions of trust. No incidences of words are linked with negative emotions. Maximum 3,2,1 existences of words in positive emotions. The subsequent phase is to generate charts to help visually examine the emotions of students. The below chart shows the entire amount of occurrences of words in the text, related to each of the eight emotions.

Table 6. Data frame

S. no	Anger	Anticipation	Disgust	Fear	Joy	Sadness	Surprise	Trust	Negative	Positive
1	0	0	0	0	0	0	0	0	0	0
2	0	1	0	0	0	0	0	2	0	3
3	0	1	0	0	1	0	1	1	0	1
4	0	1	0	0	1	0	0	2	0	2
5	0	1	0	0	1	0	1	1	0	1
6	0	1	0	0	1	0	0	1	0	2

The above Fig. 1, bar plot permits a quick and easy assessment of the proportion of words linked with each emotion of students towards online teaching. The emotion "trust" has the lengthiest bar and displays that words linked with this positive emotion found just over 25% of all the expressed words expressed by the students in their feedback. The next emotion is "disgust" has the shortest bar and displays that words linked with this negative emotion found less than 1% of all the expressed words by the students in their feedback. Overall, words linked with the positive emotions of "trust" and "anticipation" account for almost 50% of the significant words in the text, and it can be interpreted as a good sign of emotion towards the online teaching.

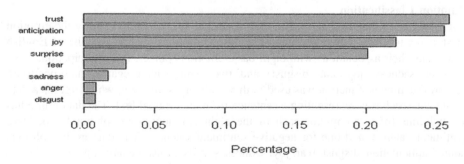

Fig. 1. Emotions in text – Bar plot

6   Insights from the Analysis

After applying machine learning algorithms and estimate sentiment score and classified the emotion of students towards online teaching., the teaching activities to be examined were identified. Potential sentimental words or related words to the online teaching identified were: good, pattern, lecture, student, interact, paper, teacher, exam, the universe, check. Detecting these words, the objective is to explore which words impact students' sentiment scores the most, and which ones provide insight into student emotion towards online teaching. Good is a vastly said word, occurring in many student responses, in positive sentiment. This could mean that online teaching is good concerning the particular faculty and hour in emotional classification Trust is the highly mentioned word, this could mean the students trusted the content and faculty. Over some time, the emotion falls under the positive category also.

7   Conclusion

This study identifies and recognizes the students' positive and negative feelings, distinguished emotions, towards online teaching. and also measured the sentimental word association and Emotional variance over online teaching. Using a lexicon sentimental analysis method and affin, bing, and syuzhet vector concept the sentiment was classified into positive and negative. The results showed from all techniques the sentiment falls under the positive side. It necessity be noted here that student feedback data are only one source of data in general towards online teaching, but syllabus/module content and delivery, and should be used in combining with other teaching and learning evaluation strategies for further study.

References

Poulos, A., Mahony, M.J.: Effectiveness of feedback: the student's perspective. Assess. Eval. High. Educ. 33(2), 143–154 (2008)

Baradwaj, B.K., Pal, S.: Mining educational data to analyze students' performance. Int. J. Adv. Comput. Sci. Appl. 2(6), 63–69 (2011)

Rogers, D., Coughlan, P., Kearney, K.: Playschool for postgrads: facilitating creativity and innovation in doctoral education using digital resources. In: The Digital Learning Revolution in Ireland: Case Studies in Practice from ndlr, pp. 165–179 (2013)

Munezero, M., Montero, C.S., Sutinen, E., Pajunen, J.: Are they different? Affect, feeling, emotion, sentiment, and opinion detection in text. IEEE Trans. Affect. Comput. 5(2), 101–111 (2014)

Munezero, M., Montero, C.S., Mozgovoy, M., Sutinen, E.: Exploiting sentiment analysis to track emotions in students' learning diaries. In: Proceedings of the 13th Koli Calling International Conference on Computing Education Research, pp. 145–152. ACM (2013)

Ortigosa, A., Martín, J.M., Carro, R.M.: Sentiment analysis in Facebook and its application to e-learning. Comput. Hum. Behav. 31, 527–541 (2014)

Cummins, S., Burd, L., Hatch, A.: Using feedback tags and sentiment analysis to generate sharable learning resources investigating automated sentiment analysis of feedback tags in a programming course. Adv. Learn. Technol. (ICALT) **10**, 653–657 (2010)

Tian, Y., Galery, T., Dulcinati, G., Molimpakis, E., Sun, C.: Facebook sentiment: reactions and emojis. In: Proceedings of the Fifth International Workshop on Natural Language Processing for Social Media, pp. 11–16 (2017)

Calders, T., Pechenizkiy, M.: Introduction to the special section on educational data mining. Assoc. Comput. Mach. Spec. Interest Group Knowl. Discov. Data Min. **13**(2), 3–6 (2012)

Troussas, C.: Advances in Social Networking-based Learning: Machine Learning-based User Modelling and Sentiment Analysis, vol. 181. Springer, Cham (2020)

Troussas, C., Espinosa, K.J., Virvou, M.: Affect recognition through Facebook for effective group profiling towards personalized instruction. Inf. Educ. **15**(1), 147–161 (2016)

Yoo, S., Song, J., Jeong, O.: Social media contents based sentiment analysis and prediction system. Expert Syst. Appl. **105**, 102–111 (2018)

Blockchain

Blockchain in Supply Chain Management: A Review of the Capability Maturity Model

R. Balakrishnan Unny[(⊠)] and Bhajan Lal

Institute of Management, Nirma University,
S G Highway, Ahmedabad 382481, Gujarat, India
balakrishnan@nirmauni.ac.in

Abstract. With the growing popularity of cryptocurrencies, Blockchain systems have found a new audience within the business environment. The decentralized ledger technology that allows the creation of verifiable transactions has extraordinary applications within business. In this paper the authors have attempted to identify the core benefits of using Blockchain technology to improve Supply Chain Management (SCM). With industry 4.0 transformation in its preliminary stages, a discussion on how Blockchain systems can benefit SCM is important. Like any other information system, Blockchain implementation is not just limited to infrastructure changes but also requires organisational wide changes to reap the benefits of the new system. The inherent technological issues associated with Blockchain are preventing many organizations from adopting Blockchain systems at a large scale. The authors have presented a model to guide the implementation of the Blockchain based systems using the industry accepted Capability Maturity Model (CMM) as the reference.

Keywords: Blockchain · Supply chain management · Capability maturity model · Information system implementation

1 Introduction

The Global Supply Chain Forum (GSCF) defines supply chain management as "the integration of key business processes from end user through original suppliers that provides products, services, and information that add value for customers and other stakeholders" [1]. Chief among the issues faced in supply chain management is the issue of business process links as they have a significant impact on the performance of the supply chain [1]. To achieve a truly integrated supply chain, commitment from all the members is essential.

To create an integrated supply chain, the buying organization has to invite its business partners into their organization. This goes beyond just sharing information about the products and requirements thereby including business partners into buying organization's operational activities. This integration does come with a challenge since there is limited reciprocity from the business partners. The business partners are provided extensive information about the inner workings of the buying organization while they can choose to remain firewalled. This is a unique problem since the objectives of both parties may not be always in line.

© IFIP International Federation for Information Processing 2020
Published by Springer Nature Switzerland AG 2020
S. K. Sharma et al. (Eds.): TDIT 2020, IFIP AICT 617, pp. 149–158, 2020.
https://doi.org/10.1007/978-3-030-64849-7_14

Additionally the creation of such an integrated supply chain often puts the buying organization at the risk of being held since there is an overwhelming reliance on the partners [2]. The sheer complexity of managing business partners through the entire supply chain is compounded by the limited willingness to create an integrated supply chain process [3].

The contemporary literature identifies various methods to implement and sustain an integrated supply chain. There is consensus that supply chain integration requires both managerial and technical solutions [4–6]. To improve the supply chain performance, contemporary organizations have been looking at technology driven solutions and they found varying amount of success.

Introduction of cyber-physical system in production and operations environment with the aim of interconnecting human beings and machines in a globally accessible network is referred to as "industry 4.0". The technologies involved in industry 4.0 include "Advanced Robotics, Artificial Intelligence, Hi-Tech Sensors, Cloud Computing, Internet of Things (IoT), Data Capture and Analytics, Digital Fabrication, Mobile Devices, Software As A Service and Blockchain" [7]. Supply chain 4.0 is the application of the above mentioned technologies in SCM to improve performance and customer satisfaction [8].

Supply chain 4.0 creates a disruption in the traditional supply chain environment which requires organizations to radically rethink and redesign their business functions That leads to leads to potential cost reduction in various domains of supply chain (7, 8). The supply chain 4.0 benefits have been achieved thus far on the traditional business intelligence infrastructure. The tradition infrastructure relies on centralized data repositories which connects all the partners of the supply chain. However centralized system could be easily manipulated by anyone rendering the data untrustworthy. With the use of Blockchain in an organization can create a decentralized platform for recording transactions that cannot be manipulated.

The supply chain 4.0 benefits have been achieved thus far on the traditional business intelligence infrastructure. The tradition infrastructure relies on centralized data repositories which connects all the partners of the supply chain. However, centralized system could be easily manipulated by anyone rendering the data untrustworthy. With the use of Blockchain in an organization can create a decentralized platform for recording transactions that cannot be manipulated.

There is also an issue of transparency which needs to be addressed. The question of "how much can I actually trust the information coming from my supply chain partner?" is a difficult question for any organization to answer. One of the solutions to such a conundrum is the use of modern technology such as Blockchain. The transparency that the Blockchain systems provide will enable organizations to improve the supply chain. Many organizations are now looking at Blockchain to ensure the validity of the information being shared across organizations. Recently Walmart had implemented Blockchain based systems in collaboration with IBM to track the movement of produce from Chinese farms to their shelves [9].

2   Blockchain Technology and Supply Chain Management

The last two decades of technological innovations in the area of peer-to-peer (P2P) networks and cryptography has led to the development of the Blockchain. The fundamental technological principle of Blockchain is the distributed, encrypted database, which cannot be reversed and is incorruptible. The following three technological concepts form the underpinnings of Blockchain technology; Decentralized Databases, Blockchain, Proof of Work/Stake [10]. Bitcoin was the first system to utilize the Blockchain data structure and has become the blueprint for future Blockchain implementations.

The starting point of the Blockchain is the concept of Distributed Ledger Technology in which each participant of the P2P network has access to a shared ledger. This provides a secure environment to perform transactions without relying on a third-party service provider [11]. Every transaction performed in the network uses public key encryption and digital signatures to validate the transaction.

The process of validation of the transaction is based on decentralized consensus. Instead of the traditional centralized consensus which was built based on database rules; authority and trust of ensuring validity of a transaction is moved to the decentralized network. Each node in the network is enabled to record transactions continuously and sequentially in a public "block" creating a unique "chain". Each successive block contains the unique fingerprint of the previous block in an encrypted format (hash). This combination of cryptography and Blockchain system removes the need for a centralized intermediary for authentication of transactions [12].

In order to ensure the validity of information being created by the nodes, Blockchain can use the network security protocol called "proof of work". This protocol essentially prevents attackers from creating transactions which are not authenticated. This protocol uses computational power from all the nodes to solve a complex mathematical function which serves as the prerequisite for the Proof of Work scheme. Proof of Stake scheme serves as an alternative to Proof of Work scheme which revolves around the entities that holds stake within the network. In certain conditions a hybrid of both the schemes can also be used to authenticate the transactions [10].

Contemporary literature is littered with examples of how Blockchain systems can be used to create a digital platform where authenticated transactions and records could be created [13]. We can classify the areas in which Blockchain has been implement into 10 overall themes namely "Finance, Citizenship Services, Integrity Verification, E-Governance, IoT, Healthcare, Privacy & Security, Business, Education and Data management" [14]. The Estonian government has created a Blockchain based e-residency program [15]. In the Indian context, the Government of Andhra Pradesh has launched an ambitious scheme to use Blockchain technology to manage land records and streamlining vehicle registrations [16]. The impact of Blockchain technology on financial services industry beyond cryptocurrencies [17, 18]. Blockchain could modernize the utilities grid to create a new era of decentralized power [19]. The Blockchain based sharing services can benefit smart cities as well [20]. Blockchain can also be considered as a general-purpose technology i.e. it can be used to create a platform without a powerful intermediary wherein the privacy risk and censorship risk is drastically reduced thereby reducing the cost of networking [21, 22]. In all the above examples, the traditional centralized intermediary based authentication is replaced with Blockchain. In all cases the authors have identified that the ability to create transaction which are authenticated increases the transparency of the transaction and the underlying service as well. In creating the transparency in transactional systems, the Blockchain has business value in record keeping of static information and maintaining a registry of tradeable information [23] (Fig. 1).

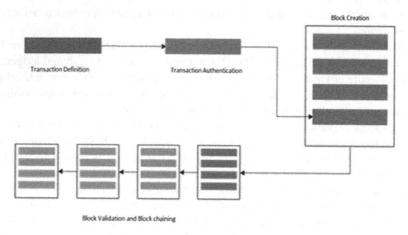

Fig. 1. Blockchain process

The Blockchain based systems are able to ease paperwork processing, identify counterfeit products, facilitate origin tracking thereby transforming enterprise supply chains [24, 25]. The container logistics company A.P. Moller – Maersk is using a Blockchain based system to reduce the paperwork and associated cost for container shipment [26]. The Blockchain enabled supply chain have the potential to improve the strategic performance dimensions including Risk reduction, Sustainability and Flexibility [27, 28].

The following studies have shown the potential benefits of using Blockchain to improve supply chain management. The first study, explains the use of Blockchain system in Pharma supply chain [29]. In their work, the authors were able to present the case of a start-up that uses IoT sensor devices to leverage Blockchain technology to bring about the benefits of fraud detection and identity management. The second study, detailed the utilization and development of RFID based Blockchain system to build agri-food supply chain traceability [30]. A similar conceptual study was conducted that detailed how Blockchain system could be used to modernize the halal supply chain [31]. All three studies look into the different parts of the supply chain's transparency issue. The benefits of Blockchain technology are not limited to transparency alone but also include durability, immutability and process integrity [32]. For example, use of Blockchain makes it much more difficult for illicit or counterfeit products to enter an otherwise legitimate supply chain [33, 34]. Having a transparent supply chain enables an organization to plan better. In a typical supply chain, multiple parties are involved and this generates extensive amounts of documentation. Small error in the paper documents may result in delays or hold up of payments. Blockchain eliminates this chance of an error thereby reducing the extra price of verification which is required for paper-based systems. Blockchain based systems can also reduce the procure-to-pay gaps with the use of smart contracts. This validated data storage provides organizations ability to create better data analysis platforms which can reduce the inventory cost by better forecasting.

One of the critical challenges involved in the implementation of Blockchain systems is the cost. As discussed before Blockchain systems require complete overhaul ng of the IT infrastructure which is expensive [35]. The second challenge is with the technology itself; the network-based validation reduces the throughput of Blockchain transactions as well as latency. With the current setup of Blockchain achieving the performance parameters of centrally controlled systems is extremely difficult [36]. The regulatory uncertainty is definitely a challenge within the Indian context as the India Government has recently decided not to recognize cryptocurrencies which is based on Blockchain. The fact that Blockchain implementation involves multiple business partners is a barrier to the implementation of the project. Combined with the lack of acceptance within the industry driven primarily by the uncertainty of benefits makes the implementation project extremely challenging [24]. Even with these challenges the benefit of creating a transparent supply chain is pushing major players in the market to adopt Blockchain as a viable alternative to traditional information systems.

3   The Capability Maturity Model for Implementing Blockchain

The Capability Maturity Model for Blockchain implementation has four categories and their corresponding maturity levels [37] and the authors have added a fifth category namely "Skills" to the existing model.

First of the categories is network; with the Blockchain, organizations will have to transform their existing centralized networks to enable peer to peer communication. Additionally, along ensuring the reliability of the network and load management it is important to ensure that proper hybrid network is designed. It is impractical to replace the entire client- server architecture with the P2P architecture. So, while designing the network there should be synergy with the operations of the organization [38–40].

Second category is the information systems wherein both technical and managerial considerations are required. The chief among the technical considerations is the requirement of upgrading the infrastructure which includes the computer systems, interfaces and storage. There is also requirement that Blockchain system should not be standalone which requires extensive integration across the legacy systems. While considering adoption of Blockchain based information systems it's important for an organization to understand the business requirement. Therefore, the information technology strategy and organizational strategy should have a convergence as well [41–44].

Third category deals with the computing methodologies. With Blockchain, generating standards that are acceptable across companies is a challenge [35]. The computational complexity involved in managing a complex Blockchain is not just limited to the volume and the speed it extends to ensuring data accuracy as well.

Fourth category is the security and privacy. Using a public Blockchain would render confidential information at risk of exposure. The complexity of securing all the nodes in the network is also extensive [45–47]. Like any information system the security of the network is dependent on the security of each device [48]. At the same time a technological solutions alone are insufficient in creating a resilient environment therefore it requires an enterprise level integration of active, passive and recovery mechanisms [49].

Fifth category in the proposed model is Skills. With the complete redesign of the supply chain environment the employees within all the participating organizations have to develop new skills to leverage the benefits of Blockchain. Improved cross functional communication and leadership skills would strengthen the collaboration between the relevant parties and prepare the organization for the digital transformation which is required. CMM for People (P- CMM) created by the Software Engineering Institute of United States Carnegie Mellon university is designed to judge the maturity of enterprise human resource processes [50]. Using the P-CMM as a reference we have identified the maturity levels for the development of the skills required in implementing and maintaining Blockchain based systems. The starting stage is having the requisite training for employees and there after identifying the competencies required and thereby ensuring that competencies are mapped and continues improved [51]. The updated CMM for Blockchain with additional parameters is represented in Fig. 2. For a successful implementation of Blockchain systems, organizations have to display maturity in all categories described above along with a clear business rationale for the implementation.

	Initial (stage 1)	Repeatable (stage 2)	Defined (stage 3)	Managed (stage 4)	Optimizing (stage 5)
Network		Network load	Reliability	Network Design	
Information systems	• Architecture • Upgrading • Integration	• Storage • Scalability • Maintenance		Business Efficiency	Strategic convergence
Computing methodologies	Standardization	Computational anxiety			
Security and Privacy	• Authentication • Node Security	Security Management System	Privacy	• Data security • Transaction security	Enterprise security integration
Skills		Training and development	Competency Development	Competency Integration	Continuous capability improvement

Source: Adapted from Wang, H., Chen, K., & Xu, D. (2016). A maturity model for blockchain adoption. Financial Innovation, 2(1), 12.

Added by the authors to the existing model

Fig. 2. Capability maturity model for blockchain implementation

4 Discussion and Future Work

Digital transformation of the entire supply chain involves both high complexity as well as high novelty whereas single use systems require far less effort from the organizations [52]. Blockchain Technology has value in business functions that have been struggling to create a system of recording and validating transactions without an intermediary. Blockchain based systems require an enterprise level transformation for a successful implementation. However, comparison between the approaches used in implementing Blockchain based systems and traditional approaches is challenging [53].

The number of organizations that have implemented Blockchain based systems is limited. Hence an empirical validation of the model will be challenging. However, a case study-based validation of the model may be considered. Also, the CMM proposed in the present study needs to be expanded to include the other management categories as well.

References

1. Lambert, D.M., Cooper, M.: Issues in supply chain management. Ind. Mark. Manag. **29**(1), 65–83 (2000)
2. Tan, K.C.: Supply chain management: practices, concerns, and performance issues. J. Supply Chain Manag. **38**, 42–53 (2002)
3. Lambert, D.M., Enz, M.G.: Issues in supply chain management: progress and potential. Ind. Mark. Manag. **62**, 1–16 (2017)
4. Turkulainen, V., Roh, J., Whipple, J.M., Swink, M.: Managing internal supply chain integration: integration mechanisms and requirements. J. Bus. Logist. **38**(4), 290–309 (2017)
5. Gunasekaran, A., Subramanian, N., Rahman, S.: Improving supply chain performance through management capabilities. Prod. Plan. Control **28**(6–8), 473–477 (2017)
6. Lambert, D.M., Cooper, M.C., Pagh, J.D.: Supply chain management: implementation issues and research opportunities. Int. J. Logist. Manag. **9**(2), 1–20 (2000)
7. Tjahjono, B., Esplugues, C., Ares, E., Pelaez, G.: What does Industry 4.0 mean to supply chain? Procedia Manuf. **13**, 1175–1182 (2017)
8. Alicke, K., Rachor, J., Seyfert, A.: Supply Chain 4.0 – the next-generation digital supply chain. McKinsey & Company (2016)
9. Jing, M.: Here's a peek at Walmart's game-changing plan to trace food from China's farms to store shelves. South China Morning Post (2017)
10. Morabito, V.: Business Innovation Through Blockchain. Springer, Cham (2017)
11. Ølnes, S., Ubacht, J., Janssen, M.: Blockchain in government: benefits and implications of distributed ledger technology for information sharing. Gov. Inf. Q. **34**(3), 355–364 (2017)
12. Mougayar, W.: The Business Blockchain: Promise, Practice, and Application of the Next Internet Technology. Wiley, Hoboken (2016)
13. Lemieux, V.L.: Trusting records: is blockchain technology the answer? Rec. Manag. J. **26**(2), 110–139 (2016)
14. Casino, F., Dasaklis, T.K., Patsakis, C.: A systematic literature review of blockchain-based applications: current status, classification and open issues. Telemat. Inform. **36**, 55–81 (2019). https://doi.org/10.1016/j.tele.2018.11.006
15. Sullivan, C., Burger, E.: E-residency and blockchain. Comput. Law Secur. Rev. **33**(4), 470–481 (2017)

16. Haridas, S.: This Indian City is Embracing BlockChain Technology – Here's Why. Forbes, Jersey City (2018)
17. Guo, Y., Liang, C.: Blockchain application and outlook in the banking industry. Financ. Innov. **2**(1), 1–12 (2016). https://doi.org/10.1186/s40854-016-0034-9
18. Petersen, O., Jansson, F.: Blockchain Technology in Supply Chain Traceability Systems: Developing a Framework for Evaluating the Applicability. Lund University, Lund (2017)
19. Basden, J., Cottrell, M.: How utilities are using blockchain to modernize the grid. Energy J. **3**, 7–9 (2017)
20. Sun, J., Yan, J., Zhang, K.Z.K.: Blockchain-based sharing services: what blockchain technology can contribute to smart cities. Financ. Innov. **2**(1), 1–9 (2016). https://doi.org/10.1186/s40854-016-0040-y
21. Catalini, C., Gans, J.S.: Some simple economics of the blockchain. National Bureau of Economic Research (2016)
22. Chen, Y.: Blockchain tokens and the potential democratization of entrepreneurship and innovation. Bus. Horiz. **61**(4), 567–575 (2018)
23. Carson, B., Romanelli, G., Walsh, P., Zhumaev, A.: Blockchain beyond the hype: what is the strategic business value? Digital McKinsey (2018)
24. Kersten, W., Blecker, T., Ringle, C.M., Hackius, N., Petersen, M.: Blockchain in logistics and supply chain: trick or treat? In: Digitalization in Supply Chain Management and Logistics, (Proceedings of the Hamburg International Conference of Logistics (HICL)), p. 18 (2017). https://doi.org/10.15480/882.1444, ISBN 978-3-7450-4328-0
25. Lee, J.H., Pilkington, M.: How the blockchain revolution will reshape the consumer electronics industry [future directions]. IEEE Consum. Electron. Mag. **6**(3), 19–23 (2017). https://doi.org/10.1109/MCE.2017.2684916
26. Moller – Maersk, A.P.: TradeLens blockchain-enabled digital shipping platform continues expansion with addition of major ocean carriers Hapag-Lloyd and Ocean Network Express (2019). Accessed 5 June 2020. https://www.maersk.com/news/articles/2019/07/02/hapag-lloyd-and-ocean-network-express-join-tradelens
27. Madhwal, Y., Panfilov, P.B.: Blockchain and supply chain management: aircrafts' parts' business case. In: 28TH DAAAM International Symposium on Intelligent Manufacturing and Automation, pp. 1051–1056 (2017). https://doi.org/10.2507/28th.daaam.proceedings.146
28. Kshetri, N.: 1 Blockchain's roles in meeting key supply chain management objectives. Int. J. Inf. Manag. **39**, 80–89 (2018). https://doi.org/10.1016/j.ijinfomgt.2017.12.005
29. Bocek, T., Rodrigues, B.B., Strasser, T., Stiller, B.: Blockchains everywhere - a use-case of blockchains in the pharma supply-chain. In: IFIP/IEEE International Symposium on Integrated Network and Service Management, pp. 772–777 (2017)
30. Tian, F.: An agri-food supply chain traceability system for china based on RFID & blockchain technology. In: 13th International Conference on Service Systems and Service Management, pp. 1–6 (2016)
31. Tieman, M., Darun, M.R.: Leveraging blockchain technology for halal supply chains. Islam Civilis. Renew. **8**(4), 547–550 (2017)
32. Abeyratne, S.A., Monfared, R.P.: Blockchain ready manufacturing supply chain using distributed ledger. Int. J. Res. Eng. **05**(09), 1–10 (2016)
33. Apte, S., Petrovsky, N.: Will blockchain technology revolutionize excipient supply chain management? J. Excip. Food Chem. **7**(3), 76–78 (2016)
34. Lu, Q., Xu, X.: Adaptable blockchain-based systems: a case study for product traceability. IEEE Softw. **34**(6), 21–27 (2017)
35. Alicke, K., Davies, A., Leopoldseder, M., Niemeyer, A.: Blockchain technology for supply chains—a must or a maybe? McKinsey & Company Operations Extranet, pp. 1–10 (2017)

36. Mendling, J., et al.: Blockchains for business process management - challenges and opportunities. ACM Trans. Manag. Inf. Syst. **9**(1), 1–16 (2018)
37. Wang, H., Chen, K., Xu, D.: A maturity model for blockchain adoption. Financ. Innov. **2**(1), 1–5 (2016). https://doi.org/10.1186/s40854-016-0031-z
38. Loo, B.T., Huebsch, R., Stoica, I., Hellerstein, J.M.: The case for a hybrid P2P search infrastructure. In: Voelker, G.M., Shenker, S. (eds.) IPTPS 2004. LNCS, vol. 3279, pp. 141–150. Springer, Heidelberg (2005). https://doi.org/10.1007/978-3-540-30183-7_14
39. Hoogeweegen, M.R., Teunissen, W.J.M., Vervest, P.H.M., Wagenaar, R.W.: Modular network design: using information and communication technology to allocate production tasks in a virtual organization. Decis. Sci. **30**(4), 1073–1103 (1999). https://doi.org/10.1111/j.1540-5915.1999.tb00919.x
40. Diabat, A., Jabbarzadeh, A., Khosrojerdi, A.: A perishable product supply chain network design problem with reliability and disruption considerations. Int. J. Prod. Econ. **212**, 125–138 (2019). https://doi.org/10.1016/j.ijpe.2018.09.018
41. Tan, C.W., Pan, S.L., Lim, E.T.K.: E-governance: towards a strategic convergence of stakeholder interests. In: ECIS 2003 Proceedings, (January) 1913–1929 (2003). http://is2.lse.ac.uk/asp/aspecis/20030154.pdfs
42. Drnevich, P.L., Croson, D.C.: Information technology and business-level strategy: toward an integrated theoretical perspective. MIS Q. **37**(2), 483–509 (2013)
43. Clohessy, T., Acton, T., Morgan, L.: (De)Mystifying the information and communication technology business model concept. Int. J. Netw. Virtual Organ. **21**(3), 1 (2019). https://doi.org/10.1504/ijnvo.2019.10007891
44. Clohessy, T., Acton, T., Morgan, L.: Contemporary digital business model decision making: a cloud computing supply-side perspective. Int. J. Netw. Virtual Organ. **19**(1), 1 (2019). https://doi.org/10.1504/ijnvo.2019.10003812
45. Lin, I.C., Liao, T.C.: A survey of blockchain security issues and challenges. Int. J. Netw. Secur. **19**(5), 653–659 (2017). https://doi.org/10.6633/IJNS.201709.19(5).01
46. Prashanth Joshi, A., Han, M., Wang, Y.: A survey on security and privacy issues of blockchain technology. Math. Found. Comput. **1**(2), 121–147 (2018). https://doi.org/10.3934/mfc.2018007
47. Li, X., Jiang, P., Chen, T., Luo, X., Wen, Q.: A survey on the security of blockchain systems. Future Gener. Syst. **107**, 841–853 (2020). https://doi.org/10.1016/j.future.2017.08.020
48. Sharma, K., Gupta, V., Verma, S., Avikal, S.: Study and implementation of face detection algorithm using Matlab. In: 2018 International Conference on Recent Innovations in Electrical, Electronics and Communication Engineering, ICRIEECE 2018, pp. 2745–2748. Institute of Electrical and Electronics Engineers Inc. (2018). https://doi.org/10.1109/ICRIEECE44171.2018.9008990
49. Unny, R.B., Mishra, G., Bhatt, N.: Strategies for improving cyber resilience of data intensive business information systems. In: Mishra, B.K., Kumar, R., Zaman, N., Khari, M., JoSo, T., Manuel, R.S., (eds.), Handbook of E-Business Security, pp. 285–312. Auerbach Publications, Boca Raton (2019)
50. Zhang, C.: Design of human capability maturity analysis system online P-CMM model. In: Proceedings - 2015 International Conference on Intelligent Transportation, Big Data and Smart City, ICITBS 2015, pp. 302–305 (2016). https://doi.org/10.1109/ICITBS.2015.81
51. Curtis, B., Hefley, B., Miller, S.: People capability maturity model (P-CMM). Software Engineering Institute (2009). https://doi.org/ReportCMU/SRI-2001-MM-001

52. Iansiti, M., Lakhani, K.R., Mohamed, H.: The truth about blockchain. Harv. Bus. Rev. **95**(1), 118–127 (2017)
53. Wang, C.M., Xu, B.B., Zhang, S.J., Chen, Y.Q.: Influence of personality and risk propensity on risk perception of Chinese construction project managers. Int. J. Proj. Manag. **34**(7), 1294–1304 (2016)

Indian MSME's Sustainable Adoption of Blockchain Technology for Supply Chain Management: A Socio-Technical Perspective

Vineet Paliwal[1]([⊠]) [iD], Shalini Chandra[2] [iD], and Suneel Sharma[1] [iD]

[1] S P Jain School of Global Management, Mumbai 400070, Maharashtra, India
vineet.dml8dba016@spjain.org
[2] S P Jain School of Global Management, Singapore 119579, Singapore

Abstract. This article studies the adoption of blockchain technology in Indian Micro, Small, and Medium Enterprises (MSME) in the context of innovations in supply chain management (SCM) using blockchain technology. Besides finance, SCM is one of the main areas where disruptive innovations based on blockchain technology are going to be deployed. Blockchain technology's unique proposition lies in the attributes of trust, transparency, traceability, immutability, and decentralization. MSME's form the backbone of the Indian economy. This article provides a socio-technical factors-based analysis of the adoption of blockchain technology in Indian MSME, particularly in a SCM context. Sustainability is an important variable that is expected to moderate the relationship between socio-technical factors and large-scale adoption. The relationships are tested via a survey of professionals in MSMEs in India who are both familiar with blockchain technology and sustainable SCM. This study shall offer a deeper understanding of the application of socio-technical systems theory for the adoption of blockchain technologies by MSMEs in India.

Keywords: Blockchain · Supply chain management · Adoption · Sustainability · Socio-technical theory · MSME

1 Introduction

The majority of the Indian population, comprising of 1.2 billion people, lives in rural India and the economic development of rural India requires connecting remote villages to local and global supply chains [1]. Micro, Small, and Medium Enterprises (MSME) contribute significantly to the Indian economy in terms of Gross Domestic Product (GDP), exports, and employment generation. Though MSME sector is extensively regarded as the instrument of growth in the industrial progress of India [2], it comes with its unique challenges such as the absence of adequate and timely banking finance, limited capital and knowledge, non-availability of suitable technology, low production capacity, ineffective marketing strategy, constraints on modernization & expansions, non-availability of skilled labor at affordable cost, and follow up with various government agencies to resolve problems due to lack manpower and knowledge, outdated and incompatible technologies and many more challenges [2]. This calls for the

© IFIP International Federation for Information Processing 2020
Published by Springer Nature Switzerland AG 2020
S. K. Sharma et al. (Eds.): TDIT 2020, IFIP AICT 617, pp. 159–165, 2020.
https://doi.org/10.1007/978-3-030-64849-7_15

adoption of technologies that can facilitate the development of MSME and maximize business opportunities.

Blockchain technology, because of its unique traits and beneficial features, is suitable to overcome most of the challenges which MSME are currently facing. We believe that the extent to which the MSME will be willing to adopt this new innovative technology will depend on various socio-technical factors which revolve around *people* (such as availability of skilled labor and education), *processes* (such as enterprise strategy and market opportunities), and *technology* (such as technological infrastructure and technological capabilities). The behavioral adoption of blockchain and the drivers for its adoption in the context of Indian MSME supply chain remains sparsely investigated. Guided by theses rationales, taking socio-technical systems theory as the theoretical lens, our first research question is: #RQ1: What factors influence the adoption intention of blockchain technology by Indian MSMEs?

Sustainability of blockchain technology (technological sustainability) refers to the long-term viability of the technology in terms of social, economic, and environmental performance. Prior research has highlighted the key role of technological sustainability in influencing the socio-technical systems [3]. Moreover, technological sustainability may facilitate MSMEs to stay competitive in the market [4]. We posit that technological sustainability would play a moderating role in influencing the relationships between people, process, and technology characteristics and intention to adopt blockchains. Thus, our second research question which we aim to answer is: #RQ2: Does the sustainability of blockchain technology influence the socio-technical characteristics to enable the adoption intention by Indian MSMEs?

2   Research Model, Theory and Hypotheses

Situating our arguments in the socio-technical theory, we suggest that people (social aspects of MSME employees), process (the aspect of blockchain technology processes as practiced by the MSMEs), and technology (technological aspects of blockchain technologies) will have a direct influence on adoption intention of blockchain technologies by MSMEs. Furthermore, sustainability will play a moderating role in explaining the relationship between socio-technical aspects and adoption intention (see Fig. 1).

2.1   Socio-Technical Theory for Adoption of Blockchain Technology

This research is contextualized specifically to the adoption of blockchain technologies for supply chain management by the Indian MSMEs. MSMEs in India don't have a high level of technology orientation or technology budgets. Large software enterprises were previously not focusing on MSME's, and therefore, good solutions were costly. But these days, software as a service (SaaS) based solutions is made for MSME. This calls to look at the socio-technical aspects for adoption. Therefore, it is necessary to draw on the social and technical perspectives and its interaction with the sustainability to understand the adoption of blockchain by MSMEs.

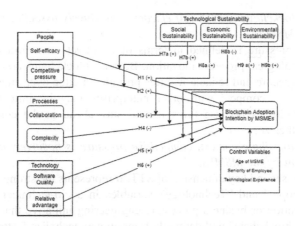

Fig. 1. Blockchain adoption model by MSMEs

Ehrenberg and King [5] advocates the use of socio-technical theory (STT) to analyze blockchain technologies. STT notes the interaction between people and technology in any organizational development. It takes an ecological view and emphasizes the interaction between society's complex infrastructure and human behavior. STT thus underscores technology implementations as an ongoing social process, thereby reiterating the technological interaction system and social system [6]. STT is based on the key principles of human values, continuous improvement, social behaviors in addition to technical aspects of storage and control of information by people [7]. Thus, socio-technical refers to the accordance between the social and technical aspects of any organization. Prior research has employed STT for distinct studies such as the broad study of Information and Communications Technologies (ICT) [8], and the study of standard tool models vis-à-vis socio-technical models [8]. Guided by these research directions, we base our conceptualization on socio-technical theory to conduct an empirical analysis of the adoption of blockchain technology by MSMEs. STT revolves around its three key dimensions of people, process, and technology, which we discuss in the following sections.

People is the first key dimension of STT. The two variables considered under this dimension are the self-efficacy and competitive pressure of the people (society in general) dealing with the blockchain technology.

Self-efficacy is defined as beliefs in one's capabilities to meet given situational demands. Self-efficacy predicts several important work-related outcomes like proficiency, attitude, and performance at the job. Compeau and Higgins [9] note that although information systems can increase organizational effectiveness, this does not always translate into utilization. They highlighted the key role of the self-efficacy of the people for the successful implementation of technology in any organization. Prior studies [9] have examined the role of self-efficacy of people for technology use. If the users learn and master the revolutionary technology such as blockchain, they can adopt it with ease. Hence, we hypothesize,

H1: In the blockchain context, self-efficacy is positively associated with adoption intention by the MSMEs.

Competitive pressure is defined in terms of its effect on a firm's incentives to initiate any technological process innovation. Because blockchains are immutable and tamper-proof, its secure and reliable features provide an edge over others to compete. MSMEs striving to compete with other enterprises may be influenced to adopt blockchain technologies because firms like to stay ahead in the competition [10]. Hence, we hypothesize,

H2: In the blockchain context, competitive pressure is positively associated with adoption intention by the MSMEs.

Process is the second key dimension of STT. It represents the strong glue that holds together the "People" and "Technology" variables in socio-technical analysis. Any digital transformation or business process re-engineering initiative that brings in new technology like "blockchain" will definitely bring in new technical features and change the interactional as well as collaborative behavior of people with technology. These new processes introduced may simplify previous processes. On the contrary, it may introduce more complex but powerful features for more people or stakeholders involved. These may inhibit people from adopting new technology. Guided by these rationales, we posit collaboration and complexity as two key factors within the dimension of the process.

Collaboration in supply chains works across multiple organizations. In order to create more value addition for the consumer and bring in more productivity, collaboration is of the utmost importance. Prior research has highlighted the key role of collaboration among partners with different goals and priorities for effective supply chain integration [11]. Because blockchains are essentially decentralized, its adoption is likely to be influenced by the collaboration among its partners. Hence, we hypothesize,

H3: In the blockchain context, collaboration is positively associated with adoption intention by the MSMEs.

Complexity refers to the complexity of technology implementation in the business processes of an organization. A high degree of complexity confuses users and causes them to have difficulty in implementing new business processes, which in turn adversely impacts its adoption decision. Since complexity can be a deterrent to successful implementation, followed by the use of innovation, it is usually negatively associated with adoption [12]. Blockchains, designed as a complex interplay of characteristics such as immutability and decentralization, may impede its adoption. Hence, we hypothesize,

H4: In the blockchain context, complexity is negatively associated with adoption intention by the MSMEs.

Technology is the third dimension of STT. New technologies are often disruptive. We have used two variables, "Software Quality" and "Relative Advantage," to describe the key idea behind the use of technology. New technology must bring some relative advantage for it to justify its adoption. Also, the new technology should adhere to certain software quality standards.

Software quality refers to the ISO 9126-1 software quality model. The model identifies six main quality characteristics, namely: Functionality, Reliability, Usability, Efficiency, Maintainability, Portability [13]. For the technology to be adopted and deployed across organizations and across various stakeholders of the supply chain, it is required that the blockchain technology-based software has long passed the Proof of Concept phase and has a high software quality based on the ISO 9126 metrics.

H5: In the blockchain context, software quality is positively associated with adoption intention by the MSMEs.

Relative advantage is the degree to which an innovation is beneficial to the competition. The perceived benefits of blockchain will provide an incentive for technology adoption. Past research indicates a positive relationship between the perceived advantage of using the technology over competition (relative advantage) and the adoption of IS innovations. Blockchain technology brings unique benefits of traceability and trust. With these benefits, blockchain is likely to affect key supply chains management objectives such as cost, quality, and sustainability [14]. This leads us to our next hypothesis:

H6: In the blockchain context, the relative advantage is positively associated with adoption intention by the MSMEs.

2.2 Sustainability

Sustainability stands on the three pillars of social, economic, and environmental performance.

Social sustainability offered by blockchains like trust, transparency, equal opportunities to participate in the supply chain, and improved job opportunities raise the self-confidence of the stakeholders [15]. Therefore, self-efficacy acts with boosted confidence at the individual level, which causes a greater effect on the adoption intention. Also, social sustainability implies that even though one remains aware of the competitive pressure, it does not turn into stress [15]. Hence, stakeholders can take informed action according to the changing business environment. Therefore, social sustainability afforded by blockchains increases the chance of "competitive pressure," turning into a "great opportunity". Hence, we hypothesize,

H7a: In the blockchain context, social sustainability positively moderates the relationship between self-efficacy of the MSMEs and their adoption intention such that the relationship becomes stronger for higher levels of social sustainability.

H7b: In the blockchain context, social sustainability positively moderates the relationship between the competitive pressure of the MSMEs and their adoption intention such that the relationship becomes stronger for higher levels of social sustainability.

Economic sustainability implies that the initiative should be profitable so that it can continue without being a burden on an organization, company, or the government. Profitability is important for sustained operations of the initiative. Effective collaboration is an important means of raising the productivity. However, a complex process that may come with new technology implementation in the organization can create hiccups. When most IT implementations partially or completely fail, complexity is often the key reason behind failure. Therefore, economic sustainability offered by blockchains is expected to moderate the relationship between "process" (collaboration and complexity) and adoption intention.

H8a: In the blockchain context, economic sustainability positively moderates the relationship between the collaboration of the MSMEs and their adoption intention such that the relationship becomes stronger for higher levels of economic sustainability.

H8b: In the blockchain context, economic sustainability negatively moderates the relationship between complexity and the adoption intention by MSMEs such that the relationship becomes weaker for higher levels of economic sustainability.

Environmental sustainability in the context of blockchains implies that the technology should be environment friendly. For example, if an initiative is creating pollution in disproportionate amounts, then scaling that initiative into something huge and global will neither be possible nor desirable. Such an initiative is likely to soon come under the governmental regulatory bodies scanner and be banned. Therefore, the quality of software and relative advantage afforded by blockchains will translate into adoption only when the roadmap of widescale adoption is clear in terms of environmental friendliness.

H9a: In the blockchain context, environmental sustainability positively moderates the relationship between software quality and the adoption intention by MSMEs such that the relationship becomes stronger for higher levels of environmental sustainability.

H9b: In the blockchain context, environmental sustainability positively moderates the relationship between relative advantage and the adoption intention by MSMEs such that the relationship becomes stronger for higher levels of environmental sustainability.

3   Proposed Methodology and Future Work

We are using a survey methodology for data collection from MSMEs across India. We have used measures and scales based on past validated scales from existing literature. We adapted the scales to our research context. The questionnaires created the use of a 5-point Likert scale. The questionnaires have been circulated online in Indian MSMEs and addressed to senior managers in those organizations. An online survey has been conducted, and the respondents were informed about the research ethics, which we are taking care of in this survey. The data collected initially was examined and found to have satisfactory factor structure and psychometric properties. We shall be doing a detailed analysis to test our proposed hypotheses so that the final results will be ready to share at IFIP WG8.6 Working Conference 2020.

4   Expected Contribution

In this research, we have explored factors for the adoption of blockchain technologies in supply chain management by MSMEs in India based on the foundations of STT. This research-in-progress paper is expected to make several theoretical and practical contributions. Theoretically, to the best of our knowledge, this is one of the first empirical studies on blockchain technology adoption, which is guided by STT. In addition, this study highlights the key moderating role of sustainability with socio-technical features and for the adoption of blockchain technology. Future research can add new factors thereby extending the research model. From the viewpoint of the practitioners, the results of the study will be useful for MSMEs who need to focus on the right set of factors to create their technology roadmap and corporate strategy. A well-focused and implemented technology roadmap plan can lead to successful blockchain technology adoption to gain sustainable competitive advantage.

References

1. Schuetz, S., Venkatesh, V.: Blockchain, adoption, and financial inclusion in India: research opportunities. Int. J. Inf. Manage. **52**(101936), 8 (2020)
2. Challenges to MSME. https://www.indiansmechamber.com/challenges_to_msme.php (2020). Accessed 30 July 2020
3. Savaget, P., et al.: The theoretical foundations of sociotechnical systems change for sustainability: a systematic literature review. J. Clean. Prod. **206**, 15 (2019)
4. Queiroz, M.M., Wamba, S.F.: Blockchain adoption challenges in supply chain: an empirical investigation of the main drivers in India and the USA. Int. J. Inf. Manage. **46**, 13 (2019)
5. Ehrenberg, A.J., King, J.L.: Blockchain in context. Inf. Syst. Front. **22**, 7 (2020)
6. Lee, A.: Editor's comments. MIS Q. **25**(1), 4 (2001)
7. Cherns, A.: The principles of sociotechnical design. Hum. Relat. **29**(8), 10 (1976)
8. Kling, R., Lamb, R.: IT and organizational change in digital economies: a socio-technical approach. Comput. Soci. **29**, 9 (1999)
9. Compeau, D.R., Higgins, C.A.: Computer self-efficacy: development of a measure and initial test. MIS Q. **19**(2), 23 (1995)
10. Chandra, S., Nanda Kumar, K.: Exploring factors influencing organizational adoption of augmented reality in e-commerce: empirical analysis using technology-organization-environment model. J. Electron. Commer. Res. **19**(3), 237-265 (2018)
11. Kouhizadeh, M., Saberi, S., Sarkis, J.: Blockchain technology and the sustainable supply chain: theoretically exploring adoption barriers. Int. J. Prod. Econ. **231**(107831), 21 (2021)
12. Bhattacharya, M., Wamba, S.F.: A conceptual framework of RFID adoption in retail using TOE framework. Int. J. Technol. Diffus. **6**(1), 32 (2015)
13. ISO 9216 Software Quality Characteristics. http://www.sqa.net/iso9126.html (2020). Accessed 4 Aug 2020
14. Kshetri, N.: Blockchain's roles in meeting key supply chain management objectives. Int. J. Inf. Manage. **39**, 10 (2018)
15. Singh, S.K., et al.: Self-efficacy and workplace well-being: moderating role of sustainability practices. Benchmarking Int. J. **26**(6), 17 (2019)

A Study on Calendar Anomalies
in the Cryptocurrency Market

D. Susana$^{(\boxtimes)}$, S. Sreejith, and J. K. Kavisanmathi

KCT Business School, Kumaraguru College of Technology,
Coimbatore 641049, India
susana@kctbs.ac.in, {sreejith.19mba,
kavisanmathi.19mba}@kct.ac.in

Abstract. Cryptocurrencies are sub-classes of digital currencies. Trading of these currencies have gained momentum during the past few years and have become new investment avenues for investors. An understanding on the market anomalies, which are patterns in asset prices would help the investors to adopt suitable strategies while trading in this asset class. This study aims to examine the presence of three calendar anomalies, day of the week, turn of the month, and year end effect in the cryptocurrencies. The top five cryptocurrencies which constitute a major share of the market capitalization value are selected for the study and the period of study is from July 23, 2017 to July 9, 2020. Dummy Variable Regression using GARCH (1, 1) model was employed on the log value of returns of the cryptocurrencies. The study provides evidence on the existence of anomalies during Thursdays, the months March and April, and at the turn of the year.

Keywords: Cryptocurrency · Efficient market hypothesis · Calendar anomalies

1 Introduction

Cryptocurrencies are subsets of the digital currencies [1] which gained prominence as an important type of digital currency during recent years. It has also become a new investment option for investors and trading in these cryptocurrencies have become colossal. There are more than 3500 types of cryptocurrencies being traded with an overall market capitalization of approximately \$350 billion as on August 5, 2020 (Source: Coinmarketcap.com). Among the cryptocurrencies, Bitcoin began operational in the year 2009 as the first decentralised cryptocurrency. It remains as the market leader in terms of trading with a market capitalization of \$208 billion as of August 5, 2020 constituting 60% of the total market share. Cryptocurrencies introduced subsequently are primarily clones of Bitcoin and other major cryptocurrencies and have novel features and certain fundamental differences. These cryptocurrencies have forayed into the market share of Bitcoin which has decreased from 86% (March 2015) to 60% (August 2020). While regulatory frameworks of cryptocurrencies are debated by policy makers across several countries, cryptocurrencies have also garnered interest of researchers. Several dimensions of the cryptocurrencies were studied by researchers, the asset class of cryptocurrencies [2], volatility of cryptocurrencies [3], dynamic

© IFIP International Federation for Information Processing 2020
Published by Springer Nature Switzerland AG 2020
S. K. Sharma et al. (Eds.): TDIT 2020, IFIP AICT 617, pp. 166–177, 2020.
https://doi.org/10.1007/978-3-030-64849-7_16

linkages of cryptocurrencies [4], investment options [5] and market anomalies [6]. The Efficient Market Hypothesis (EMH) laid on the foundations of the financial theories pertaining to market efficiency states that the asset prices reflect all available information [19]. However, in real time situations the functioning of market deviates from the rules of EMH and these deviations are called anomalies. Anomalies may occur once and disappear or could occur repeatedly. Furthermore, these anomalies are categorized as fundamental anomalies, technical anomalies, and calendar anomalies. A calendar anomaly is a type of market anomaly that considers various stock markets behavior or economic effect related to the calendar, such as the day of the week, turn of the month and so on. Information on the calendar anomalies would be beneficial to investors and they can study these patterns and deploy suitable strategies to make profits. This study aims to investigate the presence of three calendar anomalies in the cryptocurrencies, the day of the week, turn of the month, and year end anomalies during the period July 23, 2017 to July 9, 2020.

2   Literature Review

A market anomaly refers to the difference in the performance of assets from its expected or assumed price path as defined by the EMH [20]. Market anomalies and EMH are applicable to both stock and cryptocurrency market. Several studies have examined the presence of market anomalies in stock markets [7–11].

Studies related to calendar anomalies in the equity markets have revealed several patterns on the returns of indices and stock price movements at specific time frame owing to various reasons. Chandra [7] studied the calendar effect in the Indian Bombay Stock Exchange (BSE)-Sensex on basis of the turn of the month effect and timing of the month effect. Daily logarithmic market returns for ten years were analysed using the Dummy Variable Regression model. The analysis revealed that turn of the month effect as well as time of the month effect were present in the BSE-SENSEX. Market inefficiency was also established in this study. Deyshappriya [8] examined the Colombo Stock Exchange (CSE) for the presence of day of the week effect and monthly effect market anomalies from January 1, 2004 to June 28, 2013 using daily and monthly return data and grouping in two sub-sample periods comprising of pre - war period and post-war period. Ordinary Least Square (OLS) and Generalized Auto Regressive Conditional Heteroskedasticity GARCH (1, 1) regression models were employed for analysis. The stock market anomalies, both day of the week effect and monthly effect were found to exist during the war period. Safeer & Kevin [9] investigated the presence of market anomalies on the five select companies of the BSE Sensex during the period January 2008 to December 2012. The anomalies included weekend effect, turn of the month effect, turn of the year effect in terms of price and volume and stock split effect. The presence of Monday effect was found to exist in the BSE indices from January 2008 to December 2012. However, the turn of the month effect was found to be insignificant. Shakila et al. [10] studied the semi-monthly effect in the BSE Sensex using the daily stock returns of five sectoral indices namely Standards and Poor (S&P) BSE Auto Index, S&P BSE Bank Index, S&P BSE Consumer Durables Index, S&P BSE FMCG Index, and S&P BSE Health Care Index. The study found no evidence of semi-monthly effect in the selected sectoral indices from April 1, 2007 to March 31, 2017. Rossi and Gunardi [11] studied the presence of calendar anomalies, the January, and the weekdays' effects in the Stock Exchange Indices of France, Germany, Italy, and Spain. OLS and GARCH models were used to examine the Indices from 2001 to 2010 and the findings did not reveal existence of any significant calendar effect in these stock markets. The review from these studies showed mixed evidence on the presence of calendar anomalies on the stock markets.

The emergence of cryptocurrencies with novel features and the trading of these currencies which constitutes to very high market capitalization value has gained the attention of researchers to explore the presence of market anomalies in these currencies. Different facets of market anomalies studied by researchers in recent years include day of the week effect [6, 12], month of the year effect [11], persistence [13] and price over-reactions [14]. Cryptocurrency market constitute of more than three thousand cryptocurrencies but only a few top currencies contribute to major part of the market capitalization and the studies on market anomalies were focused either on Bitcoin or a particular type of calendar anomaly. Kurihara and Fukushima [15] investigated the market efficiency of Bitcoin concentrating on the weekly anomaly from July 17, 2010 to December 29, 2016 using OLS regression. This sample period was divided into two halves and the results showed that the Bitcoin market was inefficient for weekly anomaly. Caporalea and Plastunb [6] examined the presence of day of the week anomaly in the four cryptocurrencies Bitcoin, Ripple, Dash, and Litecoin for the period 2013 to 2017. Student's t-test, ANOVA, Kruskal–Wallis, Mann–Whitney, and OLS Dummy Variable Regression tests were used to analyse the entire sample period, and the sub-sample periods and evidence for Monday anomalies were found to exist only in Bitcoin currency. Kurihara and Fukushima [15] in their study found that the cryptocurrency market was inefficient but focused only on Bitcoin which was not necessarily representative of the entire cryptocurrency market and only the day of the week effect in the cryptocurrency market was examined. It can be observed from the literature review that only few studies have examined the calendar anomalies and only a particular type of calendar anomalies was studied in the cryptocurrency market. Hence this paper aims to fill this gap in the literature by examining the three calendar anomalies, the day of the week effect, month of the year effect, and turn of the year in the cryptocurrency market.

3 Data and Methodology

In this study the leading five cryptocurrencies Bitcoin, Ethereum, Tether, XRP, and Bitcoin cash were chosen for examination on the presence of calendar anomalies. These currencies constitute 80% of the total market capitalization value of the cryptocurrency market as of August 5, 2020 (coinmarketcap.com). The sample period considered for the study was three years from July 23, 2017 to July 9, 2020 based on the introduction of Bitcoin Cash on July 23, 2017. Data observations consisted of 1083 trading days the largest available data period for the chosen cryptocurrencies. Data relevant to the daily closing prices for selected cryptocurrencies were sourced from the website coinmaketcap.com. In general, the time series data are generally portrayed by typical distributions which are used to examine its properties and to decide on the suitable statistical tests for analysis. The characteristics for the selected cryptocurrencies were examined for Normality using Jarque Bera Statistics, Stationarity using Augmented Dickey Fuller (ADF), and Kwiatkowski–Phillips–Schmidt–Shin (KPSS) tests. The ADF test examines the null hypothesis as time series is not stationary. The KPSS test examines the null hypothesis as time series is stationary versus an alternative hypothesis that the series has a unit root. The unit root tests are examined without time series trend and intercept as the time series plot does not exhibit any specific trend (Fig. 1). For longer sample periods the returns for the selected cryptocurrencies may not be normally distributed and regularly tend to show excess kurtosis and skewness which are basic with financial parameters [16] and hence, logarithmic returns of the time series data are used for further analysis.

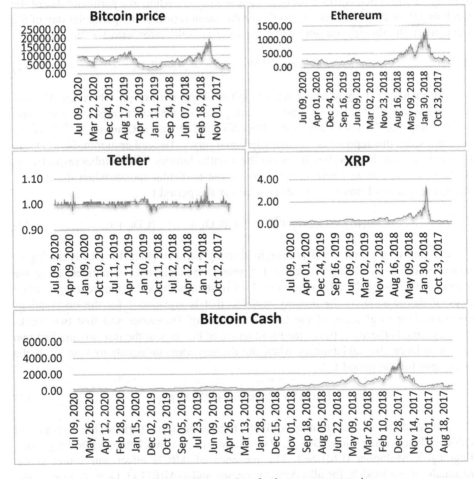

Fig. 1. Times series graphs of select cryptocurrencies

In an efficient market the stock prices are expected to adjust to anomalies or new information very rapidly and the volatilities tend to return to its normal level [16]. Studies on calendar anomalies both in stock markets [7–9, 11] and cryptocurrencies market [6, 15, 17] have used Dummy Variable OLS Regression. In this study the Dummy Variable Regression is structured to analyse calendar anomalies by adopting the rationale of Caporale and Plastun [6] for the day of the week effect, Plastun et al. [17] for month of the year and turn of the year effects in the cryptocurrency market. The size, sign, and statistical significance of the dummy coefficients provide information about the respective calendar anomalies. Equation (1) presents the Dummy Variable Regression model to examine the day of the week effect on cryptocurrencies where Ln (R_i) is the log of return of the daily closing prices of the select cryptocurrency computed using the formula Ln(Closing Price/Closing Price-1), $\text{Constant}^{\text{Sunday}}$ is the constant value which captures the presence of Sunday anomaly, D_1 to D_n are the dummy variables that equals 1 for observations corresponding to a particular day of the week and 0 for the other days, β_1 to β_n are the mean return of the particular day of the week when the dummy variable equals to 1and ε_t is the error term for the period t.

$$Ln\,(R_i) = \text{Constant}^{\text{Sunday}} + \beta_1 D_1 + \ldots + \beta_n D_n + \varepsilon_t \tag{1}$$

The month of the year effect was examined using the Eq. (2) where Ln (R_i) represents the log of return of the daily closing prices of the select cryptocurrency computed using the formula Ln(Closing Price/Closing Price-1), $\text{Constant}^{\text{December}}$ is the constant value that represents the anomaly pertaining to December month, D_1 to D_n are the dummy variables used for all days of the months January to November respectively, β_1 to β_n are the mean return of the days of the particular month when the dummy variable equals to 1 and ε_t is the error term for the period t.

$$Ln(R_i) = \text{Constant}^{\text{December}} + \beta_1 D_1 + \ldots + \beta_n D_n + \varepsilon_t \tag{2}$$

The turn of the year effect is examined using Eq. (3) where Ln (R_i) is the log of return of the daily closing prices of the select cryptocurrency computed using the formula Ln(Closing Price/Closing Price-1), Constant is the value that represents other days of the year, D_1 is the dummy variable that is equal to 1 for the observations corresponding to all days of the last two weeks of December and first two weeks January, and 0 otherwise, β_1 are the mean return of the days of the last two and first two weeks of December and January when the dummy variable equals to 1 and ε_t is the error term for the period t.

$$Ln(R_i) = \text{Constant} + \beta_1 D_1 + \varepsilon_t \tag{3}$$

The residuals of the Dummy variable regression were verified for presence of autocorrelation using Ljung-Box (L-B) portmanteau test and heteroskedasticity using Lagrange's Multiplier (LM) test. The presence of ARCH effect was found in the residuals of the models for all cryptocurrencies and GARCH (1,1) regression model was used for the analysis of the anomalies. The results of Ljung-Box (L-B) portmanteau test exhibited the presence of autocorrelations in the residuals of the regression model pertaining to the cryptocurrency Tether and hence, Auto Regressive Moving Average (ARMA) model was used for further analysis.

4 Findings and Discussions

The time series graphs and the descriptive statistics of the select cryptocurrencies provided preliminary evidence of the behaviour of the close price for the selected cryptocurrencies. From the visual analysis of the graph (Fig. 1) it can be seen that all cryptocurrencies witnessed sharp increase in their prices during December 2017 and January 2018, however only Bitcoin and Ethereum showed increase during subsequent turn of the year time periods for the years 2019 and 2020. Based on the sample period, it can be observed that Bitcoin experienced a fall and subsequent rise in prices during the months March and April of all the years in the sample period, whereas it was not observed in other cryptocurrencies. Clustering of prices can be observed in Tether while other cryptocurrencies showed no specific trend in their price movements. It can be inferred from the values of skewness and kurtosis that the daily closing prices and log return of cryptocurrencies does not confirm to normal distribution. The log return of Bitcoin and Ethereum series showed that it was negatively skewed and the kurtosis value was much higher than 3 representing that the distribution is leptokurtic with fat tails indicating that the index posted negative returns during the sample period while other cryptocurrencies displayed positive returns. Normality of the cryptocurrencies was further statistically examined using Jarque - Bera statistics (Table 1). The statistic values for the cryptocurrencies were found to be significant at 5% level of significance during the entire sample period implying that series does not meet the normality assumptions. In practice, a leptokurtic distribution is far more likely to characterize financial time series, and the residuals from a financial time series model. Brooks [18] recommends the usage of natural logarithmic transformations to meet the normality assumption as it can help to make a skewed distribution closer to a normal distribution. Hence, non-normal data series has been transformed into a normally distributed data series by applying the natural log transformation and used for further analysis.

The stationarity of the closing prices of the crypto currencies were examined using unit root tests ADF and KPSS (Table 1). The critical values of the closing prices of the crypto currencies did not meet the criteria of the ADF and the KPSS test and were found to be non-stationary. The ADF results of the log returns of the cryptocurrencies showed that the t-statistic values were lesser than the critical values -1.9411 at 5% significance level. Results implied that the Null Hypothesis (Ho) was not accepted, and the series was stationary. The KPSS test statistic values were found to be lower than the critical value 0.463 at 5% significance level. The Null Hypothesis (Ho) was not rejected, and the log returns of cryptocurrencies were found to be stationary. The stationarity of the log returns of cryptocurrencies were established and were used for further analysis.

Table 1. Characteristics of cryptocurrencies

	Bitcoin	ETH	Tether	XRP	Bitcoin Cash	Bitcoin	ETH	Tether	XRP	Bitcoin cash
	Daily closing prices					Log normal values				
Mean	7597.8	314.38	1.002	0.414	561.54	0.0011	0.0001	0.000	0.000	−0.001
Median	7459.6	225.63	1.00	0.309	354.46	0.0013	−0.0001	0.000	−0.002	−0.003
Maximum	19497	1396.4	1.08	3.380	3923.1	0.2251	0.234	0.0572	0.607	0.432
Minimum	2529.4	84.310	0.967	0.140	77.37	−0.465	−0.551	−0.049	−0.399	−0.561
Std. Dev.	2796.3	231.1	0.008	0.357	534.7	0.044	0.053	0.007	0.062	0.077
Skewness	0.754	1.913	1.45	4.026	2.366	−1.032	−1.214	0.297	1.551	0.254
Kurtosis	4.406	6.48	15.31	24.96	9.62	16.94	15.659	14.804	21.739	12.48
Observations	1083	1083	1083	1083	1083	1082	1082	1082	1082	1082
Normality - Jarque Bera Statistics										
Jarque-Bera	**191.76**	**1208**	**7216.1**	**2468.1**	**2987.6**	**8949.7**	**7490.8**	**6297.9**	**1625.8**	**4065.9**
Stationarity – ADF Test results										
ADF t-Stat.	−0.44	−1.004	−0.90	−2.18	−1.434	**−33.95**	**−34.88**	**−20.27**	**−20.88**	**−30.68**
P. value	0.52	0.28	0.68	0.62	0.141	0	0	0.048	0	0
KPSS t-Stat.	0.3	1.77	0.08	1.02	1.02	0.146	0.106	0.106	0.105	0.07

*Bold indicates significance at 5% level

4.1 Day of the Week Anomaly

The day of the week anomalies were studied by assigning value 1 for the first dummy variable on all Mondays of the sample period and 0 for other days in Eq. 1. Similarly, value 1 was assigned for all Tuesdays and 0 for other days. Sundays were not assigned values 1 since Sunday was taken as the reference variable and was represented by the constant term. The preliminary results of the Dummy Variable OLS regression equation revealed that the residuals were heteroskedastic and hence, GARCH (1, 1) models were applied to examine the day of the week anomaly for all cryptocurrencies. Clustering effect of the closing prices of Tether was observed in the Fig. 1 and the residuals of GARCH (1, 1) model applied for Tether cryptocurrency also showed presence of autocorrelation. Hence, GARCH (1, 1): ARMA (1, 1) model was used to examine presence of day of the week anomaly in Tether cryptocurrency. The results of GARCH (1, 1) models are provided in Table 2 and it can be observed that coefficients of Thursday were negative and significant for the cryptocurrencies Bitcoin (−0.008), Ethereum (−0.011), XRP (−0.010), Bitcoin Cash (0.017). The findings provided existence of Thursday anomalies for the four cryptocurrencies. Negative sign of the coefficient indicated that the cryptocurrencies had negative returns on Thursdays. In case of Tether, the day of the week anomaly was not significant for any of the weekdays. Adjusted r square values of GARCH (1, 1) model improved from the OLS models suggested that the GARCH (1, 1) model was a better fit model to study calendar anomalies. The Ljung-Box Q-statistics, LB (36) statistic tests the null hypothesis that autocorrelations up to lag 36 equals zero implying that the residuals and squared residuals are random and independent up to 36 lags. The values of Q (36) and Q^2 (36) of the Ljung-Box Q-statistics for the standardized and squared residuals were found to be insignificant and hence the residuals were uncorrelated. The ARCH LM test is a Lagrange multiplier test to assess the significance of ARCH effects or whether the residuals are exhibiting heteroskedasticity. The ARCH LM statistic was found to be insignificant at 5% significance level, confirming the removal of heteroskedasticity in the residuals. The ARCH and GARCH terms in variance equation were positive and significant at 1% level, suggesting that once a shock has occurred, volatility tend to persist for longer periods. The findings differed from the studies by Caporale et al. [13] and Caporale and Plastun [6] who showed that Bitcoin exhibited Monday anomalies having abnormal positive returns. The difference may be accounted for the high market volatility on the cryptocurrency market from December 2019 owing to the COVID - 19 pandemic and the persistence of volatility due to shocks were statistically confirmed in the ARCH and GARCH terms of the GARCH(1, 1) model.

Table 2. Results of Day of the Week anomaly of select cryptocurrencies

	Bitcoin		Ethereum		Tether		XRP		Bitcoin Cash	
Mean equation										
Variable	Coeff.	Prob	Coeff.	Prob.	Coeff.	Prob	Coeff.	Prob	Coeff.	Prob
C	0.00	0.335	0.00	0.98	0.00	0.47	−0.0	0.34	−0.0	0.75
Monday	0.00	0.726	0.00	0.73	0.00	0.83	0.01	0.07	0.01	0.35
Tuesday	−0.00	0.605	0.00	0.86	0.00	0.17	0.01	0.12	0.0	0.93
Wednesday	−0.00	0.562	−0.00	0.59	0.00	0.99	0.00	0.91	−0.0	0.82
Thursday	**−0.01**	0.032	**−0.01**	0.02	0.00	0.28	**−0.01**	0.02	**−0.02**	0.00
Friday	0.00	0.891	0.006	0.33	0.00	0.79	0.00	0.71	0.01	0.21
Saturday	0.00	0.764	0.008	0.21	0.00	0.29	0.01	0.25	0.01	0.19
AR (1)					0.08	0.15				
MA (1)					−0.8	0.0				
Variance equation										
C	0.000	0.0	0.000	0.0	0.000	0.0	0.000	0.0	0.000	0.0
ARCH	0.133	0.0	0.101	0.0	0.150	0.0	0.145	0.0	0.120	0.0
GARCH	0.813	0.0	0.830	0.0	0.600	0.0	0.832	0.0	0.828	0.0
Adj R-sq.	−0.003		0.003		0.293		−0.012		0.002	
LB Q (36)	0.853		0.261		0.134		0.814		0.777	
LB Q^2(36)	1.000		0.721		0.901		0.975		1.000	
Arch effect	0.912		0.758		0.883		0.238		0.566	

4.2   Month of the Year Anomaly

The month of the year anomaly was examined by assigning value 1 to dummy variable for January and 0 for other months and the process was repeated for subsequent months in Eq. 2. The month of December was used as the reference variable and was represented in the constant term. The results of GARCH (1, 1) models applied for Bitcoin, XRP, Ethereum and Bitcoin cash cryptocurrencies and GARCH (1, 1) ARMA model for Tether are provided in Table 3. As observed from the Table 3, Bitcoin was the only cryptocurrency that had positive significant values during the months March (0.016) and April (0.011) and therefore provided evidence for market anomalies during March and April. The positive value of the coefficient indicated that positive returns were earned in Bitcoin currencies and also confirmed the month anomaly during March and April. Plastun et al. [17] has found that Bitcoin had the lowest returns during the months of July and August. Other cryptocurrencies used in this study did not show any evidence for month anomalies. It can be surmised that Bitcoin which had higher risk return characteristics (Table 1) exhibited negative Thursday and positive March-April anomalies. Hence, market inefficiency for this cryptocurrency was evident. The traders can employ suitable trading strategies to generate abnormal profits in this asset class. Residual tests to examine the presence of ARCH effect was carried out and the insignificant values indicated the removal of ARCH effects. The statistics of Q(36) and $Q^2(36)$ of the Ljung-Box Q-statistics also confirmed the absence of autocorrelation in the residuals for the models of Bitcoin, XRP, Ethereum, and Bitcoin cash. The significant values of AR (1), MA (1) terms of Tether model GARCH (1, 1): ARMA (1,1) confirmed the absence of autocorrelations in the residuals.

Table 3. Results of month of the year anomaly of select cryptocurrencies

	Bitcoin		ETH		Tether		XRP		Bitcoin Cash	
Mean equation										
Variable	Coeff.	Prob.	Coeff.	Prob.	Coeff.	Prob.	Coeff.	Prob.	Coeff.	Prob.
C	0.00	0.96	0.01	0.59	0.00	0.51	0.00	0.98	0.00	0.80
January	0.00	0.88	0.00	0.98	−0.00	0.13	0.00	0.80	0.00	0.82
February	0.00	0.62	0.00	0.81	0.00	0.94	0.00	0.86	0.00	0.78
March	**0.02**	0.00	−0.02	0.22	0.00	0.74	−0.00	0.61	−0.00	0.92
April	**0.01**	0.05	0.01	0.66	−0.00	0.38	0.01	0.42	0.02	0.15
May	0.00	0.81	−0.00	0.96	−0.00	0.69	−0.00	0.81	0.00	0.73
June	−0.00	0.71	−0.01	0.64	0.00	0.60	−0.01	0.27	−0.00	0.78
July	0.00	0.68	−0.01	0.56	−0.00	0.44	−0.00	0.71	0.00	0.82
August	0.00	0.64	−0.01	0.71	0.00	0.91	0.00	0.98	−0.00	0.78
September	−0.00	0.77	−0.01	0.49	−0.00	0.64	0.00	0.77	−0.00	0.95
October	0.00	0.62	−0.01	0.70	−0.00	0.60	0.00	0.96	0.00	0.95
November	−0.01	0.38	−0.01	0.54	0.00	0.82	−0.01	0.42	−0.00	0.82
AR (1)					0.06	0.28				
MA (1)					−0.77	0.00				
Variance equation										
C	0.00	0.0	0.00	0.0	0.00	0.0	0.00	0.0	0.00	0.00
ARCH	0.16	0.0	0.15	0.0	0.16	0.0	0.13	0.0	0.10	0.00
GARCH	0.80	0.0	0.60	0.0	0.81	0.0	0.84	0.0	0.85	0.00
Adj R-sq	−0.03		0.00		−0.00		−0.01		−0.01	
LB Q (36)			0.44		0.28		0.93		0.88	
LB $Q^2(36)$			0.91		1.00		0.99		1.00	
LM Arch			0.93		0.83		0.24		0.52	

4.3 Turn of the Year Anomaly

The turn of the year anomaly on cryptocurrencies was analyzed using value 1 to dummy variables for the last two and first two weeks of December and January and 0 for other weeks of the year in Eq. 3. Results of GARCH (1, 1) models are provided in Table 4.

Table 4. Results of turn of the year effect

	Bitcoin		ETH		Tether		XRP		Bitcoin cash	
Mean equation										
Variable	Coeff.	Prob.	Coeff.	Prob.	Coeff.	Prob.	Coeff.	Prob.	Coeff.	Prob.
C	0.00	0.297	−0.001	0.7	0.0	0.5	0.0	0.2	−0.002	0.46
Turn of the Year	0.01	0.414	**0.01**	0.0	0.0	0.8	0.01	0.1	**0.018**	0.03
AR (1)					0.03	0.0				
MA (1)					−0.7	0.0				
Variance equation										
C	0.000	0.000	0.00	0.0	0.00	0.0	0.00	0.0	0.000	0.00
ARCH	0.136	0.000	0.09	0.0	0.14	0.0	0.13	0.0	0.100	0.00
GARCH	0.805	0.000	0.83	0.0	0.81	0.0	0.84	0.0	0.849	0.00
Adj R-sq.	−0.01		0.01		0.29		0.00		0.003	
LB Q (36)	0.884		0.45		0.46		0.89		0.872	
LB Q^2(36)	1.000		0.81		1.00		0.98		1.000	
LB Arch	0.904		0.79		0.83		0.23		0.518	

*Bold indicates significance at 5% level

Results indicate that Ethereum (0.013) and Bitcoin Cash (0.018) are the two cryptocurrencies that have positive and significant values for turn of the year effect. The value of the ARCH LM statistic was found to be insignificant and the absence of ARCH effects in the residuals was confirmed. The statistics of Q (36) and Q^2(36) of the Ljung-Box Q-statistics for the model standardized and squared standardized residuals were insignificant at 36 lags and hence the residuals were not serially correlated. Positive value of the coefficient indicates that there is a positive impact on the cryptocurrencies by the arrival of a new year. Other cryptocurrencies, namely Bitcoin, Tether and XRP were not affected by the turn of the year effect. Bitcoin cash and Ethereum were found to exhibit Thursday anomalies and turn of the year anomalies. Hence, the traders can employ trading strategy that involves short positions on Thursdays and close them at the end of this day. They can take long positions during the turn of the year except for Thursdays.

5 Conclusion

This paper examines the day of the week, month of the year and turn of the year calendar anomalies of the cryptocurrencies Bitcoin, Ethereum, Tether, XRP and Bitcoin Cash using Dummy variable GARCH regression. The study provides evidence for presence of the calendar anomalies during the sample period July 23, 2017 through July 9, 2020 and confirms market inefficiency in the cryptocurrency market. The findings of the study show that Bitcoin, Ethereum, XRP, Bitcoin Cash made negative returns on Thursdays. It may be attributed to the fact that Thursday falling in the middle of the week. Investors may have presumed that less volatility would result in less returns during this time and would have planned trading activities during the beginning and end of the week to make profits. Bitcoin also exhibited March and April month anomaly with positive returns. The months March and April are the end and start of a fiscal year and it may be suggested that investors can plan their investments especially in Bitcoin cryptocurrency for reaping more profits. Ethereum and Bitcoin were the only two cryptocurrencies effected by the turn of the year effect with positive returns caused by the change in the year. This may be due to the positive sentiment of the New Year. Tether was the only cryptocurrency that was not affected by any of the calendar anomalies examined in this paper and may be attributed to the clustering or persistence in price movements. Descriptive statistics of Bitcoin and Ethereum showed negative returns during the entire sample period. Thursday anomalies showed negative returns for these two cryptocurrencies, whereas turn of the month showed positive returns for Bitcoin and year end anomaly showed positive returns for Ethereum. It may be presumed that the occurrences of the negative returns on Thursdays were more frequent than the turn of the month and year end and hence, was reflected in the entire sample period. The findings would be beneficial to the investors and traders who can make use of these anomalies to adopt suitable trading strategies and achieve higher returns in the digital currency arena. The research in cryptocurrency is burgeoning and this study identifies the various calendar anomalies in this market and would benefit researchers by providing insights on market inefficiencies for developing models on volatility and forecasting. The cause of these anomalies may be due to volatility spill over from other global markets, political uncertainties, and news events or tweets and it can be taken into consideration for future scope of this study.

References

1. Lee, D.K.C.: Handbook of Digital Currency. Elsevier, San Diego (2015)
2. Corbet, S., Lucey, B., Urquhart, A., Yarovaya, L.: Cryptocurrencies as a financial asset: A systematic analysis. International Review of Financial Analysis **62**, 182–199 (2019)
3. Conrad, C., Custovic, A., Ghysels, E.: Long-and short-term cryptocurrency volatility components: A GARCH-MIDAS analysis. Journal of Risk and Financial Management **11** (2), 23 (2018)
4. Corbet, S., Meegan, A., Larkin, C., Lucey, B., Yarovaya, L.: Exploring the dynamic relationships between cryptocurrencies and other financial assets. Economics Letters **165**, 28–34 (2018)

5. Shahzad, S.J.H., Bouri, E., Roubaud, D., Kristoufek, L., Lucey, B.: Is Bitcoin a better safe – haven investment than gold and commodities? International Review of Financial Analysis **63**, 322–330 (2019)
6. Caporale, G.M., Plastun, A.: The day of the week effect in the cryptocurrency market. Finance Research Letters, 31 (2019)
7. Chandra, A.: Stock market anomalies: A survey of calendar Effect in BSE-SENSEX. Indian Journal of Finance, 5 (2009)
8. Deyshappriya, N.R.: An empirical investigation on stock market anomalies: The evidence from Colombo Stock Exchange in Sri Lanka. International Journal of Economics and Finance **6**(3), 177–187 (2014)
9. Safeer, M., Kevin, S.: A study on market anomalies in Indian stock market. Int. J. Bus. Admin. Res. Rev **1**, 128–137 (2014)
10. Shakila, B., Pinto, P., Hawaldar, I.T.: Semi-monthly effect in stock returns: new evidence from Bombay Stock Exchange. Investment management and financial innovations, (14, № 3 (contin. 1)), 160–172 (2017)
11. Rossi, M., Gunardi, A.: Efficient market hypothesis and stock market anomalies: empirical evidence in four European countries. J. Appl. Bus. Res. (JABR) **34**(1), 183–192 (2018)
12. Plastun, O.L., Kozmenko, S.M., Plastun, V., Filatova, H.P.: Market anomalies and data persistence: the case of the day-of-the-week effect. J. Int. Stud. **12**(3) (2019)
13. Caporale, G.M., Gil-Alana, L., Plastun, A.: Persistence in the cryptocurrency market. Res. Int. Bus. Finan. **46**, 141–148 (2018)
14. Caporale, G.M., Plastun, A.: Price overreactions in the cryptocurrency market. J. Econ. Stud. **46**(5), 1137–1155 (2019)
15. Kurihara, Y., Fukushima, A.: The market efficiency of Bitcoin: a weekly anomaly perspective. J. Appl. Finan. Bank. **7**(3), 57 (2017)
16. McDonald, J.B., Turley, P.: Distributional characteristics: just a few more moments. The American Statistician **65**(2), 96–103 (2011)
17. Plastun, A., Drofa, A.O., Klyushnik, T.V.: Month of the year effect in the cryptocurrency market and portfolio management. Eur. J. Manage. Issues **27**(1–2), 29–35 (2019)
18. Brooks, C.: Introductory Econometrics for Finance. Cambridge University Press, United Kingdom (2014)
19. Fama, E.F.: Efficient capital markets: II. J. Finan. **46**(5), 1575–1617 (1991)
20. Latif, M., Arshad, S., Fatima, M., Farooq, S.: Market efficiency, market anomalies, causes, evidences, and some behavioural aspects of market anomalies. Res. J. Finan. Acc. **2**(9), 1–13 (2011)

Does Herding Behaviour Among Traders Increase During Covid 19 Pandemic? Evidence from the Cryptocurrency Market

D. Susana$^{(\boxtimes)}$, J. K. Kavisanmathi, and S. Sreejith

KCT Business School, Kumaraguru College of Technology,
Coimbatore 641049, India
susana@kctbs.ac.in,
{kavisanmathi.19mba,sreejith.19mba}@kct.ac.in

Abstract. Cryptocurrencies are digital currencies and trading these currencies have gained huge momentum in recent years. The sophisticated features, complexities on regulatory framework, and high volatility of Cryptocurrencies would pose trading challenges to new investors and/or investors with limited knowledge. Investors generally are influenced by fund managers, financial analysts or other investors who are considered as well informed and highly knowledgeable peers. Investors mimic their behaviour to perform trading activities and such behaviour is termed as Herding. Covid 19 pandemic triggered severe uncertainties in the cryptocurrencies market and has led to wide fluctuations in prices causing severe volatility and market crashes. This paper aims to examine the herding behaviour in cryptocurrency market during the pre Covid 19 and Covid 19 pandemic period using the Cross-Sectional Standard Deviation (CSSD) approach. The findings of the paper reveal that herding was evident among all the ten crypto-currencies in normal market conditions of the entire sample period but not during market upswing or downswing. However, the herding behaviour was present in the cryptocurrencies Litecoin, Cardano and Dash during the Covid 19 pandemic period in all market conditions.

Keywords: Cryptocurrency · Herding behavior · CSSD

1 Introduction

Cryptocurrency, a phenomenal financial and technological innovation has become a key investment option for traders in recent years. With the introduction of Bitcoin in the year 2009 and its wide acceptance, an array of other cryptocurrencies was introduced in the market. Cryptocurrencies subsequently launched was tailored to adapt to Bitcoin and other leading cryptocurrencies characteristics while having to demarcation on certain unique characteristics on its own. As of August 5, 2020, top hundred cryptocurrency trading volume was $83 billion (coinmarketcap.com) which indicate an increased participation and trading activity among the investors. Cryptocurrencies does not have fundamental value and hence their prices do not reflect all the information [1]. Cryptocurrencies also exhibit exceptional returns coupled with high volatility [2]. Being an under-regulated crypto market with lack of transparency in information, naïve

© IFIP International Federation for Information Processing 2020
Published by Springer Nature Switzerland AG 2020
S. K. Sharma et al. (Eds.): TDIT 2020, IFIP AICT 617, pp. 178–189, 2020.
https://doi.org/10.1007/978-3-030-64849-7_17

traders and investors may venture into this market without realizing the risks associated on their investment. The novel features, ambiguity in information, high volatilities in the cryptocurrency market may cause the investors to rely on the judgments on financial advisors or fund managers or other investing forum. In financial theories, herding behaviour of investors relate to their trading decisions based on the views and actions on others. Lack of confidence, fear or anxiety in the investors may also lead them to mimic the trading behavior and decisions or other investors or fund managers. This behaviour may have several consequences such as price instability, higher volatility, market bubbles or crashes [3].

The financial markets are susceptible to unprecedented calamities, natural disasters, war, and pandemics leading to market crashes and financial crisis. In the case of pandemics/epidemic crisis, the previous occurrences such as the HIV/AIDS, SARS, Ebola and H1N1 which posed a threat to the lives of individuals had impacted the global financial markets and economy [4]. However, the severity in case of the recent Covid 19 pandemic is much higher in the financial markets which has disrupted the global economic activity as a whole causing collapse of several global economies and causing global stock market crashes. Yarovaya et al. [5] has noted that experts opine that Covid 19 may lead to financial crisis and may be predicted as a "black swan event", an event which is unpredictable and has not occurred earlier. Such events may impose challenges on model predictions and calculate risk assessment measures. Hence, investors trading in cryptocurrencies are confronted with uncertainties due to the Covid 19 pandemic which may lead to herd behaviour. The stock market crash and relevant investor uncertainties causes investors to deviate from their rational behaviour and exhibit biases and herding [6]. Overexcitement among investors leading to high volume trading causes herding behaviour in extreme volatile conditions [7] and the cryptocurrency prices are driven by herding behaviour [8]. Hence, examination of herding behaviour in cryptocurrency market is important during uncertain market conditions. In particular, when market crashed due to Covid 19 pandemic, herding behavioral characteristics could be a potential contributor on cryptocurrencies price variations and trading volume and its associated liquidity. On this context, this study examines the herding behaviour in the cryptocurrency market prior to Covid 19 pandemic and whether this trend has increased during the pandemic period.

2 Literature Review

Several researchers have tried to explore the dynamics of various market crashes particularly in the equity markets. Presence of herding behaviour in stock markets during the crisis period has been investigated in stock markets [3]. Investors tend to herd or mimic other investors during extreme volatile conditions in the markets hoping to make profits [9]. Studies by Lao and Singh [10], Hammami and Boujelbene [11], Jlassi and Naoui [12], Clements et al. [13], Demirer et al. [14] and Bansal [15] have confirmed the herding behaviour during market turbulence or crisis period whereas studies by Ahsan and Sarkar [16] have provided evidence of non-existence of herding behaviour as well.

Given the market severity and volatility during crisis period, investigation on herding behavior of investors becomes vital. Sophisticated features of cryptocurrencies [17] and its extreme volatile nature may cause herding activity among investors particularly during extreme and volatile market conditions. Herding behaviour in cryptocurrency markets were examined during different market conditions. Conrad et al. [18] examined herding behaviour in cryptocurrency market using CSSD, Cross Sectional Absolute Deviation of returns (CSAD) and Markov-Switching model, and found that herding existed in extreme market conditions. Silvia et al. [19] studied herding formation using modified CSAD model on select 50 cryptocurrencies based on liquidity and market capitalization. The study revealed that severe herd behaviour was exhibited during extreme periods. Vidal- Thomas et al. [20] examined herding using static, rolling, and logistic regression model and reported that herding activity increased with market uncertainty. Ballis and Drakos [21] employed GARCH models to examine herding behaviour on top five cryptocurrencies, and found herding existed during market up and down periods. Poyser [9] used Markov-Switching approach and reported that herding existed during different market regimes. Jalal et al. [8] confirmed the presence of herding behaviour in the extreme conditions of bullish and high volatility market situations of major cryptocurrencies listed in CCI30 index and sub-major cryptocurrencies and major stock returns listed in Dow-Jones Industrial Average Index, from 2015 to 2018. Junior et al. [22] noted a positive relationship between herding and market stress conditions. The studies on herding behaviour in the cryptocurrency market had established the presence of herding activity among investors during uncertain market conditions.

Covid 19 pandemic has caused uncertainty across the globe leading to falling economies, market crashes, unemployment, and other unexpected uncertainties. Previous pandemics/epidemics including the Spanish flu, SARS, HINI, HIV/AIDS had caused impact on financial markets. But in the case of Covid 19 pandemic, the lockdown restrictions and the halt of several global industrial and economic activities led to a significant impact on the financial markets [23]. Ma et al. [24] and Baker et al. [25] noted severity in economic impact and Eichenbaum et al. [26] on the huge loss in lives, Under such uncertain economic and high volatile conditions in cryptocurrency markets due to the pandemic, the herding behaviour in investors may tend to increase as established by several researchers. Kizysa et al. [27] have noted that the Government and regulatory restraints imposed to control the transmission of Covid 19 within and across countries can ease the investor herding behavior in international stock markets. Few studies have examined the herding behaviour in cryptocurrency markets during the Covid 19 pandemic. In case of cryptocurrencies, Yarovaya [6] reported that Covid 19 does not significantly amplify herding in the markets whereas Mnif et al. [28] found herding behaviour reduced after Coronovirus outbreak. Most of the studies on cryptocurrency market have tried to capture the herding behaviour in different market conditions. The limited evidences of Yarovaya [6] and Mnif et al. [28] have mixed indication on herding behaviour during Covid - 19 pandemic. Hence this study aims to justify a potential research gap by examining the herding behaviour during the pre-Covid 19 and Covid 19 pandemic period.

3 Methodology

This study aims to examine the herding behaviour in top ten cryptocurrencies. The ten cryptocurrencies used for this study are Bitcoin, Ripple, Ethereum, Bitcoin cash, EOS, Litecoin, Monera, Cardano, IOTA, and Dash. Crypto10 Index. The market index chosen was BITA Crypto10 (B10) Index, provided by the company BITA, a German-based Fintech company was introduced on 20th September 2018. The Crypto10 Index is calculated in US dollars (USD) and calculated on a daily basis. It represents the performance of the 10 largest cryptocurrencies based on the market capitalization. Daily closing prices of the Index and the ten cryptocurrencies (from BITA crpto-10 Index) are sourced from bitadata.com and coinmarketcap.com are used for the analysis. The sample period considered for this study is from July 29, 2019 to July 28, 2020 comprising of the pre Covid 19 and Covid 19 period. The BITA Crypto 10 Index returns are examined for normality and stationarity for usage in subsequent analysis.

The best possible approach to test herding is to directly observe the investor's actions. But in cryptocurrencies, it is almost impossible because of its privacy and so different proxies are developed to detect herding behavior of the crypto market based on returns' regression rate. Hence this study employs the methodology adopted by Chang et al. [29] an improvement from the original methodology offered by Christie and Huang [30]. Christie and Huang [30] suggested the use of Cross-Sectional Standard Deviation of returns (CSSD) to identify herding behavior in financial markets.

$$CSSD = \sqrt{\{(((\text{Bitcoin return} - \text{Average of B10 return})2)/N - 1\}} \qquad (1)$$

where, Bitcoin return is computed using the formula (Today's closing price – previous day closing price)/previous day closing price, B10 return is computed using (Today's index value – previous day index value)/previous day index value, and N is the number of days taken for the study.

According to Christie and Huang [30] herding can be tested when there are upswings and downswings (under market stress events) by exploiting investors' tendency to overturn their private beliefs in favor of the market consensus. The Capital Asset Pricing Model (CAPM) predicts that the dispersion will increase with the absolute value of the market return since individual assets differ in their sensitivity to the market return. And also, if herding exists, individual returns will not differ greatly from the market results. The CSSD refers to the average proximity of individuals' returns to the mean and will always be equal greater than zero. The value in the lowest bound signifies when all the returns converge while a deviation from the zero represents dispersion. The herding behaviour in the cryptocurrencies are studied using Dummy variable Ordinary Least Square (OLS) regression model as shown in Eq. 2.

$$Log (CSSDi) = c + dl + du \qquad (2)$$

where, CSSDi is the CSSD of the log return of the individual cryptocurrency, dl is 1 if market return lies on the lowest side of the distribution and 0 otherwise, du is 1 if market return lies on the upper side of the distribution and 0 otherwise. The residuals of the equation are examined for autocorrelation and heteroskedasticity. The residuals of the Dummy variable regression were verified for presence of autocorrelation using Ljung-Box (L-B) portmanteau test and heteroskedasticity using Lagrange's Multiplier (LM) test for ARCH-effect. Where the presence of ARCH effects in the currency returns GARCH (1, 1) regression models was used for the analysis.

4 Analysis and Findings

The time series graphs of the ten cryptocurrencies are illustrated in Fig. 1 plotted with prices on Y axis and days on X axis. It can be observed that all the cryptocurrencies witnessed a massive fall in their prices during the months December 2019 and March 2020.The fall in December 2019 prices may be attributed to the event when the outbreak of Coronavirus at Wuhan, China was announced. The subsequent major fall in prices during March 2020 may be due to the nationwide lockdown imposed across several global countries to contain the spread of the virus in their respective countries. The global financial markets were forced to stop trading due to the steep fall in prices and the markets moved to bear trend. It may be inferred that in such market stress situations investors uncertainty and panic would have led them exhibit herding behaviour. CSSD series for longer sample periods may not be normally distributed and

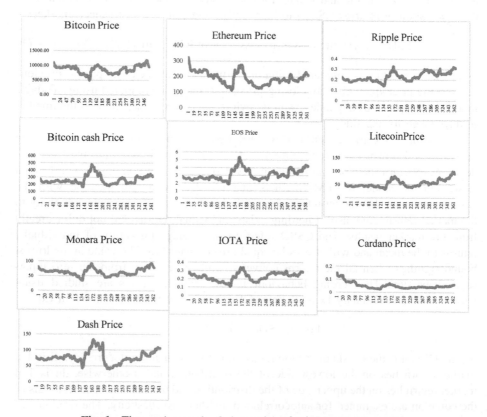

Fig. 1. Time series graph of close price of select cryptocurrencies.

regularly tend to show excess kurtosis and skewness which are basic with financial parameter [31]. Brooks [32] recommends the usage of natural logarithmic transformations to meet the normality assumption as it can help to make a skewed distribution closer to a normal distribution. The results of the log CSSD value of the cryptocurrencies carried out using ADF test showed that the t-statistic values were lesser than the critical values −2.88 at 5% significance level during both pre-Covid 19 and Covid 19 and were stationary.

4.1 Herding Behaviour During Pre-covid 19

The results of the Dummy variable OLS regression model for the ten cryptocurrencies during pre-Covid 19 periods using Eq. 2 are provided in Table 1. The residuals of these models were examined for presence of autocorrelation and heteroskedasticity. The residuals of the Ethereum CSSD regression was found to be autocorrelated and hence AR (1) term was added in the model. The residuals of the Bitcoin CSSD and EOS CSSD regression had ARCH effects and hence GARCH (1, 1) model was employed. It can be observed from Table 1, the coefficients of dl in the models for the cryptocurrencies Bitcoin (1.1252), Ethereum (1.2068), Ripple (1.1607), Bitcoin cash (1.3006), EOS (1.1954) were positive and significant. According to Christie and Huang [30], a positive and significant coefficient indicates absence of herding behaviour. It can be inferred that during market downswing or when the market returns were negative there was no existence of herding activity. However, for the cryptocurrencies Litecoin (−0.2790), Monera (−0.5218), Cardano (−0.1918), IOTA (−0.4949) and Dash (−0.3103) the coefficients of dl were found to be negative and significant. A statistically significant negative coefficient indicates presence of herding activity in the market downswing period. It can also be inferred that herding activity was not evident for the top five cryptocurrencies during market downswing, whereas the investors trading in the next five cryptocurrencies exhibited herding behaviour during this market condition. The constant term of all the cryptocurrencies which represent the normal market condition were found to be statistically significant and negative for all cryptocurrencies. It can be surmised that during normal market conditions herding activity were present. However, the coefficient du was found to be statistically insignificant and herding behaviour was not present among investors during market upswing. The residuals were examined for the presence of autocorrelation. The Ljung-Box Q-statistics, LB (36) statistic tests the null hypothesis that autocorrelations up to lag 36 equals zero implying that the residuals and squared residuals are random and independent up to 36 lags. The values of Q (36) of the Ljung-Box Q-statistics for the standardized residuals for the OLS models of the cryptocurrencies Ethereum, Ripple, Bitcoin Cash, Litecoin, Monera, Cardano, IOTA and DASH were found to be insignificant and hence the residuals were uncorrelated. The values of Q (36) and Q^2 (36) for the models Bitcoin and EOS for the standardized and squared residuals were found to be insignificant and hence the residuals were not serially correlated. The ARCH LM test is a Lagrange multiplier test to assess the significance of ARCH effects or whether the residuals are exhibiting heteroskedasticity. The ARCH LM statistic was found to be insignificant at

5% level, confirming the removal of heteroskedasticity in the residuals. The ARCH and GARCH terms in variance equation of the models of Bitcoin and EOS were positive and significant at 5% level, suggesting persistence of volatility for longer period when a shock had occurred.

Table 1. Dummy Variable OLS Regression results for herding behaviour on pre-Covid 19

Cryptocurrencies	Log Bitcoin CSSD		Log Ethereum CSSD		Log Ripple CSSD		Log Bitcoincash CSSD		Log EOS CSSD	
Variable	Coeff.	Prob.	Coeff.	Prob.	Coeff.	Prob.	Coeff.	Prob.	Coeff.	Prob.
Mean equation										
C	**−6.820**	0.000	**−6.873**	0.000	**−6.783**	0.000	**−6.880**	0.000	**−6.808**	0.00
Dl	**1.125**	0.001	**1.207**	0.018	**1.161**	0.001	**1.301**	0.000	**1.195**	0.01
Du	−0.113	0.841	0.493	0.115	−0.468	0.157	−0.338	0.351	−0.034	0.88
AR (1)			0.231	0.009						
Variance equation										
C	0.817	0.009							0.692	0.011
ArchTerm	0.131	0.166							0.343	0.071
GARCH	−0.17	0.678							−0.337	0.302
Adj R−sq	0.062		0.125		0.079		0.074		0.084	
LB Q (36)	0.115		0.204		0.970		0.288		0.529	
LB Q^2(36)	0.840								0.610	
LM Arch	0.824		0.845		0.347		0.572		0.432	
Cryptocurrencies	Log Litecoin CSSD		Log Monera CSSD		Log Cardano CSSD		Log IOTA CSSD		Log Dash CSSD	
C	**−6.79**	0.00	**−6.792**	0.000	**−6.808**	0.000	**−6.805**	0.000	**−6.807**	0.000
Dl	**−0.27**	0.000	**−0.522**	0.000	**−0.192**	0.00	**−0.495**	0.000	**−0.310**	0.000
Du	−0.03	0.503	−0.037	0.417	0.003	0.932	0.023	0.750	0.002	0.960
Adj R-sq	0.193		0.457		0.122		0.231		0.202	
LB Q(36)	0.054		0.996		0.430		0.999		0.705	
LB Q^2(36)	0.632		0.745		0.882		0.949		0.857	

* Bold indicates significance at 5% level

4.2 Herding Behaviour During Covid 19

The presence of herding behaviour during Covid 19 period was examined using Dummy variable OLS regression model and the results are shown in Table 2. The residual for the Bitcoin Cash CSSD and Dash CSSD regressions was found to be autocorrelated. AR(1) and MA(1) terms was added to the model of Bitcoin Cash CSSD and AR(1), AR(2), MA(1) and MA(2) terms were added in the model of Dash CSSD. The residuals for Bitcoin cash CSSD and EOS CSSD and IOTA CSSD had ARCH effects and hence GARCH (1, 1) model was used. It can be seen from Table 2, that the coefficient of dl (downswing market) were positive and significant for Bitcoin (1.3349), Ethereum (1.2920), Ripple (1.7878), Bitcoin cash (1.4481), EOS (1.6419). Hence herding behavior was not evident among the investors during market upturn. The coefficient of du (upswing market) were found to be negative and significant for the cryptocurrencies Litecoin (−0.2449), Monera (−0.3705), Cardano (−0.6634), IOTA (−0.3648) and Dash (−0.4589) and the presence of herding activity was found in these cryptocurrencies. The constant term representing the herding behaviour during normal market conditions for all cryptocurrencies were found to be statistically significant and negative and the presence of herding among investors was found. Similar to the pre-Covid 19 period, the coefficients of du were positive and insignificant for Bitcoin (0.4383), Ethereum (0.4110), Ripple (0.4499), Bitcoin cash (0.0347) absence of herding was observed. However, it can be seen that the coefficients of du for the cryptocurrencies Litecoin (−0.0870), Cardano (−0.1958) and Dash (−0.3977) were negative and significant indicating that the herding behavior existed when there was upswing in the market and has negative impact on cryptocurrencies. The cryptocurrencies Monera (−0.0927) and IOTA (−0.0493) coefficients were negative and insignificant and EOS (0.7405) coefficient was positive and significant which implied absence of herd behavior. The residual statistics were verified for the presence of autocorrelation and heteroskedasticity. The insignificant values of LB Q (36) and LB Q^2 (36) showed the absence of autocorrelations in the residuals of the models. The statistic values of the ARCH effect were found to be insignificant and the absence of ARCH effects were statistically confirmed. The previous studies by Gumus et al. [33] found absence of herding behaviour for the cryptocurrencies Bitcoin, Litecoin, Stellar, Monero, Dogecoin and Dash using CCI 30 Index as market proxy whereas Silva et al. [19] detected the presence of herding in 50 cryptocurrencies especially in the market stress conditions. The only study during Covid - 19 by Mnif et al. [28] showed that herding decreased during Covid 19. The findings of this study differed by the results of Mnif et al. [28] wherein it was found that similar herding behaviour was found seven cryptocurrencies Bitcoin, Ethereum, Ripple, Bitcoin cash, EOS, Monera and IOTA during pre Covid 19 and Covid 19 periods. However, the investors trading in Litecoin, Cardano, and Dash exhibited herding behaviour during market upswing, downswing, and normal conditions in the Covid 19 period. The fear and uncertainty among the investors trading in these currencies would have led them to imitate the trading behaviour of others anticipating positive returns during the market upswing. It can be presumed that these investors demonstrated excessive herding behaviour due to fear of losing money in the Covid 19 period due to the market crashes, economic downturn, and uncertainty across global economies. Studies by Conrad et al. [18], Silvia et al. [19], Vidal- Thomas et al. [20], Junior et al. [22], Jalal et al. [7] also confirmed the presence of herding behaviour during extreme market conditions.

Table 2. Dummy Variable OLS regression results for herding behaviour on Covid 19

Cryptocurrencies	Log Bitcoin CSSD		Log Ethereum CSSD		Log Ripple CSSD		Log Bitcoincash CSSD		Log EOS CSSD	
Variable	Coeff.	Prob.	Coeff.	Prob.	Coeff.	Prob.	Coeff.	Prob.	Coeff.	Prob.
Mean equation										
C	**−7.006**	0.00	**−6.930**	0.00	**−7.040**	0.000	**−6.968**	0.000	**−6.892**	0.000
Dl	**1.335**	0.00	**1.292**	0.00	**1.788**	0.000	**1.448**	0.041	**1.642**	0.000
Du	0.438	0.18	0.411	0.17	0.450	0.241	0.035	0.919	**0.741**	0.034
AR (1)							0.909	0.000		
MA (1)							−0.823	0.000		
Variance equation										
C							0.230	0.362		
Arch Term							−0.024	0.313		
GARCH							0.798	0.001		
Adj R-sq	0.070		0.079		0.090		0.111		0.102	
LB Q (36)		0.42		0.359		0.317		0.226		0.472
LB Q^2(36)								0.148		
LM Arch		0.42		0.788		0.341		0.800		0.818
Cryptocurrencies	Log Litecoin CSSD		Log Monera CSSD		Log Cardano CSSD		Log IOTA CSSD		Log Dash CSSD	
Mean equation										
C	**−6.791**	0.00	**−6.799**	0.00	**−6.795**	0.000	**−6.787**	0.000	**−6.812**	0.000
Dl	**−0.245**	0.00	**−0.371**	0.00	**−0.663**	0.000	**−0.365**	0.000	**−0.459**	0.000
Du	**−0.087**	0.04	−0.093	0.12	**−0.196**	0.010	−0.049	0.238	**−0.398**	0.000
AR(1)									1.448	0.000
MA(1)									−0.920	0.000
AR(2)									−1.429	0.000
MA(2)									0.974	0.000
Variance equation										
C							0.001	0.005		
Arch term							0.161	0.000		
GARCH							0.822	0.000		
Adj R-sq	0.141		0.159		0.278		0.151		0.218	
LB Q(36)		0.481		0.139		0.998		0.119		0.084
LB Q^2(36)								0.873		0.927
LM Arch		0.076		0.148		0.860		0.401		0.854

* Bold indicates significance at 5% level

5   Discussions and Conclusion

Financial markets react to natural calamities, epidemics political elections, news announcements. The outbreak of Covid 19 pandemic and the rapid transmission of coronavirus across global economies have caused an adverse effect on the global economy and has disrupted the lives of people across the globe. While several epidemics such as the influenza, SARS, Ebola, HINI, HIV/AIDS have posed challenges in terms of lives of people and the economic activity, the impact of Covid 19 pandemic is found to be much severe. The lockdown restrictions imposed by several countries during March 2020 to contain the spread of the virus has brought the economic activity and the lives of people to a standstill which has further aggravated the severity in global economic condition. The impact was reflected in financial markets and the market crash and halt of trading activities of several global financial markets was witnessed during this time. The cryptocurrency market which gained momentum in terms of trading during recent times also experienced the impact of Covid 19 pandemic. The investors tend to herd during situations of uncertainty and extreme volatile conditions. The reasons may be attributed to investor fear or motive to gain profits in volatile conditions. In this context, this study was carried out to examine the presence of herding activity of investors during the pre-Covid 19 and Covid 19 period. The leading ten cryptocurrencies in terms of market capitalization value was chosen and CSSD approach was employed to examine the herding behaviour of investors. The findings of the study revealed that all the ten cryptocurrencies exhibited herding behaviour during normal market conditions during the entire sample period. Herding behaviour was not evident in top five cryptocurrencies Bitcoin, Ethereum, Ripple, Bitcoin cash and EOS under situations of market upswing and downswing during the pre Covid 19 and Covid 19 period. Herding was present during market downswing in the next five cryptocurrencies Litecoin, Monera, Cardano, IOTA, and DASH during the pre Covid 19 and Covid 19 period. It can be inferred from the above findings that the regular pattern of herding existed in the top five cryptocurrencies and Monera and IOTA cryptocurrencies. The highly technological features of the cryptocurrencies, mixed views on regulatory framework may be presumed as reasons to cause investors to herd in normal market conditions. The time series graphs of the cryptocurrencies showed a gradual fall in prices during the six months of pre Covid 19 period which may be due to the fall in global economic activities. Hence investors would have followed the trading pattern of other investors in normal market conditions. They would have tended to avoid risk and hence may not have exhibited herd behaviour during market downswing. Herding was seen in the cryptocurrencies Litecoin, Cardano and Dash during the Covid 19 pandemic period in all market conditions. It can be observed from the time series graphs that two adverse falls in prices of cryptocurrencies occurred during December 2019 and March 2020 when the outbreak of the Corona virus and the lockdown restrictions were announced. The subsequent rise in prices was also observed in the cryptocurrencies. The investors trading in Litecoin, Cardano, and Dash started to herd in all market conditions during Covid 19 period. It may be reasoned that the investors trading in these cryptocurrencies would have sought to make profits in the extreme volatility in prices. The fear of losing money may also have induced the investors to herd during the Covid 19 pandemic period. The findings would be useful to investors, academicians, and researchers. The study showed the existence and pattern of herding in the cryptocurrencies during extreme market conditions. The novel features of cryptocurrencies would cause less participation in trading of cryptocurrencies and this study shows that herding behaviour is present in all cryptocurrencies in normal market conditions. Investors can make use of this finding for their trading strategies. The research in cryptocurrency is an emerging area in the field of Technology and Finance and the study would be beneficial to academicians in both these areas and gain insights on the functioning of the cryptocurrency market. The findings of this study provide evidence on the presence of an important behavioural bias of investors, herding in the cryptocurrency market particularly during the pandemic crisis situation. There are limited studies on the behaviour of financial markets in pandemic situations and this study would be beneficial to researchers. The realization of profits due to herding in the cryptocurrency market can be taken as a future scope of this study.

References

1. Cheah, E.T., Fry, J.: Speculative bubbles in bitcoin markets? an empirical investigation into the fundamental value of Bitcoin. Econ. Lett. **130**, 32–36 (2015)
2. Bouri, E., Gupta, R., Roubaud, D.: Herding behaviour in cryptocurrencies. Finan. Res. Lett. **29**, 216–221 (2019)
3. Hwang, S., Salmon, M.: Market stress and herding. J. Empir. Finan. **11**(4), 585–616 (2004)
4. Jamison, D.T., et al.: Disease Control Priorities: Improving Health and Reducing Poverty, vol. 9. The World Bank, Washington, DC (2017)
5. Yarovaya, L., Matkovskyy, R., Jalan, A.: The effects of a 'Black Swan' event (COVID-19) on herding behavior in cryptocurrency markets: evidence from Cryptocurrency USD, EUR, JPY and KRW Markets. EUR, JPY, and KRW Markets, 27 Apr 2020
6. Calderón, O.P.: Herding behavior in cryptocurrency markets. arXiv preprint arXiv:1806. 11348 (2018)
7. Jalal, R.N.U.D., Sargiacomo, M., Sahar, N.U., Fayyaz, U.E.: Herding behaviour and cryptocurrency: market asymmetries, inter-dependency and intra-dependency. J. Asian Finan. Econ. Bus. **7**(7), 27–34 (2020)
8. Poyser, O.: Herding behavior in cryptocurrency markets. arXiv preprint arXiv:1806.11348 (2018)
9. Kallinterakis, V., Ferreira, M.P.L.: Herding and feedback trading: evidence on their relationship at the macro level. SSRN Electron. J. (2007). https://doi.org/10.2139/ssrn. 984681
10. Lao, P., Singh, H.: Herding behaviour in the Chinese and Indian stock markets. J. Asian Econ. **22**(6), 495–506 (2011)
11. Hammami, H., Boujelbene, Y.: Investor herding behavior and its effect on stock market boom-bust cycles. IUP J. Appl. Finan. **21**(1), 38–53 (2015)
12. Jlassi, M., Naoui, K.: Herding behaviour and market dynamic volatility: evidence from the US stock markets. Am. J. Finan. Account. **4**(1), 70–91 (2015)
13. Clements, A., Hurn, S., Shi, S.: An empirical investigation of herding in the US stock market. Econ. Model. **67**, 184–192 (2017)
14. Demirer, R., Leggio, K.B., Lien, D.: Herding and flash events: evidence from the 2010 flash crash. Finan. Res. Lett. **31**, 476–479 (2019)
15. Bansal, T.: Behavioral finance and COVID-19: cognitive errors that determine the financial future. SSRN (2020). Doi.org\\
16. Ahsan, A.F.M., Sarkar, A.H.: Herding in Dhaka stock exchange. J. Appl. Bus. Econ. **14**(2), 11–19 (2013)
17. Krueckeberg, S., Scholz, P.: Cryptocurrencies as an asset class. In: Goutte, S., Guesmi, K., Saadi, S. (eds.) Cryptofinance and Mechanisms of Exchange. Contributions to Management Science, vol. XX, pp. 1–28. Springer, Cham (2019)
18. Conrad, C., Custovic, A., Ghysels, E.: Long-and short-term cryptocurrency volatility components: A GARCH-MIDAS analysis. J. Risk Finan. Manage. **11**(2), 23 (2018)

19. da Gama Silva, P.V.J., Klotzle, M.C., Pinto, A.C.F., Gomes, L.L.: Herding behaviour and contagion in the cryptocurrency market. J. Behav. Exp. Finan. **22**, 41–50 (2019)
20. Vidal-Tomás, D., Ibáñez, A.M., Farinós, J.E.: Herding in the cryptocurrency market: CSSD and CSAD approaches. Finan. Res. Lett. **30**, 181–186 (2019)
21. Ballis, A., Drakos, K.: Testing for herding in the cryptocurrency market. Finan. Res. Lett. **33**, 101210 (2020)
22. de Souza Raimundo Júnior, G., Palazzi, R.B., de Souza Tavares, R., Klotzle, M.C.: Market stress and herding: a new approach to the cryptocurrency market. J. Behav. Finan. 1–15 (2020)
23. Baker, S.R., Bloom, N., Davis, S.J., Kost, K., Sammon, M., Viratyosin, T.: The unprecedented stock market reaction to COVID-19. Rev. Asset Pricing Stud. (2020)
24. Ma, C., Rogers, J.H., Zhou, S.: Global economic and financial effects of 21st century pandemics and epidemics. SSRN (2020)
25. Baker, S.R., Bloom, N., Davis, S.J., Terry, S.J.: Covid-induced economic uncertainty (No. w26983). Nat. Bureau Econ. Res. (2020)
26. Eichenbaum, M.S., Rebelo, S., Trabandt, M.: The Macroeconomics of epidemics. Nat. Bureau Econ. Res. 26882 (2020)
27. Kizys, R., Tzouvanas, P., Donadelli, M.: From COVID-19 herd immunity to investor herding in international stock markets: the role of government and regulatory restrictions. SSRN 3597354 (2020)
28. Mnif, E., Jarboui, A., Mouakhar, K.: How the cryptocurrency market has performed during COVID 19? a multifractal analysis. Finan. Res. Lett. 101647 (2020)
29. Chang, E.C., Cheng, J.W., Khorana, A.: An examination of herd behavior in equity markets: an international perspective. J. Bank. Finan. **24**(10), 1651–1679 (2000)
30. Christie, W.G., Huang, R.D.: Following the pied piper: do individual re-turns herd around the market? Finan. Anal. J. **51**(4), 31–37 (1995)
31. McDonald, J.B., Turley, P.: Distributional characteristics: just a few more moments. Am. Stat. **65**(2), 96–103 (2011)
32. Brooks, C.: Introductory Econometrics for Finance. Cambridge University Press, United Kingdom (2014)
33. Kurt Gümüş, G., Gümüş, Y., Çimen, A.: Herding behaviour in cryptocurrency market: CSSD and CSAD analysis. In: Hacioglu, U. (ed.) Blockchain Economics and Financial Market Innovation. CE, pp. 103–114. Springer, Cham (2019). https://doi.org/10.1007/978-3-030-25275-5_6

Diffusion and Adoption Technology

Investigating the Effect of User Reviews on Mobile Apps: The Role of Customer Led Innovation

Miriam Erne[1], Zhiying Jiang[2], and Vanessa Liu[2(✉)]

[1] Erasmus University Rotterdam,
Burgemeester Oudlaan 50, 3062 PA Rotterdam, The Netherlands
[2] Singapore University of Social Sciences,
463 Clementi Rd, Singapore 599494, Singapore
vanessaliusw@suss.edu.sg

Abstract. User involvement has been made easy and common in the context of mobile applications (apps), where user reviews were often collected to enlighten apps developers on novel features. However, users might not always possess the required technical expertise to make commercially feasible suggestions. The value of user reviews also varied due to their unmanageable volume and content irrelevance. In this study, over 40,000 user reviews with 50 apps were analyzed to empirically examine the association between customer led innovation and the revenues from the apps. Our findings indicated that customer led innovation alone did not lead to significant changes in revenues. Its impact was only significant if the developers responded to the user reviews faster. These results contributed to the user involvement literature by highlighting the importance of the moderating effect of developer responsiveness. Apps developers could also benefit from our empirical evidence that proved the value of user involvement that enhanced innovativeness.

Keywords: Mobile apps · User involvement · Customer led innovation · User reviews

1 Introduction

Nowadays application distribution platforms such as Apple App Store and Google Play provide millions of different mobile applications (apps) to users. As of the fourth quarter of 2019, there were around 2.57 million apps for android users and 1.84 million apps for App Store users available [22]. Survival in such a "hyper-competitive" mobile market was challenging to apps developers [7]. Unwanted or unpopular apps could be phased out very shortly after launch, resulting in a waste of development cost and effort. To sustain competitiveness, it is therefore becoming increasingly important for apps developers to launch novel features that meet customer needs (e.g., see [5, 17, 18]).

One key channel for customers to voice out their feedback is through user reviews. Indeed, most apps actively elicit customer comments as they are enlightening to the apps developers in terms of novel features. As user needs vary significantly and the

S. K. Sharma et al. (Eds.): TDIT 2020, IFIP AICT 617, pp. 193–200, 2020.
https://doi.org/10.1007/978-3-030-64849-7_18

usage of the apps could differ across contexts, users may be a good source of creative ideas for development of innovative functionalities.

Despite its potential usefulness for performance enhancement, screening through user reviews could be challenging. For instance, online gurus like Facebook could generate as high as at least 2,000 user reviews per day [5]. The aspects covered in the reviews could be highly diverse, ranging from complaints about the price of the apps to the frequency of advertisements. Manual processing of these reviews is simply impossible. Management of user reviews could be overwhelming and costly to apps developers. Tools have accordingly been developed to enable automated categorization and mining of customer reviews [17, 18]. However, following up on user reviews remains highly time- and money-consuming. Is it really worth the resources to act upon the user reviews? Considering not all users are technically knowledgeable about apps development, could their involvement really offer constructive and commercially feasible suggestions for apps improvement?

User involvement is only appropriate if certain involvement roles and development conditions are fulfilled [12]. These conditions include, who should be involved, which type of software with which the users should be involved, and in which stage (i.e., when) of the software development the users should be involved. User involvement could be totally undesirable when technical expertise is needed. While the potential value of user feedback is not deniable, it may not always be economically justified for developers to translate user feedback into actual software features [12].

Our study therefore aims to empirically investigate the impact of user involvement (in the form of user reviews) on apps performance. Most prior researchers focused on the development of analytical tools for categorization of user reviews (e.g., [17, 18]), seldom questioning the actual benefits of the ideas from the user on apps development, presuming that users could always provide useful feedback. In this study, we categorized and analyzed over 40,000 user reviews associated with about 50 apps to verify the impact on user involvement on apps performance. Specifically, we conceptualized user reviews with innovative suggestions as "customer led innovation" and examined its impact on revenues of apps. We also took into consideration the time taken for apps developers to respond to the user reviews. The value of the innovativeness of user inputs may depreciate over time as other competitors might have already launched similar features onto the market. We hence included developers' responsiveness as a moderator on the relationship between customer led innovation and apps performance. In other words, the effect of user reviews on apps performance would be significantly greater if the developers were more responsive and attend to the user feedback faster.

The remainder of this paper is structured as follows: first, we will explain the conceptual framework and the related past studies. The research methodology and the data analysis procedure will then be presented. Finally, the findings will be discussed and the theoretical and managerial implications will be drawn.

2   Conceptual Framework

Our research model is presented in Fig. 1.

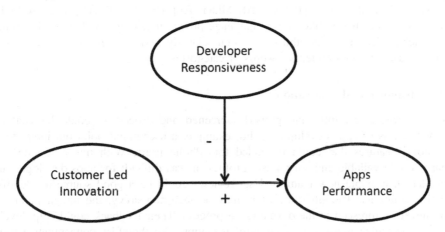

Fig. 1. The research model

2.1   User Involvement

The notion of user involvement was well documented in the literature, referring to the level of personal relevance and importance attached by users to the system [2]. In broad terms, it is defined as "direct contact with users" [15]. Recently, it was observed that customers had become more and more involved in the product development [21]. User involvement was essential and indispensable for system/software developers as it helped to collect more accurate user requirements and enable quality improvement, resulting in better fulfillment of user needs and higher user satisfaction [13, 16]. User involvement was therefore recognized by previous researchers as beneficial to the improvement of quality and performance [4]. Terms such as co-creation or co-design had emerged to describe the collaboration between developers and users. Other terms included quality function deployment (QFD), user-oriented product development, concept testing, Beta testing, consumer idealized design, lead user method and participatory ergonomics [13]. In the collaborative process, users may assume the roles of providers of information, commentators or objects for observations.

In the context of mobile apps, users and apps developers may exchange ideas on shared platforms such as the App stores. Users could submit their desirable new features or functionalities [14, 20]. Complaints from users on lack of certain features could shed light on potential new apps development [3]. However, the number of user reviews received could be immeasurable and unmanageable. More importantly, not all feedback is useful. Almost 65% of apps reviews were found to be noisy and irrelevant [5]. Some suggestions might be solely emotional and commercially infeasible for implementation.

Many tools were therefore developed to aid the search, screening, and extraction of useful information from user reviews. A review of the current literature showed that different tools were built with different mining objectives. Examples included MARK (Mining and Analyzing Reviews by Keywords) [24], MARA (Mobile App Review Analyzer) [11], ALERTme [10], and AR-Miner (App Review Miner) [5]. These tools made use of techniques like natural language processing, topic modeling, clustering and machine learning algorithms to search, classify, extract, group and rank user reviews based on pre-defined keywords or categories.

2.2 Customer Led Innovation

User reviews, if carefully and properly screened and processed, could be vital to innovativeness of apps development. For example, a user might point out interesting and novel features that could be added for iPhone users. With many varieties of smartphones available and varied user profiles, it was difficult for apps developers to consider all possible new features. User reviews could be a good source to identify creative solutions. Though some users may be tech-non-savvy, the imaginativeness may never be foreseen in the development process. Their feedback could help developers to visualize innovative features of the apps. We therefore conceptualize user reviews with new feature requests as customer led innovation. It denotes requests from users on new features to be added to the apps or new apps development. Customer led innovation offer insights to developers to add novel features, resulting in greater efficiency of development and higher user satisfaction [16]. Accordingly, we hypothesize that:

H1: Customer led innovation has a significant and positive impact on apps performance.

2.3 Developer Responsiveness to User Reviews

The time taken by developers to respond to user reviews on apps innovation may matter [23]. After a user submitted his/her feedback, he/she may tend to expect the developer to address the suggestion quickly. If the developer response is slow, other competing apps in the market might have already introduced the new feature and the degree of novelty to users would be diminished. Conversely, users may tend to be more positive about the apps if their ideas were implemented promptly. The new features would also be perceived as more novel with their first time to market. Developers should, however, be cautioned about the frequency of apps dates. Frequent issuance of updates upon novel features may actually cause disruptions to users. In general, reasonable responsiveness to creative solutions should lead to better quality and performance of apps [1]. The shorter the time taken to respond to user reviews, the greater the effect is the reviews of new features on apps performance. Accordingly, we hypothesize that:

H2: Developer responsiveness significantly and negatively moderates the relationship between customer led innovation and apps performance.

3 Research Methodology

3.1 Research Context

The data was collected through App Annie, a business intelligence company. It stored data on a collection of health and fitness apps, including the apps user reviews and revenues generated from each app. In our study, only apps that had been active for at least one year were included in the sampling. Active apps should provide more valid results as it was common in the mobile apps industry that numerous apps could have been removed before their official launch. A total of 50 apps were selected for our analysis as their revenue constituted almost 75% of the total revenue in the health and fitness apps market. There were 189,527 user reviews available for these selected apps.

In order to measure the effect of user reviews on apps performance, a specific research time frame was defined. Only reviews posted after the second last updated version and before the latest version of the apps were included in our samples. This enabled us to examine whether the user reviews led to development of new features in the resultant update of the apps. The final sample consisted of a total of 40,619 user reviews, representing 21.4% of the total reviews associated with the selected apps.

3.2 Measurement

Customer Led Innovation

User reviews were used as proxies for innovations suggested by customers. A subtraction and categorization process were conducted to identify the reviews that specifically pertained to innovation suggestions.

First, generic reviews were subtracted to isolate the specific reviews [5]. Generic reviews were noisy and irrelevant reviews that did not provide any information on creative solutions. Examples of such review were "by far the best app on meditation!" and "I love this app and have done since the moment I started using it. Potentially helped me get through a period of anxiety…". Specific reviews, on the other hand, were those that stated a wish or a new feature request, that is, a specific function that the app developer can add or incorporate in the new version of the apps. A total of 7,654 specific reviews were identified.

Next, the specific reviews were categorized to shortlist the innovation-related reviews. Consistent with previous studies, reviews concerning a new feature request were considered customer led innovation reviews [17, 18].

A feature request refers to the wish or idea proposed by users on a new functionality that should be added but does not exist yet [6, 25]. Examples of such review were "Needs to have a value for calories burned for strength training too" and "Missing a compatible version for Apple Watch". Keywords used to screen for bug reviews were "add", "please", "need", "prefer", "request", "suggest", and "wish" [17].

Developer Responsiveness

Developer responsiveness was measured by the time interval (number of days) from the first posted date of the user review to the update date when the bug was fixed or the advertisements were removed.

Apps Performance

Apps performance could be operationalized in a number of ways such as the number of downloads and apps ratings etc. In this study, apps performance was measured using the revenue generated from the apps during the research time frame. This allowed us to examine the financial impact on the apps developers more directly. Revenues could include purchases of apps, micro-transactions within an app or in-app advertisement (IADV) [8]. The revenues for each app was computed by a summation of the daily revenues for the research time frame.

3.3   Data Analysis

Regression Analysis was conducted to analyze the correlations in the measurement model. It enabled us to examine the significance and the magnitude of the impact from the independent variable (customer led innovation) on the dependent variable (performance in terms of revenues) [19].

As the data for customer led innovation took the form of written user reviews, steps were taken to convert the text data into numerical data. Each review was enumerated with a Python code respectively according to its match with the category of "feature request".

4   Findings

The results of the regression analysis were presented in Table 1 below.

Table 1. Results

	Unstand. Coefficients		Stand. Coefficients		
	B	Std. Error	Beta	t	Sig
Model 1 – Customer Led Innovation	7,761.506	8,906.398	.154	.871	.388
Model 2 – Customer Led Innovation	14,198.564	11,458.130	.281	−1.239	.021
Moderator of Customer Led Innovation	−37.904	14.565	−.590	2.602	.012

The overall model was significant with a p-value of 0.007. The overall R-square was 0.190, which was satisfactory and typical for exploratory research [19]. H1 was rejected (0.388), meaning that customer led innovation does not have a significant impact on apps performance in terms of revenues.

The moderating effect of developer responsiveness was supported (.012). It was negatively associated with the link between customer led innovation and apps revenues. With shortened response time, the impact of customer led innovation might increase the revenues further.

5 Discussion and Conclusion

User involvement has been well documented in the extant literature that the role of users plays an important part in enhancing the quality of software development. This presumption might not hold in the context of mobile apps, where hundreds or thousands of users may easily participate in the apps design through submitting reviews online. The volumes of user reviews might be hardly manageable and the usefulness of the reviews might also be impaired by the users' lack of technical expertise. It was questionable whether the users' creative solutions could lead to actual improvement of the apps performance. Our study therefore attempted to fill this gap in the literature and empirically examined the effect of customer led innovation over apps performance in terms of revenues.

Our findings provided empirical evidence on the value of user reviews on innovativeness of apps development. It was challenging for apps developers to imagine an exhaustive list of user wishes on new features. It was cost-effective to draw on user reviews to gain insights into novel features desirable by users. As customers acquired hands on experience with usage of the apps, they were more able to suggestion creative solutions. In other words, co-creation of apps with users should be encouraged to enhance innovativeness and hence the apps performance [9].

We also tested the moderating effect of developer responsiveness on the relationship between customer led innovation and apps performance. Though significant, the effect was not very strong. One plausible explanation is that developers may have to launch apps updates very frequently after addressing each new feature suggested by users. The recurring need to update the apps may be annoying to users [23] and discourage them from the continued usage of the apps. On the other hand, users might also grow impatient if new features took excessive time to be launched. Apps developers should therefore ensure user reviews on innovation were properly addressed within a reasonable time frame.

References

1. Armerding, T.: Why Users Don't Often Upgrade Software When They Should (2012). https://www.csoonline.com/article/2132061/security-awareness/References48why-users-don-t-often-upgrade-software-when-they-should.html
2. Barki, H., Hartwick, J.: Rethinking the concept of user involvement. MIS Q. 3–63 (1989)
3. Barlow, J., Møller, C.: A Complaint Is A Gift: Using Customer Feedback As A Strategic Tool. Berrett-Koehler Publishers, Oakland (1996)
4. Berger, C., Möslein, K., Piller, F., Reichwald, R.: Co-designing modes of cooperation at the customer interface: learning from exploratory research. Eur. Manag. Rev. **21**, 70–87 (2005)
5. Chen, N., Lin, J., Hoi, S., Xiao, X., Zhang, B.: AR-miner: mining informative reviews for developers from mobile app marketplace. In: Proceedings of the 36th International Conference on Software Engineering, pp. 767–778 (2014)
6. Cheung, K.W.: A Feature Request Is A Bug…Is a Dumb Detail (2013). https://www.getdonedone.com/a-feature-request-is-a-bug-is-a-task-is-a-to-do-is-a-dumb-detail/
7. Comino, S., Manenti, F. M., Mariuzzo, F.: Updates Management in Mobile Applications. iTunes vs google play (2016)

8. Ghose, A., Han, S.P.: Estimating demand for mobile applications in the new economy. Manage. Sci. **606**, 1470–1488 (2014)
9. Gustafsson, A., Kristensson, P., Witell, L.: Customer co-creation in service innovation: a matter of communication? J. Serv. Manag. **23**, 311–327 (2012)
10. Guzman, E., Ibrahim, M., Glinz, M.: A little bird told me: mining tweets for requirements and software evolution. In: 2017 IEEE 25th International Requirements Engineering Conference, pp. 11–20 (2017)
11. Iacob, C., Harrison, R.: Retrieving and analyzing mobile apps feature requests from online reviews. In: 2013 10th IEEE Working Conference on Mining Software Repositories MSR, pp. 41–44 (2013)
12. Ives, B., Olson, M.H.: User involvement and MIS success: a review of research. Manage. Sci. **305**, 586–603 (1984)
13. Kaulio, M.A.: Customer, consumer and user involvement in product development: a framework and a review of selected methods. Total Qual. Manag. **91**, 141–149 (1998)
14. Khalid, M., Asif, M., Shehzaib, U.: Towards improving the quality of mobile app reviews. Int. J. Inform. Technol. Comput. Sci. **710**, 35 (2015)
15. Kujala, S.: User involvement: a review of the Benefits and challenges. Behav. Inform. Technol. **221**, 1–16 (2003)
16. Kujala, S.: Effective user involvement in product development by improving the analysis of user needs. Behav. Inform. Technol. **276**, 457–473 (2008)
17. Maalej, W., Hadeer, N.: Bug report, feature request, or simply praise? On automatically classifying app reviews. In: 2015 IEEE 23rd International Requirements Engineering Conference (2015)
18. Maalej, W., Kurtanović, Z., Nabil, H., Stanik, C.: On the automatic classification of app reviews. Requir. Eng. **213**, 311–331 (2016)
19. Mooi, E., Sarstedt, M.: A Concise Guide to Market Research. Springer, Berlin Heidelberg (2011)
20. Panichella, S., Di Sorbo, A., Guzman, E., Visaggio, C.A., Canfora, G., Gall, H.C.: How can I improve my app? Classifying user reviews for software maintenance and evolution. In: 2015 IEEE International Conference on Software Maintenance and Evolution ICSME, pp. 281–290 (2015)
21. Prahalad, C.K., Ramaswamy, V.: The Future of Competition: Co-Creating Unique Value with Customers. Harvard Business Press, Boston (2013)
22. Statista: Number of Apps Available In Leading App Stores AS of 4th Quarter (2019). https://www.statista.com/statistics/276623/number-of-apps-available-in-leading-app-stores/
23. Vaniea, K., Rashidi, Y.: Tales of software updates: software. In: Proceedings of the 2016 CHI Conference on Human Factors in Computing Systems, pp. 3215–3226 (2016)
24. Vu, P.M., Nguyen, T.T., Pham, H.V., Nguyen, T.T.: Mining user opinions in mobile app reviews: a keyword-based approach. In: 2015 30th IEEE/ACM International Conference on Automated Software Engineering ASE, pp. 749–759 (2015)
25. Wiggins, N.: The Difference Between a Bug, Error and Feature. https://www.webigence.com/blog/the-difference-between-a-bug-error-and-feature

Education Transformation Using Block Chain Technology - A Student Centric Model

Shankar Subramanian Iyer[1](✉), A. Seetharaman[2], and K. Maddulety[3]

[1] S.P Jain School of Global Management, Dubai Campus, UAE
shankar.dsl9dba002@spjain.org
[2] S.P Jain School of Global Management, Singapore, Singapore
[3] S.P Jain School of Global Management, Mumbai, India

Abstract. The Education sector is undergoing transformation-using technology. The virtual classrooms are replacing the traditional classrooms. The proposed model envisaged is student-centric, where the student has the choice to model his curriculum depending on the student interests and area to work and not follow the usual model, using credits from micro-credentials added per unit. The challenge is to use the features, benefits of Blockchain to introduce this new Education model technology to improve efficiency by reducing cost and improving accountability. The transformation in Education Framework can revolutionize the future Learning, teaching Industry to reduce cost and time. This revolution will also lead to improved chances for Learners to be employable. The Research paper proposes to use the Modified ADKAR Change Management Model to validate this Research study and will be a significant contribution to the research topic and the Theory known.

Keywords: Block chain technology · Smart education · Education transformation · Education · Education model · Modern technologies

1 Introduction

The current existing Education System does not satisfy the aspirations of the Learners as is evident from the deteriorating employment rates of the majority of the Countries (Peugny, 2019); (Taylor et al.2020). The fees charged are most Universities so high the Learners cannot afford it. Secondly, even the University Degree does not guarantee jobs except to just a small fraction of the intake. The skills imparted to the Learners are not good enough for the industry, and most of the corporates need to impart training to the recruits. The skills imparted has been discussed by most credible Magazines like Forbes, Gartner and Education experts.

1.1 **The transformation of the current Education model to the Student-centric education model** is happening daily. The dissent from the Learners on the current courses, which is not giving employment guarantees and the increased cost of studies. The traditional Education model has pressurized the parents, the learners, the bankers and society due to the unemployment rate increases across the globe. Hence, adapting the Customer-centric model, which focusses on the Customer, the students and their needs is a necessity (Grech et al. 2017). The main point is

© IFIP International Federation for Information Processing 2020
Published by Springer Nature Switzerland AG 2020
S. K. Sharma et al. (Eds.): TDIT 2020, IFIP AICT 617, pp. 201–217, 2020.
https://doi.org/10.1007/978-3-030-64849-7_19

that the current education system is not student-centric. Still, the actual position is "Current education system is not very useful to create better employable students for future"(Arnaudov et al. 2017).

1.2 **Technologies** used for Education are Artificial Intelligence, Virtual reality, Augmented Reality, Machine Learning, Blockchain technology, to name a few. The Technologies and tools have augmented the Classroom Management, Blended Learning, Inclusive Learning to make education to give the Teachers and Learners better experiences. The future years will see more technologies to make Learning better.

1.3 **Blockchain** is a distributed Public Ledger that can automatically record and verify records which is an essential requirement of Education system where the transcripts, certificates need authentication for the employment procedure. Blockchain can facilitate most of the crucial element for educational institutes. The Education Framework needs most of the advantages of Blockchain Technology except for some challenges that can be modified to be useful (Viriyasitavat et al. 2019). The An employer to verify the same can view certificates. (Crosby et al. 2016). Blockchain technology can improve the way the education system works and improvise the future due to its unique features of decentralization, traceability, immutability, and currency properties; and significant advantages such as reliability, trust, security and efficiency are the needs of the education (Jirgensons et al. 2018), (Chen et al. 2018).

The need for transformation in the education sector is evident as the current system is not meeting the aspirations of the Learners due to the lack of achieving employability skills. Blockchain Technology analyzing its features, benefits, and challenges can most readily achieve this. Other technologies like VR, ML, IoT, AI can complement these implementations (Ali 2018). It seems that Technology adaption theory is applicable as new technology like Blockchain needs acceptance, the environment of the Organization and the User perception, count. So, the above theories TAM-TOE is relevant, and the change Management theory ADKAR is relevant. Initially, each of them is inadequate for the current situation of the Blockchain implementation to education.

2 Scope of Research

The main scope in the current situation is the need for a new educational framework, so the focus of this paper will address is followed by the evaluation of Blockchain for suitability to this sector. The research will involve the study of the benefits, features and challenges associated with the Blockchain and match it with the needs of the modern new educational model envisaged. It also involves knowing the lacuna of the current Education system. The paper looks at suggesting an education model which is a student-centric model. It also addresses the benefits and features of using such a model and the challenges, issues the transformation can face. There has been an effort to suggest other areas of work for research.

3   Research Questions

a. How can the Current Education Model be altered to suit the needs of the current and future Education?
b. How the features, challenges and benefits of the Blockchain be useful to the proposed Future New Education Model?

4   Research Objectives

a. Review the current Education model to adopt a new Education Model suiting the need of Learners
b. To employ/implement Blockchain Technology in Education Domain

5   Literature Survey & Review

5.1   Existing Higher Education System- Drivers and Barriers

Most Universities aim to enhance student learning through the use of learning technologies in learning, teaching, and assessment strategy, particularly concerning student-centered and flexible learning (Davies et al. 2006). The Higher Education system currently driven by commercial interests and not societal needs which have made it vulnerable to profiteering rather than working towards the Learner requirements. Quality has been lately questionable as most University graduates are not able to get jobs to their liking or no jobs at all. The ILO report, the World bank report and UN report have all expressed the concern of high unemployment rates across the globe barring a few areas like Sweden, Norway (ILO report, 2019); (Mackeogh et al. 2009). The barriers are mainly the mindset of people involved, the users, the technology availability and infrastructure.

5.2   Proposed Education System Features Based on Literature- Student Centric Model Features- ADKAR

The theory study reveals that the ADKAR Change Management Model, probably with some modification and the TOE is applicable. Conceptual Model of TOE framework adapted for analyzing Technology adoption. The proposed education is inclined to the Student Centric Model, whose features ensure that the learner is the center of the model. The learner decides the curriculum required to go through, the style of delivery, the place and location of study, the technology to be used. The above will make the Learners satisfied with their needs and probably meet their employability needs (Aithal 2016).

5.3   Technology Influence and Blockchain Features- Technology Organization Environment Model

Blockchain is a modern technology which uses decentralized ledgers or parts of the chain called blocks and linked using cryptography. Each transaction of the block recollects the previous one, unauthorized adjustments immediately blocked. The Blockchain works as a decentralized sign up that store records at the Internet with an open get right of entry to the public. Today, education occurs increasingly more out of doors the brick-and-mortar lecture hall universities: it happens on on-line platforms, within communities (Tolbatov et al. 2018).

6   Conceptual Research Framework and Research Methodology

The ADKAR Change Management Model and the TOE- Technology, Organization and Environment Model are very relevant and will be used with some modifications to validate the Educational Transformation suggested above (Gutierrez et al. 2015). The Researcher will test it Quantitatively by Survey Questionnaire based on a Population based in UAE, India, Australia, Singapore, Malaysia and Pakistan. The Researcher would target 385 Respondents as Sample size. The Sampling strategy applicable Stratified, Cluster, Random Convenient simple Sampling conducted via electronic media, mainly in India, UAE. The Hypotheses will be formulated as below and tested, validated using Adanco.

H1: Perceived usefulness of technology by Stakeholders significantly influence the adoption of Blockchain technology for Education transformation

H2: Technology readiness of the Organization significantly influence the adoption of Blockchain for Education transformation

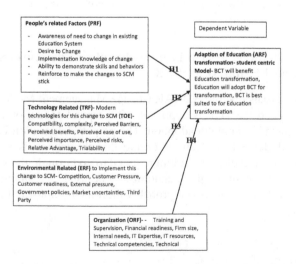

Fig. 1. Conceptual Framework- Integrated extended ADKAR-TAM-TOE Model.

H3: Disaster or Social distancing (remote working) situations influence significantly the usefulness of Blockchain technology for the adoption of Education transformation

H4: Organization Readiness and Competencies influences significantly, the using of the Blockchain technology for Education transformation

7 Findings, Analysis and Implementation

7.1 Details of the Current Education Model in Higher Education

The current Education is more University centric, and not Student Centric. Universities offer preapproved Programs from the Awarding Body, and the Student has to select out of the fixed programs (Khoon et al. 2012). The Learner is not motivated, sometimes not interested in the total program, at the best some parts of the program is useful to the Learner. However, the Student forced to take the full program irrespective of whether it is useful to him or not or get the student employment. It is evident across the global economies, and most education systems are not in a position to reduce unemployment (Kromydas, 2017). The current Education Model cannot guarantee Jobs nor guarantee full employment (Núñez et al. 2010); (ILO report, 2019).

This disruption is happening due to several factors coming together: the ever-rising college fees, which is not sustainable nor affordable for the Learners (Khalid et al. 2018). A change in Learner expectation, needs and mindset, declining consumer demand among prospective students, extreme lack of the work readiness of fresh college graduates, a rhetoric of what makes college useful (workplace-integrated and team relationship), and emerging talent attraction and development strategies by employers (Brandon Busteed 2019, Liu and Zhou 2018).

7.2 The Changing Education Scenario

In the Student Centric Education Model mentioned above, the student can choose the course curriculum, the University, the Awarding Body, the type of classroom, delivery type, the course material provided on a single Platform. It might not mean that the Learner can choose for their best; however, it leads to their making a choice and not blame others for it. The above model is very much possible using Blockchain Technology. The cost will be very reasonable, as the Universities do not incur the cost of Infrastructure, Lecturers. Universities get more Learners across the globe, and depending on their reputation will get profitable Business to make this Investment viable (Aithal et al. 2016). Most of the Quality institutions should strategize to transform students into life-long learners and innovators by enabling them to think critically, and to encourage them to scientific research (Kennedy et al. 2019).

Change Management model ADKAR Model can be applied here as it discusses the details of change management to be adapted. Once the implementation is started or set in place, it needs to be monitored closely (Tang, 2019). The TOE Theory of Environment also applies as the Educational Environment and Organization. The Change Management – ADKAR Change Management Model will be validated statistically using Qualitative data collection, survey Questionnaire. It involves testing and evaluating of the Structural Equation Model on Adanco, testing the correlation.

7.3   The Suggested Needs of the Student-Centric Education Model in Current Scenario

The Learner centric Learning focuses on flexibility in the choice of subjects to study, select their curriculum, identify the best timeline, schedule in completing their program. The student can select the mode of learning like direct learning in classrooms, virtual classroom using technology online. They have the flexibility in selecting the evaluation system and the examination system (Henderson et al. 2019), (Seechaliao, 2017). This model can allow Learners to add more credit papers as the course progresses, even more than the minimum requirement. Workplace Learning allows the students to earn while studying, so the burden on the financial need reduced, and the defaults on student loans avoided (Fernando, 2018).The Workforce indulges in more comfortable and faster ways of performing work by adopting technology (Komori, 2018).

The new Learner is impatient and does not want to wait for employment to pay off the loans borrowed for financing these courses. The current Scenario is due to lack of well-paying jobs even after guarantees from the best Colleges across the globe (Mikkonen et al. 2017). The academic units and workplace learning blending happen under the expertise of the Classroom Lecturer and the Workplace Manager (Pylväs et al. 2018); (Donald et al. 2018).

7.4   How the Block Chain Will Help Implement the New Education Model- Student Centric Approach

The primary requirements of the New Education Model- Student Centric Approach has cost reduction, enhanced efficiency, immediate authentication, transparency, security, faster operation speeds, low cost of processing and decentralized ledgers avoids hacking and loss of data and safeguard of confidentiality of stored data, which can be easily retrieved. All these are the useful features of Blockchain technology (Xie et al. 2019); (Msomi et al. 2018); (Grech et al. 2017).

These are the benefits required for the Education Domain, as this will ensure transactions and information to be secured and time-stamped. It can be then encrypted in codes and stored for further reference. The Certificates authentication happens with the click of the mouse (Chen et al. 2019); (Arnaudov et al. 2017). The usefulness of Blockchain, Artificial Intelligence, Virtual Learning, Machine Learning, Virtual Reality is quite interesting to study and apply to the Education Domain (Kolekar et al. 2019).

8 Adanco Model, Findings and Discussions

The quantitative approach is deductive research which utilizes a structured approach, statistics, and large sample size to analyze data. Looking at the sampling methodology, the population of this research is India, UAE, Singapore, Malaysia and other parts of the World. Most of the studies conducted in other countries focused on the town or city of the country; therefore, the UAE being the location of research. Based on sampling methodology, this research uses simple random sampling methodology (Sa'ait et al. 2016; Huyen and Costello 2017). The data collection process conducted among a population of 20 million who were able to access the Federal Territory of UAE through online distribution. According to Raosoft Inc (2018), the results from Raosoft Sample Size Calculator suggested that 386 is the minimum sample size of the survey (margin of error 5 percent; confident level 95 percent). The total number of respondents targeted was 385. The inclusion criterion in respondent selection is that the individual had to be a student, Teacher, the user of Blockchain, Consultant, Educationists. This research uses the five-point Likert scale for the survey statements. Besides, according to Sarstedt et al. (2014), PLS-SEM is a useful tool for family business research, and this model widely used in many fields of business research. PLS-SEM was used to measure and evaluate the reflective measurement and structural measurement. There are two stages for this model; stage one is to measure the reflective model (Nimako et al. 2014). In the beginning, indicators reliability, internal consistency reliability, convergent validity, and discriminant validity assessed in a reflective model. It is important also to measure the collinearity, predictive relevance, significance, and relevance of path coefficients in the context to the overall structural measurement of the model.

8.1 Data Validation and Analysis

Respondents' characteristics

Table 1 shows the profile of respondents who had participated in the online survey. A total of 886 survey questionnaires were distributed to millennials in Federal Territory of UAE, Indian cities, Malaysia and Singapore electronically using emails, WhatsApp and other social media means, but only 386 (43.3 percent) of respondents participated in this research. In this research, the male respondents were 238 (61.73 percent), while female respondents were 148 (38.27 percent). Besides, as this study focused on millennials, the terms of age group were limited and divided into two groups, which were 18–27, 28–36 and 36-44. Based on the results from Table 1, the majority of the respondents aged between 18 to 44 years (80 percent, 308 respondents), while only 81 respondents aged beyond 46 years. As for the nationality, all the respondents were majorly Indian, UAE, Pakistani, Malaysian and Singaporeans, which fulfilled the essential requirement of the research. In terms of education level, majority of the respondents were Postgraduates (182; 47.1 percent). Respondents in Graduate were 136 (35.3 percent), Doctorates were 39 (10.1 percent), and rest were 29 (7.6 percent). The descriptive statistics showed that the majority of the millennials that participated in this research were undergraduates.

Table 1. Demographics

Demographic Variable	Category	Percentage
Age Group	18-25	24.4
	26-35	32.8
	36-45	21.8
	46-55	14.3
	56+	6.7
Gender	Male	61.73
	Female	38.27

Demographic Variable	Category	Percentage	Demographic Variable	Category	Percentage
Education	Highschool	1.7 (6)	Income Level	Under 5000 AED	28.8
	Undergraduate	5.9 (23)		5001-10000 AED	16.1
	Graduate	35.3 (136)		10001-15000 AED	15.3
	Masters	47.1(182)		15001-20000 AED	10.5
	Doctoral	10.1 (39)		Above 20001	30.5

Demographic Variable	Category	Percentage	Actual Numbers
Usage of Smart Phones and other Devices on regular basis (Total Respondents= 3 and multiple answers as same respondent uses many of these devices)	SmartPhones	97.33	376
	iPad	46.2	178
	PC's	93.27	360
	Smart TV	50.1	195
	Accessories working on Blue tooth	67.22	259

Overall Model- all path coefficients have *** indicating all of them are significant and consistent to the SEM. Overall R^2 of 0.641 means that 64.1% of the relations and correlations between the constructs have been explained satisfactorily which is considered good statistically (Table 2).

Table 2 Goodness of model fit (saturated model)

	Value	HI95	HI99
SRMR	0.0716	0.0391	0.0416
d_{ULS}	1.1852	0.3539	0.3992
d_G	0.7556	0.2686	0.2930

A cut-off value SMRM of 0.08, as proposed by Hu & Bentler (1999), appears to be better for variance-based SEM and met by this Model. ADANCO 2.0.1 uses bootstrapping to provide the 95%-percentile ("HI95") and the 99%- percentile ("HI99") for the d_{ULS} if the theoretical model was true. (If the d_{ULS} exceeds these values, it is unlikely that the model is true.) In our results the generated values are within the values of the d_{ULS} which indicates that the model is likely to be true as per Dijkstra & Henseler (2016).

8.2   Reflective Measurement Model

The reflective measurement is the first stage of examining the reliability and validity of the measurement model. This section will be divided into several subtopics: (1) indicator reliability (loadings), (2) construct reliability, (3) convergent validity and, (4) discriminant validity (Sarstedt et al. 2014).

8.2.1   Indicator Reliability (Loadings)
Examining the indicator loadings was the first step in the reflective measurement, and the loadings score above 0.7 represented that the construct explained more than 50 percent of a variable (Sarstedt et al. 2014). Based on Table 3, the results showed that all the indicators were over 0.7.

8.2.2   Internal consistency reliability
Internal consistency reliability was used to examine the reflective measurement model, where previous studies stated that the higher the value indicator, the higher the degree of reliability (Joseph et al. 2010). Also, Jöreskog's rho (ρc) was the standard method used to evaluate the internal consistency reliability. The minimum acceptable value for internal consistency reliability was 0.6, as the value below was considered as having low significance or weak reliability. The maximum value was considered as 0.95 as the value over it was considered as problematic, or the indicator was redundant (Sarstedt et al. 2014). Based on Table 3, the result showed that the Jöreskog's rho (ρc) values for each construct, that is, People Related Factors (0.9244), Technology related factors (0.9270), Environmental related factors (0.9158), Organizational related factors (0.9243), and Adaption related factors (0.9440), ranged within 0.6 and 0.95. Therefore, all the Jöreskog's rho (ρc) values in this research were considered as "satisfactory to good," and all of the indicators in this research were significant and reliable for the internal consistency reliability.

8.2.3   Construct Reliability
For the extent of internal consistency reliability and construct reliability, Cronbach's alpha was used to measure and examine the reliability for all the constructs. The minimum acceptable Cronbach's alpha is 0.7 or above and the higher the Cronbach's alpha, the higher the reliability of multiple measures for the measurement of each construct (Joseph et al. 2010). Based on the results from Table 4, all the constructs were higher than the standard requirement (0.7) with People Related Factors as 0.8927, Technology related factors as 0.8819, Environmental related factors as 0.8843, Organizational related factors 0.8982, and Adaption related factors as 0.9438.

Table 3 Indicator loadings

Indicator	People Related Factors	Technology Related factors	Environmental related factors	Organizational related factors	Adaption related factors
PRF 1	0.7120				
PRF 2	0.7626				
PRF 3	0.6599				
PRF 4	0.6093				
PRF 5	0.7473				
TRF 1		0.8192			
TRF 2		0.8505			
TRF 3		0.7574			
ERF 1			0.8059		
ERF 2			0.6748		
ERF 3			0.5393		
ERF 4			0.7313		
ERF 5			0.6790		
ORF 1				0.6637	
ORF 2				0.7589	
ORF 3				0.7739	
ORF 4				0.6630	
ORF 5				0.6892	
ARF 1					0.9142
ARF 2					0.9367
ARF 3					0.8469

Table 4 Construct reliability

Construct	Dijkstra-Henseler's rho (ρ_A)	Jöreskog's rho (ρ_c)	Cronbach's alpha(α)
People related Factors	0.9069	0.9203	0.8927
Technology related factors	0.8868	0.9270	0.8819
Environmental related factors	0.8912	0.9158	0.8843
Organizational related factors	0.9054	0.9243	0.8982
Adaption related factors	0.9472	0.9440	0.9438

8.2.4   Convergent Validity

Convergent validity is used to measure and examine the extent that a construct converges with the specific construct's indicators by explaining the items' variance (Hair et al. 2011; Sarstedt et al. 2014). Commonly, the average variance extracted (AVE) will be used to measure for all items associated with each construct. The mean of the squared loadings for all indicators associated with the construct is the calculation method to calculate the value of AVE (Cheah et al. 2018). Besides, the minimum acceptable value for AVE is 0.5, and if the value is more than 0.5, the result represented that the construct explains more than 50 percent of the variance of items. Based on the result, all the AVE values for the constructs in this research were exceeding 0.5, which were People Related Factors (0.6982), Technology related factors (0.8090),

Environmental related factors (0.6861), Organizational related factors (0.7097), and Adaption related factors (0.8992). As all the AVE values were exceeding 0.5, the convergent validity was established in this research.

8.2.5   Discriminant Validity

Discriminant validity was the final step in the reflective measurement model after the indicator reliability, internal consistency reliability, and convergent validity were successfully established. Discriminant validity methods used to measure the different constructs differ in terms of how much a variable correlates with other variables and how much the indicators represent only a single variable. There are two methods to measure and evaluate the discriminant validity: Fornell-Larcker criterion and cross-loadings (Hair et al. 2013; Sarstedt et al. 2014).

Based on the results, the AVE value of People Related Factors with the construct of People Related Factors was 0.6982, the AVE value of technology functionality with the construct of technology functionality was 0.7867, the AVE value of perceived usefulness with the construct of perceived usefulness was 0.7479, the AVE value of perceived ease of use with the construct of perceived ease of use was 0.8285, and the AVE value of adoption intention with the construct of adoption intention was 0.797 (Table 5).

Table 5 Discriminant validity: Fornell-Larcker criterion

Construct	People Related Factors	Technology related factors	Environmental related factors	Organizational related factors	Adaption related factors
People Related Factors	0.6982				
Technology Related factors	0.5774	0.6290			
Environmental Related factors	0.4414	0.4643	0.6861		
Organizational Related factors	0.3660	0.5453	0.5415	0.7097	
Adaption Related factors	0.3263	0.5333	0.5205	0.6758	0.8992

8.3   Structural Model Assessment

Before the structural model assessment, the potential collinearity between the predictor constructs must be tested to ensure the quality of the results. Therefore, this section will be divided into several subtopics: (1) collinearity, (2) predictive relevance and, (3) significance and relevance of path coefficients.

8.3.1   Collinearity

In order to ensure the results were not biased by collinearity issues, variance inflation factor (VIF) was used to measure for each indicator in the construction. Usually, the value of VIF less than 5 is acceptable and assumed to be safe for avoiding any collinearity issues, but there could be exceptions (Benitez et al. 2020). Based on the results, all the indicators' VIF values were below five which is acceptable. This result represented that there were no significant collinearity issues observed in this model.

8.3.2   Predictive Relevance (R^2)

The coefficient of determination (R^2) was used to measure how well the construct was explained toward all the constructs in the research. According to some researchers, the minimum requirement of R^2 was 0.2, and the construct was relevant and significant if the value of R^2 exceeded 0.2 (Hair et al. 2011). Based on the result, the value of R^2 of adoption intention was 0.6414, which represented that the construct was relevant and significant, and considered as moderately high in explaining all the variables in the research.

8.4   Significance and Relevance of Path Coefficients

The final step in the structural model assessment was significance and relevance of path coefficients. According to Sarstedt et al. (2014), the researchers stated that the standard range for path coefficient values was from-1 to +1 one, while the value closer to +1 represented strong positive relationship, and the value closer to-1 represented strong negative relationship. The results from the bootstrapping procedure (386 cases, 1000 samples, no sign changes option) reveal that all four structural relationships were significant (p $\leq$ 0.05). The results showed that all the independent constructs had positive and significant relationship toward Blockchain technology adaption to Education, and the results represented that all of the hypotheses were authenticated and supported by data (Table 6).

Table 6   Direct effects inference

Effect	Original coefficient	Standard bootstrap results					Percentile bootstrap quantiles			
		Mean value	Standard error	t-value	p-value (2-sided)	p-value (1-sided)	0.5%	2.5%	97.5%	99.5%
People Related Factors -> Adaption related factors	0.1092	0.1116	0.0365	5.9890	0.0028	0.0014	0.0102	0.0385	0.1826	0.2013
Technology related factors -> Adaption related factors	0.3630	0.3618	0.0474	7.6632	0.0000	0.0000	0.2400	0.2706	0.4581	0.4917
Environmental factors -> Adaption related factors	0.2893	0.2874	0.0580	4.9888	0.0000	0.0000	0.1333	0.1755	0.3996	0.4370
Organizational factors -> Adaption related factors	0.1525	0.1556	0.0475	6.2108	0.0013	0.0007	0.0273	0.0606	0.2478	0.2749

The results showed that all the independent constructs had a positive and significant relationship with Blockchain Technology's adaption for Education. The results represented that all of the hypotheses were authenticated and supported by the data.

The research objective of this study was to identify the relationship between constructs of technology-related factors, People's related Factors, Environmental related Factors, Organizational related factors and Adaption of Blockchain Technology for Education. All the hypotheses are accepted, and the relationships are statistically established through this study to achieve the primary objective (Fig. 2).

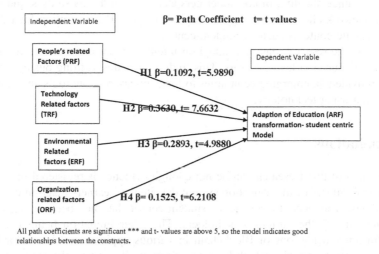

All path coefficients are significant *** and t- values are above 5, so the model indicates good relationships between the constructs.

Fig. 2 PLS-SEM Validation

ADKAR Change Management Model, Transformation Theory, TAM-TOE, individually seem inadequate for the current COVID, economic, technology bound situation. An integrated model using some of these identified constructs with more relevant factors considered seem appropriate. So, the above research framework was developed and tested for validity and reliability using PLS-SEM has been a useful contribution of this research paper and by getting a consensus of 386 respondents- stakeholders of the Blockchain education application. The methodology followed goes a long way in addressing the scarcity of relevant data for future researchers and lay the path for further research by developing on this model or such similar models. The above-cited theories have their importance in a particular situation in stable economies, equal education opportunities, infrastructure availability. However, in recession, COVID, sanction regimes, these above theories seem lacking to explain many factors. Hence a concrete, a sound research-based framework has been developed to contribute to further work.

9 Contributions

9.1 Research Implications

The research study indicates that extending the technology acceptance model along with Change Management model while measuring the User's adoption intention. The validated hybrid model through SEM-PLS provides a better understanding to researchers and practitioners why individuals choose technology for Education Purpose.

9.2 Managerial Implications

The technology managers who are investing in BCT for knowledge workers would gain a better understanding of consumer perspective through this study's finding. The hybrid framework allows technology managers to assess BCT adaption for Education through specific contexts such as Student-centric Model.

Based on the research data, the adoption intention must not focus on a particular age group or education level of users. This finding provides a strong business case for solution providers in emerging economies to focus on appropriate tools and features to be rolled out using technology.

10 Limitations

The limitation of this Research can be not enough evidence is registered or discussed on the actual failures of the education system despite the Learners disgruntled with the shortcomings. The need to change to student-centric has not been addressed in a significant way by the various stakeholders. The other limitation being the lack of successful implementations of Blockchain in various applications except for Bitcoin and other crypto Currencies which have some lacuna. So, at best the exposure can be called Smart system which passed off as blockchain technology which it is not as all the participants are not at the same operating level. Second, the volumes of scale do not justify the spends on the BCT as the energy requirements, and initial Investments are enormous to get ROI. The lack of Sponsor Organization and Regulatory body is not able to give the BCT application the credibility. Blockchain technology claims of successful implementation in the education sector tested.

11 Conclusion

The student-centric education model is the future of Global Education. The Model is going to be powered by modern technologies like Blockchain Technology, Artificial Intelligence, Machine Learning, Virtual Imaging, Virtual Reality. It will reduce the cost, efforts, staff hour needs and security of the new education system. A smart city like Dubai is well poised to take this route due to the availability of the Infrastructure, the political will and the skilled workforce. Education student-centric model in smart cities like Dubai is going to make it the future. The investment and the process are well on its way for this educational transformation. The success of the implementation of the new Model will depend on how Management able to handle these factors properly and control the interplay (Dutta, 2018).

References

Aithal, S., Aithal, P.S.: Student centric learning through planned hard work-an innovative model. International Journal of Scientific Research and Modern Education (IJSRME) ISSN, 2455–5630 (2016)

Ali, M., Hassan, A.M.: Developing applications for voice enabled IoT devices to improve classroom activities. In: 2018 21st International Conference of Computer and Information Technology (ICCIT), Dhaka, Bangladesh, pp. 1–4 (2018). https://doi.org/10.1109/ICCITECHN.2018.8631906

Arnaudov, S., Yoon, H., Hwang, J.: Technology implementation success model designed for educational organizations. In: 2017 International Conference on Platform Technology and Service (PlatCon), pp. 15. IEEE (2017)

Benitez, J., Henseler, J., Castillo, A., Schuberth, F.: How to perform and report an impactful analysis using partial least squares: guidelines for confirmatory and explanatory IS research. Inf. Manag. 2(57), 103168 (2020). https://doi.org/10.1016/j.im.2019.05.003

Busteed, B.: Why Goodwill (Not Udacity, EdX Or Coursera) May Be The World 's Biggest MOOC. Forbes, 26, 2019 (2019)

Chen, G., Xu, B., Lu, M., Chen, N.-S.: Exploring blockchain technology and its potential applications for education. Smart Learn. Environ. 5(1), 1–10 (2018). https://doi.org/10.1186/s40561-017-0050-x

Cheah, J.H., Memon, M.A., Chuah, F., Ting, H., Ramayah, T.: Assessing reflective models in marketing research: a comparison between PLS and PLSc estimates. Int. J. Bus. Soc. 19(1), 139–160 (2018)

Crosby, M., Pattanayak, P., Verma, S., Kalyanaraman, V.: Blockchain technology: beyond bitcoin. Appl. Innov. 2(6–10), 71 (2016)

Davies, A., Smith, K.: Drivers and barriers to the uptake of learning technologies: staff experiences in a research-led university. In: Technology Supported Learning and Teaching: A Staff Perspective, pp. 125–145. IGI Global (2006)

Donald, W. E., Ashleigh, M.J., Baruch, Y.: Students' perceptions of education and employability. Career Develop. Int. (2018)

Dutta, S.K.: Strategic Change and Transformation: Managing Renewal in Organisations. Routledge, Abingdon (2018)

Fernando, M.G.N.A.S.: Teaching, learning and evaluation enhancement of information communication technology education in schools through pedagogical and e-learning techniques in the Sri Lankan context. Eng. Technol. Int. J. Educ. Pedagogical Sci. 5(6), 3–22 (2018)

Grech, A., Camilleri, A.F.: Blockchain in Education. Publications Office of the European Union, Luxembourg (2017). https://doi.org/10.2760/60649. (132 S. - (JRC Science for Policy Report) - URN: urn:nbn:de:0111-pedocs-150132)

Gutierrez, A., Boukrami, E., Lumsden, R.: Technological, organisational and environmental factors influencing managers' decision to adopt cloud computing in the UK. J. Enterpr. Inf. Manag. 28(6), 788–807 (2015)

Hair, J.F., Ringle, C.M., Sarstedt, M.: PLS-SEM: indeed a silver bullet. J. Mark. Theory Pract. 9(2), 139–151 (2011)

Hair, J.F., Ringle, C.M., Sarstedt, M.: Partial least squares structural equation modeling: rigorous applications, better results and higher acceptance. Long Range Plan. 46(2), 1–12 (2013)

Henderson, M., Selwyn, N., Aston, R.: What works and why? Student perceptions of 'useful' digital technology in university teaching and learning. Stud. High. Educ. 42(8), 1567–1579 (2017)

Henseler, J., Hubona, G., Ray, P.A.: Using PLS path modeling in new technology research: updated guidelines. Ind. Manag. Data Syst. 116(1), 2–20 (2016). https://doi.org/10.1108/IMDS-09-2015-0382

Huyen, T.T., Costello, J.: Quality versus quantity: an investigation into electronic word of mouth's influence on consumer buying intention. J. Promot. Commun. 5(2) (2017)

Joseph, F.H., Black, W.C., Babin, B.J., Anderson, R.E.: Multivariate Data Analysis, 7th edn. Pearson Prentice Hall, Upper Saddle River (2010)

Jirgensons, M., Kapenieks, J.: Blockchain and the future of digital learning credential assessment and management. J. Teach. Educ. Sustain. **20**(1), 145–156 (2018)

Kennedy, C.E., Beeney, A., Macer, B., Dunn, S., McKerlie, R.A.: Staff/student partnership to encourage active and blended learning. In: Association for Learning Technology Conference (ALT-C) 2019, Edinburgh, UK, 03–05 Sep 2019 (2019)

Khalid, J., Ram, B.R., Soliman, M., Ali, A.J., Khaleel, M., Islam, M.S.: Promising digital university: a pivotal need for higher education transformation. Int. J. Manag. Educ. **12**(3), 264–275 (2018)

Kolekar, S.V., Pai, R.M., M. M., M.P.: Rule based adaptive user interface for adaptive E-learning system. Educ. Inform. Technol. **24**(1), 613–641 (2018). https://doi.org/10.1007/s10639-018-9788-1

Komori-Glatz, M.: Multilingual ELF interaction in multicultural student teamwork at Europe's largest business university. Using English as a Lingua Franca in Education in Europe: English in Europe, vol. 4, p. 150 (2018)

Kromydas, T.: Rethinking higher education and its relationship with social inequalities: past knowledge, present state and future potential. Palgrave Commun. **3**(1), 1–12 (2017)

Liu, Y., Zhou, L.: Research on the current situation and problems of the transformation and development of local undergraduate universities. In: 2018 International Conference on Educational Research, Economics, Management and Social Sciences (EREMS 2018) (2018). https://webofproceedings.org/proceedings_series/ESSP/EREMS%202018/EREMS18253.pdf

MacKeogh, K., Fox, S.: Strategies for embedding e-learning in traditional universities: drivers and barriers. Electron. J. E-learn. **7**(2), 147–154 (2009)

Mikkonen, S., Pylväs, L., Rintala, H., Nokelainen, P., Postareff, L.: Guiding workplace learning in vocational education and training: a literature review. Empirical Res. Vocat. Educ. Train. **9** (1), 9 (2017)

Min, S., Khoon, C.C., Tan, B.L.: Motives, expectations, perceptions and satisfaction of international students pursuing private higher education in Singapore. Int. J. Mark. Stud. **4**(6), 122 (2012)

Msomi, A. P., Hoque, M.: The role of stakeholders for e-Learning success in higher education. In: European Conference on e-Learning, pp. 679-XVII. Academic Conferences International Limited (2018)

Nimako, S.G., Kwesi, F.B., Owusu, E.K.: The impact of PLS-SEM training on faculty staff intention to use PLS software in a public university in Ghana. Int. J. Bus. Econ. Res. **3**(2), 42–49 (2014)

Núñez, I., Livanos, I.: Higher education and unemployment in Europe: an analysis of the academic subject and national effects. High. Educ. **59**(4), 475–487 (2010)

Peugny, C.: The decline in middle-skilled employment in 12 European countries: New evidence for job polarisation. Res. Polit. **6**(1), 2053168018823131 (2019)

Pylväs, L., Nokelainen, P., Rintala, H.: Finnish apprenticeship training stakeholders' perceptions of vocational expertise and experiences of workplace learning and guidance. Vocat. Learn. **11**(2), 223–243 (2018)

Raosoft Inc: Raosoft Sample Size Calculator (2018). http://www.raosoft.com/samplesize.html. Accessed 20 Feb 2020

Sa'ait, N., Kanyan, A., Nazrin, M.F.: The effect of E-WOM on customer purchase intention. Int. Acad. Res. J. Soc. Sci. **2**(1), 73–80 (2016)

Sarstedt, M., Christian, M., Ringle, D.S., Reams, R.: Partial least squares structural equation modeling (PLS-SEM): a useful tool for family business researchers. J. Fam. Bus. Strategy **5**, 105–115 (2014)

Seechaliao, T.: Instructional strategies to support creativity and innovation in education. J. Educ. Learn. **6**(4), 201–208 (2017)

Tang, K.N.: Change management. Leadership and Change Management. Springer Briefs in Business, pp. 47–55. Springer, Singapore (2019)

Taylor, L., Ömer, Ö.: Where do profits and jobs come from? Employment and distribution in the US economy. Rev. Soc. Econ. **78**(1), 98–117 (2020)

Tolbatov, A.V., Ahadzhanova, S.V., Viunenko, A.B., Tolbatov, V.A. Using blockchain technology for E-learning (2018)

Viriyasitavat, W., Hoonsopon, D.: Blockchain characteristics and consensus in modern business processes. J. Indust. Inform. Integ. **13**, 32–39 (2019)

Xie, J., Tang, H., Huang, T., Yu, F.R., Xie, R., Liu, J., Liu, Y.: A survey of blockchain technology applied to smart cities: Research issues and challenges. IEEE Commun. Surv. Tutorials **21**(3), 2794–2830 (2019)

Adopting Learning Analytics to Inform Postgraduate Curriculum Design

Denis Dennehy[1(✉)], Kieran Conboy[1], Jaganath Babu[1],
Johannes Schneider[2], Joshua Handali[2], Jan vom Brocke[2],
Benedikt Hoffmeister[3], and Armin Stein[3]

[1] NUI Galway, Galway, Ireland
denis.dennehy@nuigalway.ie
[2] University of Liechtenstein, Vaduz, Liechtenstein
[3] University of Münster, Münster, Germany

Abstract. Understanding students' sentiment is valuable to understanding the changes that could or should be made in curriculum design at third level. Learning analytics has shown potential for improving student learning experiences and supporting teacher inquiry. Yet, there is limited research that reports on the adoption and actual use of learning analytics to support teacher inquiry. This study captures sentiment of postgraduate students by integrating learning analytics with the steps of teacher inquiry. This study makes two important contributions to teaching and learning literature. First, it reports on the use of learning analytics to support teacher inquiry over three iterations of a business analytics programme between 2016 and 2019. Second, evidence-based recommendations on how to optimise learning analytics to support teacher inquiry are provided.

Keywords: Learning analytics · Sentiment analysis · Curriculum design

1 Introduction

Students' sentiment have increasingly received attention by researchers in higher education because understanding sentiment is valuable to understanding the changes that could or should be made in curriculum design [1, 2]. Students' sentiment is recognised as an integral part of student learning and a critical element in the learning process [3, 4]. Sentiment is closely intertwined with students' motivations and strategies for learning, and self-regulation [5–7]. Sentiment has a considerable impact on students' performance and it influences students' academic achievements [6]. There are concerns, however, that research on student sentiment in higher education is disjointed [6]. A focus on the perspectives of students is essential to the development of analytics related to their needs, rather than to the needs of institutions [8].

Yet, third level education, 'a field that gathers an astonishing array of data about its "customers," has traditionally been inefficient in its data use, often operating with substantial delays in analyzing data and feedback' [9]. Learning analytics has emerged as an area with high potential for improving student learning experiences and curriculum design [4, 8]. Learning analytics involves the use of *"analytic techniques*

© IFIP International Federation for Information Processing 2020
Published by Springer Nature Switzerland AG 2020
S. K. Sharma et al. (Eds.): TDIT 2020, IFIP AICT 617, pp. 218–230, 2020.
https://doi.org/10.1007/978-3-030-64849-7_20

integrated with learning outcomes assessment to better understand student learning and more efficiently and meaningfully target instruction, curricula and support" [10, p. 2]. Integrating learning analytics with teacher inquiry has been identified as critically important [11, 12]. There is however, a scarcity of research that examines the adoption and use of learning analytics to support teacher inquiry [13, 15].

The overarching aim of this study is to *'explore how adopting learning analytics can be used to understand students' sentiment and to use this understanding to inform curriculum design.'*

Understanding how students' sentiment can inform teacher inquiry is important for two key reasons. *First*, a systematic literature review on the use of learning analytics by [15] concluded that *"little research attention has been placed on 'providing recommendations to educators for translating the analysed data to actionable actions on their educational design and delivery* (p. 20)."* We provide such recommendations, which is important because the process of obtaining actionable insights for curriculum design is generally considered to be a time-consuming activity for educators [14–16]. *Second*, although learning analytics has been traditionally applied to understand and optimise the learning process at module level, it can also be used to understand and optimise learning at the program level [17]. This study adopts analytical techniques to understand the learning process at programme level.

The remainder of this paper is structured as follows. First, theoretical background to learning analytics and teacher inquiry is presented. Next, the research method and background to the case studied is provided. Then, the findings and analysis are presented, followed by discussion and recommendations. The paper ends with a conclusion, limitations, and future research.

2   Theoretical Background

Academic analytics refers to the use of analytics within academic settings and may be applied at the level of the institution, the department, or the learner, depending on the goals and objectives of the analysis [1, 18]. The term 'analytics' holds different meaning for people across the various academic departments and business units, as well as their use of analytics within the university. Nevertheless, the use of analytics in education must be used to transform curriculum design [9].

Academic analytics consist of two types of applied analytics called 'institutional analytics' and 'learning analytics' [1]. *Institutional analytics* is generally used to understand factors that relate to running the business of the university i.e. predicting student success and retention rates [19]. *Learning analytics* focuses specifically on students and their learning behaviors [9, 18]. Learning analytics defined as *"the measurement, collection, analysis and reporting of data about learners and their contexts, for purposes of understanding and optimising learning and the environments in which it occurs"* [8]. This definition includes techniques such as predictive modeling, social network analysis, concept analysis, and sentiment analysis [20]. [9] outline the differences between academic analytics and learning analytics (see Table 1).

The link between learning analytics and curriculum design is based on the premise that data collection and analysis is conducted at various levels (i.e. module,

Table 1. Differences between academic and learning analytics

Type	Level or object of analysis	Who benefits?
Academic analytics	Institutional: learner profiles, performance of academics, knowledge flow	Administrators, funders, marketing
	Regional (state/provincial): comparisons between systems	Funders, administrators
	National and international	Governments, education authorities
Learning analytics	Course-level: social networks, sentiments, discourse analysis	Learners, faculty
	Departmental: predictive modeling, patterns of success/failure	Learners, faculty

programme) to inform the; (i) learning experience, (ii) design process, and (iii) community of curriculum designers [21].

2.1   Mapping Teacher Inquiry with Learning Analytics

Teacher inquiring is defined as a cyclical process in which *"teachers identify questions for investigation in their practice and then design a process for collecting evidence about student learning that informs their subsequent educational designs"* [22, pp. 249–250]. Teacher inquiry is a process that can guide reflection and enhancements in a systematic and evidence-based approach [23]. Despite the critical importance of integrating learning analytics with teacher enquiry [12, 24], there is limited research that reports on the actual use of learning analytics to support teacher enquiry [13, 15, 24]. Most concerning is that learning analytics are increasingly being implemented in different educational settings, often without the guidance of a research base [20]. There is also a scarcity of research on how to analyze the learning process at the program level in order to guide the design or redesign of a program [25].

Research does suggest, however, that educators may lack the skills to formulate questions and identify solutions [26, 27] or they be unable to make sense of the data in order to inform curriculum redesign [26, 28, 29]. While many analytics studies identify patterns in students' learning behaviour, understanding of the pedagogical context that influences student activities is lacking [12, 30]. A related issue is the need to use the insights generated from the use of learning analytics to make interventions to improve learning and generate 'actionable insights' [31, 32].

Evidence-based insights generated by learning analytics provides support for educators to reflect on and improve curriculum design and delivery [15, 24, 33].

Therefore, it supports the concept of teacher inquiry [14] and can be linked to the teacher inquiry cycle [15]. Table 1 maps learning analytics with the steps of teacher inquiry. To the best of our knowledge, this is the first study to integrate sentiment analytics, a form of learning analytics, with teacher inquiry (Table 2).

Table 2. Mapping learning analytics with the steps of teacher inquiry

Step	Teacher inquiry cycle	Description [15]	Mapping learning analytics with teacher inquiry	Literature sources
1	Problem identification	Identification of a specific aspect of educational design (i.e. module, programme) and/or delivery to be evaluated in order to improve it	Can be used to measure, collect, analyse and report on students' learning experience and the context of their learning	[8, 34]
2	Develop inquiry questions	Specific questions, data to be collected, and the method for data collection is established	Can be used to identify specific problems related to the module/programme	[14, 15]
3	Educational design	Formulation of educational design in which the teacher will deliver in order to implement their inquiry	Can be used to improve the learning experience for individual learners or groups of learners	[8, 24, 34]
4	Deliver educational design and collect data	Delivering the educational design to the learners and collects the educational data using the collection method	Can be used to collect the educational data that have been defined to answer their inquiry question	[15, 34]
5	Analyse educational data	Data is analysed in order to elicit insights to answer the inquiry questions	Can be used to analyse and report on the collected data and facilitate sense-making	[15, 23, 34]
6	Reflect on data	The analysed data are used in order to answer the defined inquiry question and revise the practice in which the educational design and/or delivery is practiced	Can be used as an evidence-based approach to guide reflection	[23, 24, 33]

3   Research Method

The research described in this paper follows the principles of a case study method [35], focused on postgraduate students completing a one-year fulltime masters programme in business analytics at a university in Ireland. The specific case was purposefully chosen because, (i) reputation of the course was important as it is the largest masters programme in business analytics in Ireland, (ii) monitoring student sentiment was critical as the programme underwent significant growth with annual student enrolment, increasing from 12 to 102 students within 3-years, (iii) ensuring the course was designed for inclusive teaching was important as a diverse student population (i.e. 8 different nationalities, varying academic backgrounds), and (iv) the researchers had continuous direct access to the students and alumni.

Programme Learning Outcomes: The following learning outcomes are intended to equip students with the required industry-standard skills and knowledge: (A) Understand and be able to use specific IT which is used in developing business analytics. (B) Analyse and solve business problems using applied data analytics tools and techniques. (C) Understand and apply techniques for managing IT in organisations. (D) Identify, analyse and solve applied problems in individual and team-based settings. (E) Apply effective data-driven decision-making to global business and social problems.

Programme Growth: The programme commenced in the 2015–16 academic year with 12 students and has increased student enrolment for the subsequent academic years, namely, 2016–17: 36 students, 2017–18: 57 students, and 2018–19: 102 students. Students from Ireland, India, UK, France, Pakistan, Nigeria, China, USA, Germany, and Malaysia are represented on the programme.

3.1   Data Collection and Analysis

Cross Industry Standard Process for Data Mining (CRISP-DM) is an industry standard methodology that prescribes a set of guidelines to guide the efficient extraction of information from data (Chapman et al., 2000; Shearer, 2000). The CRISP-DM methodology consists of six cyclical steps, namely (i) Business Understanding, (ii) Data Understanding, (iii) Data Preparation, (iv) Modeling, (v) Evaluation, and (vi) Deployment. We adapt this process methodology to suit the context of our research, which includes four cyclical phases (see Fig. 1). The adapted model (Fig. 1) does not exclude any of the six phases of CRISP-DM, instead, it merges them into four inter-related activities, namely, (i) Business and Data Understanding, (ii) Modeling, (iii) Evaluation, and (iv) Actionable Intelligence.

Business and Data Understanding: In this phase, business understanding focused on the context, aim and business problem in order to align with the project objectives, and data understanding provided an understanding of the data that needed to be analysed, identify potential issues (i.e. quality) and prepare for modeling. Input data comprised of (i) three years of module data (e.g. 12 modules per year), (ii) two end of year programme reviews, and (iii) interview data.

Data Preparation: This phase included deciding what needed to be included in the dataset, cleaning the data and all other activities that needed to be done to process data which served as an input to the modeling tool in the next step. Data extraction and integration using Python scripts whereby messages were converted from RAR file format into .CSV file format. Text was then converted into Pandas DataFrame format for compatibility purposes with the sentiment analysis algorithm.

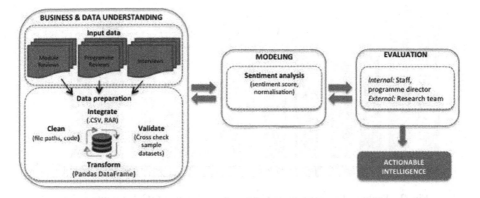

Fig. 1. Process of data preparation and sentiment analysis

Modeling: Essentially, this phase performed sentiment analysis across three consecutive academic years, namely, 2016–17, 2017–18, and 2018–19. To ensure high response rates, all responses were anonymised. The response rate for each end of year programme review was 72% (2016–17), 96% (2017–18), and 70% (2018–19). As the response rate varied across the academic years, a number of analytical techniques were applied to calculate an overall rating scale of 0 to 5. Zero being the lowest overall score the programme could receive and five been the highest rating. *Evaluation:* In this iterative phase, the model, data, and emerging findings were analysed in relation to the business and data understanding (e.g. learning outcomes). This involved regular meetings with staff and the research team. This iterative process ensured that the emerging findings and 'actionable intelligence' supported the business understanding (e.g. to inform curriculum design of the programme). These findings are presented in the next section.

4   Findings and Analysis

The findings presented in this section are intended to provide insight of how student sentiment influenced curriculum redesign rather than compare teaching staff. The end of year programme review for 2016–2017 was the starting point of our empirical analysis as (i) this was the first programme review conducted since the programme commenced, (ii) the programme review was conducted by the newly appointed programme director, and (iii) this dataset provided a baseline from which to establish student sentiment and to identify potential curriculum design issues that can be monitored in subsequent reviews. First, we were keen to understand if students were aware of the learning outcomes of the programme (Q1), if the programme delivered the expected learning outcomes (Q2), if the assessment and examination requirements were clearly communicated (Q3), and if the modules on the programme were linked effectively (Q4). The sentiment for each of these questions is presented in Fig. 2. There was concern about disconnect between stated (see purple lines in Fig. 2) and realised learning outcomes (see yellow lines in Fig. 2).

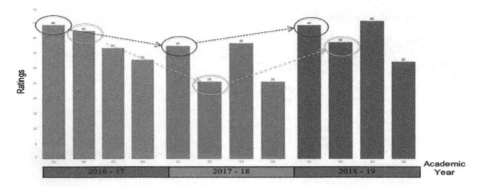

Fig. 2. Sentiment of learning outcomes and assessment (Color figure online)

To gain deeper insight of the ratings identified from the baseline data, engagement with students was necessary in order to distinguish if there was a recurring pattern relating to curriculum design issues or if it was unique to the 2016–17 class. Engagement with students revealed that the majority of students did not distinguish between programme and module learning outcomes (Q1, Q2) and many students admitted that they did not know the programme learning outcomes or where to find them.

A number of initiatives were implemented that has positively increased student sentiment for the 2018–19 academic year (see Fig. 4). These included (i) a standard template was designed for module descriptions with no more than five learning outcomes linked to a module, (ii) learning outcomes were based on Bloom's taxonomy, (iii) learning outcomes of the programme and module descriptions with the associated learning outcomes were made available on the college website, and (iv) the programme learning outcomes were incorporated into the programme orientation. The impact of these curriculum changes had a positive impact on student sentiment (see Fig. 3). Using the 2016–17 programme as a baseline rate of 3.89 out of 5, sentiment increased to 4.02 in 2018–19 academic year. While sentiment for the overall programme rating moved in a positive direction (see amber square in Fig. 3.), there was a concern that students (2016–17, 2017–18) did not find the programme intellectually stimulating (Q7). The response to this question is presented in Fig. 3 (see purple circles and lines).

Students also reported that they did not receive helpful and timely feedback during the programme (Q8). This was surprising considering there were only 36 students in the 2016–17 cohort. Yet, this sentiment remained the same (25 out of 50 points) for the subsequent academic year. Interviews with students indicated that students were unable to identify when educators were providing 'formative' assessment. Staff now explicitly inform students when they are providing formative assessment, and this had a considerable impact on student sentiment in the 2018–19 academic year, despite growth in student enrolment (see yellow circles in Fig. 3).

Figure 4 presents the sentiment trend over three academic years. To help students 'connect the dots' between modules and to get a new perspective on threshold concepts, the programme director initiated and supported a number of curriculum design

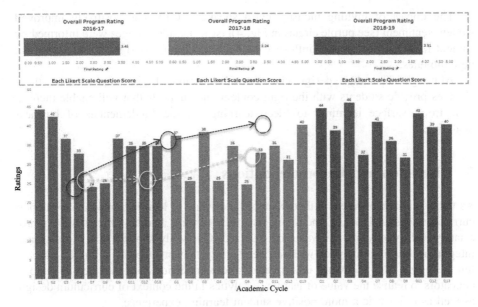

Fig. 3. Annual sentiment analysis (Color figure online)

changes. These included, inviting industry experts, setting up a business analytics society, and appointing an Honorary Professorship to Bill Schmarzo, Chief Innovation Officer, Hitachi Vantara. Schmarzo visits the university to deliver a number of workshops and lectures in order to demonstrate how his data science teams apply 'Design Thinking' in the context of business analytics.

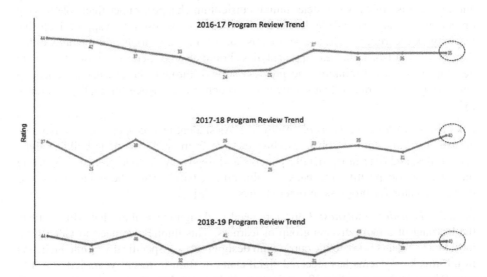

Fig. 4. Sentiment trend over three academic year (Color figure online)

The impact of inviting industry guest speakers (Q13) has positively improved student sentiment (see purple circles in Fig. 4). New module changes were informed by student feedback and used to influence staff responsible for designing and approving new modules.

Although curriculum design changes will continue to be implemented, these changes provide students with the right content and supports that will enable them to shift from 'surface learning' to 'deep learning' of the fundamentals of business analytics.

5 Discussion and Recommendations

As there is a lack of research that examines the value of learning analytics to support curriculum design [13–15], there is a risk that learning analytics is not used appropriately and thereby, its real value not realized. Our study showed that adopting and integrating learning analytics with teacher inquiry, advantageously informed curriculum redesign. The following inter-related recommendations are intended to support educators to realise the value of learning analytics in the context of curriculum design, as well as to provide a more positive student learning experience.

Creating a Learning Analytics Culture: Support educators to adapt, apply, and integrate learning analytics into their teacher inquiry. This implies that educators will require training in the use of analytical tools and analysis of data. Tailored training is important as [36] highlights that learning analytics solutions that do not incorporate diverse "alternates for action" might not achieve the desired results for students and educators.

Using Learning Analytics in Context: Understanding the contextual factors of teaching and learning is critical when determining curriculum changes, rather than sole relying on learning analytics. While learning analytics can be used to support inclusive teaching and learning, it should be used as part of a suite of tools and methods rather than be used in isolation. Learning analytics should also be used to support students to develop their critical thinking and problem solving through the process of reflecting and acting on data, rather than simply a tool to generate evidence for quality assurance [37].

Establishing of Baseline Learning Analytics: As student feedback can be emotive, it is critical that educators establish baseline metrics from which to their build analytic capabilities, and over time, identify patterns and trends, rather than prematurely acting on negative and positive feedback. Establishing a baseline has been identified as a useful indicator for progress in other studies [cf. 38].

Inclusive Learning Analytics: Educators need to design curriculum that will facilitate the learning of a more diverse group of learners. This implies we need to value what individual students bring to the curriculum design process. Specifically, while inclusion in information systems has received significant attention in recent years [c.f. 39, 40], research on inclusion within IS curriculum design and delivery has not received sufficient attention.

Differentiating Features of Sentiment Data: This study showed that sentiment analysis adds data points and information that adds different value to other types of information from and on students and their learning. Sentiment analysis can sense issues the students themselves may not even be aware of or know how to articulate themselves through the traditional survey. Traditional surveys are limited in that they only elicit what the survey designer asks, and so may miss crucial issues or issues that emerge after the survey was designed. Sentiment analysis can track emerging behaviours and use of keywords in an organic and grounded manner. However, we recommend that lecturers and educators consider these differences, use these instruments accordingly, and ensure they consider these differences when acting on the emerging sentiment feedback.

We believe that a real contribution of these recommendations is the ease at which they can be tailored and applied to other educational contexts.

6 Conclusions, Limitations, and Future Research

Learning analytics is an emerging research field that aims to support educators during the process of inquiry. This study reported the value of using sentiment analytics as a form of learning analytics to improve student-learning experiences and inform curriculum design. Sentiment analytics offers a dynamic and evidence-based approach to guide teacher inquiry and inform curriculum design. However, it assumes that educators have the ability to use these types of analytical tools and techniques and align these with their teacher inquiry. This is most likely not the case in many universities, due to a range of factors including, (i) the capacity of the discipline, (ii) availability of funding, (iii) tailored training in the use of learning analytics, and, (iv) continuous support in the use of learning analytics and curriculum design.

We acknowledge that the recommendations provided are not exhaustive but they do however contribute to the wider discourse on the need for more academic research that provides recommendations (c.f. Sergis and Sampson [15] to educators in order to maximise the use of sentiment analytics, and other learning analytics tools and techniques.

Indeed, all research has limitations and we acknowledge three limitations of this research. First, conventional textual sentiment analysis was not conducted due to limited data points, making it difficult for the reliable predictions for open-ended questions. Second, the findings are based on a single case which by nature, limits generalisability. However, the data gathered was based on three iterations (e.g. within case analyses) of a one-year master's programme and in-depth background to the case studied and rich contextual data was provided, which can help readers to relate the findings to their own educational context. Third, while learning analytics has become increasingly popular, it is only one approach to inform curriculum design. It should, therefore, not be used in isolation but rather to complement other data sources (i.e. academic analytics) and the knowledge possessed by educators and curriculum designers.

In terms of next steps, future researchers could (i) study the sentiment of students across multiple postgraduate programmes within the same university or across universities for the purpose of generalisability, and (ii) combine sentiment analytics with academic analytics for the purpose of policy changes relating to teacher inquiry and curriculum design.

References

1. Dunbar, R.L., Dingel, M.J., Prat-Resina, X.: Connecting analytics and curriculum design: process and outcomes of building a tool to browse data relevant to course designers. J. Learn. Anal. **1**(3), 223–243 (2014)
2. Baxter Magolda, M.B.: Identity and learning: student affairs' role in transforming higher education. J. Coll. Stu. Develop. **44**(2), 231–247 (2003)
3. Linnenbrink-Garcia, L., Pekrun, R.: Students' emotions and academic engagement: introduction to the special issue. Contemp. Educ. Psychol. **36**(1), 1–3 (2011)
4. Henritius, E., Löfström, E., Hannula, M.S.: University students' emotions in virtual learning: a review of empirical research in the 21st century. Br. J. Edu. Technol. **50**(1), 80–100 (2019)
5. Mainhard, T., et al.: Student emotions in class: the relative importance of teachers and their interpersonal relations with students. Learn. Instr. **53**, 109119 (2018)
6. Mega, C., Ronconi, L., De Beni, R.: What makes a good student? How emotions, self-regulated learning, and motivation contribute to academic achievement. J. Educ. Psychol. **106**(1), 121 (2014)
7. Pekrun, R., et al.: Academic emotions in students' self-regulated learning and achievement: a program of qualitative and quantitative research. Educ. Psychol. **37**(2), 91–105 (2002)
8. Ferguson, R.: Learning analytics: drivers, developments and challenges. Int. J. Technol. Enhanced Learn. **4**(5/6), 304–317 (2012)
9. Siemens, G., Long, P.: Penetrating the fog: Analytics in learning and education. EDUCAUSE Rev. **46**(5), 30 (2011)
10. Bach, C.: Learning analytics: targeting instruction, curricula and student support. Office of the Provost, Drexel University (2010)
11. Bos, N., Brand-Gruwel, S.: Student differences in regulation strategies and their use of learning resources: implications for educational design. In: Proceedings of the 6th International Conference on Learning Analytics & Knowledge, pp. 344–353. ACM, New York (2016)
12. Lockyer, L., Heathcote, E., Dawson, S.: Informing pedagogical action: aligning learning analytics with learning design. Am. Behav. Sci. **57**, 1439–1459 (2013)
13. Dyckhoff, A.L., et al.: Supporting action research with learning analytics. In: Proceedings of the 3rd International Conference on Learning Analytics and Knowledge, pp. 220–229. ACM, New York (2013)
14. Mor, Y., Ferguson, R., Wasson, B.: Learning design, teacher inquiry into student learning and learning analytics: a call for action. Br. J. Edu. Technol. **46**, 221–229 (2015)
15. Sergis, S., Sampson, D.G.: Teaching and learning analytics to support teacher inquiry: a systematic literature review. In: Peña-Ayala, A. (ed.) Learning Analytics: Fundaments, Applications, and Trends. SSDC, vol. 94, pp. 25–63. Springer, Cham (2017). https://doi.org/10.1007/978-3-319-52977-6_2
16. Marsh, J.-A., Farrell, C.-C.: How leaders can support teachers with data-driven decision making: a framework for understanding capacity building. Educ. Manage. Adm. Leadersh. **43**, 269–289 (2014)
17. Ochoa, X.: Simple metrics for curricular analytics. In: Proceedings of the 1st Learning Analytics for Curriculum and Program Quality Improvement Workshop (2016)

18. Van Barneveld, A., Arnold, K.E., Campbell, J.P.: Analytics in higher education: establishing a common language. EDUCAUSE Learn. Initiat. **1**(1), 1–11 (2012)
19. Oblinger, D.G.: Let's talk... analytics. EDUCAUSE Rev. **47**(4), 10–13 (2012)
20. Siemens, G.: Learning analytics: envisioning a research discipline and a domain of practice. In Proceedings of the 2nd International Conference on Learning Analytics and Knowledge, pp. 4–8 (2012)
21. Hernández-Leo, D., et al.: Analytics for learning design: a layered framework and tools. Br. J. Edu. Technol. **50**(1), 139–152 (2019)
22. Avramides, K., et al.: A method for teacher inquiry in cross-curricular projects: lessons from a case study. Br. J. Edu. Technol. **46**(2), 249264 (2015)
23. Dana, N., Yendol-Hoppey, D.: The Reflective Educator's Guide to Classroom Research: Learning to Teach and Teaching to Learn Through Practitioner Inquiry. Corwin Press, London (2014)
24. Bakharia, A., et al.: A conceptual framework linking learning design with learning analytics. In: Proceedings of the 6th International Conference on Learning Analytics & Knowledge, pp. 329–338.ACM, New York (2016)
25. Méndez, G., Ochoa, X., Chiluiza, K.: Techniques for data-driven curriculum analysis. In: Proceedings of the 4th International Conference on Learning Analytics and Knowledge, pp. 148–157 (2014)
26. Olah, L., Lawrence, N., Riggan, M.: Learning to learn from benchmark assessment data: how teachers analyze results. Peabody J. Educ. **85**(1), 226–245 (2010)
27. Means, B., et al.: Teachers' Ability to Use Data to Inform Instruction: Challenges and Supports. Office of Planning, Evaluation and Policy Development, US Department of Education (2011)
28. Heritage, M., et al.: From evidence to action: a seamless process in formative assessment? Educ. Meas. Issues Pract. **28**(3), 24–31 (2009)
29. Young, V., Kim, D.: Using assessments for instructional improvement: a literature review. Educ. Policy Anal. Arch. **18**(19) (2010). http://epaa.asu.edu/ojs/article/view/809. Accessed Feb 2020
30. Gašević, D., et al.: Learning analytics should not promote one size fits all: the effects of instructional conditions in predicting academic success. Internet High. Educ. **28**, 68–84 (2016)
31. Campbell, F., et al.: Hearing the student voice: Final report. HEA, Subject Centre for Education, Napier University (2007). http://dera.ioe.ac.uk/13053/2/3911.pdf
32. Clow, D.: The learning analytics cycle: closing the loop effectively. In: Proceedings of the 2nd International Conference on Learning Analytics and Knowledge, pp. 134–138 (2012)
33. Greller, W., Ebner, M., Schön, M.: Learning analytics: from theory to practice – data support for learning and teaching. In: Kalz, M., Ras, E. (eds.) CAA 2014. CCIS, vol. 439, pp. 79–87. Springer, Cham (2014). https://doi.org/10.1007/978-3-319-08657-6_8
34. Papamitsiou, Z., Economides, A.: Learning analytics and educational data mining in practice: a systematic literature review of empirical evidence. Educ. Technol. Soc. **17**(4), 49–64 (2014)
35. Yin, R.K.: Case Study Research: Design and Methods, vol. 5. Sage publications Inc., Thousand Oaks (2009)
36. Vatrapu, R.: Cultural considerations in learning analytics. In: Proceedings of the 1st International Conference on Learning Analytics and Knowledge, pp. 127–133 (February 2011)
37. Tsai, Y.S., Poquet, O., Gašević, D., Dawson, S., Pardo, A.: Complexity leadership in learning analytics: drivers, challenges and opportunities. Br. J. Edu. Technol. **50**(6), 2839–2854 (2019)

38. Rehrey, G., Shepard, L., Hostetter, C., Reynolds, A.M., Groth, D.: Engaging faculty in learning analytics: agents of institutional culture change. J. Learn. Anal. **6**(2), 86–94 (2019)
39. Coleman, E., Carter, M., Davison, R.M., Chigona, W., Urquhart, C.: Social Inclusion in the AIS Community: What, Why and How? (2017)
40. Trauth, E.: A research agenda for social inclusion in information systems. ACM SIGMIS Database Database Adv. Inf. Syst. **48**(2), 9–20 (2017)

User Adoption of eHRM - An Empirical Investigation of Individual Adoption Factors Using Technology Acceptance Model

Suryanarayan Iyer[1]($^{(\boxtimes)}$), Ashis K. Pani[2], and L. Gurunathan[3]

[1] XLRI – Xavier School of Management, Jamshedpur, India
surya1968@yahoo.com
[2] Information Systems, XLRI - Xavier School of Management,
Jamshedpur, India
[3] HRM Area, XLRI – Xavier School of Management, Jamshedpur, India

Abstract. Organizations would reap the intended benefits of Electronic Human Resource Management (eHRM) implementations through its sustained usage and adoption by individuals. This study is centered on the view that actual usage behavior is critical to studying eHRM adoption and needs to be measured in the context of the intended eHRM outcomes; operational, relational and transformational. Using a 10-item scale to measure eHRM usage behavior in a research framework grounded in Technology Acceptance Model (TAM2), this study investigates the factors influencing eHRM adoption in terms of "intention to use" and "actual usage behavior". Results indicate support for most TAM2 hypotheses. The study also enriches our understanding of organizational context factors; scope of implementation influencing Image-Usefulness relationship and post implementation stage influencing Ease of use-Intention to use relationship.

Keywords: eHRM adoption · eHRM usage behavior · TAM2

1 Introduction

Electronic Human Resource Management (eHRM), a critical element of digital transformation of the Human Resource (HR) function has been a topic of considerable interest in recent times. eHRM is the e-enablement of the HR function that is posited to help organizations achieve cost reduction and efficiency improvement of the HR function, increased service responsiveness towards employees and improving HR's strategic orientation (Lepak and Snell 1998; Lengnick-Hall and Moritz 2003; Ruel et al. 2004). Extant literature classifies these outcomes into 3 eHRM types; Operational eHRM (cost reduction), Relational eHRM (increased service responsiveness) and Transformational eHRM (improving HR's strategic orientation).

As the world sprints towards organizations digitally connecting their people and adapting to newer ways of working (remote logins, working from home, virtual meetings, online content co-creation, etc.), the paradigm for organizations shifts towards how easy-to-use, intuitive and engaging these digital HR technologies are for their employees. Consequently, eHRM adoption takes a front seat with both researchers

© IFIP International Federation for Information Processing 2020
Published by Springer Nature Switzerland AG 2020
S. K. Sharma et al. (Eds.): TDIT 2020, IFIP AICT 617, pp. 231–248, 2020.
https://doi.org/10.1007/978-3-030-64849-7_21

and practitioners alike, because it is in the holistic adoption of these technologies lies the true benefits for organizations As we trace back the last 3 decades, it is important to recognize those points of inflexion that have shaped the innovations in the eHRM space and therefore, the optimism, promise and expectations from eHRM in driving an organization's HR transformation journey (Iyer 2019). **One,** the rapid proliferation of the Internet and its capacity to integrate businesses; internally and externally. This e-enablement of the HR function has immense potential to help drive cost competitiveness and increase service responsiveness towards employees (Ulrich 1997; Martin and Reddington 2010). **Two,** globalization of the world economy wherein market place imperatives drive organizations to focus on people and their talent – knowledge, skill, abilities and other attributes as key competitive differentiators (Ulrich 2001). As Lepak and Snell (1998) say, *"Firms compete less on products and markets and more on competencies, relationships and new ideas"*. Therefore, HR innovation in terms of adapting to new competencies, newer ways of connecting people and newer ways of working through adoption of digital technologies derive prominence while continuously focusing on people productivity, engagement and their development. **Three,** the emergence of collaborative (wikis, blogs, discussion forums – linkedin, facebook, twitter, etc.) and workplace (Zoom, Slack, Workplace, etc.) technologies. Collaborative technologies have enabled organizations to socialize, provide avenues for employee "voice" and access to engagement platforms to share, co-create and collaborate their learnings (Martin et al. 2009). Workplace technologies on the other hand provide employee with the necessary productivity tools to connect remotely, work from home and seamlessly conduct business meetings, attend conference calls/webinars, knowledge sharing/brainstorming sessions and various other day-to-day work related activities. **Four,** the advent of Artificial Intelligence (AI) and Machine Learning (ML) technologies, its increasing applications in HR services and people decision making. These AI/ML based technologies also known as BOTS or digital assistants help address employee queries, drive HR process efficiencies by automating repetitive tasks and are optimistically posited to provide cognitive innovations using Natural Language Processing like persona based contextual responses to employee queries (Iyer 2019).

2 eHRM Adoption

Literature suggests that, the performance gains and strategic advantages of technological innovation are often obstructed by user willingness to accept and use the systems (Young 1984; Bowen 1986). eHRM is no exception to this challenge and it has been posited that "user satisfaction" and "actual system usage" provide a more complete picture of the eHRM system's success than if either measure were applied in isolation (Haines and Petit 1997). In extant literature, eHRM adoption studies are in 2 categories viz. organizational adoption factors and individual adoption factors. There are a lot of studies on organizational factors influencing eHRM adoption. On the other hand, studies on individual eHRM adoption are few. Some significant studies on individual eHRM adoption have employed Technology Adoption Model (Davis 1989). Marler, Liang and Dulebohn (2006) studied the effect of "extent of training" and "quality of training" on outcome variables such as "perceived ease of use", "perceived usefulness", "employee resources" and "intention to use" new software. They concluded that employee resources mediated the relationship between the extent of training and intention to use new technology. Raaij and Schepers (2008) tested the acceptance of virtual learning environments in China using the extended TAM 2 model. Marler et al. (2009) added a few additional constructs like perceived organization support (POS), managerial pressure to the standard TAM constructs; perceived usefulness, perceived ease of use and attitude towards using the system.

A key point to note in these individual adoption studies is that, the outcome variable in most cases is "Intention to use" and not "Actual Usage". Even though a few studies have incorporated "Actual Use" as the outcome variable, they have measured it using a single item *"On average, how much time do you spend on the system every day. ___hours and ___ minutes"*. In the words of Marler et al. (2009), *"including an objective measure of user behavior would enhance the validity of the results and allow us to directly examine the relationship between perceived resources and system use"*. eHRM is a business application with intended operational, relational and transformational goals and outcomes at the individual HR process level (e.g. recruiting, employee and manager self-service, employee portal, leave management, performance management, competency management, learning management, career & succession management). There would be differing levels of individual motivation and employees' attitude toward using the eHRM system depending on the type of eHRM outcome. Therefore, actual usage of eHRM needs to be measured at the individual submodule level (or HR process level) corresponding to the respective intended eHRM outcomes. The primary purpose of this study therefore, is to identify and explain the factors influencing user adoption of eHRM in terms of user acceptance (intention to use) and actual usage (Actual Behavior) at granular eHRM outcome level.

This study makes two important contributions; first, we have attempted to measure eHRM usage behavior in greater depth which is synergistic with the eHRM goals of cost reduction and productivity (operational eHRM), increasing service responsiveness (relational eHRM) and improving HR's strategic orientation (transformational eHRM). eHRM being a business application solution with multiple intended outcomes (Operational, Relational, Transformational), there would be differing levels of individual motivation to use the eHRM system. It is therefore, important to measure eHRM usage behavior for each type of eHRM outcome rather than measuring it at an overall level. We have operationalized the eHRM usage behavior construct with 10 items covering specific employee facing eHRM areas like employee records, employee portal, employee help desk, social collaboration and networking, goal setting and performance management, skill and competency management, career planning and training and development. Second, the research identifies and reinforces that "organizational context" should be considered when studying the factors influencing eHRM adoption (Marler et al. 2009). This study identifies two such factors relating to organizational context, "scope of implementation" and "stage of implementation" that is suggested to be taken up in future research.

3 Proposed Hypothesis

We have adopted one of the most established Technology Acceptance Model (TAM2) for our study (Venkatesh and Davis 2000). Before testing the eHRM adoption to additional constructs in TAM 2, it is important to consider the original TAM for testing eHRM adoption. The original TAM (Davis 1989) has been empirically tested in multiple settings and applications and found to be relevant thereby establishing the robustness of its theoretical foundation (Adams et al. 1992; Legris et al. 2003). We further rely on studies relevant to eHRM field viz., eLearning system adoption (Selim 2003; Ong et al. 2004; Raiij and Schepers 2008) which have been empirically tested for the constructs in the original TAM viz., Perceived Usefulness (USE) and Perceived Ease of Use (EASE) which have a significant influence on an individual's intention to use (INT) a technology. According to TAM, an individual's behavioral intention to use a system is determined by two beliefs; "perceived usefulness" defined as the extent to which a person believes that using a system will enhance his or her job performance and "perceived ease of use" defined as the extent to which a person believes that the system usage be free of effort. TAM also theorizes that 'perceived usefulness" is influenced by "perceived ease of use" because all things being equal, the easier the system to use, and the more useful it will be (Venkatesh and Davis 2000). For example, Individuals may resist updating their training and certification details if on one hand they find that the "learning management system" is not "easy to use" (involving too many clicks, too much mandatory information to be provided, inflexible). On the other hand, even if the system were made "easy to use", their "intention to use" and "actual usage" will be negatively impacted if individuals perceive that their training history/certification status is not considered during potential assessments, career planning or creating development plans. In line with TAM, we hypothesize;

H1:   Perceived Usefulness of the eHRM system (USE) will have a significant positive effect on Intention to Use the eHRM system (INT).

H2:   Perceived Ease of Use of the eHRM system (EASE) will have a significant positive effect on Perceived Usefulness of the eHRM system (USE).

H3:   Perceived Ease of Use of the eHRM system (EASE) will have a significant positive effect on Intention to Use the eHRM system (INT).

H4:   Intention to Use the eHRM system (INT) will have a significant positive effect on actual eHRM usage behavior (USAGE).

Social Influence Processes. TAM2 discusses two basic constructs with reference to social processes influencing behavioral intention viz., Subjective Norm (SN) and Image.

Subjective Norm. In Theory of Reasoned Action (Fishbein and Ajzen 1975) and Theory of Planned Behavior (Ajzen 1991), the theoretical underpinning for understanding the social influence on behavioral intention, Subjective Norm has been defined as "a person's perception that most people who are important to them think that they should or should not perform a behavior in question. In other words, as stated by

Venkatesh and Davis (2000), "the rationale for a direct effect of subjective norm on behavioral intention is that people may choose to perform a behavior even if they are not themselves favorable towards the behavior or its consequences, if they believe that one or more important referents think that they should and they are sufficiently motivated to comply with the referents". We therefore, hypothesize:

H5:   Subjective Norm (SN) will have a positive direct effect on perceived usefulness of the eHRM system (USE)

H6:   Subjective Norm (SN) will have a positive direct effect on intention to use the eHRM system (INT)

Image and Social Influence. "In a typical work environment with a high degree of interdependence with other social actors in carrying out ones duties, increased status within the group is a basis of power and influence via processes such as social exchange, coalition formation and resource allocation" (Blau 1964; Pfeffer 1981, 1982). "By performing behaviors that are consistent with group norms, an individual achieves membership and the associated social support. This results in increased power and influence that provides a general basis for greater productivity" (Pfeffer 1982). As a result, an individual may perceive that using the eHRM system will lead to performance improvements indirectly due to image enhancement over and above the performance benefits attributable to the system itself. For example, individuals who are a part of specialist communities (compensation and rewards, innovation, research & development, etc.) would perceive themselves as having a better image than others for being a part of an elite group. The member individuals in addition would also perceive benefits at the prospect of collaborative learning from the elite community thereby; forming positive perceptions related to image and improved job performance (perceived usefulness). We therefore, hypothesize that:

H7:   Subjective Norm (SN) will have a positive effect on image perception towards the eHRM system (IMAGE)

H8:   Image will have a positive effect on perceived usefulness of the eHRM system (USE).

Cognitive Instrumental Processes. TAM 2 theorizes four cognitive instrumental determinants of perceived usefulness viz., job relevance (JR), output quality (OQ), result demonstrability (RD) and perceived ease of use. These cognitive instrumental constructs have been theorized by Venkatesh and Davis (2000) after carefully studying multiple theoretical foundations viz. Work Motivation theory (Vroom 1964), Action theory from social psychology (Fishbein and Ajzen 1975) and Task-contingent decision making from behavioral decision theory (Beach and Mitchell 1978). Based on their extensive study of the above theories, they posited that "people use mental representation for assessing the match between important work goals and consequences of performing the act of using a system as a basis for forming judgments about the use-performance contingency. We therefore, hypothesize;

H9:   Job Relevance (JR) will have a positive effect on the perceived usefulness of the eHRM system (USE).

H10:   Output Quality (OQ) will have a positive effect on perceived usefulness of the eHRM system (USE).

H11:   Result Demonstrability (RD) will have a positive effect on perceived usefulness of the eHRM system (USE)

4   Research Methods

4.1   Measures – TAM 2

For the present study, all the nine constructs of the TAM2 (Venkatesh and Davis 2000) viz., Subjective Norm, Image, Job Relevance, Output Quality, Result Demonstrability, Perceived Usefulness, Perceived Ease of Use, Intention to Use and Actual Usage Behavior were considered as a part of the eHRM adoption model to be tested and were measured using 26 items as proposed in the original model by Venkatesh and Davis (2000). The TAM 2 measures used in the study are shown in Appendix 1.

4.2   Measures –eHRM Usage Behaviour

The final outcome construct of TAM 2 viz., usage behaviour was specifically developed for the current research. Though Venkatesh and Davis (2000) have indicated that they measured "usage behaviour" by asking a single question, "*On average, how much time do you spend on the system everyday?-__hours and __ minutes*", it was felt during the design phase for the current research that a mere duration of use does not capture the entire domain of eHRM actual usage behaviour. eHRM is a business application with intended operational, relational and transformational goals and outcomes at the individual HR process level (e.g. recruiting, employee and manager self-service, employee portal, leave management, performance management, competency management, learning management, career & succession management). There would be differing levels of individual motivation and employees' attitude toward using the eHRM system depending on the type of eHRM outcome. We therefore, argue that actual usage of eHRM needs to be measured at the individual submodule level (or HR process level) corresponding to the respective intended eHRM outcomes.

   Accordingly, 10 items were created for the 3 attributes of eHRM usage behavior viz., operational (2 items), relational (4 items) and transformational (4 items). These 10 items representing eHRM usage is provided in Table 4. The combinations of items borrowed from the original TAM and the 10 items created for "eHRM usage behavior" were subject to scale validity check viz., face validity and construct validity. We also subjected the scale items to other forms of robust validation checks such as discriminant, convergent and predictive validity in order to confirm construct validity (Hardesty and Bearden 2004).

4.3   Data Collection and Sampling

Primary data was collected through structured undisguised questionnaires administered to the respondents. The questionnaires were administered through individual face to face meetings or through e-mail as per the convenience of the respondents at home or in office. The 26 items from the TAM 2 scale were measured on a 5-point Likert scale (5 - Strongly Agree to 1 - Strongly Disagree) while the 10 items pertaining to eHRM usage behaviour were measured on a 4 - point scale (0 - Don't use, 1 - Low usage, 2 - Medium usage and 3 - High usage). A total of 249 correct responses were received and considered for further analysis. It was found from the initial review of the responses that most of the organizations had implemented the following eHRM processes viz., HR automation of employee records, leave, payroll, time accounting and performance management. Therefore, in order to measure eHRM usage behavior correctly, we selected only the response of three items (u1, u2 and u8 – refer Table 4) of eHRM usage behavior corresponding to the above implementation scope for inclusion in the structural model and further analysis.

4.4   Response Bias

The existence of response bias for the present research was assessed by performing a t-test on the responses collected from 2 modes of survey viz. personal administration and email. The t-test results indicate that there is no significant difference between the responses obtained by these 2 modes of administration indicating that the responses obtained are not susceptible to the "response bias" owing to different data collection methods adopted except for 2 constructs viz., OQ and Image.

4.5   Analysis

We have applied Structural Equation Modeling (SEM), a second-generation analytical technique (Iyer and Israel 2012) as the analytical tool of analysis and maximum likelihood estimation method for examining the proposed hypothesis. Taking support from the studies by various researchers who have used similar analytical tool (e.g., Anderson and Gerbing 1988), we chose a two-step analysis method. In the first step, we conduct a Confirmatory Factor Analysis (CFA) of the overall measurement model based on the correlation coefficient matrix of each factor of eHRM adoption in TAM2 and usage behaviour developed exclusively for the current study. This helps in confirming the fitness of the 9 constructs in terms of composite reliability, convergent and discriminant validity. In the second step, the structural model is further examined based on the covariance matrix and the hypotheses of the study tested for the entire eHRM adoption/usage behaviour model.

5   Results

5.1   Exploratory Factor Analysis and Reliability

Before proceeding with assessment of model of the present study, it was decided to test the univariate normality pattern of the study variables. Accordingly, we computed skewness and kurtosis for each of the variables of the TAM 2 model. All the variables have passed the stipulated criterion of ± 2 value for skewness and kurtosis (Hair et al. 2010). Having assessed that the data collected do not indicate any sign of non-normality, we proceeded with performing an Exploratory Factor Analysis (EFA). The factor analysis (varimax rotated) results of all the 26 items for a 9-factor solution extracted 9 factors with the respective items clearly loading onto their corresponding factors. The KMO measure of sampling adequacy was 0.825 and the Bartlet's test of sphericity ($\chi 2$ value of 4765.5, df = 406) was significant at 0.001 level. All the 9 factors extracted resulted in a total variance of 80.327. Upon confirming the existence of clear dimensions of TAM2 components in the EFA study, we moved on to assess the consistency of the data pertaining to each of the 9 components extracted separately. The Cronbach α reliability coefficients were greater than the acceptable limit of 0.7 for each of the TAM2 components (dimensions) as prescribed by Nunnally (1978).

5.2   Common Method Variance

Common Method Variance was not found to be a significant threat in the present research because the results of the EFA of all the study variables brought out 9 factors with 80% total variance explained with the first factor explaining 27% of the total variance (unrotated) and 12.14% of total variance (varimax rotated) fulfilling Harman's single factor solution criteria.

5.3   TAM 2 Measurement Model for EHRM Adoption

A first order Confirmatory Factor Analysis (CFA) was conducted to confirm the fitness of the measurement model. The measurement model test results shown in Table 1 indicate that the factor loadings of most of the items were above 0.7 (except four items where the factor loading was marginally less at 0.65 and 0.68). These items were retained because they were very critical to the study and the judges who validated the scales confirmed their relevance and importance for the study. One usage behavior item, "I use the eHRM system for my goal/key result area (KRA) setting process and entering my self-evaluation, achievements and training needs" had a factor loading of 0.59. This was deliberated upon by the researchers and primary analysis showed that this item is critical to the study since majority of the organizations who were covered in the study had implemented performance management process in their organizations and it was felt important to capture the actual usage behavior for this vital HR process. Further, removal of the item was also not significantly improving the model fit. Therefore, we retained this item in the final analysis. The critical ratio (CR) values of all the items reached the significant level (p < .001). We further analyzed the composite reliability for each of the constructs and found them all to be greater than 0.7

Table 1. Constructs & Indicators of measurement items of eHRM adoption – First Order

Measurement Item	Factor loading	Standard error	Error variance	CR value	Construct Alpha*	AVE
USE					**0.93**	**0.76**
(a1)	0.91	0.10	0.82	14.84		
(a2)	0.93	0.09	0.86	15.19		
(a3)	0.90	0.10	0.80	14.68		
(a4)	0.74	0.05	0.55			
EASE					**0.86**	**0.61**
(a5)	0.73	0.07	0.54	11.56		
(a6)	0.82	0.07	0.67	12.95		
(a7)	0.79	0.07	0.62	12.52		
(a8)	0.78	0.09	0.61			
SN					**0.92**	**0.85**
(a9)	0.88	0.06	0.77	15.15		
(a10)	0.96	0.07	0.93			
IMAGE					**0.87**	**0.70**
(a14)	0.68	0.07	0.47	12.24		
(a15)	0.93	0.06	0.86	17.81		
(a16)	0.87	0.05	0.76			
JR					**0.88**	**0.79**
(a17)	0.91	0.08	0.82	15.29		
(a18)	0.87	0.06	0.75			
OQ					**0.69**	**0.53**
(a19)	0.80	0.12	0.63	8.77		
(a20)	0.65	0.11	0.43			
RD					**0.88**	**0.66**
(a21)	0.78	0.05	0.61	16.01		
(a22)	0.83	0.05	0.69	17.93		
(a23)	0.92	0.11	0.85			
(a24R)	0.68	0.06	0.46	12.73		
INT					**0.89**	**0.81**
(a25)	0.88		0.77			
(a26)	0.92	0.08	0.84	14.51		
USAGE					**0.72**	**0.47**
(u1)	0.77	0.13	0.59			
(u2)	0.68	0.13	0.46	7.79		
(u8)	0.59	0.11	0.35	7.28		
Fit Index Chi-Square (df)	**623.39**	**263.00**				
CFI	**0.914**					
RMSEA	**0.074**					

(*) Composite Reliability

except for one factor, "Output Quality" which was marginally lower at 0.69. This implies that all the components exhibit a good internal consistency as the composite reliability coefficients are greater than 0.6 as recommended by Bagozzi and Yi (1990). We calculated the Average Variance Extracted (AVE) estimates for each of the factors and all of them are nearly equal to or greater than 0.5 (Hair et al. 2010) thereby confirming the convergent validity of the factors in the model. The AVE of each construct was further compared with the squared correlations of all other construct combinations (Table 2). The AVE of all the constructs was found to be greater than the squared correlations of the other construct combinations revealing the independent nature of each of the TAM2 constructs. Overall, the above results provide adequate evidence of convergent validity, discriminant validity and composite reliability of the model adopted for the study. The other key model fit statistics and values of the CFA, CFI = 0.914 and RMSEA = 0.074 indicate an acceptable level of model fit.

5.4   Testing TAM 2 Structural Model for EHRM Adoption – I

The results of the Structural Model for testing eHRM adoption are shown in Table 3. The TAM 2 model for eHRM adoption was tested using Structural Equation Modeling (SEM). In this study, we have simultaneously tested all the nine constructs of the TAM 2 in our structural model. The results are shown in Table 3. Looking at the results therein, we find that the overall fit using CFI criteria was 0.828, RMSEA = 0.10, $\chi2/df$ = 3.493, indicating the poor fit of the model. A perusal of the structure coefficients and their corresponding significance in Table 3 indicated that paths OQ $\rightarrow$ USE, Image $\rightarrow$ USE and Ease $\rightarrow$ INT were not significant. This being the case, a scrutiny of factor loadings (lambda coefficients) of the corresponding items on their respective factors indicated that only item a19, The quality of the output I get from the eHRM system is high" belonging to OQ had a non-significant and poor loading of 0.07 and warranted removal from the overall model. Hence, it was decided to discard the same and re-run the model. Although we felt the need to retain atleast one item related to OQ, modification indices indicated that $\chi2$ value would be reduced by 21.838 if the item a20 of OQ is merged with RD. A discussion with the experts also indicated that clubbing of item a20 of OQ was meaningful as the content of a20 was similar to the contents of RD. Further discussion with experts also revealed that the perceived closeness of meaning by the respondents can be attributed to the words "output" (for items in OQ) and "results (for items in RD) and probably this is the reason why modification indices of SEM indicated the need for linking item a20 with RD. Further, this study pertains to user adoption of eHRM systems and OQ discusses that "given a choice set of multiple relevant systems, an individual would be inclined to choose a system that delivers highest quality". In the context of eHRM systems, individuals seldom have a choice of multiple eHRM systems to base a comparative preference with regard to OQ. Hence, there is a good possibility that the respondents perceived the items with reference to increasing their job performance rather than the overall quality of the system itself. We therefore, decided to remove OQ and its item a19 from the model and club item a20 with RD for the next SEM run.

Table 2. Mean, Standard Deviation, Squared Correlations and AVE for the model constructs compared with squared correlations of other constructs

	Mean	SD	USE	EASE	SN	IMAGE	JR	OQ	RD	INT	USAGE
USE	4.12	0.704	**0.757**								
EASE	4.05	0.644	0.338	**0.608**							
SN	3.55	0.860	0.151	0.089	**0.846**						
IMAGE	2.37	1.028	0.034	0.010	0.225	**0.695**					
JR	3.90	0.848	0.286	0.124	0.095	0.078	**0.788**				
OQ	3.62	0.784	0.229	0.287	0.062	0.001	0.348	**0.531**			
RD	3.73	0.720	0.104	0.090	0.040	0.110	0.362	0.371	**0.656**		
INT	3.93	0.708	0.113	0.061	0.172	0.264	0.194	0.028	0.206	**0.807**	
USAGE	2.72	0.664	0.000	0.001	0.003	0.099	0.030	0.000	0.126	0.032	**0.466**

Values in bold shown diagonally in the table indicate the Average Variance Extracted.
Values shown below the diagonal are squared correlations.

5.5   Testing TAM 2 Structural Model for EHRM Adoption - II

Results of TAM2 after removal of OQ and addition of a20 with RD in the model yielded model fit indices of CFI = 0.857, RMSEA = 0.093, $\chi2$ = 835.93 (df = 265), $\chi2$/df = 3.154. All this indicated that removal of OQ as a separate component of TAM2 has significantly improved the model fit ($\Delta \chi2$ = 162.92, Δ df = 23). However, a perusal of structural path coefficients between Image → USE, Ease → INT and RD USE were found insignificant. A scrutiny of modification indices revealed that the $\chi2$ statistic can be reduced by 69.97 by linking RD to JR. Discussion on the relevance of connecting the path from RD → JR led us to the reasoning that since eHRM is a business application and its adoption and usage by individuals could be purely for the purpose of performing in their current and potential jobs, users would consider as important and project only those results that are relevant to their current and future jobs. This reasoning corroborates with Venkatesh and Davis (2000) view that: "If a system produces effective job-relevant results desired by the user, but does so in an obscure fashion, users of the system are unlikely to understand how useful such a system really is (p. 192)." This led us to the reasoning that the results from the eHRM system would benefit individuals in either reducing their administrative burden or lead to higher productivity and flexibility due to presence of automated workflow driven self-service. Further, individuals would benefit from competency building, greater knowledge exchange and thereby advance themselves towards career growth in their respective organizations. It was hence, reasoned that Results Demonstrability has an influence on "perceived usefulness" for individuals, if realized in the context of their performance in their current jobs and building competencies towards advancement into future jobs ("job relevance"). Hence, it was decided to test the model of TAM2 with RD connected to JR as it was convincing as stated above.

Table 3. Structural Model for testing eHRM Adoption using TAM2

Model	Standardized Coefficient	χ2	df	χ2/df	CFI	RMSEA
Model – 1		**1005.855**	**288**	**3.493**	**0.828**	**0.1**
SN → Image	0.476 ***					
Image → Use	−0.083					
SN → Use	0.187**					
SN → INT	0.331 ***					
JR → Use	0.343***					
OQ → Use	−0.027					
RD → Use	0.111**					
Ease → Use	0.477***					
Use → INT	0.198 **					
INT → Usage	0.16 **					
Ease → INT	0.031					
Model - 2	**Standardized Coefficient**	**χ2**	**df**	**χ2/df**	**CFI**	**RMSEA**
		835.93	**265**	**3.154**	**0.857**	**0.093**
SN → Image	0.477***					
Image → Use	−0.031					
SN → Use	0.197**					
SN → INT	0.334***					
JR → Use	0.397***					
RD → Use	−0.25					
Ease → Use	0.466***					
Use → INT	0.192**					
INT → Usage	0.161**					
Ease → INT	0.037					
Model - 3	**Standardized Coefficient**	**χ2**	**df**	**χ2/df**	**CFI**	**RMSEA**
		644.133	**252**	**2.556**	**0.902**	**0.079**
SN → Image	0.483***					
Image → Use	−0.046					
SN → Use	0.220***					
SN → INT	0.332***					
JR → Use	0.422***					
RD → Use	−0.049					
Ease → Use	0.471***					
Use → INT	0.182**					
INT → Usage	0.161**					
Ease → INT	0.052					
RD → JR	0.601***					

*** $p < .001$ ** $p < .01$ * $p < .05$

5.6 Testing TAM 2 Structural Model for EHRM Adoption - III

In the third SEM run, as anticipated, we found significant impact of RD on JR with a structure coefficient of 0.6, while the relationship between RD to Perceived Usefulness was found to be insignificant. The model fit statistics also improved considerably viz., CFI = 0.902, RMSEA = 0.079, $\chi 2$ = 644.13 (df = 252), $\chi 2$/df = 2.556 (Table 3). The modification indices also did not indicate any major reduction in $\chi 2$ for further modifications to the model and hence is validated in the current study. Nonetheless, the relationship between TAM2 components viz., Image and Perceived Usefulness was again found insignificant. We analyzed this also closely and felt that since the sample population comes from organizations that have implemented the basic eHRM system components viz., employee records, employee lifecycle events, payroll, benefits, time and attendance and performance management the sample population could not perceive these transactional process as being a source of status or prestige in the organization. Probably, these results would have been different if the sample population included organizations that had implemented Integrated Talent Management Systems (especially Career and Succession Planning, Competency Management, Learning and Knowledge Management) or Web 2.0 collaboration based Social Networking initiatives in the organization. Usage of these systems are either related to an individuals' career growth (in the case of Talent Management Systems) or related to contemporary technologies (Web 2.0 collaboration and social networking) both of which could potentially drive "internalization" and "individualization" amongst individuals. The potential of these systems, especially, Web 2.0 and social networking in the context of social exchange and social interdependence is perceived as a source of power, influence and enhanced status by individuals. We therefore, argue that image will positively impact perceived usefulness for individuals from organizations that have implemented talent management systems and social networking processes.

Another TAM 2 relationship that was found non-significant was "perceived ease of use" and "intention to use". This finding was consistent with the results from recent research (Szajna 1996; Chau and Hu 2002; Selim 2003; Wu and Wang 2005). A very significant reasoning by Raiij and Schepers (2008) explains this phenomenon of non-significance fundamentally. They state that TAM 2 (Venkatesh and Davis 2000) did not find any direct post-implementation effects of "perceived ease of use" on "intention to use". On the contrary, the direct effect posited in TAM 2 was in the context of pre-implementation stage. Therefore, in accordance with Raiij and Schepers (2008), we also reason that "as users gain experience with a new eHRM system, perceived ease of use becomes less profound since instrumentality overshadows concerns about the eHRM system's ease of use (Adams et al. 1992; Straub et al. 1997). All the other hypotheses of the study were supported and found significant. The overall model fit statistics viz., CFI = 0.902, RMSEA = 0.079, $\chi 2$ = 644.13 (df = 252), $\chi 2$/df = 2.556 (Table 3) indicates an acceptable level of model fit (Hair et al. 2010).

Table 4. Items for measuring Actual eHRM Usage Behavior

#	eHRM process	
u1	I use the eHRM system to view and update my personnel records like change of address, marital status, contact details, dependent/beneficiary information and tax declarations	O
u2	I use the eHRM system to apply for leave, compensatory off, applying for change of department or location or any other job related attribute	O
u3	I use the eHRM system to review and apply for jobs through Internal Job postings and refer job postings to my friends under the company's employee referral scheme	R
u4	I use the eHRM – employee portal to check the company directory and organization structure and to update myself on company communication, policies & guidelines	R
u5	I use the eHRM – Help desk functionality to log in requests for resolution of any job related issues, for e.g. Leave regularization, payroll corrections, performance rating related, or any other personal or job related issues	R
u6	I participate in "in-company" eHRM Web 2.0 collaboration initiatives (e.g. blogging, discussion boards) by actively voicing my opinions and sharing my knowledge and experience.	R
u7	I use the eHRM system to update my skills and competencies and review my competency improvement areas	T
u8	I use the eHRM system for my Goal/KRA setting process and entering my self-evaluation, achievements and training needs	T
u9	I carefully review the career paths available on the eHRM system and work with my manager to design development plans to help me grow up the career ladder	T
u10	I use the eHRM system for all my training needs e.g. Enrolling into a course, launching and attending the course, entering feedback and cost details, etc.	T

O – Operational eHRM, R – Relational eHRM, T – Transformational eHRM.

6   Discussion

Through an in-depth study of a large sample population covering individuals from organizations across all major industries, we have understood the factors affecting eHRM adoption through one of the most accepted Technology Acceptance Model – TAM2 (Venkatesh and Davis 2000). Overall, the hypothesized model fit the data well and most of the TAM2 hypotheses were supported in the study. We did not find support for hypotheses H3, H8 and H11 though. However, a more detailed analysis led us to enrich our understanding of the role played by organizational context factors in explaining the relationships mentioned in H3, H8 and H11.

Hypotheses H3, the effect of eHRM's perceived ease of use on intention to use was not supported. On careful analysis, we realized that most of the respondents belonged to organizations where eHRM was in the post-implementation phase. Raiij and Schepers (2008) also found a similar phenomenon in their study of acceptance of virtual learning environments and reasoned that TAM2 did not find any direct post-implementation effects of "perceived ease of use" on "intention to use". Marler et al. (2009) also found similar results in their study of Employee Self Service (ESS) technology adoption wherein they observed a marked change in the relationship between ease of use and attitude in the post implementation scenario and suggested that ease of use becomes redundant with perceived usefulness, post implementation. We make an important inference that as individuals gain experience of continuously using eHRM systems, post implementation, instrumentality overshadows concerns about ease of use. Therefore, unless new eHRM system alternatives offer significantly better ease of use as compared to what the users are already comfortable with and habituated to –"intention to use" will not be significantly impacted by "perceived ease of use". Future research should consider "stage of implementation" – an organization context while studying the relationship between ease of use and intention to use.

Hypothesis H8, the effect of "image" on "perceived usefulness" was not supported. On careful analysis, we realized that the sample population belonged to organizations who had implemented only the core eHRM components like employee records, life-cycle events, payroll, time and attendance and performance management. These organizations had not implemented the other eHRM processes like integrated talent management (career and succession planning, learning and development) and Web 2.0 technologies (social networking, collaboration). Though we had not included this aspect in our main hypothesis, we probably would have got support for the "image" to "perceived usefulness" relationship if the sample organizations had implemented integrated talent management, social networking and web 2.0 collaboration. The potential of these systems, especially, in the context of social exchange and social interdependence is perceived as a source of power, influence and status by individuals. We therefore, suggest that future research focus on the relationship between "image" and "perceived usefulness" in the context of "implementation scope and coverage".

Hypothesis H11, the effect of "results demonstrability" to "perceived usefulness" was also not supported. We carefully, analyzed the results and found a link between "results demonstrability" and "job relevance". This led us to probe further into its significance, though we had not hypothesized the relationship. We infer that eHRM is a business application and individuals' perception of its usefulness would largely depend on its ability to demonstrate results that are relevant in the context of an individual's performance in their current or potential jobs. Therefore, results demonstrability in the context of "job relevance" makes more meaning in the study of its relationship with perceived usefulness. This probably explains our finding of significant support for the "results demonstrability" linkage with "job relevance".

7 Contributions and Implications

This study makes two significant contributions. First, this research reinforces the organizational context angle to be considered when studying the factors influencing eHRM adoption (Marler et al. 2009). In this study, we have identified two such factors of organizational context – "scope of implementation" (effect of Image on perceived usefulness) and "stage of implementation" (effect of ease of use on intention to use). Second, we have called for measuring "eHRM usage behavior" in a detailed manner rather than measuring it at an overall level. We argue that eHRM is a business application with differing outcomes at operational, relational and transformational stages of eHRM evolution. Organizations who implement eHRM are at various stages of maturity in terms of eHRM adoption and hence, measuring eHRM usage behavior at an overall level does not seem logical. There seems to be a clear gap in literature in the way eHRM usage is measured. As a first step, therefore, we have attempted to create a scale to measure eHRM usage behavior with a 10 point scale spanning the three eHRM types stated in literature – operational, relational and transformational). Our 10 point eHRM usage scale focuses on individuals (in effect we can say Employee Self-Service - ESS) and covers employee records, leave, mobility, internal job postings (Operational eHRM), employee portal, helpdesk, Web 2.0 collaboration, social networks (Relational eHRM) and competencies, goal setting, performance reviews, career planning, learning and development (Transformational eHRM). Though we created this 10-point scale and administered it all the respondents, we got responses only for 3 items which covered employee records, leave and performance management. This was because most of the organizations from where we got individual responses had not implemented the other eHRM processes – a clear case of organizational context of "implementation scope". Therefore, though we could not test the entire 10-point scale, we believe we have initiated a serious discussion on measuring eHRM usage behavior more objectively and in greater detail. Future research should identify a more comprehensive and innovative sampling procedure to cover those organizations which have implemented all the eHRM types to test eHRM adoption and in particular, eHRM usage behavior.

Appendix 1. TAM 2 Measures Used in the Study

Item	Description
USE	
(a1)	Using the eHRM system improves my performance in my job
(a2)	Using the eHRM system in my job increases my productivity
(a3)	Using the eHRM system enhances my effectiveness in my job
(a4)	I find the eHRM system to useful in my job
EASE	
(a5)	My interaction with the eHRM system is clear and understandable
(a6)	Interacting with the eHRM system does not require a lot of my mental effort
(a7)	I find the eHRM system easy to use
(a8)	I find it easy to get the eHRM system to do what I want it to do
SN	
(a9)	People who influence my behavior think that I should use the eHRM system
(a10)	People who are important to me think that I should use the eHRM system
IMAGE	
(a14)	People in my organization who use the eHRM system have more prestige than those who do not
(a15)	People in my organization who use the eHRM system have a high profile
(a16)	Using the eHRM system is a status symbol in my organization

(continued)

(continued)

Item	Description
JR	
(a17)	In my job, usage of the eHRM system is important
(a18)	In my job, usage of the eHRM system is relevant
OQ	
(a19)	The quality of the output I get from the eHRM system is high
(a20)	I have no problem with the quality of the eHRM system's output
RD	
(a21)	I have no difficulty telling others about the results of using the eHRM system
(a22)	I believe I could communicate to others the consequences of using the eHRM system
(a23)	The results of using the eHRM system are apparent to me
(a24R)	I would have difficulty explaining why using the eHRM system may or may not be beneficial
INT	
(a25)	Assuming I have access to the eHRM system, I intend to use it
(a26)	Given that I have access to the eHRM system, I predict that I would use it

References

Adams, D.A., Nelson, R.R., Todd, P.A.: Perceived usefulness, ease of use and usage of information technology. MIS Q. **16**, 227–248 (1992)

Anderson, J.C., Gerbing, D.W.: Structured Equation Modeling in practice: a review and recommended two-step approach. Psychol. Bull. **103**(3), 411–423 (1988)

Azjen, I.: The theory of planned behavior. Organ. Behav. Hum. Decis. Process. **50**, 179–211 (1991)

Bagozzi, R.P., Yi, Y.: Assessing method variance in multitrait–multimethod matrices: the case of self-reported affect and perceptions at work. J. Appl. Psychol. **75**, 547–560 (1990)

Beach, L.R., Mitchell, T.R.: A contingency model for selection of decision strategies. Acad. Manag. Rev. **3**(3), 439–449 (1978)

Blau, P.M.: Exchange and Power in Social Life. Wiley, New York (1964)

Bowen, W.: The puny payoff from office computers. Fortune, pp. 20–24 (1986)

Chau, P.Y.K., Hu, P.J.H.: Investigating healthcare professionals' decisions to accept telemedicine technology: an empirical test of competing theories. Inf. Manag. **39**, 297–311 (2002)

Davis, F.D.: Perceived usefulness, perceived ease of use and user acceptance of technology. MIS Q. **13**, 319–339 (1989)

Fishbein, M., Ajzen, I.: Belief, Attitude, Intention and Behavior: An Introduction to Theory and Research. Addison-Wesley, Reading (1975)

Hair, F.H., Black, W.C., Babin, B.J., Anderson, R.E.: Multivariate Data Analysis, 7th edn. Prentice-Hall, Upper Saddle River (2010)

Haines, V.Y., Petit, A.: Conditions for successful human resource information systems. Hum. Resour. Manag. **36**(2), 261–275 (1997)

Hardesty, D.M., Bearden, W.O.: The use of expert judges in scale development. Implications for improving face validity of measure of unobservable constructs. J. Bus. Res. **57**, 98–107 (2004)

Iyer, S.: Understanding the eHRM promise and adoption imperatives. NHRD Netw. J., 1–10 (2019)

Iyer, S., Israel, D.: Structural equation modeling to test the impact of organization communication satisfaction on employee engagement. South Asian J. Manag. **19**(1), 51–81 (2012)

Legris, P., Ingham, J., Collerette, P.: Why do people use information technology? A critical review of the technology acceptance model. Inf. Manag. **40**, 191–204 (2003)

Lepak, D.P., Snell, S.A.: Virtual HR: strategic human resource management in the 21st century. Hum. Resour. Manag. Rev. **8**(3), 215–234 (1998)

Lengnick-Hall, M.L., Moritz, S.: The impact of e-HR on the human resource management function. J. Labor Res. **24**(3), 365–379 (2003)

Marler, J.H., Fisher, S.L., Ke, W.: Employee self-service technology acceptance: a comparison of pre-implementation and post-implementation relationships. Pers. Psychol. **62**(2), 327–358 (2009)

Marler, J.H., Liang, X., Dulebohn, J.H.: Training and effective employee information technology use. J. Manag. **32**(5), 721–743 (2006)

Martin, G., Reddington, M., Kneafsey, M.B.: Web 2.0 and Human Resources: Groundswell or Hype? Research Report. Chartered Institute of Personnel and Development, London (2009)

Martin, G., Reddington, M.: Theorizing the links between e-HR and strategic HRM: a model, case illustration and reflections. Int. J. Hum. Resour. Manag. **21**, 1553–1574 (2010)

Nunnally, J.C.: Psychometric Theory, 2nd edn. McGraw-Hill, New York (1978)

Ong, C.S., Lai, J.-Y., Wang, Y.-S.: Factors affecting engineers' acceptance of asynchronous e-Learning systems in high-tech companies. Inf. Manag. **41**, 795–804 (2004)

Pfeffer, J.: Power in Organizations. Ballinger, Cambridge, MA (1981)

Pfeffer, J.: Organizations and Organizations Theory. Pitman, Marshfield (1982)

Raiij, E.M.V., Schepers, J.J.L.: The acceptance and use of a virtual learning environment in China. Comput. Educ. **50**, 838–852 (2008)

Ruel, H.J.M., Bondarouk, T.V., Looise, J.K.: eHRM-innovation or irritation: an explorative empirical study in five large companies on web-based HRM. Manag. Rev. **15**(3), 364–381 (2004)

Szajna, B.: Empirical evaluation of the revised technology acceptance model. Manag. Sci. **42**, 85–92 (1996)

Selim, H.M.: An empirical investigation of student acceptance of course websites. Comput. Educ. **40**, 343–360 (2003)

Straub, D.W., Keil, M., Brenner, W.H.: Testing the technology acceptance model across cultures: a three country study. Inf. Manag. **33**, 1–11 (1997)

Ulrich, D.: The changing nature of human resources: a model for multiple roles. In: Ulrich, D. (ed.) Human Resource Champions. Harvard Business School Press, Boston, MA (1997)

Ulrich, D.: From eBusiness to e-HR. Hum. Resour. Plann. J. **5**, 90–97 (2001). International Association for Human Resources Information Management (IHRIM)

Venkatesh, V., Davis, F.D.: A theoretical extension of the technology acceptance model. Four Longitudinal field studies. Manage. Sci. **45**(2), 186–204 (2000)

Vroom, V.H.: Work and Motivation. Wiley, New York (1964)

Wu, J.H., Wang, S.C.: What drives mobile commerce?: an empirical investigation of the revised technology acceptance model. Inf. Manag. **42**, 719–729 (2005)

Young, T.R.: The lonely micro. Datamation **30**, 100–114 (1984)

Micro-foundations of Artificial Intelligence Adoption in Business: Making the Shift

Amit Kumar Kushwaha[✉] and Arpan Kumar Kar

Department of Management Studies,
Indian Institute of Technology Delhi, New Delhi 110016, India
kushwaha.amitkumar@gmail.com, arpan_kar@yahoo.co.in

Abstract. Artificial Intelligence has gradually materialized as an independent research field within information systems and business domains. The new forms of work evolving in the business require substantial experimentation, lead generations, and real-time recommendations. This has driven the extraordinary increase in the adoption of Artificial Intelligence technologies. Even with front runner organizations across the domain envisioning the advantages of early adoption of Artificial Intelligence technologies, some organizations scuffle the adoption owing to various barriers. This paper analyzes the characteristics that lead to and factors inhibiting the adoption of Artificial Intelligence at the organization-level. Through this paper, we report the results of Twitter conversations involving small and medium scale organizations about their level of adoption of Artificial Intelligence and barriers that they are facing. Through this analysis, we provide insights and agenda to help the executives of small and medium scale organizations to prepare for the adoption of Artificial Intelligence.

Keywords: Information systems · Artificial Intelligence · Adoption · Barriers · Chatbots · Roboadvisor

1 Introduction

The overall rise of the digital transformations among business houses fueled by Artificial Intelligence (AI) [1] has become one of the crucial drivers of scalability, flexibility, and real-time business operations. These operations range from catering the customers with appropriate promotional strategies, live support, real-time recommendations, and a personalized bundle of products. This has led the investments in AI across the world to grow at an astonishing rate. A report by Gartner in 2016 reported the adoption of AI by 9% of the organizations. By the end of 2019, AI adoption and productionalization have increased by 25% in the business organizations and are set to double itself in the next five years [2]. This shows the pace at which the organizations are embracing AI as part of business objectives.

Today AI comes as one of the critical innovation objectives and key results (OKR) when it comes to organizational goal settings [3]. With the advancements in the data storage and processing capability, AI has been driving the digital transformation OKRs. The view of organizations has evolved from looking AI as an innovation cost center to an essential business solution. Large scale organizations were the first ones to

© IFIP International Federation for Information Processing 2020
Published by Springer Nature Switzerland AG 2020
S. K. Sharma et al. (Eds.): TDIT 2020, IFIP AICT 617, pp. 249–260, 2020.
https://doi.org/10.1007/978-3-030-64849-7_22

adopt while small (start-ups or boutique consulting firms), and medium (service-based) enterprise organizations (SMO) have now started [4] seeing AI has a business necessity. What comes as an interesting report published by PwC is that AI will contribute up to $15.7 trillion to the global economy in 2030 [5]. A handful of industry reports suggests [6] that adoption of AI will give organizations to improve operations performance across lead generation, marketing, catering customers by creating a competitive advantage. Hence in totality, all these lead us to believe that the adoption of AI leads to an organizational increase in revenues, reduction in costs, and improved business efficiency.

However, many business organizations are still unclear on or are at the stage of deciding the business use case for the application of AI adoption. These organizations also struggle in identifying the right skill-sets needed for an entire pipeline of evaluating, building, and deploying AI solutions. Although several organizations across the globe are adopting AI, little research exists in the domain of adoption drivers and barriers [7]. Furthermore, a study of these drivers and barriers at the business organization level has remained marginally represented in the literature [8]. The proposed research is one of the first studies that analyze the adoption drivers and barriers and contributes towards the Information Systems (IS) literature a framework, which can be used by existing or start-up business houses to do a value assessment and roadblocks which can slow down the adoption of AI.

In this context, we propose a unique framework of an amalgamation of customer experience theories [9], with every potential business house being referred to as a customer of AI solutions and experience(good or bad) as drivers or barriers of adoption. Moreover, this research also provides empirical evidence that overcoming the not so good experiences (barriers) of AI adoption leads to a higher degree of AI practicing. The current research focusses on the state of the art AI technologies as products like chatbots, roboadvisors, virtual reality, augmented reality, recommendation engine has driven digital marketing, deep learning.

The prime objective of this study is to identify the factors responsible for impacting the advocacy of AI from the lens of adoption experiences. We use social media analytics (SMA) framework applied to the conversations and experiences shared on social media platforms (SMP) like Twitter by technical stakeholders in SMO by mining the original tweets posted by them. We further use the opinion mining approaches like topic modeling and sentiment mining. To guide our research analysis, we have undertaken two research questions:

RQ1: How stable is the identity and scope of the definition of AI technologies?
RQ2: What are the drivers, barriers, and initial experience towards AI adoption among the organizations and the users of these technologies?

The rest of the paper is organized into four sections. In the second section, we provide a methodological overview of the related literature. In the third section, we explain the research questions and formulate hypotheses. In the fourth section, we describe the methodology of the research undertaken. Furthermore, in the fifth and sixth section, we discuss the findings, interpretations, and conclude with the future research directions.

2 Prior Literature

The literature review consists of the following subsections: we start with defining state of the art AI technologies, AI adoption and barrier theories, and customer experience frameworks.

2.1 Artificial Intelligence

The notion of AI is not entirely new; it was first developed around 1950s in the computer science discipline with the primary focus towards automation [10]. It has ever remained persistent ever since Professor John McCarthy has described AI as "science and engineering making the machines do the repetitive task of humans" [11]. In the early 1980s, Lighthill [12] proposed the usage of AI addressing the problem of automation using robots with fundamental logical programming. In current times, the application of the AI is a lot wider than what it was proposed forty years back. It has started to become an essential component of any business by providing solutions like chatbots [13], robo advisors [14], virtual reality [15] shaping, and helping marketing, product, and customer service teams. AI encircles several frameworks to produce these techniques like deep learning [16, 17] expert systems, and recommendation engines.

The prior work done in the field of AI represented through the literature highlighted in the previous paragraph focusses on data, tools, and techniques of AI that can be used to strengthen the performance of the current system employed in the domain. Most of these works of literature are focused on the end implementation of AI techniques considered in silos in various domains. However, very little work exists in the domain of IS literature, suggesting the initial opinions, sentiments, and learnings while pursuing the path of AI adoption. We feel that there is a need to create work around these pivots, which can be used as a case study for the future SMO as they embark on their journey of AI adoption. We intent on filling this gap with the proposed work.

2.2 AI Adoption and Barrier Theories

The adoption of any innovation technique in an organization goes through various stages. There are three broad stages: initiation, adoption, and implementation. Rogers [18] have proposed various sub-phases within the adoption stage and has been proven across various domains and techniques. Pierce and Delbecq [19] have proposed the sociological theory of innovation, which starts with the 'pressure to change.' This makes the organizations identify the problem and to learn technology and acquire resources to make the changes for the better good. Authors [20] in the domain of adoption of innovative techniques have further proven that late adopters of the techniques have been at a loss. There exists a gap in the IS literature to understand the adoption of AI through the lens of innovation adoption theories.

To this date of writing the current manuscript, there exists a considerable number of research in IS, learning the barriers of adoption of various technologies like a cloud [21], blockchain [22, 23], mobile commerce [24], internet banking [25]. These studies pivot the barriers faced by the policy-makers in a business organization to political, economical, return on investments (ROI), skill gap, and overall experience. Reviewing the barrier literature in the IS domain reveals that these factors must be considered differently when adoption is to take place in a business house. For instance, the political barrier translates to support from top management towards adoptions [26, 27], economic barriers translate to initial cost of set-up and privacy risks [27, 28], skill gap translates to lack of skilled employees [28] and overall experience translates to resistance by the employees to up-shill themselves or to change [27, 29]. However, we feel that there is a need to explore further the barriers in the adoption of AI by business organizations, which will widen the IS literature.

2.3   Experience of AI Adoption

The employees of the business organization using AI techniques and technologies are primarily the end-users. Hence it is an exciting aspect to view their experiences of using AI from sociological theories. With a thorough review of the literature, we interpret that two most qualifying candidates emerge as premises, experience as a response of using technology as an offering [30, 31] or as a response to an assessment of the quality of the technology [32]. Extending these premises further, some of the studies [33] see the experience driven by characteristics of the technology rather than customer's (user's) response to use the technology.

   These studies have primarily focused on the extraordinary, different from regular or ordinary as the characteristics of the technology. Basis these characteristics of the technologies, the experience can range anything from weak to strong. The literature follows to explain that these experiences ranges are a continuum and cannot be tested as a dichotomy. At the time of developing this manuscript, to the best of our knowledge, there is no or minimal literature that tests the characteristics of AI on the experience of the employee (user of AI). We feel that there is a need to widen this literature, and the proposed research will help to fill this.

3   Hypothesis Development

3.1   Opportunities and Benefits of AI for the Business Sector

Rogers [18], in his theory, has proposed the importance of communication channels as an essential element in adoption where the adopters share their experiences and information. In the social media space, we use Twitter as the channel for sharing our experiences and information for others to learn and adopt. Literature [34] on AI suggests that business decisions are based on intuitions, and intuitions are based on patterns and trends learned through simulations on a large scale of data using AI techniques like deep learning. If so, then the business executives attend the real-time questions aided by intuitions, which are driven by AI. This leads us to believe that AI becomes an identity of business decisions.

   There can be different identities of AI when it comes to business applications like perceived usefulness, cost, affordability, more real-time. When organizations perceive the use of AI, they tend to adopt this technology quickly. Post-adoption, the organizations which know start innovating through AI. As the degree of adoption or diffusion of AI increases, it eventually takes the shape of an identity of the business house with perceived use and advantage. This leads us to form our first hypothesis to answer RQ1.

H(1): The operational improvement and enablement is leading the AI to become the identity of SMO.

3.2 Adoption Barriers of AI for the Business Sector

The findings of the literature show that there could be multiple barriers of adoption of an innovation pivoted around cost [28], privacy [27], the resistance of the employees to embrace [28]. Furthermore, few of the business houses feel that they are not getting the complete ROI from the technology. These barriers can further be translated as transformational and incremental barriers. There is also evidence that these techniques, if not supported by the right pieces of training of the employees, might turn out to be a barrier for adoption. This leads us to form our second hypothesis to answer the first part of RQ2.

H(2): The unsurety and unclearness of the advantages of AI might be a barrier towards adoption.

3.3 Experience as a Barrier of AI for the Business Sector

Employees of an organization perceive every technology differently. This partly drives the experience [32, 33] of using these techniques and technologies. The overall organization's adoption is built on the experience of the end-users (employees) of the technology. It is a perceptual issue that could arise out of firsthand experience and emotions of these issues. User (employee) friendliness is a noteworthy element to be tested when it comes to the adoption of AI at the organization level. This leads us to form our third hypothesis to answer the second part of RQ2.

H(3): A negative employee experience towards using AI might be a barrier towards adoption in a business organization.

4 Research Methodology

4.1 Research Instrument

This study investigates the drivers, barriers, and experiences of organizations towards the adoption of AI. For this, we have used Twitter as the channel of communication and the tweets posted as the instrument and words as a unit of analysis.

4.2 Data Collection

We have collected tweets around trending hashtags like #ArtificialIntelligence, #AI, #Chatbots, #Virtualreality, #Augmentedreality, #industry4.0, #roboadvisor.

The associated hashtags of #ArtificialIntelligence were determined based on collection of first 1000 tweets and mining it for hastag association rules. The resulting dataset consisted of 3,54,782 tweets posted by 60,142 users. We have further deployed some control mechanisms to make sure that the tweets are posted by actual users and not bots by pulling few historical tweets of these users and looking at the trend of posting these tweets in terms of hour of the day, day of the week. We have further dropped any tweet which had either only media embedded or an HTTP URL or was less than ten characters. This gave us a dataset of tweets with optimal length. We have further removed any stopwords from the tweets. This step is important as tweets are the unit of analysis.

We have further created a subset of the dataset by restricting our analysis to the SMO. For this, the tweets posted could be from the representatives of these firms like "principal engineer," "technical architects," "principal data scientists," product managers," "customer support heads." This subset was created in a two-phase manner. The first phase consisted of selecting users who have more than 10,000 followers and following. In the second phase, we have downloaded the user account level information from Twitter, and only accounts chosen to be part of the subset were those which had an association with any organizations and have a designation as part of their profile information. The resultant dataset for the analysis was reduced to 1,56,345 tweets posted by 46,302 users.

4.3 The Social Media Analytics Framework

With the words of the tweets posted by the users as the unit of analysis, we primarily use the content analysis tools of the social media analytics framework (SMAF). Content analysis tools and techniques have been accepted in the IS literature for mapping words to the sentiment and the more comprehensive theory testing and development [16, 35]. The primary and the most significant outcome of the content analysis is the sentiment polarity score [36]. These polarity scores can further be divided into negative, positive, and neutral. For the current research to analyze the drivers, barriers, and experiences, we are restricting to positive and negative sentiments. To interpret the meaningful insights from the large volume of texts, we are using word clouds [37] for each group of users (positive and negative sentiments). Latent Dirichlet Allocation (LDA) [38] has been used for topic modeling as it provides a way to control the number of words and identify the emerging theme within groups. There were 100 topics of 10 words, each of which were computed with LDA.

5 Findings

In the current research undertaken, collected data (tweets) were analyzed to identify experience and sentiments towards adoption and usage of AI using a mix of methods adopted from SMAF, which are rooted in computer science theories and inferential statistical analysis in the social science domain. We start by first illustrating a comparative view of the sentiments (polarity scores) of the tweets in the overall group (3,50,000 tweets from 60,000 users) and the focused SMO considered for this analysis (1,56,345 tweets posted by 46,302 users) (Fig. 1).

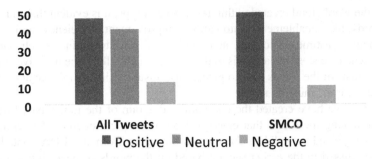

Fig. 1. Percentage polarity in groups

In general, it can be interpreted that more tweets are with positive sentiments towards AI. However, there is a considerable size of the group, which is neutral and a negative group. A manual investigation of the neutral tweets indicated that the SMOs are still not sure about the advantages of AI or are not confident in adopting owing to the current skill-set gap of the employees. The negative group might see some barriers to using AI technologies. With industry 4.0 around the corner, SMO falling in the neutral and negative group must learn from the experience of the SMO in the positive group and embark on the journey of adoption before it becomes a necessary commodity. The outcome of the current research will act as a contribution towards the literature of the success stories of AI adoption in IS, which can be used by SMO thinking to take the route of AI.

Subsequently, we attempted to visualize the 100 topics that were identified using LDA within respective groups. The most occurring topics identified from LDA on tweets basis the frequency of their occurrence in each group are plotted using the word cloud. A manual framework was also deployed to remove any verb part of the speech to make sure that we do not loose on identifying any important emotion, experience related words. This framework was tested for intercoder reliability and validity. Further, the incomplete words in the frequency map, which had spelling mistakes, were also corrected before this analysis. In this approach, the topics that occur more frequently among the respective groups will have a larger font size as compared to the words that occur less number of times among the group (Fig. 2).

Fig. 2. Word cloud of LDA topics

From the word cloud created within respective groups, it is evident that much focus is on words like enablement, automation, improvement, efficiency and efficient, advancement, real-time customers, autonomous system streamline, reach and need. However, when we steer the analysis to the SMO, which falls in the negative sentiment group, the focus of the words shift to precarious, unsure, skills, employee and emotion, large, bearish, cost, must be secure.

After that, we have created the community diagram of the topics based upon the association among the topics that emerged from the topic modeling. The community diagram is expected to validate the themes emerging from the LDA rooted in the literature discussed in the earlier section based on the words co-occurring in the same community. In the community diagram, the classes are represented by respective colors, and each class in a silo represents a theme (Fig. 3).

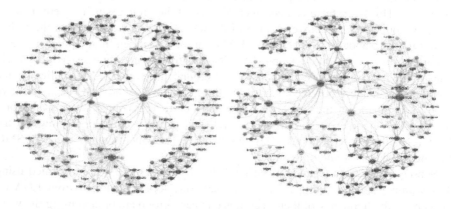

Fig. 3. Word community diagram in positive and negative respectively

From the community diagram, there are 16 themes developed with the positive SMO groups, which are: time, research, market, need, industry, accelerate, efficient, safe, and more. These 16 themes of the words association can act as premises for further hypothesis development and can be tied back to different theories highlighted in the literature. Few of these themes are further connected, highlighting that multiple premises support each other for the adoption of AI.

While analyzing the community diagram of the SMOs falling in the negative group that is emerging is the employee-emotion. This theme can act as a separate premise for hypothesis development and be linked back to the employee user experience. Other themes that emerge are skills, unsurety, and safety. These themes can be further used to explain the theoretical model explained in the introduction section to develop deep-dive research into barriers of adoption.

6 Discussion

H(1):   The operational improvement and enablement is leading the AI to become the identity of SMO

Our first finding indicates the evidence of improvements in operational efficiency in the SMOs who have adopted AI technologies. These have specific proofs of topics like quick to market, automation, and real-time customer recommendation and support, which helps businesses to make informed decisions [34]. With the inferential interpretation of these insights, we can accept the hypothesis 1 in favor of AI improving and enabling efficiency and automation.

H(2):   The unsurety and unclearness of the advantages of AI might be a barrier towards adoption

Our second finding indicates the evidence of cost, unsurety, and skills being the barriers of AI adoption in AI. Findings of IS [27] literature for the adoption of other innovations have historical evidence of cost being the most significant barrier. Being unsure is partially related to cost in terms of ROI and security. With these pieces of evidence in the current analysis, we accept the hypothesis 2 in favor of cost, unsurety, insecurity, and skills being barriers for SMOs to adopt AI.

H(3):   A negative employee experience towards using AI might be a barrier towards adoption in a business organization

Our third finding through the topic modeling and community diagram is the employees motion and experience. Employees [32, 33], irrespective of SMO or significant business organizations, look at the perceived benefit and experience they like to have while using a particular technology. Through topic modeling, employee-emotions is a separate pivot emerging from the discussions of SMOs within the negative group. In the community diagram, this theme is connected to the 'not-sure' cluster. Using this evidences, we can accept hypothesis 3 in favor of employee emotions as another barrier in the adoption of AI.

7 Conclusion and Future Scope of Research

This research aims to explore the drivers, barriers, and experiences of the adoption of AI in the SMO. An inferential SMA framework has been utilized to validate the hypothesis answering the research questions around what is driving the adoption of AI and the barriers hindering. If these factors are addressed with factors like knowledge, training, trust, security, making sure that employees do not feel outdated with the adoption of state of the art AI techniques will make the adoption a smooth process. As AI is increasingly being used in industries, studies are required to understand determinants which facilitate or impede adoption [39].

As the future scope of work, we would like further develop the hypotheses rooted more firmly in the theories which revolve more around socio-cultural elements of human encounters with an innovation like AI. Further IS researchers can also refer to the current paper as a starting point to build the initial theoretical blocks for the adoption of AI.

References

1. Agrawal, A., Gans, J., Goldfarb, A.: The simple economics of machine intelligence. Harv. Bus. Rev., 17 November 2016
2. Lerner, S.: The evolution of artificial intelligence. Enterp. Digitalization, 11 February 2019
3. Gartner's Top 10 Strategic Technology Trends for 2017. www.gartner.com/smarterwithgartner/gartners-top-10-technology-trends-2017
4. 06-technology-background.pdf. https://www.calpers.ca.gov/docs/board-agendas/201801/full/day1/06-technology-background.pdf
5. PricewaterhouseCoopers: PwC's Global Artificial Intelligence Study: Sizing the prize. PwC. https://www.pwc.com/gx/en/issues/data-and-analytics/publications/artificial-intelligence-study.html
6. Applying Artificial Intelligence to Drive Business Transformation: A Gartner Trend Insight Report
7. Alsheibani, S., Cheung, Y., Messom, C.: Artificial intelligence adoption: AI-readiness at firm-level, p. 9 (2018)
8. Perc, M., Ozer, M., Hojnik, J.: Social and juristic challenges of artificial intelligence. Palgrave Commun. 5(1), 61 (2019). https://doi.org/10.1057/s41599-0190278-x
9. Becker, L., Jaakkola, E.: Customer experience: fundamental premises and implications for research. J. Acad. Mark. Sci. 48(4), 630–648 (2020). https://doi.org/10.1007/s11747-019-00718-x
10. Kar, A.K.: Bio inspired computing – a review of algorithms and scope of applications. Exp. Syst. Appl. 59, 20–32 (2016). https://doi.org/10.1016/j.eswa.2016.04.018
11. McCarthy, J., Hayes, P.J.: Some philosophical problems from the standpoint of artificial intelligence. In: Webber, B.L., Nilsson, N.J. (eds.) Readings in Artificial Intelligence, pp. 431–450. Morgan Kaufmann (1981)
12. Lighthill, M.J.: Large-amplitude elongated-body theory of fish locomotion. Proc. R. Soc. Lond. B Biol. Sci. 179(1055), 125–138 (1971)
13. Miner, A.S., Laranjo, L., Kocaballi, A.B.: Chatbots in the fight against the COVID-19 pandemic. Digit. Med. 3(1), 65 (2020). https://doi.org/10.1038/s41746-0200280-0
14. Imerman, M.B., Fabozzi, F.J.: Cashing in on innovation: a taxonomy of FinTech. J. Asset. Manag. 21(3), 167–177 (2020). https://doi.org/10.1057/s41260-020-00163-4
15. Marín-Morales, J., et al.: Affective computing in virtual reality: emotion recognition from brain and heartbeat dynamics using wearable sensors. Sci. Rep. 8(1), 13657 (2018). https://doi.org/10.1038/s41598-018-32063-4
16. Kushwaha, A.K., Kar, A.K., Vigneswara Ilavarasan, P.: Predicting information diffusion on Twitter a deep learning neural network model using custom weighted word features. In: Hattingh, M., et al. (eds.) I3E 2020. LNCS, vol. 12066, pp. 456–468. Springer, Cham (2020). https://doi.org/10.1007/978-3-030-44999-5_38
17. Topol, E.J.: High-performance medicine: the convergence of human and artificial intelligence. Nat. Med. 25(1), 44–56 (2019). https://doi.org/10.1038/s41591-018-0300-7

18. Rogers, E.M.: Diffusion of innovations: modifications of a model for telecommunications. In: Stoetzer, M.W., Mahler, A. (eds.) Die Diffusion von Innovationen in der Telekommunikation. Schriftenreihe des Wissenschaftlichen Instituts für Kommunikationsdienste, vol. 17, pp. 25–38. Springer, Heidelberg (1995). https://doi.org/10.1007/978-3-642-79868-9_2

19. Pierce, J.L., Delbecq, A.L.: Organization structure, individual attitudes and innovation. AMR 2(1), 27–37 (1977). https://doi.org/10.5465/amr.1977.4409154

20. Cebon, P., Love, E.G.: Why do late adopters perform poorly: symbolic adoption, or cultural incongruity? Acad. Manage. Proc. 2002(1), I1–I6 (2002). https://doi.org/10.5465/apbpp.2002.7518359

21. Doherty, E., Carcary, M., Conway, G.: Migrating to the cloud: examining the drivers and barriers to adoption of cloud computing by SMEs in Ireland: an exploratory study. J. Small Bus. Enterp. Dev. 22(3), 512–527 (2015). https://doi.org/10.1108/jsbed-05-2013-0069

22. Cennamo, C., Marchesi, C., Meyer, T.: Two sides of the same coin? Decentralized versus proprietary blockchains and the performance of digital currencies. AMD (2020). https://doi.org/10.5465/amd.2019.0044

23. Sadhya, V., Sadhya, H.: Barriers to adoption of Blockchain technology. In: AMCIS 2018 Proceedings, August 2018

24. Pankomera, R., van Greunen, D.: Opportunities, barriers, and adoption factors of mobile commerce for the informal sector in developing countries in Africa: a systematic review. Electron. J. Inf. Syst. Dev. Ctries. 85(5), e12096 (2019). https://doi.org/10.1002/isd2.12096

25. Arif, I., Aslam, W., Hwang, Y.: Barriers in adoption of internet banking: A structural equation modeling - neural network approach. Technol. Soc. 61, 101231 (2020). https://doi.org/10.1016/j.techsoc.2020.101231

26. Cox, B., Ghoneim, S.: Drivers and barriers to adopting EDI: a sector analysis of UK industry. Eur. J. Inf. Syst. 5(1), 24–33 (1996). https://doi.org/10.1057/ejis.1996.9

27. Mergel, I.: Open innovation in the public sector: drivers and barriers for the adoption of Challenge.gov. Pub. Manage. Rev. 20(5), 726–745 (2018). https://doi.org/10.1080/14719037.2017.1320044

28. Ransbotham, S., Kiron, D., Gerbert, P., Reeves, M.: Reshaping Business With Artificial Intelligence: Closing the Gap Between Ambition and Action. MIT Sloan Management Review; Cambridge, vol. 59, no. 1 (2017)

29. Kruse, C.S., Kristof, C., Jones, B., Mitchell, E., Martinez, A.: Barriers to electronic health record adoption: a systematic literature review. J. Med. Syst. 40(12), 1–7 (2016). https://doi.org/10.1007/s10916-016-0628-9

30. Aswani, R., Ghrera, S.P., Kar, A.K., Chandra, S.: Identifying buzz in social media: a hybrid approach using artificial bee colony and k-nearest neighbors for outlier detection. Soc. Netw. Anal. Min. 7(1), 1–10 (2017). https://doi.org/10.1007/s13278-017-0461-2

31. Grover, P., Kar, A.K., Vigneswara Ilavarasan, P.: Blockchain for businesses: a systematic literature review. In: Al-Sharhan, Salah A., et al. (eds.) I3E 2018. LNCS, vol. 11195, pp. 325–336. Springer, Cham (2018). https://doi.org/10.1007/978-3-030-02131-3_29

32. Kumar, V., Umashankar, N., Kim, K.H., Bhagwat, Y.: Assessing the influence of economic and customer experience factors on service purchase behaviors. Mark. Sci. 33(5), 673–692 (2014)

33. Pine II, B.J., Gilmore, J.H.: Welcome to the experience economy. Harv. Bus. Rev. (1998). (From the July–August 1998 Issue)

34. Eisenhardt, K.M.: Making fast strategic decisions in high-velocity environments. AMJ 32(3), 543–576 (1989). https://doi.org/10.5465/256434

35. Grover, P., Kar, A.K., Dwivedi, Y.K., Janssen, M.: Polarization and acculturation in US Election 2016 outcomes – can twitter analytics predict changes in voting preferences. Technol. Forecast. Soc. Chang. 145, 438–460 (2019)

36. Kassarjian, H.H.: Content analysis in consumer research. J. Consum. Res. 4(1), 8–18 (1977). https://doi.org/10.1086/208674
37. Nooralahzadeh, F., Arunachalam, V., Chiru, C.-G.: 2012 presidential elections on Twitter – an analysis of how the US and French election were reflected in tweets. https://doi.org/10.1109/cscs.2013.72
38. Blei, D.M., Ng, A.Y., Jordan, M.I.: Latent dirichlet allocation. J. Mach. Learn. Res. 3, 993–1022 (2003)
39. Kar, A.K.: 5 Present-Day Applications of Artificial Intelligence – Tech Talk. https://techtalk.org/2018/02/16/5-present-day-applications-of-artificial-intelligence

Pandemic Pandemonium and Remote Working: An Investigation of Determinants and Their Contextual Behavior in Virtualization of Work-From-Home (WFH) Process

Kalyan Prasad Agrawal[1]([⊠]) [iD], Ashis K. Pani[2], and Rajeev Sharma[2]

[1] Chandragupt Institute of Management Patna, Patna, India
kalyan@cimp.ac.in
[2] Xavier School of Management (XLRI), Jamshedpur, India

Abstract. Disruption at the physical workplace, developed by threats like the coronavirus, triggers revisiting old assumptions and exploring opportunities for new ways of remote working. With the global epidemic spreading, businesses are gearing up with the managers and their respective teams to work from home (WFH). This research has offered a setting for advancing understanding of virtualization of WFH process by exploring the factors that enable or constrain the information and communication technology (ICT) enabled virtualization of processes in employee's WFH process through empirical support for the process virtualization theory (PVT). Setting pandemic outbreak as a context, outcome of this research is reliant on two independent studies conducted to examine the influencing factors. First study conducted just before the onset of pandemic outbreak, found that parts of the constructs proposed in the PVT had expected outcomes regarding the characteristics of process virtualization. Contrary to this, second study conducted after pandemic outbreak found that major constructs proposed in the PVT behaved otherwise regarding the characteristics of process virtualization. To fill the gaps in empirical knowledge, the enablers and inhibitors so found together may be motivations to anticipate business organizations and their workforces to experiment with this form of work process, predominantly improved flexibility for organizations and employees, improved productivity, quicker responsiveness to the needs and unexpected man-made and natural disasters, lower absenteeism, improved employee retention, greater cost control, along with more general social benefits.

Keywords: Work from home (WFH) process · Information and communication technology (ICT) · Process virtualization theory (PVT)

1 Introduction

Disruption at physical work place, developed by threats like the coronavirus, triggers revisiting old assumptions and exploring opportunities for new ways of remote working to stay ahead. With the global epidemic spreading, businesses are gearing up

© IFIP International Federation for Information Processing 2020
Published by Springer Nature Switzerland AG 2020
S. K. Sharma et al. (Eds.): TDIT 2020, IFIP AICT 617, pp. 261–273, 2020.
https://doi.org/10.1007/978-3-030-64849-7_23

with the managers and their respective teams to work from home (WFH). The vision of having to work from home is becoming progressively more likely for a comprehensive swath of employees resulting into the disruption of modes and means of communication, team dynamics, work patterns etc. Although all processes do not qualify to be virtualized (Overby 2008), imagination of life has now become implausible discounting online processes (Balci and Rosenkranz 2014). Extant literature has acknowledged multiple factors influencing the IT-enabled virtualization of several services by extensively adopting various theoretical lenses like, the diffusion of innovation theory (Roberts and Daker 2004; Beaudry and Pinsonneault 2005; Agrawal 2015), the technology acceptance model (Davis 1989; Baker et al. 2007), the unified theory of acceptance and use of technology (Davis 1989; Venkatesh et al. 2003; Kim and Kankanhalli 2009; Dwivedi et al. 2017), the task-technology fit theory (Goodhue and Thompson 1995; Dennis et al. 2001), and the theory of planned behavior (Ajzen and Driver 1992; Kim and Karpova 2010). There have been extensive use of these theoretical lenses in association with the acceptance of ICT-enabled activities for an individual level. Information systems (IS) literature is silent in measuring the process level and its associated requirements in remote working context.

Initially, this study began just before the onset of pandemic outbreak to understand the influencing factors on the ICT-enabled virtualization of WFH process but soon after the announcement of COVID-19 as a pandemic by World Health Organization (WHO), further extended to examine the behavior of identified factors at the intersection of separate contexts, first in pre-pandemic time and second after pandemic outbreak. This research also intends to assess whether derived factors behave as context-resistant stable factor(s) or context-driven dynamic factor(s) that can contribute to the body of knowledge in dynamic capability of firms, especially relating to remote working. These lead to the research questions *(i) what are the factors that influence the ICT-enabled virtualization of processes in employees' work-from-home (WFH) process?, and (ii) is/are the assessed factor(s) context resistant stable factor(s) or context driven dynamic factor(s)?*

Drawing upon the process virtualization theory (PVT) for evaluating determinants quantitatively, current study is investigating the factors that impact the ICT-enabled virtualization of processes in employee's WFH process. The rationale behind choosing it as analytical lens is grounded on its explaining and worthy concepts to measure which physical processes can (not) be virtualized and are (not) appropriate for online platforms than others (Overby 2008). Outcomes are expected to add valuable insight in to the current body of knowledge in literature pertaining to PVT and remote working.

2   Theoretical Background

Historically, replacements to traditional commuting immediately became important subsequent to the world oil crisis of 1970 when the concept of technology enabled remote working process became a widespread focus for academic debate (Baruch and Yuen 2000). Development of technologies in the last quarter of twentieth century facilitated the commercial usage of the Internet along with email and other communication tools and made the commuting more sustainable (Siha and Monroe 2006).

Rapid developments in technologies and associated IT infrastructure in this century has made it more affordable and accessible thereby accelerating attention towards the technology enabled virtual working process (van Winden and Woets 2004; Roukis 2006). In order to be successful, organizations in current times need to respond and operate in a dynamic work environment by offering better service beyond traditional business hours, attracting and retaining capable workforce in a close fitting labor market and reacting to the changing global demographic with respect to the workforce (Scholefield and Peel 2009).

Disaster, like Covid-19, is a sudden event with widespread disruptive consequences. It has disrupted the setting of work, creating an ethos of ambiguity with shifting priorities for individuals as well as organizations. Technology enabled work from home (WFH), when considered in current context, is gradually endorsed as an effective means to restore and ensure operational capacity in complicated disaster environments (Alvaro et al. 2011). Moreover, it enables a relocation of available work tasks across distributed workforces when allocated work locations are inaccessible (due to geographical lockdown) and hazardous (due to virus transmission). For organizations that operate under such circumstances, WFH plays a critical role in ensuring the continuation of tasks at hand (Donnelly and Sarah 2015). Influential factors for ICT-enabled virtualization of WFH process is arguably non-existent in academic research. As current study first aims to investigate the factors that impact the ICT-enabled virtualization of processes in employees' WFH process, the term 'work-from-home (WFH)' in this study is used in alignment with the terms used by other scholars in the literature (Morgan 2004; Sanchez et al. 2007) and express it as 'full-time paid employees conducting their jobs from home using information and communication technologies (ICT).'

3 Research Model

A process, as defined in the literature of PVT, is a group of multiple steps meant to accomplish an objective of a phenomenon (Overby 2008). It is either physical or virtual. In physical process there is physical interaction between people or between people and objects. On the other hand in virtual process there is no physical interaction between people or between people and objects. Process virtualization is the setting in which a physical process shifts to a virtual process. The rationale behind choosing PVT as analytical lens is grounded on its explaining and worthy concepts to measure which physical processes can (not) be virtualized and are (not) appropriate for being conducted online than others (Overby 2008). Few studies (Balci and Rosenkranz 2014; Graupner and Maedche 2015; Ofoeda et al. 2018) have been identified from the literature for its applicability in several other contexts. Thus it provides the ideal beginning point for investigating the WFH process between employee and employer.

Process virtualization theory proposes the independent variables in two groups, first group constitutes the characteristics of the process and second group constitutes the characteristics of the virtualization mechanism. First group is further comprised of sensory requirements, relationship requirements, synchronism requirements, and identification and control requirements. Considering all other things constant, these constructs are perceived to have resistance on process virtualizability. Here sensory requirements refer to the "need for process participants to be able to enjoy a full sensory experience of the process and the other process participants and objects. Sensory experience of the process includes seeing, hearing, smelling, touching, and tasting" (Overby 2008). The lesser the sensory requirements of a process, the greater is the amenability of the process to being conducted virtually and vice-versa. Below hypothesis is established.

H1: The higher the sensory requirements of the WFH process, the lower is the amenability to being conducted virtually and vice versa.

Relationship requirements state "the need for process participants to interact with each other in a social or professional context" (Overby 2008). Social interactions among people leverage knowledge, grow trust and develop friendship (Overby 2008). In general, relationships in physical settings are resilient and more advanced and therefore negatively influence the intention to practice processes online (Balci and Rosenkranz 2014). Building upon these results, below hypothesis is established.

H2: The higher the relationship requirements of the WFH process, the lower is the amenability to being conducted virtually and vice versa.

Synchronism requirements refers "the degree to which the activities relating to a process need to follow immediately with minimal delay" (Overby 2008). In physical process participants and objects can interact usually without any delay. Therefore more the synchronism requirements relating to a process, less likely the process is to being conducted virtually and vice versa. Building upon all these outcomes into the WFH perspective, below hypothesis is established.

H3: The higher the synchronism requirements of the WFH process, the lower is the amenability to being conducted virtually and vice versa.

Next independent variable representing the characteristics of the virtualization mechanism is identification and control requirements. It refers "the degree to which process participants need credentials of other process participants and the capability to regulate their behavior" (Overby 2008). As physical inspection of others to endorse their identity cannot be done by process participants in processes which are virtual they are susceptible to identity deception and control difficulties. Building upon these, following hypotheses are established (Fig. 1).

H4: The higher the identification requirements of the WFH process, the lower is the amenability to being conducted virtually and vice versa.
H5: The higher the control requirements of the WFH process, the lower is the amenability to being conducted virtually and vice versa.

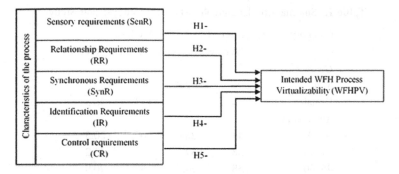

Fig. 1. Research model for WFH process virtualization (adapted and modified from Overby 2008)

4 Research Methodology

Measurement items for this research were adapted from the review of extant literature (Balci and Rosenkranz 2014b; Barth and Veit 2011b; Overby 2008; Overby et al. 2010; Balci et al. 2014; Venkatesh et al. 2003; Graupner and Maedche 2015) with appropriate revision to ensure the consistency of the survey items in line with the setting of current study. For the purpose of this study all measurement items were developed and ranked on a five-point Likert scale from strongly disagree (1) to strongly agree (5) (Likert 1932).

Post pilot study, for the exploration of the PVT in the employee's work from home context, final sample data using same survey instrument for both studies, Study-1 and Study-2, were collected through online setting from managers and business executives representing leading service sector organizations across India. To have a representative sample for the Study-1 (pre-pandemic time), 154 (40.2%) questionnaires out of 383 were received (Oct–Nov 2019) and for Study-2 (representing pandemic time), a total of 516 participants were targeted (Apr–May 2020) and 296 (57.4%) questionnaires were considered further.

5 Data Analysis and Findings

Table 1 represents the demographic distribution and sample characteristics of the respondents involved in both studies. Structural equation modelling (SEM) with partial least squares (PLS) regression is used for the evaluation of proposed model in SmartPLS 3.0 (Hair et al. 2017), as presented in Tables 2, 3 and 4.

In the model (Figs. 2 and 3), results show that all hypothesized paths in both studies are significant. As shown in Table 5, identification requirements and control requirements are found to have significant positive effects on intended WFH process virtualization. Further, the R-square value of 0.574 demonstrates that good variance can be explained.

Table 1. Summary of demographic statistics (Study-1 and Study-2)

Category	Study-1		Study-2	
	Number	Percent	Number	Percent
Gender				
Male	96	62.3	153	51.7
Female	58	37.7	143	48.3
Age (years)				
≤ 30	44	28.6	60	20.3
31–45	58	37.7	128	43.2
46–60	38	24.7	62	20.9
>60	14	9.1	45	15.2
Education				
Professional	36	23.4	55	18.6
Masters	54	35.1	130	43.9
Bachelors	47	30.5	60	20.3
Others	17	11.0	51	17.2
Work experience (years)				
≤ 10	99	64.3	172	58.1
>10	55	35.7	124	41.9

Firm age (years)	*Percent (%)*	
	Study-1	Study-2
≤ 10	29.2	22.6
11–20	27.9	38.9
21–30	26.6	25.3
>30	16.2	13.2

Table 2. Constructs, item description, and factor loading (Study-1 and Study-2)

Construct and item description	Factor loading (***p < 0.001)	
	Study-1	Study-2
Sensory requirements (SenR)		
SenR1: While working on official assignments it is important to me to see the relevant documents holding their hardcopies in hand	0.980***	0.876***
SenR2: I intend to see and listen to the concerned office colleagues and clients physically while working on official assignments	0.982***	0.733***
SenR3: It is not important to me to utilize office infrastructure while performing my job duties (reverse)	0.943***	0.947***
Relationship requirements (RR)		
RR1: To me, the social and professional interaction with the concerned office colleagues and clients is necessary and important	0.906***	0.793***
RR2: I like seeing and talking to the concerned office colleagues and/or clients	0.899***	0.759***

(*continued*)

Table 2. (*continued*)

Construct and item description	Factor loading (***p < 0.001)	
	Study-1	Study-2
RR3: I intend to establish a personal relationship with my office colleagues and/or clients	0.906***	0.893***
RR4: Individual interaction with my office colleagues and/or clients is not important to me while following the WFH process	0.900***	0.888***
Synchronism requirements (SynR)		
SynR1: I get bothered if the processing does not start straightaway with the availability of input	0.934***	0.981***
SynR2: I like to receive immediate confirmation of the input submission without delay via any form of mail or acknowledgements	0.957***	0.972***
Identification requirements (IR)		
IR1: To me, it is necessary to verify my identity while conducting ICT-enabled WFH process	0.985***	0.907***
IR2: Authentication tools are important to me in ICT-enabled WFH process	0.979***	0.923***
Control requirements (CR)		
CR1: I have restricted command over my official data and information while conducting the ICT-enabled WFH process	0.952***	0.927***
CR2: When conducting the ICT-enabled WFH process I get worried to think about losing my personal/official data and information by clicking the inappropriate link(s)	0.937***	0.944***
Intended ICT-enabled virtualization of WFH process (WFHPV)		
WFHPV1: In future I expect to use the ICT for the WFH process	0.868***	0.864***
WFHPV2: In future I intend to explore the ICT use for the WFH process	0.948***	0.950***
WFHPV3: Given a choice I would like to use the ICT while conducting the WFH process	0.700***	0.690***
WFHPV4: I will rate the ICT use for the WFH process as satisfactory	0.944***	0.946***

Table 3. Outcomes of Cronbach's α, Composite Reliability and AVE (Study-1 and Study-2)

Constructs	Study-1			Study-2		
	α	CR	AVE	α	CR	AVE
SR	0.879	0.943	0.892	0.822	0.891	0.734
RR	0.963	0.982	0.964	0.858	0.902	0.698
SynR	0.896	0.925	0.759	0.952	0.976	0.953
IR	0.926	0.947	0.816	0.806	0.911	0.837
CR	0.967	0.979	0.938	0.858	0.933	0.875
WFHPV	0.882	0.944	0.894	0.893	0.924	0.754

CR = Control requirements; IR = Identification requirements; SynR = Synchronous requirements; RR = Relationship requirements; SenR = Sensory requirements; WFHPV = WFH process virtualization

Table 4. Outcome of discriminant validity (Study-1 and Study-2)

Constructs	Study-1						Study-2					
	CR	IR	SynR	RR	SenR	WFHPV	CR	IR	SynR	RR	SenR	WFHPV
CR	.944						.935					
IR	.387	.982					.434	.915				
SynR	.603	.419	.945				.050	.323	.976			
RR	-.007	-.079	-.192	.903			.033	-.008	.473	.835		
SenR	.605	.438	-.158	.054	.969		-.028	-.231	.416	.052	.857	
WFHPV	.303	.477	-.162	.075	.944	.871	-.139	-.281	-.150	.616	-.087	.868

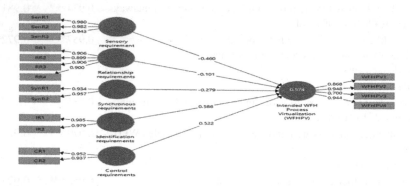

Fig. 2. PLS-SEM result showing β-coefficient and R-square values (Study-1)

As shown in Fig. 3 and represented in Table 6, sensory requirements, relationship requirements and identification requirements are found to have significant positive effects on WFHPV. The R-square value of 0.658 demonstrates that good variance can be explained in the dependent variable.

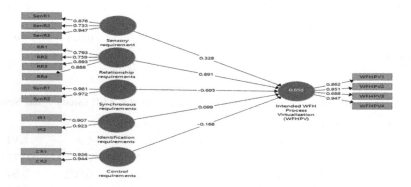

Fig. 3. PLS-SEM result showing β-coefficient and R-square values (Study-2)

Table 5. Statistical analysis outcome (Study-1)

Constructs	β coefficients	P-value	Result
SR -> WFHPV	−0.460	<0.001	H1:Supported
RR -> WFHPV	−0.097	<0.05	H2:Supported
SynR -> WFHPV	−0.280	<0.05	H3:Supported
IR -> WFHPV	0.586	<0.001	H4:Not supported
CR -> WFHPV	0.522	<0.001	H5:Not supported

Table 6. Statistical analysis outcome (Study-2)

Constructs	β coefficients	P-value	Result
SR -> WFHPV	0.328	<0.001	H1:Not supported
RR -> WFHPV	0.891	<0.001	H2:Not supported
SynR -> WFHPV	−0.695	<0.001	H3:Supported
IR -> WFHPV	0.099	<0.01	H4:Not supported
CR -> WFHPV	−0.168	<0.001	H5:Supported

6 Discussion

This paper takes the increasing use of ICT-enabled virtualization of WFH as motivation and uses a theoretical foundation of PVT to understand the context driven dynamic factors influencing intended virtualization of WFH process. Being one of the recent IS theories, this research provides novel empirical setting for a native IS theoretical lens that remains untested so far in WFH context in general and in particular assesses the context driven dynamic factors influencing intended virtualization of WFH process. Upon analysis, findings from Study-1 are mostly in agreement to the original PVT and other prior studies (Barth and Veit 2011b; Overby 2008; Balci et al. 2013; Balci and Rosenkranz 2014). Whereas results from Study-2 show that sensory requirements, relationship requirements and identification requirements are enablers of intended virtualization of WFH process. Although one of the previous studies (Graupner and Maedche 2015) found positive relation for synchronism requirements construct but outcomes of the Study-2 are in contrast to the original PVT and other prior studies (Barth and Veit 2011b; Overby 2008; Balci et al. 2013; Balci and Rosenkranz 2014) which have reported negative relations for above constructs.

The result is intelligible for a WFH process virtualization context. Conventionally, presence and need of physical interaction discourages a participant in a virtual process to establish a sensory connection to objects and/or participants (Overby 2008). This is well supported in Study-1 relating to sensory requirements. In pandemic era, the nature of work is increasingly remote, online, stress free and safer. Considering the mandate to maintain physical distancing (Harris et al. 2020) as one of the evident choices left before organizations in the pandemic age, higher sensory requirements, as found in Study-2, relating to touch, see, hear, smell, and taste rather facilitated the ICT-enabled virtualization of WFH process. Likewise, as a general acceptance, physical environments usually have established and stronger relationships. This is well supported in Study-1 relating to relationship requirements. Considering social distancing (Harris et al. 2020), which refers in this context a set of measures established to avoid the spread of a contagious disease by keeping a physical distance among people and decreasing the frequency of people coming into close contact with one another especially at workplace, as an obvious choice available for organizations amid corona crisis, higher relationship requirements, as found in Study-2, rather turned as enabler to the ICT-enabled virtualization of WFH process. As defined in original PVT (Overby 2008), synchronism requirements is the degree to which the activities in a process need to occur quickly with minimal delay. Both the studies have found worthy support to this end.

Increasing adoption of various face to face communication technologies by organizations in recent times has narrowed the scope of identity spoofing and real time recognition system has also diluted several identification issues integrated in the organizational work portfolio. The hypothesis relating to identification requirements is therefore stable and not supported in both the studies. As hypothesized, Study-2 found support for control requirements which demonstrates that capability to regulate the behavior of WFH process participants outweigh the degree to which process participants need credentials of other process participants.

To effectively increase technology enabled virtualization, organizations should understand the type of determinants that drive and motivate employees to conduct services through WFH virtualized process. As such, availability of single pane of glass access to all services, intensive networking and socializing, seamless access to data, upgraded equipment and Internet connectivity, all the support when and where needed, strong security, ability to use any app, on any device, anytime, from anywhere without inconvenience altogether seem to have diluted the motivation of resistance of discussed constructs to ICT-enabled intended virtualization of WFH process.

6.1   Theoretical Contributions and Practical Implications

Present study aims to contribute to the restricted number of studies on virtualization of processes (Barth and Veit 2011a and b; Balci and Rosenkranz 2014; Graupner and Maedche 2015; Ofoeda et al. 2018). Specifically, this is the first study to contribute elaborated insights on ICT-enabled virtualization of work-from-home process, largely to the body of knowledge on virtualization of processes, workforce engagement, and associated factors like sensory, relationship, synchronous, identification and control requirements on the remote working. By exploring the behavior of context dependent determinants relating to process virtualization in remote working, the learning outcomes also deepen deliberations on the quality, involvement, delivery and execution of virtual processes across firms. To this end, present study contributes greatly to the body of knowledge in remote working under full virtual setting with emphasis on extended flexibility for employees and organizations, improved productivity, lower absenteeism, better employee retention, extended cost control, along with more general social benefits. This benefits scholars understand behavior of each construct separately as no evidence exists about their interrelationships. Moreover, this research also assesses the behavior of derived factors and categorizes them into context-resistant stable factor(s) and context-driven dynamic factor(s), thereby contributing to the body of knowledge in dynamic capability of firms, especially relating to remote working. Such dynamic capabilities, if attained by the organizations, in terms of crafting, fine-tuning, implementation, and renovation into the design and set-up of business models, may exploit their ability to assimilate, build, and reconfigure internal competences leading to changes in the business environment thereby making them able to redesign and adjust business models and preserve cost-effectiveness over the long term (Teece 2018). Other than research, this study, by informing the management of organizations and key policymakers, also provided significant contributions to practice as it could equip practitioners with extended information on what employees intend virtualization of processes and how they can maximize benefit out of it, both under normal circumstances and in context driven testing times. At present, pandemic has augmented the volatility, uncertainty, complexity and ambiguity (VUCA) all around the technological as well as social setting (Saleh and Watson 2017). Since VUCA landscape is still unpredictable (Fletcher and Griffiths 2020), so practitioners, amid pandemic crisis, can also utilize the discussed setting to measure varying processes and sub-processes under WFH virtualization for their amenability by considering their process characteristics.

6.2 Limitations and Directions for Future Research

Given the context driven dynamic nature of factors proposed in PVT, future research can complement the model proposed here to conceptualize and validate the discussed relationships in the virtualization of similar processes under different contexts. Moreover, scholars could also examine the impact of demographic characteristics relating to different firms across industries on the process virtualization of remote working. Furthermore, future studies can assess the generalizability of findings of this study under 'new normal' settings. Finally, the outcomes of this study can be useful to explore other settings where complete physical process can be virtualized using information and communication technology, like in service sector organizations.

7 Conclusion

Primarily, to fill the gaps in empirical knowledge, this research has established a setting for advancing understanding of virtualization of work from home (WFH) process using process virtualization theory (PVT). Pandemic has made process virtualization obligatory for all sectors, especially business organizations. ICT-enabled virtualization of processes is not considered now as an option or an available add-on that may be used when required rather it is becoming a need towards attaining digital maturity as early as possible. Therefore the enablers and inhibitors found in this study together may be motivations to anticipate business organizations and their workforces to experiment with this form of work process, predominantly given the speedy growth of advance information and communication technologies. These motivations include improved flexibility for organizations and employees, improved productivity, quicker responsiveness to the needs and unexpected man-made and natural disasters, lower absenteeism, improved employee retention, greater cost control, along with more general social benefits. Being only empirical study conducted so far in this context, the results enrich the existing knowledge domain by providing unique and elaborated understanding of the context dependent influencing factors that impact intended ICT-enabled virtualization of processes in employee's WFH process. Other than research, this study also provided significant contributions to practice as it could equip practitioners with extended information on what employees intend virtualization of processes and how they can maximize benefit out of it, especially in testing times. Practitioners, amid COVID-19 crisis, can also utilize the discussed model to measure varying processes and sub-processes under WFH virtualization for their amenability by considering their process characteristics.

References

Agrawal, K.: Investigating the determinants of big data analytics (BDA) adoption in emerging economies. Acad. Manag. Proc. **2015**(1), 11290 (2015)

Ajzen, I., Driver, B.L.: Application of the theory of planned behavior in leisure choice. J. Leisure Res. **24**, 207–224 (1992)

Alvaro, M., de Assis, G., Fernando, L.: Lessons learned from September 11th: telework as an organizational resource to the business continuity planning. Jpn. J. Telework **1**, 46–51 (2011)

Baker, E., Avery, G.C., Crawford, J.: Satisfaction and perceived productivity when professionals work from home. Res. Pract. Hum. Resour. Manag. **15**(1), 37–62 (2007)

Balci, B., Rosenkranz, C.: Virtual or material, what do you prefer? In: Twenty Second European Conference on Information Systems, Tel Aviv (2014)

Barth, M., Veit, D.: Electronic service delivery in the public sector: understanding the variance of citizens' resistance. In: Hawaii International Conference on System Sciences, Kauai, Hawaii, pp. 1–11 (2011a)

Barth, M., Veit, D.: Which processes do users not want online?: extending the process virtualization theory. In: Thirty Second International Conference on Information Systems, Shanghai (2011b)

Baruch, Y., Yuen, Y.: Inclination to opt for teleworking – a comparative analysis of United Kingdom versus Hong Kong employees. Int. J. Manpower **21**(7), 521–539 (2000)

Beaudry, A., Pinsonneault, A.: Understanding user responses to information technology: a coping model of user adaptation. MIS Q. **29**(3), 493–524 (2005)

Davis, F.D.: Perceived usefulness, perceived ease of use, and user acceptance of information technology. MIS Q. **13**(3), 319–340 (1989)

Dennis, A.R., Wixom, B.H., Vandenberg, R.J.: Understanding fit and appropriation effects in group support systems via meta-analysis. Manag. Inf. Syst. Q. **25**(2), 167–193 (2001)

Dwivedi, Y.K., Rana, N.P., Jeyaraj, A., et al.: Re-examining the unified theory of acceptance and use of technology (UTAUT): towards a revised theoretical model. Inf. Syst. Front. **21**, 719–734 (2017). https://doi.org/10.1007/s10796-017-9774-y

Fletcher, G., Griffiths, M.: Digital transformation during a lockdown. Int. J. Inf. Manag. (2020). https://doi.org/10.1016/j.ijinfomgt.2020.102185

Goodhue, D.L., Thompson, R.L.: Task-technology fit and individual performance. MIS Q. **19**(2), 213–236 (1995)

Graupner, E., Maedche, A.: Process digitisation in retail banking: an empirical examination of process virtualization theory. Int. J. Electron. Bus. **12**(4), 364–379 (2015)

Hair, J.F., Hult, G.T.M., Ringle, C.M., Sarstedt, M.: A Primer on Partial Least Squares Structural Equation Modeling (PLS-SEM), 2nd edn. Sage, Thousand Oaks (2017)

Harris et al.: COVID-19 (PDF). World Health Organization. Archived (PDF) from the original on 25 March 2020 (2020). Accessed 29 Mar 2020

Kim, H., Karpova, E.: Consumer attitudes toward fashion counterfeits: application of the theory of planned behaviour. Cloth. Text. Res. J. **28**(2), 79–94 (2010)

Kim, H.-W., Kankanhalli, A.: Investigating user resistance to information systems implementation: a status quo bias perspective. MIS Q. **33**(3), 567–582 (2009)

Likert, R.: A technique for the measurement of attitudes. Archives of Psychology (1932)

Morgan, R.: Teleworking: an assessment of the benefits and challenges. Eur. Bus. Rev. **16**(4), 344–357 (2004)

Donnelly, N., Sarah, B.: Disrupted work: home-based teleworking (HbTW) in the aftermath of a natural disaster. New Technol. Work Employ. **30**, 47–61 (2015). https://doi.org/10.1111/ntwe.12040

Ofoeda, J., et al.: Virtualization of government-to-citizen engagement process: enablers and constraints. Electron. J. Inf. Syst. Dev. Countries **84**, 1–16 (2018). https://doi.org/10.1002/isd2.12037

Overby, E.: Process virtualization theory and the impact of information technology. Organ. Sci. **19**(2), 277–291 (2008). https://doi.org/10.1287/orsc.1070.0316

Overby, E., Slaughter, S., Konsynski, B.: The design, use, and consequences of virtual processes. Inf. Syst. Res. **21**(4), 700–710 (2010)

Roukis, G.: Globalization, organizational opaqueness and conspiracy. J. Manag. Dev. **25**(10), 970–980 (2006)

Roberts, S., Daker, I.: Using information and innovation to reduce costs and enable better solutions. J. Corp. Real Estate **6**(3), 227–236 (2004)

Saleh, A., Watson, R.: Business excellence in a volatile, uncertain, complex and ambiguous environment (BEVUCA). TQM J. **29**(5), 705–724 (2017)

Sanchez, A., Perez, M., Luis Carnicer, P., Jimenez, M.: Teleworking and workplace flexibility: a study of impact on firm performance. Pers. Rev. **36**(1), 42–64 (2007)

Scholefield, G., Peel, S.: Managers' attitudes to teleworking. N. Z. J. Employ. Relat. **34**(3), 1–13 (2009)

Siha, S., Monroe, R.: Telecommuting's Past and future: a research agenda. Bus. Process Manag. J. **12**(4), 455–482 (2006)

Teece, D.J.: Business models and dynamic capabilities. Long Range Plan. **51**, 40–49 (2018)

van Winden, W., Woets, P.: Urban broadband internet policies in Europe: a critical review. Urban Stud. **41**(10), 2043–2059 (2004)

Venkatesh, V., Morris, M.G., Davis, G.B., Davis, F.D.: User acceptance of information technology: toward a unified view. MIS Q. **27**(3), 425–478 (2003)

Psychological Determinants of Consumer's Usage, Satisfaction, and Word-of-Mouth Recommendations Toward Smart Voice Assistants

Anubhav Mishra[1]([⊠]) [iD] and Anuja Shukla[2] [iD]

[1] Jaipuria Institute of Management, Lucknow, India
anu.mishra@gmail.com, Anubhav.mishra@jaipuria.ac.in
[2] Noida International University, Greater Noida, India
anuja.gshukla@gmail.com

Abstract. AI-based voice assistant (VA) technologies are facing an unprecedented growth. VA are available as a standalone device like Amazon Echo dot or Google home and also as an extension such as Google maps and OK Google. Extant research has mostly focused on the device specific characteristics to explain the adoption of VA. In this research, we take a different approach and examine the psychological determinants of VA adoption. We look at how factors such as playfulness, escapism, anthropomorphism, and visual appeal of VA influence the attitudes (hedonic and utilitarian) of consumers. Moreover, we also examine the effects of psychological characteristics of VA on usage intentions and satisfaction, which lead to a favorable word-of-mouth (WOM) behavior that is critical for adoption of a technology. Using a structural equation modeling approach, our results suggest that psychological factors have a significant positive influence on both attitudes. Hedonic attitude further influences satisfaction and utilitarian attitude positively impacts usage and satisfaction, which have a positive association with WOM. Our research offers useful insights to marketers to increase the VA adoption and makes contributions to the literature.

Keywords: Smart voice assistant · Psychological factors · Word-of-mouth

1 Introduction

Rapid technological advancements have given rise to various innovative products which fulfils the need of the modern era consumer. Every decade sees a change in how humans interact with the technology. The journey has computers has followed evolution from desktop to world wide web, to mobile phones, to touch screen and now smart phones and smart devices to block chain technology (Hughes et al. 2019). The penetration level of these smart products differ according to the adoption and diffusion rate of these technologies in developing and developed economies across the globe. After the COVID-19 pandemic the dependence of human race on AI (Artificial Intelligence) based products and services have increased many fold due to social

© IFIP International Federation for Information Processing 2020
Published by Springer Nature Switzerland AG 2020
S. K. Sharma et al. (Eds.): TDIT 2020, IFIP AICT 617, pp. 274–283, 2020.
https://doi.org/10.1007/978-3-030-64849-7_24

distancing norms, sanitization issues and growth in work from home culture. The role of AI has significantly increased in the field of management (Dwivedi et al. 2019) and marketing in the recent times although it is widely used in other sciences for more than half a century (Jarek and Mazurek 2019). The large amount of data present online through smart phone devices or big data systems makes AI an important part of marketing research conducted by various online shopping or service providers portal. According to Oxford Dictionary, AI is "the theory and development of computer systems able to perform tasks normally requiring human intelligence, such as visual perception, speech recognition, decision-making, and translation between languages" ("Definition of artificial intelligence in English by Oxford Dictionaries", 2019). With the development in the field of artificial intelligence new technologies are being offered to the consumers in the form of voice, text and image recognition, autonomous vehicles and robots. The practical application of voice recognition is available in smart phones (e.g. Google Assistant). The current research focuses on smart Voice-interaction technologies such as smart speakers like Google Home and Alexa. The word "Smart" refers to "self-monitoring analysis and reporting technology."

Extant research in technology adoption mostly focuses on the usefulness and ease of use factors that are specific to device characteristics (Alalwan et al. 2017). In a recent research, Dwivedi et al. (2019) propose that attitudinal disposition toward technology is vital in influencing the behavioral tendencies to adopt technology. Psychological factors that appeal to hedonic experience (e.g., visual appeal or playfulness) significantly influence the adoption of emerging technologies like virtual reality and augmented reality (Demirkan and Spohrer 2014). However, research on impact of such factors in context of smart voice assistant is in nascent stage (Hughes et al. 2019). We try to address this research gap in present study. We look at the antecedents to the attitudes (hedonic and utilitarian) to examine the adoption and usage behavior. The purpose of this research is to investigate the impact of psychological factors such as anthropomorphism, playfulness, visual appeal, and escapism on usage and satisfaction with smart voice assistants. Furthermore, we also look at the word of mouth (WOM) recommendation, because a positive WOM increases the changes of technology diffusion (Dwivedi et al. 2019).

2   Literature Review

2.1   Smart Consumers

Consumers are co creating and experiencing the latest smart technologies in services context like hospitality and tourism (Neuhofer et al. 2015) and retail (Pantano and Naccarato 2010). The term 'Smart' represents the social, economic and technological advancements driven by rapid innovations in information and communication and connected technologies (Demirkan and Spohrer 2014). Smart technology is defined as 'value-creating connected and synchronised smart objects or devices that interact with one another, sense the environment, and guide and control their functions autonomously' (Roy et al. 2017). The active users who voluntarily extend efforts to directly help others in the smart service scape are referred to as 'smart consumers'. The extant literature have been developed to understand the variables of consumer experience co-creation. However, the literature is still at an initial stage in understanding the conceptual relationships of 'smart consumer' experience co-creation. Although there has been a lot of research concerning brand equity and customer experience (Kumar et al. 2018), none has been able to connect it to the smart services context and specifically to smart consumers.

2.2   Smart Technologies

Infusion of smartness into different contexts has been a recent trend, with some prominent examples including smart tourism (Neuhofer et al. 2015), smart retailing (Roy et al. 2017), smart cities (Letaifa 2015). The extant marketing literature defines the smart technology environment as the platform where several smart devices are consistently working for consumers to live with greater comfort (Cook and Das 2004). But in fact at the heart of the smart environment is not the devices, but the users, referred to as smart consumers (Mavrommati and Darzentas 2006). Chen et al. (2018) define smart consumers as those consumers who voluntarily engage and are competent to participate in experience sharing. User experience sharing behaviour may be defined as 'customers initiation effort made for the direct benefit of others in their service network' (Chen et al. 2018).

2.3   Smart Voice Assistant and Psychological Factors

Smart voice assistants play an important role in understanding consumer the consumer faces several trust issues in its adoption (Foehr and Germelmann 2020). Smart voice assistants work on the philosophy of capability, context, dependence, multidimensionality, separability, and applicability (Alter 2019). A voice assistant may be termed as smart voice assistant if it can: Capture information, Transmit information, Store information, Retrieve information, Manipulate information, Display information (Alter 2019). Chatbots provides engaging and interactive customer service (Chung et al. 2018). Smart voice interaction technologies (SVIT) are also termed as voice user interfaces (Kendall et al. 2020). Consumers use SVIT for three kinds of interaction: looking up, learning and leisure (Kendall et al. 2020).

Research has shown that today, consumers are not only willing to accept SVITs but also build various types of relationships with the devices. At the same time, prominent SVITs like smart speakers (e.g., Amazon Echo, Google Home) have sparked privacy and data security concerns of consumers, suggesting that the adoption of such smart technologies require considerable levels of consumer trust. Although research shows a considerable understanding of factors influencing smart technology adoption and the relationship types that result from consumer–smart technology interaction, implications on how consumers initially develop and afterwards maintain trust in these smart technologies is scarce.

Despite the recent research interest in SVITs in the fields of human-computer–interaction, consumer behaviour, and marketing (e.g., Ehret and Wirtz 2017; Verhoef et al. 2017), the definition for smart technology with voice - interaction functions is not very clear. Researchers are having different opinions for it. From the literature three categories of definitions can be identified. First, there are definitions that conceptualize SVITs mainly with reference to their underlying software components or computational infrastructure, for example, natural language processing, artificial intelligence (AI), or cloud computing (e.g., Luger and Sellen 2016; Cho 2018; Lopatovska and Williams 2018; Myers et al. 2018). Second, researchers conceptualize SVITs by discovering their possible range of abilities (e.g., online shopping or controlling other smart devices; Cowan et al. 2017; Li and Lee 2017; Manikonda et al. 2017; Porcheron et al. 2017; Chen and Wang 2018; Knote et al. 2018; Santos et al. 2018). Third, another category of definitions conceptualizes SVITs by relating the concept with consumer technologies available in the market, such as Amazon's Alexa or Apple's Siri (Moorthy and Vu 2014; Kiseleva et al. 2016; Vyturina et al. 2017; Lopatovska et al. 2018).

To respond to their users' vocal requests, SVITs are equipped with highly sensitive always-on microphones that scan their spatial environment for predefined activation terms (e.g., "Alexa", "Hey, Google"). This always-on feature of SVITs has raised serious privacy and data security concerns. It has thus been argued by researchers that SVITs constitute an element within a larger economic order of what has been termed "surveillance capitalism". Anthropomorphism is another psychological mechanism explaining the adoption and diffusion of smart speakers can be found in the voice based interaction mode between consumers and SVITs (Bort 2016). Consumers tend to anthropomorphize objects and products, meaning that they ascribe uniquely human like attributes, cognitive patterns, intentions, motivations, and emotions to non-human entities, such as technology. Consumers have been found to exhibit a tendency to anthropomorphize objects particularly if they are alone (i.e., if they desire social interaction) and have a need for affection toward their environment. With regard to SVITs, this latter motivation is of particular importance, it is closely connected with consumers' desire to explain, predict and eventually master a technology within its environment. This means that SVIT users who are not aware or bothered about the privacy concerns while interacting with them are more likely to anthropomorphize the technology.

In response to consumer tendencies to humanize SVITs, marketers of smart technologies implemented tactics in their persuasion repertoire that facilitate the anthropomorphism of products (Aggarwal and McGill 2011). Researchers argue that this is also the case for SVITs such as smart speakers. First, the voice-based mode of consumer–technology interaction facilitates consumer tendencies to anthropomorphize the technology, given that this mode of interaction is usually reserved for human-to-human exchange. Second, the naming of the voice-interaction software with which users of smart speakers interact, often suggests human like associations, like "Alexa" or "Siri". While Amazon's software developers justify their choice of the term "Alexa" as a "wake word" (note the anthropomorphic suggestion implicitly included here) because of its rarity as a first name and its special combination of soft vowels and the letter x (Bort 2016), the fact that the software was given a female first name particularly activates anthropomorphism. These anthropomorphic associations are emphasized in advertising of the Alexa. In video commercials, the smart speakers are not marketed on the basis of their technical specifications. Instead, the idea of SVIT as a helpful humanoid is conveyed. "Alexa" is thus portrayed as more than essentially a collection of software codes, constituting a "happy helper" within the private parts of consumers' day-to-day lives (Phan 2018).

In humanizing technology, consumers not only consider anthropomorphic cues but regard technologies as social actors with which they form interpersonal relationships. Consumer culture theory has recently shown increased interest in the characteristics and dynamics of these interpersonal consumer–smart technology relationships Although Schweitzer et al.'s work (2019) provides a good overview of the different types of relationships between consumers and SVIT, it disregards contextual influences on consumer–smart technology relationships (as proposed in Verhoef et al. 2017 and Woodall et al. 2018) and does not explain how trust in smart technologies and relationships may co-develop.

3   Conceptual Model

Recent research suggests that attitude is a critical antecedent to technology usage and adoption behavior (Dwivedi et al. 2019). In our research we include two aspects of attitude – hedonic and utilitarian to examine the influence of both attitudes on usage and satisfaction with technology (see Fig. 1). In this study, we explore the device characteristics and psychological benefits of using voice assisted devices that form the attitude which leads to usage and satisfaction with the technology (Alalwan et al. 2017). Moreover, word-of-mouth recommendations are vital for information diffusion and technology adoption (Mishra et al. 2018). We also analyze the impact of usage behavior and satisfaction on WOM intentions that may help us to understand the further adoption of voice assistants.

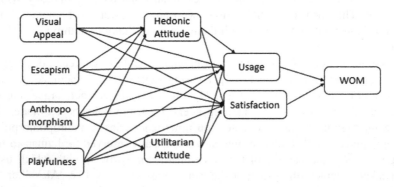

Fig. 1. Conceptual model

We propose the following hypotheses based on the conceptual model-

H1: Visual appeal is positively related with (a) Hedonic Attitude, (b) Usage, and (c) Satisfaction.
H2: Escapism is positively related with (a) Hedonic Attitude, (b) Usage, and (c) Satisfaction.

H3: Anthropomorphism is positively related with (a) Hedonic Attitude, (b) Utilitarian Attitude, (c) Usage, and (d) Satisfaction.

H4: Playfulness is positively related with (a) Hedonic Attitude, (b) Utilitarian Attitude, (c) Usage, and (d) Satisfaction.

H5: Hedonic attitude is positively related with (a) Usage and (b) Satisfaction.

H6: Utilitarian attitude is positively related with (a) Usage and (b) Satisfaction.

H7: Usage behavior is positively related to word-of-mouth intentions.

H8: Satisfaction is positively related to word-of-mouth intentions.

4   Research Methodology

The questionnaire was designed using standard items from the past literature. The data was collected online. Two video that reflect the meaning of smart voice assistant were inserted in the google form. The data was analyzed using PLS SEM technique. A total of 120 valid responses have been used in the analysis (65% males, average age 25.5 years). We used income and employment status as control variables in this study.

5   Data Analysis

5.1   Measurement Model

We tested for reliability and validity indices as recommended in extant research. All the outer loadings are above 0.8, AVE is above 0.5, and Composite reliability is more than 0.7 (Hair et al. 2016). All VIF values are less than 5, and HTMT values (discriminant validity) are less than 0.9 (Hair et al. 2016). Thus, we conclude that the measurement model is valid and reliable.

5.2   Structural Model

The structural model was evaluated using bias corrected bootstrapping resampling procedure at 5000 sub samples. The results are given in Table 1. First hypothesis had three sub parts. Impact of visual appeal on hedonic attitude (H1a, $\beta = 0.01$, p = 0.97) was found to be insignificant where as other two hypotheses (H1b, H1c) which suggested impact of visual appeal on Usage ($\beta = 0.18, p = 0.08$) and satisfaction ($\beta = 0.3$, p = 0.02) were found to be significant. Escapism significantly impacted hedonic attitude (H2a, $\beta = 0.18$, p = 0.03) and satisfaction (H2b, $\beta = 0.22, p = 0.02$) but had no impact on usage ($\beta = 0.1$, p = 0.16). Hedonic and utilitarian attitude was significantly impacted by Anthromorphism (H3a, $\beta = 0.29$, p = 0.049; H4a, $\beta = 0.37$, p = 0.003) and playfulness (H3b, $\beta = 0.37$, p = 0.003, H4c, $\beta = 0.53$, p < .001). Impact of Anthromorphism was not significant on usage (H3c, $\beta = -0.07$, p = 0.57) but impact of playfulness was found to be significant on usage (H4c, $\beta = 0.53$, p < .001). H3d and H5awere insignificant whereas H4b, H4d, H5b, H6a, H6b, H7 and H8 were supported (see Table 1).

Table 1. Hypothesis results

Hypo.	Relationship	Path coefficient	p value	Supported
H1a	Visual Appeal -> Hedonic Attitude	0.01	0.97	No
H1b	Visual Appeal -> Usage	0.18	0.08	Yes
H1c	Visual Appeal -> Satisfaction	0.3	0.02	Yes
H2a	Escapism -> Hedonic Attitude	0.18	0.03	Yes
H2b	Escapism -> Usage	0.10	0.16	No
H2c	Escapism -> Satisfaction	0.22	0.02	Yes
H3a	Anthropomorphism -> Hedonic Attitude	0.29	0.049	Yes
H3b	Anthropomorphism -> Utilitarian Attitude	0.37	0.003	Yes
H3c	Anthropomorphism -> Usage	−0.07	0.57	No
H3d	Anthropomorphism -> Satisfaction	0.01	0.96	No
H4a	Playfulness -> Hedonic Attitude	0.27	0.05	Yes
H4b	Playfulness -> Utilitarian Attitude	0.25	0.03	Yes
H4c	Playfulness -> Usage	0.53	<.001	Yes
H4d	Playfulness -> Satisfaction	0.36	0.002	Yes
H5a	Hedonic Attitude -> Usage	−0.22	0.12	No
H5b	Hedonic Attitude -> Satisfaction	0.33	0.01	Yes
H6a	Utilitarian Attitude -> Usage	0.34	0.02	Yes
H6b	Utilitarian Attitude -> Satisfaction	0.21	0.08	Yes
H7	Usage -> WOM	0.24	0.03	Yes
H8	Satisfaction -> WOM	0.56	<.001	Yes

6   Discussion and Implications

Prior research suggests that smart voice interaction technology (SVIT) is more used by the smart phone users in comparison to smart speaker users (Foehr and Germelmann 2020). The number of individuals who have tried voice assistants on smart phones is 146.6 million compared to more than 50 million for smart speakers (Voice assistant consumer adoption report 2018). Consumers view voice assistants on smart phones as utilities first, for example, the convenience of voice interactions for searching or asking for directions has replaced the touch interaction with the smart phones.

The findings suggest that psychological acceptance and gratifications derived from SVITs are critical antecedents to the hedonic and utilitarian attitude toward technology usage. Users find SVITs playful, they enjoy the experience, and use SVIT as an escape mechanism. Users perceive these devices having certain element of human and interact accordingly. The results reveal that hedonic attitude may not lead to usage but influence satisfaction, whereas utilitarian attitude lead to usage and satisfaction. Users are more likely to recommend SVIT when they are satisfied with the device.

Our study reaffirms the findings of Dwivedi et al. (2019) about the importance of attitude in technology usage behavior. The novel contribution of this study is to cement the role of psychological aspects in technology usage. We integrate elements from sociology and psychology research to arrive at antecedents to attitudinal parameters.

The design and human like appeal of SVIT can improve the chances of adoption. Hence, we suggest marketers to stress these two aspects in their communication to users for increasing the usage and satisfaction. Voice assistants provide elements of playfulness and a new fantasy world where users talk to them as humans. We believe that firms should try to make the interactions with SVIT more human like to make consumers engages and satisfied.

7 Limitations

Out study has certain limitations. We accept that the sample size is low, but since the data collection is still in process, we are hopeful to have a relatively larger sample size in few weeks that should add to robustness and generalizability of results. We did not specifically looked at the language aspect of voice assistants. In India, users use a variety of languages, which SVIT may not be able to interpret at times leading to dissatisfaction. Further research can examine the role of interactions using multiple languages. Another interesting extension could be the impact of gender of voice assistant and how it affects the users' attitudes and behavior.

References

Alalwan, A.A., Dwivedi, Y.K., Rana, N.P.: Factors influencing adoption of mobile banking by Jordanian bank customers: extending UTAUT2 with trust. Int. J. Inf. Manag. **37**(3), 99–110 (2017)

Aggarwal, P., McGill, A.L.: When brands seem human, do humans act like brands? Automatic behavioral priming effects and brand anthropomorphism. J. Consum. Res. **39**(2), 307–323 (2011)

Alter, S.: Making sense of smartness in the context of smart devices and smart systems. Inf. Syst. Front. **22**, 1–13 (2019)

Bort, B.: Amazon engineers had one good reason and one geeky reason for choosing the name Alexa. Business Insider (2016). https://www.businessinsider.de/why-amazon-called-it-alexa-2016-7?r=US&IR=T. Accessed 27 July 2019

Chen, M.-L., Wang, H.-C.: How personal experience and technical knowledge affect using conversational agents. In: IUI 2018 Companion Proceedings of the 23rd International Conference on Intelligent User Interfaces Companion, Article 53. ACM, New York (2018)

Cho, J.: Mental models and home virtual assistants (HVAs). In: Regan, M., Mark, H. (eds.) CHI EA 2018 Extended Abstracts of the 2018 CHI Conference on Human Factors in Computing Systems, Paper No. SRC05. ACM, New York (2018)

Chung, M., Ko, E., Joung, H., Kim, S.J.: Chatbot e-service and customer satisfaction regarding luxury brands. J. Bus. Res. **117**, 587–595 (2018)

Cook, D., Das, S.K.: Smart Environments: Technology, Protocols, and Applications, vol. 43. Wiley (2004)

Cowan, B.R., et al.: 'What can i help you with?': Infrequent users' experiences of intelligent personal assistants. In: Jones, M., Tscheligi, M. (eds.) MobileHCI 2017 Proceedings of the 19th International Conference on Human-Computer Interaction with Mobile Devices and Services, Article Number 43. ACM, New York (2017)

Demirkan, H., Spohrer, J.: Developing a framework to improve virtual shopping in digital malls with intelligent self-service systems. J. Retail. Consum. Serv. **21**(5), 860–868 (2014)

Dwivedi, Y.K., et al.: Artificial Intelligence (AI): multidisciplinary perspectives on emerging challenges, opportunities, and agenda for research, practice and policy. Int. J. Inf. Manag. 101994 (2019). https://www.sciencedirect.com/science/article/abs/pii/S026840121930917X

Dwivedi, Y.K., Rana, N.P., Jeyaraj, A., Clement, M., Williams, M.D.L.: Re-examining the unified theory of acceptance and use of technology (UTAUT): towards a revised theoretical model. Inf. Syst. Front. **21**(3), 719–734 (2019)

Ehret, M., Wirtz, J.: Unlocking value from machines: business models and the industrial Internet of Things. J. Mark. Manag. **33**(1–2), 111–130 (2017)

Foehr, J., Germelmann, C.C.: Alexa, can I trust you? Exploring consumer paths to trust in smart voice-interaction technologies. J. Assoc. Consum. Res. **5**(2), 181–205 (2020)

Hair Jr., J.F., Hult, G.T.M., Ringle, C., Sarstedt, M.: A Primer on Partial Least Squares Structural Equation Modeling (PLS-SEM). Sage Publications, Newcastle upon Tyne (2016)

Hughes, L., Dwivedi, Y.K., Misra, S.K., Rana, N.P., Raghavan, V., Akella, V.: Block-chain research, practice and policy: applications, benefits, limitations, emerging research themes and research agenda. Int. J. Inf. Manag. **49**, 114–129 (2019)

Jarek, K., Mazurek, G.: Marketing and artificial intelligence. Cent. Eur. Bus. Rev. **8**(2), 46–55 (2019)

Kendall, L., Chaudhuri, B., Bhalla, A.: Understanding technology as situated practice: everyday use of voice user interfaces among diverse groups of users in urban India. Inf. Syst. Front. **22**, 1–21 (2020)

Kiseleva, J., et al.: Understanding user satisfaction with intelligent assistants. In: Kelly, D., Capra, R. (eds.) CHIIR 2016 Proceedings of the 2016 ACM on Conference on Human Information Interaction and Retrieval, pp. 121–30. ACM, New York (2016)

Knote, R., Janson, A., Eigenbrod, L., Söllner, M.: The what and how of smart personal assistants: principles and application domains for IS research (2018)

Kumar, R.S., Dash, S., Malhotra, N.K.: The impact of marketing activities on service brand equity. Eur. J. Mark. **52**, 596–618 (2018)

Letaifa, S.B.: How to strategize smart cities: revealing the SMART model. J. Bus. Res. **68**(7), 1414–1419 (2015)

Li, J., Lee, Y.Y.: Multimodal interaction and believability: how can we design and evaluate the next generation of IPA? In: Hall, L.E., Flint, T., O'Hara, S., Turner, P. (eds.) Proceedings of the 31st International BCS Human Computer Interaction Conference (HCI 2017), Sunderland (2017). https://dblp.org/db/conf/bcshci/bcshci2017

Lopatovska, I., Williams, H.: Personification of the Amazon Alexa: BFF or a mindless companion. In: Shah, C., Belkin, N.J., Byström, K., Huang, J., Scholer, F. (eds.) Proceedings of the 2018 Conference on Human Information Interaction and Retrieval, pp. 265–68. ACM, New York (2018)

Luger, E., Sellen, A.: "Like having a really bad PA" the gulf between user expectation and experience of conversational agents. In: Proceedings of the 2016 CHI Conference on Human Factors in Computing Systems, pp. 5286–5297, May 2016

Manikonda, L., De Choudhury, M.: Modeling and understanding visual attributes of mental health disclosures in social media. In: Proceedings of the 2017 CHI Conference on Human Factors in Computing Systems, pp. 170–181 (2017)

Mavrommati, I., John, D.: An overview of AMI from a user centered design perspective. In: IET Proceedings of IE 2006, Athens (2006)

Moorthy, A.E., Vu, K.-P.L.: Voice activated personal assistant: acceptability of use in the public space. In: Yamamoto, S. (ed.) HCI 2014. LNCS, vol. 8522, pp. 324–334. Springer, Cham (2014). https://doi.org/10.1007/978-3-319-07863-2_32

Myers, C., Furqan, A., Nebolsky, J., Caro, K., Zhu, J.: Patterns for how users overcame obstacles in voice user interfaces. In: Regan, M., Mark, H. (eds.) CHI 2018 Proceedings of the 2018 CHI Conference on Human Factors in Computing Systems, Paper Number 6. ACM, New York (2018)

Mishra, A., Maheswarappa, S.S., Maity, M., Samu, S.: Adolescent's eWOM intentions: an investigation into the roles of peers, the Internet and gender. J. Bus. Res. **86**, 394–405 (2018)

Neuhofer, B., Buhalis, D., Ladkin, A.: Smart technologies for personalized experiences: a case study in the hospitality domain. Electron. Mark. **25**(3), 243–254 (2015)

Pantano, E., Naccarato, G.: Entertainment in retailing: the influences of advanced technologies. J. Retail. Consum. Serv. **17**(3), 200–204 (2010)

Phan, T.: Amazon echo and the aesthetics of whiteness, catalyst: feminism. Theory Technosci. **5**(1), 1–38 (2018)

Porcheron, M., Fischer, J.E., Sharples, S.: "Do animals have accents?" Talking with agents in multi-party conversation. In: Proceedings of the 2017 ACM Conference on Computer Supported Cooperative Work and Social Computing, pp. 207–219, February 2017

Roy, S.K., Balaji, M.S., Sadeque, S., Nguyen, B., Melewar, T.C.: Constituents and consequences of smart customer experience in retailing. Technol. Forecast. Soc. Change **124**, 257–270 (2017)

Santos, J., Rodrigues, J.J.P.C., Casal, J., Saleem, K., Denisov, V.: Intelligent personal assistants based on Internet of Things approaches. IEEE Syst. J. **12**(2), 1793–1802 (2018)

Verhoef, P.C., et al.: Consumer connectivity in a complex, technology-enabled, and mobile-oriented world with smart products. J. Interact. Mark. **40**, 1–8 (2017)

Voice assistant consumer adoption November: Rain Agency (2018). https://voicebot.ai/wp-content/uploads/2018/11/voice-assistant-consumer-adoption-report-2018-voicebot.pdf

Vyturina, A., Savenkov, D., Agichtein, E., Clarke, C.L.A.: Exploring conversational search with humans, assistants, and wizards. In: CHI EA 2017 Proceedings of the 2017 CHI Conference Extended Abstracts on Human Factors in Computing Systems, pp. 2187–2193. ACM, New York (2017)

Woodall, T., Julie, R., John, H.: Proposal, project, practice, pause: developing a framework for evaluating smart domestic product engagement. AMS Rev. **8**(1–2), 58–74 (2018)

Antecedents to Continuance Intention to Use eGovernment Services in India

Brinda Sampat[1]([⊠]) [iD] and Kali Charan Sabat[2] [iD]

[1] NMIMS Global Access School for Continuing Education, NMIMS University, V. L. Mehta Road, Vile Parle West, Mumbai, Maharashtra, India
brinda.sampat@nmims.edu
[2] GD Goenka University, GD Goenka Education City, Sohna—Gurgaon Rd., Sohna, Haryana, India
kalicharan.sabat@gmail.com

Abstract There are several studies that have examined the factors that determine users' attitude to adopt eGovernment services. However, there are not many studies that have explored what makes users continue to use these services. The purpose of this paper is to identify the most salient factors that influence users to continue to use eGovernment services in India. To achieve this, the paper examines the role of confirmation and satisfaction in influencing citizens' attitude leading to intention to continue using eGovernment services. In order to investigate the key factors that affect an individual's use of Information and Communication Technology (ICT) within the context of electronic government, a framework combining Expectation Confirmation Theory and Technology Acceptance Model is used to investigate satisfaction and continuity of use of eGovernment services.

Keywords: eGovernment · Satisfaction · Continuance intention · Trust · Attitude · India · Expectation confirmation theory · Technology acceptance model

1 Introduction

The term electronic Government or eGovernment refers to the use of Information and Communication Technology (ICT) to disseminate information and services to the citizens, businesses' and government agencies [15]. eGovernment is an initiative that provides a single point of access to all digital services [3]. eGovernment initiatives provide enormous benefits, but to realize these benefits citizens need to adopt these initiatives and continue to use them [11, 16]. Lack of adoption of these services hinders the benefits these services aim to provide [13]. There are certain challenges in implementing and rolling out eGovernment initiatives in India. There are a few studies that have empirically examined the factors influencing citizens' adoption of eGovernment systems [4]. Realizing a research gap in terms of an inclusive Information Technology (IT)/Information Systems (IS) research model that can help to understand the factors that help in continued usage of eGovernment services, this study aims to fill the gap. The present study attempts to identify the various factors which influence the intention of users to continue using eGovernment services.

© IFIP International Federation for Information Processing 2020
Published by Springer Nature Switzerland AG 2020
S. K. Sharma et al. (Eds.): TDIT 2020, IFIP AICT 617, pp. 284–291, 2020.
https://doi.org/10.1007/978-3-030-64849-7_25

The rest of the paper is organized as follows: The following section covers the literature review from recent studies in the context of eGovernment implementation. The next section covers the research methodology, analysis of the results and discussion. It also provides an agenda for future research.

2 Literature Review

The IS Continuance Model has been used to explore users continued use of an IS. A study by Bhattacherjee [14] revised the expectation confirmation theory (ECT) and included Perceived Usefulness from the Technology Acceptance Model (TAM) and users' satisfaction to predict continuance of eGovernment services. The TAM is the most extensively and dominant theoretical model for examining the individual's acceptance of information systems [12]. Perceived Usefulness (PU) and Perceived Ease of Use (PEOU) have consistently shown of having a positive and significant effect on shaping users' attitude, thereby affecting continuance intention. These two constructs have been included in the research model. Perceived Usefulness (PU) of an eGovernment service is the extent to which a citizen believes that using the online service will enhance his/her performance and efficiency. PU and PEOU have shown a positive effect on Attitude [13] leading to continuance Intention and Satisfaction [10]. This leads the researchers to hypothesize,

H1: Perceived Usefulness has a positive and significant effect on Satisfaction
H2: Perceived Usefulness has a positive and significant effect on Attitude
H3: Perceived Usefulness has a positive and significant effect on Continued Intention

Perceived Ease of Use (PEOU) of an eGovernment service is the extent to which a citizen believes that using an eGovernment service will be easy and will require less effort in performing any tasks. Many researchers have established a positive relation between PEOU and Perceived Usefulness [1] and PEOU and Attitude [6]. Thus, the researchers hypothesize,

H4: Perceived Ease of Use has a positive and significant effect on Perceived Usefulness
H5: Perceived Ease of Use has a positive and significant effect on Attitude

In ECT it has been proved via empirical studies that confirmation leads to satisfaction. His results suggested that it was feasible to apply ECT to the web context. Some related hypotheses were therefore formulated based on the baseline model of ECT.

H6: Confirmation has a positive and significant effect on Perceived Usefulness
H7: Confirmation has a positive and significant effect on Satisfaction

Satisfaction (SAT) is referred to as Users' feelings about prior eGovernment services use. Welch [18] found that government website use is positively associated with e-government satisfaction. Thus, the following hypotheses are proposed

H8: Satisfaction has a positive and significant effect on Attitude to use eGovernment services

H9: Satisfaction has a positive and significant effect on Continuance Intention to use eGovernment services

Attitude (ATT) is defined as "one's overall evaluation of self-performance regarding a particular behaviour". The favorable or unfavorable attitude affects the users' adoption intention regarding the outcome. BI was originally developed in the Theory of Planned Behavior (TPB) and Theory of Reasoned Action (TRA). When citizens hold a positive attitude towards using online service, they are more likely to express their willingness to use it. Hence, the researchers hypothesize,

H10: Attitude has a positive and significant effect on Continued Intention to use eGovernment services

Self-efficacy is the ability to carry out a task without anyone's help. It means a user is confident of carrying out his tasks of using the system on his own and that he need not depend on anyone. A citizen would thus choose to use eGovernment services, if he believes he has the knowledge and skills to carry out tasks using eGovernment services. This leads the researchers to hypothesize,

H11: Self-efficacy has a positive and significant effect on Continued Intention to use eGovernment services

Trust in eGovernment refers to the overall individual's reliability on eGovernment services. Lack of trust in an online system may hinder the adoption and continued use of online services. If a user trusts an eGovernment services, he/she will be more willing to avail the service and carry out transactions on it online. Studies in online adoption of services have demonstrated that trust enables people to exchange information online, share their personal details which will lead to greater adoption [2, 19]. Thus the researchers hypothesize,

H12: Trust in eGovernment has a positive and significant effect on Continued Intention to use eGovernment services

Figure 1 presents the conceptual model.

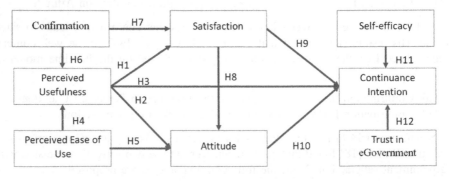

Fig. 1. Proposed research model

3   Methodology

This study aims to identify the factors that lead to users' continuance intention to use e-government services in India. To identify the drivers for the usage e-government services a conceptual model was developed by extending TAM to include confirmation, trust and social influence. The research process comprised of three steps. In the first step, a comprehensive literature review was performed to find appropriate variables that could extend TAM to better understand the consumers' continuance intention to use e-government services. Followed by the review of literature in the second step, an online survey instrument was developed and sent to randomly selected participants across the country. In the third step, a Partial Least Squares Structural Equation Model (PLS-SEM) was developed and tested using the Smart PLS 3 software.

For developing the data collection instrument for this study, established scale items were adopted from existing literature on online government services and TAM. These adopted scale items were further refined to fit into the context of this study. Before launching the survey the data collection instrument was pilot tested with few selected respondents. Based on the feedback received during the pilot testing the instrument was simplified for the better understanding of scale items by the respondents. After excluding a few items the final survey tool comprised of 32 items related to eight constructs were retained. All the items were measured using a five—point Likert scale, with anchors ranging from "Strongly disagree" (1) to "Strongly agree" (5).

The online survey was randomly distributed to 2000 individuals across the country. To improve the response rate, the initial mailing of surveys was followed by periodic reminder e-mails. Finally, 243 responses (a 12% response rate) were obtained. After rejecting 34 inappropriately filled responses, 209 filtered responses were separated for the purpose of data analysis. There are seven predictor variables (independent variables) in this study. According to Stevens [17], the sample size for social science research should be greater than 15 times the number of predictor variables. Hence, the required sample size should be greater than 105 (7×15). The number of filtered responses was twice the required sample size.

After screening the data, the study constructs were tested for the presence of multicollinearity, reliability and validity. To inspect if multicollinearity exists amongst the independent variables the inner and outer VIF values were calculated. All the VIF values for both the inner and outer model were well below the threshold value of 5 [15]. The inner VIF values are presented in Table 1 and the outer VIF values are presented in Table 2.

The evidence of construct reliability and validity is demonstrated in Table 3. The measure for consistent reliability coefficient Rho_A vary from 0.847 to 0.923 was consistently greater than the recommended value of 0.7, which indicates acceptable internal reliability for the dimensions [5]. The reliability levels (Cronbach's Alpha (CA) and Composite Reliability (CR)) of all the individual constructs exceeded the acceptable level greater than 0.75 demonstrating high internal consistency of the constructs [9]. The average of the item-to-factor loadings are higher than 0.70 [9] and the constructs indicated an Average Variance Extracted (AVE) value varying from 0.725 to 0.866, greater than the threshold value of 0.5, indicating convergent validity [7].

Table 1. Inner VIF

	Attitude	Continuance intention	Perceived usefulness	Satisfaction
Attitude		1.944		
Confirmation			1.648	
Continuance intention				
Perceived usefulness	1.575	2.417		1.000
Perceived ease of use			1.648	
Satisfaction	1.575	1.816		
Self efficacy		2.006		
Trust in eGovernment		1.768		

Table 2. Outer VIF

Items	VIF
ATT1	3.277
ATT2	3.721
ATT3	3.404
BI1	2.663
BI2	3.477
BI3	3.365
BI4	2.437
CON1	1.790
CON2	2.206
CON3	2.127
PEOU1	3.040
PEOU2	2.876
PEOU3	2.346
PEOU4	2.628
PEOU5	2.604
PU1	2.814
PU2	3.458
PU3	3.074
PU4	1.967
PU5	2.305
SAT1	2.651
SAT2	3.277
SAT3	3.171
SAT4	3.147
SEF1	2.221
SEF2	2.182
SEF3	2.180
SEF4	2.843
TRG1	2.857
TRG2	3.641
TRG3	2.707
TRG4	3.230

Table 3. Construct reliability and validity

Constructs	Cronbach's Alpha	Rho_A	Composite reliability	Average variance extracted (AVE)
Attitude	0.923	0.923	0.951	0.866
Confirmation	0.841	0.847	0.904	0.759
Continuance intention	0.915	0.915	0.940	0.796
Percieved usefulness	0.907	0.910	0.931	0.730
Percieved ease of use	0.908	0.909	0.932	0.732
Satisfaction	0.916	0.916	0.941	0.799
Self efficacy	0.874	0.878	0.913	0.725
Trust in eGovernment	0.915	0.921	0.940	0.797

To prove Discriminant validity the correlation between any two latent variables should be lower than the reliability of each of those variables [8]. The square root of AVE is used as the measure of reliability. All the latent variables for the conceptualized model had reliabilities greater than the correlations between any two constructs, indicating that each construct in the model was unique and distinct (Refer to Table 4).

Table 4. The Fornell-Larker criterion for discriminant validity

	Attitude	Confirmation	Continuance Intention	Perceived Usefulness	Perceived ease of use	Satisfaction	Self Efficacy	Trust in eGovernment
Attitude	**0.931***							
Confirmation	0.365	**0.871***						
Continuance Intention	0.620	0.527	**0.892***					
Perceived Usefulness	0.633	0.606	0.759	**0.855***				
Perceived ease of use	0.437	0.627	0.594	0.652	**0.855***			
Satisfaction	0.367	0.744	0.569	0.604	0.687	**0.894***		
Self Efficacy	0.578	0.467	0.661	0.610	0.658	0.517	**0.852***	
Trust in eGovernment	0.503	0.443	0.494	0.533	0.500	0.528	0.564	**0.893***

* Square root of AVE

After establishing the reliability and validity of constructs, the hypothesized relations in the model were tested using PLS-SEM. The path coefficients and the corresponding p-values are presented in Fig. 2.

The results support the hypotheses 4 and hypotheses 6 which indicated confirmation and perceived ease of use positively and directly influence perceived usefulness. It further establishes the role of perceived usefulness in shaping the users' attitude and

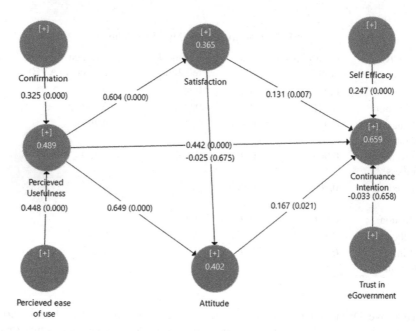

Fig. 2. Hypotheses testing and path analysis

satisfaction from the use of egovernment services (hypotheses 1 and 2). Perceived usefulness also directly leads to users' continuance intention (hypothesis 3). The results fail to support the relationship between satisfaction and attitude (hypothesis 8). But, attitude and satisfaction together with perceived usefulness and self efficacy can support the users' intention to continue with egovernment services (hypotheses 3, 9, 10 and 11). The results also fail to establish any relationship between trust in egovernment and continuance intention (hypothesis 12).

References

1. Abdullah, F., Ward, R., Ahmed, E.: Investigating the influence of the most commonly used external variables of TAM on students' perceived ease of use (PEOU) and perceived usefulness (PU) of e-portfolios. Comput. Hum. Behav. **63**, 75–90 (2016)
2. Al-Hajri, S.: The Adoption of e-Banking: The case of omani banks. Intern. Rev. Bus. Res. Pap. **4**(4), 120–128 (2008)
3. Anthopoulos, L., Siozos, P., Tsoukalas, I.: Applying participatory design and collaboration in digital public services for discovering and re-designing e-Government services. Gov. Inf. Q. **24**, 353–376 (2007)
4. Bhattacherjee, A.: Understanding information systems continuance: An expectation-confirmation model. MIS Q. **25**, 351 (2001)
5. Dijkstra, T., Henseler, J.: Consistent partial least squares path modeling. MIS Q. **39**, 297–316 (2015)

6. ELKheshin, S., Saleeb, N.: Assessing the adoption of e-government using tam model: Case of Egypt. Intern. J. Manag. Inf. Technol. **12**, 1–14 (2020)

7. Fornell, C., Larcker, D.: Structural equation models with unobservable variables and measurement error: Algebra and statistics. J. Mark. Res. **18**, 382 (1981)

8. Gaski, J., Nevin, J.: The differential effects of exercised and unexercised power sources in a marketing channel. J. Mark. Res. **22**, 130–142 (1985)

9. Hair, J., Ringle, C., Sarstedt, M.: PLS-SEM: Indeed a silver bullet. J. Mark. Theory. Pract. **19**, 139–152 (2011)

10. Kim, Y., Lee, H.: Quality, perceived usefulness, user satisfaction, and intention to use: an empirical study of ubiquitous personal robot service. Asian Soc. Sci. **10**, 1–16 (2014)

11. Lallmahomed, M., Lallmahomed, N., Lallmahomed, G.: Factors influencing the adoption of e-Government services in Mauritius. Telemat. Inform. **34**, 57–72 (2017)

12. Lee, Y., Kozar, K., Larsen, K.: The technology acceptance model: Past, present, and future. Commun. Assoc. Inf. Syst., **12** (2003)

13. Ozkan, S., Kanat, I.: e-Government adoption model based on theory of planned behavior: Empirical validation. Gov. Inf. Q. **28**, 503–513 (2011)

14. Rana, N., Dwivedi, Y., Williams, M.: Evaluating alternative theoretical models for examining citizen centric adoption of e-government. Transform. Govern.: People Process Policy. **7**, 27–49 (2013)

15. Rose, J., Persson, J., Heeager, L., Irani, Z.: Managing e-Government: value positions and relationships. Inf. Syst. J. **25**, 531–571 (2014)

16. Shareef, M., Kumar, V., Kumar, U., Dwivedi, Y.: e-Government adoption model (GAM): Differing service maturity levels. Govern. Inf. Q. **28**, 17–35 (2011)

17. Stevens, J.: Applied Multivariate Statistics for the Social Sciences. Routledge, Taylor & Francis Group, New York (2012)

18. Welch, E.: Linking citizen satisfaction with e-Government and trust in government. J. Public Adm. Res. Theor. **15**, 371–391 (2004)

19. Yu, C., Asgarkhani, M.: An investigation of trust in e-banking. Manag. Res. Rev. **38**, 1267–1284 (2015)

Re-imagining the Use of Data Standards for Retail Products: The Case of GS1 Through a Service-Dominant Logic

Shirish C. Srivastava[1]([⊠]) [iD] and Stéphane Cren[2]

[1] HEC Paris, Jouy-En-Josas, France
srivastava@hec.edu
[2] GS1, Paris, France

Abstract. Though technological advancements offer a host of emergent opportunities, they also introduce fresh challenges for organizations. To overcome these challenges, organizations need to be sensitive to the evolving business needs and growing expectations of the customers. In this research-in-progress paper, through the case of GS1, we demonstrate that even for a seemingly stable business, there is a need to continuously evaluate the influence of changes in the situating technological environment, which may lead to changes in the societal demands. GS1, a non-profit organization that develops and maintains global standards for business communication is redefining itself in the face of e-commerce impacted supply chains and evolving customer needs. We posit that organizations need to espouse a service dominant logic mindset, which can help them continually assess and redefine their business models to address the evolving ecological requirements. Our ongoing work aims to identify a set of lessons for firms to tackle this perpetual challenge.

Keywords: Data standards · Omni channel · Barcode · Supply chain · Data as a service · Service dominant logic

1 Introduction

In the current times organizations are becoming increasingly dependent on information technology (IT). From a mere support function, IT has evolved into becoming the bedrock of organization's business strategies [1]. Whether it is the quest for exploring new strategic opportunities enabled by artificial intelligence and social media analytics, or enrichment of the ongoing business operations through efficient enterprise resource planning systems, the role of IT is now deeply intertwined with the core business. Given the rapid rate at which IT is advancing, and the close interdependence between the IT and business strategy, results in both opportunities and challenges for organizations—opportunities to tap into the capabilities of the technological advancements and challenges to keep pace with the rapidly evolving technological landscape that can sometimes tend to impact the underlying logic on which the organization is premised. It will be theoretically and practically interesting to examine how agile organizations are

© IFIP International Federation for Information Processing 2020
Published by Springer Nature Switzerland AG 2020
S. K. Sharma et al. (Eds.): TDIT 2020, IFIP AICT 617, pp. 292–297, 2020.
https://doi.org/10.1007/978-3-030-64849-7_26

able to continuously redefine their strategies in the face of a continuously changing technological environment.

The next big obstacle after the industrial revolution was the need to develop a supply chain that could effectively and efficiently handle the distribution of the large variety of products manufactured in the numerous factories. In the non-Internet era, the retail supply chain relied on intermediaries such as warehouses, wholesales, and the retailers who were the final touch points with the end customers. However, as the number of products increased there was a growing need to *standardize* the "identification" of the products to ensure their error free traceability throughout the supply chain [2]. This pressing supply chain need was precipitated in the US where the retail industry was searching for ways to speed-up the checkout process at the point-of-sales. After the establishment of the ad hoc committee for a uniform grocery product identification code in 1969, it was not until 1973 when the Universal Product Code (UPC) was selected as the first single standard for unique product identification. In 1974, a pack of Wrigley's chewing gum became the first ever product with a bar code to be scanned in a shop [3]. Because of the grassroots need to exchange product related data in the retail market around the globe, a non-profit organization called GS1 gradually emerged as the nodal agency that served as a platform for fulfilling the need of *providing standards for product data exchange* for a seamless flow of products across supply chain partners to the end customers. However, with the growth of technological capabilities for data exchange, communication and the Internet, the data related needs of the supply chain partners and customers also evolved. Instead of viewing product related barcode data merely for "identification" to ensure *physical traceability*, supply chain partners started looking for enhanced "description" of the products to establish *informational traceability* for recombing this product related information with other informational sources to create value for different customers (supply chain partners and end customers).

We examine this evolution in the needs of the supply chain customers through the lens of GS1, which is a non-profit organization that develops and maintains global standards for business communication. GS1 presents a unique study context for two reasons (1) maintaining standards, by definition appears to be a static concept with seemingly stable business logic, and (2) customers for such a business also appear to be relatively fixed. However, as aforementioned, we observe that both the *standards* and the *customers* of product supply chain standards have been evolving. GS1 has been endeavoring to meticulously address the changing demands in this evolutionary journey. Consequently, through the case of GS1 we examine the following research questions:

1. How can the technological advancements impact a seemingly stable business logic?
2. How can organizations premised on principles of stability instill agility in their organizations in response to the evolving business logic?

Grounding our study in service-dominant logic (SDL) literature and adopting a case study research approach we examine how the definition and need for data exchange evolved over time. And how because of this evolution, GS1, the organization providing the platform and standards for data exchange had to incorporate appropriate changes in its business model through innovative solutions such as CodeOnline by GS1 France.

The case reiterates the importance of examining the seemingly product-centric business models through a service-centric lens. We observe that because of technological evolution, data standards, which are seemingly static attributes of products could be used for providing value added services. In addition, the study reiterates the importance of instilling agility into traditional product centric organizations that may be impacted by the enhanced informational connectivity and other technological advancements.

2   Theoretical Background and Study Context

Business models are premised on value creation for the key stakeholders. Traditional models of value creation are based on the goods-dominant (G-D) logic, in which a firm's output is the source of value creation. G-D logic is based on a push philosophy, viewing produced goods as the source of value for the consumer. The value produced is thus "value-in-exchange," where the product is the starting point for value creation and the product is expected to create value for the consumer when they are consumed. G-D logic thus views producers and consumers as separate entities with distinct roles in the value creation process. Producer playing the key role, conceptualized "as a series of activities performed by the firm" [4, p. 146]. The consumer is only expected to benefit from the value created by the producer. Going by the described G-D logic, GS1 as the platform for the provision of data standards to the supply chain partners is supposed to provide the rules and a classification system (e.g. in the form of barcodes) that provides a language of communication across supply chain partners for seamless exchange of physical products. By definition, the application and usage of the formulated data standard rules are expected to be static over time and the primary use that could be imagined by the GS1 users is to have an error free "identification" of the physical products as they move from the producer to the end customer through the supply chain partners such as wholesalers and retailers.

Vargo and Lusch [4, 5] proposed an alternative view, a service-dominant (S-D) logic in which the roles of producers and consumers in the value creation process are intertwined rather than distinct. The focus is on the requirements of the service consumers (users) and the offerings of service producers (providers) that aim at creating "value-in-use." Value in the S-D logic is created jointly and reciprocally through mutual interactions, facilitating integration of resources among the producers and consumers [4]. This new pull-based S-D logic has a user-centric perspective in which the producer and the consumer together create value by designing processes that mutually leverage available resources [6–8]. However, service provision entails greater use of intangible resources such as knowledge and skills for value creation, in addition to tangible resources such as technology or standards. Thus, in contrast to G-D logic, S-D logic emphasizes an appropriate configuration of resources—intangibles along with tangibles—to create value for consumers. In the case of GS1, the data standards are the rules that define the basis of data exchange across the supply chain partners. The implementation of these rules of standardization was left to the supply chain partners specifically the brand owners who were interested in a smooth supply chain journey for their products. However, with the growth of Internet and e-commerce there were two challenges for GS1. First, to make the data standards *accessible* to all the possibly interested players in the product supply chain, e.g. the small and medium enterprises (SMEs) who could now benefit from the Internet enabled supply chains. Such a shift entailed GS1 adopting a service-centric mindset to provide not only the 'data standards' but also the necessary 'toolkit' to implement these data standards. Second, because of the ease of access to information, the end customers want customized product related solutions which could be orchestrated by combining specific product related infor-mation with other contextual information e.g. to have a lunch menu based on the nutritional properties of the packaged food products. Such value-added solutions require GS1 to capture and provide the appropriate product related "information" to the ecosystem partners to enable them design customer-centric solutions.

The need to provide value-added solutions to different customer segments signifies the growing importance of operant resources in the current supply chain context. *Operand resources* represent tangible assets, for example, in the case of GS1 these were the rules for data standards linked with the Global Trade Item Numbers (GTIN) and bar codes for identifying products in the supply chains [9]. However, now GS1 sees a need to shift to develop *operant resources*, which are generally invisible and intangible and shaped out of knowledge and recombined capacities, for example, the GTIN implementation tool kit or customized product related solutions. In our study, we examine this shift and also identify the practices that GS1 adopted to overcome the challenges for developing the operant resources.

3 Method

This research aims at identifying the specific actions that GS1 took to overcome the challenges imposed on it because of the growing importance of e-commerce and online supply chains. Specifically, we first identify the challenges faced by GS1 and then examine the key actions taken by GS1 to overcome the identified challenges. We adopt a systematic retrospective longitudinal case study research approach to examine how the definition and need for product data exchange evolved over time and how because of this evolution, GS1 had to incorporate appropriate changes in its business model through innovative solutions such as CodeOnline for providing access to an enhanced set of supply chain partners, or initiating efforts to capture product related data which could perhaps be used by ecosystem partners for providing value added customer-centric solutions.

Consistent with the case study research approach, we will provide an overview of some of the streams of research that will contribute to our analysis, namely, service dominant logic in conjunction with literature on operand and operant resources [8, 10, 11].

Our study uses a mix of primary and secondary data to analyze the research questions. We have already conducted 5 interviews and have attended several pre-sentations given by the ecosystem partners and management team at GS1. Some of the key respondents were interviewed multiple times to clarify the facts as they emerged during the data collection process. We have audio recorded and transcribed all the interviews conducted thus far, which provided us with about 100 pages of single-spaced transcripts. We also took detailed notes during all interviews. For secondary data, we went through the organizations' activity reports, websites, published articles, internal reports, and video clips. We are using a longitudinal process view to analyze the data, aimed at understanding the actions taken in response to the specific challenges encountered [12–14]. In the coming months, we intend to interview two other categories of GS1 stakeholders (1) supply chain partners who are using GS1 services directly, and (2) final consumers of products, who need new value-added services.

4 Preliminary Findings and Expected Implications

Technological advancements do offer new opportunities but may also be instrumental in inducing unprecedented challenges even for traditionally product-centric organizations. GS1, a global non-profit organization, established for determining and maintaining commonly agreed data standards for product identification, faced challenges with the growth of Internet in two ways.

First, the growth of Internet heralded the use of e-commerce which initially connected the big brands directly to the end-customers. However, with the passage of time marketplace platforms such as Amazon, replaced the direct sales from the brand owners. Such marketplaces are very similar to the physical supermarkets with some major differences: (1) the products sold through marketplaces do not need to be physically scanned at the checkout, which obviates the need for barcodes, (2) marketplaces could stock and sell white-labelled goods from unknown suppliers, which may not have a GS1 allocated GTIN, (3) marketplaces could stock and sell integrated/assembled products from different sub-suppliers where the individual sub-components may have different GTINs.

Second, because of the increased Internet enabled connectivity end consumers have increased access to information. The product needs for these informed consumers has become more sophisticated with the growing demand for customized products. Consumers would need more information about the products before purchasing them e.g. nutritional value related information for food products. In fact, if such product related information is readily available, entrepreneurs could work out customized solutions for specific consumers based on their tastes and preferences e.g. proposing a nutritious vegetarian meal to a diabetic consumer.

From the two aforementioned challenges, it is clear that GS1 product data standards, which were till now required primarily for an error free product identification and used mainly by big brands, needs to be reimagined in two ways (a) the GTIN standards need to made *accessible* to all possible users of e-commerce supply chain such as owners of SMEs and white-labelled product manufactures, and (2) GS1 needs to provide more *product related information* so that customized value added solutions can be proposed to different consumer segments by GS1 or its ecosystem partners.

Hence, there is a definite shift in the use of data by GS1 from a mere "identification" of products to getting detailed "information" about the products, which can be used to create value-added solutions for the consumers. GS1 is currently focused on overcoming these challenges through various initiatives such as CodeOnline and involvement of ecosystem partners to offer customizable solutions to different customer segments. In our study, we are delving deeper into the different actions taken by GS1 in this transformational journey from "data as a product" to "data as a service". Our study hopes to unearth specific lessons for traditionally product-centric organizations contemplating a shift to the emerging service-centric milieu because of the enhanced technological connectivity and information access.

References

1. Huang, M.-H., Rust, R.T.: Technology-driven service strategy. J. Acad. Mark. Sci. **45**(6), 906–924 (2017). https://doi.org/10.1007/s11747-017-0545-6
2. Teo, T.S.H., Ranganathan, C., Srivastava, S.C., Loo, J.W.K.: Fostering IT-enabled business innovation at YCH group. MIS Q. Executive **6**(4), 211–223 (2007)
3. GS1 details (2020). https://en.wikipedia.org/wiki/GS1. Accessed 4 Aug 2020
4. Vargo, S.L., Lusch, R.F.: Service-dominant logic: continuing the evolution. J. Acad. Mark. Sci. **36**(1), 1–10 (2008)
5. Vargo, S.L., Lusch, R.F.: Evolving to a new dominant logic for marketing. J. Mark. **68**, 1–17 (2004)
6. Sheth, J., Parvatiyar, A.: Relationship marketing in consumer markets: antecedents and consequences. In: Sheth, J., Parvatiyar, A. (eds.) Handbook of Relationship Marketing. Sage Publications, Thousand Oaks (2000)
7. Teo, T.S.H., Srivastava, S.C., C.K., Ho.: The trident model for customer-centric enterprise system at comfort transportation, Singapore. MIS Q. Executive **5**(3), 109–124 (2006)
8. Srivastava, S.C., Shainesh, G.: Bridging the service divide through digitally enabled service innovations: evidence from indian healthcare service providers. MIS Q. **39**(1), 245–267 (2015)
9. GS1 GTIN (2020). https://www.gs1.org/standards/id-keys/gtin. Accessed 4 Aug 2020
10. Nambisan, S.: Information technology and product/service innovation: a brief assessment and some suggestions for future research. J. Assoc. Inf. Syst. **14**(4), 1 (2013)
11. Madhavaram, S., Hunt, S.D.: The service-dominant logic and a hierarchy of operant resources: developing masterful operant resources and implications for marketing strategy. J. Acad. Mark. Sci. **36**(1), 67–82 (2008)
12. Teo, T.S.H., Srivastava, S.C., Ranganathan, C., Loo, J.W.K.: A Framework for stakeholder oriented mindfulness: case of RFID implementation at YCH Group, Singapore. Eur. J. Inf. Syst. **20**, 201–220 (2011)
13. Chakraborty, S., Sarker, S., Sarker, S.: An exploration into the process requirements elicitation: a grounded approach. J. Assoc. Inf. Syst. **11**(4), 212–249 (2010). https://doi.org/10.17705/1jais.00225
14. Lyytinen, K., Newman, M.: Explaining information system change: a punctuated socio-technical change model. Eur. J. Inf. Syst. **17**(6), 589–613 (2008). https://doi.org/10.1057/ejis.2008.50

Adoption of Digital Innovation in Crop Insurance - A Data Analytics Based Benchmarking Study of Samrakshane Portal in Karnataka

Madhuchhanda Das Aundhe, Jang Bahadur Singh[(✉)], N. Ramesh, and M. Vimalkumar

IIM Tiruchirappalli, Tiruchirappalli, Tamil Nadu, India
madhu.das@gmail.com, nramesh23@gmail.com,
jbs@iimtrichy.ac.in

Abstract. Agriculture in India is prone to a lot of uncertainties and different types of risks. Crop insurance is a mechanism hedge against such contingencies. Though many governments in the past had introduced various crop insurance schemes, the penetration rate was shallow, and there were no private players. Thus, the current Govt introduced PMFBM, which can be a game-changer. Karnataka went a step ahead and implemented an end to end technology platform – Samrakshane - to promote and manage the crop insurance. Samrakshane, being an innovative technology platform enabling the complete automation of crop insurance adoption. The objective of this study is to understand and measure the innovation adoption impact of the crop insurance scheme. In this short paper, we present a conceptual outline of our ongoing research.

Keywords: Samrakshane · Agri-insurance · Digital innovation · E-Gov portal

1 Introduction

Agriculture is the most climate sensitive sector, and India is among the most vulnerable countries in South Asia, due to the dependence of the majority of its population on this sector for their livelihood [1]. Agriculture contributes to 22 percent of GDP, provides 58 percent of employment, sustains 69 percent of population, produces all the food and nutritional requirements of the nation, important raw materials for some major industries, and accounts for about 14 percent of exports [1]. The agricultural activity is carried out on 60% of the total land area of India, 60% of which is dependent on seasonal rains for its irrigation [2]. Thus, agricultural sector is recognized as a national priority by the government of India and constitutes a politically articulate and powerful constituency wooed by practically political parties of all hues. Agriculture is inherently a risky venture. Agricultural risk and fluctuations pose the biggest threat to the large majority of Indian farmers who have small and marginal land holdings (less than 5 acres of land). Risks in agriculture can be classified as:

- Idiosyncratic risks that usually affect only individual farms or firms (e.g., plant and animal pests and diseases, illnesses of the owner or laborers);

S. K. Sharma et al. (Eds.): TDIT 2020, IFIP AICT 617, pp. 298–306, 2020.
https://doi.org/10.1007/978-3-030-64849-7_27

- Covariate risks that affect many enterprises simultaneously (e.g., major droughts or floods, fluctuating market prices).

The high propensity of covariate risks in rural areas is a major reason that informal risk management arrangements break down and that formal locally based financial institutions are hesitant to provide commercial loans for agriculture [3, 4]. Jaffee and Siegel [5] list all possible sources of risk potentially affecting agricultural value chains. They identify seven categories: weather-related risks (especially those related to hail and wind damage and to high humidity or excess rain), natural disasters like floods, tsunami, earthquakes can affect agricultural supply chains for multiple growing seasons and/or production cycles, biological and environmental risks refer to presence of certain plant pests or livestock diseases, market-related risks existing for inputs and outputs and for the critical services that support supply chains, such as finance and logistics, agricultural supply chains increasingly face risks related to logistics and infrastructure, managerial and operational risks, which are closely associated with human judgment and response, public policy and institutional risks also have systemic impacts on decision making and productivity, as well as on market options. Traditionally developing countries have been using long-standing tools like interventions by governments, management of strategic food reserves, implementation of price stabilization schemes, heavily subsidized crop insurance, and credit guarantee programs for managing risks. These approaches to risk management can be further articulated as ex-ante or ex-post strategies.

1.1 Agricultural Risk Management: Individual and Institutional

One of the key objectives (globally) of agricultural risk management is stabilisation of the incomes of farmers. It is not only the low income of the farmer, but the fluctuations in income that cause hardships by affecting the stability between income and consumption requirements during the periods of crop loss or failure. This stabilisation, at an individual farmer level can happen through various ways – (i) managing the agricultural supply chain, (ii) extending the market, (iii) agricultural research (individual experimentation and innovation), (iv) crop insurance. Risks related to logistics and infrastructure are addressed by improving the distribution network for the supply of inputs, and improving the agricultural extension system. Market related risks are mitigated through support/procurement prices provided by the government. Crop insurance, as a risk management alternative, provides cover only against yield risk and hence income fluctuations arising from fluctuations in yield. Where income variability is due to price fluctuations or due to untimely or irregular supply of inputs and information, crop insurance is not the solution. Therefore, crop insurance serves as a means to mitigate weather related risks, natural disasters, and biological and environmental risks. The financial and other capabilities involved in the first three ways of risk management mentioned above may be daunting for small and marginal farmers. Therefore, crop insurance is, seemingly, important for stabilisation of incomes of small and marginal farmers [6]. Crop Insurance is an ex-ante action that may transfer certain risks to other parties (i.e. insurance agencies). Another perspective of managing risk, consists of risk minimising practices generally adopted by farmers are diversification of resources - vertical, horizontal and temporal—and adjustments within the cropping systems. The vertical diversification refers to the broader baskets of agricultural assets, i.e. animal/poultry farming that the farmer adopts to mitigate his croprelated risks. The horizontal and temporal aspects refer to both spatial and crop diversification, and these are widely used in semi-arid regions. The studies by the International Crops Research Institute for the Semi-Arid topics (ICRISAT) has proved the superiority of crop diversification over spatial diversification in reducing the income instability of farmers. However, even the usefulness of crop diversification was limited as it failed to adequately protect the farmers from risk. Adjustments within the cropping system, e.g. inter-cropping of sorghum and pearl millet, also proved ineffective as was evident from the positive and significant correlation between their yields. Since the risk minimising practices are largely related to the yield of the crops, crop insurance serves as an important risk mitigation mechanism. It has a more important role to play in countries where traditional strategies (e.g. price stabilisation schemes, supply chain management etc.) to manage risks are inefficient or ineffective. Crop insurances may, further, be of two types – multiple risk or specific risk. The fact that multiple-risk crop insurance is not a commercially viable proposition and that its existence depends on liberal subsidies from the government is further underlined by the situation in Australia. Farm incomes in Australia are notoriously volatile. The insurance of crops is undertaken by large insurance bodies in the private sector which offer insurance cover against specific risks such as hail and fire. Lloyd and Mauldon recount the failure of various attempts made in Australia to introduce multiplerisk insurance on a commercial basis [6]. Besides, contributing to income stabilisation, the provision of insurance may enable the farmers to adopt riskier innovations e.g. modern agronomic practices, riskier crops. An indirect benefit of crop insurance may be on the agricultural labour market where the incomes of labourers may stabilise as small and marginal farmers will no longer be compelled to join the ranks of agricultural labourers and push down the wage rate following a failure of crops. Given that crop insurance has an important role to play in the agricultural sector of developing countries, it is important to understand its impact on farmers. The effectiveness of crop insurance in India has been a bit dubious, given the very low rate of its adoption by farmers. Further, from an insurance agencies' point of view, Binswanger [7] points to the information asymmetry, moral hazard and adverse selection problems faced by them. The indexed approach minimises the transaction costs based on the individual basis. Incentive and information problems which are similar to both credit and insurance services act as severe obstacles to actuarial calculations. Hence, not many private insurance companies are keen to provide farmers cover for their crop yield.

1.2 Indian Scenario

In India, the efforts to introduce crop insurance date back to the years immediately after attaining independence when some state governments evinced an interest in introducing the scheme. But the schemes, since 1985 when the Comprehensive Crop Insurance Scheme (CCIS) was launched, have not been gaining the expected traction among the farmers. The Gross Cropped Areai (GCA) covered under crop insurance - touched 28% in 2016-17, then dropped to 26% in 2017–18, has remained far below the target of 50% projected by 2018–19 [8]). This is despite several attempts at changing the schemes – from individual based (72–78) to area-based (79–84: Pilot Crop Insurance Scheme- PCIS); making Crop Insurance mandatory for the loanee-farmers since 1985; fully subsidized scheme (97–98 - Experimental Crop Insurance Scheme – ECIS); share croppers were covered for the first time in NAIS– 1999–2016; farm income, rather than cost of cultivation, was insured (2003–04: Farm Income Insurance Scheme – FIIS); WBCIS based on the deviation in the rainfall (2007 – till date); Private sector was encouraged to participate and immediate partial payment to affected farmers was introduced (Modified NAIS, 2010–16) and finally PMFBY wherein Premium rates were lowered (2.5% to 1.5% for Kharif, rabi – remains at 2%) and use of technology was emphasized and covered more risks such as prevented sowing and post-harvest losses.

1.3   Crop Insurance Implementation

A recent survey by the Comptroller and Auditor General of India (CAG) revealed that the coverage of farmers, particularly small and marginal ones, under the insurance schemes was very low compared to the population of farmers as per Census 2011, the report said [9]. Duplicate claims by some farmers, manipulation in Crop Cutting Experiments (CCE), laxity in the exercise of due diligence by the bankers in the verification of documents pertaining to the identity and the Record of Rights (RoR), have been reported to have plagued the execution of the crop insurance schemes in India. To address these challenges the PMFBY Guidelines emphasize the "adoption of new technology for early loss assessment and better administration of scheme" [OPERATIONAL GUIDELINES, PMBFY, p. 48]. Technology initiatives like the Crop Insurance Mobile App[1] are being attempted. It is widely expected that deployment of ICT, as part of e-Governance, would significantly influence the effectiveness and efficiency of administration of the Crop Insurance Schemes in realizing their key objectives and the potential to impact the lives of millions of farmers while safeguarding the interests of all the stakeholders.

The crop insurance scheme with a noble intention to protect farmers can succeed only if operational guidelines are strictly followed and cut off dates are not extended frequently as was done in Kharif 2016. One of the reasons for high actuarial premium rates quoted by the reinsurance companies was the extension of cut off dates. Moreover, timely submission of yield data of CCEs and payment of premium subsidy to insurance companies will smoothen and fasten the process of claim settlements as done by Tamil Nadu in Rabi 2016–17, Tamil Nadu when they experienced one of the worst droughts. There were allegations of data manipulations while conducting CCEs like the yield of groundnut of Rajkot district in Gujarat in Kharif 2016.

---

[1] http://digitalindia.gov.in/content/crop-insurance-mobile-app visited on 17-01-2018, This Mobile App can be used to calculate the Insurance Premium for notified crops based on area, coverage amount and loan amount in case of loanee farmer. It can also be used to get details of normal sum insured, extended sum insured, premium details and subsidy information of any notified crop in any notified area.

The litmus test of any crop insurance scheme, therefore, depends on quick assessment of crop damage and payment of claim into farmers' bank account. The infrastructure to make this scheme fully operational is still inadequate. Timely submission of yield data by State government to the insurance companies is necessary so that they can finalise the claims expeditiously and pay the claims to farmers. The Indian crop insurance scenario has been beset with several problems such as lack of transparency, high premium, delay in conducting crop cutting experiments and non-payment/delayed payment of claims to farmers and delay in payment of the premium subsidy by the governments to the insurance company.

Although the policy w.r.t. Indian crop insurance schemes have undergone several changes over the last 3 decades, there has been little attention given to the process aspects (cost and efficiency) of the various schemes. Therefore, the transparency, accountability and efficiency of the administrative processes of the crop insurance schemes have not seen as much improvement or reforms, as the specific features and benefits of the schemes.

1.4   Technology Adoption in Crop Insurance Implementation in Karnataka

Karnataka has been among the leading states in the adoption of crop insurance. The state has achieved significant increase in the enrollment of farmers in the crop insurance scheme- from 8.72 lakh farmers in Kharif 2015 to 20 lakh farmers in Rabi 2017. Though, the idea of automating the crop insurance scheme using ICT is not new, Karnataka developed an end-to-end software application, christened SAMRAK-SHANE, meaning 'Protection', with many advanced features and was ahead in the implementation of such a software. This technology platform developed by National Informatics Centre (NIC), Karnataka, was rolled out in June 2016. Samrakshane, is a unified portal, and provides comprehensive support to the state Agriculture and Horticulture departments in managing the entire value chain of crop insurance under both Modified Weather-Based Crop Insurance Scheme (MWBCIS) & Prime Minister Fasal Bima Yojna (PMFBY) – from enrolment of farmers to the final payout of insurance claims through a unified portal [10]. It enables enrolment of crop insurance through multiple channels - the banks for the loanee farmers, and the Raitha Sampark Kendras (RSK) & Village Level Entrepreneurs (VLE) at the Citizen Service Centers (CSC), for the non-loanee farmers. Samrakshane is an e-governance tool to create a transparent, accountable, at the same time farmer friendly system of administration of the crop insurance schemes, with a great promise and potential to usher in radical change benefitting not only farmers, but all the key stakeholders – the insurance agencies, banks and the government. This paper aims to study the technology adoption success of the crop-insurance schemes enabled by the digital initiative SAMRAKSHANE. Of late, Karnataka has also gone ahead and made compulsory use of mobile phones while conducting the CCE. In order to address the insurance process issues from farmers' point of view, and take care of the problems faced by the private sector insurance agencies.

2   Study Objectives

The objectives of this study would be to understand and measure the innovation adoption impact of the crop insurance scheme as outlined below:

- Adoption success metrics at the level of individual farmer and village level entrepreneur (cost of service, quality of service, personal development, feeling of protection).
- Adoption success metrics at Community level (e.g. crop sustainability, crop diversification, agronomic practices, income stability).
- Adoption success metrics on Governance (efficiency and effectiveness).
- Recommendations for process improvements to enhance adoption success (enrollment, claims, proposal verification and validation, additional data capture).
- Recommendations for technological innovations in Crop cutting experiments.
- Recommendations for successful adoption of digital technology innovations for

3   Methodology for Measuring Innovation Adoption Success

We propose to adopt a robust assessment strategy for adoption success evaluation [11]. The evaluation would be done at two levels:

3.1   The Broader Impact of Crop Insurance on the Farmer Community

This Community impact is an outcome-oriented measure for Government impact, and would consist of data collected at a citizen level. The impact indices would help to understand

1. The farmers (i.e. their profiles, incomes, and farming techniques etc.) who benefit from the scheme
2. The crops (i.e. their sustainability, diversification etc.) that are supported by the scheme
3. Allied community developments (i.e. feeling of protection, development based on achievement of aspirations etc.) due to crop insurance availability.

3.2   The Specific Impact of the Software Application (Samrakshane Portal) on Governance Processes Through Two Kinds of Measures

1. Efficiency gains e.g. time taken for enrolment of Loanee/Non-loanee farmers in the scheme; time taken for claims process etc.
2. Effectiveness gains e.g. Reduction in errors in due diligence and verification of farmer records; Reduction in manipulations e.g. duplication in land records, benami enrolment; Reduction in Crop cutting experiment manipulations; Penetration of scheme; Quality of governance (transparency, accountability, participation etc.)

The evaluation would be conducted in two parts as depicted in Fig. 1 below. The first part of the study would consist of the use of Data Analytics on the database built by the Samrakshane project.

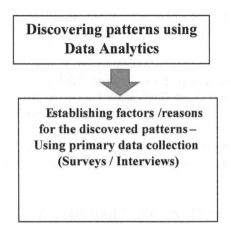

Fig. 1. Method of adoption success evaluation

Some indicative Analytics techniques that can be used are the following. However, the appropriate techniques will be decided upon accessing the Samrakshane historical data stored.

1. Descriptive (based on Statistical Analysis)

   • Farmer profile (region, caste community, economic background)
   • Crop profiles (area, season, insured amount, premium paid)
   • Insurance Unit profiles

2. Prescriptive (based on Optimization)

   • Trend Analysis of yield in a particular region for a particular crop can give an expected range, which can be used to identify any ambiguity during Crop Cutting Experiments.
   • These techniques would also help the government arrive at scientific figures for indemnity levels, average yields, threshold yield, sum insured, premium rates, seasonality discipline, coverage of risks and exclusions etc.

3. Predictive (based on Machine Learning)

   • Propensity of farmers/crops in enrolling for crop insurance/making insurance claims.

The second part of the study (as shown in Fig. 1) would consist of study of factors/reasons for the discovered patterns. This part of the study would be done based on primary data collected (i.e. Surveys/Interviews) from farmers, VLEs and RSKs, bank officials, and insurance company employees.

4   Research Progress and Expected Outcomes

The project began in April 2019 with an extensive literature survey along with contacting state officials for traces data of the protal. The objective of the literature review was to understand the types of risk faced by the farmers and the development of crop insurance schemes in India. We understood from the survey that the agriculture in India, kind of gamble and prone to multiple types of risks. Though the agriculture crop insurance to hedge against risks of farming was introduced right after the insurance, a serious step towards the implementation was took place after 1985. However, the adoption rate was shallow, and there were no private players in the crop insurance market. Thus, the current Govt introduced PMFBM, which can be a game-changer. Karnataka went a step ahead and implemented an end to end technology platform to promote and manage the crop insurance. In the literature review section, we have traced the entire evaluation of crop insurance to date.

Once we understood landscape, we scheduled meeting with NIC, Karnataka and the horticulture department to understand the intricacies of the Samrakshane platform and nature of agriculture in the state. We had regular interaction with state departments, and the department was very cooperative in supporting our research. Projects investigators continuously held various meetings with state horticulture and agriculture department officials to understand the crop insurance digital solution platform Samrakshane. The both the department were involved in the implementation of the Samrakshane portal.

Subsequently, team requested National Informatics Center, NIC to provide us with the crop insurance raw data, up to the individual level enrolled to Samrakshane platform. The department honoured our request and facilitated us with the complete raw data of three years' (nine seasons). The contained around 80,00,000 enrolments during this period, with more than 40,00,000 unique land parcels being insuring. We have performed preliminary descriptive/exploratory data analysis this entire dataset, and the same is provided in the second chapter.

We had observed different types of adopters. Some of them are early adopters but didn't turn up in the later years. Some of them have adopted in the later years and stayed back. There some formers who have enrolled in all the three years. The preliminary data analysis also shows patterns in terms of agro-climatic regions and crops.

Thus, as the next step, we had plans of visiting the fields to explore these different patters by interacting with the farmers directly. We had scheduled the visits in late March 2020 till May 2020, during the academic break. However, due to the pandemic, we couldn't interact with the farmers, and the field work has been halted from March 2020. Hopefully, we will be able to restore the data collection from September 2020.

Acknowledgement. We thank the IIMA – Idea Telecom Center of Excellence for generously funding this project. We also thank NIC – Karnataka, Horticulture department and Agriculture Department for providing us with the access to the necessary data and information required for this project.

References

1. Swain, M.: Crop insurance for adaptation to climate change in India (2014)
2. ETOnline: What crop insurance? India's farmers have no clue about the covers Centre doles out for them - The Economic Times (2017). https://economictimes.indiatimes.com/news/economy/agriculture/what-crop-insurance-indias-farmers-have-no-clue-about-the-covers-centre-doles-out-for-them/articleshow/59735439.cms
3. Skees, J., Hazell, P.B.R., Miranda, M.: New approaches to crop yield insurance in developing countries (1999)
4. Skees, J.R., Barnett, B.J.: Conceptual and practical considerations for sharing catastrophic/systemic risks. Appl. Econ. Perspect. Policy 21, 424–441 (1999). https://doi.org/10.2307/1349889
5. Jaffee, S., Siegel, P., Andrews, C.: Rapid Agricultural Supply Chain Risk Assessment: A Conceptual Framework (2010)
6. Prabhu, K.S.: Crop insurance: the international experience. Econ. Polit. Wkly. 23, 833–836 (1988)
7. Binswanger-Mkhize, H.P.: Is there too much hype about index-based agricultural insurance? J. Dev. Stud. 48, 187–200 (2012). https://doi.org/10.1080/00220388.2011.625411
8. Rajeev, M., Nagendran, P.: Where do we stand? crop insurance in India. Econ. Polit. Wkly. 54, 28–35 (2019)
9. ET: What crop insurance ? India ' s farmers have no clue about the covers Centre doles out for them
10. Gulati, A., Terway, P., Hussain, S.: Crop Insurance in India: Key Issues and Way Forward. Indian Council for Research on International Economic Relations (2018)
11. Gallivan, M.J.: Organizational adoption and assimilation of complex technological innovations: development and application of a new framework. Data Base Adv. Inf. Syst. 32, 51–85 (2001). https://doi.org/10.1145/506724.506729

Re-imagining Technology Adoption Research Beyond Development and Implementation: ITOps as the New Frontier of IS Research

Archimedes T. Apronti[✉] and Amany Elbanna

Royal Holloway, University of London, Egham TW20 0EX, UK
Archimedes.Apronti.2014@live.rhul.ac.uk,
Amany.Elbanna@rhul.ac.uk

Abstract. IT operations (ITOps) is a key function in IS organisations. To manage and ensure the availability and reliability of the plethora of new/emerging and complex technologies that organisations increasingly adopt, ITOps had undergone significant changes and is currently going through major transformations. This paper assesses the current status of ITOps research. It reviews the literature across the AIS basket of eight journals, specifically over the last four decades. The analysis highlights the key areas in need of updating and research effort. The paper concludes that ITOps is ripe for further research and it is timely for IS research to update its knowledge base on the management of IT including ITOps, considering the significance of emerging technologies in the IT landscape.

Keywords: IT adoption · IT operations · ITOps · IT infrastructure · IT availability · IT reliability · Predictive maintenance · Data analytics

1 Introduction

Information systems adoption and diffusion research covers a broad area, from conceptualisation to development through to use and operations (Dwivedi et al. 2010). Whilst much of IS adoption research focuses on development and use, keeping IS operational; i.e. available, reliable, resilient and responsive to users after initial installation is critical to organisations. However, it is widely recognised as expensive (Swanson, 1999, Tambo and Filtenborg 2019). It consumes over half of IS implementation costs and IT decision-makers are under pressure to further escalate spending on IT systems and services, to ensure operational continuity and success (Reisinger 2013; Tsunoda et al. 2017). It is also challenging, as transitioning IT from development to operations involves complex technological and organisational processes, various stakeholders/teams and a wide range of technologies that offer round the clock system monitoring and real-time interactions between different organisational functions.

It also involves a wide range of activities including system maintenance, configuration management, change/risk management, incident management, service management, process management, customer support, system audit, tools management and knowledge/skillsets management (Abeck and Mayerl 1999; Taylor et al. 1997;

© IFIP International Federation for Information Processing 2020
Published by Springer Nature Switzerland AG 2020
S. K. Sharma et al. (Eds.): TDIT 2020, IFIP AICT 617, pp. 307–319, 2020.
https://doi.org/10.1007/978-3-030-64849-7_28

Edwards 1984; Banker and Slaughter 2000; Krishnan et al. 2004; Nelson et al. 2000; Shaft and Vessey 2006). Thus, as a function, IT operations (ITOps) constitute a complex knowledge ecosystem involving several social and technical domains (Ramakrishnan et al. 2018), and is considered as one of the dynamic capabilities that help organisations to rely on IT for business (Cetindamar et al. 2009).

Currently, ITOps is undergoing major transformation including deployment of AI, IoT, digital platform technologies, data analytics and intelligent software, in addition to new methodologies like DevOps. In this regard, the ITOps management market increased by 10% in 2019 from the previous year to over $30 billion and the IT performance analysis software market also reached over $12 billion (Gartner 2020). Importantly, ITOps have shifted from domain-centric applications that focus on one area like network traffic to a more product-centric and services view that show the impact of application performance on end-users and business outcomes (Gartner 2020).

Considering its importance in keeping IT operational and the on-going transformation in the domain, this study assesses the status of research in ITOps. It questions how ITOps had been treated and which aspects had been studied? To answer these questions, we reviewed relevant articles in the AIS Senior Scholars Basket of eight journals from 1980 to 2020. This revealed the extent of ITOps research and provided grounds for suggesting future research. The rest of the paper is structured as follows. Section two presents an overview of the key aspects of ITOps followed by a description of the research method. A summary of the findings and discussion on their implications for future IS research is then presented. The paper then concludes by noting that it is timely to update the knowledge base of ITOps and the management of IT.

2   IT Operations

2.1   Key Aspects

ITOps is responsible for the smooth functioning of IT infrastructures and the operational environments that support IT service delivery and application deployment, including network management and customer support (Hetvik 2014). It is part of IS life cycle and follows the IS development phase as depicted in Fig. 1 below.

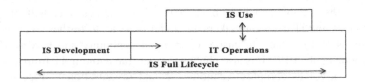

Fig. 1. Relationship between IS development and operations

ITOps thus cover a wide range of knowledge base and activities that could be categorised into day-to-day operational tasks, problem-solving/error handling and processing user change requests (Abeck and Mayerl 1999). Day-to-day operational tasks include system and user support. Problem-solving tasks include error detection/troubleshooting, incident management, software code validation, system audit and corrective/adaptive maintenance. Processing user change requests include attending to service complaints and performing preventive maintenance to address risks. They could also be categorised as technical, application development and system maintenance (Nelson et al. 2000). Technical tasks include system configuration and capacity management. Application development tasks include requirement analysis and validation. System maintenance tasks include adaptive, corrective and preventive maintenance. ITOps tasks had also been categorised as proactive, preventive and reactive (Jamieson and Low 1990; Caralli et al. 2010). Proactive tasks include system performance monitoring and process management. Reactive tasks include incident response and emergency changes. Table 1 enumerates the differences between IS development and ITOps.

Table 1. Differences between IS development and operations

	IS development	IT operations
1.	Responsible for IT design and development by producing new artefacts	Responsible for operating old/new IT Also retires legacy/defunct artefacts
2.	Delivers new IT artefacts to operations to run in production	Receives new IT artefacts from development to run in production
3.	Focus on producing new technical artefacts/systems	Focus on running existing systems at optimal levels and non-stop
4.	Design and builds technical artefacts in non-prod environment	Manages and troubleshoots failures in systems designed by others
5.	Commissions a small group of users to test system functionality	Services are deployed to a large constituent of end-users
6.	Failures in functionality may be oblivious to end-users as there are no SLAs	Live services are strictly monitored and active SLAs, SLOs or OLAs are in place.
7.	Focus on developing one or few systems/services at a time.	Operates and manages multiple systems/services at any given time
8	Teams competence focus on emerging/new technologies	Teams competence focus on both established and emerging technologies
9	Recognised project delivery models are followed to produce new artefacts	Best practices and good judgment facilitate reliable system operations
10	Requirements are well-defined	Requirements are fuzzy
11.	Does not operate the technical artefacts they design and develops	Operates technical artefacts that were designed and developed by others
12	Tolerant non-production environment for development activities	Unforgiving production environment with live systems running
13	Could easily modify or discard problematic artefacts as user-base is small	Tedious troubleshooting of artefacts and services to support growing user-base

(*continued*)

Table 1. (*continued*)

	IS development	IT operations
14	Developments are often time bounded and budgeted for in advance	Tasks are difficult to budget for in advance and incidents are common.
15	Working hours are usually sufficient since, services are not live	Round the clock coverage of live services, as failure could occur anytime
16	Failures are predictable and could wait for next available engineer	Instant failure detection, tracking and management are required
17	Configuration changes/upgrades are often planned in advanced	Configurations changes/upgrades may be urgent to counter failures
18	Tasks are often linear/clearer	Tasks are often non-linear/complex
19	Success/failure are predictable	Success/failures are unpredictable
20	Development of artefacts could be cancelled without impact on users	Abandoning production systems/artefacts have implications for users
21	Performance benefits could be projected with relative ease	performance benefits are difficult to predict due to mix of old/new kits
22.	Artefact development strategy and design could easily be changed	Artefact designs are inherited from development and thus locked-in

In practice, ITOps is guided by industry frameworks like ITIL, COBIT, ISO27000, TOGAF and Six Sigma (Herrera and Van Hillegersberg 2019) that focus on processes, procedures and governance. Although, organisations are increasingly paying more attention to automation and optimisation to improve reliability and control costs.

2.2   Organisational Reliance on ITOps and Its Critical Importance

As organisations and society increasingly rely on complex IT systems and infrastructures, ITOps had become more critical. The financial and social losses that are experienced during IT failures compel organisations to invest more in ITOps. There is an abundance of cases where IT outages had resulted in millions of dollars in loss. These include many high profile cases like WhatsApp's global IT outage in July 2020, Lloyds Bank's IT outage in January 2020, Travelex's global IT outage in January 2020, Delta, Southwest, American Airlines' IT outage in December 2019, Sydney trains' IT outage in February 2019, Air India's IT failure in April 2019, Amtrak's Signal System Failure in March 2019, Amazon's IT outage in June 2019, Google's login system outage in April 2019, Visa's IT outage in June 2018, Microsoft's Azure outage in September 2017 and New York Stock Exchange's IT outage in July 2015. Table 2 presents three cases in the UK to highlight the scale of negative impact and financial loss.

Table 2. Financial costs of three recent incidents in the UK

IT Incident	User impact	Financial impact
1. RBS IT incident in June 2012 (Financial Conduct Authority 2014)	– 6.5 million customers were unable to access ATMs and online accounts – Prevented some from making timely mortgage payments – Prevented business account holders from honouring their payroll	– A total of £42 million fine was imposed on RBS, NatWest and Ulster Bank by the UK's financial regulator (Financial Conduct Authority 2014)
2. TSB IT incident in April 2018 (Financial Times, 2018)	– Botched migration of database affected 1.9 million customers who lost access to online bank accounts – Business accounts were unable to fulfil payroll responsibilities on time – CEO resigned (BBC News, 2018b)	– FCA enquiry (BBC, 2018c) – Compensation for customers totaling £176.4 million (TSB Bank, 2018), including cancelling £10 million overdraft fees and interests worth £30 m
3. O2 and Ericsson IT Outage in Dec 2018 (Reuters 2018, Ericsson 2018)	– 25 million O2 and 7 million Sky, Giffgaff & TalkTalk data customers – 8,500 time schedule displays on London buses (Bloomberg 2018) – 11,500 bikes connected to O2 payment terminals (Bloomberg 2018) – Deliveroo (Bloomberg 2018)	– Projected compensation of about £100 million from Ericsson (Telegraph 2018) – Offered 2 days air time credit for contract holders and 10% off credit for affected pay as you go users (BBC News 2018a)

3 Methodology

To address the research question, we conducted a literature review that focused on publications from 1980 to 2020. Whilst selection of journals play a key role in the assessment of past research, "there are no established criteria that govern the choice of journals" (Robey et al. 2008; Straub 2006). However, we followed Robey et al. (2008) criteria of selecting IS journals based on reputation in the IS field. Hence, we selected the AIS senior scholars' basket of eight journals that are recognised for their rigorous review processes. This includes MISQ, ISR, JIT, JMIS, EJIS, JAIS, JSIS and ISJ.

We identified the initial set of articles through a combination of title, keyword and abstract searches, as well as reviews of research questions. We used keywords like IT operations and maintenance to search. The inclusion criterion was for the papers to directly examine an aspect of ITOps. This approach yielded 29 papers from the basket of eight IS journals. Table 3 shows a breakdown of the reviewed papers.

Table 3. IT operations literature organised by Journal (between 1980–2020)

Journals (AIS Basket of Eight)	No. of Papers	Percent
MIS Quarterly (MISQ)	7	24.14%
Information Systems Research (ISR)	4	13.79%
Journal of Information Technology (JIT)	6	20.69%
Journal of Management Information Systems (JMIS)	6	20.69%
European Journal of Information Systems (EJIS)	5	17.24%
Journal of the Association for Information Systems (JAIS)	1	3.45%
Journal of Strategic Information Systems (JSIS)	0	0
Information Systems Journal (ISJ)	0	0
Total	**29**	**100%**

Regarding analysis, we identified and analysed articles in two phases. In the first phase, we distilled the activities associated with ITOps and identified ten broad categories. We then classified the 29 articles based on these.

Table 4. IT operations literature organised by research theme (between 1980–2020)

ITOps aspects	1980s	1990s	2000s	2010s	Percent
1. System Maintenance	(Edwards 1984), (Kim & Westin 1988), (Ives & Vitale 1988), (Rozensh-tein & Minsky 1986)	(Dekleva, 1992), (Dekleva & Drehmer 1997), (Hipkin, 1996), (Tan & Gable, 1997), (Kaasbøll, 1997) (Moreton, 1990)	(Swanson & Dans 2000), (Krishnan et al, 2004), (Banker & Slaughter 2000), (Min Khoo & Robey 2007), (Shaft&Vessey 2006)	(Choudhary & Zhang 2015), (Dennis et al. 2014), (Edberg et al. 2012)	18 (62.1%)
2. Config Management					0%
3. Change/Risk Management			(Goldstein et al. 2011)		1 (3.5%)
4. Incident Management					0%
5. Service Management		(Rands, 1992), (Griffin & Sumichrast, 1994)		(Wiedemann et al. 2020)	3 (10.3%)

(continued)

Table 4. *(continued)*

ITOps aspects	1980s	1990s	2000s	2010s	Percent
6. Process Management	(Paddock, 1985)				1 (3.5%)
7. Customer Support					0%
8. System Audit		(Jamieson & Low 1990)			1 (3.5%)
9. Tools Management	(Moreton, 1992)				1 (3.5%)
10. Knowledge/Skillsets Management	(Goldstein 1989)	(Taylor et al. 1997); (Shaft & Vessey 1998)	(Nelson et al, 2000)		4 (13.8%)
Percent	**7 papers (24.1%)**	**11 papers (37.9%)**	**7 papers (24.1%)**	**4 papers (13.8)**	**29 (100%)**

In the second phase, all the 29 articles were re-categorised by publication year/decade to glean insight into whether particular aspects of ITOps or themes were dominant in each decade or not. Table 4 above shows the breakdown per decade.

4   Assessment of the Literature

4.1   Disproportionate Focus on System/Software Maintenance

The analysis presented in Table 4 above shows that across the four decades between 1980 and 2020, ITOps articles that were published in the AIS basket had a total of eighteen articles, representing 62.1% that focused on maintenance. Four articles, representing 13.79% focused on Knowledge/Skillsets Management. Three articles, representing 10.34% focused on Service Management. One article each, representing 3.45% focused on Change/Risk Management, Process Management, and Tools Management. No articles were published in three ITOps aspects, notably Configuration Management, Incident Management and Customer Support.

4.2   Lack of Contemporary View of IT Operations

The analysis revealed that most of ITOps literature dates back to the 1980s and 1990s where IT systems were more simplistic, compared to today's complex and powerful IT systems and infrastructures. This pattern is evident across the last four decades. The 1990s witnessed the highest level of interest in ITOps with 11 articles, representing 37.93% followed by the 1980s and 2000s with 7 articles, representing 24.14 each. The 2010s came last with 4 articles, representing 13.79%. This trend is surprising considering that the vast majority of the innovations and advancements behind today's complex IT systems occurred in the last decade, with a corresponding increase in ITOps management software, budgets and demands on ITOps professionals (Gartner 2020). The 1980s and 1990s were characterised by much simpler/isolated systems. However, from the 2000s, complex and integrated systems like ERP, CRM, mobile computing, virtualisation, digital platforms, cloud computing and other modern technologies emerged that changed the IT landscape (Gartner 2020).

4.3   Decline of IT Operations in Top IS Journals

Lastly, our analysis shows that each of the four decades between 1980 and 2020 witnessed significant interest in System Maintenance. This is followed by Knowledge and Skillsets Management, which had publications in three decades, except the 2010s. This is followed by 'Service Management' which had publications in two decades, the 1990s and 2010s. In terms of total breakdown, as per Table 5 below, the 1980s saw publications in four ITOps aspects (System Maintenance, Process Management, Tools Management, and Knowledge/Skillsets Management). The 1990s also saw publications in four ITOps aspects (System Maintenance, Service Management, System Audit, and Knowledge/Skillsets Management). The 2000s saw publications in three ITOps aspects (System Maintenance, Change/Risk Management, and Knowledge and Skillsets Management). Finally, the 2010s saw publications in two ITOps aspects (System Maintenance and Service Management). This pattern again points to a decline in ITOps research, particularly in recent times where there is a greater need for such researches.

Table 5. IT operations literature total breakdown (between 1980–2020)

IT Ops Aspects	1980s (40 yrs)	1990s (30 yrs)	2000s (20 yrs)	2010s (10 yrs)	Percent
1. System Maintenance	4	6	5	3	18 (62.1%)
2. Config Management					0%
3. Change/Risk Mgmt			1		1 (3.5%)
4. Incident Management					0%
5. Service Management		2		1	3 (10.3%)
6. Process Management	1				1 (3.5%)
7. Customer Support					0%
8. System Audit		1			1 (3.5%)
9. Tools Management	1				1 (3.5%)
10. Knowledge/Skillsets Management	1	2	1		4 (13.8%)
Percent	**7 papers (24.1%)**	**11 papers (37.9%)**	**7 papers (24.1%)**	**4 papers (13.8)**	**29 (100%)**

5 Discussion: Assessing the Status of Current Research and Agenda for the Future

The previous section showed that there is an uneven pattern in ITOps research, where some aspects are overlooked. In this section, we discuss the possible reasons and propose directions for future research.

5.1 Wider Perspective on IT Operations

The literature review revealed that research on ITOps disproportionately focused on software maintenance. One reason for this is that IS adoption research often considered IS development and use, with little attention to IT operations. Also, in practice, most organisations do not acknowledge operational costs when deciding on new systems (Berghout ct al. 2011). Further, outsourcing and cloud computing have shifted some aspects of ITOps to third parties.

Since ITOps is at the forefront of IT adoption and use, it is a fertile ground for taking IT seriously and opening its blackbox (Orlikowski and Iacono 2001). In this regard, the context of ITOps provides a unique opportunity for sociotechnical and sociomaterial researches to explore the interactions between human and non-human actors from various perspectives. This could be achieved by targeting configuration management, incident management and customer support.

The scope of ITOps literature could also be widened to include aspects like IT incident management. This is needed because the majority of IT budget/resources in IT organisations are dedicated to ITOps activities (Goldstein et al. 2011). Also, the relationship between vendors, contractors and internal operational teams is yet to be examined thoroughly although, many organisations adopt smart IT systems and analytic tools developed by vendors to manage their complex IT systems and infrastructures.

5.2 IT Operations and Adoption of Intelligent Technologies

ITOps is undergoing major transformations, with the adoption of novel/predictive data analytics approaches and fast-speed IoT connected devices that are enabled by AI. This presents a high level of social and technological complexity worthy of examination, despite difficulties with site access. From our experience, access to such operational environments is often restricted by organisations owing to their sensitive nature and contractual agreements with clients and vendors who have economic interests in protecting their innovations. Similarly, they are keen to ensure that system flaws are not publicised, to give them a chance to address them without the prying eyes of outsiders.

Nonetheless, it is important for IS research to pay attention to ITOps because it is an important field where the majority of IT professionals work. Further, considering that ITOps environments are replete with advance technologies, it is difficult to completely separate social and technological actors since IT is ubiquitous and manifestly act in ways that make a difference in the world. This should allow IS researchers to readily explore the advanced IT that pervade organisations (Orlikowski and Iacono 2001).

Further, since ITOps environments are at the forefront of IT innovation, adoption and use, they provide an ideal context for IS innovation researchers to broaden their scope beyond start-ups. By also exploring established IT organisations that are at the forefront of large-scale IT development, to for instance explicate how new technologies are integrated with existing technologies or how organisations transition from one technology to another. Such insights would help to shed more light on why some IT adoption initiatives are successful, whilst others fail. This would also help to shift the focus of IT adoption research to the long-term, rather than just the short term as is typical when such researches focus on the development phase, which is relatively short.

5.3   Theorisation on IT Operations

The interactions that unfold between human and non-human actors and their respective agencies, and how these collaborate within AI, IoT and sensor-based systems that are currently on the rise had led to the phenomenon of 'IT for IT management'. Whereby one form of IT manages another autonomously as is typical in IT operations, where intelligent IT sensors and tools routinely scan the health of interconnected IT systems to detect and report emerging signs of failure or performance abnormality. This informs other smart IT tools to intervene or alert ITOps engineers where necessary.

This and other similar trends that are facilitated by smart IT deserves research attention to help advance IS theorization, regarding the role of intelligent IT systems in organising. Examining ITOps in such contexts also opens up opportunities for revisiting our understanding of concepts like **'organising'** and **'work'** and who performs them and how or for what purposes (Elbanna et al. 2020).

5.4   Complex/Multidisciplinary Knowledge Ecosystem

ITOps is rich in both organisational processes and technical knowledge that emanates from diverse disciplines and technological ecosystems. This makes ITOps "knowledge ecosystem" dynamic whilst also traversing different boundaries and knowledge domains (Ramakrishnan et al. 2018), as depicted in Fig. 2 below. This includes both open-source and proprietary knowledge that are tied to various network protocols, vendor products and software applications. From this perspective, the knowledge base of ITOps departments is distributive. Further, with every new product release or customer provisioning comes new configurations that require existing knowledge to be updated to effectively integrate new configurations (Abeck and Mayerl 1999).

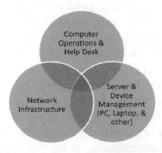

Fig. 2. ITOps knowledge domains (From: (Hetvik 2014))

Today, the complexity and dynamism of IT systems and infrastructures imposes additional demands, in terms of the management of ITOps skillset and knowledge base. This calls for further research to unearth how organisations manage their diverse and decentralised knowledge ecosystems. This is an important endeavour because whilst there is extensive literature on knowledge management (Hawk et al. 2009; Gupta et al. 2009; Orlikowski 2006; Suchman 2000), these mainly assume that organisations have full and centralized control over their operational knowledge.

However, the complexity of modern IT systems partly stems from the fact that often different vendors and third-party solution providers with proprietary knowledge, inter-disciplinary teams with domain knowledge, clients and regulatory agencies all need to collaborate to deploy and operate these systems. From this perspective, the associated knowledge is very distributed. This opens up opportunities for exploring distributed work performance from a modern perspective. Future researches could also examine the associated complex and multidisciplinary 'knowledge ecosystem' to for instance address how reliable performance is attained within such complex organising contexts.

Also, whilst the traditional notion of teams generally refers to a collection of people, in the context of ITOps, this understanding seems limited because non-human actors also participant in the performance of operational tasks. From this perspective, the constitution of teams in ITOps departs from the typical/human-centred view. This presents opportunities to revisit the notion of teams from the perspective of modern organisations that are equally reliant on intelligent technologies.

6 Conclusion

IT operations is a critical function in modern organisations. Following a review of IT operations literature in eight top IS journals, the current paper revealed three main findings, notably the disproportionate focus on System/Software Maintenance, lack of contemporary view of ITOps, and a decline of ITOps in Top IS Journals. The paper proposes four main future research directions that would help enrich ITOps literature and make it more relevant to contemporary IS organisations.

References

Abeck, S., Mayerl, C.: Modeling IT operations to derive provider-accepted management tools. In: Proceedings of the Sixth IFIP/IEEE International Symposium on Integrated Network Management, pp. 843–856. IEEE (1999)

Banker, R.D., Slaughter, S.A.: The moderating effects of structure on volatility & complexity in software enhancement. Inf. Syst. Res. 11, 219–240 (2000)

Berghout, E., Nijland, M., Powell, P.: Management of lifecycle costs and benefits: Lessons from IS practice. Comput. Ind. 62, 755–764 (2011)

Caralli, R., Allen, J.H., Curtis, P.D., White, D.W., Young, L.R.: Improving operational resilience processes: the CERT resilience management model. In: IEEE 2nd International Conference on Social Computing (SocialCom), pp 1165–1170. IEEE (2010)

Cetindamar, D., Phaal, R., Probert, D.: Understanding technology management as a dynamic capability: a framework for technology management activities. Technovation **29**, 237–246 (2009)

Dwivedi, Y.K., Levine, L., Williams, M.D., Singh, M., Wastell, D.G., Bunker, D.: Toward an understanding of the evolution of IFIP WG 8.6 research. In: IFIP Working Conference on Human Benefit through the Diffusion of Information Systems Design Science Research, pp. 225–242. Springer (2010)

Edwards, C.: Information systems maintenance: an integrated perspective. MIS Q. **8**, 237-256 (1984)

Elbanna, A.R., Dwivedi, Y., Bunker, D., Wastell, D.: The search for smartness in working, living and organising: beyond the 'Technomagic'. Inf. Syst. Frontiers **22**, 275–280 (2020)

Financial conduct authority: FCA fines RBS, NatWest and Ulster Bank Ltd £42 million for IT failures. (2014). http://www.fca.org.uk/news/fca-fines-rbs-natwest-and-ulster-bank-ltd-42m-for-it-failures

Gartner: Gartner Top 10 Trends Impacting Infrastructure & Operations for 2020 (2019). https://www.gartner.com/smarterwithgartner/gartner-top-10-trends-impacting-infrastructure-operations-for-2020

Gartner: Market Share: IT Operations Management, Worldwide, 2019 (2020). Gartner Information Technology Research. https://www.gartner.com/en/documents/3984399

Goldstein, J., Chernobai, A., Benaroch, M.: An event study analysis of the economic impact of IT operational risk and its subcategories. J. Assoc. Inf. Syst. **12**, 606–631 (2011)

Gupta, R., Prasad, K.H., Luan, L., Rosu, D., Ward, C.: Multi-dimensional knowledge integration for efficient incident management in a services cloud. In: SCC 2009. IEEE International Conference on Services Computing, pp. 57–64. IEEE (2009)

Hawk, S., Weijun, Z., Zmud, R.W.: Overcoming knowledge-transfer barriers in infrastructure management outsourcing: lessons from a case study. MIS Q. Executive **8**, 123–139 (2009)

Herrera, M., Van Hillegersberg, J.: Using metamodeling to represent lean six sigma for IT service improvement. In: IEEE 21st Conference on Business Informatics (CBI), pp 241–248. IEEE (2019)

Hetvik, J.: What Does IT Operations Management Do? (2014). https://joehertvik.com/operations-management/

Jamieson, R., Low, G.: Local area network operations: a security, control and audit perspective. J. Inf. Technol. **5**, 63–72 (1990)

Krishnan, M.S., Mukhopadhyay, T., Kriebel, C.H.: A decision model for software maintenance. Inf. Syst. Res. **15**, 396–412 (2004)

Nelson, K.M., Nadkarni, S., Narayanan, V.K., Ghods, M.: Understanding software operations support expertise: a revealed causal mapping approach. MIS Q. **24**, 475–507 (2000)

Orlikowski, W.J.: Material knowing: the scaffolding of human knowledgeability. Eur. J. Inf. Syst. **15**, 460–466 (2006)

Orlikowski, W.J., Iacono, C.S.: Desperately seeking the 'IT' in IT research: a call to theorizing the IT artifact. Information Systems Research (2001)

Ramakrishnan, M., Shrestha, A., Cater-Steel, A., Soar, J.: IT service management knowledge ecosystem–literature review and a conceptual model. Australasian Conference on Information Systems. Sydney, Australia (2018)

Reisinger, D.: How to Reduce IT Operational Costs. CIO Insight (2013). https://www.cioinsight.com/it-management/it-budgets/slideshows/how-to-reduce-it-operational-costs-05

Robey, D., Im, G., Wareham, J.D.: Theoretical foundations of empirical research on interorganizational systems: assessing past contributions and guiding future directions. J. Assoc. Inf. Syst. **9**, 4 (2008)

Shaft, T.M., Vessey, I.: The role of cognitive fit in the relationship between software comprehension and modification. MIS Q. **30**, 29–55 (2006)

Straub, D.: The value of scientometric studies: An introduction to a debate on IS as a reference discipline. J. Assoc. Inf. Syst. **7**, 241 (2006)

Suchman, L.: Making a case: 'knowledge' and 'routine' work in document production. Workplace studies: Recovering work practice and informing system design, pp. 29–45 (2000)

Swanson, E.B.: IS maintainability: should it reduce the maintenance effort? In: Proceedings of the 1999 ACM SIGCPR Conference on Computer Personnel Research, pp 164–173 (1999)

Tambo, T., Filtenborg, J.: Digital services governance: IT4IT for management of technology. J. Manuf. Technol. Manag. (2019)

Taylor, M., Moynihan, E., Wood-Harper, T.: Knowledge for software maintenance. J.Inf. Technol. **12**, 155–166 (1997)

Tsunoda, M., Monden, A., Matsumoto, K., Ohiwa, S., Oshino, T.: Benchmarking IT operations cost based on working time and unit cost. Sci. Comput. Program. **135**, 75–87 (2017)

Working from Home During Covid-19: How Do We 'Do' Social Interaction at a Distance?

Banita Lal[1], Yogesh K. Dwivedi[2], and Markus Haag[3(✉)]

[1] University of Bradford, Richmond Road, Bradford BD7 1DP, UK
[2] Swansea University, Fabian Bay, Swansea SA1 8EN, UK
[3] University of Bedfordshire, University Square, Luton LU1 3JU, UK
markus.haag@beds.ac.uk

Abstract. With the rapid adoption of homeworking by organisations across the world owing to Covid-19, employees have been separated from their informal, social networks in the traditional office space. This paper explores how individuals maintain social interaction with colleagues when working remotely. A diary study technique was employed and snowball sampling was used. Initial results from the diaries of 29 participants are presented. The findings highlight various challenges that homeworkers face, including task-related inefficiencies relating to technology-enabled communications in the absence of face-to-face interaction. The paper ends by briefly highlighting how the study analysis will proceed.

Keywords: Homeworking · Social interaction · Distance working

1 Introduction

'Homeworking' picked up pace in the 1990s with developments in Information and Communication Technologies (ICTs) and with organisations offering more flexible styles of working to their employees. Essentially, 'homeworking' is where traditionally office-based workers now work from home via means of ICTs. Fast forward to 2020, we see that the Covid-19 pandemic has really shaken up the definition of concepts such as the 'workplace', 'organisation', 'teamworking' and 'colleagues' [5] due to the sudden shift from office-based working to homeworking for a large percentage of the global white-collar workforce.

There is a notable amount of literature on homeworking in fields such as Human Resource Management, focusing on issues such as remote working and increased employee flexibility, wellbeing and productivity [7], stress, job satisfaction and costs [18], as well as homeworkers' ability to segment and balance their work-home lives [11, 22, 25]. However, the topic never garnered much interest in the Information Systems field aside from a limited number of studies [e.g. 3, 12, 13]. Thus, there are still important issues requiring further investigation. For example, how homeworkers adjust, adapt and manage their use of technology – increasingly mobile in nature – for various purposes within the home-workplace. Furthermore, how individuals manage their social interactions with colleagues via technology when working remotely is

© IFIP International Federation for Information Processing 2020
Published by Springer Nature Switzerland AG 2020
S. K. Sharma et al. (Eds.): TDIT 2020, IFIP AICT 617, pp. 320–328, 2020.
https://doi.org/10.1007/978-3-030-64849-7_29

under-researched. Such topics are gaining interest in the popular press. However, empirical evidence into these topics is scarce.

The aim of this paper is to *investigate how homeworkers engage in technology-enabled social interactions with colleagues when working from home*. This paper presents some initial findings from a study that we are currently working on. Please note that the paper provides initial findings following the first-round of analysis of data that has been collected. Thus, we do not aim to make bold assertions, but aim to provide insights into the types of patterns that appear to be emerging from the literature. The paper is structured as follows: an overview of the literature in relation to homeworking and social isolation is firstly presented, followed by the methodology. The latter includes the analysis techniques employed for the first-round of data analysis. This is followed by a brief discussion followed by a conclusion which expands on how we intend to extend the analysis going forward.

2 Literature Review

Traditionally, the 'workplace' equated to, and in the main still refers to, a specific place to which an individual travels in order to fulfil their work obligations within a specified period of time [6]. Owing to the recent global changes caused by the pandemic, this has clearly changed. Previous arguments that the extent and benefits of homeworking are rhetoric as opposed to reality [2], working from home is not useful for all organisations [23], and organisations have been slow at adopting flexible working styles [15] are called into question as industries across the world have experienced a surge in homeworking.

A considerable amount of research has examined how homeworkers have tackled the issue of no longer having spatial and temporal distinctions between their work and home lives by reconstructing these boundaries in the home-work place [4]. There has also been some research on how homeworkers construct boundaries in relation to mobile devices [3, 9, 10]. However, lesser-researched topics focus on how homeworkers are able to manage their social interactions with colleagues in order to avoid feelings of social isolation in the absence of the day-today socialisation and relationship-building communication shared in the traditional office space [12]. It is a basic human need to want to associate and identify with others via long-term, positive relationships: not having face-to-face social interaction can affect communication and camaraderie, interpersonal networking and the sharing of work-related information and gossip fwhich has the effect of enabling employees to create identification with the company [12]. The proliferation of more advanced ICTs since the early days of homeworking suggests that homeworkers should be able to retain communication via different technological means, allowing individuals to feel more 'socially present' [5].

The topic of homeworking and social interaction/isolation is, at best, briefly included as part of a wider study examining the implications of flexible working [16] where it was found that half of respondents felt that 'no professional/social interaction' was a pre-telework concern. However, the study did not expand on actual experiences of such interaction once the change in work style had been made. Below we present details of three studies that do provide some explicit insights into homeworkers and feelings of social isolation; as mentioned above, such studies are very limited in number.

In a study of sales staff working from home [8], it was found that 63% of home-workers said they felt isolated since starting homeworking, stating that they felt for-gotten and left to muddle through when working remotely. Homeworkers felt that the lack of timely and tangible company action to support them was due to a lack of employer concern, subsequently resulting in a detrimental impact on trust and rela-tionship with their employer. Within the year, labour within the sales team increased to nearly 20%: the previous annual average was 6%. Lack of in-person interaction resulted in a reduction in the speed of problem-solving and knowing what was going on as it became more difficult to share experiences. Further, infrequent team meetings were described as formal with full agendas and little scope for informal discussions with employees feeling invisible.

In their study [14], it was found that 67% of individuals working remotely acknowledged feeling loneliness, compared to 0% of office-based counterparts. The lack of face-to-face communication was an issue: there was no-one to talk to at the end of a difficult day and homeworkers would go out to the shops to have face-to-face interaction with somebody. Further, increased use of Computer-Mediated Communi-cation (CMC) reduced feelings of belonging with the company which is necessary for creating loyalty to colleagues and the organisation, and homeworkers lacked social support which could give rise to other emotions such as feelings of insecurity and lack of confidence in their abilities. The authors assert that the social interaction of the workplace is "utterly important" and homeworkers feel the stress of separation from colleagues and social banter within the office (p. 208).

Our study [12] found that homeworkers were provided with work mobile phones and social interaction via these devices could be managed to keep work and home lives distinct. Three main types of information were exchanged: general gossip about other colleagues, information about developments/changes in the company and advice on how certain work tasks could be completed. The study highlighted that homeworkers would seek social interaction with family members to compensate for the lack of social interaction with colleagues. Furthermore, the sender of the message thought carefully about the best mode of communication (e.g. a SMS was less intrusive at the weekend than a call), and that a small network of close colleagues was key both for work support and social interaction. Very few studies investigating how homeworkers use/manage their technologies, particularly mobile technology, in the home-work place have been conducted since the study by Lal and Dwivedi [12] in 2009 [e.g. 10].

Other issues faced by homeworkers included feelings of loss of career opportunities due to lower visibility, loss of organisational identity and the fact that coping strategies needed to be developed when work comes home [25].

Considering the above, there is little doubt that maintaining social interactions with colleagues is important on many levels. Technology offers promise in terms of enabling homeworkers to retain some level of social interaction with colleagues. However, as aforementioned, empirical evidence in terms of how this is done is limited. The fol-lowing section provides details of the methodology employed in investigating how homeworkers engage in technology-enabled social interactions with colleagues when working from home.

3   Methodology

This study was an exploratory study utilising the diary-keeping technique. Diary studies tend to be used more commonly in areas such as social and personality psychology [20] and the sciences. There were key reasons as to why diary studies were selected. Diaries allow researchers to gather data on participants' natural life contexts such as at home or in the workplace: this data can take the form of events, behaviours, feelings and thoughts [21]. In this study, the aim of the diary was to get an insight into participants' behaviours in terms of their social interaction with colleagues.

We requested participants to complete daily diary entries over a period of ten working days. Not only did this offer an insight into participants' everyday lives as it naturally unfolded [19], but respondents were able to record responses on the day. Diaries were kept between May and June during the height of the lockdown. There were six standard questions that participants had to consider daily: (i) their working hours; (ii) how they felt personally/professionally while working remotely; (iii) whether they had any social interaction with colleagues; (iv) if 'yes' to (iii), then the method of communication used, information exchanged and time of interaction; (v) whether they did any non-work-related activities to keep positive, and (vi) any other comments they wanted to make. The questions were intentionally kept simple so participants did not perceive completing them a daily chore, to reduce the likelihood of participants dropping out of the study and, owing to the exploratory nature of the study, enabled participants to record what was important for them. Participants were also asked to complete an additional information sheet which provided details such as demographic data.

Participants were recruited using a snowball sampling technique. This entailed the researchers initially contacting individuals they knew had recently transitioned to full-time homeworking due to the pandemic, and then these participants recommending other potential participants. Diaries were completed by a total of 29 participants.

Data was analysed as follows, following guidelines by Miles and Huberman [17]: a contact summary sheet was created for each participant. This entailed going through the ten days' diary entries in order to summarise the data provided. Codes were applied to the data which was the first stage of analysis: we did not have a start list of pre-existing codes prior to the data collection that we were trying to match to participants' data as this study was more exploratory in nature and there is currently limited empirical data which can be used to formulate pre-existing codes. A complete list of codes was also separately created. Codes were revised as necessary.

Having a record of daily experiences and the additional information sheet helped us to build a better picture of the participants which helped to develop more of a context to their responses. Thus, we could interpret the codes and data in the given context. This led onto provisional pattern codes being developed. Please note that for the purpose of this study, we have done a first-round of descriptive and interpretive coding, with initial insights into patterns (key themes and links) that emerged.

4 Initial Findings

This section provides some initial findings based on the initial first-round level of analysis. There were 15 males and 14 females who participated in this study. Occupations of participants were varied and included: Web Administrator and Digital Marketer, Software Developers, Academics, Science Policy Analyst and Sales Account Executive. 19 participants used either solely personal devices or personal plus work devices provided by their company for work. 10 participants used only devices provided by the company. 9 participants had never worked from home before the pandemic, whereas 20 participants had.

4.1 The Meaning of 'Social Interaction'

Participants were asked whether they had any social interaction with colleagues on each day they kept a diary. We intentionally did not define what 'social interaction' was in order to understand how participants defined it. In most cases, social interaction was defined by participants as *any type of communication with colleagues*, whether this was work or non-work related.

There was no doubt that social interaction had reduced because of working from home:

"I feel like the proportion of casual/personal conversations I am having with colleagues is a lot smaller when working from home (i.e. nearly all conversations are about work matters). For example, today all messages I exchanged with colleagues were about work. Without the casual conversations to break the day up, it can give the work day a more serious feel." (p. 14)

4.2 Absence of Face-to-Face Interaction

Less than a half of participants stated that they missed face-to-face interactions with colleagues for social banter:

"I do miss my office, interacting with colleagues, and just the separation between Office and home... This human interaction, work chats, corridor talks and laughs...are the best part of my job which I miss." (p. 18)

Some participants missed in-person interaction; however, the overall benefits of working from home appeared to outweigh the drawbacks:

"I do not miss the 'norm'. But I started to think about the things I did at work that I enjoyed and miss: 1. The staff member you encounter at the kitchen or the hallway... 2. Going to the gym at lunch time and have a quick chat at the changing room, 3. The person you consistently encounter on the way to the office...you would exchange greetings or a joke or a nice gesture that makes you feel nice... On the other hand, I have much longer time with my family." (p. 2)

Approximately two thirds of participants stated that the reason for missing face-to-face interaction was more work-related: working from home could sometimes prove inefficient for getting work done. This was especially the case when needing to work with others. However, again, some offset the drawbacks with the positives of working from home.

4.3   How Social Interaction Is 'Done'

Participants tended to communicate via Zoom, Microsoft Teams, Slack, Google Chat/Meet. These were used for individual chat, group chat, video and voice calls related to work and non-work. Other communication methods were also used, although to a lesser degree, including: e-mail, telephone, WhatsApp, Facebook, FaceTime, Xbox Live and SMS.

Non-work discussion was built into work meetings, often for a few minutes before/after a meeting. This limited social interaction was not cited as a problem. There were very few participants who had time specifically dedicated for social interaction:

"I also had a coffee chat with another department I work with so that we have that level of social interaction as we have while at work...discussing what we are doing to stay sane and active. And catching up what we did the previous week. Also we see each others pets or show our shopping." (p. 12)

4.4   Amount of Work and Communication

Virtually every participant appeared to be very busy, which could explain the longer hours many were working. Subsequently, some participants highlighted that working from home was beneficial as it enabled them to avoid distractions typically experienced in the office and instead concentrate on their work. Again, the benefits of working from home could potentially outweigh the drawbacks:

"I do miss some face-to-face discussion. On the other hand working without walk-in traffic does not feel too bad" (p. 15)

Although participants could avoid in-person distractions, this was not necessarily the case with technology. Homeworking naturally emphasises the role of technology in completing work tasks and communications. This appeared to be taking its toll on homeworkers:

"[Since working from home, there has been a] significant increase in time dedicated for meetings, skype, video calls...This in turn leaves lesser time to focus on your own work for which one needs thorough concentration and hence end up sitting back late or outside business hours to get it completed." (p. 27)

"it was a long day and I felt tired after back to back video calls throughout the day. I needed some time by myself so that I could sit for an hour quietly while working before speaking to members of my household at the end of the day." (p. 30)

Alongside the above, several other key trends started to appear from the data. These included: interpretation of online communications and related issues, the 'rules' of online communications which includes thinking about whether you are bothering colleagues by contacting them, the issues relating to online social interaction including some people taking over the conversation, technology issues which affect communication and productivity, and mixed feelings towards video calls which had become mandatory for many participants. Additionally, the turbulent environment created by the pandemic resulted in different pressures for all participants such as increased workloads and fear of redundancies. These factors will be investigated with further analysis.

5   Discussion and Conclusion

Previous empirical research on how homeworkers interact socially via technology is very limited, which means any insights on this topic are potentially new insights. Regarding the aim of this paper, how homeworkers engage in technology-enabled social interactions with colleagues when working from home, what can be deduced from the initial findings is that social interaction is declining for the majority of homeworkers and work communication dominates virtually all communications with colleagues. This, in turn, removes some of the casual conversations typically had in the office and results in the working day feeling more formal. Few participants have time especially dedicated for social interaction and, in the majority of cases, social interaction was built into formal communication – such as jovial banter for three minutes before the start of a meeting - and this did not appear to raise any issues. There were very few participants who could dedicate time for a catch-up with their colleagues either via a video call or online gaming with colleagues during their lunch break.

An interesting finding was that in contrast to the findings of [8, 14] where it was found that a significant portion of homeworkers felt socially isolated from their workplace, this study suggests that approximately only one third of homeworkers stated that they missed social interaction with colleagues in the traditional workplace. It appears that some participants offset the negatives of working from home with the positives; for example, they missed in-person interaction but valued the extra time they had with their family. In fact, the findings suggest that in-person social interaction was perceived as a distraction which some participants were happy to avoid as this enabled them to concentrate on their work. Face-to-face interaction was missed more for work purposes than for social interaction as working remotely made it inefficient to complete certain tasks, particularly those requiring discussions with colleagues. A noticeable pattern that was emerging was that a number of participants stated that they were experiencing communication overload which was tiring, affected their productivity and subsequently ate into their personal time, as well as potentially affecting their interactions with individuals in their home. One may suggest that such a situation could explain why few participants were not inclined to spend more time on technology for social interaction with colleagues. However, this is subject to further analysis.

Overall, the literature suggests that social isolation is felt by the majority of homeworkers which can have an array of negative implications, ranging from loneliness to trust in their employer. Thus, social interaction is regarded as key for staff wellbeing and their relationship with their employer. Although the findings of our study are provisional and the data is subject to further analysis and scrutiny, initial analysis does suggest some divergence from the literature, particularly in terms of what 'social interaction' means to a full-time homeworker who has no option to meet colleagues face-to-face during the lockdown, and how much they miss traditional office banter. This may be considered surprising given that the lockdown meant social distancing from colleagues, friends and family, which had the prospect of heightening feelings of social isolation. Nevertheless, the context of homeworking during Covid-19 is very different to homeworking prior to the pandemic: there is less social interaction with other people, yet at the same time the pressures have increased with participants citing increased work and stress due to redundancies, cost-cutting and other changes within their organisations. Such factors, which require further analysis, could explain issues such as communications overload and perhaps a lower inclination to want to socially interact with colleagues. Moving forwards, the researchers will conduct deeper analysis in defining patterns within the data from which to draw affirmative conclusions.

References

1. Bolger, N., Davis, A., Rafaeli, E.: Diary methods: capturing life as it is lived. Annu. Rev. Psychol. **54**, 579–616 (2002)
2. Brocklehurst, M.: Homeworking and the new technology: the reality and the rhetoric. Personnel Rev. **18**(2), 1–70 (1989)
3. Cousins, K., Robey, D.: Managing work-life boundaries with mobile technologies. Inf. Technol. People **28**(1), 34–71 (2015)
4. Desrochers, S., Sargent, L.D.: Boundary/border theory and work-family integration (2003). http://wfnetwork.bc.edu/encyclopedia_entry.php?id=220
5. Dwivedi, Y.K., Hughes, D.L., Coombs, C., et al.: Impact of COVID-19 pandemic on information management research and practice: transforming education, work and life. Int. J. Inf. Manage. **102211**. https://doi.org/10.1016/j.ijinfomgt.2020.102211 (2020 upcoming)
6. Fitzgerald, M.A., Winter, M.: The intrusiveness of home-based work on family life. J. Fam. Econ. Issues **22**(1), 75–92 (2001)
7. Grant, C.A., Wallace, L.M., Spurgeon, P.C.: An exploration of the psychological factors affecting remote e-worker's job effectiveness, well-being and work-life balance. Employee Relations **35**(5), 527–546 (2013)
8. Harris, L.: Home-based teleworking and the employment relationship: managerial challenges and dilemmas. Pers. Rev. **32**(4), 422–437 (2003)
9. Hislop, D., Bosch-Sijtsema, P.: Zimmermann: Introduction for special themed section: information and communication technologies and the work-life boundary. New Technol. Work Employ. **28**(3), 177–178 (2013)
10. Hislop, D., Axtell, C., Collins, A., Daniels, K., Glover, J., Niven, K.: Variability in the use of mobile ICTs by homeworkers and its consequences for boundary management and social isolation. Inf. Organ. **25**(4), 222–232 (2015)
11. Kreiner, G.E., Hollensbe, E.C., Sheep, M.L.: Balancing borders and bridges: negotiating the work-home interface via boundary work tactics. Acad. Manag. J. **52**(4), 704–730 (2009)
12. Lal, B., Dwivedi, Y.K.: Homeworkers' usage of mobile phones; social isolation in the home-workplace. J. Enterprise Inf. Manage. **22**(3), 257–274 (2009)
13. Lal, B., Dwivedi, Y.K.: Investigating homeworkers' inclination to remain connected to work at "anytime, anywhere" via mobile phones. J. Enterp. Inf. Manage. **23**(6), 759–774 (2010)
14. Mann, S., Holdsworth, L.: The psychological impact of teleworking: stress, emotions and health. New Technol. Work Employ. **18**(3), 196–211 (2003)
15. Martin, B.H., MacDonnell, R.: Is telework effective for organizations? Manage. Res. Rev. **35**(7), 602–616 (2012)
16. Maruyama, T., Tietze, S.: From anxiety to assurance: concerns and outcomes of telework. Pers. Rev. **41**(4), 450–469 (2012)
17. Miles, M.B., Huberman, A.M.: Qualitative Data Analysis: An Expanded Sourcebook. Second edition, SAGE Publications Inc., California (1994)
18. Nakrošienė, A., Bučiūnienė, I., Goštautaitė, B.: Working from home: characteristics and outcomes of telework. Int. J. Manpower **40**(1), 87–101 (2019)

19. Neupert, S.D., Bellingtier, J.A.: The Ups and Downs of Daily Diary Research. SAGE Research Methods Cases in Psychology (2018). http://methods.sagepub.com/case/the-ups-and-downs-of-daily-diary-research
20. Nezlek, J.B.: Diary Methods for Social and Personality Psychology. Sage Publications Ltd. (2012)
21. Ohly, S., Sonnentag, S., Niessen, C., Zapf, D.: Diary Studies in Organizational Research: an introduction and some practical recommendations. J. Pers. Psychol. 9(2), 79–93 (2010)
22. Park, Y.H., Fritz, C., Jex, S.M.: Relationships between work-home segmentation and psychological detachment from work: the role of communication technology use at home. J. Occup. Health Psychol. 16(4), 457–467 (2011)
23. Pathak, A.A., Bathini, D.R., Kandathil, G.M.: The ban on working from home makes sense for Yahoo: It needs the innovation and speed of delivery that come from office-based employees. Hum. Resour. Manage. Int. Digest 23(3), 12–14 (2015)
24. Sohn, T., Li, K.A., Griswold, W.G., Hollan, J.D.: In: Proceedings of the 26th ACM SIGCHI Conference on Human Factors in Computing Systems, Florence, Italy, 5–10 April, pp. 433–442 (2008)
25. Tietze, S.: When "work" comes "home": coping strategies of teleworkers and their families. J. Bus. Ethics 41(4), 385–396 (2002)

CIPPUA: Towards Coherence and Impact in ICT4D/IS

A. Kayode Adesemowo$^{(\boxtimes)}$ 🆔

Nelson Mandela University, Port Elizabeth, South Africa
kadesemowo@soams.co.za, kayode@mandela.ac.za

Abstract. Nonetheless, the many developments occasioned by and through information and communication technology (ICT), the plethora of debates on what 'development' means persist. Researchers, practitioners, policy makers and stakeholders of ICTs for Development (ICT4D) have a good understanding of ICT4D, yet their views differ when it comes to the 'development'. The ICT (as an entity), do not get interrogated well enough as a research reality or phenomenon in itself. Differing opinions persist. Without a common understanding, diffusion and adoption of ICT4D will continue fragmented. In continuing the conversation, one area to reimagine is the ICT and digital technologies in ICT4D or information systems. This paper revisits Walsham's ("ICT4D research: reflections on history and future agenda") 2017 paper, as a backdrop to elucidate the emancipatory ethos of critical realism and introduce the conceptual CIPPUA model. Through explanatory stratified ontological review of the position, nature and identity of digital technologies/objects, this paper contributes to the ongoing discourse on critical realism in digital development, especially the connection of ICT to development. More so, this paper with the conceptual CIPPUA model, contributes in part to the discourse of operationalizing critical realism in practice.

Keywords: Coherence · Critical realism · Emancipatory · Digital objects · Development, CIPPUA

1 Introduction

The debate of 'development' has been well discussed and yet on-going. It is one that keeps diverging at every converging state [1]. In essence, researchers, practitioners, policy makers and stakeholders of Information Systems (IS) and ICT for Development (ICT4D) have a good understanding of ICT4D (or ICTD, subject to the discourse on ICT4D, ICTD or digital development). Ironically, they have varying views of what 'development' is [2]. This follows through to common understanding of diffusion and/or adoption not only in ICT4D but also IS, such as in digital transformation [3].

Walsham [4] captures this succinctly, "[I]t may not be possible to agree on a shared definition of development but an alternative approach to coherence for the ICT4D research field, ... may be by *developing a shared conceptual framework for the ICT4D field*". This indicate a need for further research. What might come to mind is: what further research is required? What type of shared conceptual framework is required?

© IFIP International Federation for Information Processing 2020
Published by Springer Nature Switzerland AG 2020
S. K. Sharma et al. (Eds.): TDIT 2020, IFIP AICT 617, pp. 329–340, 2020.
https://doi.org/10.1007/978-3-030-64849-7_30

A need for re-interrogation of ICT and development is required, and thus *the potential for enhanced research impact* [4]. A need for common understanding to better appreciate the impact of ICT4D. As a starter, a year on after Walsham's paper, Thapa and Omland [2], outlined three key problems:

- Development outcomes struggle to provide clear attribution of the role played by ICTs in those outcomes;
- Contribution of ICT does not explain the connection of ICT to development;
- Connection between ICTs and development pitched only at the level of juxtaposition rather than causal link;

These contestations resonate with the notion of 'development' in itself [1], as a contested idea with diverse views of what development was, what development is, and what development should be. Whilst De´ et al., stated that "[T]he controversies and debates regarding a normative view of development, however, did not deter ICT4D researchers to broadly conclude that ICTs indeed contributed to development", ICT4D researchers and practitioners remain divided on 'ICT' and 'development'. This carries through to the "digital development" paradigm where ICTs are no longer just tools to enable particular aspects of development, but the platform that mediates development [5], just as digital technologies transforms organizations in digital transformation [3].

Part of the challenge of making correlations between 'ICT' and 'D' (Development), it would seem, is grasping the depth and linkage of the nature of ICT (technology) to the sociotechnical nature of ICT4D and IS research [2, 6]. Artefact in design science [6, 7], and objects in activity theory [8, 9], have been used to draw inference, reference and causal relationship. Yet, the underlying questions of how and why ICTs lead to development, remained largely unanswered. Therefore, they are matters requiring further inquiry. Even more so, as Mungai [6] raised a concern about the specific role of technology in mechanisms: the issue that "ICT-based cases involve social and technical entities, which creates the need to identify the elements of socio-technical mechanisms and how such mechanisms interact".

The question is; how are we going to approach the notion of ICT as a (research) reality towards a shared conceptual framework for the ICT4D and IS field? Possibly, through critical realism with its philosophical and ontological nature [1, 2, 10–12]. It is in this regard and context that this paper revisits the nature of digital objects/digital technologies and emancipatory ethos of critical realism as essential fabric towards shared conceptual framework for the 'development' in ICT4D. In this paper, IT, ICT, technology, technological objects, digital technologies and digital objects are used loosely, and where needed, emphasis or distinction are made.

1.1 Structure of the Paper

The introduction provides the background to the 'ICT' reality in ICT4D as a building block towards shared conceptual framework for 'development' in ICT4D and IS, introduces the author's view of ICT4D as a precursor to the research approach. Thereafter the paper presents an approach to evaluating critical realism (CR) components and concludes with a way forward.

2   Research Domain

2.1   View on ICT4D

Walsham [4], in his paper "ICT4D research: reflections on history and future agenda" reflected on where we were coming from and possible direction for future engagement in ICT4D. Typical of Walsham philosophical positioning [13], he outlined coherence challenges [4]. At the root of this is the diverging view of what 'development' and 'ICT' means for practitioners and stakeholders within ICT4D and IS. It is on this premise that these questions come to mind, namely:

1. How do we view the 'by', 'through', 'with', and 'of' ICT 'for' development within ICT4D? Put simply, how do we view the 'ICT' in/of ICT4D/IS?
2. How do we view and interact with the nature of ICT as digital objects?
3. How do we approach ICT4D geared for micro level and yet (might) have macro or global impact/influence due to the global village nature of the world we live in?

Invariably, must we only look at ICT4D at community, or national or international level before it can be deemed to be ICT4D or can the approaches and principles of ICT4D be applied to projects 'narrow' in scope [4]? These questions will assist in the ontological study of 'ICT' and 'development' in ICT4D. This paper narrows down to offering insight into, *in what way(s) can we achieve coherence and impact in ICT4D and IS?*

This paper's notion of emancipatory derives from the views of Roy Bhaskar's critical realism [14–16], as opposed to critical theory/critical realist [16]. CR's emancipatory values and components though relating, is distinct dialectically from emancipation and emancipation action. The concept of emancipatory is in providing explanatory understanding of how structures and mechanisms interlace toward impactful change [10].

2.2   Basis for Research and Related Work

The research philosophy is based on critical realism as opposed to interpretivism. In postulating a critical realism philosophy for identifying mechanisms of ICT4D, Thapa and Omland [2], also revisited Walsham's [4] fundamental question, "to what extent are ICTs contributing to development". Bennett, et al. [17], leveraged on critical realism to explore information technology as digital objects from the lens of hylomorphism.

Positivism and interpretivism limit ontological interrogation of ICT research realities in themselves [6, 15], and critically examining underlying structures of ICT as digital objects [18], in order to 'bring back' the observation and re-examination thereof. CR provide for this by its 'retroduction' process or steps [10, 15, 19].

CR inherently requires pluralism towards validity of insights into events and underlying mechanisms [10]. This paper plural (multi-method) approach, adapted CR's describe, identify, 'retroduction' approach [2], and are as follows:

1. Exploratory scoping: Interrogation of ICT4D research reality vis-à-vis critical realism's identify and describe [10, 20] vis-à-vis review of the paper: "ICT4D research:

   • reflections on history and future agenda" [4]; and
   • Session with author of the reviewed paper: Geoff Walsham in Cambridge;

2. Iteration: further interrogation of ICT4D reality;

   • "Critical realism and ICT4D research" [10];

3. Explanatory/Argumentative retroduction: critical realism components [21];

   • Extracting the CIPPUA from interrogation of critical realism's emancipatory components and technological/digital object;
   • Brief discussion of (CIPPUA) evaluation aspects [22].

The choice of Walsham's 2017 paper is at best 'convenience' (in sampling parlance) and the augmenting papers follow a spider-crawl (or linking). It is impossible for a paper of this nature to fully cover the spectrum of ICT4D theories, processes and actions, nor under-labour critical realism [23, 24]. CR in ICT4D research and IS are well discussed in literature [10, 31]. Readers are referred to them. For this paper, it is imperative to state that CR unlike (direct) realism, reason-back the experiences and consideration of the 'reality' – in what is called 'retroduction' [19].

2.3   Research Realities in ICT4D

This paper has indicated a lack of coherence in ICT4D as it relates to development. It has indicated that the ICT in ICT4D is not just an enabler of "D", but that it is a research reality in itself. The reality is the understanding (or lack of understanding) of the nature of 'ICT' and alongside investigation of identity, functional and societal context. Three research realities in ICT4D are identified: ICT as digital technologies/objects (technological objects), non-coherence, and critical realism emancipatory ethos/components.

ICT as Digital/Technological Objects

Within ICT4D and IS generally, there has been much focus on the human, community, organisational, reference and mid-range theory, societal engagements and consequences of (and/or with) technological entities [2, 4, 9, 11, 26, 27] or as instruments of technical rationality [28]. However, not much has been researched into the 'technology' in themselves as research entities of their own [2, 17, 18, 29]. What happens is that technologies are interacted with as part of the research or development process. This neglects the view of intricacies of technologies as technological entities. What if technologies have a life of their own? *A priori*, attempts have been made to theorise technology [27, 30] and to view mechanism of technology as interacting with social space over time domain See Archer in [31, p. 798].

Bennett et al, [17] stance is that reality construct of digital technologies/objects is the starting position from … "where we can ask how can information systems improve our lives". Faulkner and Runde [18], Bennett et al., and Adesemowo [29] views of IT/ICT, digital technologies/objects, ensembled IT assets can be said to hold true, because as objects, they conform to structured continuants or dynamic structure. This paper therefore adopts their view as those of what ICT means. Explanatory is important as *matters* (and any form of dynamic structure) can be complex [21]. Walsham [4] in highlighting the danger of disciplinary stereotyping in ICT4D research projects, pointed out a lack of understanding of the nature of 'ICT' and 'development' outside researchers' and practitioners' discipline It is essential and healthy to engage in this debate of rediscovering and theorising IT/ICT [26].

Non-coherence
The other danger that Walsham highlighted is non-coherence in interdisciplinary or transdisciplinary ICT4D research (research projects). That of wanting to bring together varying disciplinary approaches under one methodological or theoretical umbrella. To borrow from physical sciences, it is like achieving coherency with multiple wavelengths in optics [32], or in artificial intelligence, having multiple overlapping nodes or computing agents acting with limited view of the overall task but cooperating coherently in distributed problem-solving [33].

Retrospectively, at the onset of coining 'information technology', there were many disciplines. This was perhaps lost along the line and must be revisited. This paper does not provide a bullet-proof answer. It, nonetheless, brings a fresh perspective, of adumbrating the re-interrogation of IT/ICT as technological objects or digital technologies or digital objects and engaging with ICT as such.

Critical Realism Emancipatory Values/Ethos and Components
Drawing from the realities of ICT/digital technologies/objects, and non-coherence, this paper explores 'emancipatory' in critical realism; derives and provides for in-depth explanatory understanding of how structures and mechanisms interlace toward impactful change of ICT4D projects.

Whilst noting critical realism is emancipatory in a number of ways, the notion of emancipatory examined in this paper emanates and revolves around Bhaskar's transformational model of social action – TMSA [16, 31]. Without delving into details, emancipatory values/ethos evolve from transformation of structures with commonality of mechanisms [16, 17], and emergent causal powers [17]. Consequently, it follows that the impact of ICT4D and IS researches must be felt and seen in the broad development they bring, irrespective of narrow micro or broader/global macro views.

A View into Critical Realism TMSA
Discussing TMSA comes at the risk of underlabouring or entering the fray of debate on TMSA and Giddens' structuration theory, or TMSA and Archer's morphogenetic/morphostatic (M/M). In a nutshell, resolution of the antinomy of structure and agency is at the heart of TMSA with morphogenetic being an approach of development [24]. Archer herself, puts this to rest by advocating M/M as methodological complement to TMSA [21].

Integral to TMSA are the following:

- *a priori* structures [15];
- social ontology, structures and agency [15, 18, 24];
- ontological and social contexts [15];
- positioning [15];
- mediating concepts/process [15];
- structuring and re-structuring process [15];
- explanatory structure/reasoning/critique [15, 24];
- emergence, change [15, 17];
- Reproduction/transformation [15];

TMSA advocate material effectivity of the emergent properties of structures within a time and context constraint. As ICT4D and IS practitioners, we invariably work within TMSA ourselves. That being the aspects of the social and technical domain: human agency, (social) structures, and the intra and inter-relationship between them [11]. It then implies that social structures of themselves exist to be identified, reproduced and transformed. From TMSA viewpoint, we do not necessarily 'create them', even though we might create them as part of the TMSA social action. Loosely speaking, it is just as we use artefact or create or perceive them from our understanding [34].

Within critical realism, structures and mechanisms carry a form of domain, being the overlapping domains of the empirical, the actual, and the real [14]. It is within this interplay of domains that structures, and mechanisms emerge from: hence IT/ICT, digital technologies/objects are structured continuants or dynamic structure that can be interrogated as structures and mechanisms having technical identities and occupying social position(s) and not just artefacts or objects of use.

Thus, *conceptualisation* (of ICT4D/IS) must have a real effect on *applicability* within the (social-technical community) *positioning*. The social-technical dynamics of ICT development points toward 'real' domain and reality that is built on *coherence* of *concepts* and *understanding* [15]. They provide much needed lens to critically, ontologically interrogate coherence and impact in ICT4D and IS. They provide insights into the probing questions of 'of', 'by', 'with', ICT for development. The author is of the strong view that we must engage critically with the technology we are working with or 'developing', to ensure they are placed within the social space (as would be seen later in the section on CIPPUA). This will assist researchers working from the concept of IT artefacts, as they will be better placed to locate IT artefacts as embedded in some time, place, discourse, structure and community [27].

3   CIPPUA's Lens to Critical Realisms Values and Components for ICT4D Impact

Houston [35], alluded to identifying oppressive or restricting agents and then activating enabling or liberating agents. Likewise, Walsham enjoined 'development' in ICT4D to impact, as in address or at least reduce inequalities within society. More often than not, in calling for new ICTs-enabled models in transforming the processes and structures of development [4], corresponding calls for engaging the ICTs themselves are limited. More especially those relating to structures, conditions and other mechanisms [2]. It seems implied though! This is partly seen in how Walsham described the Ushahidi system [4]. The call for further research into the effect of ICTs-enabled model on developments can be met through technical identity. It is by theorising and considering the nature, forms, functions, structure, mechanism and positioning of digital technologies/objects [17, 18, 26, 29]. It is through this intransitive and stratified dimension that knowledge is gained [31] towards impact, diffusion and adoption.

3.1   CIPPUA Lens

In practical terms, how can this be enabled? In line with the critical realism's philosophy, this paper through identification, exploratory/explanatory reasoning proposes a conscious and purposeful interrogating at the intersection of two dimensions of '*conceptualisation*', '*ICT/IS development*' and '*position*' vis-à-vis '*purpose*', '*usability*' and '*applicability*' (CIPPUA), as depicted in Table 1. Undoubtedly, the degree of intersection will vary from project to project and the nature of digital technologies/objects at play. For instance, *position* might only be considered for *applicability* and not necessarily *purpose* and *usability*. When digital technologies find *usability* outside of their envisaged *applicability* or *position*, they take on new technical identity, usage/purpose.

Table 1. CIPPUA: A conceptual view of enabling and interrogating critical realism's emancipatory and technological objects.

	Conceptualisation (challenge)	ICTs/IS development (problem solving, enhancement, opportunity)	Position (Local, Society, Nation, Global)
Purpose (initiation)	... ...	...	...
Usability (experience, learning, skilling)	...	... ...	...
Applicability (knowledge, impact;)	...	...	... ...

3.2   Deriving the CIPPUA

Without rehashing the many 'concepts' that have been engaged and discussed in this paper, the CIPPUA founds its roots in demi-regularities identified in this paper. These identified nuances and demi-regularities on the nature of PhD by publication flowed from the underpinning critical realism research philosophy that this paper hinged on. The emergent generative mechanisms are ICT development, TMSA/emancipatory ethos, digital technologies/object and technical identity.

Briefly, ICT/IS development are conceptualised for development and use in and at a location (position). The usage (usability) finds applicability in the purpose for which it was intended or conceptualised. The ICT or ICT development project (or ICT4D in itself), can be seen as digital technologies/objects. Their 'components' can also be broken down into digital technologies/objects of their own [18]. Technical identity is shaped not just by the view of developers, but rather by the placement and interaction of the position they are located or placed in. Knowledge is gained through these transitive dimensions and emancipatory ethos come alive in the intersection of the true applicability and purpose.

Bennett's [9], explication of events showed how *purpose*, *usability* and *applicability* of devices and learning management systems mutate across *position* and *ICT development*. Similar explication can be seen in Iannacci [36] causal linkages between legislative and IT artefacts over time in the emancipatory transformation of police–prosecutor routines. Legislative and IT artefacts work across micro and macro levels. This is the tenet of the CIPPUA model represented in Table 1. It reinforces Njihia and Merali [37], view of critical realism causally telling us with good reason from the real domain, "why things are as they are now and where they could be heading".

CIPPUA Scenario-Play

To conclude, three ICT4D research projects are placed 'retrospectively' within the proposed conceptual CIPPUA model. The scenario-based approach [22] is a foretelling of its potential use and adoption.

Ushahidi

Whilst reviewing the Ushahidi project, Walsham [4], called for a need for some solid research as to what exactly are the effects of these ICT-enabled models. An approach would be the CIPPUA matrix. Without doubt, the Ushahidi has mutated and transformed overtime. The *position* keeps evolving, as do the *ICT development* and *applicability*, which expands the *purpose* horizon. This calls for relook of the *conceptualisation* and *usability* experience.

Zenzeleni

Zenzeleni started out as a research test bed (in the Eastern Cape province of South Africa), to become a full-fledged, self-sustaining community network [38]. Its *purpose* and *conceptualisation* has moved from testing to practice [39]. Zenzeleni's *applicability* and *ICT development* has transformed from innovation to impact [39, 40]. Zenzeleni's intersection of *applicability* and *ICT development* has seen blending of knowledge transfer, uptake and transferring of skills with indigenous knowledge, as well as, burgeoning growth, community ownership and empowerment.

ICT Network Calculator (Codename LVIII)

ICT Network is and will remain a bedrock of the fourth industrial revolution, knowledge economy and beyond. Skills shortage has been projected in ICT [41], including ICT Networking as a critical skill [42]. The *position* and *usability* of the ICT Network Calculator shifted from windows-based application within a department to web-based globally available and relevant solution [43]. The *ICT Development* has moved on to it being recognised with global award. The *applicability* is no longer just an ICT calculator tool but becoming a virtual learning environment in use as learning scaffolding. Students are now being empowered with purposeful usage.

The three ICT4D projects appraised above, based on the author's familiarity with them, are just representative of many others for which CIPPUA model can play a role in multi-dimensional evaluation.

4 Conclusion

Just as in the discussion between the author and Prof Walsham, and as evidenced in this paper, the intent is not to replace the 'artefact' focus of design science in IS-based ICT4D research projects nor tools in activity theory, neither does it intent to *impose* the digital technologies/objects emancipatory components of CR. The goal is to offer alternative and contribute to coherence, impact, diffusion and adoption.

The problem of coherence in ICT4D would appear to be, not so much of lack of appropriate methodology within each discipline (encompassing ICT4D and IS) but rather reaching-over and bringing other 'ways' into each research discipline, without losing out on common understanding of and theorising on ICT. Whilst it could be argued that existing methodologies exist, we must heed to Walsham [4] warning us, shouldn't we be looking at better approach towards coherence of ICT4D goal and working together across disciplines for better impact? Grover and Lyytinen [26] were clear on the danger of overly focusing on mid-range and referential theories in information systems at the expense of understanding and theorising 'IT' that is at the core of information systems. More so, shouldn't we be taking philosophical emancipatory view, irrespective of whether the ICT4D/IS project is deemed to be micro, macro or global? In any case, by following a digital technologies/objects approach to digital development and IS, a micro can actually be global, and macro can be micro, depending on the CIPPUA views that are at play at a particular time, space and position.

A limitation of this paper overly focusing on Walsham's paper [4], has been compensated with a cursory glance at other relevant literatures: Bennett et al. [17], Faulker and Runde [11], Faulkner and Runde [18], Fletcher [12], Heeks and Wall [10], Iannacci [36], Minger et al. [31], Mungai [6], Njihia [44], Orlikowski and Iacono [27], and Pourreau [45], and Vandenberghe [16].

I close with Bhaskar's adumbration of CR as agent of emancipatory change [24]: *"If this is so, an underlabouring philosophy such as critical realism, seriously committed to the project of universal human flourishing, can aspire to be more than a nuisance, a Nietzschean gadfly on the neck of the powers that be; it can become a spark, a liberation, lifting the weight of the (Lockean) rubbish that mires us. This is philosophy as enlightened common sense and as midwife, an agent of emancipatory change."*

Acknowledgements. The author acknowledges Profs Geoff Walsham, Khaled Abou El-Hossein for their feedback on earlier draft of the manuscript. The invaluable feedback of the anonymous reviewers is duly acknowledged. Many thanks to Desiree dos Santos for the linguistic four eyes review.

References

1. De, R., Pal, A., Sethi, R., Reddy, S.K., Chitre, C.: ICT4D research: a call for a strong critical approach. Inf. Technol. Dev. 24, 63–94 (2018). https://doi.org/10.1080/02681102.2017.1286284
2. Thapa, D., Omland, H.O.: Four steps to identify mechanisms of ICT4D: a critical realismbased methodology. Electron. J. Inf. Syst. Dev. Ctries. 84, e12054 (2018). https://doi.org/10.1002/isd2.12054
3. Wessel, L., Baiyere, A., Ologeanu-Taddei, R., Cha, J., Jensen, T.B.: Unpacking the difference between digital transformation and IT-enabled organizational transformation. J. Assoc. Inf. Syst. (2020)
4. Walsham, G.: ICT4D research: reflections on history and future agenda. Inf. Technol. Dev. 23, 18–41 (2017). https://doi.org/10.1080/02681102.2016.1246406
5. Heeks, R.: ICT4D 3.0? Part 2—The patterns of an emerging "digital for development" paradigm. Electron. J. Inf. Syst. Dev. Ctries. 86, e12123 (2020). https://doi.org/10.1002/isd2.12123
6. Mungai, P.W.: Causal mechanisms and institutionalisation of open government data in Kenya. Electron. J. Inf. Syst. Dev. Ctries. 84, e12056 (2018). https://doi.org/10.1002/isd2.12056
7. Kuechler, W., Vaishnavi, V.: A framework for theory development in design science research: multiple perspectives. J. Assoc. Inf. Syst. 13, 395–423 (2012). https://doi.org/10.17705/1jais.00300
8. Ladel, S., Kortenkamp, U.: Artifact-centric activity theory—a framework for the analysis of the design and use of virtual manipulatives. In: Moyer-Packenham, P.S.S. (ed.) International Perspectives on Teaching and Learning Mathematics with Virtual Manipulatives. MEDE, vol. 7, pp. 25–40. Springer, Cham (2016). https://doi.org/10.1007/978-3-319-32718-1_2
9. Bennett, L.A.: Capturing information technology use by senior secondary school students in New Zealand. In: Proceedings of the 28th Australasian Conference on Information Systems (ACIS 2017). AAIS: Australasian Association for Information Systems, Hobart, Australia (2017)
10. Heeks, R., Wall, P.J.: Critical realism and ICT4D research. Electron. J. Inf. Syst. Dev. Ctries. 84, e12051 (2018). https://doi.org/10.1002/isd2.12051
11. Faulkner, P., Runde, J.: Technological objects, social positions, and the transformational model of social activity. MIS Q. 37, 803–818 (2013)
12. Fletcher, A.J.: Applying critical realism in qualitative research: methodology meets method. Int. J. Soc. Res. Methodol. 20, 181–194 (2017). https://doi.org/10.1080/13645579.2016.1144401
13. Walsham, G.: Interpretive case studies in IS research: nature and method. Eur. J. Inf. Syst. 4, 74–81 (1995). https://doi.org/10.1057/ejis.1995.9
14. Bhaskar, R.: A Realist Theory of Science. Routledge, Oxon (2013)
15. Archer, M.S., Bhaskar, Roy, Collier, Andrew, Lawson, T., Norrie, A. (eds.) Critical Realism: Essential Readings. Routledge (2013). https://doi.org/10.4324/9781315008592
16. Vandenberghe, F., (ed.): What's Critical About Critical Realism?: Essays in Reconstructive Social Theory. Routledge, Oxon OX14 4RN (2013). https://doi.org/10.4324/9780203798508

17. Bennett, L.A., Toland, J., Howell, B., Tate, M.: Revisiting hylomorphism: what can it contribute to our understanding of information systems? In: 30th Australasian Conference on Information Systems 2019 (ACIS 2019), pp. 173–179. Australasian Association for Information Systems, Fremantle, Perth, Western Australia, Australia (2019)

18. Faulkner, P., Runde, J.: Theorizing the digital object. Manag. Inf. Syst. Q. **43**, 1279–1302 (2019). https://doi.org/10.25300/MISQ/2019/13136

19. Saunders, M.N.K., Lewis, P., Thornhill, A.: Chapter 4: understanding research philosophy and approaches to theory development. In: Research Methods for Business Students, pp. 128–170. Pearson, Harlow, England (2019)

20. Arksey, H., O'Malley, L.: Scoping studies: towards a methodological framework. Int. J. Soc. Res. Methodol. **8**, 19–32 (2005). https://doi.org/10.1080/1364557032000119616

21. Archer, M.S.: The morphogenetic approach; critical realism's explanatory framework approach. In: Róna, P., Zsolnai, L. (eds.) Agency and Causal Explanation in Economics. VE, vol. 5, pp. 137–150. Springer, Cham (2020). https://doi.org/10.1007/978-3-030-26114-6_9

22. Wright, G., Cairns, G., Bradfield, R.: Scenario methodology: new developments in theory and practice. Technol. Forecast. Soc. Change. **80**, 561–565 (2013). https://doi.org/10.1016/j.techfore.2012.11.011

23. Price, L., Martin, L.: Introduction to the special issue: applied critical realism in the social sciences. J. Crit. Realis. **17**, 89–96 (2018). https://doi.org/10.1080/14767430.2018.1468148

24. Bhaskar, R.: Enlightened Common Sense: The Philosophy of Critical Realism. Ontological. Routledge, New York (2016). https://doi.org/10.4324/9781315542942

25. Heeks, R., Thapa, D., Wall, P.J.: Critical realism and ICT4D: editorial introduction to the special issue of EJISDC. Electron. J. Inf. Syst. Dev. Ctries. **84**, e12050 (2018). https://doi.org/10.1002/isd2.12050

26. Grover, V., Lyytinen, K.: New state of play in information systems research: the push to the edges. MIS Q. **39**, 271–296 (2015). https://doi.org/10.25300/MISQ/2015/39.2.01

27. Orlikowski, W.J., Iacono, C.S.: Research commentary: desperately seeking the "IT" in IT research—a call to theorizing the IT artifact. Inf. Syst. Res. **12**, 121–134 (2001). https://doi.org/10.1287/isre.12.2.121.9700

28. Noir, C., Walsham, G.: The great legitimizer: ICT as myth and ceremony in the Indian healthcare sector. Inf. Technol. People. **20**, 313–333 (2007). https://doi.org/10.1108/09593840710839770

29. Adesemowo, A.K.: A rethink of the nature and value of IT assets – critical realism approach. In: Dwivedi, Y., Ayaburi, E., Boateng, R., Effah, J. (eds.) TDIT 2019. IAICT, vol. 558, pp. 402–414. Springer, Cham (2019). https://doi.org/10.1007/978-3-030-20671-0_27

30. Faulkner, P., Lawson, C., Runde, J.: Theorising technology. Cambridge. J. Econ. **34**, 1–16 (2010). https://doi.org/10.1093/cje/bep084

31. Mingers, J., Mutch, A., Willcocks, L.: Critical realism in information systems research. MIS Q. **37**, 795–802 (2013)

32. Hobbs, J.R.: Coherence and Coreference. Cogn. Sci. **3**, 67–90 (1979). https://doi.org/10.1207/s15516709cog0301_4

33. Durfee, E.H., Lesser, V.R., Corkill, D.D.: Coherent cooperation among communicating problem solvers. IEEE Trans. Comput. **C-36**, 1275–1291 (1987). https://doi.org/10.1109/TC.1987.5009468

34. Fjeld, M., Lauche, K., Bichsel, M., Voorhorst, F., Krueger, H., Rauterberg, M.: Physical and virtual tools: activity theory applied to the design of groupware. Comput. Support. Coop. Work **11**, 153–180 (2002). https://doi.org/10.1023/A:1015269228596

35. Houston, S.: Prising open the black box. Qual. Soc. Work Res. Pract. **9**, 73–91 (2010). https://doi.org/10.1177/1473325009355622
36. Iannacci, F.: Routines, artefacts and technological change: investigating the transformation of criminal justice in england and wales. J. Inf. Technol. **29**, 294–311 (2014). https://doi.org/10.1057/jit.2014.10
37. Njihia, J.M., Merali, Y.: The broader context for ICT4D projects: a morphogenetic analysis. MIS Q. **37**, 881–905 (2013). https://doi.org/10.25300/MISQ/2013/37.3.10
38. Rey-Moreno, C., Roro, Z., Tucker, W.D., Siya, M.J., Bidwell, N.J., Simo-Reigadas, J.: Experiences, challenges and lessons from rolling out a rural WiFi mesh network. In: Proceedings of the 3rd ACM Symposium on Computing for Development - ACM DEV '13, p. 1. ACM Press, New York (2013). https://doi.org/10.1145/2442882.2442897
39. Rey-Moreno, C., Blignaut, R., Tucker, W.D., May, J.: An in-depth study of the ICT ecosystem in a South African rural community: unveiling expenditure and communication patterns. Inf. Technol. Dev. **22**, 101–120 (2016). https://doi.org/10.1080/02681102.2016.1155145
40. Takavarasha Jr., S., Adams, C., Cilliers, L.: Community networks for addressing affordability of ICT access in African rural areas. In: Takavarasha Jr, S., Adams, C. (eds.) Affordability Issues Surrounding the Use of ICT for Development and Poverty Reduction, pp. 1–27. IGI Global (2018). https://doi.org/10.4018/978-1-5225-3179-1.ch001
41. Mikroyannidis, A., Gómez-Goiri, A., Smith, A., Domingue, J.: PT Anywhere: a mobile environment for practical learning of network engineering. Interact. Learn. Environ., 1–15 (2018). https://doi.org/10.1080/10494820.2018.1541911
42. Adesemowo, A.K., Oyedele , Y., Oyedele, O.: Text-based sustainable assessment: a case of first-year information and communication technology networking students. Stud. Educ. Eval. **55**, 1–8 (2017). https://doi.org/10.1016/j.stueduc.2017.04.005
43. Adesemowo, A.K., Msikinya, D., Nikitha, M., Darier, J., Tekeni, L.: L8 NetCalc: ICT network calculator. In: Remenyi, D. (ed.) The e-Learning Excellence Awards 2017: An Anthology of Case Histories, pp. 1–10. ACPIL: Academic Conferences and Publishing International, Porto (2017)
44. Njihia, J.M.: Critical realism and its prospects for African development research and policy. Thought Pract. A J. Philos. Assoc. Kenya. **3**, 61–85 (2011). https://doi.org/10.4314/tp.v3i1.70985
45. Pourreau, L.: Technology, power, and leadership: recommendations for preserving faculty autonomy in the 21st century. Siegel Inst. J. Appl. Ethics. **5**, 1–23 (2017)

Exploring Causal Factors Influencing Enterprise Architecture Failure

Yiwei Gong[1]([⊠]) and Marijn Janssen[2]

[1] School of Information Management, Wuhan University,
Wuhan 430072, China
yiweigong@whu.edu.cn
[2] Faculty of Technology, Policy and Management,
Delft University of Technology, Jaffalaan 5, 2628 BX Delft, The Netherlands
M.F.W.H.A.Janssen@tudelft.nl

Abstract. Organizations have adopted Enterprise Architecture (EA) for managing their IT-landscape and ensuring coherence among projects and activities. There is much work about approaches, methods, and tools for EA based on the assumption that their use will create business value. However, the failure of many EA efforts results in the need to investigate the factors influencing EA failure in practice. In this paper, we used a literature review to identify ten EA failure factors. Then we employed the grey-DEMATEL method to explore and analyze the influence of the ten EA failure factors based on the input of five EA experts. The result shows that failure factors are not in isolation, and they can be divided into either causal or effect factors. The factors do not have equal importance but differ in the levels of influence. For the causal factors, the ranking from most to least important is the inability to handle complexity, lack of proven EA methodology, lack of EA knowledge, lack of communication, and lack of tools. For the effect factors, the factors are a lack of support, too high effort, lack of motivation, parallel processes, and unused artifacts. We recommend practitioners to pay more attention to the five causal factors in their EA efforts. Further research is needed to generalize the findings, to understand the dependencies among factors, and to take into account situational dependency of EA failure.

Keywords: Enterprise Architecture · IT architecture · IT failure · Value · Multi-criteria decision-making · Grey-DEMATEL

1 Introduction

Enterprise Architecture (EA) has been heralded for the many benefits that it can bring to organizations. EA can bring agility [1] and interoperability [2], facilitate decision-making in IT investments [3], reduce IT costs [4], and so on. Today, EA is widely used in industry and government to manage the IT-landscape, as a continuously changing process for organizations [5].

Although many benefits are accounted for by EA, these benefits are difficult to measure in practice [4], and many business operations managers do not see the value returned from their EA investments [6]. In the literature, there are limited empirical

© IFIP International Federation for Information Processing 2020
Published by Springer Nature Switzerland AG 2020
S. K. Sharma et al. (Eds.): TDIT 2020, IFIP AICT 617, pp. 341–352, 2020.
https://doi.org/10.1007/978-3-030-64849-7_31

studies that address the benefits of EA by providing reliable evidence. In contrast, many claims of EA benefits are given without any support, resulting in ill-understanding of and many myths about EA [7, 8]. In the end, EA as a means, becomes a goal in itself.

Consultancy reports have indicated that two-third of EA initiatives failed in the past [9], and about 40% of EA programs were shut down within three years [10]. More recently, many organizations are either unable to implement their EA plans or only able to implement a part of their plans [11]. EA has shown to be countered with effectiveness and has even been blamed for failure. In this sense, avoiding failure should be first considered instead of achieving success, especially for the practitioners and organizations with limited EA experience.

Many studies have addressed the challenges and issues in EA management, but their practical help is limited. For example, many studies only proposed taxonomies without going further to guide EA practice [12]. Much research is about how to achieve the benefits of EA, but scant attention is given to EA failure [13]. Despite its importance, EA failure is undertheorized. This study aims to explore and better understand the factors failing EA initiatives. The study is explorative in nature, as this is one of the first studies in this area. For this, we employed the grey-DEMATEL method to analyze inputs from five EA experts. The findings provide practitioners and researchers with the identified factors determining the failure or success of EA implementation, provide insights into improving EA practice, and result in several further research directions.

The paper is structured as follows. In Sect. 2, we briefly discuss the background of EA failure. Thereafter, the research method is explained in Sect. 3. In Sect. 4 we present research findings of failure factors in practice and discuss the implications and recommendations for practitioners. Section 5 contains the conclusion and future research agenda.

2   Background

For investigating the failure of EA efforts, we will use normative literature about IT-project failure as the categorical base. The underlying premise is that EA implementation can be considered as a special kind of IT-project, and the categorization of IT-project failures can be used for mapping the failures of EA implementation. IT-project failure factors can be categorized int people, process, product, and technology [14]. Nelson [15] list of classical project management mistakes contains factors in each category influencing IT-projects. Recent empirical research in EA also indicates that the scope of EA covers these aspects [16]. From Nelson's list, complexity, uncertainty, scope creep, opposing stakeholder requirements, lack of top-management support, and resistance are frequently mentioned in the literature as factors that contribute to IT-project failure [15, 17–20].

In contrast to IT-projects, EA initiatives focus on the enterprise as a whole and should ensure coherency among projects, ensuring a flexible and adaptive IT-landscape, the alignment between IT and business, and so on. While IT-project failures are general to various occasions of IT-implementations, EA failures are specific to an architect's effort, and concern often many projects. EA has a wider scope and objectives than IT-projects. Hence, it is not surprising that EA failure factors can be different from those influencing IT-project failures. In the literature, there are only a few publications about the failure of EA. Table 1 summarizes the factors of EA failures from literature based on Nelson's categorization of classical IT-project failure factors.

Table 1. EA failure factors from literature

Label	EA failure factor	Source	Category
F1	Lack of communication and collaboration leads to an EA project failure	[12, 21]	People
F2	The EA development project does not have enough support from the management	[12, 22]	
F3	Lack of motivation among personnel hinders EA development projects	[12]	
F4	High-level managers do not understand the benefits of EA	[12]	
F5	EA initiatives set up processes for managing the EA life cycle parallel to the established IT processes, resulting in coordination problems	[22]	Process
F6	EA approach is highly complex, preventing it from achieving its objectives	[23]	
F7	Requiring too high effort regarding the initial EA documentation hampers the willingness to further maintain the EA artifacts	[22]	Product
F8	Existing EA artifacts remain unused in daily work and decision-making due to the poor quality	[22]	
F9	Lack of accurate and smart modeling tools makes the EA development inefficient	[24]	Technology
F10	Lack of clear methodologies for EA implementation projects makes the EA development inefficient	[24, 25]	

According to Banaeianjahromi and Smolander [12], lack of communication and collaboration refers to a type of the cause influencing the failure of EA efforts. Specifically, it refers to the lack of knowledge and support inside organizations or issues imposed by external parties, such as supply chain partners or government oversight organizations. In practice, enterprise architects are required to liaise with business and technology stakeholders. If the architects are not able to bridge the gap between themselves and their stakeholders, it will be hard to obtain support for and commitment to the implementation of EA [21]. At the root, the organizational culture turned out to be an issue that influences communication and collaboration during EA implementation.

EA is often regarded as a separate and parallel initiative, although it needs to be embedded in the established management processes. This often results in coordination problems requiring additional adjustments effort, which in turn decreased the EA initiatives' acceptance [22]. For example, a lack of coordination between the EA initiative and a parallel ITIL initiative created contradictory perceptions and redundant documentation.

EA products are the outcome artifacts of EA development, which can refer to EA models, policies, standards, and principles. EA products are intended to be used to enable organization's events, processes, and activities. But when they become complex, they constraint the same activities that it was meant to support and enable [23]. Complete EA products are not feasible due to the many stakeholders, the high organizational complexity, the continuous change, and the large scope. Even worse, organizations often do not update EA documents continuously. EA repositories gradually become outdated and are perceived as being of low quality. The poor quality of EA artifacts makes it remaining unused in daily work and decision-making [22].

Factors in the category of technology, such as the lack of accurate and smart modeling tools and lack of clear methodologies for EA implementation, are often considered as risks rather than the reasons of failures [24]. According to Hope, Chew and Sharma [11], these factors were found reflecting the technical sophistication of EA tools rather than that they determine project success. In their case studies, they found EA failures were more likely caused by communication and commitment problems. In contrast, Nam, Oh, Kim, Goo and Khan [25] argued that EA methodology applied to a single organization tends to fail when EA is applied at the national level by the central government to aggregate diverse agencies and organizations.

There are limited studies in literature focusing on the failures of EA implementation. Often, various factors influencing EA implementation are discussed as challenges [e.g. 22] or risks [e.g. 24]. Some factors are even arguable on their validity [11]. Furthermore, existing studies are either ignoring or not able to identify the interrelationships between factors, and consequently, they do not reveal the importance of different factors. This motivates our study on clarifying these ten factors of EA failures and their interrelationships. Such clarification and discussion should help enterprise architects to ensure the survival of their EA initiatives by understanding and tackling the root cause of failure.

3   Research Method

Our study is explorative in nature, and our aim is to better understand the interrelationship between EA failure factors. To analysis the correlations between the ten factors that are derived from EA literature, we employed the grey-DEMATEL method. Among the many multi-criteria decision-making methodologies, the Decision-making Trial and Evaluation Laboratory (DEMATEL) is best suited for analyzing the interrelationships and interdependencies when having a small sample size [26, 27]. The grey-DEMATEL method combines the Grey Set Theory and DEMATEL method to improve the analysis by resisting human biases, incomplete information, and uncertainty [28]. Especially, the grey-DEMATEL method includes a sensitivity analysis to help researchers in determining where their calculation results are significantly impacted by the weights assigned to different inputs.

We conducted the grey-DEMATEL method by the following steps in the three stages: 1) data collection, 2) the grey-DEMATEL analysis, and 3) sensitivity analysis.

3.1 Data Collection

The five experts from the Netherlands with rich knowledge and experience in a diversity of EA initiatives were selected and invited to fill in the questionnaire. Table 2 provides an overview of their background. We first introduced our study and explained the factors, as listed in Table 1, to the experts. After that, we asked them to complete a direct-relation matrix by indicating their opinions about the degree of influence between factors, using a five-level measurement from "no influence" to "very high influence". Their personal views relating to these factors were also captured after they filled in the matrix.

Table 2. Background and experience of EA experts

	Industry	Years of experience
Expert1	Consultancy	9
Expert2	Consultancy	21
Expert3	Government	15
Expert4	Academia	12
Expert5	Academia	5

3.2 Grey-DEMATEL Analysis

The grey-DEMATEL analysis in our study was conducted according to the following six basic steps [26, 28]:

Step 1: Construct the initial EA failure factors interaction matrix, based on the Grey Set Theory and using the five-level measurement. Grey Linguistic Scale from "No influence" to "Very high influence" as shown in Table 3.

Table 3. Linguistic scale for assigning greyscale and crisp values

Linguistic assessment	Crisp values	Grey scale
No influence	0	[0, 0]
Very low influence	1	[0, 1]
Low influence	2	[1, 2]
High influence	3	[2, 3]
Very high influence	4	[3, 4]

Step 2: Transform the average grey matrix into crisp numbers by using a modified defuzzification method.

Step 3: Assign weights to respondents based on their expertise and experience. Initially, the weights of each of the experts were equally assigned, as the experts were selected for their profound knowledge of the area. The weighted average method is applied to come up with an overall crisp direct-relation matrix from the individual direct-relation matrices.

Step 4: Develop the *normalized direct relation matrix* (N) by multiplying the matrix in Step 3 using a multiplier, which is the minimum value of the inverse of the max of the sum of a row. Then calculate the total relation matrix by multiplying N with the inverse matrix of the difference of N and the identity matrix.

Step 5: Calculate the causal parameters "R" and "D" which define the summation of all the rows and the summation of all the columns for each of the variables.

Step 6: For a given Factor i, calculate Pi which means R + D and Ei which means R-D. Then use them as x-axis and y-axis to develop the causal diagram. R + D is called "prominence" which denotes the total effect received or given by any factor. R-D is called "relation" of every factor to the other factors. Thereafter perform the *principal component analysis* to derive factors for both causal and effect factors. The greater the value of Pi, the greater the overall prominence (i.e. the influence or importance) of Factor i in terms of the overall relationships with other factors. If Ei > 0, then Factor i is a net cause or the foundation for other factors. If Ei < 0, then Factor i is the net effect of other factors. For each factor the values can then be plotted on a two-dimensional axis.

Table 4 presents the results of the calculation after following the above steps. In total, five factors were identified as causal factors (as R − D > 0) and the other five factors as their effect (as R − D < 0). The digraph is drawn using the Cartesian Coordinate System, based on R-D as Y-axis and R + D as X-axis, as shown in Fig. 1.

Table 4. The prominence and net cause or effect for EA failure factors

Factor	R	D	R + D	R − D
F1	1.972	1.687	3.660	0.285
F2	1.798	1.806	3.604	−0.007
F3	1.329	1.885	3.213	−0.556
F4	2.257	1.550	3.806	0.707
F5	1.524	2.237	3.760	−0.713
F6	2.487	1.749	4.237	0.738
F7	1.852	2.079	3.931	−0.227
F8	1.478	2.555	4.034	−1.077
F9	2.033	1.892	3.925	0.141
F10	2.869	2.160	5.029	0.708

3.3 Sensitivity Analysis

We carried out the initial calculation by assigning equal weights to all the experts. However, results may suffer from biases due to the difference in their expertise and experience. To check the robustness of the results, we carried out a sensitivity analysis to check if there is a significant change in the pattern of the responses depending on different weights given to the experts. We generated four different scenarios by

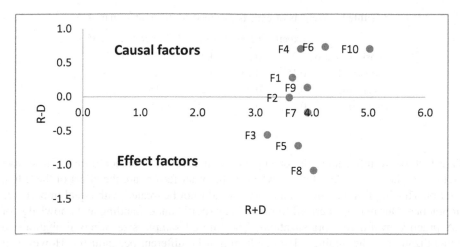

Fig. 1. Prominence-causal diagram for EA failure factors

significantly changing the level of weights assigned to different experts. Table 5 shows the assigned weights for sensitivity analysis in each scenario. Figure 2 presents the results of sensitivity analysis. By this sensitivity analysis, we found that the patterns of all the factors are similar for all the scenarios with small deviations. This indicates that our results are robust.

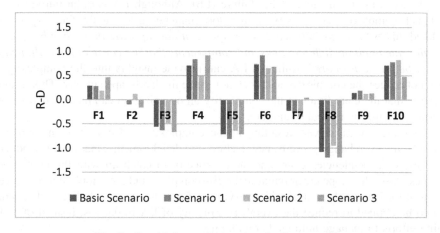

Fig. 2. Sensitivity analysis using the four scenarios

4   Findings and Discussion

There could be many reasons why an EA initiative fails in practice. Literature indicates ten main factors influence EA failure. Our grey-DEMATEL analysis further shows that those factors are not in isolation and they do not have the same importance as well.

Table 5. Weights of experts assigned to different scenarios

	Expert1	Expert2	Expert3	Expert4	Expert5
Basic scenario	0.2	0.2	0.2	0.2	0.2
Scenario1	0.15	0.15	0.25	0.2	0.25
Scenario2	0.3	0.2	0.2	0.15	0.15
Scenario3	0.1	0.25	0.15	0.25	0.25

Five factors are influencing the others, and their level of influence differs. These five factors are the cause of EA failure, whereas the other factors are the effect of these five factors. This implies that those ten factors should not be treated with equal importance in practice. Our findings derived from the EA experts' understanding and knowledge of EA practice in different organizations. The limited sample size brings limitations to generalization of the findings. The results might be different per industry. However, it reflects the common existence of the interdependencies between EA failure factors in different contexts. In this section, we present and discuss the five causal factors which are viewed as the main causes of EA failure.

4.1   Inability to Handle Complexity by EA

EA should be able to deal with a complex landscape of systems that is continuously changing. Complexity often results in IT-project failure, and our study also found that complexity is the main cause of EA failure (F6). Although EA is often introduced to deal with complexity, complexity is often too challenging to handle. One expert formulated this as *"EA was initiated 2 years ago ... it now appears that it has become so complex due to all the different links and components that the cause of the malfunction cannot be found anymore"*. Although EA can provide insights into the complexity, it does not reduce the complexity and does not make the landscape simpler. This finding suggests that there are limits to the complexity an organization can handle, despite the various instruments to deal with them.

There are several drivers resulting in the complexity of EA implementation. For example, the everchanging needs, new technology developments, inadequate products, changing of dependencies over time, and difficulty to catch-up with the continuous changes. Also, the scope creep might make EA complex, and EA should not be viewed as a tool for being able to deal with everything. EA is not a silver bullet, and scoping should be applied to reduce the overall complexity of EA initiatives, instead of dedicating efforts to manage unlimited complexity.

4.2   Lack of Proven Methodology

Given the many years practice by sharing knowledge from well-known EA frameworks such as TOGAF, Zachman, and FEAF, EA practitioners are still not clear which methods work in practice and create business value. The many competing EA methods might hinder the understanding of what works and what does not.

Lack of actionable methodology (F10) is considered the second top influencing factor for EA failure. The mainstream EA frameworks are general, but each industry has its own characteristics in IT landscape and management. Between the general EA frameworks and specific EA for a certain organization, domain-oriented reference architectures are needed, and there is much more work to be done in the development of more solid knowledge base of EA for each industry. Industry-specific EA framework would help architects better in designing their organization-specific EA.

This factor also reflects that organizations need talents who know how to make use of existing EA knowledge and are able to translate the strategic goal into tactical planning. Enterprise architecting is context-depending and requires architects having the ability to contextualize the working EA processes and routine.

4.3 Lack of EA Knowledge

Top management often has limited knowledge of EA (F4). The lack of knowledge constricts the use of EA in their decision-making and weakens their motivation in continuous investment to EA development. Furthermore, EA knowledge is often not widespread in the organization, leaving the architects on their own. One expert stated, *"For me in my daily work, I experience setting up, executing and maturing EA as a 'difficult to perform assignment,' especially in an organization that has been doing well according to its own insight and movement for 150 years"*. Organization staff should understand EA and its functions and roles to avoid failure. Although there some training and certifications for practitioners to learn EA systematically, these are not sufficient for their own organizations to understand EA. Improving the top management's learning and understanding of EA has become imperative for further improving EA practice.

EA professional readings are often too technical or operational-oriented and use vocabularies developed in the EA world, but hardly understandable by people outside this world. EA consultancy, communities, and consortiums have generated many industrial reports or white papers to advocate the value of EA. But those are often in fragmentation, superficial, and marketing-oriented. The CXOs need a more solid, convincing, and strategy-oriented knowledge about EA.

4.4 Lack of Communication

Architects are not able to communicate and collaborate with business people resulting in EA failure (F1). They take the seat of the business persons, without really understanding them. Such a mentality results in low acceptance of architects and their methods and tools. EA should align IT and business, but architects taking on the seat of the business people only enlarges the gap.

Architects and EA consultants are expected to have strong communication skills. This is often mentioned in white papers or handbooks of EA, but suitable approaches to improve communication are hardly provided. In contrast, widely used management approaches often emphasize their specific way of communication. For example, Lean management approach advocates value stream mapping to improve communication and collaboration across different business units and puts the responsibility to the staff instead of to the lean experts [29]. EA can embrace a similar approach by empowering staff instead of telling them what to do. For implementation, it would be useful to develop its specific value-creation-oriented communication approach.

4.5   Lack of EA Tools

Last but not least, the lack of suitable EA tools can result in EA implementation failures (F9). Existing tools focus on the modeling of EA artifacts with limited support on other daily works of EA development, including change management, compliance check, impact analysis, comparison of alternative solutions, and so on.

EA has a strong technical origin, and many EA professionals have a technical background. For a long time, the EA practitioners and researchers emphasized on the modeling tools for creating EA models, for example, the ArchiMate language. These are used by experts and cannot be used by the staff like value stream mapping in the Lean management approach. This results in a reliance on a few people and unclarity whether the models represent reality. Furthermore, by relying on a few persons, the maintenance and use of the EA models become challenging. This implies that the threshold for using EA tools should be lowered. The development of smart EA tools should be balanced with consideration of both EA creation and utilization.

5   Conclusions and Future Research Agenda

In this study, we extracted ten factors that influencing EA failure from the literature. To explore and understand these factors, the grey-DEMATEL method was employed to analyze the input of five EA experts. The findings indicate that the ten factors are not equally important, and they could be divided into causal or effect types of factors. The five causal factors, listed by their level of influence from high to low, are the inability to handle complexity, a lack of proven EA methodology, lack of EA knowledge, lack of communication, and lack of EA tools. The inability to deal with a high complexity seems to be a root cause of EA failure. The five effect factors are lack of support, too high effort, lack of motivation, parallel processes, and unused artifacts. The improvement of EA practices should focus on the five causal factors, as they are the very foundation of EA failure. This implies that EA initiatives should start with reducing complexity by scoping, instead of managing unlimited complexity. Instead of developing yet another framework, research should focus on identifying practices that work and result in business benefits. Staff should understand the nature and use of EA. EA methodologies should provide corresponding communication methods. Finally, the threshold of using EA and EA tools should be reduced to empower staff and to avoid overreliance on a few persons. Further research is needed to detail the causes and to understand them better.

EA is likely dependent on the context, and failure factors might be different per situation. This study has its limitation of having a limited number of experts to provide input, which might not fully reflect the EA practice in different industries. In addition, we focused on the discussion of the five causal factors and not on the five effect factors. The number of factors can be extended in further research, and the relationship between cause and effect can be researched. In future research, a diversity of EA initiatives can be investigated within different contexts. Context and situations differ, resulting in different ways EA is employed and different levels of complexity to deal with. This requires the involvement of more EA experts with diverse industrial background to generalize the findings. In addition, further investigation of the interdependencies between factors is needed to generate more insights into the EA failure in practice and how failure can be avoided. To establish the generalizability of these findings, future study should involve a theorization towards the development of a framework to explain the causal relationships of the factors.

References

1. Smith, H.A., Watson, R.T.: The jewel in the crown – enterprise architecture at Chubb. MIS Q. Executive **14**, 195–209 (2015)
2. Janssen, M.: Sociopolitical aspects of interoperability and enterprise architecture in e-government. Soc. Sci. Comput. Rev. **30**, 24–36 (2012)
3. Tamm, T., Seddon, P.B., Shanks, G., Reynolds, P., Frampton, K.: How an Australian retailer enabled business transformation through enterprise architecture. MIS Q. Executive **14**, 181–193 (2015)
4. Schmidt, C., Buxmann, P.: Outcomes and success factors of enterprise IT architecture management: empirical insight from the international financial services industry. Eur. J. Inf. Syst. **20**, 168–185 (2011)
5. Perez-Castillo, R., Ruiz, F., Piattini, M., Ebert, C.: Enterprise architecture. IEEE Softw. **36**, 12–19 (2019)
6. Kaisler, S.H., Armour, F.: 15 years of enterprise architecting at HICSS: revisiting the critical problems. In: The 50th Hawaii International Conference on System Sciences, pp. 4808–4816 (2017)
7. Gong, Y., Janssen, M.: The value of and myths about enterprise architecture. Int. J. Inf. Manage. **46**, 1–9 (2019)
8. Shanks, G., Gloet, M., Someh, I.A., Frampton, K., Tamm, T.: Achieving benefits with enterprise architecture. J. Strateg. Inf. Syst. **27**, 139–156 (2018)
9. Roeleven, S.: Why Two Thirds of Enterprise Architecture Projects Fail. Software AG (2010)
10. Sessions, R.: The IT complexity crisis: danger and opportunity. ObjectWatch (2009)
11. Hope, T., Chew, E., Sharma, R.: The failure of success factors: lessons from success and failure cases of enterprise architecture implementation. In: Proceedings of the 2017 ACM SIGMIS Conference on Computers and People Research, pp. 21–27. ACM (2017)
12. Banaeianjahromi, N., Smolander, K.: Lack of communication and collaboration in enterprise architecture development. Inf. Syst. Front. **21**(4), 877–908 (2017). https://doi.org/10.1007/s10796-017-9779-6
13. Kotusev, S.: Enterprise architecture: what did we study? Int. J. Coop. Inf. Syst. **26**, 1730002 (2017)
14. McConnell, S.: Rapid Development. Microsoft Press, Redmond (1996)
15. Nelson, R.R.: IT-project management: infamous failures, classic mistakes and best practices. MIS Q. Executive **6**, 67–78 (2007)
16. Gong, Y., Yang, J., Shi, X.: Towards a comprehensive understanding of digital transformation in government: analysis of flexibility and enterprise architecture. Gov. Inf. Q. **37**, 101487 (2020)

17. Lu, X., Liu, H., Ye, W.: Analysis failure factors for small & medium software projects based on PLS method In: The 2nd IEEE International Conference on Information Management and Engineering (ICIME), pp. 676–680. IEEE (2010)
18. Yeo, K.T.: Critical failure factors in information systems projects. Int. J. Project Manage. **20**, 241–246 (2002)
19. Pinto, J.K., Mantel Jr., S.J.: The causes of project failure. IEEE Trans. Eng. Manage. **37**, 269–276 (1990)
20. Daniels, C.B., LaMarsh, W.J.: Complexity as a cause of failure in information technology project management. In: IEEE International Conference on System of Systems Engineering (SoSE 2007), pp. 1–7. IEEE (2007)
21. Dale, M., Scheepers, H.: Enterprise architecture implementation as interpersonal connection: building support and commitment. Inf. Syst. J. **30** (1), 150–184 (2020)
22. Löhe, J., Legner, C.: Overcoming implementation challenges in enterprise architecture management: a design theory for architecture-driven IT Management (ADRIMA). IseB **12** (1), 101–137 (2013). https://doi.org/10.1007/s10257-012-0211-y
23. Iyamu, T.: Understanding the complexities of enterprise architecture through structuration theory. J. Comput. Inf. Syst. **59**, 287–295 (2019)
24. Safari, H., Faraji, Z., Majidian, S.: Identifying and evaluating enterprise architecture risks using FMEA and fuzzy VIKOR. J. Intell. Manuf. **27**(2), 475–486 (2014). https://doi.org/10.1007/s10845-014-0880-0
25. Nam, K., Oh, S.W., Kim, S.K., Goo, J., Khan, M.S.: Dynamics of enterprise architecture in the Korean public sector: transformational change vs. transactional change. Sustainability **8**, 1074 (2016)
26. Govindan, K., Chaudhuri, A.: Interrelationships of risks faced by third party logistics service providers: a DEMATEL based approach. Transp. Res. Part E Logist. Transp. Rev. **90**, 177–195 (2016)
27. Lee, H.-S., Tzeng, G.-H., Yeih, W., Wang, Y.-J., Yang, S.-C.: Revised DEMATEL: resolving the infeasibility of DEMATEL. Appl. Math. Model. **37**, 6746–6757 (2013)
28. Cui, L., Chan, H.K., Zhou, Y., Dai, J., Lim, J.J.: Exploring critical factors of green business failure based on Grey-Decision-making Trial and Evaluation Laboratory (DEMATEL). J. Bus. Res. **98**, 450–461 (2019)
29. Gong, Y., Blijleven, V.: The role of Lean principles in supporting knowledge management in IT outsourcing relationships. Knowl. Manag. Res. Pract. **15**, 533–541 (2017)

Comparative Study of Nature-Inspired Algorithms

Mohammad Abdullah Tahir$^{(\boxtimes)}$, Hasan Faraz Khan,
and Mohammad Mohsin Khan

Aligarh Muslim University, Aligarh, India
abdullahtahir919@gmail.com, farazkhan138@gmail.com,
mkbusiness255@gmail.com

Abstract. Nature-inspired algorithms are problem-solving tactics and methodologies and have been gaining much recognition for their competence. These algorithms have gained massive acclaim in the last few years to solve puzzling real-world (Nondeterministic polynomial-hard and Nondeterministic polynomial-complete) problems and solve complex optimization problems and functions whose exact solution doesn't exist. These are the algorithms that are inspired by natural processes and phenomena. The nature-inspired algorithm can be categorized based on some biological processes or any other phenomena which happen in nature. So, in this paper, we have classified some popular nature-inspired algorithms such as Genetic algorithm, Simulated Annealing, harmony search, Black hole, and many more. Based on four parameters from which the first parameter is Subject from which they were inspired. The second parameter is the optimization technique i.e. Stochastic or Deterministic. The third parameter of our classification is the number of solutions they maintain i.e. population-based or trajectory-based. And the last parameter of this categorization is memory i.e. algorithm is memory-based or memory less.

Keywords: Nature-inspired algorithms · Stochastic algorithms · Deterministic algorithms · Memory based algorithms · Memory-less algorithms

1 Introduction

1.1 Previous Classifications

Nature-inspired computing is a discipline that develops new computing techniques by observing how nature behaves to solve existing complex problems in different environmental situations. Algorithms that are inspired by natural problems are known as Nature-Inspired Algorithms. These algorithms have gained much popularity as real-world problems are becoming more and more complex and extensively large in contrast with past computing techniques. Nature-inspired algorithms are applied mostly to optimization problems and are used to give feasible and acceptable solutions to optimization problems rather than guaranteed optimal solution within a reasonable amount of time. Nature-inspired algorithms are broadly classified into four major categories which are evolution-based, swarm intelligence based algorithms, physics based algorithms, and human-based algorithms [1].

© IFIP International Federation for Information Processing 2020
Published by Springer Nature Switzerland AG 2020
S. K. Sharma et al. (Eds.): TDIT 2020, IFIP AICT 617, pp. 353–361, 2020.
https://doi.org/10.1007/978-3-030-64849-7_32

Evolution-based algorithms are inspired by the evolutionary behavior of natural systems and the laws of natural evolution. In these algorithms, a set of the population is stochastically selected and is processed over successive generations through evolutionary operations. The best individuals are selected are sent through the next generation process and this process is continued until the optimal solution is obtained or the termination criteria are reached. These algorithms are inspired by Charles Darwin Theory [2, 3] e.g. - Genetic Algorithm (GA), Differential Evolution (DE), etc. Swarm-based intelligence (SI), which is also known as Swarm optimization techniques [4], is inspired by the collective behavior of natural swarms. The working process of swarm-based algorithms is that they mimic the social behavior of groups on animals. Like particle swarm optimization [5], artificial bee colony algorithm [5, 6], and ant colony optimization algorithm [7]. One of the most popular Swarm based algorithms is Particle Swarm Optimization which was developed by James Kennedy and Russell C. Eberhart. It mimics the behavior of bird flocks and fish schooling. Physics-based nature-inspired algorithms are those algorithms that are inspired by physical processes in nature. Some common examples of physics-based algorithms are Simulate Annealing (SA) [8], Gravitational Search Algorithm (GSA) [9], Central Force Optimization (CFO) [10] and Black Hole (BH) algorithm [11], etc. While Human-based nature-inspired algorithms are inspired by human behaviors and try to imitate human characteristics. The most common example of human-based algorithms is the Harmony Search algorithm (HS) [12]. Besides this very simple categorization, nature-inspired algorithms are further classified into many categories based on their working process, mathematical functions, searching methods, and capability of finding optimal solutions.

1.2   History of Nature – Inspired Computing

Another reason why we use nature-inspired algorithms is the fact that these algorithms are inspired by nature itself. Nature is amazing and it has always been a source of inspiration for scientists and researchers. Besides these visible natural phenomena, there are numerous of invisible events and marvels that our scientists are still trying to explain. For centuries, scientists and philosophers are observing natural occurrences and trying to emulate and adapt these processes. There are already numerous researches proving that nature-inspired algorithms are much efficient and have a competitive edge over deterministic methods. In today's world where real-world problems are getting complex day-by-day and extensively large due to scientific advancements, nature-inspired computing can be exceptionally beneficial. Real-world problems have innumerable search spaces with countless difficulties, a large number of variables, and multiple dimensions. These real-world problems enhance and elucidate multiobjective functions and solve NP-hard problems. Thus, demand for resolving these complications has engaged many scientists and researchers to come down with much faster, precise, explicitly powerful nature-inspired optimization algorithms. The revolutionary period for nature-inspired algorithms started when evolution-based algorithms came into existence. In 1950, Alan Turing proposed a machine that was inspired and emulated based on principles of evolution. 1960–1970 was the most crucial decade for the development of these algorithms. In 1963, Rechenberg and Haul-Paul Schwefel solved complex computation problems in aerospace engineering using a searching technique called evolution strategy and it was extensively acknowledged as a feasible optimization method [13]. The Genetic Algorithm was then introduced by John Holland in the early 1970s and his book "Adaptation in Natural and Artificial Systems" [14]. Genetic Algorithm is a biologically inspired computational procedure that is inspired by Darwin's theory of evolution. It shows the ability to exploit the previous information to find the optimal result or expecting off-springs. 1980–1990s were also important decades as Simulated Annealing [8] was developed by Scott Kirkpatrick, Mario P. Vechchi, and C. DanielGellat in 1983. In 1992, Marco Dorigo proposed his work on the Ant Colony Optimization algorithm [15]. It is a swarm intelligence based algorithm inspired by the social behavior of ant colonies. In 1995, a remarkable advancement was made when John Kennedy and Russell C. Eberhart came up with Particle Swarm Optimization (PSO). Differential Evolution [16] was developed by Rainer Storm and Kenneth Price in 1997 and it turned out to be much more efficient than the Genetic Algorithm on many aspects. Xin-She Yang developed many nature-inspired algorithms like Firefly Algorithm (2007) [17], Bat Algorithm (2010) [17], Cuckoo Search (2009) [17], and Flower Pollination Algorithm in 2012 [18]. Since the 2000's many nature-inspired algorithms were developed and many of them were modified by scientists to give better solutions. The number of these algorithms in the past two decades has risen exponentially. Even in present times, this field of nature-inspired algorithms is evolving rapidly.

1.3 Uses of Nature – Inspired Algorithms

Nature-inspired algorithms are implemented and used in many fields of science and engineering. The genetic Algorithm which is an evolution-based algorithm is used for Machine Learning, Deep Learning, Computer Architecture, Bayesian Inference, etc. Swarm intelligence based algorithm i.e. Ant Colony Optimization (ACO) and Particle Swarm algorithm (PSO) are used for network routing applications [18], Neural network system design, image processing etc. [19]. Firefly algorithm, Bat Algorithm, and Cuckoo Search algorithm which were developed by Xin-She Yang are also preferred in Neural Network programming, Semantic Web, Software testing, and image clustering [20, 21]. Nature-inspired algorithms are immensely popular and preferred when dealing with multi-dimensional functions and complex problems where optimal solutions are required in a discrete search space.

1.4 Reason for Classification

In this paper, Nature-Inspired algorithms are classified into different categorize on various factors. Classification is very important because it helps us to identify and differentiate these algorithms on the basis of their searching technique, ability to provide an optimal solution, derivation, etc. It helps in a better understanding of these algorithms and to determine which technique to use for that specific operation and it also allows us to understand the mechanism of algorithms easily and efficiently either individually or in a group.

1.5 Basis of Classification

In this paper, algorithms are classified into Four major parameters which are optimization technique, population, and the number of solutions, subjects they are inspired from. Based on optimization, it is categorized into two categories which are Stochastic optimization and Deterministic optimization [1]. Stochastic Optimization generates and uses random variables. Stochastic optimization algorithms have expansive applications in problems in mathematics, computation techniques, and engineering. Deterministic global optimization focuses on finding global solutions to optimization problems. The next parameter is population-based against single solution based search [22]. Population-based algorithms execute a search with various initial points. Single solution method focus on modifying and enhancing an individual solution. The third parameter focuses on the source of inspiration and the subject from which they are derived. Besides the broad classification that we already have, it further classifies these algorithms based on the subject like biological evolution, chemical processes, physics-based, music-based and swarm behavior or social psychology. As per our knowledge, we have further distributed this paper in Sect. 2 and Sect. 3. In Sect. 2 we have described the drawbacks of the previous classifications which have been proposed earlier. Then in Sect. 3, we proposed our classification. Following which Sect. 4 concludes this paper with some related future work.

2   Drawbacks

Nothing is perfect, everything lacks something in it. As time passes by new issues and new problems arise. And thus, people keep working to turn it into the best possible version of it. Nature-inspired algorithms are developed to solve problems or to find a better solution to a problem. Today we have lots of Nature-inspired algorithms available to solve a particular problem. But how we are going to decide which would be the best algorithm to solve that problem. Though it is found that in some cases or circumstances one algorithm performs better than the other or Vice – Versa. It mainly depends on the problem, dimensions of the problem, inputs, variables, and many other factors that decide the success of the algorithm. So there is no universal algorithm that outperforms the other algorithms [23]. A best available algorithm must be effective in terms of performance and efficiency in terms of resources such as computation cost and time allowed to come up with the solution. These are important factors in deciding what algorithm to use.

While we were studying for our research work we have gone through a lot of books and research papers and we have found that a lot of researchers have classified Nature-inspired algorithms only based on their subject namely, swarm intelligence, physical or chemical-based algorithms, and evolutionary algorithms [24]. In our classification, we have also classified Nature-Inspired Algorithms based on their subject, nature of optimization, number of solutions, and also on the basis of memory, and in each category, we have arranged the list of Nature-Inspired Algorithms in their Chronological order.

3   Classification

Here we classify Natural Inspired Algorithm according to different categories which are described below one by one.

- **Inspired Subject:** In this category, we classify algorithms according to their subject from which they are inspired. Like the Gravitational Search algorithm which is inspired by Physics.
- **Number of Solutions:** In this category, we have two sub-Categories:
  - **Trajectory-Based NIA:** In this Category, we put those algorithms which use the single agent/particle/solution which get better upon iteration. And in the trajectory-based method, the initial agent/particle/solution is randomly selected.
  - **Population-Based NIA:** In this category, we put those algorithms which use the set of agent/particle/solutions which also result in obtaining the number of a solution in a particular iteration. A population-based algorithm selects the best solution among the number of solutions generated in the iterations. This is called elitism.
- **Based on optimization:** In this category also we have two sub-categories:
  - **Deterministic Algorithms:** These algorithms follow a certain procedure and provide the same solution on different runs.
  - **Stochastic Algorithms:** These algorithms possess randomness and provide different solutions on a different run. The main advantage of stochastic algorithms is the ability to explore several regions of the search space. That is the reason they can escape from the local optima to reach the global optimum.
- **Based on Memory:** In this category also we have two sub-categories:
  - **Memory-Based Algorithms:** Memory-based algorithms approach the problem by functioning over the entire dataset. The memory-based approach uses data to compute the similarity between items. These memory-based algorithms calculate the similarity between previously analyzed items and produce a prediction by taking the weighted average of all the ratings.
  - **Memory-less Algorithms:** Memory-less algorithms operate on an individual problem and its dataset to find an optimal solution rather than comparing and predicting results from previously compiled solutions (Tables 1 and 2).

Table 1. Classification table consisting of three parameters

Name	Inspired subject	Population based	Trajectory based	Stochastic	Deterministic
Simulated annealing	Physics	–	✓	✓	–
Stochastic diffusion search	Physics	✓	–	✓	–
Harmony search	Physics	✓	–	✓	–
Electro magnetism optimization	Physics	✓	–	✓	–
Big Bang Crunch	Physics	✓	–	✓	–
River formation dynamics	Physics	✓	–	✓	–
Central force	Physics	✓	–	–	✓

(*continued*)

Table 1. (*continued*)

Name	Inspired subject	Population based	Trajectory based	Stochastic	Deterministic
Intelligent water drop	Physics	✓	–	✓	–
Gravitational search	Physics	✓	–	✓	–
Charged system search	Physics	✓	–	✓	–
Spiral optimization	Physics	✓	–	✓	–
Black hole	Physics	✓	–	✓	–
Vibrating particle system	Physics	✓	–	✓	–
Chemical reaction optimization	Chemistry	✓	–	–	✓
ARCO	Chemistry	✓	–	✓	–
Artificial Immune system	Biology	✓	–	✓	–
Genetic	Biology	✓	–	✓	–
Taboo search	Biology	–	✓	–	✓
Memetic search	Biology	✓	–	✓	–
Differential evolution	Biology	✓	–	✓	–
Flower pollination	Biology	✓	–	✓	–
Invasive weed	Biology	✓	–	✓	–
Krill Herd	Biology	✓	–	✓	–
Dendritic cell	Biology	✓	–	✓	–
Deterministic dendritic cell	Biology	✓	–	–	✓
Brainstorm	Biology	✓	–	–	✓
Ant colony	Social Psychology	✓	–	✓	–
Particle swarm	Social Psychology	✓	–	✓	–
Shuffles frog leaping	Social Psychology	✓	–	✓	–
Bee algorithm	Social Psychology	✓	–	✓	–
Artificial bee colony	Social Psychology	✓	–	✓	–
Firefly algorithm	Social Psychology	✓	–	✓	–
Cuckoo search	Social Psychology	✓	–	✓	–
Fish school	Social Psychology	✓	–	✓	–
Atmosphere clouds model	Ecology	✓	–	✓	–
Biogeography based optimization	Geography	✓	–	✓	–

Table 2. Classification table consisting of memory parameter

Name	Memory based	Memory-less
Artificial bee colony	✓	–
Firefly algorithm	–	✓
Jumper firefly algorithm	✓	–
Memetic search	–	✓
Simulated annealing	–	✓
Blackhole	✓	–
Bat algorithm	✓	–
Particle swarm	✓	–
Cuckoo search	✓	–
Chemical reaction optimization	✓	–
Artificial immune system	✓	–
Harmony search	✓	–
Central force	✓	–
Differential evolution	✓	–
Dragon fly algorithm	–	✓
Taboo search	✓	–
Accelerated PSO	✓	–
Bacterial foraging	✓	–
Glowworm swarm algorithm	–	✓
Big Bang Crunch	–	✓
Gene expression	✓	–
Roach infestation algorithm	✓	–
Gravitational search	–	✓
Gravitational local search	–	✓

4 Conclusion and Future Works

As the provenance of innovation of nature-inspired algorithms are very contrasting and distinct so it is indisputable that algorithms are also varying in their nature. Hence in this paper, we classify the existing nature-inspired algorithms like genetic algorithm, Cuckoo search, Bat algorithm, Central force algorithm, Differential evolution, Genetic programming, and many other natural inspired algorithms based on four parameters. This can be a very informative source to choose the appropriate algorithm for the problem and also to form a base for further higher research.

It might be notable that the classification is not unique. But this paper seems to be effective for the researchers and a also for the common people who don't have prior knowledge about these algorithms. It is very hard to find the appropriate algorithm for the problem because there is a huge number of nature-inspired algorithms are present out there. So the main motive of the paper is to help the researcher to find the appropriate algorithm from the ocean of these algorithms. So they can solve the real-world optimization problem more effectively. As we all know that the development of nature-inspired algorithms for optimization is arising rapidly and has seen enormous growth in the past few decades.

In the future, we try to add on more parameters in the classification of naturein-spired algorithms i.e. objective function of the algorithm. But this classification can be broadened to freshly originated nature-inspired algorithms and also can be practiced for alteration and modifying already existing nature-inspired algorithms.

References

1. Birattari, M., Paquete, L., Stutzle, T., Varrentrapp, K.: Classification of metaheuristics and design of experiments for the analysis of components. Technical report, AIDA-01-05 (2001)
2. Digalakis, J.G., Margaritison, K.G.: Benchmarking functions for genetic algorithms. Int. J. Comput. Math. **00**, 1–27 (2000)
3. Tang, K.S., Man, K.F., Kwong, S., He, Q.: Genetic algorithms and their applications. IEEE Signal Process. Mag. **13**(6), 22–37 (1996)
4. Shi, Y., Eberhart, R.: A modified particle swarm optimizer. In: Proceedings of IEEE International Conference on Evolutionary Computation, pp. 69–73 (1998)
5. Kennedy, J., Eberhart, R.: Particle swarm optimization. In: Proceedings of IEEE International Conference on Neural Networks, pp. 1942–1948 (1995)
6. Karaboga, D., Basturk, B.: On the performance of artificial bee colony (ABC) algorithm. Appl. Soft Comput. **8**(1), 687–697 (2007)
7. Dorigo, M., Maniezzo, V., Colorni, A.: Ant system: optimization by a colony of cooperating agents. IEEE Trans. Syst. Man Cybern. **26**(1), 1–13 (1996)
8. Kirkpatrick, S., Gelatto, C.D., Vecchi, M.P.: Optimization by simulated annealing. Science **220**, 671–680 (1983)
9. Rashedi, E., Nezamabadi, S., Saryazdi, S.: GSA: a gravitational search algorithm. Inf. Sci. **179**(13), 2232–2248 (2009)
10. Formato, R.A.: Central force optimization: a new metaheuristic with applications in applied electromagnetics. Prog. Electromagn. Res. PIER **77**, 425–491 (2007)
11. Hatamlou, A.: Black hole: a new heuristic optimization approach for data clustering. Inf. Sci. **222**, 175–184 (2012)
12. Yang, X.-S.: Harmony search as a metaheuristic algorithm. In: Geem, Z.W. (ed.) Music-Inspired Harmony Search Algorithm. SCI, vol. 191, pp. 1–14. Springer, Heidelberg (2009). https://doi.org/10.1007/978-3-642-00185-7_1
13. Back, T., Hoffmeister, F., Shwefel, H.-P.: Application of evolutionary algorithms. Report of the System Analysis Research Group, (LS XI) SYS -2/92, University of Dortmund, Department of Computer Science (1992)
14. Goldberg, D.E.: Genetic Algorithms in Search, Optimization and Machine Learning. Addison-Wesley, Reading (1989)
15. Dorigo, M., Birattari, M., Stützle, T.: Ant colony optimization – artificial ants as a computational intelligence technique. IEEE Comput. Intell. Mag., 2839 (2006)
16. Storn, R., Price, K.: Differential evolution – a simple and efficient heuristic for global optimization over continuous spaces. J. Global Optim. **11**(4), 341–359 (1997). https://doi.org/10.1023/A:1008202821328
17. Yang, X.S., He, X.: Firefly algorithm: recent advances and applications. Int. J. Swarm Intell. **1**(1), 36–50 (2013)

18. Yang, X.-S.: Flower pollination algorithm for global optimization. In: Durand-Lose, J., Jonoska, N. (eds.) UCNC 2012. LNCS, vol. 7445, pp. 240–249. Springer, Heidelberg (2012). https://doi.org/10.1007/978-3-642-32894-7_27
19. Omran, G.M., Engelbrecht, A.P., Salman, A.: Particle swarm optimization method for image clustering. Int. J. Pattern Recognit. Artif. Intell. 19(03), 297–321 (2005)
20. Horng, M.H.: Vector quantization using the firefly algorithm for image compression. Expert Syst. Appl. 39(1), 1078–1091 (2012)
21. Valian, E., Mohanna, S., Tavakoli, S.: Improved cuckoo search algorithm for feedforward neural network training. Int. J. Artif. Intell. Appl. 2(3), 36–43 (2011)
22. Beheshti, Z., Shamsuddin, S.M.: A review of population-based meta-heuristic algorithm. Int. J. Adv. Soft Comput. Appl. 5, 1–35 (2013)
23. Adam, S.P., Alexandropoulos, S.-A.N., Pardalos, P.M., Vrahatis, M.N.: No free lunch theorem: a review. In: Demetriou, I.C., Pardalos, P.M. (eds.) Approximation and Optimization. SOIA, vol. 145, pp. 57–82. Springer, Cham (2019). https://doi.org/10.1007/978-3-030-12767-1_5
24. Yadav, S.L., Phogat, M.: Study of nature inspired algorithms. Int. J. Comput. Trends Technol. (IJCTT) 49(2), 100–105 (2017)

Emerging Technologies in e-Governance

"#Government" - Understanding Dissemination, Transparency, Participation, Collaboration and Engagement on Twitter for Citizens

Purva Grover[1]([⌧]) and Arpan Kumar Kar[2]

[1] Information Systems/IT Area, Indian Institute of Management Amritsar,
Amritsar, India
groverdpurva@gmail.com
[2] DMS, Indian Institute of Technology Delhi, New Delhi, India

Abstract. This study tries to explore how social media had been used for public administration activities across the global by analysing the tweets tagged with "#government" and "#gov". On the basis of the literature social media usage by public administration had been classified into five dimensions, namely information dissemination and broadcasting; open transparency; open participation; open collaboration; and ubiquitous engagement. The study collects 296,417 tweets (after cleaning, 174,204 tweets) tagged as "#government" and "#gov" as open government data (as data is available to everyone but managed by private organizations) and this study applies open government data activities and social media analytics to derive the insights. The article also explores how different usage of the social media is effecting sharing and liking of the tweets. The implications of these findings can be important to government of different countries. The article concludes by pointing that social media can be used by citizens for open participation which can subsequently facilitate information dissemination and ubiquitous engagement.

Keywords: Social media · Government · Twitter · Information dissemination · Transparency · Citizen participation · Citizen collaboration · Ubiquitous engagement

1 Introduction

Social media enables new forms of communication through text, images, audio and videos [4, 5] to initiate awareness, participation, collaboration and engagement among public [22]. Social media has the potential of increasing public participation by disseminating information among citizens [36]. Social media has the power of transforming relationship among governments and citizens [3]. Use of social media in public administration had increased citizen's satisfaction and trustworthiness [14, 31, 32]. Social media adoption for public administration depends on technology, environment and organizational factors [35]. Citizens can use social media for individual expression or for collaborative movement [20]. The transparency, participation and

S. K. Sharma et al. (Eds.): TDIT 2020, IFIP AICT 617, pp. 365–376, 2020.
https://doi.org/10.1007/978-3-030-64849-7_33

collaboration are three pillars of the open government [7]. Social media facilitates these pillars by increasing giving citizens the opportunities for journalism [8].

An open government maturity model for public engagement on social media had been presented in literature [20]. The model consists of five levels, initial conditioning, data transparency, open participation, open collaboration and ubiquitous engagement. The first level, initial conditioning level focuses on information broadcasting. The second level, data transparency focuses on sharing information related to government processes. Information shared openly brings transparency into the system. The third level, open participation focuses on gathering feedback, initiating interactive conversations among citizens. The fourth level, open collaboration focuses on co-creating value-added services and collaboration among citizens. The fifth and the highest level, ubiquitous engagement focuses on continuous public engagement between government and citizens.

Each level of the open government maturity model for public engagement focus on different usage. The usage of social media highlighted in the model: information broadcasting; releasing information related to processes and performance for transparency; gathering feedback and crowd sourcing; co-creating value-added services; and continuous public engagement. Social media had been used by government for different purposes: information dissemination, participation, feedback and collaboration [26].

Public sector, social media adoption has remained an under-researched domain [24, 35] which is line with our observation by reviewing the prior literature. Therefore, in this study we will explore how a social media platform has been used for various purposes in public administration domain through prior literature (Sect. 2.1 to Sect. 2.5) and by exploring how "#government" and "#gov" had been used on Twitter. For this tweets tag with "#government" and "#gov" had been analysed, which had been extracted for five months, starting from 1st January 2018 for 151 days. On the basis of the literature, social media platform had been used for: (a) information dissemination and broadcasting; (b) bringing transparency in system; (c) open participation; (d) open collaboration; and (e) ubiquitous engagement; in public administration domain.

The existing studies in literature have used surveys and interviews to validate the same. However, surveys and interviews suffer from responses having biases like social desirability, optimism and selective perception. This study also tries to statistically validate whether the tweets sharing and liking on Twitter are getting effected by the social media usage (depicted by the hashtag within the tweet). However such biases of filling out survey instruments are minimized in our approach as user generated content [17] is mined for the theory building. In particular, the following research questions are explored in this study:

RQ1: How is "#government" and "#gov" being used on Twitter?

RQ2: How does the nature of social media usage by the government impact the content sharing in social media?

RQ3: How does the nature of social media usage by the government impact the content popularity in social media?

The remaining sections are organized as follows. Section 2 is dedicated to theoretical basis and hypothesis development. Section 3 explains the research approach adopted for the study. Section 4 and 5 presents the insights and discusses the finding respectively. Subsequently this is followed by a conclusion section which discusses the limitations of the study along with future research directions.

2 Theoretical Basis and Hypothesis Development

The section had been divided into the five sub-sections on the basis of the social media usage by the public administration: information dissemination and broadcasting; bringing transparency in system; open participation; open collaboration; and ubiquitous engagement [20, 26].

2.1 Information Dissemination and Broadcasting

When public official post the information related to betterment of the society on social media platforms through their official registered accounts, citizens receives the information via the same channel. This is the way social media had been used for information dissemination and broadcasting purposes. The chance for further communication between officials and citizens is limited. Government had used social media for information dissemination and broadcasting purposes during natural disasters [16] and for health-care [13] and for improving living practices [33]. There was one study which had highlighted, that majority of messages on government microblogs were posted with self-promotion objective [39].

2.2 Open Transparency

The usage of social media by public administration comes under open transparency when public official post the information related to government processes and performances through their social media accounts and citizens receives the information via the same channel. The chance for further communication between officials and citizens is depending on the desires and needs of the public officials. Literature indicates government's usage for social media platforms for transparency is still in infancy stage [9]. This may because social media platforms has global reach. Therefore too much release of the information by governments for citizens on social media can bring transparency but at the same time it may be used by other parties as well, which in not in the favor of citizens well-being.

2.3 Open Participation

The usage of social media by public administration comes under open participation when government agencies build a social media platform for citizens to participate with the objective of gathering feedbacks on polices and for crowd sourcing information purposes [2]. The government official does not interact on the platform just initiate the participation among the citizens. Open participation had been used by the government for understanding citizens communication patterns [16, 39]; and the benefits of the same to the citizens [28].

2.4 Open Collaboration

The usage of social media by public administration comes under open collaboration when government agencies builds a social platform for citizens to participate and collaborate together. The objective of building such a platforms is to initiate collaborations among public administration and citizens for creating innovations and value added services. Social media had been used for different purposes for this such as: innovation within governments [22, 34] emergency management [27] and; for analyzing attitudinal and cognitive aspects of citizens interactions [24].

2.5 Ubiquitous Engagement

The usage of social media by public administration comes under ubiquitous engagement when government agencies focus on continuous engagement with public. Ubiquitous engagement increases transparency, participation and collaboration [20, 30]. Governments of various countries has used social media for ubiquitous engagement for following scenarios such as: handling foreign-language user-generated content [7]; participation of users in political election campaigns [6]; interaction of health ministry and citizens on infectious disease outbreaks [40]. Literature also indicates governments are failing to engage citizens [3].

2.6 Research Question and Hypothesis

This study focuses on three research questions (RQ) and try to explore how "#government" and "#gov" being used on Twitter (RQ1), how tweets used for different social media usage being shared and liked on Twitter (RQ2 and RQ3). Therefore, to statistically validate RQ1 we propose the hypothesis H1, to statistically validate RQ2 we propose the H2, and to statistically validate RQ3 we propose the H3. For framing hypothesis of the study, the study assumes Twitter had been used for all five purposes, equally.

RQ1: How is "#government" and "#gov" being used on Twitter?
H1: There is no statistically significant difference among content related to dissemination, transparency, participation, collaboration and engagement.

Positive influence of citizen engagement on transparency, efficiency and participation [11]. Social media plays a key role during crises and conflicts [25]. The popularity of the tweets can be measured in terms of how many times a tweet is being shared through its retweet count [1, 37] and how many times a tweet had attracted users that they save it for their future usage by liking it, can be determine through like count of the tweet [29]. Therefore to determine how tweets appeal to the citizens for different social media usage, we propose RQ2 and RQ3, subsequently to statistically validate H2 and H3. Liking is passive support for a piece of content on social media, whereas retweet is active support for the content for facilitating its propagation within the network.

RQ2: How does the nature of social media usage by the government impact the content sharing in social media?

H2: There is no statistically significant difference on sharing of the tweets containing content related to dissemination, transparency, participation, collaboration and engagement.

Social media allows instant access and information dissemination across the globe [15]. Social media usage in low- and middle-income countries has increased exponentially in recent years due to technological advances. Word of mouth and social media equally influence Indians to use IoT [10]. Some scholars indicate social media is used as tool for propaganda and not for engagement purposes [38] whereas other scholars indicates social media activity is positively associated with citizen engagement [38]. Therefore RQ3 and H3 tries to explore liking of social media users towards different usage.

RQ3: How does the nature of social media usage by the government impact the content popularity in social media?

H3: There is no statistically significant difference in liking of the tweets containing hashtags related to dissemination, transparency, participation, collaboration and engagement.

Figure 1 presents the conceptual concept investigated in the study. On one side hashtag usage category had been given, dissemination, transparency, participation, collaboration and engagement. On the other side social media measures such as hashtag frequency, tweet sharing and liking had been plotted. The proposed hypothesis, H1, H2 and H3 exploring relationship between the two had been pictorial presented in Fig. 1.

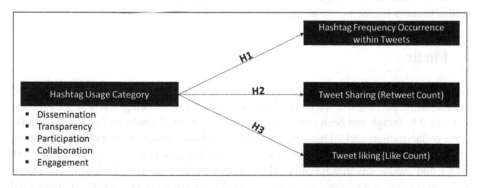

Fig. 1. Conceptual concept and investigation in the study

3   Research Methodology

Literature indicates social media data can be used for predicting commercial (i.e. product sales and stocks exchange) and public (i.e. election outcome) [6] activities [18]. This study tries to explore how Twitter had been used for public administration activities across the global by analyzing the tweets tagged with "#government" and "#gov". Social media (Twitter) data is stored and managed by the private organizations and not by the governments. Therefore to analyses the data for the study and derive insights, open government data use [40]; and capture, understand and present framework for social media analytics [12] had been used. Using the same we had tried to explore the RQ1, RQ2 and RQ3 and statistically validate H1, H2 and H3.

The "#government" and "#gov" had been used as the search terms for extracting social media data from Twitter. The data had been collected for 151 days starting from 1st January 2018. 296,417 tweets where collected along with 39 others attributes. 67% of the tweets in the sample were retweets. Therefore only unique tweets were extracted. In the sample there were around 174,204 unique tweets by 61,803 unique users. "#government" or "#gov" had been tagged with 49,659 other unique hashtags in the sample collected for the study. From these hashtags only top 100 hashtags had been considered for further analysis. Using content analysis [19] top 100 hashtags had been classified on the basis of the usage of the social media (inferred from the tweets containing these hashtags) into: (a) information dissemination and broadcasting; (b) for bringing transparency in the system; (c) open participation - gathering feedback and crowd sourcing; (d) collaboration; and (e) ubiquitous engagement. To statistically validate H1, one way anova was applied to hashtag usage category and hashtag frequency.

For each hashtag in top 100 list the tweets containing hashtag were searched. The summation of retweet count and like count for these tweets were computed and stored for each hashtag. To statistically validate H2, one way anova was applied to hashtag usage category and sum of retweet count. To statistically validate H3, one way anova was applied to hashtag usage category and sum of like count. Bar charts had been used to visualize data for frequency of the hashtags; tweets retweet ratio per hashtags for different social media usage; and tweets like ratio per hashtags for different social media usage with respect to government activities.

4   Finding

Among top 100 hashtags, 59 hashtags had been used for information dissemination and broadcasting purposes; 5 hashtags had been used for bringing transparency in the system; 9 hashtags had been used for open participation; 7 hashtags had been used for open collaboration; and 20 hashtags had been used for ubiquitous engagement. Among information dissemination and broadcasting popular hashtags are given in Fig. 2(a). News and media channel (popular #bbc and #cnn among other hashtags) are extensively reporting news related to governments. Employment issues had been considered a lot with "#government" and "#gov", therefore, #job, #hiring, #corporatocracy, #careerarc are in top hashtags used for information dissemination and broadcasting. The sample depicts tweets are showcasing how new technologies such as #blockchain and #ai can be used within public administration are being shared. As the new wave of digitalization is running across public administration it is giving rise to cyber security therefore #cybersecurity is occurring among top hashtags within information and dissemination hashtags.

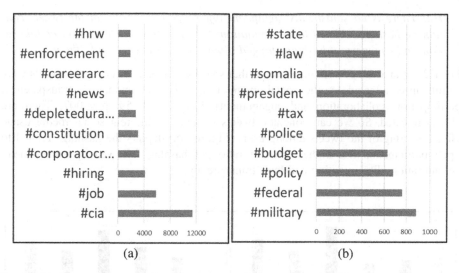

Fig. 2. (a) Information and dissemination top hashtags tagged with "government"/"gov"; (b) Ubiquitous engagement top hashtags tagged with "government"/"gov"

The popular hashtags for open transparency in sample were #justice (4793); #humanity (4551); #thaarjustice (4428); #evidence (1814); and #truth (750). The popular hashtags for open participation were related to intra and inter party's communication in different geographical locations which included the hashtags #communist, #democrat, #congress, #bjp and many more. The sample contains the hashtags related to popular political campaigns (i.e. #maga). The tweets indicates users were discussing about "#brexit" as a global event on Twitter. The healthcare policies had been discussed on Twitter a lot in context with public administration. The sample had included the hashtags related to countries like #uk, #usa/#us/#america, #india, #iraq, #russia and #china. Among ubiquitous engagement popular hashtags are given in Fig. 2(b). The sample signifies the ubiquitous engagement between public administration and citizens is going around the issues related to military, police, government policies and law, budget and tax. The null hypothesis is rejected if p < .05. The hypothesis above H1, H2 and H3 are null hypothesis. Therefore if the value of p is lesser than .05, than we will reject the hypothesis.

H1: There is no statistically significant difference on tagging "#government" and "#gov" with other hashtags related to dissemination, transparency, participation, collaboration and engagement hashtags.

For H1, an analysis of variance showed that the effect of social media usage for government activities tagged with "#government" and "#gov" was significantly different, $F(4,95) = 2.868$, $p = .027$, therefore H1 is rejected. So we can conclude that the mean tweets varies according to social media usage. It seems government hashtags are being used more for information and dissemination purposes followed by ubiquitous engagement.

H2: There is no statistically significant difference on sharing of the tweets containing hashtags related to dissemination, transparency, participation, collaboration and engagement hashtags tagged along "#government" and "#gov".

For H2, an analysis of variance showed that sharing (retweet count) of the tweets were significantly affected by the social media usage (i.e. dissemination, transparency, participation, collaboration and engagement), $F(4,95) = 3.759$, $p = .007$. Therefore H2, is rejected. So we can conclude tweets posted for different social media usage effects sharing of the tweets among users. Figure 3(a) depicts the hashtags related to open participation has highest retweet ratio per hashtag followed by engagement, collaboration, dissemination and least transparency.

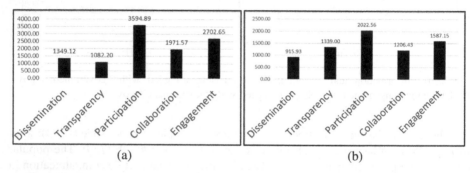

(a)   (b)

Fig. 3. (a) Tweets retweet ratio per hashtags for different social media usage; (b) Tweets like ratio per hashtags for different social media usage

H3: There is no statistically significant difference in liking of the tweets containing hashtags related to dissemination, transparency, participation, collaboration and engagement hashtags tagged along with "#government" and "#gov".

For H3, an analysis of variance showed that sharing of the tweets were affected by the social media usage (i.e. dissemination, transparency, participation, collaboration and engagement), $F(4,95) = 3.430$, $p = .012$. Therefore H3, is rejected. So we can conclude tweets posted for different social media usage effects liking of the tweets by users. Figure 3(b) depicts the hashtags related to open participation has highest like ratio per hashtag followed by engagement, transparency, collaboration, and least dissemination.

5 Discussion

Literature indicates the relationship between government and citizens can be transformed by using social media for information dissemination, transparency, participation, collaboration and ubiquitous government [3, 7, 31, 36]. According to us we feel public sector social media adoption had not been explore to great extent which is in line with literature [23, 35]. There had been studies which had explored government adoption of social media through surveys and interview but to best of our knowledge there is no study which had explored it by examining the user generated discussion in the field (social media platforms). Therefore this study tries to explore how social media had been used for various activities and how users are reacting to the tweets for different usage.

The study reports H1 is rejected on the sample collected which signifies social media had been extensively used for information dissemination and broadcasting purposes. Information dissemination had been used for news; employments, jobs and career; creating awareness about new technologies (artificial intelligence and block-chain) and their usage in public administration. In this digital age, users are concerns about their cyber security, therefore cyber security as has occurred in top hashtags.

H2 had been significantly rejected, which significances tweet usage for different social media usage effects it's sharing within the virtual communities. Figure 2(a) and Fig. 2(b) depicts a tweet related to participation as social media usage has got highest appeal of sharing and liking within the virtual communities (open participation has highest retweet and like ratio per hashtag). H3 had been significantly rejected, which significances tweet usage for different social media usage effects it's liking within the virtual world as well.

5.1 Contribution to Theory

The article on the basis of literature evidences and social media analysis presents government usage of social media for five purposes, first is for information dissemination and broadcasting purposes; second is for bringing transparency in system; third is for open participation for encouraging citizens in participating in national and global context agenda discussions; fourth is for open collaboration for betterment of the society; and lastly for ubiquitous engagement. This can be regarded as the theoretical contribution of the article towards the academic literature.

5.2 Implications for Practice

Exploration of RQ1 reveals highest number of hashtags tagged with "#government" and "#gov" had been used for information dissemination and broadcasting purposes whereas H2 and H3 reveals hashtags related to open participation has highest retweet ratio per hashtag and highest like ratio per hashtag. This signifies the tweets having participation appeal has highest penetration across the network. On the basis of the above analysis, the study briefly outlines guidelines for campaigns (hashtags usage) on social media by governments, news channels, political parties, non-governmental agencies and many more.

(a) To increase the penetration of the message on social media, the authors and distributors should try to embed the appeal of action from reader's prospective.

(b) On social media the agenda is being discussed in national or global context, so authors and distributors should always keep in mind how the message will affect the different communities present online.

(c) Authors and distributors should always be ready for rumors, if any, initiated and spread by other users present on the media.

(d) Use instructing strategy before and during the disaster and bolstering and adjusting strategy during post-disaster and recovery phase [21]. Inspired by them authors of the article will like to suggest to distributors to design the message according to situation and whether it is for information dissemination, citizen participation, citizen collaboration or citizen engagement.

6 Concluding Discussion

The study presents five uses of social media in public administration activities there are: information dissemination and broadcasting, for bringing transparency in system, participation, collaboration and engagement. The article focus on exploring three research questions, how is "#government" and "#gov" being used on Twitter and is there linkage between information sharing and liking through tweets and nature of social media usage through three hypothesis. The sample collected reveals news channels used social media extensively for information dissemination purposes. The biggest limitation of the study is that study had collected data for only 151 days and tweets only in English language had been considered for the analysis. The second biggest limitation of the study is some of the hashtags may not be necessarily from the government, it can be from individual users as well. The hashtags related to employ-ability had been extensively tagged with "#government", which signifies may be cit-izens are heavily depending on governments for earning their living. Future researchers can explore how Twitter is being used in relation with public administration and employability of citizens. Second issue which had gained lot of attention with gov-ernment hashtag is security, both physical security as well as cyber security. Researcher can explore the discussions on government and security further for deriving more insights from social media discussions.

References

1. Achananuparp, P., Lim, E.P., Jiang, J., Hoang, T.A.: Who is retweeting the tweeters? Modeling, originating, and promoting behaviors in the Twitter network. ACM Trans. Manag. Inf. Syst. (TMIS) **3**(3), 13 (2012)
2. Al–Aama, A.Y.: The use of Twitter to promote e–participation: connecting government and people. Int. J. Web Based Communities **11**(1), 73–96 (2015)
3. Aswani, R., Kar, A.K., Vigneswara Ilavarasan, P.: Detection of spammers in Twitter marketing: a hybrid approach using social media analytics and bio inspired computing. Inf. Syst. Front. **20**(3), 515–530 (2017). https://doi.org/10.1007/s10796-017-9805-8
4. Baur, A.W.: Harnessing the social web to enhance insights into people's opinions in business, government and public administration. Inf. Syst. Front. **19**(2), 231–251 (2016). https://doi.org/10.1007/s10796-016-9681-7
5. Bertot, J.C., Jaeger, P.T., Grimes, J.M.: Using ICTs to create a culture of transparency: E-government and social media as openness and anti-corruption tools for societies. Gov. Inf. Q. **27**(3), 264–271 (2010)
6. Bonsón, E., Torres, L., Royo, S., Flores, F.: Local e-government 2.0: social media and corporate transparency in municipalities. Gov. Inf. Q. **29**(2), 123–132 (2012)

7. Chatterjee, S.: Internet of Things and social platforms: an empirical analysis from Indian consumer behavioural perspective. Behav. Inf. Technol. **39**(2), 133–149 (2020)
8. Dong, C., Ji, Y.: Connecting young adults to democracy via government social network sites. Public Relat. Rev. **44**(5), 762–775 (2018)
9. Fan, W., Gordon, M.D.: The power of social media analytics. Commun. ACM **57**(6), 74–81 (2014)
10. Greene, J.A., Choudhry, N.K., Kilabuk, E., Shrank, W.H.: Online social networking by patients with diabetes: a qualitative evaluation of communication with Facebook. J. Gen. Intern. Med. **26**(3), 287–292 (2011). https://doi.org/10.1007/s11606-010-1526-3
11. Grover, P., Kar, A.K.: Big data analytics: a review on theoretical contributions and tools used in literature. Glob. J. Flex. Syst. Manag. **18**(3), 203–229 (2017). https://doi.org/10.1007/s40171-017-0159-3
12. Hagg, E., Dahinten, V.S., Currie, L.M.: The emerging use of social media for health-related purposes in low and middle-income countries: a scoping review. Int. J. Med. Informatics **115**, 92–105 (2018)
13. Hong, L., Fu, C., Wu, J., Frias-Martinez, V.: Information needs and communication gaps between citizens and local governments online during natural disasters. Inf. Syst. Front. **20**(5), 1027–1039 (2018). https://doi.org/10.1007/s10796-018-9832-0
14. Joseph, N., Kar, A.K., Ilavarasan, P.V., Ganesh, S.: Review of discussions on Internet of Things (IoT): insights from Twitter analytics. J. Glob. Inf. Manag. **25**(2), 38–51 (2017)
15. Kalampokis, E., Tambouris, E., Tarabanis, K.: Understanding the predictive power of social media. Internet Res. **23**(5), 544–559 (2013)
16. Kassarjian, H.H.: Content analysis in consumer research. J. Consum. Res. **4**(1), 8–18 (1977)
17. Lee, G., Kwak, Y.H.: An open government maturity model for social media-based public engagement. Gov. Inf. Q. **29**(4), 492–503 (2012)
18. Liu, W., Lai, C.H., Xu, W.W.: Tweeting about emergency: a semantic network analysis of government organizations' social media messaging during Hurricane Harvey. Public Relat. Rev. **44**(5), 807–819 (2018)
19. Malsbender, A., Hoffmann, S., Becker, J.: Aligning capabilities and social media affordances for open innovation in governments. Australas. J. Inf. Syst. **18**(3), 317–330 (2014)
20. Medaglia, R., Zheng, L.: Mapping government social media research and moving it forward: a framework and a research agenda. Gov. Inf. Q. **34**(3), 496–510 (2017)
21. Medaglia, R., Zhu, D.: Public deliberation on government-managed social media: a study on Weibo users in China. Gov. Inf. Q. **34**(3), 533–544 (2017)
22. Oliveira, G.H.M., Welch, E.W.: Social media use in local government: linkage of technology, task, and organizational context. Gov. Inf. Q. **30**(4), 397–405 (2013)
23. Panagiotopoulos, P., Bigdeli, A.Z., Sams, S.: Citizen–government collaboration on social media: the case of Twitter in the 2011 riots in England. Gov. Inf. Q. **31**(3), 349–357 (2014)
24. Paris, C., Nepal, S., Dennett, A.: A government-run online community to support recipients of welfare payments. Int. J. Coop. Inf. Syst. **27**(02), 1850001 (2018)
25. Perdana, R.S., Pinandito, A.: Combining likes-retweet analysis and Naive Bayes classifier within Twitter for sentiment analysis. J. Telecommun. Electron. Comput. Eng. (JTEC), **10**(1–8), 41–46 (2018)
26. Picazo-Vela, S., Gutiérrez-Martínez, I., Luna-Reyes, L.F.: Understanding risks, benefits, and strategic alternatives of social media applications in the public sector. Gov. Inf. Q. **29**(4), 504–511 (2012)
27. Porumbescu, G.A.: Linking public sector social media and e-government website use to trust in government. Gov. Inf. Q. **33**(2), 291–304 (2016)
28. Rathore, A.K., Kar, A.K., Ilavarasan, P.V.: Social media analytics: literature review and directions for future research. Decis. Anal. **14**(4), 229–249 (2017)

29. Reddick, C.G., Chatfield, A.T., Ojo, A.: A social media text analytics framework for double-loop learning for citizen-centric public services: a case study of a local government Facebook use. Gov. Inf. Q. **34**(1), 110–125 (2017)
30. Rosenberger, M., Lehrer, C., Jung, R.: Integrating data from user activities of social networks into public administrations. Inf. Syst. Front. **19**(2), 253–266 (2016). https://doi.org/10.1007/s10796-016-9682-6
31. Sharif, M.H.M., Troshani, I., Davidson, R.: Public sector adoption of social media. J. Comput. Inf. Syst. **55**(4), 53–61 (2015)
32. Snead, J.T.: Social media use in the US Executive branch. Gov. Inf. Q. **30**(1), 56–63 (2013)
33. Tang, X., Miao, Q., Quan, Y., Tang, J., Deng, K.: Predicting individual retweet behavior by user similarity: a multi-task learning approach. Knowl.-Based Syst. **89**, 681–688 (2015)
34. Uysal, N., Schroeder, J.: Turkey's Twitter public diplomacy: towards a "new" cult of personality. Public Relat. Rev. **45**(5), 101837 (2019)
35. Vakeel, K.A., Panigrahi, P.K.: Social media usage in e-government: mediating role of government participation. J. Glob. Inf. Manag. (JGIM) **26**(1), 1–19 (2018)
36. Vijaykumar, S., Meurzec, R.W., Jayasundar, K., Pagliari, C., Fernandopulle, Y.: What's buzzing on your feed? Health authorities' use of Facebook to combat Zika in Singapore. J. Am. Med. Inform. Assoc. **24**(6), 1155–1159 (2017)
37. Wang, C., Medaglia, R.: Governments' social media use for external collaboration: juggling time, task, team, and transition, with technology. Transform. Gov. People Process Policy **11**(4), 572–595 (2017)
38. Wang, L., Luo, X.: Understanding the interplay between government microblogs and citizen engagement: evidence from China. Electron. Commer. Res., 1–34 (2019). https://doi.org/10.1007/s10660-019-09376-1
39. Zheng, L., Zheng, T.: Innovation through social media in the public sector: information and interactions. Gov. Inf. Q. **31**, S106–S117 (2014)
40. Zuiderwijk, A., Janssen, M., Susha, I.: Improving the speed and ease of open data use through metadata, interaction mechanisms, and quality indicators. J. Organ. Comput. Electron. Commer. **26**(1–2), 116–146 (2016)

An Intention-Adoption Behavioral Model for Open Government Data in Pakistan's Public Sector Organizations–An Exploratory Study

Muhammad Mahboob Khurshid[1,2(✉)] 🆔, Nor Hidayati Zakaria[3],
Muhammad Irfanullah Arfeen[4], Ammar Rashid[5],
Hafiz Muhammad Faisal Shehzad[2], and Mohammad Nazir Ahmad[6]

[1] Department of Examinations, Virtual University of Pakistan, Lahore, Pakistan
mehboob.khursheed@vu.edu.pk
[2] School of Computing, Faculty of Engineering, Universiti Teknologi Malaysia,
Johor Bahru, Malaysia
mahboob.khursheed@gmail.com,
muhammad.faisal@uos.edu.pk
[3] Azman Hashim International Business School, Universiti Teknologi Malaysia,
Kuala Lumpur, Malaysia
hidayati@utm.my
[4] Quaid-i-Azam School of Management Sciences, Quaid-i-Azam University,
Islamabad, Pakistan
m.arfeen@qau.edu.pk
[5] College of IT, Ajman University, Ajman, UAE
a.rashid@ajman.ac.ae
[6] Institute of IR4.0, Universiti Kebangsaan Malaysia, 43600 Bangi,
Selangor, Malaysia
mnazir@ukm.edu.my

Abstract. Open Government Data (an innovation in the electronic government enabling public sector information accessible by the public in open formats and the ways to enable such facility) has huge potential to increase transparency, accountability, participation, efficiency in operations, data-driven/evidence-based policymaking, and trust on government institutions. Despite its potential benefits, although a few organizations are proactive and have embraced the OGD movement seriously, still OGD has not been widely adopted in Pakistan which might involve several obstacles that worked against such efforts. Driven by the nature of the research, this study conducted an exploratory field study in Pakistan by interviewing five industry experts in the e-government domain as well as attending a conference, and newspapers. This study identifies eight important antecedents to the adoption of OGD in public sector organizations and proposes future research to test their relationships. As the main theoretical contribution, this study extends organizational behavior toward technology diffusion. The findings of this study incite government, policymakers and managers to consider the factors and prepare future strategies on OGD developments.

© IFIP International Federation for Information Processing 2020
Published by Springer Nature Switzerland AG 2020
S. K. Sharma et al. (Eds.): TDIT 2020, IFIP AICT 617, pp. 377–388, 2020.
https://doi.org/10.1007/978-3-030-64849-7_34

Keywords: Open (Government) data · Adoption · Organization · Antecedents · Pakistan · Exploratory · Qualitative

1 Introduction

"Making public sector information freely available in open formats and ways that enable public access and facilitate exploitation has been termed open government data (OGD)" [1]. Open government data is a subset of open data and is simply government-related data that is made open to the public [2]. The data are public property and governments are the largest producers and collectors of data [3, 4]. These datasets are created, managed, and supplied by different government agencies. Thus, the open data process starts at the organization level. Like other developed and developing countries, there is no centralized data portal launched by the Government of Pakistan (GoP) so far, and despite this, quite a few datasets are being published by the public sector organizations on their own or other data portal like "Open Data Pakistan" launched by collaborative efforts of National Center for Big Data and Cloud Computing (NCBC), Lahore University of Management Sciences (LUMS) and Higher Education Commission (HEC). Also, very less public-sector information are being proactively released by the ministries in Pakistan [5], even the GoP has joined the Open Government Partnership in 2016 [6].

In particular, OGD research has focused more on the West, owing to the growing numbers of OGD policies in the Europe and US [7]. In developed countries, however, research on OGD is at the early stages [8].In the Pakistan context, quite a few studies are conducted i.e. OGD barriers with respect to private organizations [9], diffusion of open data in big quantities across Pakistan [10, 11], OGD adoption from academicians and citizens perspectives [12, 13], OGD impact on transparency and accountability [14], and uses and impact of open data for social sector [15]. However, the public organization's perspective is not yet explored. Therefore, this current study aims to explore the antecedents of OGD adoption in the context of public sector organizations in Pakistan. More specifically, the research question for this study is:

RQ1. What are the factors that drive or deter public sector organizations in Pakistan to adopt OGD?

To achieve this, the remaining part of this submission is structured as follows: the next section briefly describes background literature on OGD adoption, followed by research methods that are presented in Sect. 3. Section 4 outlines the explored factors, discussion in Sect. 5, and the conclusion is outlined in Sect. 6.

2 Background

The background only includes conceptual and empirically studies on organizational OGD adoption to publicize the data. Zhenbin, Kankanhalli [4] conducted a study to empirically investigating the open data sharing in Singapore by employing a resourcedependency theory and found that all the factors (including external innovator dependence, conformity need, and sensitivity of function) are supported to have their influence on sharing behavior except data quality, size of the agency, and need for transparency factors. In a study conducted by Wang and Lo [1], the adoption model of OGD in government agencies in Taiwan was developed by using TOE (Technology, Organization, Environment) theory. They found that perceived benefit, organizational readiness, and external pressure were the influencing factors on OGD adoption whereas perceived barriers factor was not supported as the influencer [1]. By employing the cognitive theory, Wirtz, Piehler [16] proposed and empirically tested the behavioral model that restricts public personnel to implement OGD. All the barriers except perceived organizational transparency had a negative influence on the OGD resistance of agencies' public officials. Grimmelikhuijsen and Feeney [17] developed and tested an integrative framework for the adoption of OGD in US local governments. Routineness and politicized environment bared the negative influential factors on open government adoption. Based on empirical investigation taking secondary data, Alderete [18] found digital adoption, and e-participation, and ICT-development indexes, and the gross domestic product had an impact on open government whereas innovation had no impact on open government. A resource-based theory was employed by Zhao and Fan [19] and empirically investigated the antecedents on OGD capacity. Moreover, an institutional theory was employed by Fan and Zhao [20] and empirically investigated the antecedents on OGD quality. By employing several theoretical models including TOE and institutional theory, the open data publication behavior among government agencies in Taiwan was examined by Yang and Wu [21]. Moreover, in a recently published study by Khurshid, Zakaria [22], a systematic literature review of theories and potential determinants that influence the OGD adoption in public sector organizations was conducted.

3   Research Method

This study explored the antecedents by employing a field-based qualitative research approach. In this way, the exploration of factors is expected to be more valuable than using only one method. Qualitative data was obtained from practitioners through interviews, attending a conference on Sustainable Development in a Digital Society (SDDS), and newspapers. Five interviews were conducted with five practitioners in public sector organizations. The interviewees were bearing different positions in public sector organizations as e-government practitioners, director/director operations, and public information officers. The semi-structured interviews were conducted between November 2019 and March 2020. The duration of each interview has lasted around 20–40 min. All interview sessions were recorded, transcribed, and presented before the interviewees for validation of the content.

Both the content and thematic analysis techniques were practiced for commonly recurring themes. However, only the deductive approach (by comparing and contrasting the same of similar conceptualizations in different regional settings) was used during the analysis phase. For instance, all the themes were more or less pre-defined constructs in earlier studies, like compliance pressure, but their nature and influence are found different in the current context and concerning OGD. In sum, selected factors were confirmed from earlier studies.

The theoretical foundation of the proposed model is based on Technology, Organization, and Environment framework (TOE) [23]. Data quality and technical interoperability fall in the technology dimension. The organization dimension covers bureaucratic culture, digitation capacity, and knowledge and understanding. The two factors political leadership and compliance pressure are observed in the environment dimension.

4   Findings

The findings of the field study and the associated links with theory are presented in the following section.

4.1   Data/Metadata Quality

The data quality bears several issues like inaccuracy, timeliness, and completeness [8], ambiguities, formats, and representation [24]. However, the quality of datasets can also be led by the poor quality of OGD infrastructure [8]. Data quality attributes have also been referred to as information/metadata quality [7, 25–27]. It is the data which is the main source and all about in the OGD initiative. The whole concept of openness rotates around data holding by public bodies. Therefore, the quality of data and information is the main concern of decision-makers to adopt OGD because the definition of open data itself is inherently influenced by the quality criteria of data [28]. This factor is not only the main concern in adoption [7] but also in the postadoption phase of openness of government data [28]. Data is also different from the government departments as another respondent highlights that

> "...the quality of data is also not very consistent. For instance, we are trying to find out about some projects, say, how many numbers of vehicles in Pakistan (3wheelers, 4-wheelers, etc. simple question. There are two or three organizations that are keeping that data. When we collect data from them, the data was different by a wide margin. One is saying Pakistan has 1-million vehicles- cars. Another will be saying 3-million cars. The third dept. may have different data. Thus, it is quite difficult for us to ascertain how many cars are there in Pakistan", (Interviewee 3)

The earlier studies outlined the poor quality of data to be the key concern in OGD adoption [29] and overall OGD initiative [7]. We propose that high quality of data will lead to increase adoption intention to open of data by the public sector organizations and thus deduce the following proposition:

Proposition 1: Data/Metadata Quality will have a positive influence on the public sector organization's intention to adopt OGD.

4.2   Technical Interoperability

Data is generated in the different public sectors at different locations such as ministries, provincial, regional, and local level departments. To exploit data by the users, these public sector organizations need to make the systems [30] and data and metadata [31] interoperable. Interoperability is considered both the technical organizational issue [32]. However, data interoperability is also often considered a bureaucratic and political issue [3, 33]. Interoperability is considered as the technical characteristic based on the argument of Hossain and Chan [34] and Sayogo and Yuli [35] such that interoperability is a technical characteristic in information systems. One of the interviewees also underlined that interoperability is the key barrier in OGD adoption outlining that

> "...The things are scattered. The offices are working in silos. One agency has the data, let say, agricultural land from the Agriculture Department. The same data and information about that particular land are also with Board of Revenue. There is no mechanism that they both should use this data, exchange this data. In IT language, we say interoperability issues. There are certain interoperability issues. Sometimes, their systems are not communicating well. So, this data remains in silos. They do not share with agencies even don't share among themselves."
> (Interviewee 1)

To make the OGD adoption successful, a combined effort by all the public organizations to make the systems and data interoperable is necessary. Thus, the higher the interoperability, the higher the OGD intention. Accordingly, we propose that data interoperability is positively related to intend to adopt OGD.

Proposition 2: Technical interoperability will have a positive influence on the public sector organization's intention to adopt OGD.

4.3   Political Leadership Commitment

Worldwide, political leaders take several initiatives: making public agencies to adopt proper measures to open the data, championing open data policy, and preparing strategy and directive for departments to act on them, carrying most of the costs for publishing data online (e.g. government of many counties including the US, Denmark, UK, Spain, and Australian carries most of the costs (such as developing and maintaining infrastructure) for publishing data online) [34, 36, 37], and preparing an open business environment where private firms and entrepreneurs can participate [34, 36, 37]. Opening data is the result of a political commitment [25]. Furthermore, the OGD initiative is supported and backed by political commitment and leadership, and this was a strong driver for OGD adoption [38]. If governments cannot see a positive impact of open data, high-level political commitment may reduce, stall, or even go backward the open data developments [39]. Leadership centrality provides shared direction and political visibility [40, 41]. Hence, it is the political leaders who institutionalized the concept of open data - their 'political movement' intended to ensure transparency and participation of citizens in governance [34]. It has been observed that political will or commitment has been an important construct as one of the respondent states that

"...degree of political will for citizens centric governance through principles of open government is a universal principle. Without political will, we are unable to make decisions. How much technology we have...". (SDDS Conference)

A lack of leadership to help drive the open data movement would be difficult because it is a critical factor [42]. Therefore, the proposition is that political leadership will have a positive influence on adoption intention of OGD in the public sector.

Proposition 3: Political leadership commitment will have a positive influence on the public sector organization's intention to adopt OGD.

4.4 Knowledge and Understanding

The government data can be used by different users including not only the politicians, public, media, private organizations but also by other government agencies. The OGD use needs statistical as well as analytical knowledge and understanding otherwise the data could be misinterpreted. Users should know to make sense or to convert into meaningful information [7]. Also, to make the sense out of the data, users are required to have the necessary resources and capabilities. On the contrary, organizations represented by the policy or decision-makers must also have an understanding of the integrity, usefulness, quantity, and diversity of government data at different locations. More specifically, in Pakistan, government organizations do not have a good idea about how much and to what extent data and information they are generating and collecting. As one interviewee indicated that

"...Computers are being used, computer operators and IT people are always in the offices. But where we [organizations] are lacking is that they [organizations] don't have a good idea that how much information they are generating and collecting. The things are scattered. In fact, the offices are working in silos". (Interviewee 1)

Accordingly, it is proposed that the more knowledge and understanding of the government data, the more will be publicized. Therefore, the following proposition has been deduced:

Proposition 4: Organization's knowledge and understanding of data will have a positive influence on their intention to adopt OGD.

4.5 Digitization Capacity

OGD is not a simple or straightforward process of publishing or releasing government data, rather its publishing goes through the laborious lifecycle [43]. Thus, making the existing data digitized so that it becomes usable involves huge efforts, requires certain conditions and resources which should be invested for such efforts. Organizations must have the capacity to make government data digitized. An organization's expert human resource is the basic technical capacity that can form the organization's digitization capacity to publish the data. Government organizations in Pakistan are lacking the digitization capacity, as one informant indicated that:

"...Agencies do not have the capacity to map the whole data, number one. They have limited capacity of digitizing this data. It is scattered in files and sometimes, you would find so many bags in sacks, the files are dumped in stores. So, Digitization is the second thing. The hurdle is when we ask them that you should digitize this...we need computers, we need huge infrastructure to digitize this...". (Interviewee 1)

"They [organizations] have not good proper technical resources who will design it and implement it. I am not saying there is no shortage of resources in organizations. I am saying that there is no shortage of resources in the market.". (Interviewee 2)

Fast generation, huge volumes, varied data, and different sources [42] make the data understanding (*"...They do share the data, but it is very difficult to get the data. It is very difficult to implement that. It is very difficult to reach there".* (Interviewee 2)), linking and management more difficult and, in turn, the OGD implementation [44]. Government institutions need new capacities and knowledge to provide integrated support to implementation and to leave no one behind [45]. Based on the aforementioned facts, it may be proposed that the more digitization capacity, the higher their adoption intention towards OGD. Therefore, the following proposition has been deduced:

Proposition 5: Digitization capacity will have a positive influence on the public sector organization's intention to adopt OGD.

4.6   Compliance Pressure

The unit of adoption can be influenced by the external arenas like a push from international organizations, regulatory agencies, peer organizations within and outside the same government or industry, higher-level authorities [21], or media and the public [46] to share the data online in open formats. The organizations are intended to achieve and obtain greater compliance with the legitimacy requirement within their institutional sphere [38, 47]. Changes and improvements in organization processes can also take place through bottom-up influence like general public and public practitioners. In this connection, one of the interviewees noted that

"...overly use of Open Data and request for under RTI Act by certain groups with vested rights. Common citizen who is a patriotic citizen could really want to use Open Government Data for positive purposes, such examples are rare." (Interviewee 1)

The empirical results also indicated that external pressures can serve as the coercive power and is a major indicator of increasing OGD adoption in the Netherlands [48], among government agencies in Taiwan [1]. Similarly, higher-level government institutions pressurize lower-level organizations to conform to the OGD policies and regulations in Singapore [4]. Therefore, we propose that compliance pressure is a predictor of OGD adoption intention and hence the proposition is deduced as:

Proposition 6: Compliance Pressure will have a positive influence on the public sector organization's intention to adopt OGD.

4.7   Bureaucratic System or Culture

The design of an organization determines its capacity as low or high. In an organization where there is centralization or culture with strong vibrant bureaucracy, the processes are highly cumbersome [19]. Moreover, the implementation of processes is highly bound with the approval of the head of the organization. In the bureaucratic type of organizational design, officials' enthusiasm and autonomy are severely affected. The bureaucratic system severely weakens the official's interest and willingness. The existence of a bureaucratic system or culture is a critical barrier in implementing the OGD initiative [17]. Since OGD can substantially change traditional organizational systems, governments are always closed and keep secrets of the public, and therefore, it is extremely difficult if the traditional bureaucratic system remains unchanged in China [49]. Such a bureaucratic system is also prevailing in Pakistan as one respondent indicated that

> "...so the problem is still these proposals are pending with ministry ... And Why? This same mindset which we perceive everything that is prevailing in the province, it is also prevailing in the center... It [Pakistan] has a long tradition and has a historic bureaucratic system. A strong vibrant bureaucracy. Very simple norm that to put confidential tag on even day to day intra-official communication... First, we have to work hard on changing mindsets of our civil servants. We have to teach them what Open Government Data is, how Open Government Data can be beneficial for public." (Interviewee 1)

Based on the previous literature and industry respondent feedback, it is proposed that the more bureaucratic culture or system is prevailing in the public organizations, the less the intention of OGD toward adoption. Hence, the proposition is deduced as:

Proposition 7: Bureaucratic culture will have a negative influence on the public sector organization's intention to adopt OGD.

4.8   Adoption Intention

Not all organizations are willing to publish their data on the Internet (Nugroho 2013) and even if organizations are willing to publish their data, there are still many barriers that counteract the publication of data [50]. Generally, the willingness of organizations would be more when barriers are less, and benefits are more visible to them. Therefore, perceptions, knowledge, and adherence to open data benefits would increase the organizations' intentions towards releasing open data [1, 51]. As one of the informants indicated that:

> "...there is not so much emphasis or eagerness to share the data". The informant mentioned that "...and willingness to share data and willingness to take responsibility for what we have done. Because the more public or open data, will give people more credible resources to hold the people and the power more accountable. And that is something which they do not want". Moreover, "We [organizations] are not saying that there is no technological lack of resources in organizations. We [organizations] have suggested that because there is no willingness to share the data... and to implement it [OGD]". (Interviewee 2)

Behavioral Intention is the level to which a person has developed conscious plans to perform or not perform some specified future behavior [52]. In previous OGD studies, behavioral intention has been found as a significant predictor of open data published by government agencies [21], as well as with similar conceptualizations such as likelihood to publish data [53], and adoption intention [34].

Proposition 8: Public sector organizations' adoption intention will have a positive influence on their adoption behavior of OGD.

5 Discussion

Several factors effect on OGD adoption. Data quality includes several dimensions/ characteristics. However, the quality of metadata or information quality is also one of the dimensions of Data Quality in the OGD perspective [7, 27]. Therefore, this exploratory study confirms that data and its relevant metadata are critical for OGD adoption. The interoperability of datasets is referred to as a technological issue that also requires different slacks such as budget and time [34]. The true and sincere efforts from the government would also be a substantial stimulus towards open data movement which this study also confirms and requires further empirical investigation. To make OGD movement momentous, technical and technological capacities are also required by the public sector administrations and confirmed by the participants during the interview session. A significant barrier which restricts the government organizations to seriously adopt OGD is the existence of so many hierarchal levels, approvals from the higher authorities, and not giving the employees autonomy in organizational decision-making.

6 Conclusion and Future Research Directions

Open Government Data is a source to increase transparency, accountability, participation, and policymaking in government institutions. This study aims to find the factors influence on OGD initiative in Pakistan. This study conducted an exploratory study by interviewing industry experts in the e-government domain, conference, and newspapers and identifies eight important factors of OGD in public sector organizations. The theoretical contribution of the study is to extend organizational behavior toward technology diffusion. The practical contribution of the study is to encourage, government, policymakers and managers to consider the addressed factors and to prepare for future strategies for OGD developments. Although this study provides useful findings it has some limitations also. The first limitation of this study is that the model was proposed by interviewing with only five interviewees. Thus, we realized that a comprehensive view might not be obtained. However, the factors are reasonably backed from the earlier studies to make them sound part of the proposed model. The infrastructure and situations may be different in each government organization and this study generally covers factors of OGD adoption. Nonetheless, it is believed that these findings can be directly applied to the whole government sector, however, the government organizations can address various factors at early stages without trial and error. The future work directions include the empirical validation of the proposed model. Also, the future work is suggested to investigate the post-adoption or implementation of OGD.

References

1. Wang, H.-J., Lo, J.: Adoption of open government data among government agencies. Gov. Inf. Q. **33**(1), 80–88 (2016)
2. Wang, V., Shepherd, D.: Exploring the extent of openness of open government data – a critique of open government datasets in the UK. Gov. Inf. Q. **37**(1), 101405 (2019)
3. Gonzalez-Zapata, F., Heeks, R.: The multiple meanings of open government data: Understanding different stakeholders and their perspectives. Gov. Inf. Q. **32**(4), 441–452 (2015)
4. Zhenbin, Y., et al.: What drives public agencies to participate in open government data initiatives? An innovation resource perspective. Inf. Manag. **57**(3), 103179 (2019)
5. Rehmat, A., Alam, M.A.: Inactive Government on Proactive Disclosure. Institute for Research, Advocacy and Development (IRADA), Islamabad (2018)
6. OGP. Open Government Partnership (2016). http://www.datastories.pk/is-pakistan-really-striving-for-open-government/
7. Janssen, M., Charalabidis, Y., Zuiderwijk, A.: Benefits, adoption barriers and myths of open data and open government. Inf. Syst. Manag. **29**(4), 258–268 (2012)
8. Shao, D.S., Saxena, S.: Barriers to open government data (OGD) initiative in Tanzania: stakeholders' perspectives. Growth Change **50**, 1–16 (2018)
9. Saxena, S., Muhammad, I.: Barriers to use open government data in private sector and NGOs in Pakistan. Inf. Disc. Deliv. **46**(1), 67–75 (2018)
10. Khurshid, M.M., Zakaria, N.H., Rashid, A., Kazmi, R., Shafique, M.N.: Diffusion of big open data policy innovation in government and public bodies in Pakistan. In: Bajwa, I.S., Kamareddine, F., Costa, A. (eds.) INTAP 2018. CCIS, vol. 932, pp. 326–337. Springer, Singapore (2019). https://doi.org/10.1007/978-981-13-6052-7_28
11. Khurshid, M.M., et al.: Analyzing diffusion patterns of big open data as policy innovation in public sector. Comput. Electr. Eng. **78**, 148161 (2019)
12. Khurshid, M.M., Zakaria, N.H., Rashid, A., Shafique, M.N., Khanna, A., Gupta, D., Ahmed, Y.A.: Proposing a framework for citizen's adoption of public-sector open IoT data (OIoTD) platform in disaster management. In: Khanna, A., Gupta, D., Bhattacharyya, S., Snasel, V., Platos, J., Hassanien, A.E. (eds.) International Conference on Innovative Computing and Communications. AISC, vol. 1059, pp. 593–601. Springer, Singapore (2020). https://doi.org/10.1007/978-981-15-0324-5_50
13. Khurshid, M.M., et al.: Examining the factors of open government data usability from academician's perspective. Int. J. Inf. Technol. Proj. Manag. **9**(3), 72–85 (2018)
14. Saxena, S., Muhammad, I.: The impact of open government data on accountability and transparency. J. Econ. Adm. Sci. **34**(3), 204–216 (2018)
15. Shabbir, T., Nadeemullah, M., Memon, S.: Uses and impact of 'open data' technology for developing social sector in Pakistan. Pak. J. Multidisc. Res. **1**(1), 50–64 (2020)
16. Wirtz, B.W., et al.: Resistance of public personnel to open government: a cognitive theory view of implementation barriers towards open government data. Public Manag. Rev. **18**(9), 1335–1364 (2016)
17. Grimmelikhuijsen, S.G., Feeney, M.K.: Developing and testing an integrative framework for open government adoption in local governments. Public Adm. Rev. **77**, 579–590 (2017)
18. Alderete, M.V.: The mediating role of ICT in the development of open government. J. Glob. Inf. Technol. Manag. **21**(3), 172–187 (2018)
19. Zhao, Y., Fan, B.: Exploring open government data capacity of government agency: based on the resource-based theory. Gov. Inf. Q. **35**(1), 1–12 (2018)

20. Fan, B., Zhao, Y.: The moderating effect of external pressure on the relationship between internal organizational factors and the quality of open government data. Gov. Inf. Q. **34**, 396–406 (2017)
21. Yang, T.-M., Wu, Y.-J.: Examining the socio-technical determinants influencing government agencies' open data publication: a study in Taiwan. Gov. Inf. Q. **33**(3), 378–392 (2016)
22. Khurshid, M.M., et al.: Modeling of open government data for public sector organizations using the potential theories and determinants—a systematic review. Informatics **7**(3), 24 (2020)
23. Tornatzky, L.G., Fleischer, M.: The Process of Technological Innovation, p. 298. Lexington Books (1990)
24. Roa, H.N., Loza-Aguirre, E., Flores, P.: A survey on the problems affecting the development of open government data initiatives. In: 2019 Sixth International Conference on eDemocracy & eGovernment (ICEDEG) (2019)
25. Martin, S., et al.: Risk analysis to overcome barriers to open data. Electron. J. e-Gov. **11**(1), 348–359 (2013)
26. Parung, G.A., et al.: Barriers and strategies of open government data adoption using fuzzy AHP-TOPSIS. Transf. Gov. People Process Policy **12**(3/4), 210–243 (2018)
27. Kubler, S., et al.: Comparison of metadata quality in open data portals using the Analytic Hierarchy Process. Gov. Inf. Q. **35**(1), 1329 (2018)
28. Mustapa, M.N., Nasaruddin, F.H.M., Hamid, S.: Post-adoption of open government data initiatives in public sectors. In: Pacific Asia Conference on Information Systems. Association for Information Systems, Langkawi (2017)
29. Haini, S.I., Rahim, N.Z.A., Zainuddin, N.M.M.: Adoption of open government data in local government context: conceptual model development. In: Proceedings of the 2019 5th International Conference on Computer and Technology Applications, pp. 193–198. ACM, Istanbul (2019)
30. Martin, C.: Barriers to the open government data agenda: taking a multi-level perspective. Policy Internet **6**(3), 217–240 (2014)
31. Susha, I., et al.: Critical factors for open data publication and use: a comparison of city-level, regional, and transnational cases. eJ. eDemocracy Open Gov. **7**(2), 94–115 (2015)
32. Maheshwari, D., Janssen, M.: Measuring organizational interoperability in practice: the case study of population welfare department of government of Sindh, Pakistan (2012)
33. Ma, R., Lam, P.T.I.: Investigating the barriers faced by stakeholders in open data development: a study on Hong Kong as a "smart city". Cities **92**, 36–46 (2019)
34. Hossain, M.A., Chan, C.: Open data adoption in Australian government agencies: an exploratory study. In: Australasian Conference on Information Systems, Adelaide (2015)
35. Sayogo, D.S., Yuli, S.B.C.: Critical success factors of open government and open data at local government level in Indonesia. Int. J. Electron. Gov. Res. **14**(2), 28–43 (2018)
36. Huijboom, N., Broek, T.V.D.: Open data: an international comparison of strategies. Eur. J. ePract. **12**, 4–16 (2011)
37. Hossain, M.A., Dwivedi, Y.K., Rana, N.P.: State-of-the-art in open data research: insights from existing literature and a research agenda. J. Organ. Comput. Electron. Commer. **26**(1–2), 14–40 (2016)
38. Altayar, M.S.: Motivations for open data adoption: an institutional theory perspective. Gov. Inf. Q. **35**(4), 633–643 (2018)
39. ODB: OpenData Barometer Global Report, World Wide Web Foundation. 2015: http://opendatabarometer.org/doc/3rdEdition/ODB-3rdEdition-GlobalReport.pdf
40. Ingrams, A.: Organizational design in open government: two cases from the United Kingdom and the United States. Public Perf. Manag. Rev. **43**, 1–26 (2019)

41. Ruvalcaba-Gomez, E.A., Criado, J.I., Gil-Garcia, J.R.: Analyzing open government policy adoption through the multiple streams framework: the roles of policy entrepreneurs in the case of Madrid. Public Policy and Administration (2020)
42. Hardy, K., Maurushat, A.: Opening up government data for Big Data analysis and public benefit. Comput. Law Secur. Rev. **33**(1), 30–37 (2017)
43. Attard, J., et al.: A systematic review of open government data initiatives. Gov. Inf. Q. **32**(4), 399–418 (2015)
44. Solar, M., Meijueiro, L., Daniels, F.: A guide to implement open data in public agencies. In: Wimmer, Maria A., Janssen, M., Scholl, Hans J. (eds.) EGOV 2013. LNCS, vol. 8074, pp. 75–86. Springer, Heidelberg (2013). https://doi.org/10.1007/978-3-642-40358-3_7
45. UN: United Nations E-Government Survey 2018, D.o.E.a.S. Affairs, Editor. United Nations, New York (2018)
46. Yang, T.-M., Lo, J., Shiang, J.: To open or not to open? determinants of open government data. J. Inf. Sci. **41**(5), 596–612 (2015)
47. Roa, Henry N., Loza-Aguirre, E., Flores, P.: Drivers and barriers for open government data adoption: an isomorphic neo-institutional perspective. In: Arai, K., Kapoor, S., Bhatia, R. (eds.) FICC 2020. AISC, vol. 1129, pp. 589–599. Springer, Cham (2020). https://doi.org/10.1007/978-3-030-39445-5_43
48. Ruijer, E., Meijer, A.: Open government data as an innovation process: lessons from a living lab experiment. Public Perf. Manag. Rev. **43**, 1–23 (2019)
49. Huang, R., Lai, T., Zhou, L.: Proposing a framework of barriers to opening government data in China. Libra. Hi Tech **35**(3), 421–438 (2017)
50. Zuiderwijk, A., Janssen, M.: Barriers and development directions for the publication and usage of open data: a socio-technical view. In: Gascó-Hernández, M. (ed.) Open Government. PAIT, vol. 4, pp. 115–135. Springer, New York (2014). https://doi.org/10.1007/978-1-4614-9563-5_8
51. Wang, H., Lo, J.: Factors influencing the adoption of open government data at the firm level. IEEE Trans. Eng. Manag. **67**, 1–13 (2019)
52. Davis, F.D.: Perceived usefulness, perceived ease of use, and user acceptance of information technology. MIS Q. **13**(3), 319–340 (1989)
53. Sayogo, D.S., Pardo, T.A.: Exploring the determinants of scientific data sharing: understanding the motivation to publish research data. Gov. Inf. Q. **30**, S19–S31 (2013)

Exploring the Adoption of Multipurpose Community Telecentres in Sub-Saharan Africa

Josue Kuika Watat(✉) (iD)

AMBERO Consulting GmbH, 61476 Kronberg im Taunus, Germany
josuewatat@gmail.com

Abstract. In several countries of the global South, hope relies heavily on technologies for economic, social, and cultural development. Multipurpose Community Telecentres have been carefully presented to disadvantaged communities as a hub to facilitate the economic and social empowerment and increase the technological skills of youths. Although several initiatives have emerged, few studies have focused on their impact in Sub-Saharan Africa. To fill the gap observed in the existing literature, this study aims to explore the key determinants associated with the acceptance of telecentres in rural municipalities in Cameroon. It intends to contextualize the Unified Theory of Acceptance and Use of technology model, branching out constructs which are specific to the study environment. This qualitative study, adopting a mixed research methodology, presents the results of needs analysis study for municipal digital services in rural areas. In addition, the study provides additional answers regarding the digital divide in rural Africa.

Keywords: Telecentre · Rural empowerment · Africa · Digital divide

1 Introduction

The Multipurpose Community telecentres project has been adopted by several countries in search of development to break the digital divide and thus dematerialize access to public services for citizens and communities living in landlocked areas [1]. The deployment of ICT infrastructures and services is aligned with the aim of promoting the multi-sectoral development of localities that have been slow to reach the digital world. Although having dedicated enormous financial resources to the deployment, acceptance and use of ICT tools, their effective use remains a big challenge in most of the countries in Sub-Saharan Africa where a large mass of people and communities reside in rural areas with limited access to technology, and a low level of digital literacy [2].

In Africa, the information society has for several years been encountering fundamental ethical problems which are undergoing rapid and exponential changes in the light of the globalization of different activities and fields [3, 4]. The use of the internet and digital tools have become substantial when we look at the place that digital occupies in modern life and society, which happens to be an important vector for the development of several sectors [5]. In addition, the exponential growth of digital tools and the digital mutations generated in daily life of humans have given rise to another level of difficulties which integrate digital inequality and social exclusion [6].

© IFIP International Federation for Information Processing 2020
Published by Springer Nature Switzerland AG 2020
S. K. Sharma et al. (Eds.): TDIT 2020, IFIP AICT 617, pp. 389–400, 2020.
https://doi.org/10.1007/978-3-030-64849-7_35

Although digital inequalities persist in sub-Saharan Africa, the gap in the appropriation of digital technologies remains large between cities and villages to date the prospects are promising for the digital economy [7]. According to United Nations, the number of people in Africa is expected to double by 2050, from more than a billion to over 2.5 billion [8]. The following Fig. 1 shows the disparities existing in the use of mobile internet in low-and-middle-income countries.

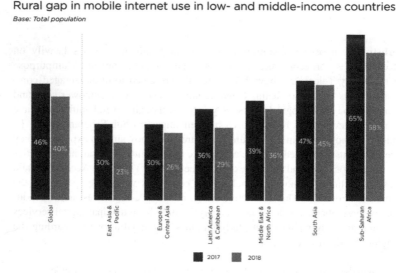

Rural gap in mobile internet use in low- and middle-income countries
Base: Total population

Global 46% 40% | East Asia & Pacific 30% 23% | Europe & Central Asia 30% 26% | Latin America & Caribbean 36% 29% | Middle East & North Africa 39% 36% | South Asia 47% 45% | Sub-Saharan Africa 65% 58%

2017   2018

Fig. 1. Rural gap in mobile internet use in low- and middle-income countries [9]

This study aims to increase the existing literature on MCTs in Africa by proposing a model that extends the Unified Theory of Acceptance and Use of Technology, contextualized to the acceptance and Use of Telecentres in a specific environment characterized by poverty, lack of technological infrastructure and the internet. The use of the UTAUT model in this context is justified because it incorporates demographic factors and experience in the generic model. Coupled with the emerging literature on Telecentres around the world and on socioeconomic and cultural specificities in Africa, we will examine the following research question: *what are the key determinants of the use and adoption of Multipurpose Community Telecentres for value creation and socio-economic development in rural areas?*

2 Conceptual Framework

This section is dedicated to the theoretical description of models and theories used to address our research objectives and thus formulate our hypotheses. We propose an extension of the Unified Theory of Acceptance and Use of Technology by branching out constructs which are specific to the context and the study environment (Fig. 2). [10] set out key constructs which constitute and contribute to the formation of UTAUT:

Performance Expectancy, effort Expectancy, Social Influence and Facilitating Conditions. The Unified Theory of Acceptance and Use of Technologies as modeled by Venkatesh, is one of the key theories when it comes to investigating the adoption of a Technology in different contexts of study [10]. To arrive at this theory, the UTAUT model went through a rigorous review and underwent significant experimental validation of eight important adoption theories [10]. The Unified Theory of Acceptance and Use of Technology (UTAUT) is used in this study because it already incorporates the demographic variables(gender, age, experience), which is not the case with the original Technology Acceptance model (TAM). In fact, most of Technology adoption model like the TAM lack a variety of constructs that can influence the study context, hence the restructuring of the study in order to be able to fit into several study contexts and thus correspond to the objectives sought [11].

2.1 Core Constructs

Performance Expectancy: "the degree an individual user believes that using the telecentre will assist in enhancing his/her performance" [10].
H1: Performance Expectancy has a positive influence on Behavioral Intention to Use Telecentre (BIU).

Effort Expectancy: refers to the level of facility in using telecentre services [10].
　　H2: Effort Expectancy has a positive influence on Behavioral Intention to Use Telecentre BIU.

Social Influence: refers to the measurement perceived by a user of the importance in the use of the telecentre by another user [10].
　　H3: Social Influence has a positive influence on BIU.

Management Effectiveness: It includes the specifications related to resolution of organizational problems and actions concerning staff management within the Telecentre [12].
　　H4: Management Effectiveness has positive influence on BIU.

Programme Effectiveness: refers to specific programs and activities that the telecentre will provide as it is set up with the aim of providing a certain number of digital services to rural communities [13].
　　H5: Program Effectiveness has positive influence on BIU.

Facilitating Conditions: is defined as the firm conviction that any user has over the existence of a technical supervision in charge of supporting the operation of the telecentre [10].
　　H6: Facilitating Conditions influence positively BIU.

2.2 Factors Used to Customized UTAUT Model

These factors are related to the specificity of the study environment as well as various development indicators of the study area. Therefore, they come as an extension of various models and theories drawn from the literature to explain and highlight the experience studied.

Awareness: It is defined as the ability to be aware of the use of a new service/product, a concept that could be beneficial in carrying out the daily tasks of a community.

H7: Awareness impact positively BIU.

Culture: Cameroon has hundreds of traditional kingdoms and more than 250 dialects in all 10 regions in the country. The official languages of are French and English. However, young people have created a complex form of slang called "camfranglais" (mixture of French, English, vernacular Cameroonian phrases and even verlan) that varies between cities [14]. Some also use the "pijin", which is a mixture of English and slang [15]. As for the traders, they negotiate very often in "pidjin" english (form of English Creole) for more than 50 years [16].

H8: Culture impact positively BIU.

Power Supply: The supply of electrical energy remains a real problem in sub-Saharan Africa, both for large cities and for rural areas. Although governments and international organizations have mobilized to be able to respond to electrical energy problems, there is still a huge gap between supply and demand [17].

H9: Power Supply has positive impact on BIU.

Government Regulatory: The Cameroonian government has set up several regulations on the management and use of telecentres through the Ministry of Posts and Telecommunications.

H10: Legal/Government regulatory has positive impact on BIU.

Accessibility: "the availability of necessary IT tools for the operation of telecentres for particular users" [18].

H11: Accessibility has a positive influence on BIU.

Trust: refers "to the intention to be voluntarily vulnerable to the actions of other users" [19].

H12: trust has positive impact on BIU.

Reliability: It refers to "the feeling possessed by individuals regarding the ability of the telecentre to perform all the missions assigned to it, without fail" [20].

H13: reliability influence positively BIU.

2.3   Control Variables

H14: control variables (**age, gender, experience, income, Education**) have positive impact to moderate core constructs (performance expectancy, effort expectancy, social influence, management effectiveness, program effectiveness, facilitating conditions) on BIU.

H15: control variables (**age, gender, experience, income, Education**) have positive impact to moderate core constructs (performance expectancy, effort expectancy, social influence, management effectiveness, program effectiveness, facilitating conditions) on Cameroon Factors (awareness, culture, power supply, government regulatory, accessibility, trust, Reliability).

Behavioral Intention to Use Telecentre: it refers to the level of the intention to manifest a specific attitude regarding the intention to use telecentre services [21].

H16: Behavioral Intention to Use Telecentre has a positive effect on Telecentre User Acceptance.

Telecentre User Acceptance: It focuses on the acceptance of the individual use of the Telecentre by users.

H17: Telecentre User Acceptance positively impact on telecentre value creation.

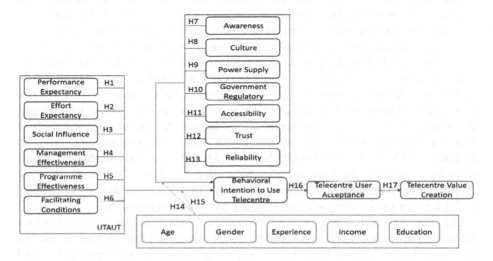

Fig. 2. Research *Model*

3 Methodology

This paper intend to use a mixed research method for testing and analyzing the proposed research [22]. It's a method based on both quantitative and qualitative approach in the same research study to provide a response to the observed deficiencies in both methods [22]. The quantitative methodology is used in this work to assess opinions, behaviors, and to induce from a much larger sample [22]. Furthermore, research on technology acceptance and Digital Divide are commonly conducted using survey questionnaires [23]. We will therefore make use of measurable data in order to be able to address the observed experience and to exhibit research trends. To obtain respondents for our study, we are planning to investigate with local actors in rural municipalities who are directly involved in the use of Multipurpose Community Telecentres (farmers, fishermen, craftspeople, youths/students, teachers, local businessmen), as well as sports associations and various cooperatives. Ideally, World Bank estimates show a target population between 15 and 70 years old in rural sub-Saharan Africa, which corresponds to the demographic sample in our study [24]. With this methodological approach, we hope to receive at least 475 respondents to be able to conduct important analyses and make projections. Thus, we have already started discussions with various stakeholders concerned by the study and so far, the feedback is rather positive as for the impact of the study at the local level (municipality), up to the national level. Several local associations have agreed to send the survey to their members, who will be able to participate either with a version of the online questionnaire or by completing the physical questionnaire which will be sent to them. The development mechanisms of the instrument is organized according to [25]. The parameters are collected on the basis of the scale existing in the emerging literature in order to consider valid allegories of each constructs so as to harmonize them with the research environment on the adoption of technologies and the digital divide [26]. Several constructs from our study are evaluated individually in order to reflect the impression of an individual using Likert scale graduated from 1 to 7. The constructs resulting from the intention to use [21], UTAUT [10], are adopted from [27], which contextualized the variables significantly in the acceptance of technologies in an environment marked by the permanent unavailability of technological infrastructures. Thereafter, constructs associated with accessibility [28], Trust [29], and reliability [30] are borrowed from [31]. They have effectively been used in the literature to investigate various barriers (emotional, structural) that can justify the non-adoption of technologies in sub-Saharan Africa [32]. This methodology implies the use of statistical tools in order to derive the results. we will use Partial Least Squares Structural Equation modelling (PLS-SEM) with SmartPLS 3.2.8 [33]. This analysis methodology will allow us to evaluate the Path models which imply the latent constructs, observed abruptly by several hierarchical constructs [34]. It will facilitate ideation of a structured model through the iterative assignment of the manifest variables [35].

After the quantitative analysis, will then proceed with a qualitative analysis which is also adapted to our study context regarding the exploration that we wish to conduct on real life in rural areas with the use of technology in order to better appreciate social phenomena [36]. It concentrates on dealing with the "how" and the "why" of social observations carried out, drawing its foundations from the experiences of individuals from rural communities as agents giving an explanation to their daily lives [36]. Also, it is a scientific research method used to gather non-numerical data and focuses on human demeanour from an agent's point of view [36]. This method is adopted in our study to explore in depth the adoption of Technologies in rural areas in a context where there is a lack of technological infrastructure, a constant absence of the internet, and also a gender difference in the use of technology due to the culture of the communities [37]. It will allow us to formulate a theory to better understand the preferences, culture, motivations and even the lifestyle of a group of target individuals regarding its mainly inductive stages. We will start with focus groups of 10 people per sector of activity (farmers, fishermen, craftspeople, youths, teachers, local businessmen) as suggested by [38] in order to obtain open responses from participants, responses which thus reflect feelings, thoughts, and experiences. The objective is to obtain more open information, regarding the unpredictable results that we can obtain at the level of quantitative analysis. This Focus group will allow the different participants to express themselves in a clear and open manner and to share opinions that could not be detected in terms of quantitative analysis [38]. Depending on the interactive nature of the focus group, the debates will therefore be more fluid, participants will be inspired by the remarks and comments of others to stimulate their own [38].

4 Results

A needs analysis study was conducted by AMBERO-Zebralog, a German consultancy firm on digitalisation needs in the North and South West regions. The purpose of this qualitative study was to be able to highlight the real needs in terms of digitalization of digital services based on the realities observed in the municipalities. A workshop was held in each municipality to which the concerned mayors or their representatives as well as a selection of municipal employees had been invited. Furthermore, several focus groups were held per municipalities with local stakeholder groups identified beforehand. The focus groups addressed local actors from different social groups, namely farmers and merchants, students and teachers, employment seekers, moto-taxi drivers as well as groups of women and young people. The focus groups were conducted to (1) discover the strengths and weaknesses of the current provision of services in the municipality from the point of view of the citizens (phase 1). (2) make the participants aware of the opportunities offered by digitalisation and the potentials of digital services for the municipality by presenting start-of-the-art digital tools to ease communication between citizens and the state (phase 2). (3) Collect ideas for new digital services and discuss conditions for their successful implementation (phase 3). (4) find out the most suitable tools and places to access these services for the users (phase 4).

Following the results, the overall use of Internet in the intervention municipalities is not very widespread. This varies slightly, for example digital literacy seems higher in urban or suburban areas (compared to rural areas) as well as in the South West (compared to the North region). Close to 50% of all participants (n = 155) of the focus groups claim that they never use the internet. Only little more than 20% state that they are regular users of the internet (Fig. 3).

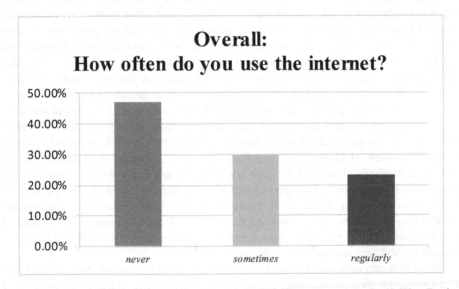

Fig. 3. Responses of participants in focus groups in both the North and the South West Region when asked about their internet use/n = 155 - September 2018

The lack of internet and adequate telecommunication infrastructure could therefore be a main obstacle for the successful implementation of new digital services. It was already in the discussion in the workshops, as the debates were sometimes extremely far away from the everyday lives of the participants. It was rather difficult to talk about potential digital services in a context where most participants lack access to the internet or digital tools. How many users will be able to value the discussed innovations, also compared to others in the same socio-professional category? The accessibility of the future services will determine its acceptability.

As the numbers collected in the workshops also show, mobile use is more common via SMS than via smartphone-powered messenger services such as WhatsApp. The preferred means of access to future digital services is by far the telecentre, followed by mobile means (mobile phone/smartphone). Telecentres are seen as an important asset for the digitalization of certain services, because they are a place that could serve both to access information on the internet but also where people can be trained can learn how to make use of digital services and, as a result, improve their digital literacy.

Hence, it might be wise to make use of tools and technologies people already use, such as mobile money services. For example, participants frequently suggest the replacing of the stamp-based payment system used in municipalities with e-payment-systems (such as mobile money). Highlights preferred means of access for future digital services for the North and South West regions.

This issue is also reflected in statements of the participants. Their most and major concern is the lack of connectivity, especially in the rural areas. Many participants state that creating access is key before developing municipal services. We concur with this assessment and suggest to first solve the problem of connectivity (e.g. through local community networks, well-equipped and functioning telecentres or a sufficient number of access points offered by private sector providers).

Interestingly, what is being prioritized in terms of "digitizable" services heavily depend on whom you ask. For example, municipal staff often thinks first of internal processes (such as archiving or electronic personnel files) and the provision of more strongly regulated services such as the provision of civil status documents. On the other hand, most citizens rather think of services that might help them in their everyday life. Among others, this concerns the delivery of information by the municipality (such as municipal website), but also affects policy areas such as health and sanitation, education, infrastructure, public safety or e-payments for a variety of municipal services.

Also, several citizens expect important benefits from the digitalization or, more precisely, the de-personalization of services. Some participants, especially young people or groups of farmers and merchants perceive a lack of transparency in the current proceedings. They feel they are not being treated fairly when it comes to the distribution of grants or social support programs. By shifting the process of application, decision-making and publication of results from a municipal agent to a transparent, electronic system, these participants see the chances of cheating, fraud, and favoritism heavily reduced. As a result, this may boost the confidence of citizens in the problem-solving capabilities and fairness of the state.

What is more, different speeds in digitalization in rural areas on the one hand and urban/suburban areas on the other account for the divergence in perceived benefits of digital services. In rural areas (such as in Bibémi or Mayo-Oulo), long trips to the town hall or other institutions can be reduced or even completely avoided by digital payment and handling systems (for permits, certificates, applications etc.). This benefit is estimated to be less pertinent in urban areas.

For citizens, it is often not self-evident which level of state is responsible for which service, especially in a decentralizing multi-level governance system such as the Cameroonian. Consequently, participants often made suggestions for changes in services that are rather in the sovereignty of the national level.

5 Implications, Limitation and Future Research Direction

This research will allow organizations and governments engaged in the process of breaking the digital divide to be equipped with concepts in order to carry out their work [39]. It will also enable future research to focus on the environmental and social and economic factors that contribute to the acceptance of telecentres in rural areas. Furthermore, several organizations will be able to understand the different approaches to increase the rate of use of technologies in disadvantaged villages and communities by offering them a catalog of services adapted to their needs. In terms of theoretical implications, the study will serve as a theoretical basis for carrying out quantitative analyzes related to the acceptance of technologies in rural areas, according to cultural indicators. The qualitative analyzes carried out will allow the next quantitative studies to adopt a better analytical approach.

However, this work has several limitations. Firstly, given the experimental nature of our study and the strong correlation between variables of the research model, expanding the sample size remains useful in order to obtain relevant results and thus ensure external validity. In the future, we plan to further expand the research model considering several technological, environmental, and psychological backgrounds. We will also study the existing disparities between men and women which are linked to current culture and practices regarding the use of ICT in households and disadvantaged communities in sub-Saharan Africa [40].

6 Conclusion

This research aims to be an addition to the emerging and existing literature by conducting empirical investigations on the key determinants of adoption and use of Multipurpose Community Telecentres to create value and contribute to economic, social and cultural development in rural areas in sub-Saharan Africa. We conducted a qualitative study (digital service needs analysis) in rural areas of North and South West Cameroon in order to be able to collect digital service needs of underprivileged communities. Also, we present a theoretical representation which is an extension of the UTAUT model, to which we have associated cultural factors. The development and deployment of digital tools and the increase of digital culture in rural areas are therefore a strong response to the various problems of rural exodus observed in villages [40]. With the arrival of digital solutions at telecentre, marginalized and disadvantaged communities will be able to take the train of digital culture, thereby developing their digital potential, important for socio-economic development and fulfilment. The Telecentres will therefore be a center for developing skills, creating value and culture for rural areas.

References

1. Dwivedi Yogesh, K., Sahu Ganesh, P., Rana Nripendra, P., Singh, M., Chandwani Rajesh, K.: Common Services Centres (CSCs) as an approach to bridge the digital divide: reflecting on challenges and obstacles. Transform. Gov. People Process Policy **10**(4), 511–525 (2016). https://doi.org/10.1108/TG-01-2016-0006
2. Mutula, S.: IT diffusion in Sub-Saharan Africa: implications for developing and managing digital libraries. New Libr. World **105**(7/8), 281–289 (2004). https://doi.org/10.1108/03074800410551039
3. Essien, E.D.: Ethical implications of the digital divide and social exclusion: imperative for cyber-security culture in Africa. Int. J. Innov. Digit. Econ. (IJIDE) **9**(1), 14–25 (2018)
4. Watat, J.K., Madina, M.: Towards an integrated theoretical model for assessing mobile banking acceptance among consumers in low income African economies. In: Themistocleous, M., Papadaki, M. (eds.) EMCIS 2019. LNBIP, vol. 381, pp. 165–178. Springer, Cham (2020). https://doi.org/10.1007/978-3-030-44322-1_13
5. Fuchs, C., Horak, E.: Africa and the digital divide. Telematics Inform. **25**(2), 99–116 (2008)
6. Oyedemi, T.D.: Digital inequalities and implications for social inequalities: a study of Internet penetration amongst university students in South Africa. Telematics Inform. **29**(3), 302–313 (2012)
7. Bahia, K., Suardi, S.: Connected society: the state of mobile internet connectivity. In: GSMA (ed.) p. 60. GSMA, London (2019)
8. UNDP: Beyond income, beyond averages, beyond today: inequalities in human development in the 21st century. In: United Nations Development Programme (ed.) Human Development Report 2019, pp. 1–366. UNDP (2019)
9. Bahia, K., Suardi, S.: Connected Society: The State of Mobile Internet Connectivity. GSMA, London (2019)
10. Venkatesh, V., Morris, M.G., Davis, G.B., Davis, F.D.: User acceptance of information technology: toward a unified view. MIS Q. **27**(3), 425–478 (2003)
11. Kim, S., Lee, K.-H., Hwang, H., Yoo, S.: Analysis of the factors influencing healthcare professionals' adoption of mobile electronic medical record (EMR) using the unified theory of acceptance and use of technology (UTAUT) in a tertiary hospital. BMC Med. Inform. Decis. Mak. **16** (2015). https://doi.org/10.1186/s12911-016-0249-8
12. Balduck, A.-L., Buelens, M.: A two-level competing values framework to measuring nonprofit organizational effectiveness. Vlerick Leuven Gent, Vlerick Leuven Gent Working Paper Series 2008/19, pp. 1–29 (2008)
13. Sowa, J.E., Selden, S.C., Sandfort, J.R.: No longer unmeasurable? A multidimensional integrated model of nonprofit organizational effectiveness. Nonprofit Volunt. Sect. Q. **33**(4), 711–728 (2004). https://doi.org/10.1177/0899764004269146
14. Vakunta, P.: On translating Camfranglais and other Camerounisms. Meta journal des traducteurs/Meta Transl. J. **53**(4), 942–947 (2008). https://doi.org/10.7202/019665ar
15. Vakunta, P.W.: The status of pidgin English in the Cameroonian Tower of Babel: an overview of the linguistic landscape of Cameroon which calls for the recognition of Cameroonian pidgin English as an official language. Engl. Today **34**(1), 20–25 (2018)

16. Ngefac, A.: The social stratification of English in Cameroon. World Engl. **27**(3–4), 407–418 (2008). https://doi.org/10.1111/j.1467-971X.2008.00575.x
17. Nfah, E., Ngundam, J., Vandenbergh, M., Schmid, J.J.R.E.: Simulation of off-grid generation options for remote villages in Cameroon. Renew. Energy **33**(5), 1064–1072 (2008)
18. Lwoga Edda, T., Chigona, W.: Perception, usage and barriers towards the utilisation of the Telecentre among rural women in Tanzania. J. Inf. Commun. Ethics Soc. **17**(1), 2–16 (2019). https://doi.org/10.1108/JICES-01-2018-0004
19. Mayer, R.C., Davis, J.H., Schoorman, F.D.: An integrative model of organizational trust. Acad. Manag. Rev. **20**(3), 709–734 (1995). https://doi.org/10.2307/258792
20. Rao, R.N., Iyer, L.: Education as a determinant of e-Governance adoption: a case study of telecenters of Karnataka. Imp. J. Interdiscip. Res. (IJIR) **2**(13), 32–38 (2016)
21. Ajzen, I.: The theory of planned behavior. Organ. Behav. Hum. Decis. Process. **50**(2), 179–211 (1991). https://doi.org/10.1016/0749-5978(91)90020-T
22. Schoonenboom, J., Johnson, R.B., Froehlich, D.E.: Combining multiple purposes of mixing within a mixed methods research design. Int. J. Mult. Res. Approaches **10**(1), 271–282 (2018)
23. Mackert, M., Mabry-Flynn, A., Champlin, S., Donovan, E.E., Pounders, K.: Health literacy and health information technology adoption: the potential for a new digital divide. J. Med. Internet Res. **18**(10), e264 (2016)
24. Sievert, M., Steinbuks, J.: Willingness to pay for electricity access in extreme poverty: evidence from sub-Saharan Africa. World Dev. **128**, 104859 (2020)
25. Moore, G.C., Benbasat, I.: Development of an instrument to measure the perceptions of adopting an information technology innovation. Inf. Syst. Res. **2**(3), 192–222 (1991)
26. Forman, C.: The corporate digital divide: determinants of Internet adoption. Manage. Sci. **51**(4), 641–654 (2005)
27. Abdulwahab, L., Dahalin, Z.M.: A conceptual model of Unified Theory of Acceptance and Use of Technology (UTAUT) modification with management effectiveness and program effectiveness in context of telecentre. Afr. Sci. **11**(4), 267–275 (2010)
28. Goncalves, G., Oliveira, T., Cruz-Jesus, F.: Understanding individual-level digital divide: evidence of an African country. Comput. Hum. Behav. **87**, 276–291 (2018). https://doi.org/10.1016/j.chb.2018.05.039
29. Datta, A., Bhatia, V., Noll, J., Dixit, S.: Bridging the digital divide: challenges in opening the digital world to the elderly, poor, and digitally illiterate. IEEE Consum. Electron. Mag. **8**(1), 78–81 (2018)
30. Shiferaw, K.B., Mehari, E.A.: Modeling predictors of acceptance and use of electronic medical record system in a resource limited setting: using modified UTAUT model. Inform. Med. Unlocked **17**, 100182 (2019)
31. Chiemeke, S., Evwiekpaefe, A.: A conceptual framework of a modified unified theory of acceptance and use of technology (UTAUT) model with Nigerian factors in E-commerce adoption. Educ. Res. **2**(12), 1719–1726 (2011)
32. Brown, I., Licker, P.: Exploring differences in Internet adoption and usage between historically advantaged and disadvantaged groups in South Africa. J. Glob. Inf. Technol. Manag. **6**(4), 6–26 (2003)
33. Hair Jr., J.F., Hult, G.T.M., Ringle, C., Sarstedt, M.: A Primer on Partial Least Squares Structural Equation Modeling (PLS-SEM). Sage Publications, Thousand Oaks (2016)
34. Chin, W.: The partial least squares approach to structural equation modeling. Mod. Methods Bus. Res. **295**(2), 295–336 (1998)
35. Hair, J.F., Sarstedt, M., Ringle, C.M., Gudergan, S.P.: Advanced Issues in Partial Least Squares Structural Equation Modeling. SAGE Publications, Thousand Oaks (2017)

36. Gill, P., Baillie, J.: Interviews and focus groups in qualitative research: an update for the digital age. Br. Dent. J. **225**(7), 668–672 (2018)
37. Patel, N.M., Kadyamatimba, A., Madzvamuse, S.: E-learning adoption in rural-based higher education institutions in South Africa. In: IEEE 2018 Open Innovations Conference (OI), pp. 320–324. IEEE (2018)
38. Guest, G., Namey, E., McKenna, K.: How many focus groups are enough? Building an evidence base for nonprobability sample sizes. Field Methods **29**(1), 3–22 (2017)
39. Kuika Watat, J., Jonathan, G.M.: Breaking the digital divide in rural Africa. Paper Presented at the 26th Americas Conference on Information Systems (AMCIS 2020), Virtual Conference, 15–17 August 2020 (2020)
40. Nasah, A., DaCosta, B., Kinsell, C., Seok, S.: The digital literacy debate: an investigation of digital propensity and information and communication technology. Education Tech. Research Dev. **58**(5), 531–555 (2010). https://doi.org/10.1007/s11423-010-9151-8

Digital Identity Evaluation Framework for Social Welfare

Umar Bashir Mir[(⊠)] [iD], Arpan Kumar Kar[(⊠)],
and Manmohan Prasad Gupta[(⊠)]

Information Systems Area, Indian Institute of Technology Delhi,
New Delhi, India
mirumar.iitd@gmail.com, arpan_kar@yahoo.co.in,
mpgupta@iitd.ac.in

Abstract. Identification systems are vital in improving efficiency and enabling innovation for public and private-sector services, such as greater efficiency in the delivery of social safety nets and facilitating the development of digital economies. With all these benefits along with the rapid improvement in the technology has led many countries to adopt a new foundational digital identity system (DIS) or retrofit the existing paper-based identity system especially in the developing economies. Apart from all these benefits, DISs has also been criticized for issues related to the security, privacy, surveillance and exclusion of people from various services they are entitled to. Considering the significant impact of DIS on the people, it is necessary to have an evaluation framework that could help understand the suitability of a DIS in a particular context. In this study, we propose a conceptual evaluation framework specifically for DISs based on the processes followed, regulations and technologies employed.

Keywords: Digital identity · Aadhaar · E-Governance · Technology assessment

1 Introduction

Digital identity (DI) is the digital counterpart to a real identity. Identity in general is comprised of various data points mingled with unique characteristics of an individual. Trustworthy digital identification is the cornerstone for a secure and sustainable digital economy. The primary purpose of identification system is to authenticate and authorize a person seeking access to a particular service. In digital space, designated bodies that provide any service – Service Providers (SP), utilise digital identification system to prevent fraudulent service access. From the public sector perspective, it is believed that digital identity system has a positive impact on the adoption of e-Government services. DISs enables people to prove they are who they say they are –authentication, which is must while opting for services provided by public or private institutions. The digitisation wave across the globe has made DI a necessity and has opened a new horizon for the development and empowerment of people. In pursuit of solving one set of problems using technological solutions often gives birth to another set of challenges. For

© IFIP International Federation for Information Processing 2020
Published by Springer Nature Switzerland AG 2020
S. K. Sharma et al. (Eds.): TDIT 2020, IFIP AICT 617, pp. 401–414, 2020.
https://doi.org/10.1007/978-3-030-64849-7_36

example IoT based systems are believed to have compromised the privacy of an individual [1] which is the basic right of a person [2].

It is important to understand that it is very difficult if not impossible for an individual to control their DI themselves considering the time and expertise it requires. There is a need of robust and consistent DIS that possesses high utility and scalability value for both public and governments. There is a lack of trust between government and people and that has resulted in various grievances and complaints about DISs. In US, Social Security Number (SSN) has been a de facto DI however there has been growing concerns about its effectiveness to deal with identity related frauds. Stakeholders have realised there is a need of better identity systems; that has better privacy and security measures; is convenient; and is trusted by users and service providers [3]. In UK national ID was seen as threat to user privacy and had to be scrapped because of the protests from public [4]. India's digital identity –Aadhaar, is world largest DIS in terms of the number of enrolments. Apart from all the benefits it has facilitated in terms of financial inclusion, public distribution system (PDS), employment and distribution of government subsidies, Aadhaar has been criticised for its effectiveness in preventing leakages in various government schemes [5]. Ideal DIS does not exist, almost all the existing DISs have been criticized for one reason or the other. We can broadly categorise these concerns into following categories: consent, surveillance, data localisation, data security, data control etc. [6]. Developing and implementing an identity system is a costly affair and requires lot of resources [7]. To avoid losses at later stages, it is advisable to evaluate identity systems for its effectiveness from a context specific view beforehand. The motivation of this study is the growing criticism of identity systems [8, 9].

All these issues have affected trust aspect of DISs which in turn is affecting the adoption of DISs. There is a need to have a mechanism to evaluate DIS beforehand that could be utilised by the people as well as governments to evaluate best suitable DIS for a particular context [7]. This study is positioned in this direction. In this study we propose an evaluation framework specifically meant for evaluating DISs. To the best of our knowledge we did not find any study that has developed a framework specifically for evaluating DISs based on processes, regulations and technologies employed. DISs have distinct characteristics and purpose as compared to generic IS or e-Government projects in terms of cost, time, utility and implementation, and hence requires a context specific evaluation approach [8]. There is a need to mitigate risks in DISs [10].

This study is grounded on the Technology Landscape for Digital Identification work of World Bank Group which analyses the relevance and effectiveness of various technologies in solving potential problems associated with user identification and authentication phenomena [11]. Needless to mention that technology is not the only factor that determines the effectiveness and adoption of massive e-government schemes like DIS [12]. In an attempt to minimise the possible damage beforehand this study attempts to develop a framework that will enable concerned authorities to evaluate a DIS. Precisely, the study focuses on the following aspects:

- Firstly, a comprehensive framework for evaluating DISs is proposed
- Next, the proposed framework is used for comparative analysis of four DISs

The remaining sections are organized as follows: Literature specific to DISs and assessment frameworks is described in Sect. 2. Section 3 describes the methodology adopted followed by findings in Sect. 4. In Sect. 5, discussion surrounding implications of this paper is presented and finally limitation and future research directions are explained in Sect. 6.

2 Literature

Electronic governance in general has garnered lot of traction in the last decade. E-Governance is an umbrella domain that includes different other research areas. Assessment of e-governance projects has been conducted either before implementation or after implementation of the project. E-governance schemes affect diverse dimensions of the society via highly complex mechanisms. Broadly, impact ranges from socio-political, socio-economic, environmental and socio-technical aspects of the society. The identification and analysis of these effects is critical when evaluating large highly complex e-government projects especially when public is involved. Evaluation is defined as the assessment of projects worth by focusing on its design, implementation and impact [13]. Subsequently, the evaluation of DIS should take into consideration: the technology employed; utility; resources required; citizen rights; and safety measures [2]. In the context of this study we have reviewed literature specific to the assessment of information technology and e-government projects.

Literature indicates that IT and e-governance act as important components for the development and change in society. The assessment of such schemes has been confined to basic instruments that could be manipulated easily [14]. Primarily researchers have focused on evaluation process and it is not always clear that what aspects of the scheme should be evaluated. Some of the assessment studies have focused on the pre and post implementation assessment of project [15]. Just knowing the changes brought by a project is not sufficient. What is more impactful is to understand what components of the project are responsible for which part of the change [16]. A comprehensive evaluation plan is required to understand the linkage between the project components and the outcome.

In [17], authors have studied the significance of interoperability in the adoption of e-government IS and identified risk management, collaboration and coordination and technical expertise as major factors that impact interoperability aspect of IS like e-government websites. Another limitation is that most of e-government systems primarily focus on the government side objectives and neglecting public aspiration by generalising highly context sensitive systems [18]. This marks another reason why a context specific assessment mechanism is required to evaluate a DIS that has significant impact on socio-political, socio-economic and cultural dimensions of the nation.

In [19] authors have evaluated digital identity systems mainly from the privacy perspective. Further, the impact of privacy on the adoption is studied with the help of a comparative analysis of four national digital identity systems. There are multiple reasons why large projects fail e.g. gaps in design and reality, unclear focus, quality of content, necessary skills, execution, regulatory issues, technical issues, lack of feedback and proper communication procedures [20]. A framework presented by World Bank in its recently published report on the technology landscape of DIS highlights the highs and lows of possible technologies that could be employed in a DIS [11]. The proposed assessment framework assesses each identification technology like biometrics, cards, protocols etc. based on six major parameters which in turn has multiple sub-parameters under each parameter. While it enables practitioners and stakeholders to evaluate available technological alternatives for identification, it does not asses non-technical parameters of identification that are equally vital for a successful DIS. In another study [10], a framework for evaluating digital identity is proposed that evaluates DIS based on its usage. The main focus of the framework is confined to the utility side of an identity system only which is just one of the many aspects of DIS. There is need of a comprehensive mechanism that would cover all the primary building blocks of DIS like technological, managerial, usage, legal and socio-political for evaluation. This article is an attempt to fill this gap. In this article, we propose a framework explicitly for evaluating DIS by taking diverse set of factors into consideration. This framework could be useful in getting first-hand experience of how strong a DIS is and will enable concerned authorities like policymakers, law makers and technology providers to align their DIS execution and implementation accordingly.

3 Methodology

We did an extensive literature review of various secondary data sources that includes research publications related to DIS and impact assessment of IS and e-Government projects from Scopus database. Scopus is one of the largest abstracts and citation repository which is being used extensively by the research community across domains. Relevant articles were selected based on the abstract and conclusion of papers which resulted in 89 articles. In some of the cases we read introduction and discussion section also to be able to clearly identify the relevance of the paper in the context of this study. Further, the corpus was narrowed down to 36 articles based on the quality of conference and publishing journal and by removing redundant articles. Apart from research articles, we also considered white papers published by World Economic Forum (WEF), United Nations (UN), National Institutes of Standards and Technology, World Bank, and official reports issued by various governments including India, Estonia, US and UK to build support and identify list of evaluation parameters for this study.

3.1 DIS Evaluation Framework

Understanding the lifecycle of a DIS enables designers, implementers, and policy developers grasp the processes followed and technologies involved in provisioning the credentials that enable identification and authorization of an individual. For example from technological perspective – iris based systems are still in its early stage where as fingerprint recognition is fairly mature and have seen wide adoption already. Based on the technologies implemented and processes followed in a DIS, we have proposed a framework as shown in Table 1 below. Each major parameter is evaluated based on specific factors. The evaluation parameters are presented below:

Table 1. Comparative Analysis using DIS Evaluation Framework

DI parameters	Reference	Factors	Scale	Aadhaar	Estonia	SSN	UK
Biometrics	[8, 21]	Physiological	Desirable	✓	✓		✓
		Behavioural	Desirable				
Governance structure	[22]	Public	Desirable	✓		✓	✓
		Private	Least Desirable				
		PPP	Desirable		✓		
Purpose	[23, 24]	Foundational	Desirable	✓	✓		✓
		Functional	Less Desirable			✓	
Instrument type	[7, 22]	Card/paper	Least Desirable			✓	✓
		Number	Desirable	✓			
		Chip	Desirable		✓		
Identity provider	[25, 26]	Government	Desirable	✓	✓	✓	✓
		Third-party	Less Desirable				
Scalability	[27, 28]	One time	Less Desirable			✓	✓
		Future-proofing	Desirable	✓	✓		
Type of identity system	[29]	Platform	Desirable	✓	✓		✓
		Software Product	Least Desirable			✓	
ID architecture	[7]	Centralized	Less Desirable	✓		✓	✓
		Decentralize	Desirable		✓		
Verification mechanism	[30]	Technology-assisted	Desirable	✓	✓	✓	✓
		Human dependence	Least Desirable				
Enrolment	[27, 31]	Fully Automatic	Desirable				
		Semi-Automatic	Less Desirable	✓	✓		✓
		Manual	Least Desirable			✓	
Data localisation	[45, 46]	Access control	Desirable		✓		✓
		Consent	Desirable		✓		✓
Relying parties	[29]	Both public and private	Desirable	✓	✓	✓	✓
		Either public or private	Less Desirable				
Adoption	[3]	Voluntarily	Desirable	✓			✓
		Mandatory	Less Desirable		✓	✓	

(*continued*)

Table 1. (*continued*)

DI parameters	Reference	Factors	Scale	Aadhaar	Estonia	SSN	UK
Eligibility	[27, 32]	For all	Desirable	✓			
		Age limit	Less Desirable		✓	✓	✓
		Category limit	Least Desirable				
Interoperability	[7, 28]	At national level	Desirable		✓		
		At state/region level	Less Desirable	✓		✓	✓
Accountability	[19, 33]	User side	Desirable		✓		
		Management side	Desirable		✓	✓	
Redressal mechanism	[26]	Online	Desirable	✓	✓	✓	✓
		Offline	Less Desirable				
Reusability of ID	[24]		Desirable				
Utility in online and offline space	[26, 27]	–	Desirable	✓	✓	✓	✓
General Data Protection Regulation (GDPR) adherence	[29]	–	Desirable		✓		✓

Biometrics. Biometric recognition uses an individual's unique physiological and behavioural attributes to identify and authenticate his or her identity. Physiological features include elements related to the shape or composition of the body, such as iris patterns, finger-prints ridges, and facial characteristics. Examples of behavioural attributes include gait, signature, keystroke patterns, and mouse usage.

Governance Structure. Governance structure depicts the powerhouse of DIS. Majority of the national identity systems are governed by the government of that particular country. However, there is a possibility that government can outsource some functionalities of the DIS management to third-party. In general, DIS could be governed by either government or by a government-approved private entity or by PPP model.

Purpose. Most of the countries have some type of DIS that is tightly coupled with some specific services and are serving an only particular section of the society. Such systems are widely known as functional systems. According to World Bank report, 18% of the developing nations have identity system that is used only for identification, 55% have identity system that is tailored for a particular accessing service like voting, subsidies, banking etc. and only 3% have an identity system that can be utilized to access a variety of online as well as offline services –Foundational systems [34].

Instrument Type. It could be a certificate, object, or a data structure that guarantees the identity of an individual via an authentication and authorization process. Digitization has revolutionized the means of verifying the legitimacy of an individual. It has significantly impacted the way proof of identity is realized. Traditional systems were based on paper-based identity instruments which were replaced by ID cards and chips. Recent technological innovations like cloud computing and blockchain have further transformed hardware-based ID instruments into software-based, e.g. numbers. Each type of ID instrument has its benefits and challenges and hence makes it an important factor in a novel DIS.

Identity Provider. Identity provider (IdP) is the heart of a DIS. It is an entity that is responsible for managing and issuing identity to an individual. IdP could be the government itself or a single specific department that works under the guidelines of government or fully independent third-party entity with its own set of rules. IdP is responsible for collecting user data like biometrics, and demographic details and links it to a unique ID which is issued to the user.

Relying Parties. Relying party (RP), also known as the service provider, is an entity that provides some services to users based on their credentials. It relies on another entity for user identification before providing access to a particular service. The information exchange between RP and IdP depends on the type of Identity management model adopted. The relation between RP and IdP could be one-to-one (traditional), one-to-many (centralized), or many-to-many (federated).

Scalability. Scalability is important from the view point of technology and backend processing. It is well known that Algorithms do not always scale gracefully. Since DIS is supposed to generate identities for large population (using biometrics for ensuring uniqueness). It is important to know if algorithms used for this process will scale up or not. Therefore, scalability, of technology and processes used to process the data and generate these unique IDs is a critical parameter in DIS.

Type of Identity System. DIS could be implemented either as a software application system or as a platform. Massive software application systems are complex and tedious to manage but require little network connectivity whereas platform is heavily dependent on network connectivity among large number of commodity devices. It is comparatively easy to secure software application system which requires less information sharing as compared to platform in which information is shared among nodes extensively.

ID Architecture. A technical framework that covers the processes of creating, managing and application of DIs is referred to as Identity and Access Management (IAM). IAM can be broadly classified into two categories: centralized and decentralized. Centralized systems were most common in the initial days of IAM wherein IAM was developed, owned, and controlled by a single organization. Centralized systems store all user credentials in a single large database which is queried during authentication and authorization processes. Decentralized systems, on the other hand, have user data scattered on multiple devices that are in sync and is usually used by multiple institutions.

Verification Mechanism. Verification of user credentials is the first step in accessing services. It has three levels; in the lowest level, the only photograph is checked whereas in highest level biometric data is also included and in some cases additional information like One-Time Password (OTP) or answer to the security question is also provided during verification process. The process of verification could happen in two ways. One where some level of human intervention is necessary to complete the verification process, second where human intervention is both minimal and not mandatory to complete the verification process.

Data Localization. In recent times, the physical location of the database in which user data is stored has become one of the hot debatable topics because of the growing concerns towards surveillance and information war among countries. On one side, cloud storage has reduced the burden of having developing infrastructure from scratch, and on the other side, it has been questioned for data leakage and data control. Governing bodies prefer full possession and control on its citizen data, and demand data is stored within the physical boundaries of the countries.

Enrolment. Users provided their credentials to enrolment agency that is responsible for recording data in the most accurate form so as to avoid any incomplete or duplicate entry in the system. Depending on the type of data recorded defines the necessary requirements from technological perspective. For example capturing biometric data requires sophisticated devices with high precision whereas recording demographic details could be done manually. Reliability of enrolment system has a significant impact on the overall efficiency of the DIS.

Adoption. Adoption is the stage where a particular technology is selected for use by an individual or an organization. The rate of adoption depends on whether DI has been made mandatory by the authorities, or it is voluntarily adopted by an individual. From the control-flow perspective, mandatory systems follow the top-to-bottom approach, whereas bottom-up is followed in voluntary systems. Adoption rate could be higher in mandatory systems, but that does not guarantee high usage. It is the public value of DIS that will drive its usage, and each individual values DIS differently based on their attitude and needs.

Eligibility. Developing an identity system is a highly complex political process. All the functional identity systems developed until now are based on some criteria. There could be multiple reasons for restricting identity to a particular section only. The most commonly found example is of voter ID that is issued only after attaining a particular age, e.g. in India, voter ID is issued if a person is above 18 years. Most of the existing Identity systems signify the eligibility and entitlements a particular user is entitled to with the help of user identity.

Interoperability. Extending utility of DI beyond today's confined range of services to a wider range of services that spans domains and sectors is highly dependent on the interoperability support. User access different types of services from private and public entities which means they may have to deal with a different set of incompatible systems that require user identity in different forms. Standardized DI that could be used across geographies and sectors will reduce the burden of keeping and managing service-specific identities.

Accountability. Success of DIS is dependent on the level of trust people have in it and accountability is one of the significant factor in building trust. Further, accountability has impact on other dimensions of DIS also like transparency, adoption, satisfaction and privacy of DIS. Personal details of an individual is extremely important and must be guarded from all forms of violations so as to ensure security and privacy. Entities that process user data should be held accountable for any misuse of data and should be penalised depending on the severity level of misuse [35].

Redressal Mechanism. Grievance Redressal is a common mechanism in the service sector. User can report grievances that can originate from various processes like information sharing, access and service consumption, the accuracy of user data, availability etc. It enables an individual to register a complaint or seek an update on the already submitted complaint. Effective Grievance Redressal mechanism enables agencies to be more transparent and responsive to their users. Complaints could be made either using online web-portal or by directly submitting it to the department.

Reusability of ID. Reusability in identity systems is relatively a new concept. Although most of the existing DIS did not focus on the reusability aspect of DIS, initially, this attitude is changing fast, considering its significant impact on the speed and cost of onboarding new users. According to a survey, some institutions spend around $500 million per year to onboard new users and $60 million in financial institutions alone.

Utility in Online and Offline Space. Internet penetration has increased exponentially in the last decade or so, which has resulted in the tremendous growth of online service delivery. Identity is a must for conducting any transaction, and it becomes even more important in case of online transactions –faceless transactions. One of the major drawbacks in traditional identities is that they lack support for interoperability and that hampers its utility in online space.

GDPR Adherence. Data breaches happen, and data gets compromised. To protect citizens' data from being violated European Union has passed a law in 2016 –GDPR. Its adherence is mandatory for companies that deal with EU citizen data. Although it does not apply to all the countries, all the companies that process EU citizen data need to follow it. It is the most versatile data protection law taking into account user consent, data anonymization, data breach update, and safe data flow across borders. Adherence to GDPR or similar regulations must be mandatory for DIS so that protection of user data is ensured.

3.2 Evaluation Scale

Proposed DI Evaluation Framework uses a three-point scale of "desirable", "less desirable" and "least desirable" to rate the significance of each factor. "Desirable" depicts that a particular factor is crucial, and its presence in DIS should be given utmost priority. "Less desirable" factors were common in traditional identity systems and were the reason behind some of the lacunas in those identity systems. Inclusion of such factors should be considered when no better alternative is available. Moreover, such factors are highly context-sensitive, and decisions regarding its inclusion should be made accordingly. "Least desirable" factors bring more hardship than benefits. Inclusion of such factors should be avoided in the best possible way.

4   Findings

The study uses national digital identity schemes of four countries as a case study for evaluation. Many countries have evaluated or implemented national identity programs in the past. Some implemented successfully, whereas few had to withdraw because of strong protests from the public. It is worthwhile to note that digital identity systems have raised strong concerns regarding privacy, security, governance mechanism and inclusion or exclusion of people from various schemes. National identity systems evaluated in this study are briefly explained below.

4.1   India – Aadhaar

Aadhaar is considered as the world largest digital identity system based on the number of enrolments which is more than 1 billion. It is a random 12 digit unique number assigned to each resident of India. It is coupled with the biometric and demographic details of an individual. It is linked across sectors including banking, healthcare, education and telecom. It is governed by the government of India and is utilized in both public and private sector for user authentication. Apart from its all promising benefits, it has been criticized for various reasons which are mainly related to the technological issues, privacy issues and monitoring issues.

4.2   Estonia

Estonia is considered to have the most advanced e-governance platform in the world. Estonian digital identity could be owned via three means: Chip-based ID card, Mobile-ID SIM card, and application-based Smart-ID. People use the ID card to avail services like healthcare, banking, travelling and shopping on a routine basis. There are approximately 600 and 2,400 e-services being offered to the citizens and businesses respectively. In 2017 around 750,000 national ID's got compromised because of a technical glitch that enabled to infer private key from users public key.

4.3   Social Security Number

Social Security Number is a 9-digit number issued by Social Security Administration to permanent and working residents of U.S. SSN is not a conventional digital identity as its primary purpose was to keep a check on taxes. Over the time it has been used for identification of an individual in the private and public sector and has become a de facto national identity of U.S. As per a report, the US has lost around $16.8 billion to identity fraud cases in 2017 and saw a 44.7% increase in data breaches. Further, reports suggest that the use of SSN as an identifier should be stopped in both the private and public sector, and a new age digital identity system should be developed [3].

4.4   UK

UK's national ID cards linked an individual's personal identification documents, and travel documents with National Identity Register. In 2011, national identity, along with its associated register, was scrapped because of public protest against it [4]. There were many reasons for the failure of national ID, which includes scalability, lack of support for interoperability, and lack of communication between public institutions and industry regarding technical aspects of the scheme [23].

We tested our proposed DI evaluation framework based on the comparative analysis of four national identity systems. The results of the study are shown in Table 1 above.

5 Discussion

With multiple technologies available, an evaluation framework can help designers, implementers, and policy developers to compare available technological alternatives, gaining a sense of how systems work, what are the strong and weak aspects in the system and how they might be useful for a particular use-case. Such mechanisms could help mitigate potential risks that could impact DIS negatively [10] and facilitate the development of better identity system [3]. Identity systems of various countries including China, UK, US, and India, have been questioned for various issues which also includes violations in security and privacy of user data. Having an identity system is not enough rather having the right identity system for a particular context is what is desirable, but there are basic minimum criteria that every identity system must meet. Apart from supporting interoperability, it will also facilitate in building trust in the system. The study is in line with the growing concerns related to identity systems and helps to understand it in a better way from process and technology relational perspective [8, 23].

Comparative analysis of four identity systems depicts the relative strengths and weakness of each identity system. ID systems that possess better data localization and interoperability support are found to be more desirable. It could be justified because of the growing concerns regarding data security and privacy issues [34] that has made people serious about their personal data. Initially, national-level interoperability was desired as the majority of the population was mostly confined within the geographical boundaries of a country. As international travelling has become more convenient and cheaper, people travelling across borders in pursuit of better growth opportunities have also increased considerably. This could be another reason why ID systems with support for international interoperability are desirable considering its potential to make international travel convenient. Type of ID system is another important factor that impacts the adoption of an ID system. Most of the traditional ID systems were centralized and software-based systems that used to suffer from issues like bugs, software crash and natural calamities which could be avoided to a great extent in platform-based systems. Platform-based ID systems are easy to maintain and scale and is another crucial factor that should be taken into consideration while evaluating an ID system. ID systems are mostly driven by public entities and may lack domain-specific technical expertise. Incorporating specialized private entities for such tasks could improve the effectiveness and efficiency of design, development and implementation of the ID system. From the comparative analysis, we can see high scored Estonia's ID system, which is considered as the world's most advanced systems is based on PPP model. Instrument type is another crucial factor and is dependent on the target population. Number based ID is preferred over chip-based ID systems for larger populations. Aadhaar is a number based ID that is presently the largest ID system in the world with more than 1 billion enrolments [8]. Also, number-based ID systems reduce the overall cost of an ID system. Voluntary adoption faces little resistance from the people, and by increasing the utility value of ID could have a positive impact on the adoption and acceptance. Aadhaar is the best example that increased adoption rate by making it voluntary and increasing utility value of the ID system. However, voluntary systems may not always achieve desired goals considering the reluctance, and digital divide among masses towards technological changes and hence require contextual considerations. Accountability upon intentional or unintentional misuse of user data should be clearly defined along with the penalty. This will enable conflict resolution in case of any data violations. Regarding international regulations about data security, GDPR is the most advanced one and has been made mandatory by the UK government for processing its citizen data within and outside the country for smooth transactions.

The study contributes to two aspects: 1) it enables concerned authorities to focus on the critical aspects of an ID system in advance that will further help in utilizing effective processes and technologies for robust and successful ID system; 2) the framework could be used in the preliminary analysis by the policymakers and evaluators for comparing the various ID systems. It could also be utilized in the feasibility phase of the ID development for an initial set of recommendations.

6 Conclusion

In this article, we identified 21 important parameters from the secondary data sources that primarily included research articles, official reports, and white papers. The findings from the comparative analysis of four DIS highlight the significance of each parameter in accordance with the best available identity system of Estonia. Parameters like governance structure, ID architecture type, data localization, interoperability, accountability, blockchain support and adherence to GDPR play a pivotal role in evaluating any DIS. In case of developing a new DIS, DIS evaluation framework could be helpful in identifying avoidable losses by dropping obsolete technologies, and inefficient processes beforehand from the proposed system. For existing DIS, it can play a vital role in deciding the success or failure reasons of the system that could act as a feedback for policymakers and DIS developers in the future. The primary limitation of this study is the type of data source –secondary in this case, from which parameters are identified. Directions for future research are to enrich the proposed DIS evaluation framework by incorporating primary data source for analysis and test the proposed framework on more DISs for better insights.

References

1. Ziegeldorf, J.H., Morchon, O.G., Wehrle, K.: Privacy in the Internet of Things: threats and challenges. Secur. Commun. Netw. **7**(12), 2728–2742 (2014)
2. United Nations: Universal Declaration of Human Rights, United Nations (1948). https://www.un.org/en/universal-declaration-human-rights/
3. The Better Identity Coalition: Better Identity in America: A Blueprint for Policymakers, pp. 1–48 (2018). https://static1.squarespace.com/static/5a7b7a8490bade8a77c07789/t/5b4fe83b1ae6cfa99e58a05d/1531963453495/Better_Identity_Coalition+Blueprint+-+July+2018.pdf
4. Travis, A.: ID cards scheme to be scrapped within 100 days. The Guardian Weekly (2010)
5. Khera, R.: The Aadhaar debate. Contrib. Indian Sociol. **52**(3), 336–342 (2018)
6. Dixon, P.: A failure to Do No Harm – India's Aadhaar biometric ID program and its inability to protect privacy in relation to measures in Europe and the U.S. Health Technol. (Bcrl) **7**(4), 539–567 (2017)
7. Mir, U.B., Kar, A.K., Dwivedi, Y.K., Gupta, M.P., Sharma, R.S.: Realizing digital identity in government: prioritizing design and implementation objectives for Aadhaar in India. Gov. Inf. Q. **37**(2), 101442 (2020)
8. Mir, U.B., Kar, A.K., Gupta, M.P., Sharma, R.S.: Prioritizing digital identity goals – the case study of Aadhaar in India. In: Digital Transformation for a Sustainable Society in the 21st Century, pp. 489–501 (2019)
9. Pinto, J.K., Mantel, S.J.: The causes of project failure. IEEE Trans. Eng. Manage. **37**(4), 269–276 (1990)
10. Bhandari, V., Trikanad, S., Sinha, A.: Governing ID: a framework for evaluation of digital identity (2020)
11. World Bank: Technology Landscape for Digital Identification (2018)
12. Mir, U.B., Sharma, S., Kar, A.K., Gupta, M.P.: Critical success factors for integrating artificial intelligence and robotics. Digit. Policy, Reg. Gov., March 2020. https://doi.org/10.1108/DPRG-03-2020-0032
13. World Bank Group: ICT for greater development impact-information and communication technology (2012)
14. Howitt, R.: Theoretical foundations. In: Vanclay, F., Esteves, A.M. (eds.) New Directions in Social Impact Assessment. EdwardElgar, pp. 3–19 (2011)
15. Heeks, R., Alemayehu, M.: Impact assessment of ICT-for-development projects: a compendium of approaches. Development Informatics Working Paper, (36) (2009)
16. Pade-Khene, C., Sewry, D.: Proposed stages of a rural ICT comprehensive evaluation framework in ICT for rural development projects. In: Proceedings of the South African Institute of Computer Scientists and Information Technologists Conference on Knowledge, Innovation and Leadership in a Diverse, Multidisciplinary Environment - SAICSIT 2011, p. 326 (2011)
17. Van Thanh, N., Yoon, H., Hwang, J.: A study on the factors affect to technological adoption of e-government information system interoperability in Vietnam. Int. Technol. Manage. Rev. **7**(2), 125 (2018)
18. Zahran, I., Al-Nuaim, H., Rutter, M., Benyon, D.: A critical analysis of e-government evaluation models at national and local municipal levels. Electron. J. e-Gov. **13**(1), 28–48 (2015)
19. Khatchatourov, A., Laurent, M., Levallois-Barth, C.: Privacy in digital identity systems: models, assessment, and user adoption. In: Electronic Government, pp. 273–290 (2015)

20. Anthopoulos, L., Reddick, C.G., Giannakidou, I., Mavridis, N.: Why e-government projects fail? An analysis of the Healthcare.gov website. Gov. Inf. Q. **33**(1), 161–173 (2016)
21. Thorat, S., Bhilare, V.: Comparative study of Indian UID Aadhar and other biometric identification techniques in different countries. Int. J. Curr. Trends Eng. Res. **2**(6), 62–72 (2016)
22. Al-Khouri, A.M.: Digital identity: transforming GCC economies. Innov. Manag. Policy Pract. **16**(2), 184–194 (2014)
23. McAfee: Modernizing the social security number (2018)
24. A frictionless future for identity management; a practical solution for Australia's digital identity challenge, no. December 2016
25. Laurent, M., Bouzefrane, S.: Digital identity management (2015)
26. Jacobsen, E.K.U.: Unique Identification: inclusion and surveillance in the Indian biometric assemblage (2012)
27. UIDAI: UIDAI strategy overview creating a unique identity number for every Resident in India, pp. 1–45 (2010)
28. Zelazny, F.: The Evolution of India's UID program lessons learned and implications for other developing countries CGD Policy Paper 008, no. August 2012
29. Segovia, A.I., Álvaro, D., Enríquez, M.: Digital identity: the current state of affairs digital identity: the current state of affairs (2018)
30. Okumura, A., Komeiji, S., Sakaguchi, M., Tabuchi, M., Hattori, H.: Identity verification using face recognition for artificial-intelligence electronic forms with speech interaction. In: HCI for Cybersecurity, Privacy and Trust, pp. 52–66 (2019)
31. Venkatanarayanan, A.: Aadhaar enrolment costs. Medium Corporation (2018). https://medium.com/karana/aadhaar-enrolment-costs-bc17f0d30018. Accessed 04 July 2019
32. WorldBank: Global ID coverage by the numbers: insights from the ID4D-Findex survey, vol. 15, no. Id, pp. 15–18 (2017)
33. Graham, S., Wood, D.: Digitizing surveillance: categorization, space, inequality. Crit. Soc. Policy **23**(2), 227–248 (2003)
34. BankWorld: World Development Report 2016: Digital Dividends. The World Bank (2016)
35. Knight, A., Saxby, S.: Identity crisis: global challenges of identity protection in a networked world. Comput. Law Secur. Rev. **30**(6), 617–632 (2014)

Exploring Net Benefits in the Context of an E-Government Project

Ambuj Anand(✉) [ID]

Indian Institute of Management Ranchi, Ranchi 834008, Jharkhand, India
`ambuj@iimranchi.ac.in`

Abstract. A typical e-Government project will undergo an impact assessment several times in its lifecycle. An important aspect of impact assessment is to measure benefits from the project, especially to the end-users. Often, when these benefits are measured, projects have positive scores, but when it comes to voluntary adoption of e-Government project on a large scale, the rate of adoption is slow. Not all the people who use it for the first time are willing to continue with the digital alternative. In this paper, we argue that one source of such contradictory findings is a unitary view of an important construct – benefits. In the extant literature, the construct – benefits - has been widely regarded as a single-dimensional construct. We propose that a multi-dimensional approach to measuring benefits will facilitate the respective government department to reach out to all the target audience with significant relative advantage. In order to identify the dimensions of benefits, we use the theory of Maslow's hierarchy of needs. Accordingly, we propose five dimensions of benefits which would cater to different kinds of individuals among the target users.

Keywords: Benefits · Conceptual analysis · E-Government · Adoption

1 Introduction

In the domain of e-Government, impact assessment has been an important area of concern for academicians and practitioners alike (Madon 2004; Bhatnagar and Singh 2010; De 2006; Lin et al. 2011). Heeks (2008) advocates a five-step approach to assess an e-Government project - identify the stakeholders, identify each stakeholder's goals for the eGovernment project, measure the achievement of each goal, identify other impacts and finally classify the project outcome. The accuracy of each of the subsequent step is dependent on the preciseness of the previous step. The first step is relatively simple. In a typical e-Government project, leadership (political and bureaucracy), government employees, citizens, technology partners, vendors, businesses, and NGOs are some of the key stakeholders. The next step is challenging. For instance, not all citizens will have the same expectations from an e-Government project. Different members of the project leadership would also have different goals from the project. Each member of this group may value one or more stated objective of the project. The challenge is to identify the goals for each group such that the goals of most

© IFIP International Federation for Information Processing 2020
Published by Springer Nature Switzerland AG 2020
S. K. Sharma et al. (Eds.): TDIT 2020, IFIP AICT 617, pp. 415–421, 2020.
https://doi.org/10.1007/978-3-030-64849-7_37

of the members are reflected in the final list. In this paper, we attempt to create one such list of goals for one of the most important stakeholders - the citizens.

Most of the theories related to adoption/diffusion of information systems deal with expected benefits as a unified construct. In the Delone and McLean success model, the construct - net benefits follow the use of the system. Similar to the expected benefits in adoption literature, Delone's model also treats net benefits as a unified single construct. In this paper, we attempt to extend these theories by identifying dimensions related to expected benefits. We believe that the dimensions of net benefits will also be the same as that of expected benefits.

Citizens would seek a variety of benefits from a typical e-Government project. Savings in terms of time, cost, the effort could be a few most commonly desired benefits. However, not all the citizens would be satisfied with mere savings along these three dimensions. It is no surprise that when a group of citizens would be asked to evaluate benefits from an e-Government project on a scale of 1 to 5, some of them would choose each of these categories on the Likert scale. In this paper, we attempt to explain this variance with the help of Maslow's hierarchy of needs (Maslow 1943). We argue that citizens seek benefits from an e-Government project along each of the dimension of Maslow's hierarchy viz. physiological, safety, love/belonging, esteem and self-actualization.

This is a theoretical paper based on conceptual analysis as defined by Järvinen (1997). Future work will involve testing the hypothesis developed in this paper. The paper is structured as follows. We discuss the key theories on the adoption of information systems. These theories also form the basis of e-Government adoption literature. Based on this discussion, we highlight the gap in the extant literature. This forms the basis of our next section - the research question. It is followed by a brief discussion of the research method. It is followed by conceptual analysis and conclusion.

2   Literature Review

In the domain of Information Systems, a popular research theme has been centred around the question of acceptance and adoption of digital systems and their continued use. In this context, several theories have been popular among researchers. Some of these theories have also borrowed from each other. In the following section, we briefly discuss five such theories.

According to the theory of reasoned action (TRA), individual behaviour in terms of use of an information system is determined by the behavioural intentions towards such a system. The behavioural intention is a function of an individual's attitude toward the behaviour and the prevalent subjective norms related to the same (Fishbein and Ajzen 1975). Among other factors that would influence the attitude towards the behaviour, expected benefits perceived by individuals would have a significant impact. However, this theory does not explicitly talk about expected benefits to the users. Theory of planned behaviour (TPB) is an extension of TRA. TPB adds a new construct - Perceived Behavioural Control - to the list of independent variables (Ajzen 1991). In the context of the information system, perceived behavioural control captures the individual's perception of the ease with which the new system can be used. To some extent, this would also capture the expected benefits from the new system. Similar to TRA, this theory also does not explicitly talks about expected benefits from the new information systems or from performing a particular behaviour. Technology acceptance model (TAM) is an adaptation of TRA to the field of Information Systems. In this model, the two independent variables are replaced by perceived usefulness and perceived ease of use (Davis 1989). Both these variables reflect some aspects of benefits to the end-users. This theory deals with all different kinds of benefits at an aggregate level. Variability of perception of expected benefits by the end-users has not been explored in this theory. We highlight this as one of the key gaps in the extant literature.

The next evolution in this domain was proposed by Venkatesh et al. (2003). This was an attempt to consolidate eight existing theories viz., the theory of reasoned action, technology acceptance model, motivational model, the theory of planned behaviour, a combined theory of planned behaviour/technology acceptance model, the model of PC utilization, innovation diffusion theory, and social cognitive theory. The consolidated model was termed as the unified theory of acceptance and use of technology (UTAUT). In this theory, the dependent variable remains same as TAM, but there is now a revised list of independent variables - performance expectancy, effort expectancy, social influence, and facilitating conditions - and four new moderating variables. In UTAUT, expected benefits are captured by performance expectancy and effort expectancy. In this paper, we argue that these two variables miss out on several possible dimensions of benefits from an e-Government project.

Delone and McLean (1992) proposed information systems success model first in 1992 and later updated it in 2002–03. Updated Information Systems Success Model (DeLone and McLean 2002; DeLone and McLean 2003) has three independent variables - information quality, system quality and service quality - also termed as the quality triad. The theory highlights that benefits are accrued from the use of information systems. Use follows the intention to use, which in turn is impacted by the quality triad. An end-user may expect certain benefits from each of these dimensions of the quality triad of Delone and McLean. For instance, better usability, extra availability, added reliability, more adaptability and superior response time are some of the potential expected benefits from an information system with greater system quality. Similarly, personalized content, complete information at one place, more crisp and relevant information, easy to understand data, and information security are some of the expected benefits from an information system with high information quality. Likewise, service quality would proxy the expected benefits related to the role of intermediaries, especially those dealing with the technical aspects of the solution. In this paper, we further explore these possible dimensions of the construct - net benefits - in the context of an e-Government project.

Most of the research that follows the above set of theories (like Prybutok et al. (2008); Bertot et al. (2008)) considers net benefits as a single unified construct. Consequently, they fail to explain the variance in citizens' perception of an e-Government project. Some scholars have used alternative approaches to capture and classify benefits from e-Government projects. These approaches are equally divergent. In the following section, we attempt to demonstrate some such variations in capturing benefits from e-Government project.

Guo (2010) identifies four aspects of benefits from e-Government projects viz., 'democratization', 'environmental bonuses', 'speed, efficiency, and convenience' and public approval. Gilbert et al. (2004) have captured 'avoid personal interaction', 'control', 'convenience', 'cost', 'personalization' and 'time' as the major benefits from the e-Government projects. If we compare the above two approaches, only one-dimension overlaps, i.e. speed, efficiency, and convenience.

3 Research Question

As discussed in the previous section, the dominant part of e-Government literature considers benefits as a single construct. Few researchers who have taken a more micro perspective at the benefits have introduced more dimension to the construct of benefits, but such efforts are far from standardization and lack theoretical grounding. Accordingly, we formulate the following research question.

Identify the key dimensions of benefits in the context of e-Government projects in India.

4 Research Method

The key research method used in this paper is conceptual analysis as defined by Jarvinen (1997). According to this conceptual-analytical approach, earlier works in the form of constructs, models, theories are analyzed considering newer realities. Generalizations of earlier empirical studies are theorized in light of new assumptions of a certain part of reality. Similar work has been done by Ives et al. (1980) to derive a comprehensive MIS research model from a review of extant literature. In this paper, we identify possible dimensions of benefits from the extant literature and further classify them based on the theory of Maslow's hierarchy of needs.

5 Conceptual Analysis

In this paper, we argue that the use of Maslow's hierarchy of needs would facilitate understanding the variance in citizens' perceived benefits from an e-Government project. It would also help in unifying various approaches that were adopted to capture and classify net benefits.

According to Maslow's Hierarchy of Needs, individuals have five different levels of needs - physiological, safety, love/belonging, esteem, and self-actualization (Maslow 1943). We argue that the benefits from an e-Government project should correspond to each of these levels. Every individual has a varying degree of these five needs. Accordingly, he/she would seek different kinds of benefits from an e-Government project. We use extant literature to classify the benefits into each of these five levels.

Physiological needs in the context of e-Government could mean convenience and cost. Convenience is a perceived attribute (Chan et al. 2010). An end-user could perceive convenience in the use of an e-Government project because of ease of use

(Berry et al. 2002) as well as ease of access (Meuter et al. 2000). Several scholars have highlighted that convenience plays an important role in helping citizens choose the digital channel over the traditional ones (Torkzadeh and Dhillon 2002; Everett and Peirce 1993). Convenience would also mean some savings in the time required to avail the service. Cost savings through the use of e-Government would also be part of physiological benefits from such projects. Such savings would not only include the direct cost of application and intermediary fees but would also include a reduction in the time cost of availing the service.

Ashaye and Irani (2014) have identified improvement in the quality of service delivery as one of the key e-Government implementation benefits. Improvement of quality of service delivery may include service guarantee and service traceability. These benefits can be mapped as safety needs. Safety needs related benefits would also include safety of transactions, privacy controls and scope of grievance redressal with respect to the above concerns.

The third level in Maslow's hierarchy of needs is love/belonging. Such need of an individual can be satisfied by facilitating connectedness. In this context, connectedness would mean allowing end-users to interact amongst themselves beyond the e-Government transactions. Benefits under this category should also involve facilitating provision for avoiding personal interactions (Chan et al. 2010) especially with government employees (applicable for interactions which are often less pleasant).

Esteem, the fourth level of the hierarchy of needs include the desire for achievement, for adequacy, for confidence, for independence, and for prestige. Citizens who are early adopters of e-Government systems may achieve a sense of achievement, confidence and prestige (Rogers 2010). Some such users also become motivators and guides for the late adopters. Thus, the use of e-Government may improve the image of the end-user in the social network. E-Government features like personalization and 24 × 7 access will give users a sense of control and hence will help them fulfil their need for esteem.

Finally, the last level of needs - self-actualization - could be fulfilled by doing what one is capable of doing. One such aspiration is to contribute to the overall development of the society (at times the nation). The perception of contributing to the reduction in overall corruption in the society, to increase the transparency and fairness in the system, and to develop overall trust among the stakeholders may help in achieving the self-actualization needs of citizens.

Thus, we argue that benefits from an e-Government system can be classified along the five dimensions emerging from Maslow's Hierarchy of Needs. Since every individual can seek different degrees of each of these five types of needs, e-Government systems should be designed such that real benefits to the citizens are realized along all these five dimensions. Such a system design would also reduce the variability in citizens' perceived net benefits.

Thus, five propositions may be developed from the above argument.

1. Physiological needs related benefit would impact the use of the e-Government application.
2. Safety needs related benefit would impact the use of the e-Government application.

3. Belonging needs related benefit would impact the use of the e-Government application.
4. Esteem needs related benefit would impact the use of the e-Government application.
5. Self-actualization needs related benefit would impact the use of the e-Government application.

6 Conclusion

Most of the e-Government projects in India are focused on providing benefits along the first two dimensions (Berry et al. 2002; Meuter et al. 2000). A few projects also provide benefits along the other three dimensions. However, benefits provided along the last three dimensions are more incidental than planned.

We argue that an e-Government project should be designed such that it provides significant benefits along all the five dimensions. The management mechanisms and the benefits listed under each of these dimensions are not exhaustive, but the dimensions themselves are exhaustive. Hence, executives and designers may focus on the five key dimensions while they plan for potential benefits to getting embedded in the new system. Two key contributions of this paper include first - identifying dimensions of net benefits in the context of the adoption of e-Government projects (DeLone and McLean 2003) and second – extending the theory of Maslow's hierarchy of needs (Maslow 1943) in the context of benefits derived from information systems project. The proposed framework is theoretical in nature. We intent to test the proposed model in our future work.

References

Ajzen, I.: The theory of planned behavior. Organ. Behav. Hum. Decis. Process. 50(2), 179–211 (1991)

Ashaye, O. R., Irani, Z.: E-government implementation benefits, risks, and barriers in developing countries: Evidence from Nigeria. US-China Educ. Rev. 4(1), 13 (2014)

Berry, L.L., Seiders, K., Grewal, D.: Understanding service convenience. J. Market. 66(3), 1–17 (2002)

Bertot, J.C., Jaeger, P.T., McClure, C.R.: Citizen-centered e-government services: benefits, costs, and research needs. In: Proceedings of the 2008 International Conference on Digital Government Research, pp. 137–142. Digital Government Society of North America, May 2008

Bhatnagar, S.C., Singh, N.: Assessing the impact of e-government: a study of projects in India. Inf. Technol. Int. Develop. 6(2), 109 (2010)

Chan, F.K., Thong, J.Y., Venkatesh, V., Brown, S.A., Hu, P.J., Tam, K.Y.: Modeling citizen satisfaction with mandatory adoption of an e-government technology. J. Assoc. Inf. Syst. 11(10), 519–549 (2010)

Davis, F.D.: Perceived usefulness, perceived ease of use, and user acceptance of information technology. MIS Q. 13(3), 319–339 (1989)

De', R.: Evaluation of e-government systems: project assessment vs development assessment. In: Wimmer, M.A., Scholl, H.J., Grönlund, Å., Andersen, K.V. (eds.) EGOV 2006. LNCS, vol. 4084, pp. 317–328. Springer, Heidelberg (2006). https://doi.org/10.1007/11823100_28

DeLone, W.H., McLean, E.R.: Information systems success: the quest for the dependent variable. Inf. Syst. Res. **3**(1), 60–95 (1992)

DeLone, W.H., McLean, E.R.: Information systems success revisited. In: Proceedings of the 35th Hawaii International Conference on System Sciences (HICSS 02), Big Island, Hawaii, pp. 238–249 (2002)

DeLone, W.H., McLean, E.R.: The DeLone and McLean model of information systems success: a ten-year update. J. Manage. Inf. Syst. **19**(4), 9–30 (2003)

Everett, J.W., Peirce, J.J.: Curbside recycling in the U.S.A.: convenience and mandatory participation. Waste Manage. Res. **11**(1), 49–61 (1993)

Fishbein, M., Ajzen, I.: Belief, Attitude, Intention, and Behavior: An Introduction to Theory and Research. Addison-Wesley Pub. Co, Don Mills (1975)

Gilbert, D., Balestrini, P., Littleboy, D.: Barriers and benefits in the adoption of e-government. Int. J. Public Sector Manage. **17**(4), 286–301 (2004)

Guo, Y.: E-government: definition, goals, benefits and risks. In: 2010 International Conference on Management and Service Science, pp. 1–4. IEEE, August 2010

Heeks, R.: Success and Failure in eGovernment Projects (2008). http://www.egov4dev.org/success/techniques/self_assessment.shtml

Ives, B., Hamilton, S., Davis, G.B.: A framework for research in computer-based management information systems. Manage. Sci. **26**(9), 910–934 (1980)

Järvinen, H.P.: The new classification of research approaches. In: Zemanek, H. (ed.) The IFIP Pink Summary-36 Years of IFIP. IFIP, Laxenburg (1997). http://www.ifip.org/36years/a51jarvi.html. Accessed 28 June 2019

Lin, F., Fofanah, S.S., Liang, D.: Assessing citizen adoption of e-government initiatives in Gambia: a validation of the technology acceptance model in information systems success. Gov. Inf. Q. **28**(2), 271–279 (2011)

Madon, S.: Evaluating the developmental impact of e-governance initiatives: an exploratory framework. Electron. J. Inf. Syst. Develop. Count. **20**(1), 1–13 (2004)

Maslow, A.H.: A theory of human motivation. Psychol. Rev. **50**, 370–396 (1943)

Meuter, M.L., Ostrom, A.L., Roundtree, R.I., Bitner, M.J.: Self-service technologies: understanding customer satisfaction with technology-based service encounters. J. Market. **64**(3), 50–64 (2000)

Prybutok, V.R., Zhang, X., Ryan, S.D.: Evaluating leadership, IT quality, and net benefits in an e-government environment. Inf. Manage. **45**(3), 143–152 (2008)

Rogers, E.M.: Diffusion of Innovations. Simon and Schuster (2010)

Torkzadeh, G., Dhillon, G.: Measuring factors that influence the success of Internet commerce. Inf. Syst. Res. **13**(2), 187–204 (2002)

Venkatesh, V., Morris, M., Davis, G., Davis, F.: User acceptance of information technology: toward a unified view. MIS Q. **27**(3), 425–478 (2003)

Emerging Technologies in Consumer Decision Making and Choice

Impact of Digital Transformation on Retail Banking Industry in the UAE

Umesh Kothari and A. Seetharaman[✉]

SP Jain School of Global Management, Dubai, United Arab Emirates
seetha.raman@spjain.org

Abstract. The UAE's banking industry has emerged as one of the most dynamic in the region, and the largest financial center in the Middle East. The industry has been confronted with 'digital disruption', 'digitization' 'digital banking'. The key reasons for digitization in addition to competitiveness include improved banking efficiency, attracting and retaining customers, improving analytics, launching innovative services and enhancing customer experience. However, organizations struggle with the implementation of digitalization initiatives and fall behind in achieving their plans. There is very limited literature written on the research to study impact of digital transformation on the retail banking industry in the UAE. Moreover, it is based on secondary research. This study aims to identify the variables that drive digital transformation and study the impact of digital transformation in Retail Banking Industry in the UAE. The results of the study show that customer needs, technology, regulation, business processes, skills and competencies impact digital transformation and should support retail banks in developing a theory of digital transformation in their journey to excel in a competitive marketplace.

Keywords: Digitization · Retail banking · Strategy · Transformation · Technology · Customer experience

1 Introduction

1.1 Digital Transformation

Digital Transformation or disturbance is not a disengaged event yet is something that has occurred since 1990s with various interruptions happening crosswise over various kinds of industry fragments (Shrivastava 2017). At first the music, photography and video were altogether upset by new participants and new players who were grasping computerized and digital innovation.

During the 2000s, another arrangement of enterprises began to be disturbed by digital revolution, such as Television, travel and enlistment (Isaksson 2018). A third surge of digital disruption has undergone especially with more changes in the retail industry post 2000s. The 2010s are undergoing a third wave of digital disruption. This can be attributed to the change in customer preferences to associate with brands (Valenduc and Vendramin 2017).

© IFIP International Federation for Information Processing 2020
Published by Springer Nature Switzerland AG 2020
S. K. Sharma et al. (Eds.): TDIT 2020, IFIP AICT 617, pp. 425–438, 2020.
https://doi.org/10.1007/978-3-030-64849-7_38

1.2   Digital Transformation – Retail Banking

Digitization is different from the customary strategies fundamentally because of new developments such as social media and use of internet (Andersson et al. 2016). This has led to changes in a wide range of businesses such as cars industry. Finance and healthcare are the next industries that are going to change as part of this ongoing disruption.

The retail banking system is facing challenges in its digital transformation journey. Inherited technology landscape, fostering agility, reducing time to market for new products and effectively using customer data to better engage customer and manage customer relationships make digitization in retail banking banks more of a necessity than a choice.

1.3   Digital Transformation – UAE

Over the years, the UAE has become known as the key financial hub for the Middle East and one of the world's leading financial centers. We have recently seen a renewed drive to move the country to a global innovation center with a number of exciting initiatives announced and embarked upon: Artificial Intelligence, Blockchain and FinTech.

2   Research Questions

The primary aim of this study is to understand the digital transformation and its impact in UAEs Retail Banking industry via the following questions.

a. What do customers expect from a digital bank?
b. What technology investments are needed by Banks to support digital transformation?
c. Does digital transformation respond to the business process and vice versa?
d. Does digital age reshape the organizational skills and competencies?
e. Do regulatory and compliance impact digital bank?

3   Research Objectives

As a solution to the above research questions the study is aimed to answer the following research objectives.

a. To explore customer needs and expectations from a digital bank
b. To understand the role of technology as an enabler in Bank's digital transformation journey
c. To diagnose the processes to be automated by digital banks

d. To recognize the skills and competencies required by a digital bank to help the bank achieve its growth plans
e. To study the regulatory and compliance requirements that could impact a digital bank

4 Scope of the Study

Over the years, the UAE has become known as the key financial hub for the Middle East and one of the world's leading financial centers. There has been a renewed drive to move the country to a global innovation center with a number of exciting initiatives announced and embarked upon: Artificial Intelligence, Blockchain and FinTech. In order to make in in-depth study, this qualitative research is confined to digital transformation in retail banking of UAE.

5 Literature Review

Digitization is modifying our daily lives in terms of how we interact with each other and handle personal data. Various organizations have essentially no other option but to adjust their customary styles and policies to digital auxiliary change (Deutsche Bank 2014). Specially financial companies face with the paradigm 'digitalize or die'.

The banking industry plays an important role in the county's economic development—around 8% of GDP, and 13% of non-oil sector domestic product.

The Central Bank of the UAE promotes financial stability, resilience in the financial system and protects consumers through effective supervision that supports economic growth. The banking sector is overbanked, with a total of 49 Banks (22 national and 27 foreign banks) operating in the UAE in 2019 (UAE Central Bank Report 2019) and a population of 9.7 million people (EIU, June 2019).

The literature review is structured according to the variables considered in this research. The dependent variable is impact of digital transformation on retail banking. The different independent variables are: (i) customer needs (ii) technology; (iii) business process; (iv) regulation; and (v) skills and competencies. The added value of this research paper lies in providing deeper understanding of the multiple aspects of digital transformation.

5.1 Customer Needs

One of the most critical areas that banks are trying to improve through digital banking is customer experience. The customer expectations are continuously being raised by the experience provided by hi-tech companies like Google, Apple, Amazon, and Facebook. Customers expect similar experiences from their financial services providers. As banking products get standardized, drivers of customer experience have changed, and consider 'service' as a key factor in selecting their financial services provider.

Banks in the UAE have begun to introduce different digital solutions in line with customer's needs to maximize customer experience.

* Emirates NBD offers new banking services through its digital channels to optimize operational efficiencies and enhance customer service.
* Mashreq provides mobile banking solutions through an application called Snapp to build on customer convenience and accessibility.
* Standard Chartered offers a mobile application that prompts users with real time and personalized offers from retailers operating nearby. This interactive solution ensures improved customer experience with the Bank.

Banks are looking at new opportunities pertaining to changes in consumer demand, the continuing technology revolution and evolving staff requirements. Banks should continue to invest in digital and electronic tools for customers and related internal processes to compete in the marketplace. New players in the payment industry has led to new competition for Banks. Footfall levels in retail branches are expected to fall thereby forcing banks to respond with a whole new model of retail banking (Austin 2014).

5.2   Technology

While technology plays a pivotal role in supporting banks to achieve their goals, banks are hampered by inflexible, legacy technology infrastructures that are making change very challenging.

The banking industry is confronting a period of disruptive change. FinTech's have been able to drive change through speed, agility and insight without the burden of legacy systems. These disruptive innovators have challenged the practices followed by Banks and have provided customers with innovative, easy-to-access and easy-to-use financial solutions that are more similar to those offered by Amazon and Apple than of a traditional banking experience. Banks are slow to respond to these changes as they face a dilemma between their well-established business models and to adapt to the rapidly evolving customer needs. The next-generation technology model that progressive banks are adopting is based on outsourcing and building relationships with strategic partners (DeLuca 2016).

Customer Engagement and Fulfillment is making an impact in the financial services value chain. The digital wave will not necessarily be a tsunami for all businesses. Some are capable of adapting to the new environment and thus able to resist. They can change their operating methods and refocus their strategy. The financial services business is customer-facing, competitive, distribution- sensitive and turnaround-time sensitive. (Shukla and Nerlekar 2019).

Banks need to be mindful of newer competition from fintech companies that have unbundled the value chain of banks by specializing in their different areas such as payments, money transfer. These new competitors are highly flexible and tend to have a low-cost structure (Giaretta and Chesini 2018). Lately, FinTech organizations and new businesses have participated in this change management process changing the banking business environment i.e. personal loans, web-based services, investment solutions in order to attract new clients along with unrivaled services and support to its existing customers.

5.3 Business Processes

It appears that Banking institutions are still operating through physical branches which is expected to be visited less by customers in the future. Some banks in Sri Lanka have started to curb expanding their branch operations. As a strategy Banks are increasingly encouraging and promoting the use of digital non-channels by its customers (Bandara 2016).

One of the main benefits of process automation is that it gives banks a competitive advantage to customize product and service offerings in line with customer needs and expectations. It also decreases costs, errors thereby increasing reliability and building on customer trust (Swacha-Lech 2017).

5.4 Regulation

Banks would subject to regulations, an area still not applicable to FinTech. However, a fully transformed bank through digital approaches could reasonably be expected when virtual cash gets true and will simplify the exchange. A strategy to blend customary banking practices with Fintech services could provide best results to the banking clients (Vasiljeva and Lukanova 2016).

The recent advanced digital models pose new threats pertaining to digital security, consumer protection, operational stability and cheating. These risks are not addressed by the existing methods in the regulatory domain. Hence there is a need to enhance the regulatory structure to include these new threats accommodating digital innovation making the banking industry more robust for the future. Digital dangers and threats may not only create economic damage but also impact the customer's confidence in accepting new technologies even if they enhance customer experience especially due to safety and security issues (González-Páramo 2017).

The banking sector expends greater amount on Information and Technology compared to other industries. The sector grapples with issues related to compliance that is estimated to cost the sector more than $100 billion annually. The continuing issues of managing and analyzing data faced by banks could lead to the use of sub optimal technology solutions with low utility to address business objectives. Regulatory Technology in the current banking environment has more potential to achieve potential gains made through digital transformation with relatively less investments in resources (Butler and O'Brien 2019).

5.5   Skills and Competencies

The digital age is reshaping the way in which organizations, recruit, select and develop skills for a new generation of employees. An important challenge for organizations is to find the right balance and incentives to develop digital skills for Generation Y members that despite the fact that are professionally well equipped they lack the ability to become real business problem solvers and to generate profit for companies (Mihalcea 2017).

Digitalization brings innovation, ease of working, new job opportunities and growth in the economy. It is not only important to have the digital tools available but also the knowledge and benefits to use them. The future of Indian Banking sector is transformative with the use of technology-based solutions to increase customer experience, cost optimization and manage organization risk (Deshpande 2018).

Digital transformation requires highly trained people with specialized expertise. The challenge is to find a structure for these partnerships that will create a compelling value proposition so that the staff are motivated not just to stay but also to do their best work (Kumar et al. 2019).

6   Research Methodology

Research Methodology helps to bridge an understanding gap in a structured and systematic manner (Saunders et al. 2016). Research Methodology is a science of studying the techniques based on which the researcher can decide what study is to be conducted. Besides it is a logical, productive and planned steps that help in a better understanding of a phenomena (Zikmund 2009).

Information for research was gathered from different sources of secondary data. Most data were collected from an online search of relevant indexed journals, industry reports and reference books. The research methodology details the existing core variables identified through an exhaustive literature survey. A simple direct relationship between five core variables - customer needs, technology, business process, skills and competencies and the impact on digital transformation is positioned in the research model.

7   Research Framework

From the literature review exercise carried out a proposed research framework is developed as shown below. The impact of the digital transformation is the dependent variable.

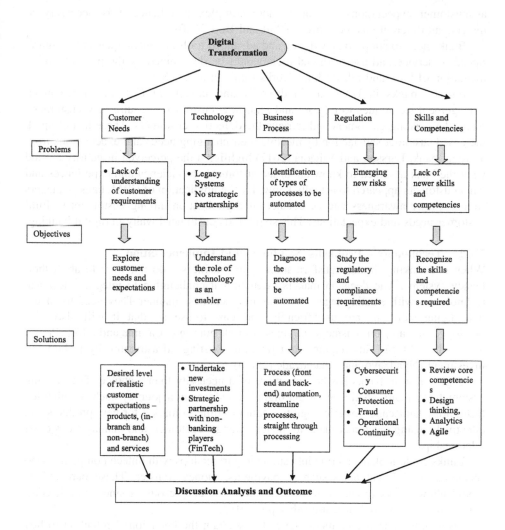

7.1 Discussion, Analysis and Outcome

7.1.1 Customer Needs – Problems, Solutions and Implementation

A study to understand the skills required by agile digital banks would benefit banks in the UAE. Moreover due to evolving customer needs and segments and increasing usage of digital tools in their day-to-day habits these customers expect the same from banks. Hence financial service institutions need to offer products and services to meet the requirements of the target segment.

Customer needs and their management are of great significance to customer service and satisfaction. There is a clear prerequisite to approach customer needs and expectations differently and proactively for professional services rendered by organizations as customer expectations are much more complex and hence it is necessary to understand different customer needs (Butt and Butt 2020).

Banks need to adopt to new digital and advanced tools and techniques in the future. Speed of service and use of digital tools would be determined by the pace of implementation of laws and related frameworks (Sajic et al. 2018).

Further, banks in UAE should discover and implement Customer relationship management techniques to explore and scan new customers, acquire new customers, retain the existing customers and retrieve the defective customers. These tactics spark increased customer satisfaction by meeting their changing needs and expectations from a digital bank. Larsson and Viitaoja (2017) highlights the perceived insecurity around what the bank assumed to know about its customer's proficiency and experiences and what customers appeared to actually know. By the application of CRM, bank managers should garner awareness and acceptance of digitalization among customers to fulfil customer needs and expectations. This step builds customer loyalty in digital banking.

7.1.2   Technology – Problems, Solutions, and Implementation

When undertaking digital transformation many businesses do not want to abort their legacy systems. The decision makers often find it challenging to integrate new age technologies with existing legacy systems in a seamless manner They need to ensure that digital solutions are user-friendly and easy-to-use so that it will also help employees to carry out business activities without putting extra time and effort (Prasad and Sridhar 2015). This requites strengthening existing infrastructure by technology investment (Nyadzayo and Khajehzadeh 2016).

Digitization in banks has become more of a necessity than a choice. The banking system faces many challenges in its digital transformation journey such as inherited technology landscape, fostering agility, reducing time to market for new products and effectively using customer data to better engage customer and manage customer relationships.

Banks could look at entering into strategic partnerships with fintech companies who specialize in different areas such as payments, money transfer. These partnerships would allow banks to capitalize on their expertise and resources since fintech companies have a low-cost structure (Shelepov 2017).

Technology acceptance model helps to ascertain the behavioural intention to buy motivated by usefulness of the digital technology and its ease of use. Basing on systems life cycle of the digital technology and time required for learning or experience curve, digitalisation is inducted with the assurance of pay back period or Net Present value of investment decisions. This ensures the role of technology as an enabler in achieving sustainable journey of digital transmission (Marangunic and Granic 2015).

7.1.3   Business Process – Problems, Solutions and Implementation

While making a digital transformation strategy organization need to focus on digitizing conventional business process efficiently and flawlessly. An organization must undertake digital transformation by automating various business activities. It needs to automate the business processes in several phases (Marques 2017).

It is necessary that the banking institutions spend on implementing solutions that are new and digitally advanced. These could be related to payments gateway, data analytics and mechanization of processing service requests. Banks must consider offering services through online channels and must have back-end activities to support the same (Vasiljeva and Lukanova 2016). Business process involves restructuring and regrouping bank resources namely men, machine, materials, methods and money.

Regrouping or restructuring of resources through cost and asset reduction to reverse declining sales and profit. Digitalization of public telecommunication services is primarily driven by technology developments within the Wide Area Networking market which could be used by speedier banking services. The few fundamental trends within this market are the advent of downsizing or right sizing (Chouhan 1994). Now, this dream of last decade of 20th century has become true in retail banking sector which is heading towards branchless banking by creation of automated digital banks.

7.1.4   Regulation – Problems, Solutions and Implementation

Security issue appears to be a key concern for customers when there is talk of taking personal and financial information online. Customers do not want to risk their privacy when using banking services which can hamper digital transformation (Belás et al. 2016).

Individuals voluntarily share a lot and different types of information on the social networking sites like Facebook, Twitter and rely on these sites as a primary communication medium of communication professionally and personally. In this process a large bunch of individual data is collected. Individuals voluntarily share personal information and a huge amount of identifiable material is gathered during the start of a business relationship. A key area of concern for social media operators is to safeguard and protect the data that is gathered from the customers and non-customers (Narayanaswamy and McGrath 2014).

Digital transformation must include a sophisticated security policy to protect the applications and data from various targeted security attacks. It must implement the latest data privacy regulations to collect and leverage customer data over a longer period. Organizations must address issues related to information security and data privacy (Bouyon and Ayoub 2018).

The adoption of Information Security Systems is looked at as a quite complex task within organizations and should adopt Cyber Security standards with clear guidelines on Information Systems Security (Gamundani et al. 2019). Legislature is expected to evolve on an on-going basis in the interest of the individuals and organizations that use automated devices in their operations.

The current state of the market for cyber safety is information security market is puerile. In this scenario comprehensive tools and technologies may not be available in the market place (Kiilu and Nzuki 2015). Banks must also take into account the stringent regulations on prudent capital requirements and payment services.

Control arises due to inherent imperfections of things and people. Voluntary and governmental regulations play a pivotal role by applying the principles underlying Information Security Control Theory. The study by Anderson et al. (2017) focuses that Information Security Control Theory offers a good framework for the information security policy development process balancing the protection of information resources with the need for sharing information in many domains including banking industry. This also fulfils regulatory and compliance requirements that could impact a digital bank.

7.1.5   Skills and Competencies – Problems, Solutions and Implementation

Banks need to adapt their existing service models to changing customer expectations and cost-awareness. It is believed that new ways of doing tasks through collaborative working would be required for companies that are undergoing a digital transformation program (Sanyal and Hisam 2018).

Banks need to develop digital skills in order to compete. While hiring is increasingly taking place by financial institutions from various external exhibitions and forums, less emphasis is given to interdisciplinary skills. This is important as functional knowledge is a minimal component of the overall skill requirement. Skills that support and transform automation to the organizational goals are critical. Moreover, people who are able to effectively use data and information to support business decisions would be demand by banks (McKinsey 2016).

The digital competencies of the workforce and the ways in which technology are used in the workplace will continue to develop and change. Organizations need to explore the technological competencies by staff alongwith optimum benefits of deploying digital tools in achieving desired outcomes (Colbert et al. 2016). With the customer in mind new developments in integrated design thinking are being considered to build on customer service (Ojasalo and Ojasalo 2018).

Digital literacy proclaims digital skills namely operational, technical and formal; information, cognition; digital communication; digital content creation; and strategic. These skills help the advancement of digitalization in several sectors (Iordache et al. 2017). This is more relevant for banking industry by recognizing the skills and competencies required by a digital bank to help the bank achieve its growth plans.

8   Research Implications

The study findings are based on qualitative research based on recent studies and validated secondary data. A meta-analysis of the study findings is provided and detailed for enhancing digital transformation within an organization. A new conceptual framework is provided and substantiated for digital transformation in retail banking in the UAE should help to apply a digital transformation theory as a holistic approach to move retail banks from traditional and simple digital efforts to managerial, cultural, procedural, technological and developmental changes of the overall bank.

Using a theory of change approach this study should derive a definition of digital transformation as an outcome variable and the necessary preconditions and activities to reach the outcome.

The research findings should help banks to determine the best answer to introduce digital transformation initiatives in UAE to satisfy customers and achieve growth objectives in the retail banking sector. This research would help to achieve a stability and consolidation digitalization in retail banking of UAE. Thus, this research contributes to banking practice.

8.1 Contribution of Theory (Theory of Transformation)

A comprehensive theory of digital transformation involves four interlinked elements namely a theory of social reproduction, a theory of the gaps and contradictions of reproduction, a theory of trajectories of unintended social change, and a theory of transformative strategies. The first of these elements provides an account of social culture of UAE by the evolving customer needs and expectations in responsiveness with social system of UAE. The second shows how in spite of environmental, emerging new risks and legacy technologies there are possibilities of digital transformation to bridge the gaps that exist in achieving business objectives of retail banking in an optimum manner in UAE. The third specifies the possibilities of developing new skills and competencies to build an agile organization in its transformation in UAE. And finally, the fourth component of transformation attempts to provide direction on formulating clear strategies, innovation, aligning business processes to smoothen digital transformation in retail banking in UAE. In this connection, Michael Porter's generic strategies namely cost leadership and differentiation can be applied. These four theoretical agendas are interrelated while digitally transforming the retail banking in UAE.

9 Limitations and Scope for Future Research

The literature studied is based on secondary data. Secondary data may be irrelevant as the data may have been collected at a time period which could be outdated. Hence the use of the information obtained may be restricted. Moreover, secondary data might be available but may not include all the required (Sreejesh et al. 2014). Secondary data has no control over its accuracy. Research conducted may be biased to support the vested interests of the source (Zikmund 2009).

There is a lot more to study and explore on this topic, especially on the different aspects that impact digital transformation among Retail Banks. In addition, further research could narrow the study down to retail banking in the UAE where customer data could be collected as secondary data is either not available or is highly confidential hence cannot be accessed. The future research can make use of primary data through surveys or interviews.

It appears that digital transformation needs to be further explored especially in the UAE and in the Retail Banking industry. The authors of the literature review exercise that have been studied digitalization in retail banking are in the developed world, emerging economies with limited studies pertaining to UAE.

The future research can make use of primary data through surveys or interviews. Limited research is carried out to correlate impact of the digital revolution within banking sectors and customer experience globally. Limitation to such empirical study is due to the slowness in the advancement of digital banking technology in this Asian region. Future survey could be carried out with a statistically robust sample (Venkathaialam and Abdulwahab 2017).

10   Conclusion

The varying dynamic demand of different customer segments that is attained to be met by banks appears to be a key challenge for financial institutions in their digitization plans. These needs range from obtaining an account balance on their mobiles to submitting a loan application to the bank through an on-line channel. Customers also prefer convenience related to payments or remittances made through the internet. In the midst of these needs of customers it is essential to consider those segments for whom a branch is preferred channel to interact with the bank and should be conveniently located. Customers believe that their needs would be addressed by financial institutions through digital tools like those adopted by companies in other industries.

In addition to the always developing customer requirements, Financial institutions are also facing stress from FinTech's to implement digital transformation approach alongwith technological advancements. It is therefore imperative that financial institutions to reexamine their business strategies and operating models. It is believed that these reviews would lead to adoption of advanced and emerging technologies.

In a data and information driven environment it is necessary for banks to focus on transparency to assure trust and reliability to its consumers. This may lead to an increase in competition among banks if consumers select products that meet their desired needs. Due to limitations of volume of data that the consumer would have to deal with through long applications and contracts resolving transparency concerns may not be simple for banks. Rhoen (2016) too, points out the importance of a logical application of consumer protection legislation that would addresses the requirements of regulatory bodies.

Agility is important for organization to ensure the right staff attitude, positive revenue and success in digital transformation. A phased approach could be adopted by financial institutions to align procedures and achieve the transformation agenda. The initial phase could be a hybrid one until digitization is achieved. Banks could execute modifications by introducing automation and advanced technologies and tools (Sajic et al. 2018).

Banks would need a set of processes that are aligned with digital interactions in order to compete successfully based on the expectations that have been set by all of the other digital brands. It is believed that the crucial activities could include customer on-boarding, request origination and value estimations. The digital transformation theory should support retail banks in the UAE to implement a comprehensive transformation program and thereby achieve their strategic goals to differentiate in the competitive Using a theory of change approach this study should derive a definition of digital transformation as an outcome variable and the necessary preconditions and activities to reach the outcome.

References

Anderson, C., Baskerville, R.L., Kaul, M.: Information security control theory: achieving a sustainable reconciliation between sharing and protecting the privacy of information. J. Manag. Inf. Syst. **34**(4), 1082–1112 (2017)

Andersson, L., Lanvin, B., Van der Heyden, L.: Digitalisation initiatives and corporate strategies: a few implications for talent. In: e Global Talent Competitiveness Index 2017, p. 51 (2016)

Kerényi, Á., Müller, J.: Brave new digital world? – Financial technology and the power of information. Financ. Econ. Rev. **18**(1), 5–32 (2019). https://doi.org/10.33893/fer.18.1.532

Mihalcea, A.D.: Employer branding and talent management in the digital age. Manag. Dyn. Knowl. Econ. **5**(2), 289–306 (2017). https://doi.org/10.25019/mdke/5.2.07

Shukla, A., Nerlekar, S.: Impact of digitization transformation on financial markets. MET Manag. Retrospect **3**(1) (2019)

Belás, J., Korauš, M., Kombo, F., Korauš, A.: Electronic banking security and customer satisfaction in commercial banks. J. Secur. Sustain. Issues (2016)

Deshpande, B.N.: Digitisation in banking sector. Int. J. Trend Sci. Res. Dev. (2018). Conference Issue

Bouyon, S., Ayoub, J.: Consumer Credit, Digitalisation and Behavioural Economics: Are new protection rules needed? (No. 13831). Centre for European Policy Studies (2018)

Butler, T., O'Brien, L.: Understanding RegTech for digital regulatory compliance. In: Lynn, T., Mooney, J.G., Rosati, P., Cummins, M. (eds.) Disrupting Finance. PSDBET, pp. 85–102. Springer, Cham (2019). https://doi.org/10.1007/978-3-030-02330-0_6

Butt, M.W., Butt, U.J.: Digitalisation of the global FinTech industry. In: Handbook of Research on Innovations in Technology and Marketing for the Connected Consumer, pp. 431–449. IGI Global (2020)

Chouhan, N.: Application of transputer links and routers in telecommunication systems. In: IEE Colloquium on T9000 Transputer, p. 3–1. IET (1994)

Colbert, A., Nick, Y., Gerard, G.: The digital workforce and the workplace of the future. Acad. Manag. J. **59**(3), 731–739 (2016). https://doi.org/10.5465/amj.2016.4003. Research Collection Lee Kong Chian School of Business

Thompson Jr, A.A., Strickland III, A.J., Gamble, J.E.: Crafting and Executing Strategy: The Quest for Competitive Advantage: Concepts and Cases, 17th edn., p. 149. McGraw-Hill/Irwin, Boston (2010). ISBN 9780073530420

Giaretta, E., Chesini, G.: Digital innovation and profitability. Evidence from European financial institutions, FM Classification code: 510 – Depository Institutions – Management. JEL classification: G21, G28, P51 (2018)

Gamundani, A., Bhunu-Shava, F., Bere, M.: A digital economy technology intergration model incorporating the cyber security layer. In: ICCWS 2019 14th International Conference on Cyber Warfare and Security: ICCWS 2019, p. 65. Academic Conferences and publishing limited (2019)

Bandara, H.M.H.: Digital banking: enhancing customer value. In: 28th Anniversary Convention (2016)

Iordache, C., Mariën, I., Baelden, D.: Developing digital skills and competences: a quick-scan analysis of 13 digital literacy models. Ital. J. Sociol. Educ. **9**(1), 6–30 (2017)

Isaksson, A.J., Harjunkoski, I., Sand, G.: The impact of digitalization on the future of control and operations. Comput. Chem. Eng. **114**, 122–129 (2018)

Bughin, J., van Zeebroeck, N.: The best response to digital disruption. MIT Sloan Manag. Rev. (2017)

González-Páramo, J.M.: Financial innovation in the digital age: challenges for regulation and supervision. Financ. Stab. Mag. **32** (2017)

Ojasalo, J., Ojasalo, K.: Service logic business model canvas. J. Res. Market. Entrep. **20**, 70–98 (2018)

Swacha-Lech, M.: The main challenges facing the retail banking industry in the era of digitalisation. J. Insur. Financ. Markets Consum. Prot. **26**, 94–116 (2017)

Marangunić, N., Granić, A.: Technology acceptance model: a literature review from 1986 to 2013. Univ. Access Inf. Soc. **14**(1), 81–95 (2015). https://doi.org/10.1007/s10209-014-0348-1

Marques, M.I.N.: Which strategy should retail banks pursue relatively to marketing automation depending on the type of customer? Doctoral dissertation (2017)

Sajic, M., Bundalo, D., Bundalo, Z., Pasali, D.: Digital technologies in transformation of classical retail bank into digital bank. Int. J. Eng. (2018)

Austin, N.: The future of the financial workplace: banks, workplace and property in a changing world. Corp. Real Estate J. **4**(2), 156–165 (2014)

DeLuca, N.J.: Smart banks can win: leveraging next-generation technology to win the battle for the customer relationship. J. Digital Bank. **2**, 51–57 (2016)

Nyadzayo, M.W., Khajehzadeh, S.: The antecedents of customer loyalty: a moderated mediation model of customer relationship management quality and brand image. J. Retail. Consum. Serv. **30**, 262–270 (2016)

Kiilu, P.K., Nzuki, D.M.: Factors affecting adoption of information security management systems: a theoretical review. Int. J. Sci. Res. **5**(12), 162–166 (2015)

Prasad, R., Sridhar, V.: The dynamics of spectrum management: legacy, technology, and economics. Management **40**(3), 388–391 (2015)

Narayanaswamy, R., McGrath, L.: A holistic study of privacy in social networking sites. Acad. Inf. Manag. Sci. J. **17**(1) (2014)

Rhoen, M.: Beyond consent: improving data protection through consumer protection law. Internet Policy Rev. **5**(1), 1–15 (2016)

Rogers, D.: The Network is Your Customer: Five Strategies to Thrive in a Digital Age, pp. Xvii–Xx. Yale University Press, New Haven, London (2010)

Saunders, M., Lewis, P., Thornhill, A.: Research Methods for Business Students, 7th edn. Pearson Education Limited, Harlow (2016)

Sanyal, S., Hisam, M.W.: Impact of training and development on the performance of employees-a comparative study on select banks in sultanate of Oman. Int. J. Sci. Res. Manag. **6**(03) (2018)

Shelepov, A.: New and traditional multilateral development banks: current and potential cooperation. Int. Organ. Res. J. **12**(1), 127–147 (2017)

Sreejesh, S., Mohapatra, S., Anusree, M.R.: Business Research Methods: An Applied Orientation. Springer, Cham (2014). https://doi.org/10.1007/978-3-319-00539-3

Shrivastava, S.: Digital disruption is redefining the customer experience: the digital transformation approach of the communications service providers. Telecom Bus. Rev. **10**(1), 41 (2017)

Vasiljeva, T., Lukanova, K.: Commercial banks and fintech companies in the digital transformation: challenges for the future. J. Bus. Manag. **11** (2016)

Valenduc, G., Vendramin, P.: Digitalisation, between disruption and evolution. Transfer Eur. Rev. Labour Res. **23**(2), 121–134 (2017)

Venkathaialam, V., Abdulwahab, A.S.: The impact of digitalization of retail banks in Malaysia on customer experience. Int. J. Account. Bus. Manag. **5**(2), 197–213 (2017)

Zikumnd, W.G., Babin, B.J., Carr, J.C., Griffin, M.: Business Research Methods, 8th edn. (2009)

Information Seeking Behaviour in Online Shopping

Christina Sanchita Shah[(⊠)] and Anindita Paul

Indian Institute of Management Kozhikode, Kozhikode, India
{christinas12fpm,apaul}@iimk.ac.in

Abstract. Prior literature has established that information seeking is crucial part of the process of online shopping. However, information seeking behaviour is usually treated as a black box and there is a dearth of studies about the information seeking behaviour of consumers during online shopping and its influence on online purchase intention. Our study aims to fill that gap by employing Ellis' model of information seeking behaviour as our theoretical lens to understand this phenomenon. Ellis' model has eight features or stages related to information seeking behaviour: starting, chaining, browsing, differentiating, monitoring, extracting, verifying and ending. We first conducted a survey to measure these features. We then constructed a measurement model to validate the survey instrument. We found that only three features passed the validity and reliability tests which were starting, monitoring and verifying. We then used structural equation modeling for hypotheses testing and found a significant relationship only for the verifying feature. In other words, only verifying was positively associated with online purchase intention.

Keywords: Information seeking behaviour · Online shopping · Ellis' model of information seeking behaviour

1 Introduction

The online experience today has brought a new dimension to our information-searching practices, providing a wide variety of options for users. A significant amount of data has moved from print media and is now electronically available for the public. Thus, several people automatically associate information and related events with the internet [1]. Understanding users' information searching behaviour is an active area of research that has broad implications on the design of information systems. Information scientists have always been interested in explaining people's information seeking behaviour as it will help in designing better information systems that are easy to use [2]. This has huge implications for both commercial and academic purposes. Understanding people's information seeking behaviour in an online context is therefore, important because it will help increase our understanding of web information spaces, its design and maintenance [1].

Online shopping has evolved dramatically over the years and has become a daily trend in various product categories owing to an increase in internet connectivity and use [3]. Global e-commerce sales reached 3.53 trillion USD in 2019 and is expected to

© IFIP International Federation for Information Processing 2020
Published by Springer Nature Switzerland AG 2020
S. K. Sharma et al. (Eds.): TDIT 2020, IFIP AICT 617, pp. 439–450, 2020.
https://doi.org/10.1007/978-3-030-64849-7_39

reach 6.54 trillion USD by 2022 [4]. Online shopping thus, has become one of the most popular online activities worldwide. Due to internet technology, people today have easy access to information available in the online domain. As the Internet increases in reach and popularity, more and more people become familiar with it and use it as a tool for information finding and online shopping [5, 6]. Previous research indicates that for many users, the Internet has become a significant source of information [7–9].

The purchasing behaviour of consumers is complex in different ways and is affected by various factors. Prior literature shows many attempts to build models for explaining consumer decisions and their decision-making process. Amongst many factors that influence a user's purchase decision, information search is widely considered as being one of the critical factors [10]. Due to its role in the process of consumer decision-making and marketing communications strategy, a number of researchers and marketing experts have long analysed consumer search behaviour before purchasing items [11–13]. Thus, information search is an essential part of consumer decision-making process and purchase behaviour.

In the context of online shopping, one relies mainly on the information provided on the website. This information can consist of brand, online advertisements, online vendor suggestions, online expert reviews and product comparison [10]. Investigating user's information seeking behaviour during online shopping is therefore crucial for understanding user's online purchase behaviour. Information search has been established in literature to be an antecedent of online purchase intention [14–18]. However, the literature does not elaborate on the process of consumers' information search behaviour. Specifically, the relationship between information seeking behaviour of users with online purchase intention. Thus, we see that there is a gap in literature in describing the details of information seeking behaviour of consumers during online shopping. Ellis' model is one of the seminal models and widely cited as best describing the ways users search for information [19, 20]. It is based on solid empirical analysis and has been subsequently validated in many studies in different contexts. Our study aims to fill the literature gap by using the Ellis' model to examine the information seeking behaviour of users when shopping online, specifically, in relation to online purchase intention.

2 Information Seeking for Online Shopping

Information seeking has seen in literature to influence online shopping in a variety of ways. For example, Chaturvedi et al. [21] reported information seeking to be an antecedent of online apparel shopping. Kang and Johnson [22] found that users who were value conscious and social browsers (people who browse for social purposes) used online social shopping for the purpose of information-seeking. Hjorthol [23] studied the relationship between online shopping, information seeking and travel activity. This research showed that different kinds of groups use the Internet to search for information in order to purchase different kinds of products. Kau et al. [24] found that most groups search for information before making an online purchase. Seock and Bailey [25] conducted a survey analysis of college students and found that the shopping orientation of the participants was substantially related to their on-line search for information for online shopping. Esch et al. [26] found that information seeking has a positive moderating effect on perceived product satisfaction during online purchasing. Finally, Zha et al. [27] found that self-efficacy in collecting information influenced perceived decision quality and satisfaction with online shopping.

However, current literature does not elaborate on the process of consumers' information search behaviour. Only few studies have attempted to capture the information seeking behaviour of users. For instance, Detlor et al. [28] studied consumer preferences for Web-based product information display across browsing and searching tasks. They found that information about price, product and vendors were essential for both searching and browsing. While searching emphasized on product information, browsing focused more on vendor information. They concluded that website design and how it displayed information could be instrumental in promoting online shopping. Benn et al. [29] studied consumers online behaviour when shopping online and found browsing was preferred over searching and pictorial information was relied upon more than textual information. Kim and Eastin [30] found that online shopping behaviour was influenced by pre-purchase browsing time and that the pre-purchase browsing time has a positive relationship with online buying frequency. The study also found a positive relationship between purchase intention and perceived quality of information. Thus, we see that there is a gap in literature in describing the information seeking behaviour of consumers during online shopping. Our study aims to fill that gap by using the widely influential and seminal Ellis' model to examine the information seeking behaviour of users when shopping online.

3 Ellis' Model of Information Seeking Behaviour

Based on the study of information seeking behaviour of academics, Ellis [19, 20] proposed a generic model of information behaviour. This model had eight "features" which were various activities involved in information seeking patterns. These included starting, chaining, browsing, differentiating, monitoring, extracting, verifying and ending [19]. Ellis studied and reported the search activity of 60 social scientists who searched for paper-based information in a library environment.

The robustness of Ellis' model was subsequently proved in multiple studies involving academics, chemists, engineers and physicists [31–38]. The information seeking behaviour model developed by Ellis was based on information seeking in library environments using paper-based information sources, not electronic or online library catalogues. However, he did not rule out the possibility of this model being applied to hypertext systems.

Various processes of Ellis' model are described below:

Starting: Starting activity is characteristic of the initial search for information and involves identifying the initial materials to search through and select starting points for the search.

Browsing: Browsing involves a semi-directed searching in an area of potential interest as a monitoring activity going through the scanning of journals and tables of contents etc., to find the something of particular interest.

Chaining: Chaining is when the information seeker follows the chains of citations or other forms of referential connection between materials to identify new sources of information. Chaining can be forwarded where the user is looking for new sources that refer to the initial source or follows footnotes and citations in an information source.

Differentiating: Differentiating is characterized by activities in which the user ranks the information sources based on their relevance and value to his or her information need.

Monitoring: Monitoring is similar to searching for the information for current awareness purposes where the user maintains an awareness of developments in his field of interest through the monitoring of particular sources.

Extracting: The user systematically works through a particular source to locate material of interest in the extracting mode. This implies the selective identification of relevant material in an information source and represents a major feature of the information-seeking patterns of many researchers.

Verifying: Verifying involves checking the accuracy of information obtained by the user from various sources.

Ending: Ending involves 'tying up the loose ends' through a final search.

This model focusses on the different characteristics of information seeking behaviour of users. These features or characteristics do not take place in any sequence and maybe performed in different patterns at different times during the information search process of a user. The strength of Ellis' model is that it is based on robust empirical research and has been tested in multiple studies subsequently [32, 40–42]. In fact, Wilson [43] also incorporated the features identified by Ellis in his model of information seeking behaviour. Thus, Ellis' model of information seeking behaviour has been influential and prompted multiple subsequent studies to understand information search behaviour of users. In this study, we aim to understand user's information search behaviour during online shopping from the lens of Ellis' model.

4   Relating Ellis' Model to Online Shopping

Ellis proposed that hypertext-based systems could perform the activities indicated by his original model. If we consider the internet as a hyperlinked network of multiple web pages, Ellis' model already supports much of the information search activities [44]. As described by Choo et al. [41]: "An individual could begin surfing the web, from one of a few, favourite starting pages or sites (starting) follow hypertextual links to related information sources, both in backward and forward linking directions (chaining); scan the web pages of the sources selected (browsing); bookmark useful sources for future reference and visits (differentiating); subscribe to e-mail based services that alert the use of new information or developments (monitoring) also search a particular source or site for all information on that site on a particular topic (extracting)." Table 1 show possible web-based extensions to Ellis' features for information seeking behaviour. The web-based activities are labelled as "Anticipated Web Moves" and compared with

Ellis' original formulations which are labelled as "Literature Search Moves" as suggested by [41].

Table 1. Information seeking behaviours and web moves [41]

	Starting	Chaining	Browsing	Differentiating	Monitoring	Extracting
Literature Search Moves (Ellis et al., 1989, 1993, 1997)	Identifying sources of interest	Following up references found in given material	Scanning tables of contents or headings	Assessing or restricting information according to their usefulness	Receiving regular reports or summaries from selected sources	Systematically working a source to identify material of interest
Anticipated web moves	Identifying web sites/pages containing or pointing to products one wishes to purchase	Following links on starting pages to other content-related pages	Scanning top-level pages: lists, headings, site maps	Selecting useful pages and sites by bookmarking, printing, copying and pasting, etc.; Choosing differentiated, preselected site	Receiving site updates using e.g. push, agents, or profiles; Revisiting 'favorite' sites	Systematically searches a local site to extract information of interest at that site

Thus, we can adapt Ellis' model easily for studying online shopping and how it influences user's purchase intention. Each of the new information-seeking behavioural features identified by Ellis can be easily adjusted in the context of online shopping when searching for pre-purchase information while retaining its original and basic function (as can be seen in Table 1).

In order to build and sustain the successful consumer relationship, an online shopping website should therefore consider the consumers ' purchasing behaviours Kim and Hong [45]. Ajzen [46] indicates that intentions are believed to reflect how eager people are towards performing a particular behaviour. Research has shown that lack of intention to purchase online is the main hindrance to e-commerce [47]. In a study by Laohapensang [48], it was seen that difficulty of shopping online was the most influential factor that affected online purchase intention. Thus, we see that there is a link between purchasing intention and actual purchasing behaviour.

It has been established in literature that users' search for information before making a purchase is critical in their decision-making process [10, 11]. Ellis' identified various features of information search process. Choo et al. [41] theoretically extended how Ellis' features could be used in an online system. By applying Ellis' model, we therefore expect that each of these features (starting, chaining, browsing, differentiating, monitoring, extracting and verifying) will directly and positively influence user's purchase intention as part of their information search activities. Purchase intention is known to be a determinant of purchase behaviour [47–50]. Therefore, we formally hypothesize for each of the features of Ellis' model:

Table 2. Factor structure

Construct	Item	Factor loading
Starting = 0.725	Before making an online purchase, I start surfing the web for finding websites which sell the product/item of my interes	.914
	I identify multiple online sources from which I could potentially purchase my item/product of interest before making the actual purchase	.816
Monitoring = 0.514	I usually keep abreast with developments for my item/product of interest by regularly visiting related web pages	.752
	I sometimes use google alert feature or push notifications to keep me updated regarding my item/product of interest	.763
Verifying = 0.653	I check the accuracy of information given by reading my item/product of interest's reviews before making an online purchase	.687
	I check the accuracy of information given by checking how many other people have bought my item/product of interest before making an online purchase	.864
Purchase Intention = 0.809	I choose to buy items/products online	.845
	I will frequently purchase product online in future	.860

H1: The starting feature of Ellis' model is positively related to online purchase intention

H2: The chaining feature of Ellis' model is positively related to online purchase intention

H3: The browsing feature of Ellis' model is positively related to online purchase intention

H4: The differentiating feature of Ellis' model is positively related to online purchase intention

H5: The monitoring feature of Ellis' model is positively related to online purchase intention

H6: The extracting feature of Ellis' model is positively related to online purchase intention

H7: The verifying feature of Ellis' model is positively related to online purchase intention

5   Research Methodology

5.1   Data Collection

Two studies were conducted to test the proposed hypotheses. Study 1 uses a survey methodology to validate the constructs in the research model and to gain some initial insight about Ellis' model of information seeking behaviour. In study 2, structural equation modelling was used for hypotheses testing.

Since there are no existing scales that measure each of the features of Ellis' model of information seeking behaviour, we designed and administered a survey, based on literature review, to capture the information search behaviour of users during online shopping and how it influences their purchase intentions. A set of measurement items was adapted to the context of this research, and a 21-item questionnaire was implemented. The responses of the survey participants to each of the items were measured on a five-point Likert scale, ranging from 1 (strongly disagree) to 5 (strongly agree). The total number of responses was 108. 66% of the respondents were male while 34% were female. 61.2% of participants were 26–30 years old, 36% participants were 20–25 years old, 5.2% were 31–35 years old and the rest were above 35 years. Of these, 41.4% shopped online every month, 26.7% shopped online every two weeks, 9.5% shopped online every week, 2.6% shopped twice a year and 0.9% shopped once a year. Thus, we see that the sample pool comprised of young people who shopped regularly and were familiar with the process of online shopping.

5.2 Data Analysis

Next, the convergent and discriminate validity of the constructs and the individual reliability for each item was established (Table 3). The convergent validity of each construct is acceptable for a loading higher than 0.505 [51]. The individual reliability for each item is given by loadings or correlations between the item and the construct. Since many items failed to meet the acceptable criteria for factor loading, they were removed.

Table 3. Validity and reliability of survey

	CR	AVE	MSV	MaxR (H)	Monitoring	Purchase intention	Starting
Monitoring	0.920	0.893	0.013	1.757	0.945		
Purchase Intention	0.820	0.697	0.206	0.865	−0.030	0.835	
Starting	1.141	1.141	0.063	1.141	−0.043		
Verifying	0.741	0.614	0.206	0.984	0.116	0.454	0.250

Only four constructs cleared the criteria for validity and reliability both which were monitoring, purchase intention, starting and verifying as shown in Table 2.

Following the establishment of reliability and validity of the constructs, the structural model is examined. It can be seen that out of seven hypotheses were constructed for each of the features of Ellis' model of information seeking behaviour. However, only four constructs were passed the validity and reliability criteria. A reason for this can be that Ellis' model is more than twenty years old and not all the features maybe relevant today in the context of online shopping. Structural equation modelling in AMOS version 23 was used to test the relationship in H1, H5 and H7. Only H7 was found to be significant (Table 4).

Table 4. Result of structural equation modelling

Variable	Estimate	S.E	P-value
PurchaseIntention ← Starting	−.072	.068	.289
PurchaseIntention ← Monitoring	−.038	.085	.659
PurchaseIntention ← Verifying	.747	.203	***
S1 ← Starting	.473	.241	.050
M1 ← Monitoring	.200	.413	.628
PI5 ← PurchaseIntention	.900	.180	***
V2 ← Verifying	1.756	.562	.002

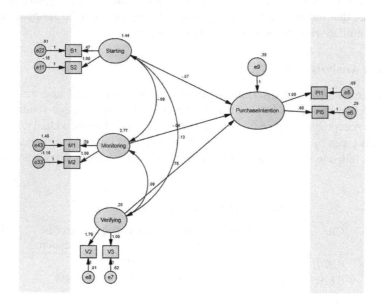

Fig. 1. Structural Model

6   Discussion and Conclusion

This purpose of this study was to understand the information seeking behaviour of consumers during online shopping, specifically in relation to online purchase intention. Prior research has established that information search behaviour is a determinant of online purchase intention. However, there is a dearth of studies about the information seeking behaviour of consumers during online shopping. Information seeking behaviour is usually treated as a black box in literature. Our study aims to shed more light on consumer's information seeking behaviour by employing Ellis' model as our theoretical lens to understand this phenomenon in the context of online shopping. Ellis' model has eight features or processes related to information seeking behaviour: starting, chaining, browsing, differentiating, monitoring, extracting, verifying and ending.

We first conducted a survey to measure these features. We then constructed a measurement model to validate the survey instrument. We found that only three features passed the validity and reliability tests which were starting, monitoring and verifying.

Next, we conducted hypothesis testing for the hypotheses relevant to starting, monitoring and verifying. We found significant relationship only for the feature verifying. In other words, only verifying was positively associated with online purchase intention.

Thus, we see that not all features of Ellis's [20] original eight feature model of information seeking behaviour are relevant today in relation to consumer's purchase intention in the context of online shopping. The information seeking behaviour model developed by Ellis [19] was based on information seeking in library environments using paper-based information sources, not electronic or online library catalogues. Hence it cannot be directly applied to the consumer's purchase intention during online shopping. Nonetheless, Ellis' model remains broadly valid even today. Three features of the model continue to be valid for consumer's purchase intention during online shopping are: starting, monitoring and verifying in the context of online shopping. Of these, only verifying is positively associated with purchase intention in the context of online shopping. This suggests that a user may start the process of information search but it may not always lead to a positive purchase intention. Furthermore, even if a user monitors a product or item of interest, it does not mean that user will definitely buy it. However, if a user is in the process of verifying the information then it implies a positive purchase intention.

The implications of this study are manifold. First, the process of looking for information, especially online, is different and more research is needed to capture the new dimensions. Second, users place a lot of focus on verification of the information. This might be because the product is being bought online and is intangible. With the changing landscape of shopping from brick and mortar to click and mortar, the information seeking behaviour of users is also changing. Third, we need a different information seeking model to capture all the dimensions of online search behaviour of users. Towards this end, Meho and Tibbo [52] revised Ellis' model and to include new features called accessing, networking, verifying and information managing. Their paper was based on the faculty of social sciences, which studied stateless nations. Although their research echoed the applicability of Ellis's model, it found that a more thorough explanation of the actions of the social scientists seeking information could be found by differentiating between processes of searching for information and activities of finding information.

This study is not without limitations. First, the sample size was small and data was collected from a largely student population. Future work can expand the sample size and collect a more geographically distributed data to ensure representativeness. Second, future work can use other models of information search behaviour such as Meho & Tibbo [52] which is more apt for the context of online shopping.

References

1. Nkomo, N., Ocholla, D., Jacobs, D.: Web information seeking behaviour of students and staff in rural and urban based universities in South Africa: a comparison analysis. Libri. **61** (4) (2011). https://doi.org/10.1515/libr.2011.024
2. Cutrell, E., Guan, Z.: What are you looking for?: an eye-tracking study of information usage in web search. In: Proceedings of the SIGCHI Conference on Human Factors in Computing Systems - CHI 2007, San Jose, California, USA, pp. 407–416 (2007). https://doi.org/10.1145/1240624.1240690
3. Lissitsa, S., Kol, O.: Generation X vs. Generation Y – a decade of online shopping. J. Retail. Consum. Serv. **31**, 304–312 (2016). https://doi.org/10.1016/j.jretconser.2016.04.015
4. Clement: Retail e-commerce sales worldwide from 2014 to 2023 (in billion U.S. dollars). Statista, 19 March 2020. https://www.statista.com/statistics/379046/worldwide-retail-e-commerce-sales/. Accessed 13 May 2020
5. Farag, S., Schwanen, T., Dijst, M., Faber, J.: Shopping online and/or in-store? A structural equation model of the relationships between e-shopping and in-store shopping. Transp. Res. Part Policy Pract. **41**(2), 125–141 (2007). https://doi.org/10.1016/j.tra.2006.02.003
6. Keisidou, E., Sarigiannidis, L., Maditinos, D.: Consumer characteristics and their effect on accepting online shopping, in the context of different product types. Int. J. Bus. Sci. Appl. Manag. **6**(2), 31–51 (2011). https://www.econstor.eu/bitstream/10419/190625/1/06_2_p31-51.pdf
7. Kim, J.S., Ratchford, B.T.: Consumer choice and use of multiple information sources for automobile purchases. Int. J. Electron. Commer. **16**(3), 7–40 (2012). https://doi.org/10.2753/JEC1086-4415160301
8. Klein, L.R., Ford, G.T.: Consumer search for information in the digital age: an empirical study of prepurchase search for automobiles. J. Interact. Mark. **17**(3), 29–49 (2003). https://doi.org/10.1002/dir.10058
9. Lee, M.-S., Ratchford, B.T., Talukdar, D.: The impact of the internet on information search for automobiles. SSRN Electron. J. (2002). https://doi.org/10.2139/ssrn.310889
10. Akalamkam, K., Mitra, J.K.: Consumer pre-purchase search in online shopping: role of offline and online information sources. Bus. Perspect. Res. **6**(1), 42–60 (2018). https://doi.org/10.1177/2278533717730448
11. Demangeot, C., Broderick, A.J.: Engaging customers during a website visit: a model of website customer engagement. Int. J. Retail Distrib. Manage. **44**(8), 814–839 (2016). https://doi.org/10.1108/IJRDM-08-2015-0124
12. Su, B.: Characteristics of consumer search on-line: how much do we search? Int. J. Electron. Commer. **13**(1), 109–129 (2008). https://doi.org/10.2753/JEC10864415130104
13. Tsao, W.C., Chang, H.R.: Exploring the impact of personality traits on online shopping behavior. Afr. J. Bus. Manage. **4**(9), 1800–1812, August 2010. http://www.academicjournals.org/app/webroot/article/article1380814476_Tsao%20and%20Chang.pdf
14. Chang, M., Cheung, W., Lai, V.: Literature derived reference models for the adoption of online shopping. Inf. Manage. **42**(4), 543–559 (2005). https://doi.org/10.1016/S03787206(04)00051-5
15. Ranganathan, C., Ganapathy, S.: Key dimensions of business-to-consumer web sites. Inf. Manage. **39**(6), 457–465 (2002). https://doi.org/10.1016/S0378-7206(01)00112-4
16. Shim, S., Eastlick, M.A., Lotz, S.L., Warrington, P.: An online prepurchase intentions model. J. Retail. **77**(3), 397–416 (2001). https://doi.org/10.1016/S00224359(01)00051-3

17. Vijayasarathy, L.R., Jones, J.M.: Print and internet catalog shopping: assessing attitudes and intentions. Internet Res. **10**(3), 191–202 (2000). https://doi.org/10.1108/1066224001 0331948
18. Zimmerman: E-commerce (a special report): selling strategies-web design: keep it simpleluxury retailers still haven't learned an important lesson for their websites: glitz is great, but not online. Wall Str. J. **15**(2), 287–296 (2002)
19. Ellis, D.: A behavioural approach to information retrieval system design. J. Doc. **45**(3), 171–212 (1989). https://doi.org/10.1108/eb026843
20. Ellis, D., Cox, D., Hall, K.: A comparison of the information seeking patterns of researchers in the physical and social sciences. J. Doc. **49**(4), 356–369 (1993). https://doi.org/10.1108/eb026919
21. Chaturvedi, S.A., Gupta, S.A., Hada, D.S.B.: Perceived risk, trust and information seeking behavior as antecedents of online apparel buying behavior in India: an exploratory study in context of Rajasthan. Int. Rev. Manage. Mark. **6**(4), 935–943 (2016). www.econjournals. com
22. Kang, J.-Y.M., Johnson, K.K.P.: F-Commerce platform for apparel online social shopping: testing a mowen's 3 M model. Int. J. Inf. Manage. **35**(6), 691–701 (2015). https://doi.org/10.1016/j.ijinfomgt.2015.07.004
23. Hjorthol, R.J.: Information searching and buying on the internet: travel-related activities? Environ. Plan. B Plan. Des. **36**(2), 229–244 (2009). https://doi.org/10.1068/b34012t
24. Keng Kau, A., Tang, Y.E., Ghose, S.: Typology of online shoppers. J. Consum. Mark. **20**(2), 139–156 (2003). https://doi.org/10.1108/07363760310464604
25. Seock, Y.-K., Bailey, L.R.: The influence of college students' shopping orientations and gender differences on online information searches and purchase behaviours. Int. J. Consum. Stud. **32**(2), 113–121 (2008). https://doi.org/10.1111/j.1470-6431.2007.00647.x
26. Van Esch, P., Northey, G., Duffy, S., Heller, J., Striluk, M.: The moderating influence of country of origin information seeking on homophily and product satisfaction. J. Promot. Manage. **24**(3), 332–348 (2018). https://doi.org/10.1080/10496491.2018.1378300
27. Zha, X., Li, J., Yan, Y.: Information self-efficacy and information channels: decision quality and online shopping satisfaction. Online Inf. Rev. **37**(6), 872–890 (2013). https://doi.org/10.1108/OIR-09-2012-0156
28. Detlor, Sproule, Gupta: Pre-purchase online information seeking: Search versus browse. J. Electron. Commer. Res. **4**(2), 72–84 (2003). http://ojs.jecr.org/jecr/sites/default/files/04_2_p03_0.pdf
29. Benn, Y., Webb, T.L., Chang, B.P.I., Reidy, J.: What information do consumers consider, and how do they look for it, when shopping for groceries online? Appetite **89**, 265–273 (2015). https://doi.org/10.1016/j.appet.2015.01.025
30. Kim, S., Eastin, M.S.: Hedonic tendencies and the online consumer: an investigation of the online shopping process. J. Internet Commer. **10**(1), 68–90 (2011). https://doi.org/10.1080/15332861.2011.558458
31. Brine, A., Feather, J.: The information needs of UK historic houses: mapping the ground. J. Doc. **66**(1), 28–45 (2010). https://doi.org/10.1108/00220411011016353
32. Ellis, D., Haugan, M.: Modelling the information seeking patterns of engineers and research scientists in an industrial environment. J. Doc. **53**(4), 384–403 (1997). https://doi.org/10.1108/EUM0000000007204
33. Salajegheh, M., Hayati, Z.: Modelling information-seeking behaviour patterns of Iranian medical school academic staff. Libri. **59**(4) (2009). https://doi.org/10.1515/libr.2009.025
34. Ellis, D., et al.: Information seeking and mediated searching. part 5. user-intermediary interaction. J. Am. Soc. Inf. Sci. Technol. **53**(11), 883–893 (2002). https://doi.org/10.1002/asi.10133

35. Ford, N., Wilson, T.D., Foster, A., Ellis, D., Spink, A.: Information seeking and mediated searching. part 4. cognitive styles in information seeking. J. Am. Soc. Inf. Sci. Technol. **53** (9), 728–735 (2002). https://doi.org/10.1002/asi.10084

36. Spink, A., Wilson, T.D., Ford, N., Foster, A., Ellis, D.: Information-seeking and mediated searching. part 1. theoretical framework and research design. J. Am. Soc. Inf. Sci. Technol. **53**(9), 695–703 (2002). https://doi.org/10.1002/asi.10081

37. Spink, A., Wilson, T.D., Ford, N., Foster, A., Ellis, D.: Information seeking and mediated searching study. part 3. successive searching. J. Am. Soc. Inf. Sci. Technol. **53**(9), 716–727 (2002). https://doi.org/10.1002/asi.10083

38. Wilson: Evolution in information behavior modeling: Wilson's model. Theor. Inf. Behav., 31–36 (2007). https://pdfs.semanticscholar.org/4d69/5d5eb58f5f269b9b0474b93a119 cadfe1aab.pdf

39. Wilson, T.D.: Human information behavior. Informing Sci. **3**(2), 49–56 (2000). https:// www.researchgate.net/profile/Tom_Wilson25/publication/270960171_Human_Information_ Behavior/links/57d32fe508ae601b39a42875/Human-Information-Behavior.pdf

40. Bates, M.J.: The design of browsing and berrypicking techniques for the online search interface. Online Rev. **13**(5), 407–424 (1989). https://doi.org/10.1108/eb024320

41. Choo, C.W., Detlor, B., Turnbull, D.: Information seeking on the web: an integrated model of browsing and searching. First Monday **5**(2) (2000). https://doi.org/10.5210/fm.v5i2.729

42. Sutton: The role of attorney mental models of law in case relevance determinations: an exploratory analysis. J. Am. Soc. Inf. Sci. **45**(3), 186–200 (1999)

43. Wilson, T.D.: Models in information behaviour research. J. Doc. **55**(3), 249–270 (1999). https://doi.org/10.1108/EUM0000000007145

44. Michael, E., Makarfi, A., Goshie, R., Jimada, A.: An overview of users information seeking behaviour on online resources. IOSR J. Humanit. Soc. Sci. **19**(1), 09–17 (2014). https://doi. org/10.9790/0837-19190917

45. Kim, E., Hong, T.: Segmenting customers in online stores from factors that affect the customer's intention to purchase. In: 2010 International Conference on Information Society, London, pp. 383–388, June 2010. https://doi.org/10.1109/i-Society16502.2010.6018733

46. Ajzen, I.: The theory of planned behavior. Organ. Behav. Hum. Decis. Process. **50**(2), 179–211 (1991)

47. He, D., Lu, Y., Zhou, D.: Empirical study of consumers' purchase intentions in C2C electronic commerce. Tsinghua Sci. Technol. **13**(3), 287–292 (2008). https://doi.org/10. 1016/S1007-0214(08)70046-4

48. Laohapensang, O.: Factors influencing internet shopping behaviour: a survey of consumers in Thailand. J. Fash. Mark. Manage. Int. J. **13**(4), 501–513 (2009). https://doi.org/10.1108/ 13612020910991367

49. Pavlou, Fygenson: Understanding and predicting electronic commerce adoption: an extension of the theory of planned behavior. MIS Q. **30**(1), 115 (2006). https://doi.org/10. 2307/25148720

50. Roca, J., José García, J., José de la Vega, J.: The importance of perceived trust, security and privacy in online trading systems. Inf. Manage. Comput. Secur. **17**(2), 96–113 (2009). https://doi.org/10.1108/09685220910963983

51. Falk, R.F., Miller, N.B.: A primer for soft modeling. Univ. Akron Press (1992)

52. Meho, L.I., Tibbo, H.R.: Modeling the information-seeking behavior of social scientists: Ellis's study revisited. J. Am. Soc. Inf. Sci. Technol. **54**(6), 570–587 (2003)https://doi.org/ 10.1002/asi.10244

Developing a Model for Green IS Adoption in Indian Banking and IT Industries

Monika Singh[1]([⊠]) and G. P. Sahu[2]

[1] Shri Ramswaroop Memorial University, Lucknow, India
`rms1502@mnnit.ac.in`
[2] Motilal Nehru National Institute of Technology Allahabad, Prayagraj, India
`gsahu@mnnit.ac.in`

Abstract. Numerous studies explore that, in current era, Banking and Information Technology (IT) services sector, in various developed/developing countries, either adopted or in the phase of Green IS adoption. Since countries, round the globe, have recognized the significance of Green IS and its impact over environment, it is now vital for every industry to implement Green IS and contribute in environment sustainability. This Research-in-Progress paper observes the effective Green IS implementation through carefully consideration of different Motivational, Technological, Organizational and Environmental factors. Subsequently, in this paper 16 different factors are revealed via Literature Review and Experts opinion and a research model is developed using Technological-Organizational-Environmental (T-O-E) theory and Unified Theory of Acceptance and Use of Technology 2 (UTAUT2) framework for effective Green IS implementation, which will be helpful for academician and practitioners in this field.

Keywords: Green IS · Environment sustainability · Information technology · TOE · UTAUT2

1 Introduction

According to Yang et al. [73], the increasing energy ingestion put heavy pressure on energy production at large scale that consequently enforces heavy compression on the atmosphere. This becomes a huge problem in case of cloud data center and required abrupt vigilant action by the researcher, practitioners and users in the IT field since these cloud data centers consumes high level energy due to resource scheduling mechanism to complete the task at high priority causing low server use ratio as well as due to requirement of cooling system that is on the basis of highest significant strategy causing extreme chilling supply, escalations in maneuver cost, and huge energy waste [46, 50, 61, 71–73]. According to WEF Report [71, 72], in the current scenario, data centers situated globally are consuming total 1.5 to 2% (two percent) of total energy and it is predicted that the consumption will rise to 140 billion kilowatt-hours per annum by 2020. Consequently, the carbon emission would be nearly 150 million metric tons yearly. Additional to this, data centers were consuming more than 1% (one percent) of the electricity in the server dense country i.e. U.S. Their combined yearly

© IFIP International Federation for Information Processing 2020
Published by Springer Nature Switzerland AG 2020
S. K. Sharma et al. (Eds.): TDIT 2020, IFIP AICT 617, pp. 451–462, 2020.
https://doi.org/10.1007/978-3-030-64849-7_40

carbon emissions of 80 metric megatons of Carbon-dioxide (CO_2) are approaching the carbon footprint of the Netherland and Argentina [3]. A computer/laptop working for over or about ten hours per day emits 1200 lb of carbon-dioxide i.e. nearly equivalent to one tenth CO_2 emitted from an automobile yearly [10, 70]. According to Belkhir and Elmeligi [4], total number of computers/laptops worldwide is expected to increase by 5.2% and will account for huge level of CO_2 emission; it signifies the concern over IT ecological footprint is valid [42].

Table 1. Need for research in Green IS area

Reasons	Context	Study
Wasteful computer energy	The computer is "on" while not in use	[8, 23, 27, 29, 42, 59, 69]
Wasteful printing	Often printing the redundant documents	[8, 42, 56]
Contamination	Emission of GHGs during manufacturing, using or disposing of electronic equipment	[8, 14, 42, 59]
Toxicity	Use of Toxic elements in manufacturing of IT equipment in mass	[8, 23, 42, 56]
High cost	Electricity bill and other charges for using computers	[8, 29, 42, 56, 59]

Issues are enlisted in Table 1, which provides the necessity of Green IS urgently day by day. As a result, various countries agreed to noteworthy reductions in GHGs emission that are the main causes of global warming, as per Paris Agreement 2015, held at Paris in 2015, to ensure that the global warming will not exceed 1.5–2.0 °C [47, 56, 65]. Additional factors enforcing organizations to adopt Green IS are the regulations and laws created by various countries to reduce their carbon footprints including the IT sector, customers and stakeholders' awareness towards social responsibility and competitive forces [30]. The literature review explores that research is in its initial stage and require more research in this area [4, 29, 56] for environment sustainability and reduction of carbon footprints. IT/S produces GHGs and carbon footprints, but IT/S use in green ways, i.e. Green IS provide the solution of the problem and reduces carbon and GHGs emission [71, 72]. Capra and Merlo [12], had defined Green IS under three areas: 1) Power competency of IT, 2) Eco-companionable life cycle management of IT, and 3) IT as a facilitator of green governance. Dedrick [20], had categorized Green IS into four main disciplines: 1) Blueprint, 2) Development, 3) Utilization and, 4) Disposal of IT equipment e.g. PCs, servers and other associated peripheral devices to gain minimal or no impact on the environment. According to Trimi and Park [63] Green IS referring to the objective of achieving energy efficiency and reduction in carbon emissions through "Greening of IT" i.e. creating Green IS products and reuse, refurbish and through "Greening by IT" as using IT to reduce environmental impacts.

In this Research in Progress paper, 16 CSFs are investigated in order to develop a research model for Green IS adoption with the aid of T-O-E and UTAUT2 frameworks. The paper presents research strategy to investigate the key factors and an experimental scheme to validate the research model, and measurement of models' robustness along with computing individual CSFs' impact over behavioral intention to adopt Green IS in Indian Banking and IT sector. The Next section presents CSFs for practicing Green IS Adoption, Research Model and Methodology, Summary, Research Contribution and Paper ended with Limitation of the Study.

2   CSF(S) for Practicing Green Is Adoption

The literature review in the area of CSFs for Green IS adoption/acceptance is limited in the present scenario. From the accessible articles/reports it is explored that different authors (like [5, 7, 26, 49, 62] etc.) has worked on the alike factors, however, categories under various themes (like economic, environmental, descriptive, injunctive etc.). To conduct the research, out of total 34 studied CSFs from literature review, 16 CSFs namely: Hedonic Motivation (HM), Habit (HA), Interoperability (IO), Energy Efficient Technology (EET), Performance Expectancy (PE), Effort Expectancy (EE), Leadership (LA), Employee Stewardship (ES), Expert Appointment (EA), Organizational Policy (OP), Facilitating Conditions (FC), Price Value (PV), Government Regulations (GR), Incentives (IC), Competitive Pressure (CP), Social Influence (SI) and Intention to Adopt Green IS in organization' (BI) have been identified on the basis of decision made after discussion with Expert's and Academician in the field of IT/Technology adoption as well as considering the modernization (inclusion of UTAUT2 theory constructs) and feasibility of the study. Table 2 reflects the 16 identified CSFs and their supporting study. Literature Review explored that, various authors (e.g. [1, 6, 16, 18]) have categorized the CSFs for Green IS effective and efficient adoption generally in four categories: Organizational factors, Economical Factors, Social-culture factors and Regulatory compliance factors. From the accessible literature review (e.g. [18, 24, 41, 51, 55]) it is explored that numerous models on adoption of Green IS have been developed on the basis of literature review in the field of IT or technology adoption. Already in the area of Green Information Systems following models have been given by different authors:

1. Bose and Luo [9] proposed and established integrative theory for recognition of key factors for Green readiness of companies and Green IS adoption, on the basis of Technology-Organization-Environment (T-O-E), Process Virtualization (PVT), and Diffusion of Innovation (DoI) theory.
2. Chen and Chang [13] established Green IS adoption model for Taiwan' administrations on the basis of Technology-Organization-Environment (T-O-E) theory along with Perceived e-Readiness Model (PERM) and identified driving forces.
3. Thomson and Belle [62] investigated the antecedents (drivers and readiness factors) for implementation of Green IS in Higher Education Institutions (HEI) of South Africa using GITAM model established by Molla (2008)

Table 2. Critical success factors for Green IS adoption

Constructs/Code	Study
Hedonic Motivation (HM)	[2, 11, 15, 22, 28, 29, 31, 32, 34–36, 45, 54, 60, 67]
Habit (HA)	[2, 21, 22, 31, 32, 36, 57, 67]
Interoperability (IO)	[9, 13, 17, 29, 35, 38, 44, 68, 74]
Energy Efficient Technologies (EET)	[9, 13, 19, 29, 35, 38, 48]
Performance Expectancy (PE)	[2, 22, 31–33, 35, 36, 48, 64, 74]
Effort Expectancy (EE)	[2, 22, 29, 31–33, 36, 48, 64, 74]
Leadership (LA)	[5, 9, 13, 19, 21, 30, 34, 35, 38, 44, 48, 52]
Employee Stewardship (ES)	[13, 21, 25, 29, 33–35]
Expert Appointment (EA)	[9, 13, 17, 21, 25, 30, 33, 35, 44, 52]
Organizational Policy (OP)	[9, 17, 29, 37, 48, 74]
Facilitating Conditions (FC)	[2, 9, 13, 17, 21, 22, 29–32, 35–37, 48, 67]
Price Value (PV)	[2, 9, 13, 22, 29, 31–33, 35, 36, 48, 67, 74]
Government Regulations (GR)	[5, 9, 11, 13, 21, 28–30, 34, 35, 37, 40, 44, 48, 74]
Incentives (IC)	[9, 13, 29, 48]
Competitive Pressure (CP)	[11, 13, 19, 28, 29, 34, 35, 48, 74]
Social Influence (SI)	[2, 13, 19, 22, 29, 31–34, 36, 67, 74]

4. Nazari and Karim [43] used both the theories T-O-E framework and DoI model together, to recognize factors inducing Green IS implementation at managerial level and advised framework that highpoints three groups of factors that affect Green IS acceptance are: Invention, Organizational and Ecological Factors.
5. Molla [39] developed Green IS Adoption Model (GITAM) based on existing innovation and adoption models e.g. TOE model.

To address the shortcomings of UTAUT, Venkatesh et al. [66, 67] developed UTAUT2, including three new constructs: hedonic motivation, price value, and habit. The literature review in the area of frameworks adopted/used for research in the area of Green IS and its' adoption unearths that T-O-E framework is the maximum used framework used by authors; however, most of the research are the qualitative research studies. Additionally, this is also unearthed that UTAUT2 is minimal times (almost not) used by any author in this area especially in the context of Indian Banking and IT industries. Consequently, this research work is based on both the theories i.e. TO-E framework and UTAUT2 theory in order to identify the CSFs for effective and efficient adoption of Green IS in Indian services sector with special reference to Indian Banking and IT industries as well as to develop a research model for the same.

3   Research Model

The research model in a study creates the base-structure of the entire study [58]. The research model represents the relationship among the constructs and subsequently facilitates hypotheses development for testing. Research model developed for this study is shown in Fig. 1. The relationships between the constructs are shown in the research. In the research model all the 16 factors (independent variables) are constructs and Age, Gender and Experience are roll out as the moderating variables. For model simplicity use behavior of consumers is abolished.

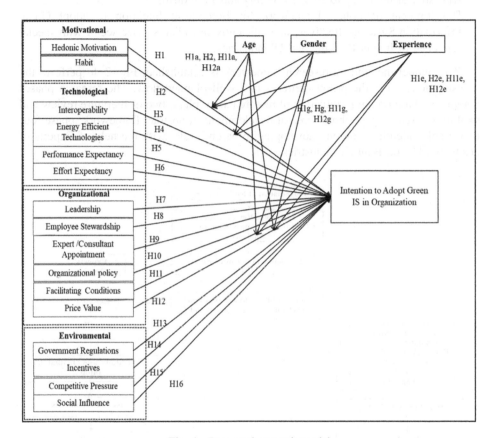

Fig. 1. Proposed research model

4   Research Methodology

Research methodology is known as systematic set of process and principles to search something. The term methodology provides set of reasonable order to researcher to attain the preset goal like facts, acumen, strategy, intermediation and revolutions. In this study, therefore, 16 CSFs i.e. HM, HA, IO, EET, PE, EE, LA, ES, EA, OP, FC, PV, GR, IC, CP and SI identified, in order to develop the research model for the study. The study and developed research model would provide answers of the following research gap:

1. The current state-of-the-art of research in the area of Green IS adoption in organizations.

2. Various CSFs that influence Behavioral Intention to adopt Green Information Systems effectively and efficiently in Indian service sector with special reference to Indian Banking and IT industries.
3. Validated model for Green Information Systems adoption in Indian service sector with special reference to Indian Banking and IT industries.
4. Development of Policy Framework for Behavioral Intention to adopt Green Information Systems effectively and efficiently in Indian service sector with special reference to Indian Banking and IT industries.

To conduct the study a research framework is established, Fig. 2, to perform the investigation within the preset premises in a well-planned flow. The research phases comprise: phase one of formulation of research area, phase two of literature review and exploring research gap, phase three of development of abstract framework; phase four of variables identification and developing research model with the help of Experts of academic, IT and Banking industries.

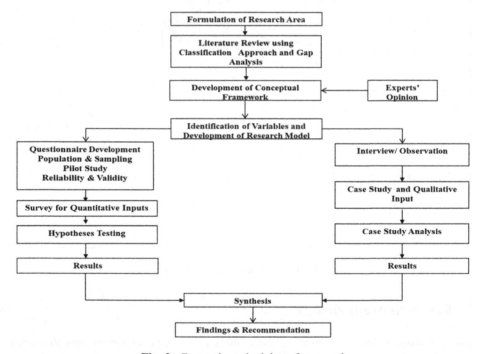

Fig. 2. Research methodology framework

For testing research model, data/information is required to validate the framed hypotheses. After phase four the research framework divided into two different approaches - 1) Quantitative approach and 2) Qualitative approach for further research tools and analysis procedure. Both the approaches will be performed simultaneously in coordination with experts of the field. The quantitative approach comprises phase five of developing hypotheses, questionnaire development and pilot testing; Phase six of survey and data collection and phase seven of hypotheses testing. On the other side, in qualitative approach, phase five comprises interview of experts and decision makers of IT departments and observation of the field area phase six of conducting case study and collecting information and phase seven comprises application of qualitative tools and techniques over the collected information and analysis of the output. Phase eight in both the approaches comprises results obtained by application of tools and techniques and analysis of the collected data/information. Phase nine will provide synthesis of the results obtained from qualitative and quantitative analysis and finally, the last step of the research framework is phase ten providing overall findings of the research recommendation for the researchers/practitioners in the same field for the future practices.

5 Instrument Design and Validation

Following the quantitative approach, survey method would be used to collect the data from IT and Banking sector. Additionally, for qualitative analysis, interview and researcher's observation would be used for data collection. A draft copy of developed of questionnaire will put in front of various experts from industry as well as academic to recognize any latent problems and check validity and reliability. For qualitative study, the main methods used are interview and researcher' observation of the experts in the organization. Convenience Sampling technique and 1000 sample size selected, based on expert's suggestions and following the recommendation provided by renowned authors. In this study Statistical Package for Social Sciences (SPSS) 21 version will be used to analyze the primary data, and Structural Equation Modeling (SEM) would be used for CFA and to validate the hypothesized model. Further, to analyze the qualitative data Interpretive Structural Modeling (ISM) technique will be used. Interpretive structural modeling (ISM) can rightly be employed under such circumstances [53].

6 Summary

This paper includes the meek investigation of CSFs for Green IS adoption in Indian services sectors with special reference to Indian Banking and IT industries. The study describes the research design of the proposed investigation with regard technology adoption using mix-method approach (qualitative as well as quantitative data analysis) and data collection techniques. This paper presents the procedures for conducting the research, which include the literature review, proposed research model and validation techniques while providing selection of model. On the basis of the research methodology research study will be conducted and empirical and non-empirical results will be provided near future.

7 Projected Support to Practice, Strategy and Research

As this study is research designed to perform imminent research and that will contribute the existing research in the area of Green IS adoption as well as will helpful for the practitioners to make/implement strategies for Green IS implementation in various organization at different regions. The investigated CSFs and validated research model will positively help decision makers/practitioners and researchers in their future works. Consequently, they will be able to influence the society and organizations to adopt Green IS in daily practices, purchasing of Green Compliant products and help in environment sustainability. Additionally, as research contribution for researchers, this study will provide literature review and research gap/scope in the area of Green IS. The research also provides unique combination of T-O-E and UTAUT2 framework development. Explicit contributions and repercussions will be accessible after accomplishment of this study.

8 Limitations of the Study

Like all research work, this proposed research work will also abide by some limitations. As to conduct the study with quantitative data approach, Convenience sampling is planned to use and filling the questionnaire since: 1) The accurate population representing sample is difficult to determine.; 2) Further, due to target respondents' hectic schedule/fear from authorities, many time they avoid to fill up the questionnaire; 3) And lastly, due to expenditure problem and limitation of interviewers' (authors) of geographically approach to conduct interviews at all target offices for qualitative study. Further, the research may face problem of generalization due to nonlongitudinal study.

References

1. Ajzen, I., Fishbein, M.: Understanding Attitudes and Predicting Social Behavior. Prentice-Hall Inc., Englewood Cliffs (1980)
2. Alharbi, N., Papadaki, M., Dowland, P.: The impact of security and its antecedents in behaviour intention of using e-government services. Behav. Inf. Technol. **36**(6), 620–636 (2017)
3. Andrae, A.S., Edler, T.: On global electricity usage of communication technology: trends to 2030. Challenges **6**(1), 117–157 (2015)
4. Belkhir, L., Elmeligi, A.: Assessing ICT global emissions footprint: trends to 2040 & recommendations. J. Clean. Prod. **177**, 448–463 (2018)
5. Bokolo, A.J., Majid, M.A.: Development of a Green ICT model for sustainable enterprise strategy. J. Soft Comput. Decis. Support Syst. **3**(3), 1–12 (2016)
6. Bokolo, A.J., Pa, N.C.: A case based reasoning architecture and component based model for Green IS implementation and diffusion in organisation. Int. J. Digit. Inf. Wirel. Commun. **6**(2), 97–112 (2016)
7. Bokolo, A.J., Majid, M.A., Romli, A.: A proposed model for green practice adoption and implementation in information technology based organizations. Problemy Ekorozwoju **13**(1), 95–112 (2018)

8. Bolla, R., Davoli, F., Bruschi, R., Christensen, K., Cucchietti, F., Singh, S.: The potential impact of green technologies in next-generation wireline networks: is there room for energy saving optimization? IEEE Commun. Mag. **49**(8), 80–86 (2011)
9. Bose, R., Luo, X.: Integrative framework for assessing firms' potential to undertake Green IT initiatives via virtualization – a theoretical perspective. J. Strateg. Inf. Syst. **20**(1), 38–54 (2011)
10. Bussel, G.V., Smit, N., Pas, J.V.D.: Digital archiving, Green IT and environment. Deleting data to manage critical effects of the data deluge. Electron. J. Inf. Syst. Eval. **18**(2), 187–198 (2015)
11. Butler, T.: Compliance with institutional imperatives on environmental sustainability: building theory on the role of Green IS. J. Strateg. Inf. Syst. **20**(1), 6–26 (2011)
12. Capra, E., Merlo, F.: Green IT: everything starts from the software. In: European Conference on Information Systems. Association for Information Systems, Verona, Italy, pp. 62–73 (2009)
13. Chen, H., Chang, J.: A study on Green IT adoption. Comput. Sci. Inf. Technol. **2**(8), 315–323 (2014)
14. Cherki, S., Idrissi, E., Laval, U., Corbett, J.: Green IS research: a modernity perspective. Commun. Assoc. Inf. Syst. **36**, 30 (2016)
15. Corbett, J.: Leaders and lemmings: organizational responses to smart grid transformation. Paper Presented at 18th Americas Conference on Information Systems, Seattle, Washington, p. 12 (2012)
16. Damanpour, F., Schneider, M.: Phases of the adoption of innovation in organizations: effects of environment, organization and top managers. Br. J. Manag. **17**(3), 215–236 (2006)
17. Dao, V., Langella, I., Carbo, J.: From green to sustainability: information technology and an integrated sustainability framework. J. Strateg. Inf. Syst. **20**(1), 63–79 (2011)
18. Davis, F.D.: Perceived usefulness, perceived ease of use, and user acceptance of information technology. MIS Q. **13**(3), 319–340 (1989)
19. De Zoysa, M., Wijayanayake, J.: The influential factors of Green IT adoption in data centres of Sri Lankan Banks. J. Emerg. Trends Comput. Inf. Sci. **4**(12), 908–915 (2013)
20. Dedrick, J.: Green IS: concepts and issues for information systems research. Commun. Assoc. Inf. Syst. **27**(1), 11–18 (2010)
21. Dolci, D.B., Lunardi, G.L., Salles, A.C., Alves, A.P.: Implementation of green IT in organizations: a structurational view. Revista de Administração de Empresas **55**(5), 486–497 (2015)
22. Dwivedi, Y.K., Shareef, M.A., Simintiras, A.C., Lal, B., Weerakkody, V.: A generalised adoption model for services: a cross-country comparison of mobile health (m-health). Gov. Inf. Q. **33**(1), 174–187 (2016)
23. GeSI: SMARTer 2020, The Role of ICT in Driving a Sustainable Future (2020)
24. Hedman, J., Henningsson, S.: Developing ecological sustainability: a green IS response model. Inf. Syst. J. **26**(3), 259–287 (2016)
25. Henningsson, S., Hedman, J.: Industry-wide supply chain information integration: the lack of management and disjoint economic responsibility. Int. J. Inf. Syst. Supply Chain Manag. **3**(1), 1–20 (2010)
26. Hernandez, A.A.: Exploring the factors to Green IT adoption in SMEs in the Philippines. Paper Presented at IST-Africa 2014 Conference, Vienna, Austria, pp. 49–66 (2018)
27. Hovorka, D.S., Corbett, J.: IS sustainability research: a trans-disciplinary framework for a 'grand challenge'. In: ICIS 2012 Proceedings, Aisel (2012)
28. Ijab, M.T., Molla, A., Cooper, V.: Green information systems (Green IS) practice in organisations: tracing its emergence and recurrent use. In: 18th Americas Conference on Information Systems Proceedings, Seattle, Washington, p. 6 (2012)

29. Jenkin, T.A., Webster, J., McShane, L.: An agenda for 'Green' information technology and systems research. Inf. Organ. **21**(1), 17–40 (2011)
30. Jung, J.J., Chang, Y.-S., Liu, Y., Wu, C.-C.: Advances in intelligent grid and cloud computing. Inf. Syst. Front. **14**(4), 823–825 (2012). https://doi.org/10.1007/s10796-012-9349-x
31. Kraljic, A., Pestek, A.: An application of UTAUT2 model in exploring the impact of quality of technology on mobile Internet. Econ. Rev. J. Econ. Bus. **14**(2), 66–76 (2016). ISSN 1512-8962, University of Tuzla, Faculty of Economics, Tuzla
32. Kupfer, A., Ableitner, L., Schöb, S., Tiefenbeck, V.: Technology adoption vs. continuous usage intention: do decision criteria change when using a technology? Paper Presented at Twenty-Second AMCIS 2016, San Diego, USA, pp. 1–10 (2016)
33. Kurkoon, P., Pimchangthong, D., Boonjing, V.: A conceptual framework for individual Green Information Technology consumption and its impact. J. Bus. Manag. **3**(3), 388–396 (2018)
34. Lei, C.F., Ngai, E.W.T.: Green IS assimilation: a theoretical framework and research agenda. In: 18th Americas Conference on Information Systems Proceedings, Seattle, Washington, p. 2 (2012)
35. Lei, C.F., Ngai, E.W.T.: Green information technologies adoption: a managerial perspective. In: PACIS 2013 Proceedings, p. 274 (2013)
36. Leong, G.W., Ping, T.A., Muthuveloo, R.: Antecedents of behavioural intention to adopt Internet of Things in the context of smart city in Malaysia. Glob. Bus. Manag. Res. **9**, 442–456 (2017)
37. Mazuru, W., Mashavira, N., Chidoko, C.: Green information technology and its implication for business strategy in the banking sector in zimbabwe. **3**(8), 351–360 (2012)
38. Moini, H., Sorensen, O.J., Moini, H., Sorensen, O.J., Szuchy-Kristiansen, E.: Adoption of green strategy by Danish firms (2014). https://doi.org/10.1108/SAMPJ-01-2013-0003
39. Molla, A.: GITAM: a model for the adoption of Green IT. In: ACIS 2008 Conference Proceedings, Christchurch, New Zealand, p. 64 (2008)
40. Molla, A., Abareshi, A.: Organizational green motivations for information technology: empirical study. J. Comput. Inf. Syst. **52**(3), 92–102 (2012)
41. Molla, A., Abareshi, A.: Green IT adoption: a motivational perspective. In: PACIS Proceedings, p. 137 (2011)
42. Nanath, K., Pillai, R.R.: A sustainability model of Green IT initiatives. Paper Presented at International Conference on Information Systems 2012, Orlando (2012)
43. Nazari, G., Karim, H.: Green IT adoption: the impact of IT on environment: a case study on Green IT adoption and underlying factors influencing it. In: 17th Conference on Electrical Power Distribution Proceedings, pp. 1–7. IEEE (2012)
44. Nedbal, D., Wetzlinger, W., Auinger, A., Wagner, G.: Sustainable IS initialization through outsourcing: a theory-based approach. In: AMCIS Proceedings, p. 255 (2011)
45. Ozturk, A., Umit, K., Medeni, I.T., Ucuncu, B., Caylan, M., Akba, F., Medeni, T.D.: Green ICT (Information and Communication Technologies): a review of academic and practitioner perspectives. Int. J. eBusiness eGovernment Stud. **3**(1), 1–16 (2011)
46. Park, J.H., Jeong, H.Y.: Cloud computing-based jam management for a manufacturing system in a green IT environment. J. Supercomput. **69**(3), 1054–1067 (2013)
47. Pasolini, G., Alexandropoulos, G., Mucchi, L., Prieto, J., Shen, Y.: Energy and Spectrum Efficient Wireless Sensor Networks, pp. 2–4 (2016)
48. Radu, L.D.: Determinants of green ICT adoption in organizations: a theoretical perspective. Sustainability **8**(8), 731 (2016)

49. Raisinghani, M.S., Idemudia, E.C.: Green information systems for sustainability. In: Khosrow-Pour, M. (ed.) Green Business: Concepts, Methodologies, Tools, and Applications, pp. 565–579. IGI Global, Hershey (2019)
50. Robey, D., Zmud, R.: Research on the organization of end-user computing: theoretical perspectives from organizational science. Inf. Technol. People **6**(1), 11–27 (1992)
51. Rogers, E.M.: Diffusion of Innovations, 4th edn. Free Press, New York (1995)
52. Sahu, G.P., Singh, M.: Green information system adoption and sustainability: a case study of select Indian Banks. In: Dwivedi, Y.K., et al. (eds.) I3E 2016. LNCS, vol. 9844, pp. 292–304. Springer, Cham (2016). https://doi.org/10.1007/978-3-319-45234-0_27
53. Salimifard, K., Abbaszadeh, M.A., Ghorbanpur, A.: Interpretive structural modeling of critical success factors in banking process re-engineering. Int. Rev. Bus. Res. Pap. **6**(2), 95–103 (2010)
54. Salimon, M.G., Yusoff, R.Z.B., Mokhtar, S.S.M.: The mediating role of hedonic motivation on the relationship between adoption of e-banking and its determinants. Int. J. Bank Mark. **35**(4), 558–582 (2017)
55. Sarkar, P., Young, L.: Managerial attitudes towards Green IT: an explorative study of policy drivers. In: Proceedings of the 13th Pacific Asia Conference on Information Systems, Hyderabad, India, p. 95 (2009)
56. Sarkis, J., Koo, C., Watson, R.T.: Green information systems & technologies – this generation and beyond: introduction to the special issue. Inf. Syst. Front. **15**(5), 695–704 (2013). https://doi.org/10.1007/s10796-013-9454-5
57. Seidel, S., Recker, J., Vom Brocke, J.: Sensemaking and sustainable practicing: functional affordances of information systems in green transformations. MIS Q. **37**(4), 1275–1299 (2013)
58. Sekaran, U.: Research Methods for Business: A Skill-Building Approach, 3rd edn. Wiley, New York (2000)
59. Soomro, T.R., Sarwar, M.: Green computing: from current to future trends. World Acad. Sci. Eng. Technol. **63**, 538–541 (2012)
60. Stevens, E.M., Dillman Carpentier, F.R.: Facing our feelings: how natural coping tendencies explain when hedonic motivation predicts media use. Commun. Res. **44**(1), 3–28 (2017)
61. GeSI: The Global e-Sustainability Initiative (GeSI) and the Climate Group Report, SMART 2020: Enabling the low carbon economy in the information age, June 2008
62. Thomson, S., van Belle, J.P.: Antecedents of Green IT adoption in South African higher education institutions. Electron. J. Inf. Syst. Eval. **18**(2), 172 (2015)
63. Trimi, S., Park, S.-H.: Green IT: practices of leading firms and NGOs. Serv. Bus. **7**(3), 363–379 (2013). https://doi.org/10.1007/s11628-012-0163-9
64. Tuskeentushi, B., Sedera, D., Recker, J.: Green IT segment analysis an academic literature review. Paper Presented at Twentieth Americas Conference on Information Systems, Georgia, USA, pp. 1–15 (2013)
65. UNFCCC: Results of the 21st Conference of the Parties (COP21) to the United Nations Framework Convention on Climate Change (2015). http://unfccc.int/resource/docs/2015/cop21/eng/10a01.pdf
66. Venkatesh, V., Morris, M., Davis, G., Davis, F.: User acceptance of information technology: toward a unified view. MIS Q. **27**(3), 425–478 (2003)
67. Venkatesh, V., Thong, J.Y., Xu, X.: Consumer acceptance and use of information technology: extending the unified theory of acceptance and use of technology. MIS Q. **36**(1), 157–178 (2012)
68. Wang, Y.S., Li, H.T., Li, C.R., Zhang, D.Z.: Factors affecting hotels' adoption of mobile reservation systems: a technology-organization-environment framework. Tour. Manag. **53**, 163–172 (2016)

69. Watson, R.T., Boudreau, M.-C., Chen, A.J.: Information systems and environmentally sustainable development: energy informatics and new directions for the IS community. MIS Q. **34**(1), 23–38 (2010)
70. Weiss, A.: Can the PC go green? networker **11**(2), 18–25 (2007)
71. World Economic Forum Report (WEF): The Global Risks Report 2019 (2019). https://www.weforum.org/reports/the-global-risks-report-2019. Accessed 26 Jan 2019
72. World Economic Forum (WEF): Two Degrees of Transformation Businesses are coming together to lead on climate change. Will you join them? (2018). http://www3.weforum.org/docs/WEF_Two_Degrees_of_Transformation.pdf. Accessed 26 Jan 2019
73. Yang, Z., Sun, J., Zhang, Y., Wang, Y.: Perceived fit between green IS and green SCM: does it matter? Inf. Manag. **56**(7), 103154 (2019)
74. Zheng, D.: The adoption of green information technology and information systems: an evidence from corporate social responsibility. In: PACIS 2014 Proceedings, p. 237 (2014)

Consumer Insight on Driverless Automobile Technology Adoption via Twitter Data: A Sentiment Analytic Approach

Michael Adu Kwarteng[1,2](✉) , Alex Ntsiful[1,2] ,
Raphael Kwaku Botchway[1,2] , Michal Pilik[1,2] ,
and Zuzana Komínková Oplatková[1,2]

[1] Faculty of Management and Economics, Tomas Bata University in Zlin,
Mostni 5139, 760 01 Zlin, Czech Republic
{Kwarteng,Ntsiful,Botchway,Pilik,Kominkova}@utb.cz
[2] Faculty of Applied Informatics, Tomas Bata University in Zlin,
Nad Stráněmi 4511, 760 05 Zlin, Czech Republic

Abstract. Technology has sped up the innovation effort in the automobile industry. Further to this automobile innovation such as intelligent climate control, adaptive cruise control, and others, we find in today's vehicles, it has been predicted that by 2030, there will be driverless vehicles, of which samples are already on the market. The news and the sights of these so-called driverless vehicles have generated mixed reactions, and this motivated our study. Hence the present study focuses on a dataset of tweets associated with driverless vehicles downloaded using the Twitter API. Valence Aware Dictionary and sentiment Reasoner (VADER), a lexicon and rule-based sentiment analysis tool were used in extracting sentiments on the tweets to gauge public opinions about the acceptance and adoption of the driverless vehicles ahead of their launch. The VADER sentiment analysis results, however, show that the general discussion on driverless vehicles was positive. Besides, we generated a word cloud to visually analyze the terms in the dataset to gain further insights and understand the messages conveyed by the tweets in other to enhance the usage and adoption of driverless vehicles. This study will enable self-driving vehicle technology service providers and autonomous vehicle manufacturers to gain more insights on how to transform the transportation sector by investing in research and technology.

Keywords: Driverless vehicle · Twitter · Sentiment analysis · Autonomous · Technology · Innovation

1 Introduction

Technology has sped up the innovation effort in the automobile industry. A shred of evidence is that most of the latest vehicles we find in town are endowed with technological advancements such as automatic braking systems, crash sensors, cruise control, auto speed control, intelligent climate control, adaptive cruise control, advanced emergency braking system, and many others. Further to these advancements,

S. K. Sharma et al. (Eds.): TDIT 2020, IFIP AICT 617, pp. 463–473, 2020.
https://doi.org/10.1007/978-3-030-64849-7_41

research indicates that by 2030, the automobile industry could fully introduce unto the market, another dynamic product-driverless vehicle (Panayiotopoulos and Dimitrakopoulos 2018) which could oust the driver from his/her seat literally. With its other variant names such as an un-crewed car, unmanned vehicle, self-drive car, robot car, and the like, driverless vehicle is a type of automobile designed and equipped with artificial intelligence (AI) in such a way that it can self-sense its environment and navigate safely to its destination. It is popularly known in the literature as autonomous vehicles (AVs) but for this paper and many variant audiences in mind, we will use a driverless vehicle. It is interesting to note that there are already some of these vehicles on the market, though most of them are being piloted. Young (2015) cites Mercedes Benz F015, General Motors GM ENV, Google self-driving car, Servvan Robotic Vehicle, BMW E-patrol, BMW Honey Comb, and the Zoox Level 4 Reversible, as examples of driverless vehicles available. Young notes that some of these vehicles are so intelligent that they could sense the driver's capabilities and decide to take over the driving when necessary.

However, it is important to note that driverless vehicles would not replace the traditional vehicles but would rather serve as an addition to the levels of vehicles we have in the automobile industry. In line with this assumption, SAE international (2016) explains that there would be five levels of vehicles with level 0 being the fleet of vehicles which is fully operated by humans and level 4 as those vehicles fully driven without any human involvement. The levels of 1–3 vehicles are classified depending on the level of their 'autonomousity' or the amount of human involvement in operating them. Extant studies have argued that the adoption of driverless vehicles on our road comes with a myriad of advantages (Piao et al. 2016; Sparrow and Howard 2017; Meyer et al. 2017). Examples of these benefits include a new line of business (Litman 2017), reduction in road accidents (KPMG International 2019; Piao et al. 2016), and new transport service, and new transport means for the aged and physically impaired (Sparrow and Howard 2017; Meyer et al. 2017). For instance, Piao et al (2016) explain that driverless vehicles could reduce road accidents by 90% because these accidents are caused by human errors due to factors such as fatigue, alcohol, carelessness, and the influence of drugs. Despite these merits, another stream of research has found that some members of society think that accepting driverless vehicles in our fleet may be problematic. They explain that the challenges, which come with the current level of automobile innovations, mentioned earlier, have not been fully resolved (Panagiotopoulos and Dimitrakopoulos 2018). For instance, studies such as (Milakis et al. 2017; Van Brummelen et al. 2018) have found that drivers have trust issues with automated system vehicles and also believe that the automated systems come with some workload and situation awareness issues for the drivers. To this end, researchers have begun to engage the public on their possible acceptance of the incoming technology and also the factors that could influence their adoption (Payre et al. 2014; Xu et al. 2018). Thus, to add to this body of initial and pre-driverless vehicle launching research is the main objective of this study. However, we approach this research task with a different method, that is, the sentiment analysis via twitter data. Specifically, the study seeks to gauge the public opinions (positive and negative) about the acceptance and adoption of the driverless vehicles ahead of their launch to offer insights to engineers, product designers, and policymakers of automobile industries, especially those specializing in unmanned vehicles, by using sentiment analysis via twitter.

We believe that both the generation Z and generation alpha, who would be ultimate users of the driverless vehicles, mostly use social media to search for information on the latest technology (Rathore et al. 2016), and that a medium such as the twitter could give reach information needed for the study. We also contend that using a survey to ask people 'on the street' about the driverless vehicle, they might have not seen a demo, a method which the previous studies used (e.g. Daziano et al. 2017; Chowdhury and Ceder 2016) may not be realistic or the best. With the sentiment analysis, we can extract, from people who have seen a demo of this yet-to-be-launched innovation, rich data of opinions, ideas, challenges, and other sentiments they may have with the technology. We also contend that the sentimental data is richer in that they are not responses to a survey question where a respondent may give socially desirable answers but we are extracting 'post-natural responses to unasked questions. Moreover, this study's population is global, as we do not use twitter sentiments from one location but all users of twitter. Our study is indeed significant for several reasons: First, we argue that, apart from the unique methodological approach highlighted above, the findings of this study will set the tone for further deductive empirical research. Second, the findings can also serve as a guide to policymakers in developing automobiles, and road and traffic management policies. Finally, the results can also guide driverless vehicle engineers to incorporate consumer preferences and challenges into driverless vehicle engineering designs.

The rest of the paper is organized as follows. Next to this introduction is the literature review, followed by a snapshot of sentiment analytic approach. Following that is the analysis of data and findings. We end the paper with a short discussion and conclusion.

2   Literature Review

2.1   Automobile Technology Adoption and Consumer Insights

Like with any other innovation, which comes to the market, customers may be skeptical of the driverless vehicle and would begin to raise questions on several issues. For instance, in Egbue and Longs (2012) study involving consumers' attitudes towards the adoption of electric vehicles, it was found that cost and performance were rated higher than environmental and sustainability benefits. Before this finding, Axsen et al. (2010) have found that limitations with battery technology and the high cost of the battery were key barriers to electric vehicle adoption. Similarly, the cost has been anticipated to be a potential barrier to adoption when driverless vehicles become fully functional (Fagnant and Kockelman 2015). They explain that driverless vehicles require technologies like sensors, software for each automobile, and communication and guidance technology, which are expensive and build up to the total cost of the vehicle. In this regard, Shchetko (2014) estimates that Light Detection and Ranging (LIDAR) systems, a common essential device for driverless vehicles, is priced between cost $30,000 to

$85,000 and this cost excludes the cost of software, sensors, software, engineering, and extra power and computing requirements.

By giving a fair idea of how much driverless vehicles may cost, we refer to Dellenback (2013) estimates of the cost of 2013 civilian and military driverless vehicles, which stood at $100,000 in 2013. Further, earlier studies have also found other adoption challenges for driverless vehicles including trust (Bansal et al. 2016; Kyriakidis et al. 2015). Although Paden et al. (2016) have highlighted high carbon emission, excessive traffic and accidents as the challenges we have with the conventional vehicles, problems which are not found with the driverless vehicle, Fagnant and Kockelman (2015)'s findings of security, trust, privacy, reliability, and liability with the autonomous vehicle cannot be discounted. By shedding more light on these concerns, Fagnant and Kockelman (2015) argue that there is the need to worry about electronic security as there are possibilities of computer hackers, terrorist organizations, and demotivated employees who could sabotage driverless vehicle and that could result in accidents and traffic on the roads. When the driverless vehicle becomes operational, data and information sharing become a common ritual and that is where privacy issues set in (Fagnant and Kockelman (2015). Despite these drawbacks, Kaur and Rampersad (2018) argue that there may be certain situations, which would make some consumers opt for driverless vehicles as compared to others, and that further research is needed to uncover those situations.

2.2 Overview of Driverless Automobile Technology

The definition for driverless vehicle ranges from a vehicle that operates without human driver (Paden et al. 2016), to a vehicle whose critical control functions such as steering, braking, throttling is managed without the driver's support (NHTSA 2013). It is envisaged that the introduction of the driverless vehicle can help reduce about 1.2 million road fatalities, which according to WHO (2015), occurs every year. Interest in this driverless automobile technology is said to have started as far back as 1939 during the World's Fair held in New York (Levy 2016). However, LeValley (2013) reports that fully developed autonomy occurred in the early 21st Century. Levy explains that the developer of these autonomous technologies took inspiration from the Defense Advanced Research Projects Agency (DARPA), which developed driverless technology for the military. According to DARPA (2014), the military driverless vehicle was intended to reduce the number of soldiers who lose their lives on the war front. Gradually, DARPA continued to develop this concept until they had a breakthrough (called the DRAPA's first Urban Challenge) in 2007 when they have autonomous vehicles, which were capable of navigating through city-like terrain, obey traffic regulations, change and merging lanes while avoiding road obstructions.

Since that breakthrough, interest in autonomous vehicles has surged up. Extant studies have it that technology giants like Google, Testa, and Uber, and well-known automobile firms like General Motors, Ford (all in the US) together with their European and Japan counterparts have made significant progress in this regard (Chehri and Mouftah 2019). As the tech and automobile giants make progress, governments and legislative bodies begin to develop strategies, promulgate laws and regulation, and build infrastructure like smart cities, to support and in ahead of the launch of the driverless vehicles. Infrastructures are very essential to its success because, according to Chehri and Mouftah (2019) autonomous vehicle uses a different range of technologies including radar, cameras, radio antennas, and the support of artificial intelligence, 5G network to safely navigate on roads. This suggests that for a country to adopt driverless vehicles certain infrastructures must be in place as well as amendments to its laws, especially those relating road and traffic issues.

To this end, Johnsen et al. (2017) indicate that German Bundestag has reviewed their Road Traffic Act given this new paradigm shift in the automobile industry. A section of the amended Road Traffic Act reads: *'The driver may turn his attention away from the traffic situation and vehicle operation if the car is in an automated or autonomous driving mode, but she/he must in principle remain vigilant so that he can immediately take control of the vehicle again, if necessary (Johnsen et al. 2017, p. 49).* Moreover, many other countries are preparing well for the task ahead in automobile technology and this has led to a periodic compilation of countries' readiness, known in literature now as Autonomous Vehicle Readiness Index (AVRI) by KPMG international since 2018. Thus, according to KPMG (2019)'s Autonomous Vehicle Readiness Index (AVRI), there are about 25 countries that are ready to embrace the driverless vehicles' agenda with Netherland leading the chart. The AVRI has four key measures and these include policy and legislation, technology and innovation, infrastructure, and consumer acceptance. Netherland leads the 2019 chart because it had 1st position in the infrastructural ranking, 2nd on consumer acceptance, 5th on policy and legislation, and 10th in technology and innovation category, culminating to total points of 25.05. Four other countries following Netherland include Singapore (2^{nd,} 24.32 points), Norway (3rd, 23.75). United States (4th, 22.58 points), and Sweden (5th, 22.48 points). For the comprehensive list of the ranking, see the KPMG AVRI report 2019.

2.3 A Snapshot of Sentiment Analytic Approach via Twitter

Sentiment analysis, popularly known as opinion mining, has been long studied in both academia and the industry (Grover and Akar 2017; Kar and Dwivedi 2020). It employs computational algorithms in the form of natural language processing bent on identifying sentiment polarity, intensity, and topics, particularly where the so-called sentiments apply (Liu et al. 2005; Chamlertwat et al. 2012). Sentiment analysis in practice turns out to automate opinion discovery and classification systems that deal with a huge amount of data by purposefully extracting and understanding complex human-generated content/judgment. (Lake 2011)

In the last decade, the concept of sentiment analysis has become one of the most topical and researched areas in machine learning (see, Agarwal et al. 2011; Whitelaw et al. 2005). Technically, sentiment analysis applies to different levels of text granularity (Agarwal et al. 2011). Thus, the scope of the sentiment analysis process involves document-level classification task to a finer-grain level of a sentence and then to the phrase level for execution. (Wilson et al. 2005). However, there are two main approaches used in sentiment analysis, and these can be categorized under the machine learning approach and Lexicon based approach. The machine learning approach works as a supervised learning approach where the training process involves classifies input into output manually. Once training data with sentiment values are captured by the process, the corresponding domain data will generate results. On the other hand, the lexicon-based approach used in this study works as an unsupervised learning approach. It works based on the features fed by the encoded sentimental lexicon score to analyze the polarity whether it is positive or negative.

Over the years, sentiment analysis has been used extensively in several areas such as deducing opinions of customers' in the banking sector (Botchway et al. 2020), products review data analysis (Fang and Zhang 2015), gaining insights in telecommunication usage in Ghana (Nabareseh et al. 2018)

2.4   Research Questions

Extant literature has shed more light on user-generated content on social media (Afful-Dadzie et al. 2016; Feldman 2013; Aggarwal et al. 2011). This paper employed opinion mining/sentiment analysis to do a rigorous analysis using unstructured textual information on Twitter sites (data). The following research questions guided the study.

1. What are the characteristics of driverless vehicle adoption tweets? Are there any patterns of negativity or positivity associated with the adoption and usage of driverless cars on twitter sites?
2. What are the sentiments of driverless vehicles tweets? How do customers feel about the use of driverless cars?

3   Methodology

3.1   Data Collection and Pre-processing

Twitter has become the most preferred social media channel with 330 million monthly active users according to Statista (2019). The dataset consists of 11,000 tweets collected between May, 20, 2020, and June 29, 2020, using the Twitter streaming Application Programming Interface (API). With the help of the python library Tweepy (Feldman 2013), we collected tweets that contained the keyword "self-driving cars" on Twitter (Fig. 1).

We then proceeded to clean the text by removing duplicate tweets, punctuations, stop words, URLs, slangs, @ symbol used to mention usernames and converted all text to lowercase. Additionally, we omit terms with low frequency and filter out meaningless words. Consequently, 9590 documents (tweets) were stored as a corpus in a comma separated value (CSV) format after the cleaning process.

3.2   Document Analysis

We used a lexicon-based sentiment analysis approach for our work (Grover et al. 2018). Although the lexicon approach is considered an unsupervised method, it is a major sentiment analysis technique that categorizes text documents into a set of predefined sentiment classes. The Valence Aware Sentiment Dictionary and Reasoner (VADER), a lexicon and rule-based tool specifically attune to sentiments expressed on

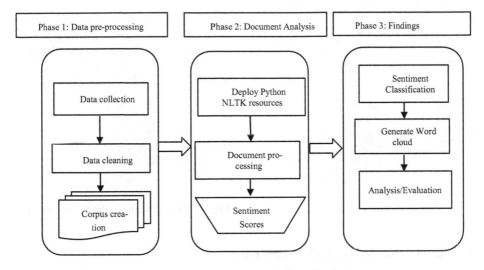

Fig. 1. Model framework of our Study

social media (Hutto and Gilbert 2014) were deployed from the python NLTK 3.4.1 toolkit. Given a document, VADER examines its lexical features to determine an initial sentiment score before applying five different rules based on grammatical conventions and syntax to amend that score. These rules handle capitalization and exclamation marks as sentiment amplifiers. Besides, they also handle negations and contrastive conjunctions well. VADER produces positive, negative, neutral, and compound scores for each tweet in the dataset. The positive, negative, and neutral scores are ratios for proportions of text that lie in these categories whereas the compound score sums up all the lexicon ratings which have been normalized between −1(most extreme negative) and +1(most extreme positive).

3.3   Findings

Our initial experiments reveal that VADER with a threshold value of 0.2 produces the best values of precision and recall, with an improvement in both classification directions (positive and negative) in terms of metrics. Hence documents (tweets) with VADER scores greater than 0.2 were classified as positive, documents with scores between 0 and 0.2 are classified and neutral with all other tweets with scores less than zero classified as negative. Out of 9590 documents (tweets), 4014, 1976, and 3600 were classified as positive, negative, and neural respectively. Figure 2 shows the proportion of sentiment classes. We generate a word cloud based on the frequencies of the words used in the dataset to determine the size of the words to gain further insights into the opinions expressed in the tweets.

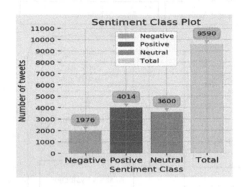

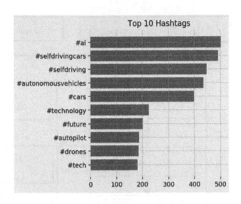

Fig. 2. Sentiment class graph   **Fig. 3.** Top 10 hashtags from the dataset

4   Short Discussion and Conclusion

In this study, we performed the sentiment analysis of 9590 tweets using the VADER lexicon. The tweets were classified into three classes namely: positive, negative, and neutral. VADER classified 4014 tweets as positive while 1611 and 3965 tweets were classified as negative and neutral respectively. The sentiment analysis results indicate that the overall discussion on self-driving cars in terms of usage and adoption involving stakeholders on Twitter was positive. This is quite encouraging judging from the increasing popularity self-driving vehicle technology is currently enjoying coupled with its huge potential to transform the transportation system (and by extension the economy and society). Analysing Fig. 3 (Top 10 hashtags) and Fig. 4 (word cloud of negative sentiments) provides further insights from different perspectives. Artificial intelligence (AI) tops the list in Fig. 3 which shows the significant impact and pioneering role of AI in autonomous vehicle development (Maayan-Wainstein 2020). An example is deep reinforcement learning (DRL), which combines strategies of deep learning and reinforcement learning to enhance the automation of training algorithms in applications used for lower-level vehicle automation. Since the bigger and bolder a word appears in a word cloud depicts the importance and frequency with which the word is mentioned within a given context, prominent words like "car", "people", "crashes", "ai", "problem" found in the negative sentiment word cloud raises safety and technology issues that require attention. Investigating the tweets containing these terms to find out the actual message they carry will go a long way to enhance the usage and adoption of autonomous vehicles. In our view, the explanation provided above adequately answers research questions 1 and 2, which also collaborates with recent studies performed by researchers (Botchway et al. 2019; Nabareseh et al. 2018; Ibrahim and Wang 2019). Ignoring non-English tweets was a major limitation to this study since their inclusion could potentially enrich the work by providing further insights that could be exploited. In the future, methods such as topic modeling and time-series amongst others could be applied to improve the analysis of tweets in the dataset.

Fig. 4. Negative sentiments word cloud

Acknowledgment. This work was supported by the research project NPU I no. MSMT-7778/2019 RVO - Digital Transformation and its Impact on Customer Behaviour and Business Processes in Traditional and Online markets and IGA/CebiaTech/2020/001. The work was further supported by the resources of A.I. Lab at the Faculty of Applied Informatics, Tomas Bata University in Zlin (ailab.fai.utb.cz).

References

Afful-Dadzie, E., Nabareseh, S., Oplatková, Z.K., Klímek, P.: Framing media coverage of the 2014 sony pictures entertainment hack: a topic modelling approach. In: Proceedings of the 11th International Conference on Cyber Warfare and Security: ICCWS 2016, p. 1 (2016)

Agarwal, A., Xie, B., Vovsha, I., Rambow, O., Passonneau, R.J.: Sentiment analysis of Twitter data. In: Proceedings of the Workshop on Language in Social Media (LSM 2011), pp. 30–38, June 2011

Axsen, J., Kurani, K.S., Burke, A.: Are batteries ready for plug-in hybrid buyers? Transp. Policy **17**(3), 173–182 (2010). https://doi.org/10.1016/j.tranpol.2010.01.004

Bansal, P., Kockelman, K.M., Singh, A.: Assessing public opinions of and interest in new vehicle technologies: an Austin perspective. Transp. Res. Part C Emerg. Technol. **67**, 1–14 (2016). https://doi.org/10.1016/j.trc.2016.01.019

Botchway, R.K., Jibril, A.B., Kwarteng, M.A., Chovancova, M., Oplatková, Z.K.: A review of social media posts from UniCredit bank in Europe: a sentiment analysis approach. In: Proceedings of the 3rd International Conference on Business and Information Management, pp. 74–79, September 2019. https://doi.org/10.1145/3361785.3361814

Botchway, R.K., Jibril, A.B., Oplatková, Z.K., Chovancová, M.: Deductions from a Sub-Saharan African Bank's Tweets: a sentiment analysis approach. Cogent Econ. Finance **8**(1), 1776006 (2020). https://doi.org/10.1080/23322039.2020.1776006

Chamlertwat, W., Bhattarakosol, P., Rungkasiri, T., Haruechaiyasak, C.: Discovering consumer insight from Twitter via sentiment analysis. J. UCS. **18**(8), 973–992 (2012)

Chehri, A., Mouftah, H.T.: Autonomous vehicles in the sustainable cities, the beginning of a green adventure. Sustain. Cities Soc. **51**, 101751 (2019). https://doi.org/10.1016/j.scs.2019.101751

Chowdhury, S., Ceder, A.A.: Users' willingness to ride an integrated public transport service: a literature review. Transp. Policy **48**, 183–195 (2016). https://doi.org/10.1016/j.tranpol.2016.03.00

Daziano, R.A., Sarrias, M., Leard, B.: Are consumers willing to pay to let cars drive for them? Analyzing response to autonomous vehicles. Transp. Res. Part C Emerg. Technol. **78**, 150–164 (2017). https://doi.org/10.1016/j.trc.2017.03.003

Dellenback, S.: Director, intelligent systems department, automation, and data systems division, southwest research institute. Communication by email, 26 May 2013

Egbue, O., Long, S.: Barriers to widespread adoption of electric vehicles: an analysis of consumer attitudes and perceptions. Energy policy **48**, 717–729 (2012)

Fagnant, D.J., Kockelman, K.: Preparing a nation for autonomous vehicles: opportunities, barriers and policy recommendations. Transp. Res. Part A Policy Pract. **77**, 167–181 (2015). https://doi.org/10.1016/j.tra.2015.04.003

Fang, X., Zhan, J.: Sentiment analysis using product review data. J. Big Data **2**(1), 1–14 (2015). https://doi.org/10.1186/s40537-015-0015-2

Feldman, R.: Techniques and applications for sentiment analysis. Commun. ACM **56**(4), 82–89 (2013). https://doi.org/10.1145/2436256.2436274

Grover, P., Kar, A.K.: Big data analytics: a review on theoretical contributions and tools used in literature. Glob. J. Flex. Syst. Manag. **18**(3), 203–229 (2017). https://doi.org/10.1007/s40171-017-0159-3

Grover, P., Kar, A.K., Davies, G.: "Technology enabled Health"–insights from Twitter analytics with a socio-technical perspective. Int. J. Inf. Manag. **43**, 85–97 (2018)

Hutto, C.J., Gilbert, E.: Vader: a parsimonious rule-based model for sentiment analysis of social media text. In: Eighth International AAAI Conference on Weblogs and Social Media, May 2014

Ibrahim, N.F., Wang, X.: Decoding the sentiment dynamics of online retailing customers: time series analysis of social media. Comput. Hum. Behav. **96**, 32–45 (2019). https://doi.org/10.1016/j.chb.2019.02.004

Johnsen, A., Strand, N., Andersson, J., Patten, C., Kraetsch, C., Takman, J.: D2. 1 Literature review on the acceptance and road safety, ethical, legal, social and economic implications of automated vehicles (2017)

Kar, A.K., Dwivedi, Y.K.: Theory building with big data-driven research–moving away from the "What" towards the "Why". Int. J. Inf. Manag. **54**, 102205 (2020)

Kaur, K., Rampersad, G.: Trust in driverless cars: Investigating key factors influencing the adoption of driverless cars. J. Eng. Tech. Manag. **48**, 87–96 (2018). https://doi.org/10.1016/j.jengtecman.2018.04.006

KPMG International: 2019 Autonomous Vehicle Readiness Index, Assessing countries preparedness for autonomous vehicles (2019)

Kyriakidis, M., Happee, R., de Winter, J.C.: Public opinion on automated driving: Results of an international questionnaire among 5000 respondents. Transp. Res. Part F Traffic Psychol. Behav. **32**, 127–140 (2015). https://doi.org/10.1016/j.jengtecman.2018.04.006

Lake, T.: Twitter Sentiment Analysis. Western Michigan University, Kalamazoo (2011)

LeValley, D.: Autonomous vehicle liability—application of common carrier liability (2013)

Levy, J.: No need to reinvent the wheel: why existing liability law does not need to be preemptively altered to cope with the debut of the driverless car. J. Bus. Entrepreneurship Law **9**, 355 (2016). http://digitalcommons.pepperdine.edu/jbel/vol9/iss2/5

Litman, T.: Autonomous vehicle implementation predictions. Victoria Transport Policy Institute, Victoria, Canada (2017)

Liu, B., Hu, M., Cheng, J.: Opinion observer: analyzing and comparing opinions on the web. In: Proceedings of the 14th International Conference on World Wide Web, pp. 342–351, May 2005

Maayan-Wainsten, L.: Four Innovations Taking Autonomous Vehicle AI to the Next Level, 6 July 2020 (2020). https://www.enterpriseai.news/2020/07/06/4-innovations-taking-autonom ous-vehicle-ai-to-thenext-level/. Accessed 7 July 2020

Meyer, J., Becker, H., Bösch, P.M., Axhausen, K.W.: Autonomous vehicles: the next jump in accessibilities? Res. Transp. Econ. **62**, 80–91 (2017). https://doi.org/10.1016/j.retrec.2017.03.005

Milakis, D., Van Arem, B., Van Wee, B.: Policy and society related implications of automated driving: a review of literature and directions for future research. J. Intell. Transp. Syst. **21**(4), 324–348(2017)

Nabareseh, S., Afful-Dadzie, E., Klimek, P.: Leveraging fine-grained sentiment analysis for competitivity. J. Inf. Knowl. Manag. **17**(02), 1850018 (2018)

National Highway Traffic Safety Administration. NHTSA: Preliminary statement of policy concerning automated vehicles, Washington, DC (2013)

Paden, B., Čáp, M., Yong, S.Z., Yershov, D., Frazzoli, E.: A survey of motion planning and control techniques for self-driving urban vehicles. IEEE Trans. Intell. Veh. **1**(1), 33–55 (2016)

Panagiotopoulos, I., Dimitrakopoulos, G.: An empirical investigation on consumers' intentions towards autonomous driving. Transp. Res. Part C Emerg. Technol. **95**, 773–784 (2018)

Payre, W., Cestac, J., Delhomme, P.: Intention to use a fully automated car: attitudes and a priori acceptability. Transp. Res. Part F Traffic Psychol. Behav. **27**, 252–263 (2014). https://doi.org/ 10.1016/j.trf.2014.04.009

Piao, J., McDonald, M., Hounsell, N., Graindorge, M., Graindorge, T., Malhene, N.: Public views towards implementation of automated vehicles in urban areas. Transp. Res. Procedia **14**, 2168–2177 (2016). https://doi.org/10.1016/j.trpro.2016.05.232

Rathore, A.K., Ilavarasan, P.V., Dwivedi, Y.K.: Social media content and product co-creation: an emerging paradigm. J. Enterp. Inf. Manag. **29**, 7–18 (2016)

SAE International: Taxonomy and definitions for terms related to driving automation systems for on-road motor vehicles. SAE International (J3016) (2016)

Shchetko, N.: Laser eyes pose price hurdle for driverless cars. Wall Street J. (2014)

Sparrow, R., Howard, M.: When human beings are like drunk robots: driverless vehicles, ethics, and the future of transport. Transp. Res. Part C Emerg. Technol. **80**, 206–215 (2017). https:// doi.org/10.1016/j.trc.2017.04.014

Statista. Number of monthly active twitter users worldwide from 1st quarter 2010 to 1st quarter 2019 (in millions) (2019). https://www.statista.com/statistics/282087/number-of-monthly-active-twitter-users

Van Brummelen, J., O'Brien, M., Gruyer, D., Najjaran, H.: Autonomous vehicle perception: the technology of today and tomorrow. Transp. Res. Part C Emerg. Technol. **89**, 384–406 (2018). https://doi.org/10.1016/j.trc.2018.02.012

Wilson, T., Wiebe, J., Hoffmann, P.: Recognizing contextual polarity in phrase-level sentiment analysis. In: Proceedings of Human Language Technology Conference and Conference on Empirical Methods in Natural Language Processing, pp. 347–354 (2015)

Whitelaw, C., Garg, N., Argamon, S.: Using appraisal groups for sentiment analysis. In: Proceedings of the 14th ACM International Conference on Information and Knowledge Management, pp. 625–631, October 2005

WHO: Global Status Report on Road Safety 2015. World Health Organization (2015). http://www. who.int/violence_injury_prevention/road_safety_status/2015/en/. Accessed 27 June 2020

Xu, Z., Zhang, K., Min, H., Wang, Z., Zhao, X., Liu, P.: What drives people to accept automated vehicles? Findings from a field experiment. Transp. Res. Part C Emerg. Technol. **95**, 320–334 (2018). https://doi.org/10.1016/j.trc.2018.07.024

Young, M.: From Motorist-Monitoring Autos to Self-Driving Trucks (2015). https://www. trendhunter.com/slideshow/autonomous-vehicles. Accessed 26 June 2020

A Study on the Factors Influencing Behavioral Intention of Indian Consumers in Adopting Voice Assistants

Dimple Kaul, Mohak Shah$^{(\boxtimes)}$, and Neeraj Dhakephalkar

K.J. Somaiya Institute of Management, Mumbai 400077, India
mohak.shah@somaiya.edu

Abstract. In the past few years, Internet of Things (IoT) has led to multiple devices interacting with humans as well as other devices, helping create a huge network of these entities that share data on a regular basis. The use cases of IoT technology have become synonymous with devices used to enable "Smart Home", wherein various applications inside the house are usually controlled using smartphones or smart speakers. These Smart Speakers and Smart Phones are enabled using Voice Assistants developed by various Tech Giants from all over the world. Various Tech Companies have developed their own Voice Assistants that are integrated in multiple devices, ranging from Smart phones, Smart Speakers to Smart TVs. Using their ability to connect to the Internet and the eco-system formed by the Tech Giants, Voice Assistants are helping to improve the quality of life.

Despite the extensive coverage in media, review of Literature showed that no such research about adoption of Voice Assistants by Indian Consumers has been conducted. There hasn't been any study that evaluates factors that influence the adoption of Voice Assistants by Indian Consumers. That is the gap which this research addresses and tries to fill. Through this study, we aim to build a model which finds out Indian consumers' acceptance of Voice Assistants for this technology to reach commercialisation.

The purpose of this study is to explore the user attitudes, satisfaction, and other factors governing and encouraging or discouraging the intention of Indian Consumers to adopt Voice Assistants. Through analysis, we can find out the inconveniences of adoption and usage process and propose the direction of product improvement.

Keywords: Internet of Things (IoT) · Voice assistants · Behavioral intention · System quality · Perceived usefulness · Perceived ease of use · Behavioral control · Intention to use

1 Introduction

In recent years, the use of devices such as Smart phones and speakers has become widespread in India. According to a recent research carried out by Edison research- a US based research firm, smart speakers are influencing a wide range of consumer habits like reduction in their time spent with screens, consumption of audio content like news,

© IFIP International Federation for Information Processing 2020
Published by Springer Nature Switzerland AG 2020
S. K. Sharma et al. (Eds.): TDIT 2020, IFIP AICT 617, pp. 474–483, 2020.
https://doi.org/10.1007/978-3-030-64849-7_42

music, documents, podcasts, commerce etc. This revolution has been accelerated by lower data costs over the past few years in the country. The market for smart speakers was established in India in 2017 with the successful launch of Amazon Echo. Since then, many companies have launched various products that compete with each other. But the response of these consumers in India hasn't been as positive as that of foreign users. It really brings up the question of whether the Voice Assistants that meet the needs and requirements of foreign users can really adapt to the Indian Market. Each country is different and the consumers differ extensively as well. If the Voice Assistant usage in India has to increase beyond the initial uptake, then companies like Amazon and Google will have to adapt for the Indian audiences to increase acceptance and improve experience. Given the huge investment that has been made by Technology Companies in creating their own respective ecosystems, it is very important to understand and explain the intention of Indian consumers to adopt Voice Assistants.

2 Literature Review

This (Berdasco et al. 2019) study evaluates two dimensions of Voice Assistants: how natural the answers sound to the users and correctness of the answers. The findings showed that Google Assistant and Alexa are way better as compared to Cortana and Siri. Cortana and Siri provided the poorest performance according to the research. Siri is one of the most popular Voice Assistants being used in the US, due to the popularity of iPhones there and yet showed poor performance as compared to Google Assistants and Alexa.

The study conducted by (Hwang 2018) examined the kind of effect that consumer satisfaction towards smart speakers may have on usage intentions and expression of loyalty towards the brand. User Satisfaction was calculated based on 2 parameters: Information Quality and System Quality of the smart speaker. The findings showed that the ones who were satisfied with smart speakers were using the service continuously and expressed loyalty towards the brand. Frequency of use of these devices also had a positive influence on intention to use.

A recent study carried out by (Xiao and Kim 2018) showed a comparison between the experience of users with two of the most popular Smart Speakers in China: MI AI Speaker and Tmall Genie. The users were found to be uncomfortable with the functional aspect of the Smart Speakers. These users also expressed their discomfort when it came to the usability aspect of these devices. The research also showed that very few participants use the smart speakers to control smart home devices due to the fact that penetration of smart home appliances in China is very meagre. This is actually a big selling point of smart speakers which cannot be made use of in China.

This study conducted by (Kowalczuk 2018) was primarily to identify the factors that motivate or discourage consumers from using Smart Speakers in their daily lives. In order to conduct this research, acceptance models were tested, whilst following a mixed approach. The study found out that enjoyment had a strong effect on usage intention of consumers. Also, the results showed that security/ privacy risk, system diversity, technology optimism of consumers, and system quality had a huge impact on consumer acceptance. Apart from these factors, perceived ease of use and perceived usefulness had effect on consumer acceptance.

(Chu 2019) conducted research in order to find out the factors that would affect a consumer's intention to adopt a smart speaker. A new model that was extended and developed using the Technology Acceptance Model (TAM) was proposed. The characteristics that were analysed in the model were product characteristics, social factors, consumer characteristics and financial factors. Some of the variables considered included attitude, enjoyment, Internet of Things (IOT) skills, social influence, cost, consumer self-innovativeness, trust, and reliability. Findings showed that Factors like Social Influence and Trust had a big impact on consumer intention to adopt smart speakers. Factors like security/privacy, IOT Skills, social influence also had an effect, Trust proved very useful in predicting attitude and perceived ease of use (PEOU).

3   Conceptual Model

The Research Model of this study uses Technology Acceptance Model (TAM) penned down by Davis in 1989 alongwith Theory of Planned Behavior (TPB) by Ajzen (1991) in order to understand and predict the behavioural Intention of Indian Consumers in regards with adoption of Voice Assistants. The following factors are examined in this Research: System Quality, Security, Perceived Cost, Self-Innovativeness, Perceived Usefulness, Perceived Ease of Use, Attitude, Social Norms, Perceived Behavioral Control and Intention to Use and their relationship with each other.

The conceptual model of study is shown as under:

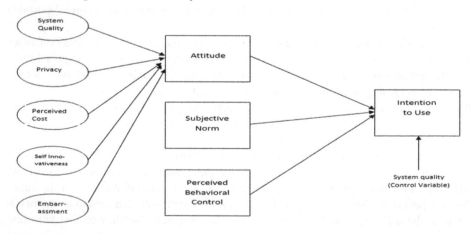

4   Research Model and Hypothesis Development

The model to be used for estimating the behavioural intentions towards usage of voice assistants and smart speakers is a hybrid model which considers the parameters of both TAM and TPB theories.

4.1   Exogenous Variables

1. System Quality

System Quality is defined as the observed quality of the various performance features of the system. The sound of the speakers, Response time, Robustness, Quality of responses etc. are the variables which contribute the system quality of smart speakers and voice assistants.

H4. System Quality is positively associated with attitudes to using smart home services.

2. Security/privacy risk:

Smart voice assistant systems collect data about residents' lifestyles, such as purchase preferences, in order to support them effectively. Consequently, these systems face the challenge of ensuring the safety of personal data (Balta-Ozkan et al. 2014). Kalakota and Whinston (1997) defined security risk as a "circumstance, condition, or event with the potential to cause economic hardship to data or network resources in the form of destruction, disclosure, modification of data, denial of service, and/or fraud, waste, and abuse." Security risk includes the risk of the violation of a user's privacy. In this study, therefore, security/privacy risk refers to voice assistant users' fear that their personal data will be leaked or that systems will be hacked by criminals.

H5. Security/privacy risk is negatively associated with attitudes toward using voice assistant services.

3. Perceived Cost

The perceived costs of systems strike a balance between the ease that a particular system caters to the price of installing the particular system. A rational person will implement a solution only if the perceived cost is less than the benefits catered by the solution. It is very difficult to enlist the benefits linked to cost or monetary savings in case of using voice assistants or smart speakers.

H6. Perceived Cost is negatively associated with the attitudes towards using smart speakers.

4. Self-Innovativeness

Self-innovativeness is the motivation (internal/external) to try using new technologies as an experiment. It is the behaviour trait where people use newer technologies on their own and find experimentation worth the time spent. The people who are innovators, having an inclination towards technology use latest technology devices.

H7. Self-innovativeness is positively associated with the attitudes towards using voice assistant.

5. Embarrassment

This is an important factor as far as using technology is considered. People face social difficulties when trying to communicate with a device in public. It's this embarrassment that restricts many people from using voice assistants in public. Man people especially in India consider talking to a voice assistant in public to be socially weird or unusual.

H8. Embarrassment is negatively associated with the attitudes towards using voice assistants.

5 Research Methodology

Primary as well as secondary research was carried out to understand the phenomenon of behavioural intention of using Voice Assistants in India.

Survey Instrument: The mentioned relationships have been examined by the means of a structured questionnaire. The questionnaire consists of 24 questions as shown in Table 7. Other demographic variables such as age, gender, profession, and level of education are also considered.

Target Respondents: The sample size consists of 100 respondents. Both males and females are taken into consideration. The respondents are included from diverse age groups, and levels of education practicing different professions.

Procedure: An online questionnaire consisting of all the questions was circulated amongst a sample set and they were asked to answer the questions. The responses were recorded for interpretation, analysis and discussion. SPSS was used to understand the effects of independent variables on the dependent ones and also to understand the strength of the relationships between the variables.

6 Data Analysis

Data Analysis was done using SPSS and AMOS20. All hypotheses relationships in this study are estimated using Structural Equation Modelling (SEM).

6.1 Validity and Reliability Check

Exploratory Factor Analysis was carried out to check reliability and validity of the model. The research instrument involved modified validated instrument scales from previous empirical studies for measuring of variables as shown in Table 7. A Likert Scale (1–7) was used to rate all the items on the scale. Principal Component Axis and Varimax Rotation were used in EFA. The Kaiser-Meyer-Olkin measure of sampling adequacy was 0.743 (greater than 0.6.) establishing sampling adequacy as shown in Table 1. The results of Bartlett's Test of Sphericity as given in Table 1 is also considered appropriate as value $p < 0.05$ indicating that the test is significant and sample is adequate.

The correlation results show that the questions are mutually exclusive, mutually independent and not leading into each other. A highest correlation of 0.641 was found which shows that those questions are similar in nature. The correlation matrix had dimensions of a higher degree.

Table 1. KMO and Bartlett's test

KMO and Bartlett's Test		
Kaiser-Meyer-Olkin Measure of Sampling Adequacy		0.743
Bartlett's Test of Sphericity	Approx. Chi-Square	974.508
	df	276
	Sig.	0.000

The extraction of the factors clearly shows that all the factors have fairly good extraction in the analysis. Some technical factors like "compatibility with other devices" have low extraction i.e. 0.367. Other factors show fairly high extraction coefficients, which depicts their significance.

The Analysis shows that 58.98% i.e. approximately 60% of the total variance can be accounted for five principal variable factors. Thus 24 questions can be grouped together into five different factors, which would properly explain the variance (Table 2).

Table 2. Communality extraction method: principal component analysis.

	Initial	Extraction
Manuall_searching_cumbersome	1.000	0.600
Likely_to_buy_new_gadget_in_market	1.000	0.749
Liking_the_ideaOfUsingVA	1.000	0.674
Time_taken_to_respond	1.000	0.762
Accuracy_in_understanding	1.000	0.696
Sound_quality	1.000	0.572
Compatibility_with_OtherDevices	1.000	0.367
AnswerAccuracy	1.000	0.543
I_AmAffraid_Other_people_may_Access	1.000	0.523
Voice_search_improves_the_quality	1.000	0.422
I_will_not_use_other_devices_before_others_use_them	1.000	0.456
Improves_productivity	1.000	0.608
Price_expensive	1.000	0.458
Risky_to_disclose_personal_information	1.000	0.571
VoiceAssistant_usage_is_benefitial	1.000	0.622
VoiceAssistant_easuTo_use	1.000	0.522
Intention_to_use_VoiceAssistants_than_alternative	1.000	0.657
Cost_to_operate_voiceAssistants	1.000	0.577
Uncomfortable_to_give_command_inFront_ofPeople	1.000	0.549
Opinions_are_valued_want_me_to_use_VA	1.000	0.570
Its_mostly_uptome_whether_to_Use_VA	1.000	0.670
Having_Resources_knowledge_ability_to_Adopt_VA	1.000	0.700
Important_people_use_VA	1.000	0.562
Intention_to_use_VA_in_month	1.000	0.726

All the models have a significance coefficient less than the determined 0.05 which shows that all the cases are statistically significant. The 6th case takes into consideration the maximum factors i.e. six. Hence we consider the model with six independent variables. The model has an R value as 0.789 and adjusted R-square 0.598, which shows that 59.8% of the variance in the dependent variable is due to the change in these independent variables as shown in Table 3 below:

Table 3. Model Summary

Model summary

Model	R	R Square	Adjusted R Sq	Std. Error of the Estimate	Change Statistics					DW
					R Sq Change	F Change	df1	df2	Sig. F Change	
1	.580[a]	0.337	0.330	0.98485	0.337	49.805	1	98	0.000	
2	.695[b]	0.484	0.473	0.87359	0.147	27.550	1	97	0.000	
3	.739[c]	0.547	0.533	0.82272	0.063	13.367	1	96	0.000	
4	.761[d]	0.578	0.561	0.79755	0.032	7.155	1	95	0.009	
5	.778[e]	0.606	0.585	0.77555	0.027	6.466	1	94	0.013	
6	.789[f]	0.623	0.598	0.76252	0.017	4.241	1	93	0.042	2.010

Predictors: (Constant), Q1, Q23, Q12, Q11, Q7, Q17

The coefficients were analysed. The multiple regression model has a p-value of 0.042 which is less than 0.05, which shows that the results are significant.

Based on the regression analysis model given, the following coefficients can be used for the regression model.

$$Y = -0.293 + 0.280X1 + 0.379X2 + 0.261X3 - 0.205X4 + 0.203X5 + 0.195X6$$

Hence, according to the model used for determination of the intention to use voice assistants, it is clear that factors like the ease of use, system quality, lack of self-innovativeness (especially in India) and subjective norm coupled with peer pressure are the significant factors, considering the Indian context.

CMIN is the chi- squared coefficient. The values of CMIN/DF must lie between 1.0 and 5.0 in terms of the acceptable limits. Here, the independence model has a ratio of CMIN/DF of 4.660 which shows that the model is a proper fit as shown in Table 4 below:

Table 4. CMIN

Model	NPAR	CMIN	DF	P	CMIN/DF
Default model	39	446.567	151	.000	2.957
Saturated model	190	.000	0		
Independence model	19	796.818	171	.000	4.660

Here we can observe in Table 5, GFI of 0.695 and 0.430 for the default model and the independence model respectively.

Table 5. RMR, GFI, FMIN

Model	RMR	GFI	AGFI	PGFI	FMIN	F0	LO 90	HI 90
Default model	.229	.695	.616	.552	4.511	2.986	2.384	3.665
Saturated model	.000	1.000			.000	.000	.000	.000
Independence model	.284	.430	.367	.387	8.049	6.321	5.473	7.246

RMSEA

Model	RMSEA	LO 90	HI 90	PCLOSE
Default model	.141	.126	.156	.000
Independence model	.192	.179	.206	.000

The result shown in Fig. 1 below indicate that all the predictor variables like attitude, subjective norm and perceived behavioural control have a direct and positive effect on the outcome variable behavioural intention.

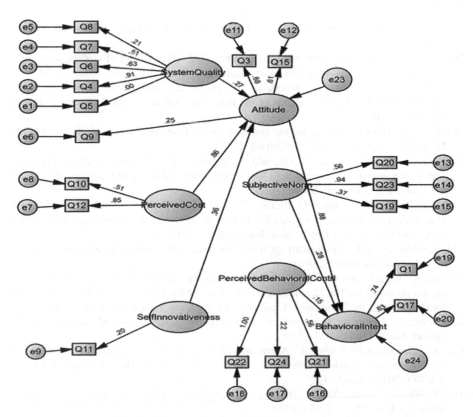

Fig. 1. Measurement model and structural model

7 Managerial Implications

Understanding consumer behaviour and it predictors can help managers in better planning and designing of products and services, especially technology products like voice assistants. The marketing strategies need to be upgraded and updated regularly to meet the fast changing needs and expectations of consumers. In the process of improving services, insights about what matters to consumers and what shapes their behaviour will go a long way in helping managers.

Theoretical Implications: This research will fill the gap that exists in the existing literature when it comes to Adoption of Voice Assistants by Indian Consumers. The research will also provide a solid research model that sheds light on the factors that influence Consumers' Intention to Adopt Voice Assistants in India.

Practical Implications: This research will give Product Managers some insights to optimize the Smart Speaker products to adapt to the needs of the Indian User, and will help Marketing Managers shape their Marketing Communication to touch Indian Audiences efficiently.

References

Ajzen, I.: The theory of planned behavior. Organ. Behav. Hum. Decis. Process **50**, 179–211 (1991)

Love, P.E.D., Irani, Z., Standing, C., Lin, C., Burn, J.M.: The enigma of evaluation: benefits, costs and risks of IT in Australian small–medium-sized enterprises. Inf. Manag., 200 (2011)

Park, E., Ohm, J.Y.: Factors influencing the public intention to use renewable energy technologies in South Korea: effects of the Fukushima nuclear accident. Energy Policy **65**, 198–211 (2014)

Goldsmith, R., Hofacker, C.: Measuring consumer innovativeness. J. Acad. Mark. Sci. **19**, 209–221 (1991). https://doi.org/10.1007/BF02726497

Berdasco, A., López, G., Diaz, I., Quesada, L., Guerrero, L.: User experience comparison of intelligent personal. Presented at the 13th International Conference on Ubiquitous Computing and Ambient Intelligence (2019)

Bickmore, T., Trinh, H., Stefan O, Rickles, N., Ricardo C.: Patient and consumer safety risks when using conversational assistants for medical information: an observational study of Siri, Alexa, and Google Assistant. J. Med. Internet Res. (2018)

Chu, L.: Why would I adopt a smart speaker? Consumers' intention to adopt smart speakers in smart home environment (2019)

Hwang, S.: Would satisfaction with smart speakers transfer into loyalty towards the smart speaker provider? In: The 22nd Biennial Conference of the International Telecommunications Society: Beyond the Boundaries: Challenges for Business, Policy and Society (2018)

Kowalczuk, P.: Consumer acceptance of smart speakers: a mixed methods approach. J. Res. Interact. Mark. **12**, 418–431 (2018)

Lau, J., Zimmerman, B., Schaub, F.: Alexa, are you listening? Privacy perceptions, concerns and privacy-seeking behaviors with smart speakers. Proc. ACM Hum.-Comput. Interact. **2** (CSCW) (2018). Article 102

Lei, X., Tu, G., Liu, A., Ali, K.: The Insecurity of Home Digital Voice Assistants – Amazon Alexa as a Case Study. CNS (2018)

Venkatesh, V., Thong, J.Y.L., Chan, F.K.Y., Hu, P.J.-H., Brown, S.A.: Extending the two-stage information systems continuance model: Incorporating UTAUT predictors and the role of context: Context, expectations and IS continuance. Inf. Syst. J. **21**, 527–555 (2011)

Xiao, X.-T., Kim, S.-I.: A study on the user experience of smart speaker in China- focused on Tmall Genie and Mi AI speaker. J. Digit. Convergence **16**, 409–414 (2018)

Whiteside, S.: How smart speakers are changing consumer behavior. WARC (2019)

Davis, F.D.: Perceived usefulness, perceived ease of use, and user acceptance of information technology. MIS Q. **13**(3), 319–340 (1989)

A Study on Attributes of Websites with Specific Reference to Online Purchase Intentions of Baby Products in Chennai

E. Pradeep$^{(\boxtimes)}$ and R. Arivazhagan

SRM School of Management, SRM Institute of Science and Technology, Kattankulathur, Chengalpattu District 603203, Tamil Nadu, India
pradeepe@srmist.edu.in

Abstract. Baby products, our area of interest, are very sensitive products which are used by tender infants and little kids. Therefore, parents exercise great care while purchasing them and only go for the best, which explains our need to study the online purchase intentions of baby products. Working women with financial resources of their own and coupled with availability of huge information on the internet have empowered them to make informed decisions while purchasing for their babies and kids. Most of the baby products are available online and customers now prefer to buy the products through online shopping websites. But product sales through online particularly relies on the trust of the company and the company website. This article tries to analyze the appearance of the website, features and other related factors of the online shopping portal and their influences on making purchase decisions for baby products among the customers in Chennai. In this regard, data were collected from 174 respondents, through a survey method, by using structured questionnaire and the judgemental sampling method was adopted. Collected data were analysed and results revealed that trust and usability factors were significant. The results also revealed the most important factors for designing a website for achieving more customer satisfaction.

Keywords: Baby products · Consumer behaviour · Online purchase · Trust and privacy · Website design

1 Introduction

Indian Economy is growing at a fast pace due to the surge in the working age population. Household incomes and therefore, spending capacity has greatly increased. Likewise, the disposable incomes of young parents have been on the steady rise and most of them live in urban areas as nuclear families. Both the parents are working and in particular, the working women are looking forward to use safer and better products for their babies. They are also willing to pay more for the premium quality. India has a huge birth rate too every year compared to other countries. Hence there is a huge potential for the baby care products' segment in India. Also CAGR has pointed out that the projected growth rate of baby care market is over 17% till 2020 [1].

© IFIP International Federation for Information Processing 2020
Published by Springer Nature Switzerland AG 2020
S. K. Sharma et al. (Eds.): TDIT 2020, IFIP AICT 617, pp. 484–492, 2020.
https://doi.org/10.1007/978-3-030-64849-7_43

There is a huge array of products available for babies like diapers, wet wipes, powders, baby baths liquids, shampoos, dresses, baby food, baby furniture, toys, books and many more. Due to the surplus of information available in the internet they are able to compare and contrast between various brands and choose the right product for their babies.

Due to the busy lives of people and hectic work schedules, there is a huge surge in e-commerce purchases. When people are already familiar with the product and there is no need to go and physically examine them before buying, people prefer to purchase them online, so that it reaches their place without the hassles of commuting to the shop. Hence online shopping now plays a pivotal role in our lives. There are a lot of online shopping portals now available. For the e-commerce website to be a huge success and reap profits, it is essential to keep the website attractive and safe for customers. Customers should feel comfortable and find it easy to purchase through online. Websites have also started to use Artificial Intelligence to effectively tap more customers.

Therefore, there is a big market for those who do online purchases, especially for baby products and hence this explains our need to study the online purchase intentions of baby products. In this study, Chennai region is alone considered as it is the hub of both buzzing technological and economic activity. Later on, this study can be expanded to other regions also.

2 Review of Literature

Online purchase is greatly influenced by perceived usefulness [2]. Findings show that the usability, entertainment, and complementarity of economy hotel websites positively affected eTrust which in turn positively influenced online booking intentions [3]. Proper design strategies pertaining to every stage of the purchase decision-making process have to be planned by the online merchants who have adopted social commerce, so that the online portals meet the needs and desires of customers [4].

Consumers' purchase intentions are greatly influenced by the website quality and it increases product appeal. Purchase intentions are increased when the trust in e-commerce sites increases and also there exists a positive relationship between quality of the website and purchase intentions [5]. Major factors which influence the development of e-loyalty are hedonism, privacy, e-satisfaction and customer service [6]. Website quality, design and information should be given more opportunity to improve website quality [7]

One of the finding says that the online purchase intentions are related to the ease of browsing and using. The added information should be true and good interactions support online purchase intentions [8]. Another study says that, Customers online purchase intentions are positively associated with website quality [9].

Cho.V, [10] said that there is a hierarchical relationship among the constructs. The most important construct was the perceived usefulness for online services. Perceived risk and trust were less important mostly on online legal services. Findings of another study show that website quality has a direct and positive impact on customer satisfaction which in turn has an impact on purchase intentions. The influence of website quality on purchase intentions significantly mediates the effect [11]. Reputation had a positive effect on consumers' emotion and negative effect on perceived risk [12].

It is a product category where parents are initially unable to judge brand performance as consumption is undertaken by babies or toddlers. Manufacturer-branded baby-care products were regarded by respondents to be of higher quality and lower perceived risk than retail-branded baby-care products [13]. Understanding the purchase pattern of parents would help firms in formulating strategies to cater to the needs of the consumer and thereby increase their market share [14].

Normative-beliefs have been found as the most significant to influence students' intention for shopping on Internet [15]. To develop a successful e-business online store, it is necessary to have a deep understanding on the trust developed and how it affects online purchase intentions [16].

Customers' perception about the website is greatly affected by trust and perceived risk which in turn their purchase intentions [17]. There is a positive correlation between the overall perceived quality and the purchase intention when considering the company's website [18].

3   Research Problem

3.1   Research Focus

While doing literature study, the researcher came across scarce literature support for baby products based studies, whereas studies related to online purchase intention and behaviour were found to have quite reasonable numbers. Baby product segment is very sensitive since new born babies are very sensitive towards accessing their products such as clothes, cosmetics, toys etc. Since the current generation is more focussed towards the single child concept, every parent is very keen on choosing their baby products. Although they have more experience on online purchase, they struggle while doing the same for purchasing baby products because they may not be aware of choosing criteria due to the single child concept and sensitive nature of new born babies. Hence the researcher would like to support and enlighten the new parent's online purchase behaviour towards baby products buying with a comfortable manner. This study also supports E-Retailers in order to design their websites in a more user friendly manner. Hence this study was conducted with the following objective.

3.2   Objective of the Study

The objective of this study is to analyse the various attributes of E-retail websites by focusing the buying behaviour of baby products.

4   Research Methodology

This research was designed based on a descriptive method. Scope of this study was confined within Chennai city. Scopes of respondents were limited to the people who are purchasing baby products online. It was not mandatory that the respondents should have kids; instead they could buy baby products for others such as other family members, relatives and friends for gifting purposes. Structured questionnaire was prepared which includes basic demography details, buying behaviour and website attributes related questions. Data were collected from 200 respondents, of which 26 were rejected due to poor and incomplete responses. Finally 174 responses were considered for data analysis. Data was collected through a survey method by using non-probability cum judgemental sampling methods, because the data collection person has to make sure, whether they have purchased any baby products online earlier, before giving the questionnaire to a respondent. Collected data were entered into the SPSS software package and analysed by using various statistical tools such as frequency analysis, factor analysis, reliability analysis and regression analysis, and results were given in the following section.

5   Data Analysis and Results

5.1   Frequency Analysis

Frequency analysis was carried out for demography details just to get basic understanding about the respondents. Data were collected from 54% of male respondents and 46% of female respondents. Among them 53% were between 21 to 30 years of age and 47% were above 30 years. This study includes 28% of unmarried respondents and 72% were married. Education qualification of the respondents was 10% Diploma holders, 60% Undergraduates, 28% Post graduates and 2% with Ph. D. Among the total respondents 13% were self-employed, 17% were homemakers, 63% private employees, 4% government employees and 3% doing various other professions. Around 69% of the respondents were below an income level of Rs. 30,000 per month and remaining 31% above Rs. 30,000 per month. This study includes 37% of respondents from North Chennai zone, 44% from Central Chennai and 19% from South Chennai zone. Among the total respondents 36% had children below 4 years and 64% didn't have kids below 4 years. Around 41% of respondents had one child less than 4 years, 4% had two children less than 4 years and 55% had children greater than 4 years. Among the total respondents around 54% of the people purchase less frequently, 20% purchase always and 26% purchase only if someone recommends. Among all respondents around 43% of the people purchased for their own kids, 30% purchase for their family members and other 27% for gifting purposes. Around 37% of respondents were using mobile phones, 48% laptops, 9% desktops and 6% tablets for purchasing baby products through online.

5.2   Factor Analysis

Factor analysis was used to minimize the multiple variables into few factors, so that variables could be categorized under specific attributes. Factor analysis was presented by using three different segments such as KMO and Bartlett's test, total variance explained and rotated component matrix. KMO test was used to justify the sampling adequacy. Table 1 shows that, sampling adequacy value of KMO test was 0.852. It denotes that sampling adequacy for this study was 85% and it was considered as adequate. Bartlett's test of factor analysis shows that significant value of all the factors which consider for this study and resulted as significant, since the significant value was 0.000 (p ≤ 0.05).

Table 1. KMO and Bartlett's test

KMO and Bartlett's test parameters		Values
Kaiser-Meyer-Olkin Measure of Sampling Adequacy.		0.852
Bartlett's Test of Sphericity	Approx. Chi-Square	619.876
	Df	136
	Sig.	0.000

The total variance explained through factor analysis by all variables was 72% (Table 2) with four different factors (components). All these four factors were extracted by using principle component analysis method. Loadings of each variable were determined and rotated by using Varimax rotation method. Rotation converged in 9 iterations. All the variables categorized under these four different factors based on the loading value of 0.5 and above.

Table 2. Total variance explained

Component	Initial Eigenvalues			Rotation sums of squared loadings		
	Total	% of variance	Cumulative %	Total	% of variance	Cumulative %
1	8.543	50.252	50.252	4.102	24.128	24.128
2	1.407	8.279	58.531	3.237	19.040	43.168
3	1.292	7.601	66.132	2.802	16.482	59.650
4	1.040	6.118	72.250	2.142	12.601	72.250
5	.755	4.442	76.693			

Table 3 shows the different variables in specific factors. First factor includes six variables such as not vulnerable to hacking, information security features, satisfied on addressing issues, proper security wall, handling financial transactions and carries out the functionalities seamlessly. This factor named as Trust. Second factor includes four other variables such as options provided, sorting filters, comparison of features and navigating the sites. This factor named as Web Design. Third factor includes four variables such as easy to use and buy, easy interaction, easy to understand and operating speed. This factor named as Usability. Finally fourth factor includes three variables such as amount of information, accuracy of the information and ease of applying the promotional offers. This factor named as Information quality.

Table 3. Rotated component matrix[a]

Variables	Factors (components)			
	Trust factor	Web design factor	Usability factor	Information quality factor
Easy to use and buy			.713	
Easy interaction			.637	
Easy to understand			.829	
Satisfied on operating speed			.831	
Options provided		.732		
Sorting filters		.596		
Comparison features		.734		
Navigating the sites		.749		
Amount of information				.715
Accuracy of the information				.621
Ease of applying the promotional offers				.515
Not vulnerable to hacking	.651			
Information security features	.810			
Satisfied on addressing issues	.826			
Proper security wall	.789			
Handling financial transactions	.658			
Carry out the functionalities seamlessly	.662			
Reliability (Chronbach's Alpha value)	.927	.779	0.738	0.801

Extraction Method: Principal Component Analysis. Rotation Method: Varimax with Kaiser Normalization.
a. Rotation converged in 9 iterations.

Reliability of these four factors were also analysed by using Cronbach's alpha value. First factors show that 93% ($\alpha = 0.927$) of reliability value. Second, third and fourth factors shows the reliability value of 80% ($\alpha = 0.779$), 74% ($\alpha = 0.738$) and 80% ($\alpha = 0.801$) respectively and these values were highly accepted.

5.3 Regression Analysis

Regression analysis was conducted by using overall satisfaction on website service as dependent variable and all seventeen website based factors considered as independent variables. Regression analysis revealed following findings. Model summary (Table 4) in regression analysis shows that R^2 value of 0.645. This justified that 64.5% of variance explained by the variables which taken in this study. ANOVA analysis (Table 5) in the regression analysis justified that all the variables which taken for regression analysis was significant, since significant value was 0.000 (p $\leq$ 0.05) (Table 6).

Table 4. Model Summary of regression analysis

Model	R	R square	Adjusted R square	Std. error of the estimate
1	.803[a]	.645	.473	.68845

a. Predictors: (Constant), Factor1, Factor3, Factor2, Factor4

Table 5. ANOVA result of regression analysis

Model		Sum of squares	Df	Mean square	F	Sig.
1	Regression	23.405	4	5.851	10.925	.000[b]
	Residual	26.243	49	.536		
	Total	49.648	53			

a. Dependent Variable: Overall satisfaction of the website service factors; b. Predictors: (Constant), Factor1, Factor2, Factor3, Factor4

Table 6. Coefficients of regression analysis

Model		Unstandardized coefficients		Standardized coefficients	t	Sig.
		B	Std. error	Beta		
1	(Constant)	−.690	.706		−.978	.333
	Trust	.135	.057	.331	2.369	.022
	Web design	.064	.057	.176	1.109	.273
	Usability	−.048	.067	−.124	−.706	.483
	Information quality	.083	.035	.393	2.363	.022

a. Dependent Variable: Overall satisfaction of the website service factors

Out of four factors, trust and information quality factors were turned to be significant factors since their significant values were 0.022 and 0.022 respectively. Influence of each factor decided based on Unstandardized Coefficients values. For example, increase of one unit in trust factor would influence 0.135 units of customer satisfaction. Similarly increase of one unit in information quality factor would increase 0.083 units of customer satisfaction. Whereas, importance of these factors were decided based on standardized coefficients. In this study Information quality factor (0.393) was identified as very important factor in customer satisfaction and followed by trust factor (0.331). Hence this study strongly recommends online retailers to concentrate more on quality of information and trust factors such as payment gateway, product quality, and safety of kids etc., while designing their websites in order to increase their customer satisfaction.

These findings were validated through literature support. Review of the literature section of this article is substantiating these findings, because most of the literatures were documented by supporting trust, quality of website and its information to be considered as most important factors while designing E-retail websites. Though these variables were given for general E-retail purposes, this study revealed that those factors not only important to general online purchase, but also significant for online buying of baby products too.

6   Conclusion

Baby care segment is in great demand due to a steadily growing economy and increase in disposable incomes. Also online shopping is more and more gaining popularity due to the ease of access in buying products. Most of the baby care products are also bought online owing to a huge segment of working mothers. Hence there is always a huge potential for purchasing baby care products, online. This study finds out that quality of information and trust based factors were identified as very important factors while designing baby products E-Retail websites in order to achieve more customer satisfaction. Moreover, the parents of first baby also could validate and choose the best websites that sells baby products online through these factors by considering respective variables mentioned in this study.

References

1. Rishu, G.: Entrepreneur India, Web online portal (2018). https://www.entrepreneur.com/article/314431
2. Chiu, Y.B., Lin, C.-P., Tang, L.-L.: Gender differs: assessing a model of online purchase intentions in e-retail service. Int. J. Serv. Ind. Manag. 16(5), 416–435 (2005)
3. Li, L., Peng, M., Jiang, N., Law, R.: An empirical study on the influence of economy hotel website quality on online booking intentions. Int. J. Hosp. Manag. 63, 1–10 (2017)
4. Huang, Z., Benyoucef, M.: The effects of social commerce design on consumer purchase decision-making: An empirical study. Electron. Commer. Res. Appl. 25, 40–58 (2017)
5. Liu, F., Xiao, B., Lim, E.T., Tan, C.W.: The art of appeal in electronic commerce: understanding the impact of product and website quality on online purchases. Internet Res. 27(4), 752–771 (2017)
6. Ahmad, A., Rahman, O., Khan, M.N.: Exploring the role of website quality and hedonism in the formation of e-satisfaction and e-loyalty: evidence from internet users in India. J. Res. Interact. Mark. 11(3), 246–267 (2017)
7. Sam, M., Fazli, M., Tahir, M.N.H.: Website quality and consumer online purchase intention of air ticket (2009)

8. Leonidio, U.D.C., Montezano, R.M.D.S., Carvalho, F.A.D.: Evaluation of perceived quality of the website of an online bookstore: an empirical application of the Barnes and Vidgen Model. JISTEM-J. Inf. Syst. Technol. Manag. **8**(1), 109–130 (2011)
9. Hasanov, J., Khalid, H.: The impact of website quality on online purchase intention of organic food in Malaysia: a web-qual model approach. Procedia Comput. Sci. **72**, 382–389 (2015)
10. Cho, V.: A study of the roles of trusts and risks in information-oriented online legal services using an integrated model. Inf. Manag. **43**(4), 502–520 (2006)
11. Bai, B., Law, R., Wen, I.: The impact of website quality on customer satisfaction and purchase intentions: evidence from Chinese online visitors. Int. J. Hosp. Manag. **27**(3), 391–402 (2008)
12. Kim, J., Lennon, S.J.: Effects of reputation and website quality on online consumers' emotion, perceived risk and purchase intention: based on the stimulus-organism-response model. J. Res. Interact. Mark. **7**(1), 33–56 (2013)
13. Broadbridge, M.: Retail-brand baby-products: what do consumers think? J. Brand Manag. **8**, 196–210 (2001). https://doi.org/10.1057/pqlgrave.bm.2540020
14. Kalaiselvi, S., Mohana, P.M.: Women's perception towards baby food with special reference to Erode town. Asia Pac. J. Mark. Manag. Rev. **2**(6) (2013). ISSN 2319-2836
15. Yulihasri, E., Md. Aminul, I., Daud, K.A.K.: Factors that influence customers' buying intention on shopping online. Int. J. Mark. Stud. **3**(1) (2011)
16. Ganguly, B., Dash, S.B., Cyr, D.: Website characteristics, trust and purchase intention in online stores:- an empirical study in the Indian context. J. Inf. Sci. Technol. **6**(2) (2009)
17. Chang, K.C., Hsu, C.L., Chen, M.C., Kuo, N.T.: How a branded website creates customer purchase intentions. Total Qual. Manag. Bus. Excellence **30**(3–4), 422–446 (2019)
18. Kourtesopoulou, A., Theodorou, S.-D., Kriemadis, A., Papaioannou, A.: The Impact of Online Travel Agencies Web Service Quality on Customer Satisfaction and Purchase Intentions. In: Katsoni, V., Segarra-Oña, M. (eds.) Smart Tourism as a Driver for Culture and Sustainability. SPBE, pp. 343–356. Springer, Cham (2019). https://doi.org/10.1007/978-3-030-03910-3_24

Customers Interest in Buying an Electric Car: An Analysis of the Indian Market

M. Prabaharan[1]([⊠]) [iD] and M. Selvalakshmi[2]([⊠]) [iD]

[1] Madurai Kamaraj University, Madurai, India
prabaharmp@gmail.com
[2] Thiagarajar School of Management, Madurai, India
selvalakshmi@tsm.ac.in

Abstract. In the automobile industry, an electric car is a vehicle impelled by the electric motors utilizing energy stored in refillable batteries, as a replacement of diesel or petrol engine. The electric car has predicted to rule the Indian market in the next few years. The study aims to know the factors which make interest in buying the electric car. Integrating the Technological acceptance and diffusion of innovation model the present research proposed extended technology acceptance model. The data were collected from 600 non-commercial car owners to test the proposed model. The findings demonstrate the perceived usefulness, perceived ease of us, and attitude are positively influence the customers' interest to buy the electric car. The relative is one of the innovation factors which have a positive effect on interest to buy the electric car. The result also shows that majority of customers are interested to buy Indian brand cars which will have a low-price range.

Keywords: Automobile industry · Electric car · Technology acceptance model · Diffusion of innovation · Customers interest

1 Introduction

An electric car is a vehicle impelled by electric motors utilizing energy stored in refillable batteries, as a replacement of diesel or petrol engine which is of three kinds such as Electric powered solar vehicle, Hybrid cars (both internal ignition and batteries) and BEV (Battery electric vehicle). Special measures have been taken in India like cutting GST on EV (Electric Vehicles) to 5% against 28% for diesel and petrol engines, also has exempted 1.5 lakh INR on loan to buy EV but only 1500 cars were sold during April - December, 2019. [1]. According to economic times survey, about 90% of Indian car customers were willing to purchase an electric car if it has good infrastructure (high cost of purchase, maintenance, charging stations) proper maintenance and support system. At present, EV market dispersion is only 1% of total sales in India [2]. But it aims to reach 30% EV dispersion by 2030. In the forthcoming five years, EV is likely to replace conservative internal ignition engines [3]. The passenger car customers are expecting safety, reliability, performance and personalization of the electric cars over combustion cars. The performance of electric vehicles is higher compared to the conventional vehicles between 100 km and 150 km. Customers welcoming the electric

© IFIP International Federation for Information Processing 2020
Published by Springer Nature Switzerland AG 2020
S. K. Sharma et al. (Eds.): TDIT 2020, IFIP AICT 617, pp. 493–509, 2020.
https://doi.org/10.1007/978-3-030-64849-7_44

cars due to lower cost with quick charging points [4]. Generally, Electric car is a major innovation to diminish energy consumption and zero-emission in the automobile segment. Initially, the electric cars will be offered at a lower price to encourage the purchase of the customer. Electric cars are environmentally friendly and the operating cost is also less compared to the combustion engine. In the subsequent few years, the leading international car brands will launch the electric cars in both cost-effective and premium price range for their customers in India. Thus, it's vital to know the customers' interest on purchasing electric cars after propelling in India.

In India 1309 (Mahindra e-Verito – 523, Tata Tigor EV – 491, Hyundai Kona EV – 280, Mahindra e20) electric cars were acquired from April to November 2019. Currently, three electric car models are available in India, they are Tata Tigor, Mahindra e-Verito and Hyundai Kona EV [5]. The Indian government aimed to make India the fourth largest for EVs by 2040, but it is very hard for customers to switch over from combustion engines to zero-emission cars. Now it's very significant to know the factors which make customers interest to buy electric cars in future.

The study objectives are 1) to deliver a theoretically acceptable research model that integrates TAM and DOI to know the factors which make interest in buying the electric car in the Indian market. 2) To identify the brand and type of electric cars which buyer interest to acquire.

2   Theoretical Model and Hypothesis Development

The electric car is an in-mint condition with zero-emission technology which is considered to be ingenious. This study is executed by integrating two well-known adaption theories.

2.1   Technology Acceptance Model (TAM)

TAM has set to foresee the acceptance of new technology. This model is grounded in the theory of reasoned action (TRA-psychological theory) by [6]. Technology Acceptance Model (TAM) is the theory which explains acquiring ability of user towards newly introduced technology. It could provide information about the relative likelihood of success of proposed systems early in their development, where such information has the greatest value [7]. Acceptance of new technology is entirely based on usage. The technology acceptance model (TAM) is a widely used and most impactful theory for describing the acceptance of information technology by an individual [8]. Technology acceptance model established user attitude [9] and perceived usefulness (PU) identified the role of perceived ease of use (PEOU) in realizing user acceptance in information systems [10, 11].

Perceived Usefulness: The two exogenous constructs of the attitude of TAM were perceived usefulness (PU) and perceived ease of use [12]. Perceived usefulness (PU) reinforces the customer's belief that using the new technology will enhance and boost the performance [13, 14]. In our research, PU denotes to the expectations of the customer, which make them interested in buying electric cars. Perceived usefulness of the electric car is based on price range, performance, tax benefits, battery cost & warranty period. The Perceived usefulness has a positive effect on purchase intention [15]. The past studies have supported the perceived usefulness have a significant positive effect on the intention to use [9, 16–23]. Hence, we propose the following hypothesis. H_2: Perceived usefulness of electric car will have a positive effect on interest to buy (ITB) electric cars.

Perceived Ease of Use: Perceived ease of use (PEOU) is defined as "the degree which a person believes that using a particular system would be free of effort" [24]. PEOU shows the frame of mind of customers towards buying and their perception about battery charging stations, recharging time, distance from home to charging station and durability assurance. Thus, the research has supported the hypothesis that the perceived ease of use will have a positive effect on attitude use [15]. Several researches had studied the PEOU have a positive effect on attitude [9, 18–20].

Therefore, we formulate the following hypothesis.

H_3: Perceived ease of use will have a significant positive effect on attitude to use.

Attitude to Use: Attitude refers to a person forming favourable or unfavourable feelings toward adopting a specific technology [20]. The attitude of an individual is not the only factor that determines the use but also influenced by system performance [16]. The attitude refers that it leads to the intention to use and adoption of a particular technology [26]. Attitude to use and intention to accept are the endogenous factors [6]. Prior studies had shown the presence effect of attitude on the intention to use of new technology. Several studies supported the hypothesis that the attitude will have a positive effect on the intention to use [18, 19, 27, 28]. Hence, we formed the following hypothesis H_4: Attitude has a direct and positive influence on customer interest to buy electric cars.

2.2 Diffusion of Innovation Theory (DOI)

The innovation diffusion theory expressed to predict and interpret how users adopt an innovation [29]. DOI Theory, proposed by E.M. Rogers in 1962 to explain to how, over time, an idea or product gains momentum and spreads through certain population or social system. The final result of the theory is that users accept a new idea, behaviour, or product [30].

Relative Advantage: The Diffusion of innovation theory enables to understand the impact of innovation characteristics. The five factors that influence the adoption of innovation are Relative advantages, Complexity, Compatibility, Observability & Trialability [31]. The relative advantage is one of the main factors of diffusion innovation theory which extend the innovation better than the idea it replaces. The greater the relative advantage of innovation the greater acceptance of new technology [32]. RA is similar to perceived usefulness in TAM. [33]. The Relative advantages (RA) has a significant positive impact on consumer attitude towards technology [34]. Customers focus on new technologies that are easy to use, low cost and deliver benefits in the future over existing technology [37]. The past researches have suggested that the relative advantages are one of the best predictors of intention to accept new technology and it is positively related to the intention to buy [25, 28, 36]. The significant relationship between relative 3 advantage and intention to accept have been studied by some of past research in different fields such as solar energy, renewable energy sources, online travel purchase. Hence, we hypothesize that,

H_5: Relative advantages have a direct and positive influence on customer interest to buy electric cars. Finally, to know the association between gender and the factors such as charging station, price range, environmentally smart and technology which customer's interest in buying the electric car [38]. Hence, we formulate the following hypothesis.

H_1: There is an association between gender and factors which make the customer interest to buy an electric car (Fig. 1).

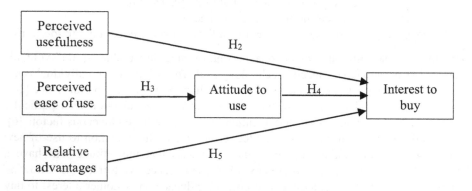

Fig. 1. Proposed conceptual model

3   Data Methodology

In this study, the research design is descriptive in nature. The purposive sampling technique had used to collect primary data from the samples. The close-ended and well-structured questions (Likert-5-point scale) had been framed to collect the data from the respondents. The questionnaire had been developed based on the Diffusion of Innovation and Technology Acceptance Model with two parts. The first part includes the degree of demographics such as gender, age, education and income slab of the respondents and the second part includes questions based on the models. The pilot was conducted among 50 non-commercial passenger car owners to check the reliability of the instrument. The data collected for this study were 660. However, 600 samples had the completed data, hence 90.9% of samples have been considered. The tools used in this research paper include percentage analysis, chi-square, correlation analysis and multiple regression with the help of IBM SPSS 20 software.

4   Literature Review

See Table 1..

Table 1. Literature review

Studies	Year	Application	Theory/Method	Samples	Constructs used	Results
[18]	2019	Uber Mobile application	Diffusion of Innovation theory & Technology acceptance model	300	Perceived Usefulness, Perceived Ease of Use, Relative advantage, Compatibility, Complexity, Observability, Social influence, Attitude & Future usage intention	Diffusion of innovation factors had effect perceived ease of use and on perceived usefulness of smartphone application
[19]	2019	Electric Vehicles	Theory of planned behavior (TPB), Technology acceptance model (TAM) & Innovation diffusion theory (IDT)	336	PU, PEOU, Compatibility, Personal innovativeness, External influence, Perceived behaviour control, Attitude, Subjective norms, Self-control, Purchase intention	The investigation revealed that the attractive battery and charging schemes are the factors which attract consumers
[39]	2019	Crowdsourcing Platform - Students	Technology acceptance model (TAM),	48	Perceived Usefulness, Perceived Ease of Use & Behavioural intention	The research exposed that perceived usefulness and perceived have significant positive association on behavioral intention
[25]	2018	Renewable energy usage	Unified theory of acceptance and use of technology (utaut)	280	Relative advantage, Awareness, Behavioral control, Moral norms, Social norms, Attitude & Intention to use	Perceived behavioral control, relative advantage, awareness, and moral norms which had statistically significant positive associations with intention
[36]	2018	Solar Energy Technology	Technology acceptance model (TAM), Diffusion of innovation (DOI) and Theory of planned behavior (TPB)	384	Relative advantage, Perceived behavioural control and Perceived ease of use	Relative advantage, perceived ease of use and perceived behavioural control had a positive effect with solar energy technology adoption
[40]	2018	Electric Vehicle	–	384	–	The research exposed 91.27% of respondents in Malaysia were interested to buy electric vehicle. The charging station offices must be available like petrol stations

(*continued*)

Table 1. (*continued*)

Studies	Year	Application	Theory/Method	Samples	Constructs used	Results
[27]	2018	Multimedia among School Teachers	Technology acceptance model (TAM)	460	Perceived Usefulness, Perceived Ease of Use, Attitude & Intention to use	Perceived ease of use would enhance the intention to use of multimedia software. The attitude toward use had a positive effect on the intention to use
[15]	2017	Apparel products	Technology acceptance model	900	Perceived Usefulness, Perceived Ease of Use, Attitude & Behvioural intentions	Perceived usefulness, perceived ease of use, attitudes, intention to purchase were related with consumers' use of sustainability standards of apparel products
[28]	2016	Purchase travel online	Innovation diffusion theory (IDT) and the technology acceptance model (TAM),	495	Relative advantages, Perceived ease of use, PU, compatibility, trust, attitude, Intention to participate, and intention to purchase	Consumers who observed the relative advantages in online travel had a positive attitude of online travel community
[41]	2015	Electric vehicle	Stated choice methods	384	–	Chinese consumers are interested to adopt Battery Electric & mid-price range of plug in hybrid electric vehicle (PHEV) and American consumers favor low-range PHEVs
[35]	2014	Mobile websites	Technology acceptance model and Trust theory	302	Perceived ease of use (PEOU), Perceived usefulness (PU) and Trust	The outcomes revealed that there had a positive association between PEOU, PU and mobile users' satisfaction. PU and trust positively associated to trust and satisfaction of mobile users
[42]	2014	New media	Unified Theory of Acceptance and Use of Technology (UTAUT)	380	Performance Expectancy, effort expectancy, social influence, Facilitating conditions.	Age and gender may not play as critical a part in new innovation utilize and appropriation
[22]	2013	Smartphone usage	Technology acceptance model (TAM) and the uses and gratifications (U&G) approach	491	Motivation for ritualized use, Motivation for instrumental use, Perceived usefulness and Perceived ease of use	The research exhibited that spread information system with innovative and features, the developer ought to pay consideration to users' natural inspirations as well as to their outward recognitions
[43]	2011	Electric cars	Stated preference methods	1152	–	Micro/city cars had showed response positively like to secondary cars. The performance was top priority to leisure, off-roaders and sports cars

5   Results and Discussion

5.1   Demographic Profile

The table shows the demographic characteristics like gender, age, education qualification and income of the respondents (Table 2).

Table 2. Demographic profile

Particulars	Levels & Percentage				
Gender	Male 58.7%	Female 41.3%			
Age	21–25 years 11.7%	26–30 years 11.7%	31–35 years 47.2%	35–40 years 17.7%	Above 40 11.8%
Education	Higher secondary 5.8%	Graduate 29.1%	Post graduate 65.1%		
Income slab	Below 5 lakhs 5.8%	5 to 10 lakhs 29.3%	10 to 15 lakhs 47.2%	15 to 20 lakhs 17.7%	>20 lakhs 5.8%

The table shows that the total sample for this study was 600. As observed, the majority of respondents (58.7%) were male and female were (41.3%). A majority of the respondents (47.2%) belonged to the age limit between 30 to 35 years, the prevailing level of education is postgraduate (65.1%) followed by graduates (29.1%). A majority of respondents had the (47.2%) income slab from 10 to 15 lakhs followed by 5 to 10 (29.3%). Overall data represents that respondents are young adults, well-educated and affluent. This might be help to know the customers interest in buying an electric car.

5.2   Descriptive Indicator of the Car of Respondents

Table 3. Descriptive indicator of the car of respondents

Table No.-2- Descriptive indicator about the respondents' interest in the electric car.						
Particulars	**Levels & Percentage**					
Numbers of Cars Owned	1 car 53.3 %	2 cars 29.2 %	3cars 11.7 %	More than three cars 5.8 %		
Type of cars	Hatchback 47.0 %	MPV 11.8 %	Sedan 29.4%	MPV 11.8 %		
How long have you been using the car	1 year 23.5 %	2 years 35.2 %	3 years 12.0 %	4 years 11.8 %	≥ 5 17.5 %	
Interested in buying an electric car	Yes 82.3 %	No 17.7 %				
Interested brand to buy electric car	Maruthi 29.5 %	Tata 9.8 %	Renault 14.1 %	Mahindra 11.2 %	Hyundai 17.5 %	Honda 12.0 %	Ford 6.0 %

The table contains descriptive indicators of particulars like number, type & brand of cars. The majority (53.3%) of respondents owned one car, 29.2% owned two cars &

11.7% owned three cars. About half of the respondents had owned a hatchback type of car. Most of the respondents (35.2%) have been using the car for two years, followed by one year (23.5%). The majority of respondents (82.5%) are interested in buying an electric car and most of the respondents preferred to buy Maruthi brand cars followed by Hyundai (See Table 3).

5.3   Reliability

Reliability test is used to measure data quality and consistency in measured items. The reliability has been tested using Cronbach's Alpha. The usually accepted value of Cronbach alpha is between 0.6 and 0.7. The Cronbach alpha value between 0.8 and 0.9 is very good level [44] (Table 4).

Table 4. Reliability test

Factors	No. of Items	Cronbach Alpha
Perceived usefulness	6	0.751
Perceived use of ease	4	0.841
Relative advantage	4	0.661
Attitude to use	6	0.717
Interest to buy	4	0.708

The value obtained for in this study was 0.909 for 24 items which are greater than 0.7, so the value is acceptable. The Cronbach alpha value for each construct (perceived usefulness, perceived use of ease, relative advantage, attitude to use and interest to buy) is more than 0.6. This value shows that the data collected for this study are reliable.

5.4   Chi-Square Test

Test-1: Gender and factors which will make the customer interest to buy an electric car (Table 5).

Table 5. Frequency table - Gender vs factors which influence the customer interest to buy.

Factors	Gender		Frequency	Percentage
	Male	Female		
Innovativeness	35	37	72	12.1
Environmentally smart	106	36	142	23.7
Low taxes over and tax deduction on loan interest	0	70	70	11.6
Fuel cost elimination	105	70	175	29.1
Technology	70	35	105	17.5
Safety in speed	36	0	36	6.0
Total	352	248	600	100

As observed, the majority of respondents (29.7%) expect the fuel cost elimination followed by (23.7%) are liked the environmentally smart factor.

The chi-square test was performed at a 5% level of significance and hypothesis was tested.

H1 – There is an association between gender and factors which make the customer interest to buy an electric car.

Table 6. Chi square values

	Value	df	Asymp. Sig. (2sided)
Pearson Chi-Square	145.576[a]	5	.000
Likelihood Ratio	183.886	5	.000
Linear-by-Linear Association	9.948	1	.002
N of Valid Cases	600		

The Table 6a shows that the significance value is 0.000 which is less than the probability value ($p < 0.05$). It supports the hypothesis hence there is a significant relationship between gender and factors which make the customer interest to buy an electric car. This result clearly shows that innovativeness, environmentally smart, low taxes, safety in speed and technology are the factors which make customers interest to buy an electric car varies significantly with gender.

5.5 Correlation Analysis

This analysis is the statistical method used to identify the correlations between the variables. It is also used to describe the strength of the correlation between the variables. Correlation analysis was tested to know the relationship among variables in the construct of the model. To identify the correlation between perceived ease of use, perceived usefulness, relative advantages, attitude and interest to use all variables were correlated by using this analysis. The average score of multiple items in each construct was calculated and used for more analysis [26]. The coefficient of correlation (r) value is considered weak when it from 0.10 to 0.29 and 0.30 to 0.49 its medium then 0.5 to 1 is considered strong [45]. To evade multicollinearity the coefficient of correlation value should be less than 0.8 [46] (Table 7).

Table 7. Pearson correlation analysis results

Constructs	PU	PEOU	RA	ATU	ITB
Perceived usefulness (PU)	1				
Perceived ease of use (PEOU)	0.705[**]	1			
Relative advantages (RA)	0.710[**]	0.612[**]	1		
Attitude to use (ATU)	0.619[**]	0.666[**]	0.603[**]	1	
Interest to buy (ITB)	0.672[**]	0.661[**]	0.618[**]	0.625[**]	1

** Correlation is significant at the 0.01 level (2-tailed), * Correlation is significant at the 0.05 level (2-tailed)

The result shows the correlation value 0.710, which is high among all variables. So, this value is smaller than 0.80. Hence, there is no multicollinearity in this study. The dimensions in the model were positively correlated with each other.

5.6   Multiple Regression Analysis

The statistical method which defines a set of predictor variables and criterion variables. It also used to understand which independent variables are related to the dependent variable. In this research, we explore the relationship among perceived usefulness, perceived use of ease, relative advantage, attitude to use and interest to buy. The proposed model was examined through the parameters such as R2, F-ratio of overall fit, residual and hypothesis testing, t-test of specific parameters. In this research, these parameters had applied to find the direct and positive effect among constructs.

Regression Analysis of Perceived Usefulness vs Interest to Buy: The hypothesis (H1) of whether the perceived usefulness will have a positive effect on interest to buy has proposed and tested results are shown in the table. The result had enumerated that the p-value was less than 0.05 ($p < 0.05$) and t-test value (8.874) which was positive. Hence so the results support the hypothesis, so the perceived usefulness will have a positive effect on interest to buy which had the ability of elucidation of 52.6%. ($R^2 = 0.526$). The result indicates that the perceived usefulness of the electric car such as price range, performance, tax benefits, battery cost & warranty period, will make customer interest to buy the car (Table 8).

Table 8. Coefficient a of perceived usefulness and interest to buy

Model	R^2 value – 0.526 (52.6%)			t-value	Sig.
	Coefficient of perceived ease of use				
	Unstandardized coefficients		Standardized coefficients		
	B	Standard Error	β		
Constant	0.585	0.066		8.874	0.000
Perceived use of ease	0.411	0.039	0.557	10.610	0.000
Dependent variable: Interest to buy					

Regression Analysis of Perceived Ease of Use vs Interest to Buy: In the testing of proposed hypotheses (H2 & H3) in the model has extended and test results are showed in the table. The result had indicated that the p-value of PEOU and attitude was less than 0.05 ($p < 0.05$) and t-test value was positive. Hence so the results support hypotheses and the interest to buy was significantly affected by both perceived ease of use and attitude to use which had the capability of elucidation of 55.0% ($R^2 = 0.550$) (Table 9).

Table 9. Coefficient a of perceived use of ease, attitude and interest to buy

R² value – 0.219 (21.9%)					
Model	Coefficient of PEOU & attitude			t-value	Sig.
	Unstandardized coefficients		Standardized coefficients		
	B	Standard Error	β		
Constant	0.482	0.081		5.988	0.000
Perceived use of ease	0.122	0.033	0.169	3.732	0.000
Attitude	0.402	0.039	0.437	10.359	0.000
Dependent variable: Interest to buy					

The result shows that the perceived ease of use such as battery charging stations, recharging time, travel distance to charge station from home and durability assurance of the electric car will influence the attitude of the customer and make interest to buy an electric car. Both PEOU and attitude have a significant and positive influence on interest to buy. Furthermore, the attitude has a strong effect (0.437) on interest to buy then perceived ease of use (0.169) (Table 10).

Table 10. Coefficient [a] of relative advantages and interest to buy

	R² value – 0.219 (21.9%)				
Model	Coefficient of relative advantage			t-value	Sig.
	Unstandardized coefficients		Standardized coefficients		
	B	Standard Error	β		
Constant	0.866	0.160		5.417	0.000
Relative advantage	0.336	0.037	0.349	9.128	0.000
Dependent variable: Interest to buy					

Regression Analysis of Relative Advantage vs Interest to Buy: The hypothesis (H3) of whether the relative advantages have a direct and positive influence on interest to buy has proffered and test results are exposed in the table. The result had enumerated that the p-value was less than 0.05 ($p < 0.05$) and t-test value (5.417) which was positive. Hence so the results sustenance the hypothesis, so the relative advantage will have a direct and positive influence on interest to buy and capability of exposition of 21.9%. ($R^2 = 0.219$).

This result shows that the relative advantages such as Maximum driving speed, environmentally-friendly, maintenance expenses and acceleration of the electric car will influence the customer interest to buy the car (Fig. 2).

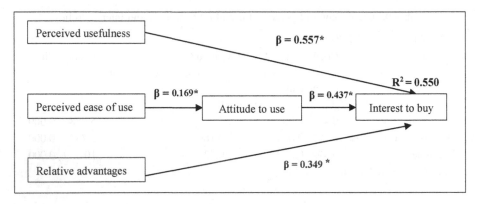

Fig. 2. Test results, *: represents significant difference p < 0.05:

6 Discussion

Our study employed two theories – TAM and DOI to analysis influence of customers interest in buying electric cars made several theoretical contributions. However, the resemblance of two theories have been recognized and the past studies linked to know the customer interest in buying the electric cars [9] and scales developed by combining two theories [33]. The high correlation between the perceived usefulness (r = 0. 0.672, p < 0.01), perceived ease of use (r = 0.672, p < 0.01), relative advantages (r = 0. 0.672, p < 0.01), attitude to use (r = 0.672, p < 0.01), and interest to buy the electric cars by customers. These results showed that the customer interest will be high based on the perceived usefulness of the electric car. The higher perceived ease of use of the electric car will have better attitude to use and willingness to buy the electric car and these findings assenting the previous studies [47]. The result exhibits that the perceived usefulness has a direct and positive effect on the customers' interest to buy electric cars. The higher usefulness such as price range, performance, tax benefits, battery cost is considered as the most useful factors which make interest to buy the electric cars resulted in higher interest to acquire electric cars. This finding is confirming the previous studies. [9, 15–17]. The test outcome indicates that the perceived ease of use had a positive effect on the attitude to use and interest to buy. The battery charging stations, recharging time, travel distance to charge station from home and durability assurance are determining factors of the ease of use which had positive effect on interest in buying the electric car. This result makes a positive agreement with past studies [15, 18, 19]. The finding reveals that relative advantage such as environmentally-friendly, maintenance expenses, maximum driving speed & acceleration of the electric car had a positive effect on the interest in buying the electric cars, confirming pervious results that relative advantage has a positive effect on intention to use [28, 36]. The chi-square results exposed that the factors influencing customers interest in buying the electric car varies significantly with gender. The price range, fuel elimination cost are important factors which makes gender sensitive. This result confirms the past research [38]. The customers are interested to buy the Indian brand manufactures like Maruthi, Mahindra.

The study finds that few customers have interest in electric cars because of innovativeness in it.

7 Scope and Limitations

This study helps the marketer to know the customers' interest in electric cars and understand the highest responsibility on bringing commercial value to an environmentally smart passenger car. It aids to know the role of various factors such as charging infrastructure, convenience in city use, tax benefits and maximum driving speed in building interest to buy an electric car, so that marketer can enhance the product and facilities that will result in maximum reach of electric cars in the Indian market. This study gives the empirical support to the vital role that perceived usefulness, perceived use of ease and relative advantage of electric cars which make customer interest to buy.

This research is restricted to the car industry in India, so this may constraint the generalizability of other overseas countries outcome. This study mainly emphasizes on the electric car (environmentally smart), so the customers' interest in the fuel based engine cars are not considered for this research. The survey data are collected only from non-commercial car owners. The study is based on the list of leading cars selling metropolitan cities report for the financial year 2019 [48] in India. The outcomes of the study should therefore be exercised with extreme cautiousness in non- metropolitan cities.

8 Conclusion

The rapid change in technology leads to introduction of electric car in alternative to fuel engine which is considered to be linchpin in the automobile industry. It is necessary for the customers to have interest towards theory of z generation before buying electric car. Customers are aware of the factors such as charging station, price range, environmentally smart and technology and they are very much ready to accept new technology with low price range. The findings of this research given greater understandings when analyzing customers interest to buy the electric car. The perceived usefulness, perceived ease of use, relative advantage, attitude and interest to buy were the factors investigated to know the interest and willingness of customers to buy the electric cars. As a result, we proposed the integration of TAM and DOI models could offer better overall outcomes. This study helps to understand the preeminent responsibility for bringing commercial value to an environmentally smart passenger car.

Appendix

Factors		Items
Perceived usefulness	PU-1	The Price range is the main factor that I will consider to buy an electric car
	PU-2	The Performance of the electric car is a factor that I will consider for purchase
	PU-3	Accept that tax benefits (Low taxes) provided by the government will encourage the electric car's sale
	PU-4	Admit that additional income tax deduction provided on the interest paid on loan taken will promote to buy an electric car
	PU-5	The battery cost is a significant factor that I will consider for purchase
	PU-6	The warranty period will help me to buy electric cars
Perceived ease of use	PEOU-1	Am willing to own the electric car if battery charging stations assigned in a high number
	PEOU-2	Consider the recharging time of the battery will play a vital role in buying an electric car
	PEOU-3	He distance from home to charging station is a factor that I will consider before purchasing an electric car
	PEOU-4	Will purchase if durability assurance is given by the car company
Attitude to use	ATU-1	Believe that charging facility of the electric car at home will convince the buyers
	ATU-2	Believe that comfort for city use is an important factor in electric car purchasing
	ATU-3	Believe that charging infrastructure in high number will encourage the customer to buy the electric car
	ATU-4	He Attractive design and style will stimulate me to acquire the electric car
	ATU-5	Believe the short driving distance of an electric car will not affect the buying interest
Relative advantages	RA-1	Maximum driving speed of the car is a significant factor that I will consider for purchase
	RA-2	Am ready to pay more for the electric car since its environmentally-friendly charging car
	RA3	Am ready to spend more money to purchase an electric car to save maintenance expenses
	RA-4	My expectation on acceleration is high on the electric car compared to fuel engines
Interest to buy	ITB -1	Am eager to buy the Indian brand electric cars
	ITB -2	Am eager to purchase an electric car as a secondary (used) car
	ITB -3	Am eager to buy luxury and sports type of electric cars
	ITB -4	Am willing to buy an electric car if the car company offers a micro car segment

References

1. Inc42. https://inc42.com/features/what-is-the-future-of-electric-cars-in-india/
2. ETAuto. https://auto.economictimes.indiatimes.com/news/passenger-vehicle/cars/90-of-car-owners-will-buy-e-car-if-right-infrastructure-is-provided-report/63611387
3. World economic forum. https://www.weforum.org/agenda/2019/10/how-can-india-transition-to-electric-vehicles-heres-a-roadmap/
4. Research&Market. https://www.researchandmarkets.com/reports/4765084/understanding-indian-consumerspriori-ties?utm_source=CI&utm_medium=PressRelease&utm_code=sw2cm4&utm_campaign=1307859++India+Hybrid+and+Electric+Vehicles+Consumers%27+Priorities%2c+Preferences+and+Willingness+to+Purchase%2c+2019+Research&utm_exec=chdo54prd
5. ETauto. https://auto.economictimes.indiatimes.com/news/passenger-vehicle/cars/e-cars-in-india-sold-only-1309-units-duringapril-nov-2019-merely-0-07-of-total-pv-sales/73007605
6. Fishbein, M., Ajzen, I.: Belief, attitude, intention, and behavior: an introduction to theory and research (1977)
7. Davis, F.D.: A technology acceptance model for empirically testing new end-user information systems: theory and results. Doctoral dissertation, Massachusetts Institute of Technology (1985)
8. Silva, P.: Davis' technology acceptance model (TAM) (1989). In Information seeking behavior and technology adoption: Theories and trends, pp. 205–219. IGI Global (2015)
9. Lee, Y.H., Hsieh, Y.C., Hsu, C.N.: Adding innovation diffusion theory to the technology acceptance model: supporting employees' intentions to use e-learning systems. J. Educ. Technol. Soc. **14**(4), 124–137 (2011)
10. Taylor, S., Todd, P.A.: Understanding information technology usage: a test of competing models. Inf. Syst. Res. **6**(2), 144–176 (1995)
11. Venkatesh, V., Davis, F.D.: A theoretical extension of the technology acceptance model: four longitudinal field studies. Manag. Sci. **46**(2), 186–204 (2000)
12. Williams, L.R., Magee, G.D., Suzuki, Y.: A multidimensional view of EDI: testing the value of EDI participation to firms. J. Bus. Logist. **19**(2), 73 (1998)
13. Davis, F.D.: User acceptance of information technology: system characteristics, user perceptions and behavioral impacts. Int. J. Man Mach. Stud. **38**, 475–487 (1993)
14. Mathwick, C., Malhotra, N., Rigdon, E.: Experiential value: conceptualization, measurement and application in the catalog and Internet shopping environment☆. J. Retail. **77**(1), 39–56 (2001)
15. Ma, Y.J., Gam, H.J., Banning, J.: Perceived ease of use and usefulness of sustainability labels on apparel products: application of the technology acceptance model. Fash. Text. **4**(1), 3 (2017)
16. Suki, N.M., Suki, N.M.: Exploring the relationship between perceived usefulness, perceived ease of use, perceived enjoyment, attitude and subscribers' intention towards using 3G mobile services. J. Inf. Technol. Manag. **22**(1), 1–7 (2011)
17. Altanopoulou, P., Tselios, N.: Assessing acceptance toward wiki technology in the context of higher education. Int. Rev. Res. Open Distrib. Learn. IRRODL **18**(6), 127–149 (2017)
18. Min, S., So, K.K.F., Jeong, M.: Consumer adoption of the Uber mobile application: insights from diffusion of innovation theory and technology acceptance model. J. Travel Tour. Mark. **36**(7), 770–783 (2019)
19. Tu, J.C., Yang, C.: Key factors influencing consumers' purchase of electric vehicles. Sustainability **11**(14), 3863 (2019)

20. Kim, Y.H.: A global analysis and market strategy in the electric vehicle battery industry. Doctoral dissertation, Massachusetts Institute of Technology (2014)
21. Ayeh, J.K.: Travellers' acceptance of consumer-generated media: an integrated model of technology acceptance and source credibility theories. Comput. Hum. Behav. **48**, 173–180 (2015)
22. Joo, J., Sang, Y.: Exploring Koreans' smartphone usage: an integrated model of the technology acceptance model and uses and gratifications theory. Comput. Hum. Behav. **29** (6), 2512–2518 (2013)
23. Persico, D., Manca, S., Pozzi, F.: Adapting the Technology Acceptance Model to evaluate the innovative potential of elearning systems. Comput. Hum. Behav. **30**, 614–622 (2014)
24. Van der Heijden, H., Verhagen, T., Creemers, M.: Understanding online purchase intentions: contributions from technology and trust perspectives. Eur. J. Inf. Syst. **12**(1), 41–48 (2003)
25. Rezaei, R., Ghofranfarid, M.: Rural households' renewable energy usage intention in Iran: extending the unified theory of acceptance and use of technology. Renew. Energy **122**, 382–391 (2018)
26. Wang, Y.S., Wu, S.C., Lin, H.H., Wang, Y.M., He, T.R.: Determinants of user adoption of web "Automatic Teller Machines': an integrated model of' Transaction Cost Theory 'and' Innovation Diffusion Theory'. Serv. Ind. J. **32**(9), 1505–1525 (2012)
27. Weng, F., Yang, R.J., Ho, H.J., Su, H.M.: A TAM-based study of the attitude towards use intention of multimedia among school teachers. Appl. Syst. Innov. **1**(3), 36 (2018)
28. Agag, G., El-Masry, A.A.: Understanding consumer intention to participate in online travel community and effects on consumer intention to purchase travel online and WOM: an integration of innovation diffusion theory and TAM with trust. Comput. Hum. Behav. **60**, 97–111 (2016)
29. Agarwal, R., Prasad, J.: A conceptual and operational definition of personal innovativeness in the domain of information technology. Inf. Syst. Res. **9**, 204–215 (1998)
30. Miller, R.L.: Rogers' innovation diffusion theory (1962, 1995). In Information seeking behavior and technology adoption: Theories and trends, pp. 261–274. IGI Global (2015)
31. Rogers, E.M., Shoemaker, F.: Diffusion of Innovation: A Cross-Cultural Approach. Free Press, New York (1983)
32. Rogers, E.M.: Diffusion of Innovations. The Free Press, New York (1983)
33. Moore, G.C., Benbasat, I.: Development of an instrument to measure the perceptions of adopting an information technology innovation. Inf. Syst. Res. **2**, 192–222 (1991)
34. Chen, L., Gillenson, M.L., Sherrell, D.L.: Enticing online consumers: an extended technology acceptance perspective. Inf. Manag. **39**, 705–709 (2002)
35. Amin, M., Rezaei, S., Abolghasemi, M.: User satisfaction with mobile websites: the impact of perceived usefulness (PU), perceived ease of use (PEOU) and trust. Nankai Bus. Rev. Int. **5**, 258–274 (2014)
36. Bandara, U.C., Amarasena, T.S.M.: Impact of relative advantage, perceived behavioural control and perceived ease of use on intention to adopt with solar energy technology in Sri Lanka. In: 2018 International Conference and Utility Exhibition on Green Energy for Sustainable Development (ICUE), pp. 1–9. IEEE, October 2018
37. Ahmad, A., Rashid, M., Omar, N.A., Alam, S.S.: Perceptions on renewable energy use in Malaysia: mediating role of attitude. Jurnal Pengurusan (UKM J. Manag.), **41**, 123–131 (2014)
38. Chiu, Y.C., Tzeng, G.H.: The market acceptance of electric motorcycles in Taiwan experience through a stated preference analysis. Transp. Res. Part D Transp. Environ. **4**(2), 127–146 (1999)

39. Mohd Amir, R.I., Mohd, I.H., Saad, S., Abu Seman, S.A., Tuan Besar, T.B.H.: Perceived ease of use, perceived usefulness, and behavioral intention: the acceptance of crowdsourcing platform by using technology acceptance model (TAM). In: Kaur, N., Ahmad, M. (eds.) Charting a Sustainable Future of ASEAN in Business and Social Sciences, pp. 403–410. Springer, Singapore (2020). https://doi.org/10.1007/978-981-15-3859-9_34
40. Firdaus, H.M.S., et al.: Acceptance of Electric Vehicle based on Pricing and Charging Station (2018)
41. Helveston, J.P., Liu, Y., Feit, E.M., Fuchs, E., Klampfl, E., Michalek, J.J.: Will subsidies drive electric vehicle adoption? Measuring consumer preferences in the US and China. Transp. Res. Part A Policy Pract. 73, 96–112 (2015)
42. Workman, M.: New media and the changing face of information technology use: the importance of task pursuit, social influence, and experience. Comput. Hum. Behav. 31, 111–117 (2014)
43. Lieven, T., Mühlmeier, S., Henkel, S., Waller, J.F.: Who will buy electric cars? An empirical study in Germany. Transp. Res. Part D Transp. Environ. 16(3), 236–243 (2011)
44. Hulin, C., Netemeyer, R., Cudeck, R.: Can a reliability coefficient be too high? J. Consum. Psychol. 10(1), 55–58 (2001)
45. Hong, W., Thong, J.Y., Wong, W.M., Tam, K.Y.: Determinants of user acceptance of digital libraries: an empirical examination of individual differences and system characteristics. J. Manag. Inf. Syst. 18(3), 97–124 (2002)
46. Kabengele, B.O., Kayembe, J.M.N., Kayembe, P.K., Kashongue, Z.M., Kaba, D.K., Akilimali, P.Z.: Factors associated with uncontrolled asthma in adult asthmatics in Kinshasa, Democratic Republic of Congo. PloS One 14(4), e0215530 (2019)
47. Huang, L.S., Huang, C.F.: A study of using technology acceptance model and its effect on improving road pavement smoothness in Taiwan. EURASIA J. Math. Sci. Technol. Educ. 13 (6), 2181–2195 (2017)
48. Drive Spark: https://www.drivespark.com/four-wheelers/2019/state-wise-car-sales-india-report-for-fy2019-details-028980.html

The Impact of Digital Marketing on Exploratory Buying Behavior Tendencies (EBBT)

K. K. Roshni[✉], T. Shobana[✉], and R. Shruthi[✉]

Ethiraj College for Women,
No; 70, Ethiraj Salai, Egmore, Chennai 600008, India
{roshni_kk,shobana_t,shruthi_r}@ethirajcollege.edu.in

Abstract. A marketing study is not complete without studying the buyer's behavior. With more people moving to the digital platform for day to day purposes, digital marketing is gaining momentum like never before. Hence this study aims to study the effect of digital marketing on Exploratory Buying Behavior Tendencies (EBBT) of the consumers. Since the ambit of digital marketing ambit is huge, only internet marketing, mobile marketing, E-Mail marketing and Social media marketing were taken for the study. Data from 110 respondents were collected and the results were analyzed using weighted average, correlation and regression. The study concludes that out of the four components in digital marketing, internet marketing has the highest influence on consumers as they buy products.

1 Introduction

In an era where information is omnipresent, digital marketing is inevitable. Digital marketing is the use of online platforms reach out to the consumers. Though are many components of digital marketing only a few of them have become the buzzword. To begin with, internet marketing is crucial as India has the second largest number of internet users after China. It concentrates on making the website attractive for consumers, posting advertisements in various sites. Mobile marketing is the next major component as the smart phone penetration is increasing day by day. Mobile marketing is done through applications, SMS and push notifications. Messages containing information regarding products and offers are sent to consumers. E-Mail marketing involves in sending personal and at times exclusive E-Mails to consumers to their mail inbox. E-Mail also contains information about new products in the form of E-Newsletters. Social media marketing is new when compared to the other three components of digital marketing. They include marketing on Facebook, Twitter, Instagram, LinkedIn, etc. This method is more attractive people tend to spend much of their online time on these social media platforms. With such digital media platforms, consumers tend to explore more products as more information is available to them in just a click. This makes them to take the risk of buying and trying unknown, other brand products. Moving on to buying behavior, exploring new products is salient factor influencing consumers. They search for innovative products offered, thereby leading to

© IFIP International Federation for Information Processing 2020
Published by Springer Nature Switzerland AG 2020
S. K. Sharma et al. (Eds.): TDIT 2020, IFIP AICT 617, pp. 510–519, 2020.
https://doi.org/10.1007/978-3-030-64849-7_45

exploratory buying behavior. The concept of Exploratory Buying Behavior Tendencies (EBBT) was proposed by Hans Baumgartner and Jan-Benedict E.M. Steenkamp in the year 1996. They identified that buying behavior can be motivated when the consumer expects that the end result of using a product will excite him. EBBT is a Two-Factor model. The first factor- Exploratory Acquisition of Products (EAP) deals with sensory stimulation of a consumer. All the five senses of a consumer i.e. sight, taste, smell, hearing and touch must be satisfied when he consumes the product. The second factor - Exploratory Information Seeking (EIS) prods the cognitive stimulation of the consumer. By getting additional information on a variety of products, he gets to choose a product which deliver his needs. As a consumer receives information on internet, mobile phone, E-Mail and social media, the artificial intelligence present in all these media brings in exact information that he needs. This thirst for exploring new products seem to be endless for consumers. For example, if a person is searching for features of a particular brand of mobile phone in internet, details regarding other models of the same brand and different brand's phones immediately pops up in other websites and social media sites. Hence, the study attempts to analyze the impact of digital marketing on EBBT.

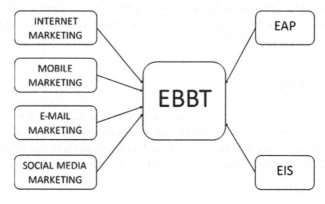

2   Review of Literature

Baumgartner and Steenkamp (1996) in paper 'Exploratory consumer buying behavior: Conceptualization and measurement' analyzed and proposed a two-factor concept of exploratory consumer buying behavior in which the authors explained that exploratory acquisition of products is different from exploratory information seeking. The method of Analysis used was correlation and two factor analysis. They narrowed down on 41 EAP factors and 28 EIS factors from 89 prospective factors. The results of six studies with students from two different countries, one a major American university and another university in the Netherlands shows that the scale has good psychometric properties and that its relationships with other constructs and actual exploratory behaviors confirm to theoretical expectations.

Waheed and Jianhua (2018) in their study 'The linkage between e-marketing and consumers' exploratory buying behavior tendencies have investigated the effect of EBBT toward E- Marketing in addition to the sub-factors of the E-Marketing model in China was inspected with gender as a moderate variable. Data from 1,600 respondents were collected over a period of 7 months. Pearson's correlation was used to analyze the data using SPSS with SEM technique. The results stated the positive relationships of EBBT toward all E-Marketing factors but relatively less positive effect than the direct effect of E-Marketing factors to EBBT.

Gañac (2018) in his paper 'Investigating Consumer Optimum Stimulation Level and Exploratory Online Buying Behavior' concentrated on elucidating the shooting increase of Internet shopping not only because of the rapid advances in technology but also due to the deep-rooted susceptibility of consumers to involve in exploratory buying and consumption. The merging of the decision-making process with exploratory buying behavior, lead to the formation of a theoretical framework for OSL driven online buying. They have made use of the generic purchase decision model as a framework to measure Internet-domain exploratory shopping behavior. The method of Analysis used was Pearson's correlation. The results exhibit that the weakest connection with exploratory buying behavior across the spread of information acquisition to purchase behavior, whereas consumer innovativeness revealed the highest correlation with impulsive buying behavior.

3   Research Gap

As digital marketing is the new normal, consumer buying behavior has drastically evolved over the period of time. Even though previous studies concentrate on Internet, mobile and E-Mail marketing, they have failed to touch upon social media marketing. Therefore, this study covers the influence of social media marketing over consumer's buying behavior.

4   Objectives

–   To find out the relationship between components of digital marketing and EBBT.
–   To analyze the key factors digital marketing and EBBT.

5   Methodology

Primary data has been collected through structured questionnaire from 110 respondents using convenience sampling technique. The data has been collected through on online survey having questions measured on five-point Likert scale ranging from strongly agree to strongly disagree. The questionnaire consists of three parts. Part- A has four statements on specific demographic variables. Part - B has 24 statements on digital marketing and 10 statements on EBBT. Part- C has questions on general demographic variables. Correlation and factor analysis have been used for analyzing data.

6 Results and Discussions

To measure the reliability and validity of the questionnaire, Cronbach's alpha, Kaiser-Meyer-Olkin (KMO) and Bartlett test were performed. The value of 0.869 for Cronbach's alpha suggests consistency of the items in the scale. The KMO measures was 0.807, which signifies that the scales of the variables in the questionnaire is understood by all the respondents and they have correctly answered. Additionally, Bartlett's test of for sphericity has a high chi-square value which justifies the sample suitability (Table 1).

Table 1. Table showing reliability and KMO analysis

Reliability statistics		
Cronbach's Alpha		N
0.868		6
Kaiser-Meyer-Olkin (KMO) and Bartlett test		
Kaiser-Meyer-Olkin Measure of Sampling Adequacy		0.807
Bartlett's test of for sphericity	Approx. Chi-Square	2367.18
	Df	561
	Sig	0

6.1 Sample Profile

The table below describes the demographic profile of the respondents with respect to gender, age, educational qualification and monthly income of 110 respondents.

Table 2. Table showing demographic variables

S. No	Demographic variables	% of respondents
General demographic variables:		
1	Gender:	
	Male	41.80%
	Female	57.30%
	Prefer not to say	0.90%
2	Age:	
	20 years–30 years	84.50%
	30 years–40 years	7.30%
	40 years–50 years	5.50%
	Above 50 years	2.70%
3	Educational status:	
	UG	49.10%
	PG	37.30%
	M.Phil./Research	2.70%
	Professional qualification	10.90%

(continued)

Table 2. (*continued*)

S. No	Demographic variables	% of respondents
4	Income:	
	Less than Rs 20,000	42.70%
	Rs 20,000–Rs 40,000	27.30%
	Rs 40,000–Rs 60,000	20.90%
	Rs 60,000–Rs 80,000	5.50%
	More than Rs 80,000	3.60%

It is inferred from the Table 2 that most of the respondents are female (57.3%). Majority (84.5%) of the respondents belong to the age group of 22-30 years and 7.3% of them belong to the age group of 30–40. 49.1% of the respondents have completed their UG and 37.3% have completed their PG. 43% of the respondents have their monthly income Rs. 20,000 and 20.9% have their monthly income from Rs. 40,000 to Rs. 60,000.

6.2   Finding of Objective 1

In order to identify the relationship between digital marketing and consumers' exploratory buying behavior tendencies (EBBT), Factor analysis of e-marketing with EBBT was examined using five factors: Internet marketing (IM), E-mail marketing (EM), mobile marketing (MM) and social media marketing (SM).

The Table 3, 4, 5 and 6 depicts that there exists a relationship between drivers of digital marketing and dimensions of EBBT. Out of the above four factors, Social Media Marketing is highly correlated with EBBT followed by E-mail marketing, internet marketing and mobile marketing.

Table 3. Correlation Matrix between Internet Marketing and EBBT

	IM Q1	IM Q2	IM Q3	IM Q4	IM Q5	IM Q6	EBBT Q1	EBBT Q2	EBBT Q3	EBBT Q4	EBBT Q5	EBBT Q6	EBBT Q7	EBBT Q8	EBBT Q9	EBBT Q10
IM Q1	1	0.414	0.486	0.498	0.47	0.36	-0.06	-0.297	0.111	0.264	-0.15	0.023		0.224	0.008	0.089
IM Q2		1	0.6	0.319	0.338	0.448	0.043	-0.176	-0.024	0.088	-0.009	-0.111	0.124	0.282	-0.033	0.113
IM Q3			1	0.506	0.328	0.407	-0.055	-0.077	0.133	0.084	0.006	0.15	0.214	0.333	-0.271	0.019
IM Q4				1	0.293	0.436	0.029	-0.141	0.249	0.076	-0.117	0.173	0.34	0.177	-0.018	-0.04
IM Q5					1	0.502	0.071	-0.269	0.068	0.293	-0.124	0.091	0.284	0.256	-0.09	-0.292
IM Q6						1	0.094	-0.217	0.065	0.093	-0.127	0.036	0.143	0.147	-0.211	-0.191
EBBT Q1	-0.06	0.043	-0.055	0.029	0.071	0.094	1	-0.173	0.307	0.213	-0.108	0.248	0.298	0.212	-0.161	-0.117
EBBT Q2	-0.297	-0.176	-0.077	-0.141	-0.269	-0.217	-0.173	1	-0.124	-0.239	0.18	-0.002	-0.382	-0.178	0.011	0.126
EBBT Q3	0.111	-0.024	0.133	0.249	0.068	0.065	0.307		1	0.359	-0.154	0.216	0.311	0.188	-0.178	-0.029
EBBT Q4	0.264	0.088	0.084	0.076	0.293	0.093	0.213			1	-0.315	0.322	0.361	0.165	-0.157	-0.12
EBBT Q5	-0.15	-0.009	0.006	-0.117	-0.124	-0.127	-0.108				1	-0.115	-0.33	-0.029	0.144	0.284
EBBT Q6	0.023	-0.111	0.15	0.173	0.091	0.036	0.248					1	0.238	0.5	-0.264	-0.173
EBBT Q7	0.29	0.124	0.214	0.34	0.284	0.143	0.298						1	0.339	-0.128	-0.133
EBBT Q8	0.224	0.282	0.333	0.177	0.256	0.147	0.212							1	-0.231	-0.029
EBBT Q9	0.008	-0.033	-0.271	-0.018	-0.09	-0.211	-0.161								1	0.5
EBBT Q10	0.089	0.113	0.019	-0.04	-0.292	-0.191	-0.117									1

Table 4. Correlation Matrix between Mobile Marketing and EBBT

	MM Q1	MM Q2	MM Q3	MM Q4	MM Q5	MM Q6	EBBT Q1	EBBT Q2	EBBT Q3	EBBT Q4	EBBT Q5	EBBT Q6	EBBT Q7	EBBT Q8	EBBT Q9	EBBT Q10
MM Q1	1	0.384	0.514	0.421	0.507	0.455	0.067	-0.177	0.236	0.271	-0.241	0.116	0.204	0.27	-0.014	0.067
MM Q2		1	0.621	0.554	0.42	0.43	0.137	0.033	0.245	0.006	-0.127	0.056	-0.016	0.293	-0.082	0.173
MM Q3			1	0.601	0.526	0.515	0.211	-0.055	0.279	0.272	-0.18	0.168	0.163	0.323	-0.072	0.042
MM Q4				1	0.74	0.524	0.152	0.007	0.315	0.237	-0.163	0.036	0.188	0.267	-0.054	-0.036
MM Q5					1	0.678	0.073	-0.127	0.287	0.273	-0.156	0.024	0.222	0.273	-0.082	0.024
MM Q6						1	0.111	-0.152	0.265	0.241	-0.155	-0.037	0.223	0.26	-0.026	0.164
EBBT Q1	0.067	0.137	0.211	0.152	0.073	0.111	1	-0.173	0.307	0.213	-0.108	0.248	0.298	0.212	-0.161	-0.117
EBBT Q2	-0.177	0.033	-0.055	0.007	-0.127	-0.152		1	-0.124	-0.239	0.18	-0.002	-0.382	-0.178	0.011	0.126
EBBT Q3	0.236	0.245	0.279	0.315	0.287	0.265			1	0.359	-0.154	0.216	0.311	0.188	-0.178	-0.029
EBBT Q4	0.271	0.006	0.272	0.237	0.273	0.241				1	-0.315	0.322	0.361	0.165	-0.157	-0.12
EBBT Q5	-0.241	-0.127	-0.18	-0.163	-0.156	-0.155					1	-0.115	-0.33	-0.029	0.144	0.284
EBBT Q6	0.116	0.056	0.168	0.036	0.024	-0.037					-0.115	1	0.238	0.5	-0.264	-0.173
EBBT Q7	0.204	-0.016	0.163	0.188	0.222	0.223						0.238	1	0.339	-0.128	-0.133
EBBT Q8	0.27	0.293	0.323	0.267	0.273	0.26								1	-0.231	-0.029
EBBT Q9	-0.014	-0.082	-0.072	-0.054	-0.082	-0.026									1	0.5
EBBT Q10	0.067	0.173	0.042	-0.036	0.024	0.164										1

Table 5. Correlation Matrix between E-Mail and EBBT

	EM Q1	EM Q2	EM Q3	EM Q4	EM Q5	EM Q6	EBBT Q1	EBBT Q2	EBBT Q3	EBBT Q4	EBBT Q5	EBBT Q6	EBBT Q7	EBBT Q8	EBBT Q9	EBBT Q10
EM Q1	1	0.819	0.719	0.64	0.707	0.675	0.157	-0.01	0.377	0.094	-0.162	0.19	0.177	0.285	-0.301	-0.161
EM Q2		1	0.826	0.616	0.752	0.718	0.166	-0.067	0.333	0.043	-0.069	0.191	0.196	0.327	-0.295	-0.079
EM Q3			1	0.611	0.689	0.633	0.218	-0.062	0.277	0.092	-0.062	0.176	0.168	0.287	-0.216	-0.098
EM Q4				1	0.611	0.559	0.148	-0.107	0.141	0.127	-0.096	0.172	0.218	0.3	-0.205	-0.13
EM Q5					1	0.807	0.271	-0.056	0.26	0.006	-0.206	0.083	0.2	0.271	-0.321	-0.148
EM Q6						1	0.192	-0.109	0.191	-0.081	-0.151	0.051	0.035	0.305	-0.247	-0.046
EBBT Q1	0.157	0.166	0.218	0.148	0.271	0.192	1	-0.173	0.307	0.213	-0.108	0.248	0.298	0.212	-0.161	-0.117
EBBT Q2	-0.01	-0.067	-0.062	-0.107	0.056	-0.109		1	-0.124	-0.239	0.18	-0.002	-0.382	-0.178	0.011	0.126
EBBT Q3	0.377	0.333	0.277	0.141	0.26	0.191			1	0.359	-0.154	0.216	0.311	0.188	-0.178	-0.029
EBBT Q4	0.094	0.043	0.092	0.127	0.006	-0.081				1	-0.315	0.322	0.361	0.165	-0.157	-0.12
EBBT Q5	-0.162	-0.069	-0.062	-0.096	-0.206	-0.151					1	-0.115	-0.33	-0.029	0.144	0.284
EBBT Q6	0.19	0.191	0.176	0.172	0.083	0.051					-0.115	1	0.238	0.5	-0.264	-0.173
EBBT Q7	0.177	0.196	0.168	0.218	0.2	0.035						0.238	1	0.339	-0.128	-0.133
EBBT Q8	0.285	0.327	0.287	0.3	0.271	0.305								1	-0.231	-0.029
EBBT Q9	-0.301	-0.295	-0.216	-0.205	-0.321	-0.247									1	0.5
EBBT Q10	-0.161	-0.079	-0.098	-0.13	-0.148	-0.046										1

Table 6. Correlation Matrix between Social Media Marketing and EBBT

	SM Q1	SM Q2	SM Q3	SM Q4	SM Q5	SM Q6	EBBT Q1	EBBT Q2	EBBT Q3	EBBT Q4	EBBT Q5	EBBT Q6	EBBT Q7	EBBT Q8	EBBT Q9	EBBT Q10
SM Q1	1	0.698	0.669	0.631	0.604	0.411	0.145	-0.13	0.177	0.187	0.016	0.162	0.158	0.324	-0.056	0.098
SM Q2		1	0.81	0.741	0.653	0.589	0.143	-0.16	0.281	0.2	-0.045	0.14	0.117	0.361	-0.146	0.134
SM Q3			1	0.65	0.719	0.547	0.18	-0.2	0.229	0.237	-0.15	0.098	0.214	0.339	-0.087	0.036
SM Q4				1	0.729	0.63	0.133	-0.07	0.271	0.226	-0.135	0.192	0.212	0.432	-0.075	0.032
SM Q5					1	0.534	0.046	-0.19	0.224	0.314	-0.08	0.1	0.254	0.272	0.016	0.058
SM Q6						1	0.179	-0.07	0.224	0.185	-0.168	-0.015	0.102	0.218	-0.124	0.004
EBBT Q1	0.145	0.143	0.18	0.133	0.046	0.179	1	-0.17	0.307	0.213	-0.108	0.248	0.298	0.212	-0.161	-0.117
EBBT Q2	-0.126	-0.164	-0.204	-0.073	-0.186	-0.072		1	-0.124	-0.239	0.18	-0.002	-0.382	-0.178	0.011	0.126
EBBT Q3	0.177	0.281	0.229	0.271	0.224	0.224			1	0.359	-0.154	0.216	0.311	0.188	-0.178	-0.029
EBBT Q4	0.187	0.2	0.237	0.226	0.314	0.185				1	-0.315	0.322	0.361	0.165	-0.157	-0.12
EBBT Q5	0.016	-0.045	-0.15	-0.135	-0.08	-0.168					1	-0.115	-0.33	-0.029	0.144	0.284
EBBT Q6	0.162	0.14	0.098	0.192	0.1	-0.015						1	0.238	0.5	-0.264	-0.173
EBBT Q7	0.158	0.117	0.214	0.212	0.254	0.102							1	0.339	-0.128	-0.133
EBBT Q8	0.324	0.361	0.339	0.432	0.272	0.218								1	-0.231	-0.029
EBBT Q9	-0.056	-0.146	-0.087	-0.075	0.016	-0.124									1	0.5
EBBT Q10	0.098	0.134	0.036	0.032	0.058	0.004									0.5	1

6.3   Findings of Objective 2

See Tables 7, 8 and 9.

The Eigen value table has been sub divided into three sections i.e. initial Eigen value, extracted sum of square loadings and rotated sum of squared loadings. The factor accounts for 69.72% of the variance extractions sum of squared loadings shows the number of rows in the panel of the table corresponding to the number of factors retained. Rotations sum of squared loadings represents the distribution of the variance after the varimax rotation. Factors are rotated for easier interpretation. The idea of rotation is to reduce the number of factors of which the variable under investigation have high loading. Exploratory Factor analysis results show that all the statements are accepted i.e. Social media motivates consumers to interact with others for information sharing has the lowest value of 0.314. The results of exploratory factor analysis reveal that Social media advertising motivates buying tendencies is 0.852 has a significant impact over exploratory buying behavior. Results also shows that digital marketing has an impact Over exploratory buying behavior tendencies.

Table 7. Total variance explained

Component	Initial eigenvalues			Extraction sums of squared loadings			Rotation sums of squared loadings		
	Total	% of Variance	Cumulative %	Total	% of Variance	Cumulative %	Total	% of Variance	Cumulative %
1	10.46	30.759	30.759	10.46	30.759	30.759	5.14	15.122	15.122
2	3.17	9.324	40.083	3.17	9.324	40.083	4.81	14.133	29.256
3	2.445	7.192	47.275	2.445	7.192	47.275	3.8	11.189	40.445
4	2.228	6.554	53.829	2.228	6.554	53.829	2.88	8.456	48.901
5	1.727	5.081	58.909	1.727	5.081	58.909	1.92	5.66	54.561
6	1.408	4.141	63.051	1.408	4.141	63.051	1.86	5.463	60.024
7	1.198	3.523	66.574	1.198	3.523	66.574	1.71	5.02	65.044
8	1.07	3.146	69.72	1.07	3.146	69.72	1.59	4.675	69.72

Extraction Method: Principal Component Analysis (Source: Research Output)

Table 8. Component Matrix[a]

	Component							
	1	2	3	4	5	6	7	8
SM Q4	0.757				0.318			
SM Q2	0.729				0.362			
SM Q3	0.705	0.407						
MM Q3	0.701			0.387				
EM Q2	0.689	−0.56						
EM Q1	0.678	−0.568						
EM Q5	0.661	−0.552						
SM Q6	0.66					−0.336		
SM Q5	0.655	0.447						
EM Q4	0.654	−0.307						
EM Q3	0.649	−0.517						
IM Q3	0.641			−0.432				
EM Q6	0.633	−0.511						
MM Q1	0.631							
SM Q1	0.628	0.39						
MM Q4	0.615			0.519				
MM Q5	0.581			0.576				
MM Q6	0.564			0.477				
IM Q6	0.549				−0.352	−0.336		
MM Q2	0.542		0.32	0.41				
IM Q4	0.537					0.379		
IM Q2	0.536	0.333		−0.336				
IM Q1	0.529	0.385			−0.337	0.322		
EBBT Q8	0.515				0.312			0.482
IM Q5	0.462	0.358	−0.322		−0.322			
EBBT Q3	0.414			0.309				
EBBT Q7	0.37		−0.597					
EBBT Q10			0.576			0.475		
EBBT Q4	0.324		−0.559					
EBBT Q6			−0.483		0.462		0.41	
EBBT Q5			0.438					
EBBT Q9		0.371	0.374			0.395	−0.332	
EBBT Q2			0.412				0.476	−0.304
EBBT Q1			−0.348		0.322		−0.372	0.367

Extraction Method: Principal Component Analysis.
[a]7 components extracted.

Table 9. Rotated Component Matrix[a]

	Component							
	1	2	3	4	5	6	7	8
EM Q2	0.884							
EM Q1	0.843							
EM Q5	0.839							
EM Q3	0.82							
EM Q6	0.807							
EM Q4	0.651							
SM Q2		0.852						
SM Q3		0.846						
SM Q5		0.788						
SM Q4	0.314	0.757						
SM Q1		0.742						
SM Q6		0.613	0.446					
MM Q5			0.815					
MM Q4			0.789					
MM Q6			0.727					
MM Q2			0.686					
MM Q3	0.314	0.318	0.652					
MM Q1			0.512	0.468				
IM Q1				0.743				
IM Q4	0.389			0.643				
IM Q3	0.398	0.396		0.57				
IM Q5				0.557		-0.405		
IM Q2		0.469		0.475	-0.326			
EBBT Q4					0.649			
EBBT Q3					0.584			
EBBT Q5					-0.496	0.359		
EBBT Q10						0.841		
EBBT Q9						0.695		
IM Q6		0.328		0.394		-0.413		
EBBT Q6							0.796	
EBBT Q8							0.736	
EBBT Q2								-0.736
EBBT Q1				-0.342				0.601
EBBT Q7				0.322	0.496			0.498

Extraction Method: Principal Component Analysis.
Rotation Method: Varimax with Kaiser Normalization.
[a.]Rotation converged in 10 iterations.

7   Conclusion

To begin with, internet marketing is crucial as India has the second largest number of internet users after China. Mobile marketing is the next major component as the smart phone penetration is increasing day by day. Social media marketing is more attractive as people tend to spend much of their online time on the social media platforms. Taking all these factors into account, the study shows that social media marketing has a tremendous impact in consumers buying behavior. Thus, companies who are already in the market or new companies entering the market can explore marketing options in various social media platform like Instagram, Facebook, WhatsApp, Twitter, LinkedIn, Pinterest and even YouTube.

As consumers move to these platforms for networking, it makes easy for them to shop as AI in these sites are easily able to identify the consumers' needs through their search results. Even though, internet shopping offers the same, consumers are directly able to interact with the sellers which is not the case in most of the internet sites. Simultaneously, the consumers are opting for detailed information of the products rather than sensory features. Therefore, consumers look out for information of various products before buying them.

References

Baumgartner, H., Steenkamp, J.E.M.: Exploratory consumer buying behavior: conceptualization and measurement. Int. J. Res. Mark. **13**, 121–137 (1996)

Waheed, A., Jianhua, Y.: Achieving consumers' attention through emerging technologies: the linkage between e-marketing and consumers' exploratory buying behavior tendencies. Baltic J. Manag. **13**(2), 209–235 (2018)

Gañac, C.G.: Investigating consumer optimum stimulation level and exploratory online buying behavior. DLSU Bus. Econ. Rev. **28**(1), 67–85 (2018)

Fin-Tech Applications

Influence of FinTech Companies on Banking Landscape an Exploratory Study in Indian Context

Parvathy Venkatachalam[(✉)]

Indian Institute of Management, Indore, India
ef20parvathyv@iimidr.ac.in

Abstract. Globally, there is a disruption in the financial sector due to the emergence of FinTech companies. The industry is changing in the way it functions. Hence, it is important to understand the changing landscape in the Indian context. The key players identified in the landscape are regulators, traditional banks, and FinTech companies. The objective of the study is to understand in Indian context 1) Role of key players in the changing landscape and 2) Influence of FinTech companies on the ecosystem. This study observes that there will be an emergence of the multi-dimensional relationship among the participants in the ecosystem and the scope of regulation will widen. This paper also observes that FinTech has a positive influence on meeting Sustainable Development Goals and the challenges of regulation considering this larger goal will vary based on the risk involved in business models and products, with technology playing a pivotal role.

Keywords: FinTech · Emerging technologies · Traditional banks · Regulator

1 Introduction

The banking and financial services (BFS) industry of India is changing rapidly with the advent of the FinTech ecosystem. Post financial crisis of 2008, it has been observed that there is decreased loyalty to a single bank, an increase in tech-savvy customer-segment, and other changing behaviours of consumers leading to innovative banking practices [1]. While the traditional banks had the advantage of trust, the fintech companies focused on value creation in terms of usage patterns, convenience, price, variety in the offering, etc. Given the changing scenario, the objective of the study is to understand 1) the Role of key players in the changing landscape and 2) the Influence of FinTech companies on the ecosystem in the Indian context. The study is exploratory in nature using secondary data for analysis. The study analyses the development, design, and diffusion of technology architecture and solutions through 1) five FinTech companies that are emerging in this decade of FinTech era 2) five financial institutions/bank and five core banking solutions that are deployed in these institutions 3) infrastructure and regulatory policies and guidelines. The study aims to understand how each one of these players in the ecosystem view technology and the challenges emerging due to the evolving landscape.

S. K. Sharma et al. (Eds.): TDIT 2020, IFIP AICT 617, pp. 523–528, 2020.
https://doi.org/10.1007/978-3-030-64849-7_46

The paper is divided into two parts: The first part briefly explains the methodology of the study and lists the key findings. In the next part, the role of each entity and the influence of FinTech companies on the ecosystem are discussed.

2   Methodology

As a first step, five traditional banks were shortlisted. Their respective websites and the annual reports of 2019–20 were taken as the reference to understand the product details. The data collected include 1) What are the collaborated offerings in the digital space 2) What features are highlighted on the product/services being offered 3) What are the underlying technology, components and layers defined in their banking technology product. As a next step, five companies that emerged as FinTech players as per the definition in this study were shortlisted. Broadly, the FinTech companies in India belong to the following categories 1) Lending 2) Payments 3) Neobank/Accounting 3) RegTech 4) Enablers 5) Financial Inclusion 6) Insurance 7) Investments. For the analysis for this study, the FinTech companies belonging to Neobank/Accounting focusing on SMB were considered. As a final step, the background information on regulatory aspects was collected from publicly available news releases and reports.

3   Findings and Analysis

3.1   Banks at the Time of FinTech

The Banking sector is disrupted by business model innovation with the advent of FinTech companies. Though FinTech companies offer innovative banking products and services through technology, there are few practical issues for them to scale. Currently, the traditional banks are licensed to integrate with the payment systems in the Indian context. But they seem to be lacking in innovation capabilities, presence of underserved customer segments, and geographical areas. With the changing business models, technology architecture has also evolved to mimic the change in business. To overcome the disadvantages on these ends, banks are observed to have adopted an increased level of collaboration. It is also seen that the banks had a partnership with an established incubator or played the role of incubator for the FinTech startups.

3.2   FinTech Companies and Their Offerings

All the FinTech samples were startups and had a venture capitalist deal. In all the samples, the utility of the product or service, the beneficiaries, and the ease of access to the product are highlighted while the details of the functionality of the product or service are often described through FAQ (Frequently Asked Questions) section. (Table 1 FinTech Segments in Indian context).

Table 1. FinTech Segments in Indian Market

Product/Service	Reason behind growth	Business Model of FinTech Players	Identified Technology
Payments	Increase in smart phones, internet connectivity, online shopping	Payment bank licenses – through hybrid model where mobile services interact with banking services	Integration of payment processing into web applications, transaction through UPI
Lending and Investment, Trade Finance, Insurance	Presence of crowd funding, financial aggregators etc.	Through portals and collaboration	Payment and Settlement systems, Robo-advisory solutions
Account Aggregators	Increased spending and financial planning requirements	NBFC (Non-banking)	Data Analytics

3.3   Regulatory Bodies in Evolving Landscape

The payment system architecture UPI (Unified Payment Interface, 2016) has made all the systems seamlessly communicate with each other serving as the major digital channel. The non-banks do not have access to these payment systems and can interact only through registered banks. In 2019, the steering committee of the Ministry of Finance of Government of India, analysed the developments in the FinTech space and published a list of recommendations.

4   Discussion

4.1   Roles of Entities

Based on the study, it is seen that 1) FinTech companies focus on innovation of financial products and generating customer experience. They penetrate new segments and markets and co-brand with a bank when required. However, underlying architecture details are not disclosed. 2) Traditional banks understand the market need and partner with FinTech companies. Their primary objective has been to meet regulatory requirements. They entrust the technology integration to system integrator that mirrors the business model using extensible technology. 3) the role of regulator is to understand the landscape and accommodates the same in the policy framework and guidelines for all regulatory bodies. This body has the holistic vision of the changes happening currently, has the responsibility to meet the policy and societal goals in enabling transformational changes.

4.2   Identity of FinTech

It should be noted that FinTech companies are operating in a crossover space between technology and financial sectors. They bring out innovative financial products through emerging technology which still is not under the purview of the regulatory framework. As a result, the identity of the FinTech companies tends to vary in comparison to traditional banks who are licensed to operate. In this case, the tendency to possess the sectoral identity of technology domain is stronger than that of the finance domain.

4.3   Challenges for Regulator

The regulatory focus has been on consumer protection and market integrity. In the current operating space, FinTech has the risk of both these factors. New technology by itself cannot be considered as risk and the enabling ability of technology has to be leveraged. Hence the focus shifts to protecting consumers and data security. Similarly, the identity dilemma of FinTech companies and their regulations are also challenging. The impact of technology innovations, its legal implications, resilience of operations due to FinTech is to be explored. The traditional banks enjoy the customer trust and therefore have access to interface with the central bank's framework. This allows them to act as front-end of FinTech companies. However, in case of breach or violations, they have to be held equally responsible and cannot blame it on failed technology. Here again, the policy makers are forced to consider the need for creating the level playing field for both banks and FinTech companies.

But it has to be understood that the innovation of the product stems from technology as against traditional product offering by banks where the offered product is configured in the technology system. Hence the policy has to adjust its boundary and provide flexibility accordingly. The failure to do so may result in the lack of development in innovations. However, lack of technical details shared for enabling the product offering is a cause for concern and the regulators have to take cognizant of the same.

4.4   Multi-dimensional Relationship of Entities

FinTech and Banks

Banks are likely to be the backbone of industry and will promote the innovative ideas of FinTech companies through collaboration. The responsibility of the technology integration may continue to lie with the bank as per the regulatory guidelines and with emerging technology total cost of ownership in the maintenance of the system might reduce. The modular architecture enables the infrastructure to grow as rapidly as that of the business model.

FinTech Companies and Technologies

Given the contribution to financial inclusion, deeper and faster penetration, FinTech's core strength is innovation. Currently, in the Indian context, startups dominate the field. However, the future of FinTech in Indian context largely lies with regulation.

FinTech and Regulator

The policies and measures are being taken to address the operational concerns; Government is focusing on technology-related infrastructure required to create the base for the expansion of FinTech services. Largely, studies [2] state that FinTech related policies can fall under three categories 1) Governing FinTech based financial services 2) Governing underlying technology of such offerings 3) Policy Initiatives. All these three are applicable in Indian context as well. There will be a need for robust policy in place for each of the categories and should be open to change continuously. The next challenge is the risk assessment that includes operational risk among banks due to third-party service providers, data protection, and security. The macro-financial risks tend to rise if there is greater fund flow in the certain segment and that is unstable.

4.5   Role of FinTech in SDGs

It can be observed that tilting focus towards consumers through deeper market penetration, new experience generation, reduced intermediaries in transactions etc., through FinTech companies aids in accelerating the Government aim in meeting financial inclusion. The digital model further aids in meeting green-based finance. The role of technology aids in achieving all these goals. However, the critical issue and risk is that of the digital divide leading to the financial divide which will be the key concern for the regulator.

5   Conclusion - Quo Vadis?

Thus, it can be observed that today, enabling technologies are the foundations for most of the innovations in the delivery of financial services. In providing products and services, the traditional banks used technology as a delivery channel but the fintech companies use technology as a value creator. There is an emergence of a multi-dimensional relationship among the entities identified. So what could be the approach the regulator is likely to explore in Indian context? Will FinTech be recognised as technology sector or as finance sector? Given the change in technology, innovation, demand, participants and their roles the scope of regulator varies which is captured through the following framework (Fig. 1):

6   Limitation and Way Forward

Post Covid-19, there is expected to have an impact on all sectors. It is speculated there will be increased financial inclusion, digital transactions, and more internet penetrations. The product innovations might increase. The level of disruption, the way the industry will react and restructure, the impact of technology on competition and consumer is not clearly defined at the moment. All these aspects are not considered in the current analysis. Similarly, Sustainable Development Goals (SDG) will undergo a revision of priority based on the pandemic impact. The socio technology perspective on the success of FinTech in the changed macro conditions is to be explored.

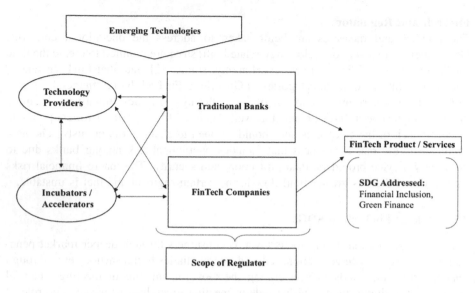

Fig. 1. Framework of FinTech Landscape in Indian Context

References

1. Hansen, T.: The role of trust in financial customer-seller relationships before and after the financial crisis. J. Consum. Behav. **13**(6), 442–452 (2014)
2. Ehrentraud, J., Ocampo, D.G., Garzoni, L., Piccolo, M.: Policy responses to fintech: a cross-country overview. FSI Insights on Policy Implementation, 23 (2020)

Is Cash Still the Enemy? The Dampening of Demonetization's Ripple Effect on Mobile Payments

U. Mahesh Balan[1] and Abhipsa Pal[2(✉)]

[1] Indian Institute of Technology Madras, 600036 Chennai, India
u.maheshbalan@gmail.com
[2] Indian Institute of Management Kozhikode, 673570 Kozhikode, India
abhipsapal@iimk.ac.in

Abstract. Technology diffusion has often been triggered unintendedly by crises and disasters, as witnessed in several cases including the demonetization cashcrisis surging mobile payment adoption in India. However, once the shock waves induced by the crisis event weakens over time, there exists a void that questions the sustenance of the technology whose diffusion was a ripple effect of the shock. This is seldom explored by the literature that focuses on the immediate aftermath of the crises. We address this limitation by examining the cash withdrawal patterns from ATMs in India post-demonetization for a continuous period of three years. The results provide strong empirical evidence to support our claims towards the dampening of demonetizations' ripple effect on mobile payments. The theoretical contributions of the study add further to the existing literature on technology diffusion and technology adoption post-crises with a focus on the digital payment systems. The findings have implications for policymakers and government concerned with the digital economy, with cash emerging as an enemy overshadowing the growth of digital payment methods.

Keywords: Mobile payments · Digital payments · Cash usage · ATM cash withdrawals · Technology diffusion

1 Introduction

Crises and disasters have often created organic changes in an environment by creating shock waves that surge technology adoptions; and eventually, these shock waves create a ripple effect that leads to a greater diffusion of the respective technology (Rasmussen and Johnson 2008). Some classic examples include diffusion of ERP systems worldwide as an aftermath of the Y2K problem (Ma-bert, Soni, and Venkataramanan 2001), expansion of information and communication technology (ICT) industry in South Korea post the East Asian financial crises (Lee 2003), and the remarkable rise in social media usage due to the Arab Spring revolution (Bruns, Highfield, and Burgess 2013). The recent banknote crises triggered by the demonetization policy in India in 2016 offered a similar scope for rapid diffusion of digital modes of payments due to the invalidation of the majority of currency notes in circulation (Chakravorti 2017). The initial spread of mobile payments was recorded by the rising statistics for usage of

© IFIP International Federation for Information Processing 2020
Published by Springer Nature Switzerland AG 2020
S. K. Sharma et al. (Eds.): TDIT 2020, IFIP AICT 617, pp. 529–540, 2020.
https://doi.org/10.1007/978-3-030-64849-7_47

unified payments interface (UPI), a common platform for mobile money transactions (NPCI Website 2020). But, is this surge in digital payments in India an illusion or a reality?

Post demonetization in India, the UPI data serves as a proxy for growth in mobile payments, raising hopes of moving towards a digital economy. However, various articles and reports claim that citizens have migrated back to cash within a year post demonetization, threatening the sustenance of the mobile payments technology (Choudhury 2018). Leaders in the digital payment domain have ex-claimed how "cash is the biggest enemy" (Nair 2016). Therefore, it is still un-clear if mobile payments are indeed on its way to become the dominant payment option or continue to be a secondary option with a cash-based economy resuming its primary stand after the demonetization cash crises ended. This leads us to our research questions: Did the cash crisis of demonetization enable mobile payments to become the primary payment mode for transactions or does cash still dominate the daily transactions? Did the ripple effect of demonetization on mobile payment diffusion sustain or dampen over time?

To answer these questions, in this study, we use a database of daily ATM withdrawals pan India provided by a large cash management service provider in India, helping load cash for most of the leading Indian banks. We use this data from 100 towns across 7 states of India, spanning across 4 years, to empirically evaluate if there are significant changes in the withdrawal patterns before and after demonetization; and the change, if exists, is sustained or dampened over time. Building on the existing knowledge from past literature on crisis-driven technology diffusion, we examine if demonetization had created a shock wave strong enough to trigger a ripple effect that sustains for a long time. Most of the literature in this area focuses on technology diffusion that occurs during or immediately post-crisis, but does not question the sustenance of such phenomenon through the tests of time (e.g., Oh, Agrawal, and Rao 2013; Zhou, Shi, Mao, Tang, and Zeng 2014). In this study, we address this limitation by providing strong empirical evidence that demonstrates the effect of demonetization on the diffusion of mobile payment technologies. This paper becomes one of the first to claim the dampening effect of mobile payment adoption post demonetization. This has various implications for literature in ICT4D and technology usage after crises.

The rest of the paper is organized as follows. We give a brief background of the demonetization and explain with evidence the rise in UPI transactions. This is followed by the past literature and the theoretical background for this study. Next, we discuss the research methods, and the findings of the study, before concluding the paper.

2 Motivation

November 2016 witnessed one of the biggest economic events in the history of the 21st century as the government of India introduced the demonetization of banknotes in circulation (Kumar 2016). The policy invalidated 500 INR and 1000 INR banknotes in circulation and exchanging them for new banknotes issued by the government. The primary intent of the decision was taken to curtail the shadow economy and curb black money and unlawful transactions, but it led to both positive and negative unintended consequences (Dutta 2018). One of the most welcome outcomes was the inevitable

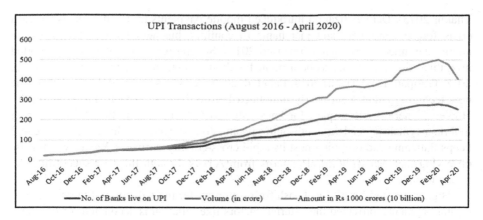

Fig. 1. UPI Transaction Statistics National Payments Corporation of India (NPCI)

transformation of the economy from physical cash to digital cash amidst the unintended severe cash crisis that the policy introduced (Mehta et al. 2016). This natural experiment on the biggest democracy of the world has received widespread attention by various scholars around the world, adding to the existing literature on the digital economy, policymaking and ICT4D (e.g., Banerjee et al. 2019, Dash 2017, Singh and Singh 2016). Many of these studies argue that there is an increase in the adoption of mobile payment technologies pan India post demonetization (e.g., Pal et al. 2020). This also has led to the launch of several digital wallets post demonetization like Google Tez, PhonePe, Airtel money, Amazon Pay, and other mobile payment technologies introduced by other banks (Bureau 2019). These various wallets and banking apps that were supported by the common platform of UPI, resulted in the wider spread of UPI (Hetavkar 2019). The flourishment of UPI was visible in the statistics reported by the National Payments Corporation of India (NPCI).

See the graph in Fig. 1 below for the steep rise in UPI adoption in the dimensions including the number of live banks, the volume of transactions, and the amount.

We can see from the graph that UPI transactions grew gradually and fast over the two years post demonetization, masquerading an effect of sustainable growth of digital payments. What went unnoticed in the growth curve is the return of the cash in circulation, specifically, the ATM withdrawals representing the cash for daily transactions. The steady decline of UPI payments two years post demonetization, as seen in the figure, is not the only evidence of the uncertain future of mobile payments, as we investigate empirically, but also the rising pattern of cash withdrawals from ATMs and posing huge threat to its sustenance.

3   Literature

Before demonetization, mobile payment and banking research in India focused on why the adoption rates in India were insignificant although the technology had been accepted in many developing economies (Bamoriya and Singh 2011, Srivastava and

Thakur 2013). Demonetization introduced mobile payments to the masses, as the cash crisis forced consumers and merchants to continue business through this seamless alternative mode of payment (Francisco 2017). Several research studies have reported how this crisis turned out to be a boon for digital payments' growth (Agarwal et al. 2018, Goriparthi and Tiwari 2017, Pal et al. 2018). Citizens reported the benefits of the new technology that went nearly unnoticed before the cash crunch (Pal et al. 2020). However, there is still a quest for knowledge to further examine the phenomenon of mobile payment spread in-depth, and specifically, answering why its growth curve keeps flattening and dropping post its rapid cross-country diffusion. We answer this by observing the cash withdrawal patterns from ATMs through the year succeeding the phenomenal event.

Higher demand for physical cash forms a proxy for the reduction of transactions in digital payments, provided the external factors like inflation is accounted for (Arango-Arango and Suárez-Ariza 2019). An individual's cash usage patterns changes with her or his digital payment usage (Stix 2004), indicating a measurable drop in the amount of cash replaced with the growth in digital payment options (Humphrey 2004). There remain various advantages of digital money including enabling convenient and seamless one-click transactions (de Kerviler et al. 2016, Mallat 2007). However, studies have also identified issues with mobile payments in terms of the risks from thefts and failures, and difficult cross-platform transferability (Luo et al. 2010, Wright 2002). With other environmental and habitual effects, the demand for cash continues to rise globally (Arango-Arango and Suárez-Ariza 2019), and particularly in India once the cash crisis started to gradually decline (Roy 2017). This paper aims to verify this ongoing concern of the rise of cash usage and the threat of decline of digital payments.

4 Theoretical Foundation on Ripple Effect

Technology adoption has been often witnessed as unintended aftermaths like the ripple effect after crisis situations including technical, social, and financial crises and disasters (James Cater III and Beal 2014). A ripple effect is defined as "a spreading, pervasive, and usually *unintentional* effect or influence" (Merriam-Webster Dictionary 2020).

Our first significant example includes the ERP systems' adoption as firms invested in the installation of ERPs to solve the sudden date format in their systems from 1900 to 2000, popularly called the Y2K problem (Chang et al. 2008, Pliskin and Zarotski 2000). As firms were threatened by their legacy system failures due to the sudden change in the historic date format, they chose the investment for new technology – the ERP systems (Themistocleous et al. 2001). This technical crisis of the Y2K problem resulted in the unanticipated diffusion of different technology. Next, we have the Arab Spring revolution creating a spark in social media usage (Bruns et al. 2013). During the insurgency in several Arab Springs' countries between 2010 and 2012, the Twitter hashtag culture expanded, and motivated technology adoption researchers (Oh et al. 2013, Rauniar et al. 2014). Another example is the 1997 East Asian financial crisis triggered aggressive ITbusiness adoption in South Korea (Jeon et al. 2006, Lee 2003). A campus shootout disaster in April 2007 on the Virginia Tech college campus led to a countrywide enhancement of the technologies for emergency procedures and response systems (Rasmussen and Johnson 2008).

Although the crises events discussed here are disparate and of varied nature and impact, there is one common phenomenon among them – the ripple effect of crises on technology adoption. In similar lines, we observe the ripple effect of demonetization on the adoption of digital payments. Research in technology adoption in the crisis domain has looked at the immediate rise in technology usage after the shock. However, we argue that the ripple effect would dampen over time, bringing the usage closer to pre-crisis levels as cash usage rises back to pre-demonetization normalcy.

5   Research Hypotheses

Demonetization created a severe cash crisis across India, with the shortage of acceptable new banknotes and long queues across banks and ATMs (Express 2016). The only way to sustain transactions for daily livelihood was shifting to alternative payment options which included digital payments like debit/credit cards and mobile payment wallets (Goriparthi and Tiwari 2017). As debit and credit card usage was limited to existing cardholders, mobile payments offered a quick installation and easy immediate payment option (Bhargava 2017). Even local merchant and small-scale vendors started depending on mobile payments for continuing businesses in the absence of cash (Bureau 2016). Therefore, we primarily hypothesize,

H1: Demonetization has a ripple effect on the adoption of digital payment technologies, as seen through the sudden dip in cash withdrawals from ATM

The adoption and diffusion of mobile payments post demonetization can, therefore, be attributed to the technology push by the crisis (Pal et al. 2018), as also seen in the crisis cases discussed above. However, as new banknotes reached the country's circulation system, citizens started reverting to the traditional cash system, often discontinuing the newly adopted mobile payments (Choudhury 2018, Mint 2017). The question remains if the ripple effect of the demonetization crisis on mobile payment technology continues to thrive or dampens over time. We posit,

H2: People will gradually revert from alternative modes like mobile payments to cash as the dominant payment mode, and withdraw cash from ATMs as high as the pre-demonetization levels.

In our study, the ripple and the dampening effect of demonetization on mobile payments are measured by dip and upsurge of ATM cash withdrawals, respectively, since cash usage can be used as a reverse proxy for digital payment diffusion (Arango-Arango and Suárez-Ariza 2019). This analysis would throw light on technology adoption after crises or disasters, as it questions the sustenance of the technology once the shock in the environment disappears and original resources and conditions are restored. Certain technologies with greater switching costs, like the ERP system, are likely to flourish. However, individual-level IT artifacts like mobile payments or social media always have the threat of discontinuance in the absence of the shock condition that led to its adoption.

6 Research Methodology

The research methodology includes the data analysis of cash withdrawals from 100 ATMs, as discussed in this section.

6.1 Data Collection

The data for this study was provided by a very large cash management services provider in India that provides ATM management for most of the leading banks in India. The data reports daily ATM cash withdrawals in 100 ATMs spanning across 100 towns and 7 states of India for 4 years, from November 2015 to November 2019. Each ATM is a representative of the highest withdrawal outlet of a town. In order to mitigate the effect of out-of-money and technical issues impacting the daily withdrawal patterns, we aggregate the data to monthly resolution, thus having 48 observations for each ATM spanning 4 years (48 months). The data was then split into 4 different buckets-based representation 4 different years before after the day of demonetization (November 8, 2016). We have 1 year of data before demonetization as a bucket and 3 years post demonetization data as 3 different buckets, which will enable us to study the sensitivity analysis on the change in withdrawal patterns on a yearly basis. We filtered out the data from November 8, 2016, and Dec 30, 2016, because the Government of India banned the loading of ATMs with cash until the new currencies (500 INR and 2000 INR) were in circulation from Jan 2, 2017. (Refer to Table 1 for the descriptive statistics).

Table 1. Descriptive statistics of the data

Total number of ATMs	100
Total number of Towns	100
Total number of States	7
Timeline of the data	Nov 2015 – Nov 2019
Average monthly withdrawal per ATM in INR (2015–2016)	4705741.69
Average monthly withdrawal per ATM in INR (2016–2017)	3456763.75
Average monthly withdrawal per ATM in INR (2017–2018)	4545057.87
Average monthly withdrawal per ATM in INR (2018–2019)	4410984.67

6.2 Data Analysis

Analysis of Variance (ANOVA) is a widely used statistical tool for the comparison of group means (Park 2009). The classical one-way ANOVA is a highly influential method in confirmatory data analysis (Hesamian 2016). For this study, ANOVA was conducted on the monthly ATM withdrawals to compare the means across 4 time periods. The analysis was further strengthened using ANCOVA, with controlling for the inflation rate and the state, to account for the external factors that could affect the cash usage measures.

7 Results

ANOVA was conducted with monthly ATM withdrawals as the dependent variable and the time-periods (4 buckets) as the independent variable. There was a significant difference in the monthly withdrawal patterns for the four time-periods [F (3, 4896) = 47.031, p < 0.001], thus supporting hypothesis H1.

To strengthen the analysis further and to control for the effects of Inflation and location, a one-way ANCOVA was conducted with monthly ATM withdrawals as the dependent variable and the time-periods (4 buckets) as the independent variable, *controlling for Inflation rate and State*. We used the Inflation rates reported by the Indian Government for every year (source: data.gov.in) and the State was used to control for the locality. The ANCOVA was significant and there was a linear relationship between Inflation, State (covariates), and monthly withdrawals (dependent variable). There was a significant change in monthly withdrawals across different time-periods, controlling for Inflation and State [F (3, 4894) = 43.551, p < 0.001]. Both the covariates, Inflation and State, were significantly related to time-period [Inflation: F (1,4894) = 30.397, p < 0.001; State: F (1,4894) = 189.406, p < 0.001]. This implies that even after controlling for Inflation and State, there exists an influence of time-period (pre/post demonetization) on monthly ATM cash withdrawals, thus strengthening support for H1.

Although the ANOVA and ANCOVA results reported significant changes in monthly withdrawal patterns, it shows evidence that at least one of the time-periods differ from each other. We investigate further using post-hoc analyses to find pair-wise differences in monthly withdrawals across all the time-periods.

The sample size in each group is almost the same (12 months *100 ATM) and hence we did a Tukey HSD post-hoc analysis to estimate pair-wise comparisons of monthly withdrawals across the 4 time-periods. The results show that the mean monthly withdrawals for 2015–2016 (T1; M = 4705741.69, SD = 2990544.408) were significantly different from 2016–2017 (T2; M = 3456763.75, SD = 2665621.900, p < 0.001). Also, the mean monthly withdrawals for 2016–2017 (T2; M = 3456763.75, SD = 2665621.900) was significantly different from 2017–2018 (T3; M = 4545057.87, SD = 3138506.664, p < 0.001). (Please see Table 2).

Table 2. Tukey HSD Test with Monthly ATM withdrawals as Dependent Variable

Group	N	Mean	SD	Tukey HSD Comparison of group mean differences (1)	(2)	(3)
2015–16(1)	300	705741.69	2990544.41			
2016–17(2)	200	456763.75	2665621.90	−1248977.94***		
2017–18(3)	200	545057.87	3138506.66	−160683.82	088294.12***	
2018–19(4)	1200	410984.67	2595645.29	−294757.03	54220.92***	134073.21

Comments: Hypothesis 2 supported, as (2,1); (3,2) and (4,2) are significant.

Note: Significance level, *p < 0.05, ** p < 0.01, *** p < 0.001

However, the mean monthly withdrawals for 2017–2018 (T3; M = 4545057.87, SD = 3138506.664) was NOT significantly different from 2018–2019 (T4; M = 4410984.67, SD = 2595645.297, p = 0.659). Also, mean monthly withdrawals for 2015–2016 (T1; M = 4705741.69, SD = 2990544.408) was NOT significantly different from 2018–2019 (T4; M = 4410984.67, SD = 2595645.297, p = 0.05) at 95% confidence.

The results of the analyses indicate that the mean monthly cash withdrawal in T2 (the immediate year post demonetization; Nov 2016–Nov 2017) is significantly *lower* than the mean monthly cash withdrawal in T1 (pre demonetization; Nov 2015–Nov 2016); further, supporting hypothesis H1.

And, the mean monthly cash withdrawal in T3 (2 years post demonetization; Nov 2017–Nov 2018) is significantly *higher* than the mean monthly cash withdrawal in T2 (the immediate year post demonetization; Nov 2016–Nov 2017); thus, supporting hypothesis H3. And there is NO significant difference between periods T3 and T4; thus, together with supporting hypothesis H3.

To summarize, there was an immediate ripple effect reflecting *lesser* monthly withdrawals in the year post-demonetization (2016–17, M = 3456763.75, SD = 2665621.900) compared to the pre-demonetization time-period (2015–16, M = 4705741.69, SD = 2990544.408). As time progressed, gradually there is a damping effect reflecting higher monthly withdrawals from post-demonetization, raising to values closer to the pre-demonetization period (2015–16; M = 4705741.69, SD = 2990544.408 and 2018–19; M = 4410984.67, SD = 2595645.297).

Table 3 presents the ANCOVA results. Refer to the Fig. 2 below for the plots of the ANCOVA results for the number of cash withdrawals versus the number of months post demonetization. The y-axis is monthly withdrawals in INR and the x-axis is the number of months starting 6 months prior demonetization. We could see a huge drop after 6 months (Nov 2016) when demonetization of banknotes was announced by the Government of India. Afterward, the daily monthly withdrawals decrease for a while and then slowly start to increase after 20 months, returning to old patterns. In the graph, the thick blue line represents the mean, and the shaded region represents the confidence interval of monthly withdrawals.

Table 3. ANCOVA results with inflation rate and state as covariates

Source	Df	Mean square	F	Sig.
Corrected Model	4	5.74×10^{14}	73.435	<0.001
Intercept	1	3.9×10^{14}	508.219	<0.001
Inflation Rate	1	2.37×10^{14}	30.397	<0001
State	1	1.48×10^{15}	189.406	<0001
Timeline (group: 4 years)	3	1.02×10^{15}	43.551	<0001
Error	4894	3.83×10^{15}		
Total	4900			

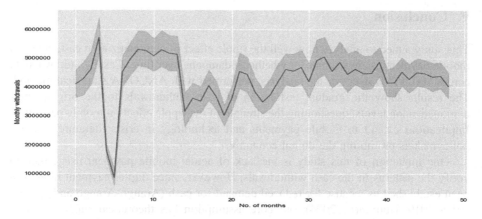

Fig. 2. Plots

8 Implications

This study contributes to the two streams of literature – mobile payment diffusion, and technology adoption post-crisis. While the evidence of this study is not adequate to completely dismiss the claims of the rise in mobile payment usage in India post demonetization (Goriparthi and Tiwari 2017, Mehta et al. 2016, Pal et al. 2020), it surely questions its future sustainability. Mobile payment and digital payment studies should once again focus on the factors beyond cash usage to understand the motivations promoting its future. On the other hand, studies on crises and technology adoption have observed and noted an upsurge in usage of certain technologies like ERP systems, social media, and security technologies, as an immediate consequence of the shock (Bruns et al. 2013, Rasmussen and Johnson 2008, Themistocleous et al. 2001). By and large, there is a lack of focus on how these technologies sustained over time. This paper offers one of the primary studies on continued observation after an economic shock to observe if the behavioral changes were long-term or short-lived for the lingering duration of the crisis.

Policymakers and the government promoting the digital economy can gain practical lessons from this study. As many critiques have claimed a failure of the digital payment agenda through demonetization (Diplomat 2017), we try to show with evidence why heavy cash dependence is the most dominant cause. However, like the nation, with a bulk of unorganized segment, continues to thrive on cash, it must be noted that developing nations with low digital penetration may find it difficult to depend on digital payments ecosystem requiring infrastructure like smartphone and Internet beyond the affordability of all (Ananth 2016). It is then, that cash is the friend of the poor, not enemy.

9   Conclusion

This study aimed to analyze how well the ripple effect of demonetization cash crisis on mobile payment usage sustains, or whether it dampens over time. Cash withdrawal data across 100 ATMs used for the analysis, performed with ANCOVA statistical method. The results show the gradual restoration of cash withdrawals to the original pre-demonetization levels, questioning the strength of the ripple effect on mobile payments. Implications extend to mobile payments and technology in crisis literature, and for policymakers promoting the digital economy.

One limitation of this study is the lack of actual mobile payment usage data to verify the patterns in the cash withdrawals. However, since digital payment usage has been established as a cause for reduced demand for cash (Arango-Arango and Suárez-Ariza 2019, Humphrey 2004), our core assumption has theoretical support. Future research could analyze the cash withdrawal patterns with other critical transaction behaviors like mobile payment transactions, card-based POS payment statistics, and other modes of cash and digital transactions to draw a thorough picture of the payment landscape post a serious economic crisis.

References

Kumar, R.P.: What is demonetisation and why was it done. The Economic Times (2016)

Dutta, P.: Demonetisation: what india gained, and lost. India Today (2018)

Mehta, S., et al.: Demonetisation: shifting gears from physical cash to digital cash. Voice Res. 5, 47–50 (2016)

Banerjee, A.V., Breza, E., Chandrasekhar, A.G., Golub, B.: When Less is More: Experimental Evidence on Information Delivery During India's Demonetization (2019). https://papers.ssrn.com/abstract=3163930, https://doi.org/10.2139/ssrn.3163930

Dash, A.: A study on socio-economic effect of demonetization in India. Int. J. Manag. Appl. Sci. 3(3), 13–15 (2017)

Singh, P., Singh, V.: Impact of demonetization on Indian economy. In: 3rd International Conference on Recent Innovation in Science, Technology, Management and Environment (2016)

Pal, A., Herath, T., De', R., Rao, H.R.: Contextual facilitators and barriers influencing the continued use of mobile payment services in a developing country: insights from adopters in India. Inform. Technol. Dev. 26(2), 1–27 (2020)

Bureau, F.E.: UPI players Google Pay, Paytm and PhonePe eye offline merchants (2019). https://www.financialexpress.com/industry/upi-players-google-pay-paytm-and-phonepeeye-offline-merchants/1590833/

Hetavkar, N.: UPI's value grew 700% in 2018 while total digital payments fell 1%. Business Standard India (2019)

Bamoriya, P.S., Singh, P.: Issues & challenges in mobile banking in india: a customers' perspective. Res. J. Finan. Account. 2, 112–120 (2011)

Srivastava, M., Thakur, R.: Customer usage intention of mobile commerce in India: an empirical study. Jnl Indian Bus. Res. 5, 52–72 (2013)

Francisco, F.B.S.: Banking\textbar Demonetization Is Catalyzing Digital Payments Growth in India (2017). https://www.frbsf.org/banking/asia-program/pacific-exchange-blog/demonetization-is-catalyzing-digital-payments-growth-in-india/

Agarwal, S., Basu, D., Ghosh, P., Pareek, B., Zhang, J.: Demonetization and Digitization (2018). https://papers.ssrn.com/abstract=3197990, https://doi.org/10.2139/ssrn.3197990

Goriparthi, R.K., Tiwari, P.: Demonetization in india an era for digital payments. Splint Int. J. Professionals: A Mon. Peer Reviewed Int. J. Manag. & IT; Bhubaneswar **4**, 40–48 (2017)

Pal, A., Herath, T., De', R., Rao, H.R.: Factors facilitating adoption of mobile payment services over Credit/Debit Cards: An Investigation after the Demonetization Policy Shock in India 9 (2018)

Arango-Arango, C.A., Suárez-Ariza, N.F.: Digital payments adoption and the demand for cash: new international evidence. Borradores de Economía 1074 (2019)

Stix, H.: How do debit cards affect cash demand? Surv. Data Evid. Empirica **31**, 93–115 (2004)

Humphrey, D.B.: Replacement of cash by cards in US consumer payments. J. Econ. Bus. **56**, 211–225 (2004)

de Kerviler, G., Demoulin, N.T.M., Zidda, P.: Adoption of in-store mobile payment: are perceived risk and convenience the only drivers? J. Retail. Consum. Serv. **31**, 334–344 (2016)

Mallat, N.: Exploring consumer adoption of mobile payments – a qualitative study. J. Strateg. Inform. Syst. **16**, 413–432 (2007)

Luo, X., Li, H., Zhang, J., Shim, J.P.: Examining multi-dimensional trust and multi-faceted risk in initial acceptance of emerging technologies: an empirical study of mobile banking services. Decis. Support Syst. **49**, 222–234 (2010)

Wright, D.: Comparative evaluation of electronic payment systems. INFOR: Inform. Syst. Oper. Res. **40**, 71–85 (2002)

Roy, A.: Cash is still king as circulation nears pre-demonetisation level: Report. Business Standard India (2017)

James Cater III, J., Beal, B.: Ripple effects on family firms from an externally induced crisis. J. Fam. Bus. Manag. **4**, 62–78 (2014)

Merriam-Webster Dictionary. Definition of RIPPLE EFFECT. Merriam-Webster Dictionary (2020). https://www.merriam-webster.com/dictionary/ripple+effect

Chang, H.-H., Yin, C.-P., Chou, H.-W.: Diffusion of enterprise resource planning systems in taiwan: influence sources and the Y2K effect. Int. J. Enterp. Inform. Syst. (IJEIS) (2008). www.igi-global.com/article/diffusion-enterprise-resource-planningsystems/2134

Pliskin, N., Zarotski, M.: Big-bang ERP implementation at a global company (2000). https://doi.org/10.4018/978-1-61520-593-6.ch013

Themistocleous, M., Irani, Z., O'Keefe, R.M.: ERP and application integration: exploratory survey. Bus. Process Mgmt J. **7**, 195–204 (2001)

Bruns, A., Highfield, T., Burgess, J.: The arab spring and social media audiences: english and arabic twitter users and their networks. Am. Behav. Sci. **57**, 871–898 (2013)

Oh, O., Agrawal, M., Rao, H.R.: Community intelligence and social media services: a rumor theoretic analysis of tweets during social crises. MIS Q. **37**, 407–426 (2013)

Rauniar, R., Rawski, G., Yang, J., Johnson, B.: Technology acceptance model (TAM) and social media usage: an empirical study on Facebook. J. Ent. Info. Manag. **27**, 6–30 (2014)

Jeon, B.N., Han, K.S., Lee, M.J.: Determining factors for the adoption of e-business: the case of SMEs in Korea. Appl. Econ. **38**, 1905–1916 (2006)

Lee, S.M.: South Korea: from the land of morning calm to ICT hotbed. Acad. Manage. Perspect. **17**, 7–18 (2003)

Rasmussen, C., Johnson, G.: The ripple effect of virginia tech: assessing the nationwide impact on campus safety and security policy and practice. Midwestern Higher Education Compact (2008)

Express, T.I.: Long queues at banks, no money in ATMs (2016). https://indianexpress.com/article/india/demonetisation-cash-crunch-long-queues-at-banks-no-money-in-atms-4405765/

Bhargava, Y.: Demonetisation made people understand mobile payments. The Hindu (2017). 37.

Bureau, M.T. Cash crunch forces local vendors to resort to e-wallet, mobile payment options (2016).   https://www.indiatoday.in/mail-today/story/local-vendors-e-wallets-mobile-payments351980-2016-11-15

Choudhury, S.R.: Cash is still king even as digital payments are set to rise, according to PayPal's CTO   (2018).   https://www.cnbc.com/2018/05/22/cash-is-still-the-biggest-threat-for-digital-payments-firms-paypal-cto.html

Mint, L.: Demonetisation anniversary: 40% of mobile wallet users shift back to cash (2017). https://www.livemint.com/Industry/GILitiFcUpCxdDLOLqnFKP/Demonetisation-anniversary-40-of-mobile-wallet-users-shift.html

Park, H.M.: Comparing Group Means: T-tests and One-way ANOVA- Using Stata, SAS, R, and SPSS* 51 (2009)

Hesamian, G.: One-way ANOVA based on interval information. Int. J. Syst. Sci. **47**, 2682–2690 (2016)

Diplomat, A.M.: The Is India's Demonetization a Failure? (2017). https://thediplomat.com/2017/09/is-indias-demonetization-a-failure/

Ananth, V.: Only 17% Indians own smartphones: survey (2016). https://www.livemint.com/Consumer/yT14OgtSC7dyywWSynWOKN/Only-17-Indians-own-smartphones-survey.html

Explaining Variation in Adoption of FinTech Products and Services Among Citizens: A Multilevel Model

Ben Krishna and Satish Krishnan$^{(\boxtimes)}$

Indian Institute of Management Kozhikode, Kozhikode, Kerala, India
{benkrishna12fpm, satishk}@iimk.ac.in

Abstract. Despite the several advantages, adoption of the FinTech services vary across individuals in different countries. This study proposes a model to examine how the country level ICT competitiveness, demographic and socio-economic factors influence the FinTech services diffusion in a country. In this study, we use Generalized Linear Mixed Model to analyze both the individual-level and country-level variables to explain the variation in the probability of individuals adopting FinTech services while accounting for the variance at each level. National ICT competitiveness especially political and regulatory environment, Infrastructure, ICT usage by firms demonstrated a stronger influence on the adoption of FinTech services. In addition, demographic variables and socio-economic status also demonstrated stronger evidence in explaining the variation in the adoption of FinTech services.

Keywords: FinTech · ICT · Diffusion

1 Introduction and Background

In 2020, half of the world will be using at least one FinTech product or service [9]. Major reason for this trend is the recent proliferation of financial technologies, such as payment service providers, aggregators and robo advisors, peer-to-peer lenders, and innovative trading platforms along with increased smartphone usage [52]. Consumers are using FinTech products to access financial services in a much cheaper and efficient way [5]. In 2015, Jim Yong Kim (World Bank Group President) announced World Bank has set an ambitious goal of universal financial access by 2020. With the continued digitalization of financial sector, both the banks and other financial institutions had made efforts to increase the consumer's adoption of FinTech products and services, capitalizing on high mobile and smartphone usage [28].

Although, more consumers worldwide are accepting FinTech applications, adoption and frequency of usage vary across countries. The 2018 National Financial Capability Study reports that 84% of the banked US respondents engage in online banking and 65% in mobile banking at least sometimes [38]. However, only nearly half of the banked US respondents use FinTech services frequently, rest presumably using other payment methods like cash, credit or checks. In contrast, in some economies, there has been a large demand for FinTech services. Countries like China, India have high rate (87%) of FinTech adoption and countries like Japan (34%) and France (35%) have low rate of adoption [17]. Even though the customer awareness of FinTech services remains high at 96% globally, average adoption rate is only 64%. Industry experts [17] point out two major reason for these variations in adoption rates (i) Lack of infrastructure and restriction or regulation of certain FinTech services (ii) Financial behaviors exhibited by consumers because of demographic and socio-economic characteristics. This is further supported by the academic literature. FinTech usage is influenced or constrained by Information communication and Technology (ICT) infrastructure, adoption in financial sector and political or regulatory environment [4, 34]. In developing economies, a gender gap of 6% points exists, 43% of men have both mobile phone and internet access, while only 37% of women have the same. In some economies like Bangladesh, Ethiopia, and India, men have access to mobile and internet twice as likely as women do. However, in China, Colombia, and South Africa, both men and women have equal access [18]. Adoption of FinTech is also driven by various factors like age, gender and social status [36, 40, 60]. Given these variations and complexities, it is important to understand what all factors could explain the variations in adoption of FinTech products and services across countries.

Because of the strong linkages between financial development and economic growth, determinants of adoption of financial technologies has been largely studied [27]. Our brief review of existing literature indicate that there are two main streams of research evident in the adoption of financial technologies literature [26]. First stream concerns with identifying determinants related to adoption of FinTech among organizations [8]. Second stream of research concerns with identifying determinants related to adoption of FinTech by end consumers [55]. In the second stream of research, most studies utilized technology adoption literature to explain the adoption of FinTech products and services. Few studies have addressed whether the national ICT level will influence adoption of FinTech [1, 20]. Several other studies focus on individual factors such as demographic variables, trust, and subjective norm to understand the diffusion of financial technologies [47, 56]. However, these studies confine within a country [51, 53] or few countries [2]. The current study aimed to fill this gap in prior research by conducting a cross-country (127 countries) analysis, including both country level (national ICT competitiveness) and individual level (demographic and socio-economic) variables in the same model to explain variation in adoption of financial technologies. To increase the understanding of the FinTech usage behavior, following research question motivated our study:

RQ: *What are the macroeconomic (ICT competitiveness related) and individual level factors that could explain the variation in adoption of FinTech products and services among citizens across countries?*

2   Theoretical Background and Hypotheses

2.1   Individual Level Difference and FinTech Adoption

Previous studies conceptualized financial technologies as technological innovation and analyzed adoption of FinTech products using various technology adoption theories

[34]. Further, the speed of diffusion of financial technologies depends on the characteristics of the technology as well as characteristics of the users to whom it is directed [14]. Various theories include UTAUT theory [62], Diffusion of Innovation theory, TAM [45] and SDT [59]. User differences plays a key role in adoption and using innovation and same goes with financial technologies as these differences result in variety of needs and expectation [47]. To increase the likelihood of the success of FinTech, FinTech firms and financial institutions should target the early and late adopters of innovation, as late adopters are potential consumers of next generation services [30]. Accordingly, grouping of the consumers based on their demographic and socio-economic status is critical to understanding the willingness to adopt Fintech. Diffusion paradigm helps to capture the distinction between different users based on their innovativeness.

Diffusion, according to Rogers [46] is a "process in which an innovation is communicated through certain channels over time among the members of a social system". Rate of adoption of innovation is determined by its characteristics. Rate of adoption is determined by the 1) perceived attributes of innovation (relative advantage, compatibility, complexity, trialability and observability). These characteristics are perceived differently based on demographic features and social-economic status [46]. Gender plays an important role in moderating the relationship between perceived ease of use and behavioral intention to use the system; as men will rate the perceived ease of use highly [36]. Previous studies found younger people are more likely to adopt innovation quickly [6]. Further, the older generation are more skeptical about digital payments or remittance as older people are more prone to financial exploitation [40]. In addition, the adoption of FinTech applications also depend on the education level and income level of the individual in the country [34]. Higher education is assumed to be improving one's knowledge, productivity, and thus speeds up the adoption of innovation-decision process [37, 46]. Further, it was found out that higher-income families use more technology than low-income families [60]. Thus, more the income of the household can increase the probability of usage of FinTech services. This is also driven by an inherent motivation inside the individual to gain social status [16]. Thus, we hypothesized that

Hypothesis 1: *Gender influence FinTech usage among individuals in a country where males adopt FinTech services more than females.*

Hypothesis 2: *Age influence FinTech usage among individuals in a country where younger adults adopt FinTech services more than older adults.*

Hypothesis 3: *Education influence the FinTech usage among individuals in a country where more educated to adopt FinTech services more than less educated.*

Hypothesis 4: *Income influence the FinTech usage among individuals in a country where high net worth individuals adopt FinTech services more than low net worth.*

2.2 ICT Competitiveness and FinTech Adoption

National ICT development assist financial sector in the form of services offered to the citizens and aid support to firms to produce FinTech products [17–19, 33]. Innovative services and digitalization of the financial market is a symbol of a well-developed economy and capital market which promotes entrepreneurship especially FinTech innovators [20]. Business innovation environment is categorized by the availability of the latest technologies, local competition, government procurement of latest technology, and more [19]. Technologies like nearfield communication (NFC), QR codes, and bluetooth enabled mobile wallet transactions helped the firms for the faster payment systems, reduced transaction costs, and improved information symmetry. Political environment plays a crucial role in implementing the favorable regulatory policies, communication channels, and business environments. Recently, scholars have identified the impact of such laws on various technology adoption of various currencies like bitcoin [4], blockchain [61], robo advisors [15], social trading platforms [13] and e-wallet and mobile payment services [35]. Venture capital investment in the FinTech start-ups is mainly determined by the differential treatment of enforcement of political laws [12]. To summarize, overall network readiness of a country indicates the modernization of society, including financial system, which will improve the adoption of FinTech products and services among citizens. Thus, we hypothesized that

Hypothesis 5: *Adoption of FinTech services among individuals occur more in countries with a political and regulatory environment that facilitate ICT penetration.*

Hypothesis 6: *Adoption of FinTech services among individuals occurs more in countries with a well-developed business innovation environment that facilitate innovation.*

Hypothesis 7: *Adoption of FinTech services among individuals occur more in countries with higher Business usage of ICT.*

Another driver of FinTech usage is the extent to which the ICT infrastructure support latest FinTech applications and services. One such example is the shift in the withdrawal of money from banks to Automatic teller machine (ATM) to mobile banking [44, 49]. Previous studies have indicated a positive correlation between mobile or internet services and financial development in a country [7, 48]. It was identified that a 1% increase in the fixed broadband number led to a 2.13% increase in financial development and a 1% increase on internet lead to a 0.097% increase in financial development [1]. In Sub-Saharan African countries, mobile phone account payments or remittance through text-based mobile services (m-pesa) has revolutionized the financial inclusion [20, 29]. Thus, we hypothesized that

Hypothesis 8: *Adoption of FinTech services among individuals occur more in countries with well-developed infrastructure for ICT.*

3   Methodology

3.1   Data Sources and Data Definition

The data sources for this research include the Global information technology report (GITR) 2016 [19] by the World Economic Forum and Global financial inclusion index (GFI) 2017 [18], and world bank datasets. After excluding the missing data and data cleaning, final sample includes 127 countries common to both data sources which include a total of 78,529 cases. GITR publishes the Networked Readiness Index (NRI), which assess the various factors that enable a country to leverage the ICT for increased competitiveness in all sectors. Global Findex database is one of the global comprehensive datasets on explains the financial inclusion of adults which include their account holding pattern, how individuals save, borrow, make payments, or send money. To ensure validity and reliability of the data, global data collection agencies like the World Economic Forum and World Bank followed various processes. For instance, to ensure reliability, GFI was created using three-level of sampling which include stratified sampling at higher, clustering at the middle and random at the bottom level to choose household. Data weighting was done to ensure database consists of national representatives from each economy and to ensure nonresponse error. To ensure the validity, questionnaires were prepared with the help of leading academic practitioners and policymakers.

Variables. This study uses ICT competitiveness (country level) and individual level variables. Country-level predictor variables include political and regulatory score, business environment score, infrastructure score, and business usage taken from GITR. The rationale for choosing these variables, as they represent the ICT competitiveness of the country. Individual-level predictor variable includes gender, age group, education, and household income taken from GFI. Individual-level control variable includes individual is a member of workforce (employed or not) and country-level variable includes income groups and logarithm of GDP.

FinTech Adoption. FinTech refers to the technology-enabled or digitalization process of finance solutions [56]. To improve validity, we burrow the concept of "bucket" from Global FinTech Adoption Index published by EY [17]. This study introduces the concept of "buckets" or "categories" and grouped similar services together. Therefore, a FinTech adopter is someone who uses two or more categories of services. This study used five categories: 1) basic access of financial services (access account through internet or mobile), 2) money transfer and payments, 3) e-commerce trade/utility bill, 4) budgeting and financial planning, 5) borrowing and insurance.

Age, Household income, Education, and Gender. Age is a nominal variable with six different age groups ranging from below 18 to 65 and above. Gender is a dichotomous variable with male coded as 1 and female as 0. Household income is a nominal variable with five different groups ranging from the poorest 20% to the richest 20%. Education is also a nominal variable with three levels ranging from primary to tertiary and more.

National Level Predictors. The political and regulatory environment consists of nine indicators that assess the environment favorable for penetration of ICT. The business and innovation environment consists of nine indicators that measure the environment favorable for entrepreneurship in terms of innovation-friendly. Infrastructure consists of four indicators that capture the country's ICT infrastructure. Business usage consists of six indicators that capture ICT usage in business.

Control Variables. Employed is a dichotomous variable, where "1" represents the individual is a member of the workforce. Income level classification is based on the World Bank classification by income. GDP indicates the country's standard of living.

Generalized Linear Mixed Model (GLMM). In the current study, we use GLMM, which is a multilevel modeling technique. GLMM examine dependent variables that is categorical in nature and predictor variables are nested within groups [44]. In this study, all the demographic and socio-economic variables are nested within a larger group (countries), thus GLMM were employed to analyze both the individual (level 1) and country-level (level 2) variables to explain the variation in the probability of individuals' adopting FinTech services while accounting for the variance at each level [24]. GLMM incorporates the necessary transformation and appropriate error distribution directly into the statistical model to mitigate violation and approximate the model to near linear [25, 32]. Further, we used robust estimation to handle violation of assumptions. GLMM was analyzed using IBM SPSS [22]. The two-level GLMM model using the logistic link function is as follows:

$$\text{Level 1: Fintechadoption}_{ij} = a_{0j} + a_{1j} * \text{edu}_{ij} + a_{2j} * \text{gender}_{ij} + a_{3j} * \text{income}_{ij} \\ + a_{4j} * \text{age\_group}_{ij} + a_{5j} * \text{employed} + r_{ij} \tag{1}$$

$$\text{Level 2: } a_{0j} = b_{00} + b_{01} * \text{PR}_j + b_{02} * \text{BI}_j + b_{03} * \text{BU}_j + b_{04} * \text{INF}_j \\ + b_{06} * \text{Inclvl}_j + b_{07} * \text{logGDP}_j + u_{0j} \tag{2}$$

$a_{1j} = b_{1j}, a_{2j} = b_{2j}, a_{3j} = b_{3j}, a_{4j} = b_{4j}, a_{5j} = b_{5j}$; *Fintechadoption$_{ij}$ is the adoption of FinTech services by the individual i in country j; b_{00} is the mean adoption of FinTech services for all of the countries in the sample; b_{1j} is the slope of education for individual in country j; b_{2j} is the slope of gender for individual in country j; b_{3j} is the slope of income for individual in country j; b_{4j} is the slope of age group for individual in country j; b_{5j} is the slope of employed for individual in country j; b_{6j} is the slope of the cross level interaction term; r_{ij} is a unique error associated with the individual i in country j,; b_{01} is the slope of political and regulatory environment value for each country; b_{02} is the slope of Business and innovation environment value for each country; b_{03} is the slope of business usage for each country; b_{04} is the slope of infrastructure level for each country; b_{06} is the slope of income group level for each country; b_{07} is the slope of logGDP for each country; and u_{0j} is a unique error to the intercept associated with country j.*

4   Results and Discussion

Null Model (model 1). The variance of the intercept has a coefficient greater than 1 (1.280) which indicates there is significant variation between countries in terms of the proportion of individuals identified as FinTech adopters. This essentially indicates that there might be other level 1 and level 2 (country) predictors that can be added to the model which can explain random variation. Thus justifies the multilevel model. The

Intraclass correlation (ICC) describes the proportion of variance that lies between countries relative to the total variance (i.e., between and within countries). The estimated ICC suggests that 33.24% of the variability in FinTech adoption exist between countries (Table 1).

Table 1. The intraclass correlation for the null model

Fixed effect	Coefficient (t)	Odds ratio	95% CI
Intercept	−0.855(8.492)***	0.425	[0.349 0.518]
Random effects			
Countrylevel effect(u_{0j})	1.280 (Z = 7.793)***		[0.995 0.518]
ICC	33.24%		

*: p < 0.05, **: p < 0.01, ***: p < 0.001.

Random Intercept Model with Level 1 and Level 2 Predictors (model 2). The estimates of the level 1 variables (Table 2) suggest that they are significant variations in the adoption of FinTech services within the both levels. The odds of adopting FinTech

Table 2. Random intercept model with Level 1 and Level 2 predictors

	Without control variables	With control variables
Fixed effect	Coefficient(t)	Coefficient(t)
Intercept	−6.184 (−9.616)***	−4.014 (−3.468)***
Gender	0.211 (7.599)***	0.165 (5.734)***
AgeGroup 65&above	−1.799 (−13.546)***	−1.691 (−12.336)***
55–64	−0.781 (−5.735)***	−851 (−6.169)***
45–54	−0.209 (−1.707)	−0.352 (−2.883)**
35–44	0.227 (1.990)*	0.076 (0.658)
25–34	0.319 (2.755)**	0.177 (1.506)
18–24	0.326 (3.104)**	0.241 (2.235)*
Income Richest 20%	0.896 (16.387)***	0.867 (16.095)***
Fourth 20%	0.578 (11.570)***	0.557 (11.262)***
Middle 20%	0.392 (8.241)***	0.379 (8.001)***
Second 20%	0.233 (5.361)***	0.225 (5.194)***
Education- Tertiary or more	1.497 (26.174)***	1.474 (25.7)***
Secondary	0.729 (15.149)***	0.722 (14.836)***
PR_value	0.558 (2.895)**	0.430(2.444)*
Infra_value	0.231 (2.767)**	−0.106 (−0.992)
Bus_usage	0.670 (13.608)***	0.652(3.078)**
Random effects		
Country level effect(u_{0j})	0.769 (Z = 7.524)***	0.615 (Z = 7.323)***

*: p < 0.05, **: p < 0.01, ***: p < 0.001. Note: Income classification based on within economy household income quin-tile and base is poorest 20%. Education base is Primary education. Age group base is below 18(15,16,17). Non-significant values and control variable values were omitted in table.

services are about 1.179 times higher for males than females, holding other factors constant. Regarding the age group, higher age groups (above 45) are less likely to adopt FinTech services as compared to lower age groups. For an individual, whose income household income is on the higher side have higher probability of adopting FinTech services. Finally, the probability of an individual who has tertiary or more education adopting FinTech service is 30.39% and the probability of an individual who has secondary education adopting FinTech service is 17.07% as compared with the individual having primary education.

Between countries, political regulatory environment and business usage are positively related to the probability of adopting FinTech services by citizens (0.401, p < .05 and 0.601, p < 0.01). This suggests that improving political and regulatory environment score (e.g., liberalizing the ICT laws) and business usage score (e.g., firm-level technology absorption) increase the probability of adopting FinTech services. An estimate of the other level 2 predictors suggest that they are insignificant in predicting the probability of adoption of FinTech service. Thus, this full model draws support for Hypotheses 1, 2, 3, 4, 5 and 7.

We run two set of sensitivity tests to improve the stability of our results. We replace one of the country-level control variable 'income group' by 'country group'. This helps to group the adoption of FinTech services based on IMF classification of various economies based on their region (e.g. Eurasia). Second, we run a regression on sub-samples where countries were randomly selected. Results show that the effect of individuallevel effects on the probability of adoption of FinTech services are more robust and country-level variables show slight deviation.

Influence of National ICT Competitiveness on FinTech Services Adoption. The positive effect of level 2 variables on the adoption of FinTech services by individuals suggests that individuals who are in countries with favorable political and regulatory environment for ICT development, favorable ICT infrastructure and higher adoption of ICT by business entities are more likely to have a higher probability of adoption of FinTech products and services. The findings in this study are consistent with the assessment of the world bank. According to the framework developed by the World Bank as a part of universal financial access by 2020 initiative [54], financial and ICT infrastructures, legal and regulatory frameworks, and public and private commitment as the potential critical enablers of the universal access to and frequent usage of transaction accounts. Further, the impact of business usage is significantly positive. Given that the business usage sub-index is an aggregate of various several indicators like firm-level technology absorption, business to consumer internet use, it is not appropriate to compare the direct influences of each indicator on the adoption of FinTech services. However, the nature of the dependent variable (see Sect. 3.1), ensures that this study did more to highlight a convincing influential pattern of several indicators of business usage on adoption of FinTech. ICT Infrastructure of a country also shows a positive influence, which shows that the probability of citizens adopting FinTech services is higher for the citizens in countries having a better ICT infrastructure environment. This can be explained based on the shortage of capital investment in ICT structure in middle income and low-income countries and they could not catch up with the pace in which high-income countries invest in ICT structures [20]. To summarize, national ICT competitiveness demonstrated a stronger influence on the adoption of FinTech services, which highlights the additional evidence for the existence of third-order digital divide (related to ICT outcome) [23, 50, 57].

Influence of Individual-level Variables on FinTech Services Adoption. The overall findings suggest a linkage between level 1 predictor variables and FinTech adoption. Males have higher probability than female to adopt FinTech services. This is consistent with the earlier findings where gender differences impact the adoption and use of ICT [11]. Further, this finding also highlights the growing recognition of a digital divide based on gender differences [57]. The findings regarding age groups suggest that older adults have lower probabilities of adopting FinTech services with respect to the younger generation. Previous research on the relation between different age groups and internet use was found to be piecewise linear, with younger people tend to more internet enthusiasts than older people [3]. A possible explanation for this digital divide is that the younger generation receives quite a lot of exposure and benefits from the ICT competitiveness of the country [49]. Regarding the socio-economic status variables education and household income level, findings indicate that individuals' having higher education and belongs to higher income levels have a higher probability for the adoption of FinTech services. Previous literature indicates that education undoubtedly has been very significant in influencing technology use [41]. Households' emphasis on better education has fostered awareness and ICT skills which invariably help individuals to adopt and use ICT for their development [21, 39]. Yang [58] have identified that income level in a household is one of the crucial determinants on internet penetration and income per capita [10] as a determinant of ICT (mobile or computer) product ownership. To summarize, demographic variables and socio-economic status demonstrated a stronger influence on the adoption of FinTech services. In addition, this study also highlights the additional evidence for the existence of the level 2 variables on the adoption of FinTech services.

5   Conclusion

By presenting a multilevel model including both the network readiness variables which represents the national ICT competitiveness and individual-level variables which represent their demography and socio-economic status, this study sheds light on the complex influences of ICT competitiveness on the probability of adoption of FinTech services by a citizen. This study synthesize literature related to diffusion paradigm, the impact of ICT on development of the financial sector and makes following contribution; First, this study adds to the literature by exploring the variation in the adoption of FinTech services using the ICT competitiveness of the country, which was not explored in the previous studies. Such findings would be very helpful in a better understanding of what will be the effect of ICT competitiveness, in this case, role of the political and regulatory environment of a country and assimilation of ICT in business within a country in predicting the adoption tendencies. Second, by employing, a new way to examine the two widely recognized indices to assess the FinTech services adoption, this study encompasses a broad spectrum of subjects across countries. Third, we used

GLMM to analyze both the individual-level and country-level variables to explain the adoption of FinTech services while accounting for the variance at each level (nested model). In terms of practical implication, the study points out a direction for national policymakers in providing a favorable political and regulatory environment as well for the FinTech firms to channel their innovation. Moreover, demographic and socio-economic status have a major influence in explaining the variation in the probability of FinTech service adoption. As a result, the findings are of particular importance for FinTech firms and national level policymakers.

References

1. Alshubiri, F., Jamil, S.A., Elheddad, M.: The impact of ICT on financial development: empirical evidence from the gulf cooperation council countries. International Journal of Engineering Business Management, 11 (2019)
2. Belanche, D., Casalo, L., Flavian, C.: Artificial intelligence in FinTech: understanding roboadvisor adoption among customers. Industrial Management & Data Systems (2019)
3. Blank, G., Graham, M., Calvino, C.: Local geographies of digital inequality. Soc. Sci. Compu. Rev. **36**(1), 82–102 (2018)
4. Böhme, R., Christin, N., Edelman, B., Moore, T.: Bitcoin: economics, technology, and governance. J. Econ. Perspect. **29**, 213–238 (2015)
5. Bruhn, M., Love, I.: The real impact of improved access to finance: evidence from Mexico. J. Finan. **69**(3), 1347–1376 (2014)
6. Carlin, B., Olafsson, A., Pagel, M.: FinTech Adoption Across Generations: Financial Fitness in the Information Age (No. w23798; p. w23798). National Bureau of Economic Research (2017)
7. Chowdhury, S.: Investments in ICT-capital and economic performance of small and medium scale enterprises in East Africa. J. Int. Dev. **18**(4), 533–552 (2006)
8. Clohessy, T., Acton, T.: Investigating the influence of organizational factors on blockchain adoption: an innovation theory perspective. Industrial Management & Data Systems (2019)
9. Consumers International (2020). https://www.consumersinternational.org/news-resources/blog/posts/10-things-consumers-need-to-know-about-fintech/. Accessed 01 April 2020
10. Cruz-Jesus, F., Oliveira, T., Bacao, F.: The global digital divide: evidence and drivers. J. Glob. Inform. Manag. (JGIM) **26**(2), 1–26 (2018)
11. Cruz-Jesus, F., Oliveira, T., Bacao, F., Irani, Z.: Assessing the pattern between economic and digital development of countries. Inform. Syst. Front. **19**(4), 835–854 (2016). https://doi.org/10.1007/s10796-016-9634-1
12. Cumming, D., Schwienbacher, A.: Fintech venture capital, SSRN Working Paper (2016)
13. Doering, P., Neumann, S., Paul, S.: A primer on social trading networks—institutional aspects and empirical evidence, SSRN Working Paper (2015)
14. Escobar-Rodríguez, T., Romero-Alonso, M.: The acceptance of information technology innovations in hospitals: differences between early and late adopters. Behav. Inform. Technol. **33**(11), 1231–1243 (2014)
15. Fein, M.L.: Robo-advisors: a closer look, SSRN Working Paper (2015)
16. Gartrell, C.D., Gartrell, J.W.: Social status and agricultural innovation: a meta-analysis. Rural Sociol. **50**(1), 38 (1985)
17. GFAI (2019). https://www.ey.com/en_gl/ey-global-fintech-adoption-index. Accessed 01 April 2020
18. GFI (2017). https://globalfindex.worldbank.org/. Accessed 01 April 2020

19. GITR   (2016).   https://reports.weforum.org/global-information-technology-report-2016/networked-readiness-index/. Accessed 01 April 2020
20. Haddad, C., Hornuf, L.: The emergence of the global fintech market: economic and technological determinants. Small Bus. Econ. **53**(1), 81–105 (2019)
21. Harwit, E.: Spreading telecommunications to developing areas in China: Telephones, the Internet and the digital divide. Chin. Q. **180**, 1010–1030 (2004)
22. Heck, R.H., Thomas, S., Tabata, L.: Multilevel Modelling of Categorical Outcomes Using IBM SPSS. Routledge Academic, Abingdon (2013)
23. Hilbert, M.: The end justifies the definition: the manifold outlooks on the digital divide and their practical usefulness for policy-making. Telecommun. Policy **35**(8), 715–736 (2011)
24. Hox, J.J.: Multilevel analyses of grouped and longitudinal data. In: Baumert, J. (ed.) Modeling Longitudinal and Multilevel Data: Practical Issues, Applied Approaches, and Specific Examples. Lawrence Erlbaum Associates, Mahwah (2000)
25. Hox, J.J., Moerbeek, M., Van de Schoot, R.: Multilevel Analysis: Techniques and Applications. Routledge, Abingdon (2010)
26. Hua, X., Huang, Y., Zheng, Y.: Current practices, new insights, and emerging trends of financial technologies. Ind. Manag. Data Syst. **119**(7), 1401–1410 (2019)
27. Ilyina, A., Samaniego, R.: Technology and financial development. J. Money Credit Bank. **43**(5), 899–921 (2011)
28. ITU (2017). https://www.worldbank.org/en/news/press-release/2015/04/15/massive-dropin-number-of-unbanked-says-new-report. Accessed 01 April 2020
29. Jack, W., Suri, T.: Mobile money: The economics of M-PESA (No. w16721). National Bureau of Economic Research (2011)
30. Jahanmir, S.F., Lages, L.F.: The late-adopter scale: a measure of late adopters of technological innovations. J. Bus. Res. **69**(5), 1701–1706 (2016)
31. Jamal, A., Kizgin, H., Rana, N.P., Laroche, M., Dwivedi, Y.K.: Impact of acculturation, online participation and involvement on voting intentions. Gov. Inform. Q. **36**(3), 510–519 (2019)
32. Lee, V.E.: Using hierarchical linear modelling to study social contexts: the case of school effects. Educ. Psychol. **35**(2), 125–141 (2000)
33. Leon, F., Zins, A.: Regional foreign banks and financial inclusion: evidence from Africa. Econ. Model. **84**, 102–116 (2020)
34. Li, B., Hanna, S.D., Kim, K.T.: Who uses mobile payments: fintech potential in users and non-users. J. Finan. Couns. Plan. **31**(1), 83–100 (2020)
35. Mallat, N., Rossi, M., Tuunainen, V.K.: Mobile banking services. Commun. ACM **47**, 42–46 (2004)
36. Moon, J.W., Kim, Y.G.: Extending the TAM for a World-Wide-Web context. Inform. Manag. **38**(4), 217–230 (2001)
37. Morgan, J., David, M.: Education and income. Q. J. Econ. **77**(3), 423–437 (1963)
38. NFSC (2018). https://www.usfinancialcapability.org/downloads/NFCS_2018_Report_Natl_Findi ngs.pdf. Accessed 01 April 2020
39. Nishida, T., Pick, J.B., Sarkar, A.: Japan' s prefectural digital divide: a multivariate and spatial analysis. Telecommun. Policy **38**(11), 992–1010 (2014)
40. O'Neill, P., Flanagan, E.: Elderly consumers are a significant market – but may need special protection. J. Retail. Bank. Serv. **20**(1), 25–33 (1998)
41. Pick, J.B., Azari, R.: A global model of utilization of technology based on governmental, social, economic, and business investment factors. J. Manag. Inform. Syst. **28**(1), 51–85 (2011)

42. Pick, J.B., Sarkar, A., Johnson, J.: United States digital divide: State level analysis of spatial clustering and multivariate determinants of ICT utilization. Soc.-Econ. Plan. Sci. **49**, 16–32 (2015)
43. Ramdhony, D., Munien, S.: An investigation on mobile banking adoption and usage: a case study of Mauritius. World. 3(3) (2013)
44. Raudenbush, S.W., Bryk, A.S.: Hierarchical Linear Models: Applications and Data Analysis Methods, 2nd edn. Sage, Thousand Oaks (2002)
45. Riquelme, H.E., Rios, R.E.: The moderating effect of gender in the adoption of mobile banking. Int. J. Bank Mark. **28**(5), 328–341 (2010)
46. Rogers, E.M.: Diffusion of Innovations, 5th edn. Free Press, New York (2003)
47. Ryu, H.-S.: What makes users willing or hesitant to use Fintech? The moderating effect of user type. Ind. Manag. Data Syst. **118**(3), 541–569 (2018)
48. Sassi, S., Goaied, M.: Financial development, ICT diffusion and economic growth: lessons from MENA region. Telecommun. Policy 37(4–5), 252–261 (2013)
49. Skryabin, M., Zhang, J., Liu, L., Zhang, D.: How the ICT development level and usage influence student achievement in reading, mathematics, and science. Comput. Educ. **85**, 49–58 (2015)
50. Song, Z., Wang, C., Bergmann, L.: China's prefectural digital divide: spatial analysis and multivariate determinants of ICT diffusion. International Journal of Information Management, 102072 (2020)
51. Soutter, L., Ferguson, K., Neubert, M.: Digital payments: impact factors and mass adoption in sub-saharan Africa. Technol. Innov. Manag. Rev. **7**(10), 41–55 (2019)
52. Statista (2019). https://www.statista.com/statistics/330695/number-of-smartphone-users-worldwide. Accessed 01 April 2020
53. Stewart, H., Jürjens, J.: Data security and consumer trust in FinTech innovation in Germany. Inform. Comput. Secur. **26**(1), 109–128 (2018)
54. UFA (2017). https://www.worldbank.org/en/topic/financialinclusion/brief/achieving-universal-financial-access-by-2020. Accessed 01 April 2020
55. Wang, T., Li, Y., Kang, M., Zheng, H.: Exploring individuals' behavioral intentions towards donation crowdfunding: evidence from China. Industrial Management & Data Systems, Forthcoming (2019)
56. Wang, Z., Zhengzhi Gordon, G.U.A.N., Hou, F., Li, B., Zhou, W.: What determines customers' continuance intention of FinTech? Evidence from YuEbao. Industrial Management & Data Systems (2019)
57. Wei, K.K., Teo, H.H., Chan, H.C., Tan, B.C.: Conceptualizing and testing a social cognitive model of the digital divide. Inform. Syst. Res. **22**(1), 170–187 (2011)
58. Yang, Y., et al.: Roots of tomorrow's digital divide: documenting computer use and internet access in China's elementary schools today. Chin. World Econ. **21**(3), 61–79 (2013)
59. Yao, H., Liu, S., Yuan, Y.: A study of user adoption factors of mobile banking services based on the trust and distrust perspective. Int. Bus. Manag. **6**(2), 914 (2013)
60. Yardi, S., Bruckman, A.: Income, race, and class: exploring socioeconomic differences in family technology use. In: Proceedings of the SIGCHI Conference on Human Factors in Computing Systems, pp. 3041–3050, May 2012
61. Yermack, D.: Corporate governance and block chains. Rev. Finan. **21**, 7–31 (2017)
62. Yu, C.S.: Factors affecting individuals to adopt mobile banking: empirical evidence from the UTAUT model. J. Electron. Commer. Res. **13**(2), 104–121 (2012)

Investor's Perception Towards Mutual Fund Investing on the Rise of Digitalization in Indian Mutual Fund Industry

K. Pushpa Raj[⊠] [ID] and B. Shyamala Devi

SRM Institute of Science and Technology, School of Management,
Chennai, TN, India
pushpapush@gmail.com, shyamalb@srmist.edu.in

Abstract. Technological advancement has been playing an essential role in the development of any sector. Even mutual fund industries are more exposed to the advent in the field of financial technology. Advancement in the FinTech arena has been witnessed in every aspect of the mutual fund industry. Asset Management Companies (AMC's) are started using robotics to increase their efficiency of fund management and ease their transaction processing or customer servicing. Investors can access the information online, track or redeem their investment any time of the day. Unified Payments Interface (UPI) and Electronic Clearing Services (ECS) are the online modes of payment facilities adopted by most fund houses. Association of Mutual Fund India (AMFI) has been consistently deploying considerable efforts to ensure that every investor has sufficient information to make informed decisions. Even the Know Your Customers (KYC) process has been completed online and more superficial than earlier days. In this paper, an effort has been made to understand the importance of Mutual Fund investments, the awareness among different investors about the mutual fund, the impact of Digitalization on mutual fund investment, and the information availability to every investor related to the mutual funds.

Keywords: Mutual funds in India · Digital payments · Digital footprint · Importance of mutual funds · Asset management · Robo advisors

1 Introduction

The Mutual Fund industry in India is undergoing tremendous growth in recent years. With the adoption of newer technologies, Asset Management Companies (AMCs) have managed to reach every corner of the nation to reach millions of investors. Digitalization has created more transparency, which has gained investors' confidence level and made them invest more confidently than before. Each investor has the freedom to get the information online and start investing online by completing a simple online eKYC process. Investors can purchase mutual funds with the click of a button through their mobile application by making electronic payments linked to their accounts. Paperless transactions are increasing, making life easier for the Investment Advisors to concentrate on the returns rather than indulging in any paperwork.

© IFIP International Federation for Information Processing 2020
Published by Springer Nature Switzerland AG 2020
S. K. Sharma et al. (Eds.): TDIT 2020, IFIP AICT 617, pp. 553–560, 2020.
https://doi.org/10.1007/978-3-030-64849-7_49

Soon, the Financial Advisors will be replaced by Robo-Advisors with access to the affluence of information online to perform the prediction based on the investors' risk appetite. Nowadays, the use of online calculators for calculating the returns yielded by any specific mutual funds can be computed efficiently. These calculators are available free of cost on every fund house's websites to make investors make confident decisions on their investments according to their future needs. The flow of information between Financial Advisors to their investors about the purchase of redemption decisions has been made easier with the technology's advent. Also, the communication between AMCs to their distributors regarding the new set of policies or product launches has been relatively more straightforward in recent days. Mutual Funds are gaining popularity among investors because of their ability to generate higher returns in the long term than any other investment avenues. Mutual Funds can yield greater returns when compared to your savings bank account or your bank fixed deposits during longer tenure. Mutual Funds can be generating higher returns based on the compounding interest. Also, the investment approach based on SIP can be providing you the advantage of rupee cost averaging, which is even more powerful. Mutual Funds are also considered as one of the less risky investment options as it utilizes the power of diversification.

2   Literature Review

A most recent study undertaken by Kishore Kumar Das and Shahnawaz Ali during [3] confirmed that the adoption of Digitalization in the mutual fund industry had shown a positive trend in the increased participation of retail investors. Distribution channels are making use of this financial advancement to make their work more efficient and investor-friendly. A study conducted by Sujit G Metre and Pranay Prashar during Jan [1] has concluded that the availability of information and knowledge about mutual funds because of Digitalization has no impact on the investor's perception of online MF investment. An investigation performed by Dikkatwar Ramakrishna, De Tonmay, and Satya Prasad T K during Dec [2] has concluded that digital interventions are mostly targeted towards distributors and large investors like corporate and other HNIs. Another research study conducted by Prasada Rao and Manda V K. during [4], the examination revealed that Blockchain technology would help every stakeholder of the mutual fund industry. It can also provide the advantage of transparency, accountability, privacy, and decentralization. These transparencies could help in increasing the confidence level among the different investors because of this Digitalization.

3   Need for the Study

Digitalization has provided an excellent platform for the Financial Services industry to operate more efficiently. This has also paved the way for the distributors' increased capacity to reach more customers without much paperwork or involving any physical transactions. Though we are already witnessing much of the digital impact on the FinTech application, much has been left over to explore shortly. With these advancements in place, are the investors taking advantage of these avenues to decide about their mutual fund investment? The perception of investors towards mutual fund investment, their knowledge level about the risk & returns relevant to their assets is still challenging for many to identify or interpret. In this study, we have attempted to understand the importance of investing in mutual funds alongside to study awareness among the investors on risk & return tradeoff based on their investments. We have also analyzed the impact of Digitalization on investors' perceptions of mutual fund investment and even their understanding of the associated fund manager.

4 Objectives of This Study

The objective of this study is

1. To analyze the importance of mutual fund investment.
2. To understand the investor's awareness about Risk and Returns in mutual fund investment.
3. To identify the impact of Digitalization on Mutual Fund investments.
4. To analyze the information available about Mutual Funds amongst investors.

5 Sampling Information

The research has been conducted with the help of Primary data. Primary data has been collected using a structured questionnaire. Statistical tools and graphical methods have been employed for data analysis. Analysis has been performed under different broad categories, as follows:

1. Importance of Mutual Fund investments
2. Investors awareness about Risk & Returns in Mutual Fund investments
3. Impact of Digitalization on Mutual Fund investments
4. Information availability about Mutual Fund amongst investors

Data is collected by distributing this questionnaire to relevant participants and getting this filled using online methods. Questions covered under this questionnaire have been based on Likert scale measurement. Likert scale is balanced on both sides of the neutral option. We used the Likert scale as the measurement unit, as this is one of the reliable techniques for understanding users' attitude or opinion. Respondents are selected based on their investing patterns. The researcher has collected the data from 144 respondents those who are already invested in mutual funds for the period of short to long term.

6 Data Analysis and Inferences

6.1 Importance of Mutual Fund Investments

Null Hypothesis (H0): Mutual Funds are considered as the safest long term investment option.

Alternative Hypothesis (H1): Mutual Funds are NOT considered as the safest long term investment option.

Mutual fund investments are considered as one of the safest investment options for long term investors. Most of the investors are parking their amount in mutual funds as long term investments. Based on the Fig. 1 below, it is evident that close to 58% of respondents are long term investors in mutual funds.

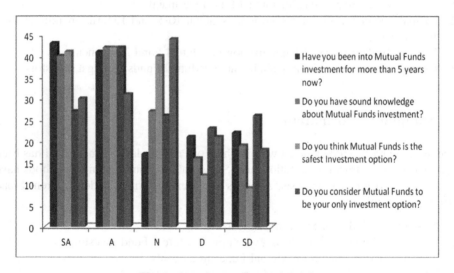

Fig. 1. Importance of mutual Funds

They believe that the returns yielded my mutual funds are superior, and hence they wanted to continue their investments into mutual funds. It has also been observed that close to 58% of respondents consider mutual fund the safest investment option. Only 15% of respondents either disagree or strongly disagree with this question. Around 48% of the respondents considered mutual funds as the only investment option. The rest of them have diversified its investment across different available options. It has also been observed that 42% of respondents considered mutual fund investment as their income's tax saving objective. While remaining people are invested primarily for generating capital gain on their invested amount. More than 53% of respondents strongly agree that mutual fund investments are essential for long term investments. Hence we accept the hypothesis and conclude that Mutual Fund investments are a crucial long-term investment option.

6.2   Investor's Awareness About Risk & Returns in Mutual Fund Investments

Null Hypothesis (H0): Investors are aware of the Risk and Returns in mutual fund investment.

Alternative Hypothesis (H1): Investors are NOT aware of the Risk and Returns in mutual fund investment.

Risks involved and the corresponding returns associated with the invested amount should be clearly communicated to the investors. This information is considered to be one of the essential things while making decisions about any investment. From Fig. 2 below, it is observed that only 36% of respondents are aware of the risk associated with mutual investments.

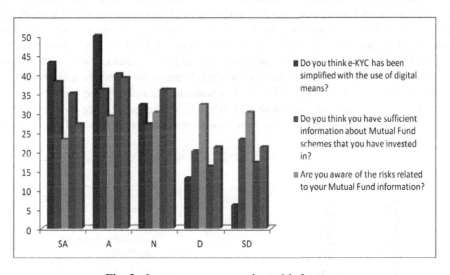

Fig. 2. Investors awareness about risk & returns

The remaining 43% of the respondents disagree, and they were still unclear about the risks associated with mutual fund investments. But on the contrary, 52% of respondents answered that they were well informed about the returns they would get at the time of maturity. Only 23% of the respondents were not very clear about the returns they will get at the time of maturity. Also, more than 50% of respondents informed us that they clearly understand the mutual fund they have invested in their money. Around 30% of the respondents were not clear about the investments they made in mutual funds. It is astonishing to see that considerably more people have invested their money without clearly understanding the scheme that they were investing their money. More than 50% of respondents Strongly Agree and Agree as they have the risk and return information about their investment in the mutual fund. Hence we accept the hypothesis and conclude that Investors are aware of the Risk and Return information of the mutual fund investment.

6.3   Impact of Digitalization on Mutual Fund Investments

Null Hypothesis (H0): Mutual fund investments have grown due to Digitalization.

Alternative Hypothesis (H1): Mutual fund investments have NOT grown due to Digitalization.

Recently Digitalization has been introduced in every financial platform. Also, we are seeing more people are interested in online payments and online investments. This is because of their convenience and to save the efforts involved in other modes of physical transactions. From Fig. 3 below, it is noticed that more than 63% of respondents consider digital payments to have more comfortable, and even they considered that their money is safe while making digital transactions. Only 22% of respondents think that digital transactions are not the safest option for them. More respondents (60%) communicated that digital transactions are faster than their physical transactions used before. It is also interesting to note that around 69% of respondents have made fresh investments into mutual fund post digitalization. Even the same amount of respondents considered that their queries related to any investments are clarified at the earliest with introducing the digital medium. Only 22% of the respondents are still not comfortable with digital transactions and the online mode of query resolutions. More than 65% of respondents Strongly Agree and Agree that mutual fund investments are increased post digitalization. Hence we accept the hypothesis and conclude that Mutual Fund investments are grown due to Digitalization.

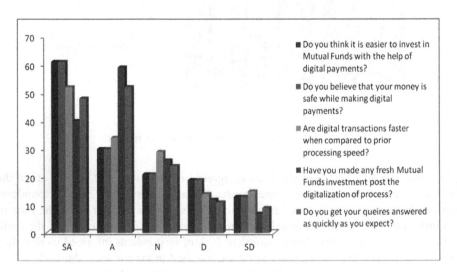

Fig. 3. Impact of digitalization on mutual funds

6.4   Information Availability About Mutual Fund Amongst Investors

Null Hypothesis (H0): All the investment information is NOT available to the mutual fund investors.

Alternative Hypothesis (H1): All the investment information is available to the mutual fund investors.

As digital technology is emerging, most people tend to get information online. They used to research online to get the information they wanted before making any decisions. With this advancement, we requested respondents about the information they have about their mutual fund investments. In Fig. 4 below, it is surprising to see that only a limited number of respondents, 42%, have informed that they believe that transparency in the information they get from mutual fund investments. Around 38% of respondents believe that there is no transparency in their knowledge about mutual fund investment. Also, 40% of the respondents did not trust AMC on the initial period's marketing information. Another vital thing to be noticed here is more than 68% of the respondents are not aware of their fund manager who manages their mutual fund investment. With the advancement in the field of digital technology, still, most of the investors are not aware of their fund managers. Even 59% of the respondents didn't trust the skills of their fund manager. They believe that fund performance is based on the market volatility and not based on their fund manager's skills. Only 21% of the respondents believe that the returns generated by their fund are because of the skills of their fund manager. More than 54% of respondents Strongly Agree and Agree as the mutual fund manager or their skills are unknown. Hence we accept the hypothesis and conclude that all the investment information is NOT available to the mutual fund investors.

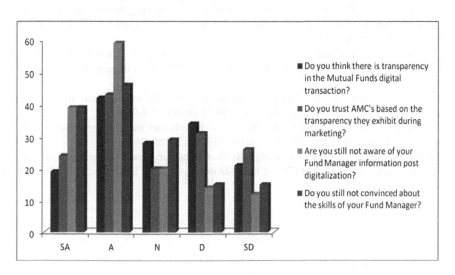

Fig. 4. Information availability of mutual funds

7 Conclusion

Based on this study, we observed that most investors are long-term investors in mutual funds. They firmly believe that Mutual Funds investments are yielding greater returns when compared to other investment avenues. They also consider mutual funds as one of the safest investment options which carry a lesser risk. Though we observe that few of the investors are not aware of the risks associated with the investment they make into mutual funds, most of the investors seem to be having the information related to their associated investment. The introduction of technological improvements in the mutual fund industry has paid significantly, making more investors drift towards mutual fund investments by making digital payments. The paperless eKYC process and the purchase, redemption, and other online activities, make investors' lives more manageable in their home comfort. With Digitalization taking deeper inroads, investors are still not aware of their Fund Manager information who manages their mutual fund. Also, the investors are not entirely in the belief that the returns generated from their investments are not associated with the fund manager's skills. Though the information's about every scheme of mutual funds is available online, the distributors and the fund houses should powerfully communicate the importance of the Fund Managers and their skills in handling the crises. We can gain the investors' confidence level to a greater extent, which in turn can result in increased participation of the investors.

References

1. Metre, S.G., Parashar, P.: Impact of digitization on mutual fund services in India. In: Proceedings of 10th International Conference on Digital Strategies for Organizational Success (2019). SSRN: https://ssrn.com/abstract=3309277, http://dx.doi.org/10.2139/ssrn.3309277
2. Ramakrishna, D., De Tanmoy, S.P.V.: Innovations & technology based initiatives in mutual fund distribution intermediation in India. Int. J. Innov. Technol. Explor. Eng. 9(2), 4747–4753 (2019). ISSN: 2278-3075
3. Das, K., Ali, S.: The role of digital technologies on growth of mutual funds industry. Int. J. Res. Bus. Soc. Sci. (2147–4478) 9(2), 171–176 (2020). https://doi.org/10.20525/ijrbs.v9i2.635
4. Manda, V.K., Rao, S.S.P.: Blockchain technology for the mutual fund industry. SSRN Electron. J., 12–17 (2018). http://dx.doi.org/10.2139/ssrn.3276492
5. Kuo, C., Lee, D., Teo, E.G.S.: Emergence of fintech and the lasic principles. J. Finan. Perspect., 1–26 (2015). http://dx.doi.org/10.2139/ssrn.2668049
6. Carbo-Valverde, S.: The impact on digitalization on banking and financial stability. J. Finan. Manag. Mark. Inst., 133–140 (2017). http://dx.doi.org/10.12831/87063:y:2017:i:1:p:133-140

Financial Inclusion via Mobile Banking – A Comparison Between Kenya and India

M. C. Arthi[1(✉)] and Kavitha Shanmugam[1,2]

[1] SRM Institute of Science and Technology, SRM Nagar, Kattankulathur, Kanchipuram, Chennai 603203, TN, India
arthimc@gmail.com
[2] Faculty of Management, SRM Institute of Science and Technology, SRM Nagar, Kattankulathur, Kanchipuram, Chennai 603203, TN, India
https://www.srmist.edu.in/

Abstract. Mobile payments in India and Kenya had grown tremendously in the last decade and this paper intend to analyze the trend, progress and achievements of both the countries in mobile payments especially focusing on socially and economically backward sections of the society. Mobile payment banking system in Kenya exists since 2007, even before digital era began in India. Payments banks in India, as a concept, envisioned in 2014, nevertheless showing lot of promising growth because of the mobile penetration in India. There are lot of similarities in the intention of both the initiatives, as they mainly focus on financial inclusion for economically poor society and rural population. M-Pesa by Safaricom had made an implausible change in Kenya, improving the labor class and rural people access to banking, reducing time spent on transactions and simplifying the process by just making cell phones as their banks. India until first decade of 20th century, was mainly dependent on postal service for rural areas as banking solution, but now rapidly moving to digital era with payment banks as a mobile enabled banking solution. The paper explains the Indian service providers like Paytm, Airtel, Jio, and Indian postal service who had already established in India were able to move to Payment bank services quicker because of the base they had established in the last decade. The paper utilizes the secondary data information extracted from published reports and reports from Reserve Bank of India, Central Bank of Kenya and other independent organizations like FSD Maps, Statista and GSMA to arrive at a comparison between the payments systems in both the countries.

Keywords: Financial inclusion · Digital payments · M-Pesa · Mobile banking · Mobile payments · Payment banks

© IFIP International Federation for Information Processing 2020
Published by Springer Nature Switzerland AG 2020
S. K. Sharma et al. (Eds.): TDIT 2020, IFIP AICT 617, pp. 561–569, 2020.
https://doi.org/10.1007/978-3-030-64849-7_50

Abbreviations

BPM	Business Process Management
ETBFSI	Economic Times Banking, financial services and insurance (E-Magazine and Newsletter)
GDP	Gross domestic product
GSMA	Global System for Mobile Communications Association
IPPB	Indian Postal Payment Bank
IT	Information Technology
PMJDY	Pradhan Mantri Jan Dhan Yojana
QR	Quick Response
RBI	Reserve Bank of India
SACCOS	Savings and Credit Cooperative Societies

1 Introduction

The need for financial inclusion and provision of digital technology to access Government services is increasingly becoming important to address social inclusion and economic uplifting of the poor. The influencers for financial inclusion are; IT & financial literacy (Kajole 2018) internet availability (Mervyn et al. 2014), relatively young population who can learn latest technology fast, smart phones at affordable prices, GDP per capita (Ndung'u 2018) and easy access to the services. In this article, we will address how the banking needs of the rural and economically weaker sections of society are taken up in India & Kenya and how effective are they in the current state of implementation. Innovative financial services enabled with technology, which provides with easy affordable access and hassle free services are adopted by both countries. It is important that customers are well educated on the values of the services offered and satisfied with them. The traditional banking services are inconvenient, more costly and inaccessible for people in the base of the economic pyramid.

In 2012, the World Bank estimated that, one in three mobile money users worldwide were in Kenya although Kenya has less than 1% of the world's population (Winn 2015).

Kenya was able to achieve financial inclusion by providing a simple remittance services that works seamlessly and reliabe on even the most basic mobile handsets. M-Pesa bypassed the complexity of modern banking at a time when traditional bricks and mortar banks in advanced market economies are finding it ever more difficult to compete with alternative financial services (Winn 2015).

For M-Pesa in Kenya, the value proposition for users was fast, cheap, reliable remittance services from urban and rural areas, while for agents it was fee income. (Winn 2015). For Payment banks in India, the value proposition for users are zero balance account, convenience, ease of transfer to any part of India, less transaction charges and security (Shrey et al. 2018).

Most M-Pesa customers said that they chose the service because of its low cost (Morawczynski and Pickens 2009) and M-Pesa's pricing structure encourages users to experiment with the service while extracting value from the transactions that customers value the most (Mas and Ng'weno 2010).

Both the services use branchless banking systems, taking advantage of increasingly universal real-time mobile communications networks to bring banking services into everyday retail stores, thereby removing the need for banking infrastructure in the communities where poor people live and work (Dermish et al. 2011).

The vision of universal branchless banking services is associated with high-volume, low-value transactions by customers using cash with values like quick, convenient, and most importantly, guaranteed service (Dermish et al. 2011).

2   Financial Inclusion in India - An Overview

2.1   Banking for the Unbanked

Financial inclusion in Indian subcontinent was one of the focus areas for the Government and it is taken up with more rigor starting 2014, thanks to the effort of the Government. Pradhan Mantri Jan Dhan Yojana (PMJDY) is an initiative taken by Government of India, which is open to all Indian citizen with the focus of affordable banking solution for the poor and needy. It aims to provide a basic bank account, remittances, credit and insurance to the citizens. This scheme was launched on 28 August 2014. A record number of 11.50 crore bank accounts opened under PMJDY as on 17th January 2015 against the original target of 7.5 Crore set by 26th January, 2015 (Soumiya Devi et al. 2015) which show the success of the scheme in India.

Due to the initiative, as of 2017 (data from Business standard), 80% of the Indian people have bank account; about same number of people use mobile phone. The economic revolution of moving away from cash and go to digital transactions have started in India for the past few years and due to COVID-19 situation in India, there is more need to do contactless transactions.

With the limitation of banks not able to open branches in all parts of India, especially rural areas, the need for quick access to bank account for payments, savings and transfer of money is to be fulfilled. With almost all Indian citizens holding mobile phone, the most economic and quicker solution for financial inclusion is to focus on mobile banking solution (Sikdar and Kumar 2017).

2.2   Payment Bank History and Current Scenario

To overcome the challenges faced due to the restrictions to use Scheduled Commercial banks, in September 2013, a "Committee on Comprehensive Financial Services for Small Businesses and Low Income Households", headed by Nachiket Mor, was formed by the RBI (RBI Press release 2013). By January 2014, the Nachiket Mor committee submitted its final report with recommendation for a new category of bank called "Payment Banks" with a condition that 25% of its branches must be in the unbanked rural area (Shrey et al. 2018). The banks must use the term "Payment Banks" in its books and files in order to differentiate it from other types of bank (RBI report 2014).

Currently there are five active Payments Banks in India namely,

- **Paytm Payment Bank:** Offers cashless payments transaction with QR codes and provide minimal banking needs to the unbanked sections of society
- **Airtel Payment Bank:** Offers 4% interest, online debit, cash deposit via nearest Airtel Banking point.
- **Indian Post Payment Bank:** Safe and secure cash transactions and banking at your doorstep and utility bill payments
- **Fino Payment Bank:** Started its services with 410 branches and 25,000 banking points in India. Fino Payment Bank won the Digital Payments Award 2018–19, ETBFSI Excellence Award and Champion of Rural Market Award for providing outstanding performance in its domain (see Fino banks Awards and Recognition, finobank.com)
- **Jio Payment Bank:** Provides basic banking services along with online utility bill payments. Ease of use via MyJio app

Fig. 1. Roadmap of payment banking system establishment in India Source: Reserve bank of India and Payment banks sites

The below figure covers the roadmap and history of payment banks in India from 2013 till 2019 (Fig. 1):

3   Financial Inclusion in Kenya - An Overview

3.1   M-Pesa - Mobile Payment Solution from Kenya

M-Pesa is a mobile payments system first developed in Kenya, which effectively offers a banking system based on mobile phones. It was started in 2007, by Vodafone Group plc and Safaricom, the largest mobile network operator in Kenya (Onsongo and Johan Schotm 2017). Since then, M-Pesa has seen a rise in popularity with over 23 million users as of the year 2019 (Vodafone, press releases 2020). The Central Bank of Kenya backed M-Pesa development and rollout, as means for financial inclusion and kept other commercial banks' opposition at bay, as financial inclusion is a higher immediate objective over the interests of the banking sector (Onsongo and Schotm 2017). It had become the widespread person-to-person transaction channel such that it accounted for 66.56 percent of the throughput volume in Kenya's National Payment System (Muthuiora 2015). It now provides services such as; Deposit and withdrawal of funds, transfer of money to users and non-users, payment of bills, gateway to loans, transfer money between services and bank accounts and purchasing airtime or what we call as mobile talk time and data (see Safaricom).

Registration for M-Pesa is simple for users with mobile phone number become account number with Safaricom. User credits amount to the account from retail outlets or authorized resellers called agents and top up their phone. A pin is used to protect the account, which can be accessed to send or receive funds (Mbiti and Weil 2011). To withdraw cash, the user visits the agents' outlet and makes the transaction (see Safaricom). According to the Central Bank of Kenya, the value of all transactions in 2019 is 44 percent of the country's GDP.

Benefits

- **Interest on savings account:** In cooperation with Safaricom M-Pesa offers savings accounts, paying 3% to 6.65% per annum interest (see Safaricom). Many people started earning interest for the first time in their lives.
- **Mobile payments:** Utility bill, cable TV rent, online purchases and supermarket shopping, can be done with M-Pesa. Money transfer to M-Pesa is simple and easy using the cell phone.
- **Cell phone becoming virtual banks:** In 2007, several million Kenyans owned a cell phone with a Safaricom number. Then this phone number actually became a virtual bank account number (Bengelstorff 2015). Rural Kenyans with no banking opportunities leaped from the agricultural age straight into the digital world of tomorrow.
- **Financial Benefit:** M-Pesa increased the volume of money flowing in and out of the communities, speeding up money velocity, which boosted local consumption. Therefore, there was an increased volume and variety of food and agricultural inputs in local markets thus bolstering food security.
- **More jobs:** More youth and women found employment (Matheson 2016) in the rapidly expanding agent network as businessperson became M-Pesa agents in addition to their core business.
- **Security**: In terms of physical security, users reported reduced muggings and thefts, and women reported being able to use M-Pesa to accumulate cash securely (Muhura 2019).

3.2 Role of Mobile Money Agents for M-Pesa

The M-Pesa agents pay a major role in serving the unbanked in Kenya by offering mobile money products and services and helping the country's GDP and increasing the income of households by bringing banks to people's doorstep especially for rural population where the need is higher (refer Fig. 2). The agents compete with other competitors like commercial banks, Cooperative societies for promoting and sustaining MPesa both in rural and urban Kenya (Muthuiora 2015). From Fig. 3, it is very clear the domination of mobile money agents and making it evident that M-Pesa growth in Kenya largely depend on the strength of the mobile money agents.

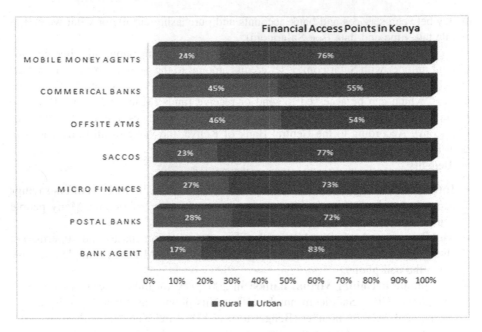

Fig. 2. Financial access points by type – rural vs urban view

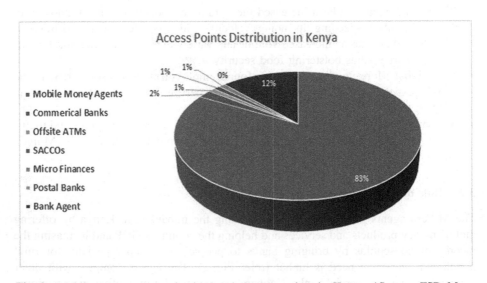

Fig. 3. Mobile money agents domination in access points in Kenya. *Source: FSD Maps, Kenya, GSMA's Mobile Money for the Unbanked (MMU)

4   Comparing Kenya's Mobile Banking Model with India Payment Bank Services

See Fig. 4.

Kenya	India
• eCitizen program for digitalization by government in 2014 • Inua Jamii benefits program - uses mobile banking platform for direct transfers • M-Pesa agents for servicing customers- currently there are more than 2 lakh+ agents in Kenya* • 135+ million transactions as of May'20 month via mobile payments* • M-Pesa is promoted via women's self help group but penetration is lower due to lower literacy rate and poverty* • Information and communication technology contribution stands at 11% of GDP*	• UMANG, Aadhar card for citizens and complete digitalization in 2017 • Direct money transfers using PYMDY program thereby encouraging financial inclusion • Five payment banks with complete mobile banking solutions with servicing via retail agent shops and service centers • Totally 1.46 billion mobile transactions of which 1.38+ million is via payment banks as of May 2020* • In India, the awareness level is higher on mobile payments but Indian women are more influenced by reference groups • The IT-BPM industry in India constitutes approx. 7.7% of India's GDP as of 2017

Fig. 4. Comparing Kenya and India on mobile banking and digitization *Source 1. Statista.com: Contribution of Indian IT Industry to India GDP. 2. FSD Maps, Kenya 3. GSMA Connected Women - Bridging the Gender Gap: Mobile access and usage in low- and middle-income countries (Santosham et al. 2015) 4. GSMA Person-to-government (P2G) payment digitization: Lessons from Kenya, Case Study (Wasunna et al. 2017)

5   Mobile Transaction Volumes and Value of Payments: Comparison Between Kenya and India

The payment bank transaction is India is comparable with the volume and value of transactions in Kenya although overall mobile transactions volume and value in India including commercial banks is more than 10 times than Kenya's transactions (refer to Fig. 5 and Fig. 6). What we can infer is that, the Kenya's transactions trend and value is more or less had become stable over the last one year, whereas in India, there is a variation still showing and we had still not reached maturity on payment banks. In addition, the current Covid-19 situation creates an uncertainty in the volume and availability of money in the hands of customers to do mobile transactions. However, considering population size of the countries, comparing to Kenya, India has to go a long way in financial inclusion as we see only two of the five payment banks are in top 10 banks in volume and value of transactions as per RBI reports.

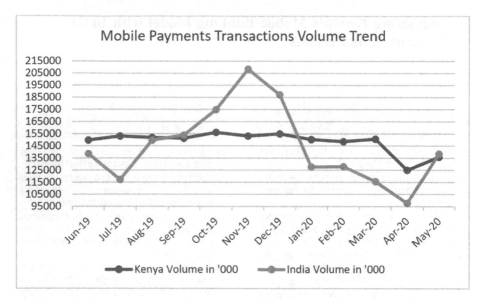

Fig. 5. Comparing the trend of mobile transaction between two countries *Source: Central Bank of Kenya, Reserve Bank of India

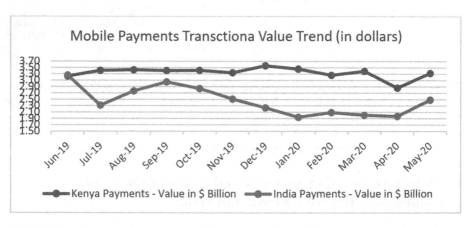

Fig. 6. Comparing mobile payments value of transactions between two countries. *Source: Central Bank of Kenya, Reserve Bank of India

6   Conclusion

We can visualize a common trend between the two countries mobile banking services (M-Pesa from Kenya and Payment banks from India), but payment banks popularity as mobile banking solution in India is still a long journey. Payment banks had to compete with schedule commercial banks whereas in Kenya, Safaricom's M-Pesa is almost a monopoly with 64% market share compared other competitors in Kenya (see Annual report, Communications Authority of Kenya). The road ahead for Payment Banks is challenge not only in terms of value or volume but also from profitability perspective. Systematic pricing structure, cross-selling products like insurance, micro finance/lending via tie-ups, are the opportunities ahead of them

References

Muhura, A.: Accelerating digital inclusion for women in Kenya, GSMA (2019)

Dermish, A., Kneiding, C., Leishman, P., Mas, I.: Branchless and Mobile Banking Solutions for the Poor: a survey of the literature. Innov. SSRN **6**, 81–98 (2011)

Bengelstorff, A.: A Global Success from Kenya. Credit Suisse news and articles (2015)

Shrey, B., Tanmayee, B., Mohak, C., Animesh, D., Geetha, I.: Role of payment banks in India: opportunities and challenges. Int. J. Adv. Manag. Econ. (2018)

Muthuiora, B.: Enabling Mobile Money Policies in Kenya, Fostering a Digital Financial Revolution, GSMA (2015)

Central Bank of Kenya, Statistics, Mobile Payments (2019)

Communications Authority of Kenya, Annual Report for the Financial Year Ended June 30th 2019, pp. 41–50 (2019)

Onsongo, E.K., Schot, J.: Inclusive Innovation and Rapid Sociotechnical Transitions: The Case of Mobile Money in Kenya. SSRN (2017)

FSD Maps Kenya, Datasets (2014)

Mas, I., Ng'weno, A.: Three keys to M-PESA's success: branding, channel management and pricing. J. Pay. Strat. Syst. **4**(4), 270–352 (2010)

Mbiti, I., Weil, D.N.: Mobile Banking: The Impact of M-Pesa in Kenya. NBER Working paper series (2011)

Winn, J.K.: Mobile Payments and Financial Inclusion: Kenya, Brazil, and India as Case Studies. SSRN - University of Washington School of Law Research Paper (2015)

Mervyn, K., Simon, A., Allen, D.: Digital inclusion and social inclusion: a tale of two cities. Inf. Commun. Soc. **17**, 1086–1104 (2104)

Soumiya Devi, M.K., Shanmugam, K., Ramya, J.: Payment banks a leap towards financial inclusion. Int. J. Sci. Technol. Manag. **4**(1), 128–136 (2015)

Kajole, N.: Factors that Matter for Financial Inclusion: Assessment of Empirical Evidences, with Special Reference to India, Abhigyan, vol. 36, no. 1. Gale Academic (2018)

Wasunna, N.: Person-to-government (P2G) payment digitization: Lessons from Kenya, Case Study, GSMA (2017)

Ndung'u, N.: Next steps for the digital revolution in Africa, Inclusive growth and job creation lessons from Kenya, African Growth Initiative, Brookings (2018)

Sikdar, P., Kumar, A.: Payment bank: a catalyst for financial inclusion. Inst. Manag. SAGE Publ. Asia-Pacific J. Manag. **12**(3–4), 1–6 (2017)

RBI Report: Committee on Comprehensive Financial Services for Small Businesses and Low Income Households (2014)

Matheson, R.: Study: Mobile-money services lift Kenyans out of poverty, MIT News (2016)

Safaricom. https://www.safaricom.co.ke/personal/m-pesa

Santosham, S., Lindsey, D.: Bridging the gender gap: Mobile access and usage in low and middle-income countries, GSMS Connected Women (2015)

Statista: Information technology/business process management sector in India as a share of India's GDP from FY 2009 to FY 2017

Morawczynski, O., Pickens, M: Poor People Using Mobile Financial Services: Observations on Customer Usage and Impact from M-PESA, CGAP (2009)

The Evolution of Causal Mechanisms that Drive the Diffusion of Platforms: Investigating Corrective Mechanisms

Abhinay Puvvala[1], Shane McLoughlin[1]([⊠]), Brian McLafferty[2], Yuliia Yehorova[3], and Brian Donnellan[1]

[1] Lero, National University of Ireland, Maynooth, Ireland
shane.mcloughlin@mu.ie
[2] School of Business, National University of Ireland, Maynooth, Ireland
[3] CONFIRM, School of Business, National University of Ireland, Maynooth, Ireland

Abstract. This study investigates the evolving nature of causal mechanisms driving the evolution of a digital platform. By drawing from a rich dataset representing the evolution of a thriving FINTECH platform (i.e. HP-EFS) over a period of 7 years, we propose to a) identify the causal mechanisms responsible for its evolution, and b) further understand the dynamic nature of these causal mechanisms. We integrate the existing literature on Generative Mechanisms with the theoretical streams of Socio-technical systems and Systems theory to address the research question. The contribution of this paper is to propose and elucidate a class of causal mechanisms, 'Corrective Mechanisms' for future IS research. We anchor this approach amongst existing IS 'Generative Mechanisms' research and argue it's utility in complementing existing research when explaining digital platform evolution.

Keywords: Generative mechanisms · Fintech · Platforms · Evolution · Causality · Corrective mechanisms · Critical realism · Abductive reasoning

1 Introduction

The emergence of platforms as building blocks for innovation redefining industry structures of products and services is a key trend defining the modern economy [1], by disrupting how organizations create and deliver value [2]. A platform is increasingly seen as an organizational form in the literature [3–5] with two key aspects: 1) technology, comprising of the core modules, interfaces and extensions to bridge with complementors [1, 6] and 2) social processes, involving such factors as governance mechanisms to coordinate the actors and interactions between them in the platform's associated ecosystem [4, 7]. These two aspects feed into each other to shape the evolution of a platform and its ecosystem, such as in social networking and P2P platforms (e.g. Facebook, Airbnb) etc. The first aspect, technology, combines two modules: a) a stable module with a set of components providing basic utilities, commonly referred to as the platform core, and b) a complementary module with a set of

© IFIP International Federation for Information Processing 2020
Published by Springer Nature Switzerland AG 2020
S. K. Sharma et al. (Eds.): TDIT 2020, IFIP AICT 617, pp. 570–580, 2020.
https://doi.org/10.1007/978-3-030-64849-7_51

components providing varied uses [8]. Such a configuration combines stability with variety to make platforms extremely evolvable. Consequently, the underlying 'mechanisms' driving their evolution is a source of intrigue for the research community.

Literature on Platform design can broadly be categorized into three approaches: (a) top-down or functional [9], (b) bottom-up or product consolidation [10] and (c) evolutionary or redesign approach [11]. Given the path-dependency nature of platforms (i.e. evolution is connected to their initial design) [12–14]) and the rapidly evolving nature of platforms within volatile environments and uncertain future states (e.g. Fintech, Smart city), the evolutionary 'redesign approach' is most fruitful to studying such platforms, yet drawn on by few studies when identifying the generative mechanisms driving platform success. As such, a recent overview of IS platform research advocated the need for longitudinal studies [15], with research examining the evolution of a) Platform's core and b) Proprietary platforms even scarcer given challenges in gaining access to empirical data [15]. Based on these identified literature gaps, whereby an understanding of the causal mechanisms driving successful platform evolution can give crucial insights for their governance that influences adoption and diffusion, we formulated the following research question: *What is the nature of evolving causal mechanisms driving a proprietary digital platform?*

More specifically, we are interested in the evolution of a proprietary platform core in context and relation to its boundary resources (e.g. APIs), periphery (e.g. complementors) and overall ecosystem (e.g. customers). Thus, we seek to both identify the causal mechanisms responsible for its evolution and understand the dynamic nature of these causal mechanisms. To address the research question, we selected and investigate the 'Hewlett Packard Enterprise Financial Services' (HPE-FS) platform across a 7-year period. The platform started as a piece of software to simplify and coordinate sale transactions and evolved into a thriving industry platform composing numerous complementors and a rich ecosystem supporting $6.2 billion in transactions annually.

The study adopts a Critical Realist view by applying abductive reasoning for developing a configurational perspective of Platform evolution. The research design drew together the theoretical and methodological guidance of a) Henfridsson and Bygstad [16] seminal work on Generative Mechanisms, and b) on socio-technical representations [17] and evolutionary process models [18]. To better understand the causality behind these key change events, we further looked to c) Systems Theory for relevant theoretical underpinnings. The contribution of this paper is to formatively propose (based on initial case analysis) that the 'second order' evolution i.e. changing nature of causal mechanisms driving platform evolution, means prevalent IS research on Generative Mechanisms alone is insufficient in painting a complete picture. By following the process of abductive reasoning, we also encountered what we refer to as 'Corrective Mechanisms', seen as a complementary lens to the existing IS focus of Generative Mechanisms. The latter currently more concerned with causal patterns behind key change events in digital platform evolution.

The paper is organized as follows – we start with a discussion on the emergence of Generative Mechanisms and its roots in Critical Realism. The subsequent sections integrate theoretical streams of Socio-technical systems and Systems Theory to the literature on Generative Mechanisms. The final two sections present the research design and discuss the initial results and the future work.

2 Emergence of Generative Mechanisms as an Analytical Lens

Critical Realism (CR), as a scientific endeavor rooted in the philosophy of (social) science, seeks to bridge the dichotomous positivism-interpretivism divide, by lending a 'middle path' addressing inherent limitations in separately pursuing positivism or interpretivism alone [19, 20]. It acknowledges a real world independent of our perception and knowledge of it [21], i.e. a realist ontology, yet rejects pure empiricism as capable of understanding the world through observation alone. Instead, it contends that reality is layered (i.e. the real, the actual and the empirical domain) and comprised of often unobservable mechanisms at work that produce and thus explain events, changes or outcomes. These mechanisms are the causal structures (e.g. social or economic competition, 'self-fulfilling prophecy' etc.) that explain certain phenomena [21]. The layers entail the real domain that includes social, cultural, psychological and physical structures and processes, and the mechanisms that emerge within/from them. The actual domain consists of 'events' that occur as a result of mechanisms from the real domain. Finally, the empirical domain includes the subset of the events occurring in the actual domain that can be perceived and experienced, i.e. observed [20]. Thus, mechanisms tend to be unobservable as we cannot perceive and experience all layers of reality. This is why the interpretivist tradition is valued for its methods of enquiry in critical realism despite not fully subscribing to their philosophical roots. In critical realism, the central task is explaining the causality of events or effects (i.e. dependent variables), by identifying causal "mechanisms" at play, considered middle-range theories or explanations.

In IS literature, the term Generative Mechanism (GM) is used in CR based studies, as it's defined as the *"causal structures that generate observable events"* [16]. The concern is to grasp, 'the real, manipulatable, internal mechanisms at the heart of CR accounts of why things are as they are' [22]. As such, generative explanations are the 'causal agent(s)' [21] assumed to have generated the relationship between entities/variables being analysed. In the case of Generative Mechanisms, what has generated (i.e. caused) the relationship between two variables (e.g. between an initial condition (independent variable) and the 'event', i.e. condition in effect (dependent variable)) is the emergent property of the mechanism at work (i.e. the parts, processes, relationships of the mechanisms structure) [23].

The search for Generative Mechanisms is a search for the most plausible explanations for distinguishing true causality (i.e. why we observe what we observe) amongst the indicators, correlations, co-incidental or spurious associations we tend to make. Searching for plausible patterns behind observable events [24], changes or outcomes, is how we surmise the mechanisms that 'explain, likely endure and can generalise' [25]. Thus, according to Mingers & Standing [25] these "mechanisms are relatively enduring in respect of the events they cause but their absolute timescale may vary immensely".

In relation to levels of analysis, Henfridsson & Bygstad [16] describe generative mechanisms as a composite of interconnected mechanisms at varying levels acting in context. The compositional view suggests micro (individuals), macro (society or organization) or both levels of analysis to describe causality [25]. It's based on Hedström and Swedberg's [26] distinction of; a) 'situational mechanisms' linking macro level (society or organization) to micro level (individual) (i.e. the whole influences actions of parts); b) 'individual action mechanisms' linking desires and beliefs with action opportunities at micro level (i.e. combining individual actions generate specific actions) and; c) 'transformational mechanisms' linking individual actions (micro level) into wider effects at the macro level (i.e. micro actions interact to generate macro actions) [26].

As an IS research inquiry, the focus of GM studies using evolutionary process theories tend to be on searching for patterns of 'punctuation' or revolutionary change events to its deep structure (as is evident from deviations to stable periods of a platform's life) [18]. This is because much IS research is particularly interested in a platform's 'generativity' in terms of its own capacity to change [27], and/or its capacity to enable periphery and ecosystem change [28, 29]. Here it should be noted that a platform's generativity is critical to its adoption & diffusion potential, though does not necessarily always equal positive outcomes [16]. Finally, IS research also looks to generative mechanisms as a composite of lower order mechanisms, on self-reinforcing mechanisms, as well as possible configurations of generative mechanisms at play [16].

A well-cited example of a generative mechanism is the 'self-fulfilling prophecy' based theory [30]. The premise is that "an initially false definition of a situation evokes behaviors that eventually make the false conception come true" [30]. A key example is a run on a bank (i.e. initial event) started by a false rumor of insolvency. This causes depositors to withdraw savings, which reinforces the belief in the rumor as (1) withdrawals damage the financial situation of the bank and (2) signal to others that something is wrong with the bank. As this situation cyclically self-reinforces, an initially solvent bank may go bankrupt (i.e. final event) when enough depositors withdraw. Thus, a false initial belief in a situation causes the situation to become true in effect. In this case, a 'belief formation mechanism' [26] is at work, unobservable but plausibly explaining the event observed.

3 Evolution of Socio-technical Systems

Leavitt's (1964) decomposition of a socio-technical system comprises of four subsystems in the form of actors, task, structure and technology that together (intertwined) form a complex ensemble. While they have been isolated for analytical convenience, there is an implicit acknowledgement the sub-systems are not intended to be isolated when determining causality of a socio-technical action [31]. Leavitt's [17] simple yet generic and inclusive model has been widely used to represent a range of socio-technical systems in IS literature. We adopt Leavitt's socio-technical view to represent platforms, themselves increasingly seen as organizational forms.

To represent the evolution of platforms, IS literature broadly branches into two paradigms – a) continuous, incremental change characterized by a slow stream of Darwinian mutations and b) episodic punctuations followed by periods of stability characterized by incremental events to bring back equilibrium in the system [12, 32, 33]. A key difference is that the former paradigm perceives change to be always progressive, while the latter explicitly states that systems are prone to both cycles of progression and deterioration along evolution. This study adopts the latter, i.e. episodic, punctuated paradigm to interpret evolution of platforms because it's more suited to the characteristics of the digital platform evolution of interest.

Further, we refer to Lyytinen and Newman's [18] seminal work, Punctuated Social IS Change (PSIC) model to explore the evolution of the HPE-FS platform. Gersick [12] suggests changes in a system's 'deep structure' are central to understanding the entirety of evolution. Deep structure refers to the set of fundamental choices a system has made in terms of its organizations, principles of interaction and activity patterns that are critical to maintain its existence [12]. These deep structures manifest themselves by providing the system with properties of memory and path dependency. This is all the more pertinent for a platform configuration where the technological core is kept relatively invariant by design. The focus on and the processes behind generating network effects is another aspect that corresponds to the deep structure in a platform setup.

Gersick's [12] and Lyytinen and Newman's [18] definitions of a punctuation although differ somewhat semantically, both emphasize the impact a punctuation has on the deep structure of a system. A successful punctuation reconfigures the deep structure with a configuration comprising new pieces while retaining some pivotal old pieces [12]. The deep structure is connected to the periods of stability systems go through. During these periods of relative stability, systems undergo limited adaptations that are generally responses to environmental perturbations [18]. These periods of stability are sustained by inertia due to routinization, cognition, motivation and obligation and the benefits of a stable environment [33]. These incremental adaptations are critical in maintaining the balance between the four sub-systems of a socio-technical system. The PSIC model offers methodological guidance in identifying these critical incidents that result in gaps which are addressed by the support systems (referred as the building system in the PSIC model) in place. These interventions result in one of the four possible outcomes – failed, incremental, punctuated interventions or further destabilization.

4   Theoretical Underpinnings of Systems Theory

Concepts such as causality, emergence, autopoiesis, homeostasis or the systemic and holistic representations that embody Critical Realism are also firmly rooted in Systems Theory [34]. Considered an output of the later phase of development in systems thinking, System Dynamics' [35] core tenets particularly align to a Critical Realist perspective. Sterman's [36] work builds on a basic premise of "behavior follows structure" to unravel underlying patterns of causal relations through which systemic behavior emerge. Further, Senge's [37], 'The Fifth Discipline' (a cornerstone publication in Systems Dynamics) proposes the idea of system archetypes which are generic templates of causal structures comprising balancing and reinforcing feedback loops, that when dominant produce patterns of systemic behavior such as "limits to growth", "eroding goals" etc. These archetypes are tantamount to mechanisms in Critical Realism [25].

Further, a mechanism in the Critical Realist view can only be recognized in the real domain on the basis of events it generates in the actual domain that in turn need to be observed in the empirical [21]. Moreover, from a systems thinking perspective, underlying causal structures are continuously at play and the net effect of these supporting and counteracting forces is responsible for the manifestation of observable events which in turn are analysed empirically to mine out mechanisms that explain systemic behaviour. Systems thinking proposes a technique called Loop Dominance Analysis (LDA) [38, 39] where the behavior of variables of interest are viewed as a sequence of atomic behavior patterns by repeatedly (de)activating sections of the causal structure.

5 Research Design

5.1 Abductive Reasoning and Retroduction

The Critical realist approach to mechanism-based research generally follows the abductive reasoning approach [40]. Abductive Reasoning is a form of logical enquiry that moves back and forth between deduction and induction. It starts with empirical observations and then tries to find the simplest and most plausible explanation for these observations, similar to a doctor trying to diagnose a group of patients with an acute and possibly unknown illness. Iterating through various cycles of theory matching, the researcher identifies relevant variables, conceptual relationships, develops plausible hypotheses to arrive at a provisional theory accounting for the original anomaly [41]. In the case of mechanism based research, hypotheses are formed as 'potential causal mechanisms' at work proposed to explain the phenomena observed [21, 25]. For example, a previously unknown virus and its spread (epidemiology) caused the illness in a group of patients several thousand miles from its origin. This process of enquiry often takes the form of Retroduction [21, 25], whereby, 'events are explained by postulating (and identifying) mechanisms which are capable of producing them' [42]. Specifically, the researcher starts with a description of significant variables or features associated with the event observed, then 'retroduces' the possible causes, eliminating less plausible alternatives and finally identifying the most plausible explanation generating the event(s), i.e. the Generative Mechanism(s) [21]. Importantly the process of hypothesizing possible causes is a weighty endeavor involving careful data collection and analysis, that can contextualise long periods of time before the event in question. In the case of the virus example given, several generative mechanisms are at work, in the severity of illness amongst patients, and in its spread to and amongst patients.

5.2 Case Selection and Data Collection

To address our research question, we selected and investigated the digital FINTECH platform of HPE-FS over a 7-year period between 2013 and 2019. This platform was selected because the HPE-FS platform is 'proprietary' and provided appropriate accessibility to sufficient case data and people, thereby enabling an excellent opportunity to learn about the complexities of the phenomena of interest [43]. Secondly, this accessibility was granted over a suitable longitudinal period of data collection, whereby a researcher (co-author) was embedded in the project during this duration. Finally, the platform offered an ideal candidate for studying 'path dependency' in 'platform redesign' as it began as a piece of software to simplify and coordinate sale transactions and evolved into a successful industry platform in that it now: a) supports $6.2 billion in transactions, b) enables 3rd party services from Adobe, FICO etc., and c) connects customers, partners, HPE and other products from other suppliers such as Dell, Apple etc.

The challenges faced in our attempts to collect the data to represent and analyze the 7-year evolution was in identifying the boundaries and defining the unit of analysis and drawing out the critical incidents/change events along the evolution of this platform.

Figure 1 outlines our methodological approach to address the research question (see introduction). We started the abduction process via observation of the case selected across the period of data collection and began to move back and forth between the data and theory to find plausible explanations (i.e. generative mechanisms) of evolutionary change by 'retroducing' observed events. However, through this process, we began to observe through the data activity and processes in the platform development not directly connected to change events observed, but yet were crucial to the platform's stability and sustainability over time. In other words, they generated changes in the platform that were much more opaque or invisible to see, but yet crucial to its continuing success.

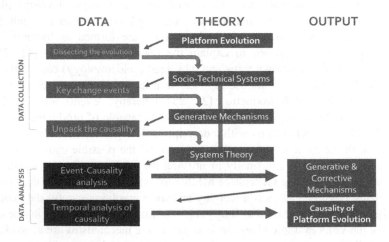

Fig. 1. Research design: abductive reasoning

6   Initial Results and Future Work

As we unpacked the causal forces behind the HPEFS platform evolution based on critical realisms fundamental stratification of reality into the domains of the "real", "actual" and "empirical" [21] - the causal mechanisms retroduced from the empirical base of observed events, i.e. the generative mechanisms began to emerge [16, 23].

However, we also unexpectedly identified a class of causal mechanisms constantly bubbling underneath the surface without ever generating any overt empirically observable change events, but yet helped account for the platform's stability and sustaining over time. We subsequently refer to these as 'Corrective Mechanisms', which we tentatively define as, *causal mechanisms that ensure periods of platform stability (keeping the deep structure intact) and/or incremental improvement without reconfiguring its underlying deep structure)*. We illustrate an example from the initial results as follows:

Analysis showed that one of the significant mechanisms behind the successful evolution of HPE-FS platform was primarily driven by Data. The platform's growth in the later years was largely driven by vast amounts of data captured from various sources igniting self-reinforcing processes leading to an increased platform appeal. While the data-driven mechanisms of its evolution became more significant in the events they produced, they had actually been in operation since the beginning. The scale, shape and purpose of data captured in the earlier years was smaller, was primarily solicited from customers by sales and marketing, and specifically used to maintain the platform's stability. As such, we see this as a mechanism that started as a Corrective Mechanism, but later observed that they had further transitioned into a Generative Mechanism as greater data was collected and exploited to evolve the platform. This is because, as the data-driven approach increased in scale and volume, it eventually went on to drive significant and clearly observable event changes, contributing to the platform's generativity.

To summarize, we propose Corrective Mechanisms as a research enquiry to explain how a state of equilibrium is ensured or re-established between/amongst the technology, actors, tasks and structural components of a socio-technical system. Further examples of activities and process revealed through case abduction which demonstrate restoration of equilibrium (between 2 or more subsystems) but yet not tied to clearly observable events include; a) adjusting (or fixing) customer matching accuracy after implementation of credit scoring, b) restricting visibility (used for internal reconciliation) of certain invoices to avoid confusing customers, c) adjusting the product type selection granularity to customers from the HPEFS partners, and d) adjusting how the eSignature step could be implemented across multiple but connected documents.

Structures to support *'Corrective Mechanisms'* include a set of resources to enact housekeeping routines and processes [44] and even carry out incremental adaptations succeeding punctuations [18]. They play a crucial but understated role in preserving stability, often exemplified in IS terms like 'maintenance' or 'normal project operation' [45, 46]. The 'events' produced as a result of these mechanisms do not necessarily surface at an empirical level, hence escaped attention of studies deploying a Generative Mechanism lens.

It is also worth noting that, homeostasis, the system property responsible for maintaining a stable equilibrium between interdependent elements [47] is an emergent property from actualization of Corrective Mechanisms. We appreciate the difficulty in capturing such mechanisms without the convenience of starting from the empirically observed events. We believe a holistic understanding of the causal structures [35], system archetypes [37] and aspects of the socio-technical system viewed in relation to the purpose/task [17] operating in the system could all prove useful in identifying

Corrective Mechanisms. As mentioned in Sect. 4, Loop Dominance Analysis (LDA) in conjunction with all the above could potentially provide further methodological guidance. Finally, as this is a study in progress, further work is needed by the authors and the IS community to elaborate and refine methods for identifying corrective mechanisms and their application in understanding the evolution of information systems.

Acknowledgement. This work was supported, in part, by Science Foundation Ireland grant 13/RC/2094, and from the European Union's Horizon 2020 research and innovation programme under the Marie Skłodowska-Curie grant agreement No. 754489.

References

1. Baldwin, C.Y., Woodward, C.J., Gawer, A.: The architecture of platforms: a unified view. In: Gawer, A. (ed.) Platforms, Markets and Innovation. Edward Elgar Publishing Limited, Cheltenham (2009)
2. Tiwana, A.: Platform synergy: architectural origins and competitive consequences. Inf. Syst. Res. **29**(4), 829–848 (2018)
3. Gawer, A., Cusumano, M.A.: Industry platforms and ecosystem innovation. J. Prod. Innov. Manag. **31**(3), 417–433 (2014)
4. Nambisan, S., Lyytinen, K., Majchrzak, A., Song, M.: Digital innovation management: reinventing innovation management research in a digital world. MIS Q. **41**(1), 223–238 (2017)
5. Saadatmand, F., Lindgren, R., Schultze, U.: Configurations of platform organizations: Implications for complementor engagement. Res. Policy **48**(8), 103770 (2019)
6. Karhu, K., Gustafsson, R., Lyytinen, K.: Exploiting and defending open digital platforms with boundary resources: Android's five platform forks. Inf. Syst. Res. **29**(2), 479–497 (2018)
7. Adner, R.: Ecosystem as structure: an actionable construct for strategy. J. Manage. **43**(1), 39–58 (2017)
8. Bresnahan, T.F., Greenstein, S.: Technological competition and the structure of the computer industry. J. Ind. Econ. **47**(1), 1–40 (2003)
9. Farrell, R.S., Simpson, T.W.: Product platform design to improve commonality in custom products. J. Intell. Manuf. **14**(6), 541–556 (2003)
10. Moore, W.L., Louviere, J.J., Verma, R.: Using conjoint analysis to help design product platforms. J. Prod. Innov. Manag. **16**(1), 27–39 (1999)
11. Meyer, M.H., Dalal, D.: Managing platform architectures and manufacturing processes for nonassembled products. J. Prod. Innov. Manag. **19**(4), 277–293 (2002)
12. Gersick, C.: Revolutionary change theories: a multilevel exploration of the punctuated equilibrium paradigm. Acad. Manag. Rev. **16**(1), 10–36 (1991)
13. Katz, M.L., Shapiro, C.: Systems competition and network effects. J. Econ. Perspect. **8**(2), 93–115 (1994)
14. Plowman, D.A., Baker, L.T., Beck, T.E., Kulkarni, M., Solansky, S.T., Travis, D.V.: Radical change accidentally: the emergence and amplification of small change. Acad. Manag. J. **50**(3), 515–543 (2007)
15. de Reuver, M., Sørensen, C., Basole, R.C.: The digital platform: a research agenda. J. Inf. Technol. **33**(2), 124–135 (2017)

16. Henfridsson, O., Bygstad, B.: The generative mechanisms of digital infrastructure evolution. MIS Q. **37**(3), 907–931 (2013)
17. Leavitt, H.J.: Applied organization change in industry: structural, technical and human approaches. In: Cooper, S., Leavitt, H.J., Shelley, K. (eds.) New Perspectives in Organizational Research, pp. 55–71. Wiley, Chichester (1964)
18. Lyytinen, K., Newman, M.: Explaining information systems change: a punctuated socio-technical change model. Eur. J. Inf. Syst. **17**(6), 589–613 (2008)
19. Smith, M.L.: Overcoming theory-practice inconsistencies: critical realism and information systems research. Inf. Organ. **16**(3), 191–211 (2006)
20. Wynn, D., Williams, C.K.: Principles for conducting critical realist case study research in information systems. MIS Q. **36**(3), 787–810 (2012)
21. Bhaskar, R.: A Realist Theory of Science, 2nd edn. Harvester Press (1978)
22. McGrath, K.: The potential of generative mechanisms for IS research. In: Thirty Fourth International Conference on Information Systems (2013)
23. Mingers, J.: A classification of the philosophical assumptions of management science methods. J. Oper. Res. Soc. **54**(6), 559–570 (2017)
24. Mingers, J.: Realizing information systems: critical realism as an underpinning philosophy for information systems. Inf. Organ. **14**(2), 87–103 (2004)
25. Mingers, J., Standing, C.: Why things happen – developing the critical realist view of causal mechanisms. Inf. Organ. **27**(3), 171–189 (2017)
26. Hedström, P., Swedberg, R.: Social mechanisms. Acta Sociol. **39**, 281–308 (1996)
27. Tilson, D., Sørensen, C., Lyytinen, K.: Platform complexity: lessons from the music industry. In: Proceedings of the Annual Hawaii International Conference on System Sciences (2013)
28. Zittrain, J.L.: The generative internet. Harv. Law Rev. (2006)
29. Cennamo, C., Santaló, J.: Generativity tension and value creation in platform ecosystems. Organ. Sci. **30**(3), 617–641 (2019)
30. Merton, R.K.: Social Theory and Social Structure. Free Press, New York (1968)
31. McLeod, L., Doolin, B.: Information systems development as situated socio-technical change: a process approach. Eur. J. Inf. Syst. **21**(2), 176–191 (2012)
32. Greenwood, R., Hinings, C.R.: Understanding radical organizational change: bringing together the old and the new institutionalism. Acad. Manag. Rev. **21**(4), 1022–1054 (1996)
33. Tushman, M.L., Romanelli, E.: Organizational evolution: a metamorphosis model of convergence and reorientation. Res. Organ. Behav. **7**, 171–222 (1985)
34. Mingers, J.: The contribution of systemic thought to critical realism. J. Crit. Realism **10**(3), 303–330 (2011)
35. Forrester, J.W.: Industry Dynamics. MIT Press, Cambridge (1961)
36. Sterman, J.D.: Business Dynamics: Systems Thinking and Modeling for a Complex World, 1st edn. McGraw-Hill, New York (2000)
37. Senge, M.P.: The fifth discipline. Meas. Bus. Excell. (1997)
38. Richardson, G.P.: Problems for the future of system dynamics. Syst. Dyn. Rev. **12**, 141–157 (1996)
39. Ford, A.: Modeling the Environment: An Introduction to System Dynamics Models of Environmental Systems. Island Press, Washington DC (1999)
40. Peirce, C.S.: Collected Papers of Charles Sanders Peirce, vol. 2. Harvard University Press, Cambridge (1960)
41. Behfar, K., Okhuysen, G.A.: Perspective—discovery within validation logic: deliberately surfacing, complementing, and substituting abductive reasoning in hypothetico-deductive inquiry. Organ. Sci. (Providence R.I.) **29**(2), 323–340 (2018)

42. Sayer, R.A.: Method in Social Science: A Realist Approach, 2nd edn. Routledge, London (1992)
43. Stake, R.E.: Qualitative research: studying how things work. In: Qualitative Research: Studying How Things Work, The Guilford. Guilford Press, New York (2010). ix, 244 pp.
44. Markus, M.: Power, politics, and MIS implementation. Commun. ACM 26(6), 430–444 (1983)
45. Lyytinen, K., Hirschheim, R.: Information systems failures—a survey and classification of the empirical literature. In: Oxford Surveys in Information Technology, vol. 4, pp. 257–309. Oxford University Press, Oxford (1988)
46. Markus, M.L., Keil, M.: If we build it, they will come: designing information systems that people want to use. Sloan Manag. Rev. 35(4), 11 (1994)
47. Von Bertalanffy, L.: An outline of general system theory. Br. J. Philos. Sci. 1, 134–165 (1950)

Performance Modelling on Banking System: A Data Envelopment Analysis-Artificial Neural Network Approach

Preeti and Supriyo Roy[(✉)]

Department of Management, BIT Mesra, Ranchi, India
supriyo.online@gmail.com

Abstract. With changing banking environment, the efficiency of the operational function of bank is of critical importance and needs timely watch. Apart from measuring the operational performance of banks using DEA approaches, the banking sector today is more inclined to predictive analytics to identify their future performance and improve their competitiveness well in advance. In this sequel, the present paper proposes hybridisation of Data Envelopment Analysis and Artificial Neural Network Approaches for operational performance measurement and prediction for Indian banks using the five-year (2015 to 2019) dataset. Non-oriented non-radial DEA model is adopted in the present study, attempting to provide decision-makers the discretion to identify slacks in performance by maximising outputs and minimising inputs. This can identify causes of inefficiency and suggest necessary steps for improvement. In addition to DEA findings, the paper performs prediction task for obtained efficiency scores. Finding of will be advantageous for policymakers, managers of banking industry for predicting future operational performance of banks until they are able to make required changes for its improvement.

Keywords: Data envelopment analysis · Artificial neural network · Operational performance · Efficiency · Banking

1 Introduction

Banking system holds immense significance in any countries economy upliftment (Bhattacharya et al. 1997). With advancement of digital banking, the competition between banks have only risen further. Banks are constantly under pressure to improve performance to withstand the change (Reserve Bank of India 2018). As a result, the performance analysis of banks has become integral issue for management concerned. Top managers are constantly putting effort to identify inefficiencies to eliminate them to achieve competitive advantage and face challenges. Moreover, operation risk management is pertinent to any commercial banks to ensure operation effectiveness and competitiveness. How to improve the operational performance of commercial banks has become an emerging question that commercial banks now faces prominently. The basic research question boils down to: *the need for performance evaluation to measure, improve and predict the operating efficiency levels of banking system.*

© IFIP International Federation for Information Processing 2020
Published by Springer Nature Switzerland AG 2020
S. K. Sharma et al. (Eds.): TDIT 2020, IFIP AICT 617, pp. 581–597, 2020.
https://doi.org/10.1007/978-3-030-64849-7_52

Traditionally, the bank managers made use of multiple ratios to analyse different aspects of banking operations. However, ratios are subjected to limited information while making economies of scale assumptions, framing benchmarking policies or estimating overall performance of banks (Yeh 1996). Alternatively, frontier approaches as opposed to ratio approaches, allows objective measurement of performance within complex operational environments. Frontier efficiency approaches, namely parametric and non-parametric, are two categories of approach differing on the basis of assumption of functional form of variables and presence of computational error (Berger and Humphrey 1997). The problem of performance measurement is well studied by using non-parametric approaches (Cooper et al. 2007). As per literature, Data Envelopment Analysis (DEA) is a non-parametric benchmarking technique to identify efficient and inefficient banks based on multiple input and output data derived from banking dataset (Charnes et al. 1978).

Apart from measuring the operational performance of banks using DEA approaches, the banking sector today is more inclined to predictive analytics to identify their future performance and improve their competitiveness well in advance. The basic capability of DEA modelling is of performance measurement, but not predictive capacity of performance. Also, DEA results do not provide potential solutions for allocation of resources to inefficient units leading to inappropriate support to managerial decision making. Therefore, there is need for flexible modelling to measure and predict performance is of significant interest for practical concerns (Wu et al. 2006). The progressive use of various machine learning approaches is proved to be indispensable. Artificial neural network, a machine learning technique is increasingly used to assist DEA findings to estimate efficiency (Wang 2003). Considering similarities between DEA and ANN, as both belong to non-parametric category as well as both approaches do not makes assumption related to functional form of inputs and output variables. At first, Athanassopoulos and Curram (1996) applied the combination of DEA and ANN to classification and prediction problems. The study revealed that DEA proves better than ANN for measurement purpose and latter can be utilised for prediction analysis. Since then, many researchers applied DEA-ANN approach towards various domains like banking, education, industries, hospitals (Sreekumar and Mahapatra 2011; Tosun 2012). To the best of our knowledge, there is limited study developing hybrid model which utilises DEA and neural network in context of Indian banks.

To summarise, the plenty of DEA-related studies is limited to measuring performance without prediction. Therefore, it is imperative to integrate DEA and data mining techniques such as ANN for Indian banking system. Present paper adopts hybrid modelling approach to estimate, improve and predict operational performance of Indian banks with a period of five years from 2015 to 2019. The two main contribution of the study can be listed as follows:

- *Development of DEA model* - Operational performance is measured and improvement identified for Indian banks
- *Development of ANN model* – ANN model is trained using five year banking dataset (2015 to 2019) with efficiency score as output and input-output variables as utilized in DEA model as inputs.

Remaining study is structured as follows. Most relevant literature pertaining to use to DEA and DEA-ANN approach in various sectors, especially banking is discussed in Sect. 2. Next, Sect. 3 describes DEA and ANN approaches explicitly. Section 4 explains data, proposed framework and empirical findings of the paper. Section 5 concludes with summary, limitations and future direction of the study.

2 Related Studies

In recent past, plenty of studies has resorted to quantitatively measure performance of banks by developing several DEA models. Although, many researchers applied DEA to estimate bank's operational performance and only few studies attempted to using Artificial Intelligence techniques like ANN to predict operational performance of banking system.

2.1 DEA Applications to Banking Sector

Initially, the stress was on development of mainly traditional (radial) DEA models suggesting proportional changes in input and output variables (Wild 2016). Sahoo and Tone (2009a) and Sahoo and Tone (2009b) introduced radial and non-radial DEA models for Indian banking system to study the effect of financial sector reforms on the efficiency growth of banks. The studies concluded that public sector banks do not reflect the learning experience compared to private sector banks. In 2016, Stewart *et al.* used radial DEA models to study the bank performance in Vietnam for the period of 1999 to 2009. The study concluded that efficiency rose over the observed period. Defung et al. (2016) studied the impact of regulatory reforms on the performance of Indonesian banking industry, confirming statistical significant relationship between regulatory reforms and technical efficiency score. Profit efficiency is compared across different Indian banking ownership groups by developing DEA model to assess the impact of Global financial crisis (Gulati and Kumar 2016). As per the findings, the Global financial crisis did not much effect the profit efficiency of Indian banks.

Kumar et al. (2016) evaluated the efficiency, productivity and return to scale of Indian banks for the period of post reform and global financial crisis. The study answered question regarding the impact of global financial crisis on the performance of banks. Azad et al. (2016) used sample of 43 Malaysian commercial banks to compare the performance across bank ownership and nature. Sathye and Sathye (2017) confirmed this relationship by testing the impact of ATM intensity, Bank size, soundness, ownership and risk on the performance of Indian banks using bootstrap DEA model. Covering the period from 2012 to 2016, the efficiency of Brazilian banks was estimated using radial DEA models (Henriques et al. 2018). The study identified the efficient and inefficient banks by estimating pure technical and scale efficiency. Most recent study (Davidovic et al. 2019) on the implementation of radial DEA model to estimate the efficiency trends of the Croatian banking industry for the period from 2006 to 2015. Variables like relative ownership structure, market size, and origin of capital are studied to test the relationship with efficiency score. Mohapatra et al. (2019) estimated the operating efficiency of Indian banks for the year 2011 to 2015 using radial DEA model. Study investigated the relationship between intellectual capital and performance of banks.

2.2   DEA-ANN

Despite of many data mining techniques that have been used in literature for predicting certain output, the ANN technique has been sporadically used in literature. Since the pioneering work of combining DEA and ANN by Athanassopoulos and Curram (1996), plenty of studies have adopted DEA-ANN approach in various field such as banking, healthcare, supply chain and manufacturing industries. After extensive literature review of studies, particularly those studies that utilised DEA in conjunction with ANN is discussed below. Wu et al. (2006) developed DEA-ANN model for branch efficiency of big Canadian banks. Based on its findings, the study offers guidelines to improve the performance of inefficient branches. Moreover, short-term efficiency prediction is performed using developed model. Emrouznejad and Shale (2009) generated back propagation neural network in conjunction with DEA to estimate efficiency scores of DMUs with large datasets with many input/output variables. This paper used five large dataset to propose that developed model is better alternative than using conventional DEA which uses large amount of computer resources like CPU time and memory.

Mostafa (2009) quantified the performance of top Arab banks using DEA-ANN approach. The study develops probabilistic neural network to perform classification function of banks depending on best accuracy score of the model. The study highlighted flexibility and robustness advantages of utilising developed model for classifying banks performance. Sreekumar and Mahapatra (2011) developed integrated DEA and neural network model for assessing performance of Indian B-school. The study identified input-output variables to measure and suggest improvement in technical efficiency of B-schools. Performance prediction using neural network is made for effective decision making. Tosun (2012) combined DEA-NN model to measure the efficiency of hospitals and overcome the limitations of DEA approach. The developed model is trained using DEA results and prediction is made on test data to categorise banks as efficient and inefficient banks. Moreover, the obtained results are compared with results using Discriminant analysis (DA). The study confirms that ANN is best approach to perform classification function compared to DA as it requires lesser computer resources and CPU time.

Barros and Wanke (2014) analysed performance of Insurance companies by developing two-stage model using DEA and neural network. The study identified ceded reinsurance as potential output for increasing efficiency score of companies and also predicted performance using the developed neural network model. Kwon and Lee (2015) enhanced the two-stage DEA model by adding predictive capacity using BPNN approach. The study applied the developed model to the datasets from large US banks to empirically demonstrate constructive performance modelling. To overcome the predictive capability of DEA model, Shokrollahpour et al. (2016) developed combined DEA and ANN model to forecast future benchmark for Iranian commercial banks. The study performed five year efficiency forecast to suggest strategies to improve efficiency and its causes. Kwon (2017) developed performance measurement and prediction model for railways using DEA and NN approach. Efficiency trend of railroad is estimated using CCR model of DEA and prediction is made for efficiency score and projected output using NN for each railroad. The proposed framework is beneficial for decision making and benchmarking prac2tises for railroads. Tavana et al. (2018) adopted two data mining models such as ANN and Bayesian networks to assess bank liquidity risk. Dataset from large US banks is utilised for implementing the proposed model for liquidity risk assessment. Petropoulos et al. (2020) adopted multiple machine learning techniques to forecast bank insolvencies of sampled US-based financial institution. The result confirmed that Random Forest as well as Neural Network are superior methods compared to others. For prediction of bank failures, the study suggested CAMELS evaluation framework offers higher marginal contribution. Le and Viviani (2018) proved that ANN is more accurate than traditional statistical technique to predict bank failure. A sample of 3000 banks was investigated for period of 5 years before bank becomes inactive. Five significant ratios that study identified as significant includes capital quality, liquidity, loan quality, operations efficiency and profitability.

Only few studies demonstrated the integration of DEA-ANN approach within banking system, particularly in Indian banking system. Most DEA related studies measured the performance based on different DEA models, only few of them included prediction of performance. Prediction of bank performance is of utmost importance to restrict banks from being insolvent or weaker. The hybrid model is developed to enhance the predictability dimension to black-box like DEA model. The empirical finding provided by DEA for performance improvement may not always be action-oriented due to lack of prediction capability. Therefore, the hybrid DEA-NN model provide managers plausible capabilities to predict optimal operational performance for setting advance improvement goals and progress. In this sequel, the objective framed for the study is as follows:

1. To *develop* DEA model to measure operational efficiency scores and identify areas of improvement of Indian banks for the period of five years.
2. To *train* ANN model using estimated operational efficiency scores and input-output variables.
3. To *predict* the operational performance of banks using developed ANN model.

3   Research Methodology

3.1   Data Envelopment Analysis

DEA, a linear programming managerial tool used for measuring productivity and efficiency for any Decision Making Units (DMU). It is excessively applied for both public and private sector including airlines, banks, hospitals, manufacturers, transportations and universities. Consequently, variations in model development, new applications, variable differences are ongoing research fields in area of DEA. As name suggests, DEA "envelops" input-output production function as closely as possible by developing efficient frontier that identifies best and worst performing DMUs. Original DEA models like, Charnes-Cooper-Rhodes model and Banker-Charnes-Cooper model measures the radial technical and pure technical efficiency of DMUs, respectively. More sophisticated model like Slack Based Measure (SBM) model, as proposed by Tone (2001), supersedes these traditional DEA models by measuring efficiency of an inefficient DMU by referring to the furthermost point on the benchmark frontier of an inefficient DMU by referring to the furthermost point on the frontier. SBM model are non-radial models measuring non-proportional input excesses and output shortfalls, unlike CCR and BCC measuring only radial (proportional) efficiencies (weaker efficiency). Certain properties that SBM model satisfies includes acceptance of semipositive data and unit invariance of variables, scalar value for reported efficiency score. Also, non-oriented modelling of SBM model allows to report inefficiencies on both side of production function - input excesses and output shortfalls.

Mathematical Equations

Notations for development of non-oriented SBM model is as under:

$$n = \text{Total DMUs each having inputs(m) and outputs(v)}; \ j = 1, 2, \ldots, n)$$

$$X = (x_{ij}) \text{ set of inputs}; \ i = 1, 2, \ldots, m$$

$$Y = (y_{uj}) \text{ set of outputs}; \ u = 1, 2, \ldots, v$$

ρ = non-radial slack indicator (efficiency value), s^- = input slack, s^+ = output slack, λ = intensity vector; $X > 0$ and $Y > 0$.

With notations as clarified, the production possibility set A for DMU (x_{i0}, y_{u0}) is defined as:

$$A = \{(x, y) | x \geq X\lambda, y \leq Y\lambda, \lambda = 1\} \tag{1}$$

Non-oriented SBM model:

$$\rho = \min \frac{1 - \frac{1}{m} \sum_{i=1}^{m} \frac{s_i^-}{x_{i0}}}{1 - \frac{1}{v} \sum_{u=1}^{v} \frac{s_u^+}{y_u 0}} \tag{2}$$

Subject to:

$$x_0 = X\lambda + s^-$$

$$y_0 = Y\lambda - s^+$$

$$\lambda = 1; s^-, s^+ \geq 0 \tag{3}$$

The objective of the study is to optimise the objective Eq. (2) subject to constraints (3) such that value of ρ is equal to 1 and value of input and output slack is 0.

3.2   Artificial Neural Network

Influenced by biological neural network, ANN is popularly known machine learning method that captures non-linear patterns in data, utilised mainly for credit rating classification problems. Such problems require big dataset, explanatory variables. Literatures arguments numerous neural networks with structural variations depending on information flow, hidden layers and algorithm differences used to train them. These layers of neural network are connected by connection weights. A typical neural network is series of interconnected neuron layers. The information transfer in neural network occurs in two ways: feedforward and back-propagation. Feed forwarding functions to processes the information from input layer to output layer resulting into error, whereas back propagation tries to optimise output by fixing errors by sending information back in the network. On designing multilayer neural network, it is pertinent to decide upon number of hidden layer. Also, the number of hidden layers depends on complexity of problem to be predicted.

Back Propagation Neural Network is considered to most popular neural network used for both classification and prediction purpose (Rumelhart et al. 1986). All ANN uses multilayer feed-forward neural network to learn the parameters to form non-linear function between input-output variables. The typical structure of ANN comprises of input layer, hidden layer and output layer. Inputs are fed into input layer simultaneously in units. Weighted output of units from input layer are fed into second layer called hidden layer. Weighted output of this hidden layer is input to second hidden layer, and so on depending on the network. The output of the hidden layer is fed as input to output layer which provides prediction for DMUs. Basically, input data related to back prorogation is fed to neural network, the output is compared to the desired output to estimate the error for each iteration. This estimated error is back propagated to adjust weights in order to decrease error for each iteration. Learning process continues till acceptable range of output error is reached after considerable weight adjustment to train the model to produce the desired output. Figure 1 illustrates the basic structure of ANN

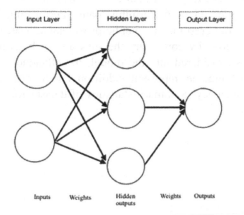

Fig. 1. Typical structure of artificial neural network

4 Empirical Analysis and Results

4.1 Data and Variables

Data on 39 Indian banks for the period of 5 years was obtained from annual publications of Reserve Bank of India and Indian Banks Association websites. Total of 39 banks from both public and private sector is involved in present analysis covering the study period of five years (2015 to 2019). As per DEA rule of thumb, minimum number of DMUs to be included in the study must be three times the sum of input-output variables (Charnes et al. 1978). Input-output dataset for 39 banks (DMUs) is used for period for 5 years (2015 to 2019) totalling to 195 observations is used to develop ANN model. The dataset is split into training and testing data in 7:3 ratio. The implementation of model includes training the model and using the developed to test the outputs. There exists no formal rule of thumb regarding optimal dataset for neural network. However, usually the training dataset should be 10 times the sum of independent variables used as inputs in the model (Kwon and Lee 2015).

For variable selection, the two approaches are mainly followed- production and intermediation. Production approach, developed by Benston (1965), consider banks as service providers for customers using physical inputs like labor, capital and assets to make services available like deposits and advances, whereas intermediation approach, as developed by Sealey and Lindley (1977) portrays the intermediary functioning of banks by collecting funds from customers and converting into loans. Berger and Humphrey (1997) and Fethi and Pasiouras (2010) advocated that intermediation approach is more appropriate for measuring performance of banking system. Considering the literature relevance, the present study follows intermediation approach in selecting variables for developing non-radial SBM DEA model.

The study uses investments, performing loans and advances, non-interest income as desirable outputs, whereas operating expenses and deposits are included as input variables. Operating expenses is one of the prominent factors that effects profitability and also improves efficiency. In intermediation function of banks, deposit is an important input factor. Investments includes sum of long-term investments as well as marketable securities. Adjusting total loan amount with non-performing loans creates new output variable referred as performing loans. Performing loans and advances represents the source of interest income that helps to maintain security and liquidity for normal banking operations by conveying the message of banking stability. If unadjusted loan amount is considered into the model, the efficiency score might be overestimated. Non-interest income- represents additional source of income for banks that helps in improving efficiency. Summary statistics of dataset for entire study period is presented in Table 1.

Table 1. Summary statistics of selected variables

Variables	Mean	Median	Minimum	Maximum
Operating expenses	5333.83	536.89	4619.32	6024.36
Deposits	230605.02	30603.16	183213.68	264097.57
Performing loans	175430.44	9260.53	166770.86	190928.55
Investments	74503.06	6814.34	67207.92	83831.35
Non-interest income	15711.55	27406.69	2912.99	64731.16

4.2   Proposed Framework

Idea behind utilising DEA in conjunction with ANN is that it can complement DEA approach by capturing the non-linear relationship between selected variables and performs optimisation. Continuous operational changes in banking environment calls for evaluation for operational performance to ensure its competitiveness, to predict its operation in delivering objective and to work upon their future development. In this sequel, the proposed hybrid model, two-stage Hybrid model including non-oriented DEA model and BPNN is used to measure the operational efficiency of banks, incorporating two inputs and three outputs. Figure 2 illustrates the framework for hybrid model. Present hybrid model is built on five datasets of 39 banks for year 2015 to 2019. The model tries to predict efficiency scores as estimated using DEA model.

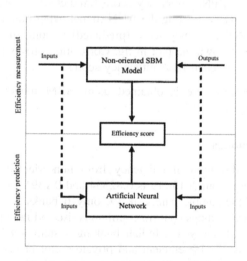

Fig. 2. Framework of hybrid modelling

Steps for Hybrid Modelling

1. *Non-oriented SBM model* - The model aims to minimise input levels as well as maximise output levels to measure the non-radial operational efficiency of banks.

2. *DEA result analysis* - Identifying benchmarks banks and performance improvement requirement for inefficient banks
3. *Data Preparation for ANN* - The sample dataset is divided into train set and test set. There exists no formal rule of thumb regarding optimal dataset for neural network. However, usually the training dataset should be 10 times the sum of independent variables used as inputs in the model (Kwon and Lee 2015). At first, 70% of data from 5-year period is used to train the model and rest 30% is used to test the prediction accuracy of the model.
4. *Data Normalisation* - As variables included in the sampled dataset differs in ranges, data must be normalised. In this study, logarithmic transformation is used to normalise the variables to be considered for ANN training.
5. *Network Structure* - Before initiating to train the sample, the network typology is pre-decided in terms of number of variables in input-layers, hidden layers and output layers. In present model, input and output variables in DEA model is fed as variables in input layer, and efficiency score is fed as only output in the output layer. The optimum number of hidden layers depends on trial and error process to minimise error and increase accuracy of trained sample.
6. *Model Training* - BPNN learns by repeated iterations on training sample and comparing the predicted efficiency scores with actual efficiency scores. Weights for each training sample is so adjusted (back propagated) to minimise mean square error between predicted efficiency scores derived from BPNN and actual efficiency score derived from DEA model.
7. *Model Validation* - BPNN efficiency score (predicted) is compared to DEA efficiency scores (actual) Validating the ANN model using random samples of banks from dataset. BPNN efficiency score (predicted) is compared to DEA efficiency scores (actual) and shown via plot in fig. Correlation proves that predicted scores are good estimate of actual DEA efficiency scores.

The DEA efficiency score is obtained using SBM model in DEA SOLVER LEARNING VERSION 13.

4.3   Empirical Findings

Mean and standard deviation of efficiency from non-oriented SBM model under variable return to scale from 2015-'19 is 0.82334 and 0.13912, respectively (Table 2) On average, out of the sample banks of 39, only 6 banks is observed to be fully efficient. The empirical findings confirm continuous rise and fall in efficiency of banks. Over the period of last five years, Indian banking system is 82.33% efficient, with public sector banks as 77.51% efficient and private sector banks as 87.41% efficient. Therefore, inefficiency present in the banks calls for in-depth analysis into inefficient input or output variables (Table 3).

Table 2. Efficiency score measurement for five years

Particulars	2015	2016	2017	2018	2019	Overall
Average efficiency score	0.8217	0.7930	0.8652	0.7354	0.8955	0.8233
Maximum efficiency score	1	1	1	1	1	1
Minimum efficiency score	0.5362	0.4610	0.4708	0.08802	0.5542	0.5061
Standard deviation	0.1667	0.1737	0.1422	0.3458	0.1416	0.1391

Table 3. DEA parameters with slack analysis

Variables	Mean
Efficient DMUs	6
Average efficiency score	0.8233
Slack value analysis (Input excesses and output shortfall):	
Operating expenses	2,300.5385
Deposits	3,60,109.7535
Performing loans	1,13,282.9135
Investments	83,320.7701
Non-interest income	1,00,305.4249

Such deviation from efficiency can be improved by working on improvable spaces as highlighted by slack values for each input-output variable. Difference between projected value and actual value is termed as slack value, particularly as input excesses and output shortfalls. For each variable, the banking system must target to reduce input values and expand output values as mentioned in Table 4. Conclusion drawn upon slack analysis gives future direction for strategic decision making.

Table 4. Comparison of different network structures

Model decision	Model network	Error	Epochs	Accuracy
Excluded	(5,5,3)	0.019	15,656	96.15%
Excluded	(5,5,5)	0.026	19,188	98.01%
Included	(15,10)	0.007	9,259	98.5%

The functional relationship that represents the developed ANN model can be interpreted as:

$$Efficiency\ score = f\left(I_{Operatingexpenses}, I_{Deposits}, O_{TotalAdvances}, O_{Investment}, O_{NonInterestIncome}\right)$$

Where, I and O stands for inputs and outputs used for non-oriented SBM model. The above production function is used to train the ANN model using input and output variables to predict the scalar efficiency scores. The package named "NeuralNet" in R software is used for developing the proposed ANN model. The most arduous task is to select the best network structure for the performance of NN model by trail-and-test method until minimum error is obtained for model training. Table 5 shows different network structures compared based on number of nodes in hidden layer, error scores and number of epochs (iterations) before finding the best trained model to predict the efficiency scores of banks. Since error is minimum with network structure (15, 10), it is considered to be the best network with 98.5% accuracy after 9,259 iterations.

Table 5. Actual and predicted operational efficiency scores

Banks	Actual	Predicted	MAE	SE	Banks	Actual	Predicted	MAE	SE
B39	0.990000	0.986001	0.000077	0.000016	**B50**	0.611896	0.568766	0.000829	0.001860
B40	0.675409	0.654931	0.000394	0.000419	**B51**	0.711288	0.699880	0.000219	0.000130
B41	0.771183	0.716970	0.001043	0.002939	**B52**	0.663660	0.600759	0.001210	0.003956
B42	0.990000	0.768494	0.004260	0.049065	**B54**	0.592869	0.615368	0.000433	0.000506
B44	0.625537	0.584095	0.000797	0.001717	**B56**	0.703195	0.708060	0.000094	0.000024
B45	0.990000	0.860430	0.002492	0.016788	**B57**	0.597082	0.584757	0.000237	0.000152
B46	0.445490	0.353427	0.001770	0.008476	**B58**	0.665522	0.623967	0.000799	0.001727
B47	0.820521	0.814866	0.000109	0.000032	**B59**	0.990000	1.053788	0.001227	0.004069
B48	0.482282	0.463190	0.000367	0.000365	**B60**	0.990000	0.948562	0.000797	0.001717
B49	0.699680	0.673277	0.000508	0.000697	**B61**	0.836759	0.794670	0.000809	0.001771
								MSE	**0.619768**
								RMSE	**0.787254**

After training of the network, it is tested with 30% of the dataset to prove generalisation capability of the developed model (Table 6). It is observed that Mean Square Error (MSE) and Root Mean Square Error (RMSE) on actual and predicted datasets with value equal to 0.6197 and 0.7872, respectively. The correlation between actual performance (DEA efficiency scores) and predicted performance (ANN predicted scores) is exhibited in Fig. 3, with pattern indicating sufficient correlation. Predictive potential of model is shown in Fig. 4, exhibiting stable mean absolute error (MAE). In conclusion, implementing the proposed ANN and using the given definition of efficiency score (Eq. (1)), we were able to predict operational efficiency with a 98.5% accuracy.

Table 6. Detail of average efficiency scores with bank codes

Bank name (public)	Bank code	Efficiency score	Bank name (private)	Bank code	Efficiency score
Allahabad Bank	B1	0.6300	City Union Bank Ltd.	B21	1.0000
Andhra Bank	B2	0.8620	Tamilnadu Mercantile Bank Ltd.	B22	0.8599
Bank of Baroda	B3	0.9530	The Catholic Syrian Bank Ltd.	B23	0.8876
Bank of India	B4	0.6838	Dhanlaxmi Bank Ltd	B24	1.0000
Bank of Maharashtra	B5	0.5659	The Federal Bank Ltd.	B25	0.7456
Canara Bank	B6	0.9188	The Jammu & Kashmir Bank Ltd.	B26	0.6431
Central Bank of India	B7	0.5299	The Karnataka Bank Ltd.	B27	0.8358
Corporation Bank	B8	0.9286	The Karur Vysya Bank Ltd.	B28	0.7406
Dena Bank	B9	0.5061	The Lakshmi Vilas Bank Ltd.	B29	0.9197
Indian Bank	B10	0.8736	RBL Bank Ltd.	B30	0.9003
Indian Overseas Bank	B11	0.6446	The South Indian Bank Ltd.	B31	0.8436
Oriental Bank of Commerce	B12	0.7711	Axis Bank Ltd.	B32	0.9204
Punjab & Sind Bank	B13	0.7817	DCB Bank Ltd.	B33	0.9352
Punjab National Bank	B14	0.7637	HDFC Bank Ltd.	B34	0.8461
Syndicate Bank	B15	0.7968	ICICI Bank Ltd.	B35	1.0000
UCO Bank	B16	1.0000	Indusind Bank Ltd.	B36	0.7950
Union Bank of India	B17	0.8775	Kotak Mahindra Bank Ltd.	B37	0.7497
United Bank of India	B18	0.7616	YES Bank Ltd.	B38	1.0000
Vijaya Bank	B19	0.6540	IDBI Ltd.	B39	0.9848
State Bank of India (SBI)	B20	1.0000			
Average efficiency score		0.7751	Average efficiency score		0.8741
Standard Deviation		0.1527			0.1047

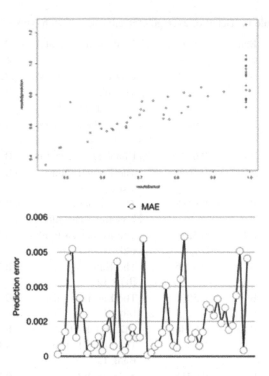

Fig. 3. Correlation and error for actual and predicted efficiency score

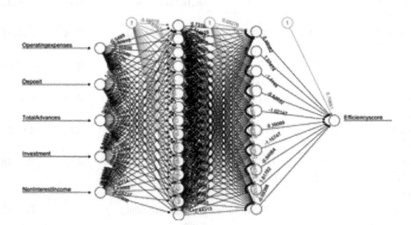

Fig. 4. Neural network structure

5   Concluding Remarks

Proposed hybrid model is basically combination of traditional approach (DEA) and non-traditional approach (Neural Network) to develop prediction model for operational performance of Indian banks. Empirical results show that proposed model possess good predictive power by having low error and high accuracy. Paper focuses on measurement and prediction of operational performance of Indian banks using DEA and ANN approaches. Firstly, the efficiency score is measured for each bank along with slack analysis. Secondly, the estimated efficiency scores are used to predict performance of banks using developed ANN model. In this paper, a Hybrid model is proposed, incorporating DEA and ANN, to estimate and predict operational performance of banks. The study addressed the problem of measuring and predicting the operational efficiency performance by using two-stage hybrid approach.

The result of the study posits important policy implications. Developed model will help banks to predict performance with different data according to their capacity to test performance. Nevertheless, the empirical findings of this study offer constructive insights to regulator and policymakers to investigate the health of banking system based individual banks and augment policy responses. The proposed model can assist in managerial decision-making process proving its practical and innovative. The study provides useful contribution in terms of utilising the proposed model for small dataset problems. Identification of benchmark banks will help to investigate best business decision, effective and innovative strategies and operating procedures. Conclusion drawn upon slack analysis gives future direction for strategic decision making. Managers can use the propose model to infer about future operational performance of banks and buy time to frame relevant strategies.

Also, the study does not include macroeconomic variable that could enhance performance prediction. Inclusion of more contextual variables into BPNN model would enhance the predicting accuracy of the developed model. Present paper postulated hybrid model only on Indian banks, thereby excluding foreign banks. Future scope of the study points to developing model on enriched dataset including foreign banks and thereby larger dataset. ANN model developed is trained on 195 observation (5-year dataset). However, use of larger datasets is recommended to avoid the problem of under training. Additionally, the future directions to present modelling framework can be explored with dynamic setting DEA models to capture more realistic performance prediction. Also, the proposed model can be expanded to other relevant sectors like manufacturing, research & development, supply chain and across different industries. To check the robustness of the developed model by testing its predictive applicability with other data mining models. Future study can utilise the existing model for benchmarking process by exploiting classification function of BPNN model. Also, to investigate the number of hidden layers and number of units in the hidden layer that further reduces prediction error of the proposed model is one of the areas for future investigation.

References

Azad, M.A.K., Munisamy, S., Masum, A.K.M., Saona, P., Wanke, P.: Bank efficiency in Malaysia: a use of malmquist meta-frontier analysis. Eurasian Bus. Rev. **7**(2), 287–311 (2016). https://doi.org/10.1007/s40821-016-0054-4

Benston, G.J.: Branch banking and economies of scale. J. Financ. **20**(2), 312–331 (1965)

Berger, A.N., Humphrey, D.B.: Efficiency of financial institutions: International survey and directions for future research. Eur. J. Oper. Res. **98**(2), 175–212 (1997)

Bhattacharyya, A., Lovell, C.K., Sahay, P.: The impact of liberalization on the productive efficiency of Indian commercial banks. Eur. J. Oper. Res. **98**(2), 332–345 (1997)

Barros, C.P., Wanke, P.: Insurance companies in Mozambique: a two-stage DEA and neural networks on efficiency and capacity slacks. Appl. Econ. **46**(29), 3591–3600 (2014)

Charnes, A., Cooper, W.W., Rhodes, E.: Measuring the efficiency of decision-making units. Eur. J. Oper. Res. **2**(6), 429–444 (1978)

Cooper, W.W., Seiford, L.M., Tone, K.: Data Envelopment Analysis: A Comprehensive Text with Models, Applications, References and DEA-Solver Software. Springer, New York (2007). https://doi.org/10.1007/978-0-387-45283-8

Cooper, W.W., Huang, Z., Li, S., Zhu, J.: A response to the critiques of DEA by Dmitruk and Koshevoy, and Bol. J. Prod. Anal. **29**(1), 15–21 (2008)

Davidovic, M., Uzelac, O., Zelenovic, V.: Efficiency dynamics of the Croatian banking industry: DEA investigation. Econ. Res.-Ekonomska istraživanja **32**(1), 33–49 (2019)

Doyle, J., Green, R.: Efficiency and cross-efficiency in DEA: derivations, meanings and uses. J. Oper. Res. Soc. **45**(5), 567–578 (1994)

Emrouznejad, A., Shale, E.: A combined neural network and DEA for measuring efficiency of large scale datasets. Comput. Ind. Eng. **56**(1), 249–254 (2009)

Fausett, L.: Fundamentals of Neural Networks: Architectures, Algorithms, and Applications. Prentice Hall, Englewood Cliffs (1994)

Fethi, M.D., Pasiouras, F.: Assessing bank efficiency and performance with operational research and artificial intelligence techniques: a survey. Eur. J. Oper. Res. **204**(2), 189–198 (2010)

Kwon, H.B., Lee, J.: Two-stage production modeling of large US banks: a DEA-neural network approach. Expert Syst. Appl. **42**(19), 6758–6766 (2015)

Kwon, H.B., Lee, J., Roh, J.J.: Best performance modeling using complementary DEA-ANN approach. Benchmarking Int. J. **23**(3), 704–721 (2016)

Kwon, H.B.: Exploring the predictive potential of artificial neural networks in conjunction with DEA in railroad performance modeling. Int. J. Prod. Econ. **183**, 159–170 (2017)

Han, Y.M., Geng, Z.Q., Zhu, Q.X.: Energy optimization and prediction of complex petrochemical industries using an improved artificial neural network approach integrating data envelopment analysis. Energy Convers. Manag. **124**, 73–83 (2016)

Henriques, I.C., Sobreiro, V.A., Kimura, H., Mariano, E.B.: Efficiency in the Brazilian banking system using data envelopment analysis. Future Bus. J. **4**(2), 157–178 (2018)

Lam, M.: Neural network techniques for financial performance prediction: integrating fundamental and technical analysis. Decis. Support Syst. **37**, 567–581 (2004)

Le, H.H., Viviani, J.L.: Predicting bank failure: an improvement by implementing a machine-learning approach to classical financial ratios. Res. Int. Bus. Financ. **44**, 16–25 (2018)

Mostafa, M.M.: Modeling the efficiency of top Arab banks: a DEA–neural network approach. Expert Syst. Appl. **36**(1), 309–320 (2009)

Petropoulos, A., Siakoulis, V., Stavroulakis, E., Vlachogiannakis, N.E.: Predicting bank insolvencies using machine learning techniques. Int. J. Forecast. **36**(3), 1092–1113 (2020)

Pendharkar, P.C., Rodger, J.A.: Technical efficiency-based selection of learning cases to improve forecasting accuracy of neural networks under monotonicity assumption. Decis. Support Syst. **36**(1), 117–136 (2003)

Reserve Bank of India, Report on Trend and Progress of Banking in India 2017–2018. https://www.rbi.org.in. Accessed 18 July 2020

Samoilenko, S., Osei-Bryson, K.-M.: Determining sources of relative inefficiency in heterogeneous samples: methodology using cluster analysis, DEA and neural networks. Eur. J. Oper. Res. **206**(2), 479–487 (2010)

Sathye, S., Sathye, M.: Do ATMs increase technical efficiency of banks in a developing country? Evidence from Indian banks. Aust. Account. Rev. **27**(1), 101–111 (2017)

Sealey Jr., C.W., Lindley, J.T.: Inputs, outputs, and a theory of production and cost at depository financial institutions. J. Financ. **32**(4), 1251–1266 (1977)

Sexton, T.R.: Data envelopment analysis: critique and extension. New Dir. Program Eval. **32**, 73–105 (1986)

Sreekumar, S., Mahapatra, S.S.: Performance modeling of Indian business schools: a DEA-neural network approach. Benchmarking Int. J. **18**(2), 221–239 (2011)

Sherman, H.D., Gold, F.: Bank branch operating efficiency: evaluation with data envelopment analysis. J. Bank. Financ. **9**(2), 297–315 (1985)

Shokrollahpour, E., Hosseinzadeh Lotfi, F., Zandieh, M.: An integrated data envelopment analysis–artificial neural network approach for benchmarking of bank branches. J. Ind. Eng. Int. **12**(2), 137–143 (2016). https://doi.org/10.1007/s40092-015-0125-7

Tavana, M., Abtahi, A.R., Di Caprio, D., Poortarigh, M.: An artificial neural network and bayesian network model for liquidity risk assessment in banking. Neurocomputing **275**, 2525–2554 (2018)

Tone, K.: A slacks-based measure of efficiency in data envelopment analysis. Eur. J. Oper. Res. **130**(3), 498–509 (2001)

Tosun, Ö.: Using data envelopment analysis–neural network model to evaluate hospital efficiency. Int. J. Prod. Qual. Manag. **9**(2), 245–257 (2012)

Tsolas, I.E., Charles, V., Gherman, T.: Supporting better practice benchmarking: a DEA-ANN approach to bank branch performance assessment. Expert Syst. Appl. **160**, 113599 (2020)

Wu, D.D., Yang, Z., Liang, L.: Using DEA-neural network approach to evaluate branch efficiency of a large Canadian bank. Expert Syst. Appl. **31**(1), 108–115 (2006)

Wu, D.: Supplier selection: a hybrid model using DEA, decision tree and neural network. Expert Syst. Appl. **36**(5), 9105–9112 (2009)

Yeh, Q.J.: The application of data envelopment analysis in conjunction with financial ratios for bank performance evaluation. J. Oper. Res. Soc. **47**(8), 980–988 (1996)

Healthcare Information Technology

Physicians' and Nurses' Perceived Threats Toward Health Information Technology: A Military Hospital Case Study

Mansor Alohali[✉], Fergal Carton, and Yvonne O'Connor

Business Information Systems, Cork University Business School,
University College Cork, Cork, Ireland
m.alohali@mu.edu.sa, {f.carton,y.oconnor}@ucc.ie

Abstract. The potential of Health Information Technology (HIT) to increase the quality of healthcare delivery is well documented but improvements can be hindered if physicians and nurses resist HIT. However, the technology is still facing resistance. The literature suggests that user resistance to HIT is predicated on their perception of its impact. However, we do not fully understand how users' perception is formed. In response, this study investigates the antecedents of perceived threats by examining the organisational factors, the personal traits of the user, HIT-related factors, and the factors related to the interaction between physicians and nurses and the organisation that lead to perceived threats. This study uses a case study of a military hospital to understand the antecedents of perceived threats and user resistance. The findings of the study indicate that dissatisfaction and risks are the main components of perceived threats of HIT for physicians and nurses. Furthermore, the study suggests that the antecedents of perceived threats are: system incompatibility, management support, related knowledge, and lack of trust. This research will contribute to identifying the core reasons for resistance and will lead to a better understanding of the phenomenon, hence, can help organisations solve the root causes of the problem.

Keywords: User resistance · Health Information Technology · Perceived threats

1 Introduction

The potential of Health Information Technology (HIT), such as Electronic Health Records (EHR), to increase the quality of healthcare delivery is well documented [1]. However, even with the recognised benefits of HIT, the technology is still facing user resistance [2] There are a number of examples of failed HIT implementation because of user resistance (c.f. [3, 4]). Furthermore, various studies have shown that user resistance is a contributor to time and budget overruns [5]. Therefore, user resistance must be taken into consideration by organisations managers and IT project implementers [10]. Awareness about the factors that influence user resistance and recognising the behaviours of resistance will enable managers to better manage new IT projects [6]. It is envisioned that such understanding will improve the likelihood of successful HIT

S. K. Sharma et al. (Eds.): TDIT 2020, IFIP AICT 617, pp. 601–613, 2020.
https://doi.org/10.1007/978-3-030-64849-7_53

implementation and continues use of the technology, thereby attaining the promised improvements in healthcare that HIT can provide.

User resistance literature indicates that resistance to HIT is predicated on users' negative perception of the technology [4, 6–8]. However, very few studies have examined and explained how user perception is formed (e.g. [9]). Additionally, a number of researchers have highlighted the need for more studies the help our understanding of the issues that lead to negative user perception and user resistance [9–11]. To address this gap in literature, this study aims to investigate the conditions that lead physicians and nurses to perceive HIT as a threat, thus leading to user resistance. This research will take place in a military hospital, which could present unique opportunities to our understanding of user resistance due to several important factors, for example: (1) Studies have shown that physicians and nurses working in military hospitals have high professional autonomy and control over work practice [5]. The introduction of HIT is likely to reduce power and autonomy; hence, physicians and nurses might perceive HIT as a threat and opt to resist the system [12]. (2) The unique relationship between management who tend to be military personnel and between physicians and nurses who are mostly civilians [5], suggesting that managing change brought by HIT can be more challenging due to the different background between management and most of the users [13]. These factors will present an interesting dynamic and will provide new insights into our understanding of user resistance.

This study examines user resistance in the healthcare sector by examining the antecedents of perceived threats and it aims to answer the following research question: What are the organisational, personal, HIT, and the factors related to the interactions among physicians, nurses, and their organisations that lead physicians and nurses to perceive HIT as a threat? Thus, the study may help hospital managers to understand user resistance better and create the right policies and actions to mitigate resistance and increase the likelihood of HIT adoption. Healthcare cost is rising [14], and in many hospitals, IT investments represent a considerable percent of hospital's budget [14]. In light of this, understanding user resistance and the antecedents of user perception is crucial since resistance is a major cause of HIT implementation failure [2].

2   Literature Review

User resistance has been the subject of much research, and in recent years IS researchers have developed various theoretical models that offer new insights and improve our understanding of user resistance. A number of these theoretical models consider the role of user perception to a new system implementation as the leading factor in user resistance, such as the role of perceived threat [7, 8, 15, 16], perceived compatibility [7, 17], perceived ease of use [7, 9, 17], and perceived dissatisfaction [4]. These theoretical models explain that users who believe that the system will negatively impact them, their work, or their status within the organisation will resist the new system [4, 15, 17]. However, few of the user resistance model explained how user perception is developed and how it affects user resistance. This study attempts to identify some of the factors that can influence perceived threats. The study will go further than existing user resistance research as it will explore the antecedents of user perception and will explain what influence user perception.

The perceived threats can be characterised as users' fear of HIT implementation because of expected negative consequences, such as fear of losing power, revenue, or control [7, 8, 11, 18]. Some researchers have shown that perceived threat can cause emotional pain or perception of an unfavourable situation; thus, it can be deemed by the user as a reason for resisting IT implementation (e.g. [7, 8, 11, 15]). Physicians and nurses are sensitive to the possible risk factors that HIT might cause, such as the fear that HIT will have negative effect on their job performance, or concern that system defects can endanger patients [6, 8]. This study aims to examine how and why physicians and nurses may perceive HIT as a threat.

A review of user resistance literature indicates that four general factors can influence perceived threats and user resistance to technology, which are personal factors, organisational factors, system factors, and the interaction between the people, the system, and the organisation. First, the personal factors refer to internal and external factors of people, such as their personality traits, cognitive style, and the natural human tendency to resist change [3, 16]. Personal traits suggest that an individual's perception of the technology can be influenced by specific characteristics such as gender, age, background, lack of confidence, and lack of IT skills [9, 18]. Studies have found that the more familiar users are with HIT, the more likely that they will feel confident using the system, whereas, users who lacked IT skills are more likely to feel anxious about the new system and be unhappy in the workplace [11]. Consequently, it likely that these users will resist the system [4]. Second, the organisational factors refer to factors related to the culture, structure, or management of the organisation [5, 10]. Introduction of large IT projects such as HIT may lead to several organisational changes in term of the general culture of the organisation, the job structure, and the work style of employee [3, 17]. These changes require organisations to have the capacity to accept such changes [19]. The case reported by Lapointe and Rivard (2005) [8] shows that physicians and nurses tend to be sensitive about changes in the work environment.

Third, HIT-related factors refer to factors related to the system itself [20]. This can include the design of the interface, system reliability [20], the complexity of the system [18], the compatibility of the system with the existing work requirements [3, 18]. Finally, the interaction factors refer to the interaction between characteristics related to the people, the organisation, and HIT [16]. It is expected that HIT implementation could change the dynamic of the organisation and lead to changes in the relationships between employees [16, 17] Typical interaction between people could affect how people perceive things; as an example, the IS literature has suggested that social influences such as the opinion of colleague and other IT users are a key predictor of user behaviour [21].

To summarise this section, user resistance literature suggests that perceived threats is influenced by personal factors, organisational factors, HIT-related factors, and factors related to the interactions among physicians, nurses, and their organisations. Section 5 identifies these factors.

3 Methods

A single exploratory case study approach was employed to meet the objective of this study - identifying and understanding the major factors that influence physician's and nurse's perceived threats of HIT. The case consists of a military hospital that has recently implemented and used HIT. The HIT is an Electronic Health Records (EHR) system that grants physicians and nurses access to patients' records. The system allows physicians and nurses to enter and retrieve data such as patient's treatment plans and medication. In addition, it allows physicians to request and obtain test results such as lab exams and X-rays. The research context and the case study will be presented in detail in Sect. 3.3.

A qualitative research method was selected because it is well-suited to answer the research questions as it facilitates for the exploration of new ideas, capture of new phenomena, and rich contextualised details of complex concepts such as physicians' and nurses' resistance [22, 23]. Furthermore, user resistance behaviour can range from cover to overt [8]. It is important for researchers and organisational managers to understand user resistance behaviour to effectively respond to user resistance. A nuanced qualitative approach is apt as it allows users to express their feelings without appearing obstructive to the organisation that was selected [23]. In addition, it will allow the researchers to better identify and understand user resistance behaviour. The study will take a post-implementation perspective (6–12 months after initial adoption). User resistance during pre-implementation and implementation phases is very high and well documented because of the widespread disruption to existing processes [3]. Furthermore, a dearth of research focuses on the post-implementation phase [24], and addressing this gap in existing research will allow us to examine the longer term and non-implementation related factors that could lead to user resistance and potential system abandonment [25]. Moreover, after their direct interaction and actual experience with the system, users will reevaluate their initial perception of the system [26], thus providing us with an opportunity to study the actual causes of user resistance.

Semi-structured interviews were conducted (May and June of 2018) with physicians and nurses in a military hospital. The interview captured socio-demographic information and was guided by the factors presented in the literature review. Open-ended questions were asked. These questions were developed from the factors disused previously in the literature review section. The questions provided valuable insight into the participants' perception of HIT. The interviews were useful in allowing people to be free to describe their perceptions [27]. Therefore, effective in allowing the researcher to comprehend the perception of physicians and nurses' and the conditions that lead them to view HIT negatively. A snowball sampling strategy was used to identify subsequent respondents, where each initial respondent was asked to suggest other physicians and nurses working in the hospital. The respondents were physicians and nurses who are familiar with the hospital HIT and represented a subset of the hospital population. The data collection process ended at the point of redundancy. In total, 13 physicians and 15 nurses across four different departments were interviewed. The study received ethical approval from University College Cork Ethics Committee.

For a comprehensive data analysis, the data were analysed based on the recommendations of Strauss and Corbin (1997) [28] - three coding procedures are used in the process of analysing qualitative data, which are open coding, axial coding, and selective coding. This approach is considered appropriate for this research because it allows for flexibility and rigour [29]. Furthermore, it provides a structured approach for analysing the phenomenon of interest [30]. Each interview was transcribed and coded on a line by line basis using NVivo 9.0 to help in the analyses of the data and to identify themes for analysis. The codes were grouped together to form categories or themes through comparative analysis across interviews. Axial coding was then used to establish relationships between categories and themes. Finally, the selective coding was used to build a story through identification of core categories and the relationship between categories and explaining the categories that need further development and refining. Moreover, the researchers utilised a chain of evidence technique to group the quotations from each physician and nurses that participated in the study. By doing this, the researchers were able to present and support their findings with data from the interviews.

3.1   Case Background

The case study was conducted at a military hospital (a pseudonym), a large 500+ bed that provides primary to tertiary care to military personnel and their families. The majority of the physicians and nurses are civilians, whereby the majority of high-level managers are military personnel.

In 2008, hospital management decided to modernise the hospital by implementing HIT and established a new IT department to develop its new HIT in-house. The first module was launched in 2010 and was very simple, as the system only issued patient's ID and stored a scanned version of doctors' notes under the patients' name. Physicians and nurses sent their notes to a scanning department, in which the notes were scanned and uploaded to the system that allowed physicians and nurses to retrieve the scanned notes. However, the system faced technical problems and was slow. Physicians and nurses were dissatisfied with the system and complained, as they did not find the system useful and it did not end their reliance on paper.

The hospital and the IT department continued to update the system, adding new features to the system. In 2018, the hospital implemented the latest update to the system which allowed physicians and nurses to write clinical notes and diagnoses in the system. Currently, the system is an automated workflow system that allowed physicians to enter, track, and retrieve notes and orders in the system: this included laboratory, X-rays, and pharmaceutical orders. The system represented a significant change from the first version of the system that was introduced in 2010. At one point, the system allowed physicians and nurses to remotely access the system which allowed them to access patient's information from home. However, this feature was later removed because of security breaches. Later, the hospital only allowed consultants to have remote access to the system.

4 Results

The results show that signs of resistance exist towards HIT among physicians and nurses in the military hospital. Various forms of resistance behaviour emerged during interviews, such as sarcasm and scepticism of the usefulness of the system, compatibility with working style, and safety of the system. This scepticism can be considered as a negative behaviour and an overt form of resistance as some users were uncooperative and forcefully complained about the system [8]. Furthermore, this scepticism led some physicians and nurses to complain about HIT during department meetings. Then again, it was not easy to identify perceived threats because users often communicated indirectly during the interviews, such as by using humour or referencing others to describe the dissatisfaction with the system. However, the results of the study indicates that perceived dissatisfaction and perceived risk are the main perceived threats to HIT, and four core categories emerged, which are considered to be antecedents to perceived dissatisfaction and perceived risk: 1) Related knowledge; 2) Management support; 3) System incompatibility; 4) Trust; The findings are subsequently presented in more detail and with empirical chains of evidence.

4.1 Personal Factors: Related Knowledge

The findings show that related knowledge of physicians and nurses influence perceived dissatisfaction, Related knowledge, in this study, refers to previous user experience with HIT and understanding of HIT concepts. Physicians and nurses who are more familiar with HIT systems such as (EHR) felt more confident and comfortable using the system. One nurse said:

"In my previous work, we had a system similar to the one we have here [in this hospital], so, for me, it was easy to learn how to use the system. I am happy that we have this system in the hospital." (Nurse 6)

Some physicians and nurses who have not used HIT before or who have insufficient computer knowledge and skill were dissatisfied with the system.

"Whatever you do, some people will never change. Maybe, they are not quite familiar with the computer; they haven't used it enough." (Physician 2)

In this instance, the lack of related knowledge of HIT led physicians and nurses to perceive it negatively.

4.2 Organisational Factors: Management Support

Management support, in this study, refers to the extent at which managers are willing to provide the necessary resources and authority or power that are important for a successful HIT implementation such as motivation and training. The results show that there is a link between lack of management support and physicians and nurses' perceived dissatisfaction. In a large IT project such as HIT, managers play a vital role in the successful development and implementation of HIT. However, in this case study, physicians and nurses felt that managers were not supportive and did not prepare them for HIT.

"We are extremely busy. I needed some time to learn how to use it and I had to stay for extra hours to teach myself. They should have given us {physicians} time to adjust and not put us under pressure to start using it almost immediately." (Physician 7)

The lack of support shown by the management caused physicians and nurses to be dissatisfied with the system, as they felt they did not have sufficient training, did not have enough time to learn and adjust to the system, and there was a lack of open and honest communication; as one nurse explained:

"It will also be good if they tell us about any new changes and explain to us why they made those changes and how the changes will help us." (Nurse 2)

This Lack of support shown by managers in the organisation lead physicians and nurses to have a feeling of irritation and frustration with HIT.

4.3 HIT Related Factors: System Incompatibility

System Incompatibility, in this study, refers to users belief that HIT does not fit with their work style, needs, and work environment. Some physicians and nurses felt that the HIT was not compatible with their work style, needs, or work environment. The findings revealed that system incompatibility is the leading HIT-related factor which influences perceive dissatisfaction. Hospitals have a large number of departments, and every department requires a specific feature in the system. For example, a physician explained:

"The neurology department might need a whole body where he can make points indicating the weakness, etc. So, every department has its requirements. For example, the Otorhinolaryn-gology department might need an image of the nose, the throat, etc. These are requirements that you need in the clinic. The Dermatology {Department} needs, for instance, specific ima-ges." (Physician 4)

The system was the same for all the departments. Hence, physicians and nurses working in departments with special requirements found the system to be limited and does not meet their needs. One nurse stressed this problem by saying:

"We have other papers that we fill. For every patient, there are 21 pages just for anaesthesia that we have to fill manually because it is not in the system." (Nurse 2)

In addition, some physicians and nurses felt that HIT affected their relationship with patients because it reduced the eye-to-eye contact with the patients.

"I've noticed that it {the system} affects communication with the patient; my eyes are focused on the device. The patient is talking and, although physically with him, he feels that I am not with him because I'm looking at the device – as I can't type without looking. So, in order to save time, I sacrifice the patient's well-being." (Physician 8)

"When you type like that {looking at the computer} and you just listen to what they say, you're not interacting eye-to-eye." (Nurse 11)

These issues caused physicians and nurses to be dissatisfied with the system as they have to work around the limitation of the system to perform their job correctly. Physicians and nurses thought the system was incompatible with their work as it did not have the charts, the forms, or the pictures they need to perform their job, and it had a negative impact on their relationship with their patients; as a result, they were dissatisfied with the system.

4.4   Interaction Factors: Lack of Trust

In this study, trust is referred to as physicians' and nurses' confidence in HIT and the organisation decisions. In this case, trust is strongly linked with perceived risk. The data analysis indicates that physicians and nurses did not have the complete trust of the organisation and management ability to develop and implement a quality HIT, which influenced their perception of HIT. The lack of trust could be because of the earlier version of the implemented HIT, which some physicians and nurses considered to be a failure and thus lead to a lack of trust. A physician express his feeling by declaring:

> *"I cannot blindly trust the system. For example, if patients result show that he is improving and the previous visits show the same, but the system gave the visits before that when they were sick. So, of course, these things influence my decision." (Physician 10)*

As outlined in the aforementioned quotes, the failure of the system to show recent visits lead users to distrust the system, feel uncertain of new changes and resist new system updates because they felt that the organisation is unable to implement complex systems, and system failure could lead them to make a wrong decision.

4.5   Perceived Threats: Perceived Dissatisfaction

Perceived dissatisfaction, in the content of this study, refers to the frustration and irritation caused by HIT. Physicians and nurses were not happy with the system and felt that it was a source of irritation and displeasure. Data analysis reveals that physicians and nurses perceived dissatisfaction of HIT directly influences user resistance. Many of the physicians and nurses felt that HIT was causing them frustration and irritation and displeasure; thus, they were showing signs of resistance. This is exemplified in the following comments:

> *"The problem it has is that it did not end our reliance on paper documents and files. Sometimes we have to go back to paper note to review a patient file. We have to write a paper note on a daily bias." (Physician 4)*

Physicians and nurses must search both paper notes and notes on HIT to acquire complete information about their patients. This duality is compounded by the workload necessary to transcribe manual notes into the HIT.

> *"Because everyone knows the load of work among nurses, honestly. The nurse in inpatient… imagine she's taking care of 6 patients and she has to leave patients to write all these 100 papers in the system." (Nurse 2)*

After the last version of the system was introduced, management issued a mandate requiring all employees to use the system. The order was not received positively among physicians and nurses and generated strong reactions. It was common for physicians and nurses, during department meetings and training sessions, to complain about the system and point in an objective manner any minor flaws in the system. Overall, most physicians and nurses reluctantly used the system after the mandate. However, the system used is not optimal, and considerable resentment and dissatisfaction persisted.

4.6 Perceived Threats: Perceived Risk

Perceived risk, in the context of this study, refers to physicians' and nurses' fear of the risk factor they associated with HIT, such as a fear that will pose risks to patients, loss of privacy, and reduce their work efficiency. Perceived risk can be considered as an element of perceived threats and it is directly linked with user resistance. Physicians and nurses are sensitive to the risk factors that HIT might cause because of the sensitive work environment that requires them to deal with people's lives. Such a risk could be the fear or belief that HIT will harm their job performance. Also, physicians and nurses fear unauthorised use of their account in HIT. One physician said,

> "They had to dismiss a physician and a pharmacist because of this issue; the doctor said that someone used his account and that it wasn't him who made the order, whereas the pharmacist claimed that he has received the order from that person and that he carried up." (Physician 9)

In the example above, both the physician and the pharmacist lost their job because of unauthorised use of HIT. According to one physician, sometimes physicians and nurses share their passwords with each other to speed up the work process, such as ordering medical exams, and this could lead to unauthorised use of HIT. Moreover, physicians and nurses felt the system does not protect the privacy of the patient.

> "Honestly... look, any patients file can be reached, and their privacy violated." (Physician 12)

These factors lead physicians and nurses to perceive the system as a threat and a risk, consequently, leading to resistance.

5 Discussion and Conclusions

The purpose of this study was to investigate the circumstances that lead physicians and nurses to perceive HIT as a threat. To this end, a case study of a military hospital that uses HIT is presented. This study provides insights into how physicians and nurses may perceive a new HIT implementation negatively. Second, the study investigates the role of the organisation, personal user traits, and HIT on physicians and nurses' perception of HIT. While previous research showed the effect of user perception on user resistance to HIT (e.g. [7, 9, 12]) this study went further to investigate the antecedents of perceived threats. The main findings of the study explain that perceived dissatisfaction and perceived risks of HIT are the main perceived threats for physicians and nurses. Furthermore, four factors that influence perceived dissatisfaction and perceived risks are identified: related knowledge, management support, system incompatibility, and lack of trust. The study explained how these factors could influence physicians and nurses perception of HIT.

The results of this research indicate that trust influences perceived risk, which influences user resistance. Some physicians and nurses expressed their concerns regarding inaccurate results in HIT, as well as privacy issues with HIT. This lack of trust expressed by physicians and nurses could be because of an internal organisation which could be due to the different background between hospital managers who have mostly military background and between employees who are mostly civilians. One way to increase physicians and nurses' trust in HIT is by providing management support. In large IT projects such as HIT, managers are responsible for supporting and ensuring a successful implementation by providing the required training to use the new system, and by allowing HIT users sufficient time to familiarise themselves with the functionality of the new system.

Many physicians and nurses felt that HIT was incompatible with their work. Most of the work that is done in hospitals follow routinised paths [31]. The introduction of HIT to physicians and nurses' work will influenced their practices and disrupted their work routines. The military hospital decided to develop and implement HIT in-house, which had some advantages and disadvantages. One of the advantages was that the system was very simple, and most physicians and nurses were happy that the system was easy to use. Nevertheless, due to lack of experience in HIT development, many felt that HIT was incompatible with their work requirements and was, therefore, dissatisfied with HIT, as it did not end their reliance on papers to complete the work requirements. Managers and HIT developer should seek to develop HIT that's customisable and compatible with physicians' and nurse's needs. Furthermore, they should consider how HIT can affect the relationship between physicians, nurses, and their patients. HIT reduces eye-to-eye contact between physicians, nurses, and their patients because physicians and nurses turn to face the computer to write their notes or order exams and medications, rather than facing the patient.

The results of this study differ from other researchers that suggested that HIT implementation could lead physicians and nurses to perceive loss of autonomy [32], loss of power [3, 8], and loss of control [8]. This could be due to the unique characteristics of a military hospital that inherited some military culture. In general, military organisations are bureaucratic, hierarchical, and meritocratic [33]. Thus, it is less likely that physicians and nurses will have significant autonomy, power, and control even before system implementation. Most of the physicians and nurses interviewed in this case were civilians but have been working in the hospital for many years, hence, it is possible that they have conformed to the bureaucratic and hierarchical culture of a military organisation. Therefore, the fear of loss of autonomy, loss of power, and loss of control was not a factor of user resistance in this case study.

5.1   Implications

This study extends the scope of existing user resistance literature (e.g., [6–9, 15]) by investigating the antecedents of perceived threats. Little research has been done to examine the antecedents of user perception. This research provides the foundation and highlights the need to further examine the core reasons of user perceptions that lead to user resistance, especially in healthcare settings. For practitioners, this study provides a better understanding of user resistance and user perception in the healthcare sectors.

This understanding will help hospital managers responsible for developing and implementing HIT to design resistance mitigation plans. Such plans should consider perceived dissatisfaction and perceived risks as a cause of user resistance; hence, it could be a cause of failure to HIT implementation. First, managers should develop HIT that is compatible with physicians' and nurses' needs while considering that each department in the hospital could have different needs. Second, managers should provide the required support to physicians and nurses to help them adapt HIT, such as providing training and quickly resolving any HIT problem. Third, trust is a crucial factor in determining the usage of HIT. Therefore, managers should seek to develop trust between physicians and nurses and HIT. Such a belief will reduce the adverse effects of perceived risk, dissatisfaction, and user resistance behaviours. It is envisioned that explicit attention paid to the factors presented in this study will reduce HIT resistance among physicians and nurses.

References

1. Carvalho, J.V., Rocha, Á., van de Wetering, R., Abreu, A.: A maturity model for hospital information systems. J. Bus. Res. **94**, 388–399 (2019). https://doi.org/10.1016/j.jbusres. 2017.12.012
2. Kruse, C.S., Kristof, C., Jones, B., Mitchell, E., Martinez, A.: Barriers to electronic health record adoption: a systematic literature review. J. Med. Syst. **40**(12), 1–7 (2016). https://doi. org/10.1007/s10916-016-0628-9
3. Bhattacherjee, A., Davis, C., Hikmet, N.: Physician reactions to healthcare IT: an activity-theoretic analysis. Paper presented at the 2013 46th Hawaii International Conference on System Sciences, January 2013
4. Ngafeeson, M.N., Midha, V.: An exploratory study of user resistance in healthcare IT. Int. J. Electron. Financ. **8**(1), 74 (2014)
5. Alshahrani, F., Banjar, H., Mahran, S.: Magnet work environment at military hospitals as perceived by registered nurses in KSA. J. Nurs. Health Sci. **7**, 1–07 (2018). https://doi.org/ 10.9790/1959-0703060107
6. Smith, T., Grant, G., Ramirez, A.: Investigating the influence of psychological ownership and resistance on usage intention among physicians. In: 2014 47th Hawaii International Conference on System Sciences, 6–9 January 2014, pp. 2808–2817 (2014)
7. Bhattacherjee, A., Hikmet, N.: Physicians' resistance toward healthcare information technology: a theoretical model and empirical test. Eur. J. Inf. Syst. (2007). https://doi. org/10.1057/palgrave.ejis.3000717
8. Lapointe, R.: A multilevel model of resistance to information technology implementation. MIS Q. **29**(3), 461 (2005). https://doi.org/10.2307/25148692
9. Laumer, S., Maier, C., Eckhardt, A., Weitzel, T.: User personality and resistance to mandatory information systems in organizations: a theoretical model and empirical test of dispositional resistance to change. J. Inf. Technol. **31**(1), 67–82 (2016). https://doi.org/10. 1057/jit.2015.17
10. Ali, M., Zhou, L., Miller, L., Ieromonachou, P.: User resistance in IT: a literature review. Int. J. Inf. Manag. **36**(1), 35–43 (2016). https://doi.org/10.1016/j.ijinfomgt.2015.09.007
11. Hsieh, P.-J., Lin, W.-S.: Explaining resistance to system usage in the PharmaCloud: a view of the dual-factor model. Inf. Manag. **55**(1), 51–63 (2018). https://doi.org/10.1016/j.im. 2017.03.008

12. Walter, Z., Lopez, M.S.: Physician acceptance of information technologies: role of perceived threat to professional autonomy. Decis. Support Syst. **46**(1), 206–215 (2008). https://doi.org/10.1016/j.dss.2008.06.004

13. Hall, L.K.: The importance of understanding military culture. Soc. Work Health Care **50**(1), 4–18 (2011). https://doi.org/10.1080/00981389.2010.513914

14. Einav, L., Finkelstein, A., Mahoney, N.: Provider incentives and healthcare costs: evidence from long-term care hospitals. Econometrica **86**(6), 2161–2219 (2018). https://doi.org/10.3982/ECTA15022

15. Lin, C., Lin, I.C., Roan, J.: Barriers to physicians' adoption of healthcare information technology: an empirical study on multiple hospitals. J. Med. Syst. **36**, 1965–1977 (2012). https://doi.org/10.1007/s10916-011-9656-7

16. Markus, M.L.: Power, politics, and MIS implementation. Commun. ACM **26**(6), 430–444 (1983). https://doi.org/10.1145/358141.358148

17. Laumer, S., Maier, C., Eckhardt, A., Weitzel, T.: Work routines as an object of resistance during information systems implementations: theoretical foundation and empirical evidence. Eur. J. Inf. Syst. **25**(4), 317–343 (2017)

18. Klaus, T., Blanton, J.E.: User resistance determinants and the psychological contract in enterprise system implementations. Eur. J. Inf. Syst. **19**, 625–636 (2010). https://doi.org/10.1057/ejis.2010.39

19. Ludwick, D.A., Doucette, J.: Adopting electronic medical records in primary care: lessons learned from health information systems implementation experience in seven countries. Int. J. Med. Inform. **78**(1), 22–31 (2009). https://doi.org/10.1016/j.ijmedinf.2008.06.005

20. Jiang, J.J., Muhanna, W.A., Klein, G.: User resistance and strategies for promoting acceptance across system types. Inf. Manag. **37**(1), 25–36 (2000)

21. Kim, K.: Investigating user resistance to information systems implementation: a status quo bias perspective. MIS Q. **33**(3), 567 (2009). https://doi.org/10.2307/20650309

22. Bhattacherjee, A.: Social Science Research Principles, Methods, and Practices (2012)

23. Cassell, C., Symon, G.: Essential guide to qualitative methods in organizational research. Athenaeum Studi Periodici Di Letteratura E Storia Dell Antichita **1**, 388 (2004)

24. Alohali, M., Connor, Y., Carton, F.: Investigating the antecedents of perceived threats and user resistance to health information technology: towards a comprehensive user resistance model. In: European Conference on Information Systems (2018)

25. Fryling, M.: Investigating the effect of customization on rework in a higher education enterprise resource planning (ERP) post-implementation environment: a system dynamics approach. J. Inf. Technol. Case Appl. Res. **17**(1), 8–40 (2015). https://doi.org/10.1080/15228053.2015.1014750

26. Saeed, K.A., Abdinnour, S., Hall, M.L., Hall, C.A.: Examining the impact of pre-implementation expectations on post-implementation use of enterprise systems: a longitudinal study. Decis. Sci. **41**, 659–688 (2010)

27. King, N.: Using interviews in qualitative research. In: Essential Guide to Qualitative Methods in Organizational Research, pp. 11–22. SAGE Publications Ltd. (2004)

28. Strauss, A., Corbin, J.M.: Grounded Theory in Practice. Sage, Thousand Oaks (1997)

29. Sarker, N., Tsudzuki, M., Nishibori, M., Yasue, H., Yamamoto, Y.: Cell-mediated and humoral immunity and phagocytic ability in chicken Lines divergently selected for serum immunoglobulin M and G levels. Poult. Sci. **79**(12), 1705–1709 (2000). https://doi.org/10.1093/ps/79.12.1705

30. Day, J.M., Junglas, I., Silva, L.: Information flow impediments in disaster relief supply chains. J. Assoc. Inf. Syst. **10**(8), 1 (2009)

31. Berg, M.: Patient care information systems and health care work: a sociotechnical approach. Int. J. Med. Inform. **55**(2), 87–101 (1999). https://doi.org/10.1016/s1386-5056(99)00011-8

32. Cresswell, K., Sheikh, A.: Organizational issues in the implementation and adoption of health information technology innovations: an interpretative review. Int. J. Med. Inform. **82** (5), e73–e86 (2013). https://doi.org/10.1016/j.ijmedinf.2012.10.007
33. Holmberg, A., Alvinius, A.: How pressure for change challenge military organizational characteristics. Def. Stud. **19**(2), 130–148 (2019)

Multiple Machine Learning Models for Detection of Alzheimer's Disease Using OASIS Dataset

Preety Baglat[1], Ahmad Waleed Salehi[2], Ankit Gupta[3],
and Gaurav Gupta[2(✉)]

[1] Universita Della Svizzera Italiana, Lugano, Switzerland
[2] Yogananda School of AI, Computers and Data Science, Shoolini University,
Himachal Pradesh 173229, India
solan.gaurav@gmail.com
[3] Interactive Technologies Institute (IT/LARSyS) and M-ITI,
9020-105 Funchal, Portugal

Abstract. Alzheimer's Disease (AD) is the most common form of dementia that can lead to a neurological brain disorder that causes progressive memory loss as a result of damaging the brain cells and the ability to perform daily activities. This disease is one of kind and fatal. Early detection of AD because of its progressive threat and patients all around the world. The early detection is promising as it can help to predetermine the condition of lot of patients they might face in the future. So, by examining the consequences of the disease, using MRI images we can get the help of Artificial intelligence (AI) technology to classify the AD patients if they have or may not have the deadly disease in future. In recent years, AI-based Machine Learning (ML) techniques are very useful for the diagnosis of AD. In this paper, we have applied different machine learning techniques such as Logistic Regression, Decision Tree, Random forest classifier, Support Vector Machine and AdaBoost for the earlier diagnosis and classification of Alzheimer's disease using Open Access Series of Imaging Studies (OASIS) dataset, in which a significant performance and result gained on classification with Random Forest classifier.

Keywords: Alzheimer's disease · Machine learning · SVM · Logistic regression · Random forest · Decision tree · AdaBoost · OASIS

1 Introduction

Alzheimer Disease (AD) is a type and the most common form of dementia that can leads to neurological or brain disorder that causes cognitive deterioration and progressive memory loss as a result of brain cells death. Normally the symptoms and signs in AD cases develop very slowly and get terrible enough that involve affecting in their daily routine life [1]. Even though the main cause of AD is not only problem with old age but as well as in its early stages, the loss of the memory is mild, and their skills ability are dramatically changed [2]. The possible effective treatment of this disease is early diagnosis. Especially at an initial stage of AD diagnosis is a challenging task.

© IFIP International Federation for Information Processing 2020
Published by Springer Nature Switzerland AG 2020
S. K. Sharma et al. (Eds.): TDIT 2020, IFIP AICT 617, pp. 614–622, 2020.
https://doi.org/10.1007/978-3-030-64849-7_54

It has been estimated that 1 out of 85 people around the world can affect with AD disease by the year 2050 [3]. Those are in the final stage of this disease are bed-bound which also require care around-the-clock.

Previous studies showed that in the most patients of AD the language function is lost. So, for early diagnosis of Alzheimer usually a neuropsychological examination is used. And the researchers believe and stated that the key for preventing from the disease is the early detection of AD [4]. The Symptoms of Alzheimer's disease vary among individuals.

1.1 Common and Initial Symptom Which Are Gradually Worsening Are [5]

- Memory loss that affect daily life
- Difficulty in completing familiar tasks
- Confusion with place or time
- Trouble in understanding of visual image and spatial relationships
- New problems and troubles with words in writing or speaking
- Misplacing in things and losing the capability to retrace steps

Diagnosing of AD requires careful and a complete medical evaluation. the psychological cognitive test accuracy is completely depends on the capability and experience of the clinician. Make use of this test with huge number of AD patients will make the use of more effort, money, and time. So, it is important to build or develop Artificial Intelligence-based automatic detection model for classification of the disease [6]. Medical specialists are responsible in analyzing the interpreted of medical data, this technique is quite hard and limited for a medical specialist to interpret the images due to image subjectivity and complexity. So, in other areas of the real-world application the usage of Artificial Intelligence (AI), Machine Learning (ML) algorithms has shown promising and accurate in providing output for medical data [7]. With the speedy growth of AI-based approaches machine learning algorithms are capable of classification, feature extraction and will also assist in the accurate diagnosing of AD patients with less amount of time using images such as MRI, PET [8].

The aimed of this paper is to train an automated model based on the combination of ML algorithms includes Support Vector Machine (SVM), Random Forest, Logistic Regression for AD subjects. The classification is based on Open Access Series of Imaging Studies (OASIS) library of MRI patient scans. In this paper, the first section includes the experimental data, method and the algorithms used for classification of AD in the second section, then followed with next section results and discussion, and the last section is the conclusion part.

2 Experimental Data

The data is from OASIS dataset MRI scans obtained from https://www.oasis-brains.org . OASIS is a project which is aimed at making and providing neuroimaging datasets of the brain available freely to the scientific researchers [9]. By collecting and distributing neuroimaging datasets freely, we hope to facilitate and help future discoveries and clinical neuroscience like other initiatives for example Alzheimer's Disease Neuroimaging Initiative (ADNI). In this study, we have describe T1-weighted MRI data from OASIS with and without AD subjects from older adults. In this MRI scans images dataset, we have taken a longitudinal collection of 150 individuals aged from 60 to 96 years (Fig. 1).

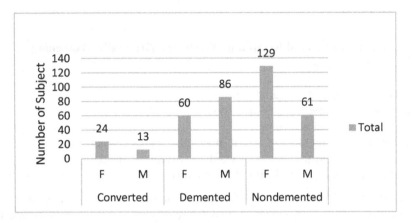

Fig. 1. Count of subject ID by group and gender (F = Female, M = Male)

3 Method and MRI Classifiers

In this work, we have implemented different machine learning models such as Logistic regression, Decision tree, Random forest classifier, Support vector machine and AdaBoost for the classification of Alzheimer's disease using Anaconda for Python and TensorFlow with 8 GB RAM and Graphics Intel HD 6000 1536 MB. 5-fold cross-validation is used due to the small dataset.

3.1 Support Vector Machine Classifier

A support vector machine is a type of supervised learning method that is used for the classification and the regression problem. Prediction of Disease the most popular binary classification algorithm SVM is used for the structural MRI scan images. SVM is machine learning derived classifiers which is used for the mapping a vector of predictors into a higher dimensional plane by either using two different linear and non-linear kernel functions. The binary classification problem these two- dimensional objects which belong to two classes (+1,−1) that are simple to find out the line that can separate them perfectly in a higher dimension hyperplane according to structural risk minimization principle [10]. The objective of SVM is to build a discriminating function that use training data which will classify new examples (m, n). When there is no training data possible for linear separation then support vector machines can work efficiently in combination with kernel models using the kernel trick. So, that hyperplane can defining the SVMs communicate to a nonlinear decision boundary. Only this way the decision function can communicate in terms of the support vectors:

$$f(m) = sign\left(\sum a_i y_i K(s_i, x) + w_0\right)$$

Where K is a kernel function and si is the support vectors and αi is a weight constant that is derived from the support vector machine [11].

3.2 Decision Tree Classifier

Decision tree classifier is a type of supervised machine learning that splits the dataset based on certain parameter that maximizes the separation of data and gives the result in the form of a tree-like structure [12]. Decision tree algorithm is used for classification and regression problem and the algorithm creates a binary tree and each node has two edges for finding the best categorical and numeric feature to split by using suitable impurity criterion. For decision tree classification, use Gini and Entropy impurity. In Gini impurity.

$$\sum_{i=1}^{C} fi(1 - fi)$$

Where n is the number of unique labels and fi is the frequency of label x at a node. In Entropy, fi is the frequency of label x at a node and n is the number of unique labels.

$$\sum_{i=1}^{C} -fi\log(fi)$$

3.3 Logistic Regression Classifier

Logistic regression is a type of machine learning which comes under the supervised learning technique. This technique is a predictive analysis and used in a way to describe data and explain the relationship between a dependent binary variable and one or more ordinal, or nominal variables [13]. The outcome is measured with a dichotomous variable [14].

$$p = b0 + b1X1 + b2X2 + odds = \frac{p}{1} - p$$
$$\log it(p) = \ln\left(\frac{p}{1} - p\right)$$

3.4 Random Forest Classifier

Random forest is an ensemble learning method used for the classification. which creates a set of decision trees together. A decision tree is the most important element in a random forest classifier which is based on bagging which is a sampling method and the same samples are using again and it will be put back into the dataset [15]. Suppose there is a dataset with n samples and if m decision tree is needed for that then m data sets for bagging will be built for training. For the decision tree, each node will be represented by the features used for the classification.

3.5 Adaptive Boosting Classifier

The Adaptive Boosting (AdaBoost) is a classifier that is based on the enhancement methods and boosting methods increase the accuracy of weak classifiers by taking the repeated iteration. Aims of every iteration are to be decreasing the classified data and increasing the weight of missorted data [16] (Fig. 2).

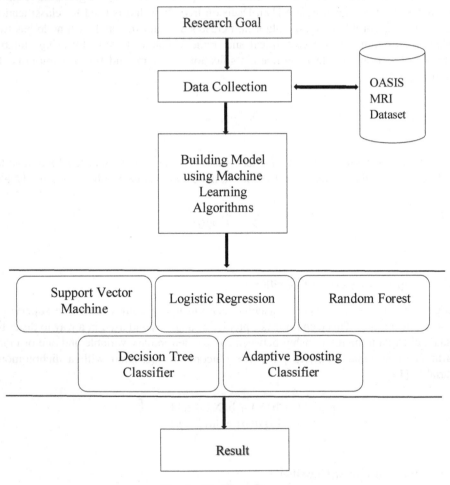

Fig. 2. Workflow diagram

4 Results

For classification of Alzheimer's disease using machine learning models on OSIAS dataset the current performance of our models using Logistic Regression with the accuracy rate of 78%, 81% form SVM, Decision tree and 86% from Random Forest and Adaptive Boosting classifier (Table 1 and Figs. 3, 4, 5 and 6).

Table 1. Performance metrics for each model.

SN	Model	Accuracy	Recall	AUC
1	Logistic regression(w/imputation)	0.789474	0.75	0.791667
2	Logistic regression(w/dropping)	0.750000	0.70	0.700000
3	SVM	0.815789	0.70	0.822222
4	Decision tree	0.815789	0.65	0.825000
5	Random forest	0.868421	0.80	0.872222

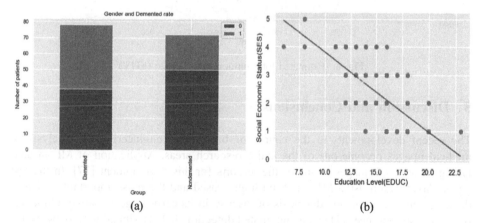

(a)   (b)

Fig. 3. a) Gender and demented rate (Male = 0, Female = 1), b) SEES and EDUC

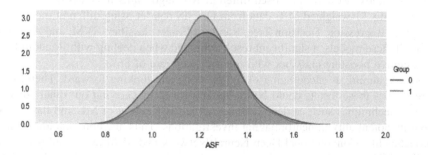

Fig. 4. Bar chart of atlas scaling factor (ASF) (nondemented = 0, demented = 1)

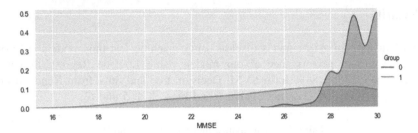

Fig. 5. Mini-mental state examination (MMSE)

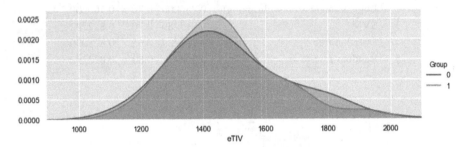

Fig. 6. Estimated total intracranial volume (eTIV)

5 Discussion and Conclusions

The recent developments in the course of biomedical engineering the analysis of medical images become one of the major research areas. Application of ML in analyzing of medical images is one of the reasons for this development [17]. In the last years classification using ML has been highly used and the most important AI-based development for automatic diagnosis of disease in its early stage to satisfy clinicians primary goals and needs [18]. An automated detection and classification framework for Alzheimer's disease using medical images is very crucial for the early detection of the AD patients.

In this study, we have proposed different ML algorithms for classification of AD patients using T1-weighted MRI data from OASIS dataset using different models such as Logistic Regression, Decision Tree, Random Forest classifier, SVM, and AdaBoost. Out of all these models, a significant result achieved when dealing with Random Forest and Adaptive boosting classifier with the accuracy rate of 86%.

We are aiming at encouraging of future work and looking forward. Therefore, in future studies these results could be further improved by carrying out other advanced AI-based techniques such as deep learning which is a subset of ML and has recently shown its potentiality in neuroimaging investigations. Thus, the combination of multi-approaches like Convolutional Deep Neural Network and SVM using multi-sites MRI data like ADNI would significantly enhance the ability of the model in early detection of disease.

References

1. Salehi, A.W., Baglat, P., Gupta, G.: Alzheimer's disease diagnosis using deep learning techniques. Int. J. Eng. Adv. Technol. **9**(3), 874–880 (2020). https://doi.org/10.35940/ijeat. c5345.029320
2. Bature, F., Guinn, B.A., Pang, D., Pappas, Y.: Signs and symptoms preceding the diagnosis of Alzheimer's disease: a systematic scoping review of literature from 1937 to 2016. BMJ Open **7**(8) (2017). https://doi.org/10.1136/bmjopen-2016-015746
3. Rathore, S., Habes, M., Iftikhar, M.Λ., Shacklett, A., Davatzikos, C.: A review on neuroimaging-based classification studies and associated feature extraction methods for Alzheimer's disease and its prodromal stages. Neuroimage **155**(April), 530–548 (2017). https://doi.org/10.1016/j.neuroimage.2017.03.057
4. Gaugler, J., James, B., Johnson, T., Scholz, K., Weuve, J.: 2016 Alzheimer's disease facts and figures. Alzheimer's Dement **12**(4), 459–509 (2016). https://doi.org/10.1016/j.jalz.2016. 03.001
5. Alzheimer's Association: "Memory Loss & 10 Early Signs of Alzheimer's," Alzheimer (2009). http://www.alz.org/alzheimers_disease_10_signs_of_alzheimers.asp
6. Lyu, G.: A review of alzheimer's disease classification using neuropsychological data and machine learning. In: Proceedings - 2018 11th International Congress on Image and Signal Processing, BioMedical Engineering and Informatics, CISP-BMEI 2018, no. 2017, pp. 1–5 (2019). https://doi.org/10.1109/cisp-bmei.2018.8633126
7. Gupta, G., Gupta, A., Jaiswal, V., Ansari, M.D.: A review and analysis of mobile health applications for Alzheimer patients and caregivers. In: 2018 5th International Conference on Parallel, Distributed and Grid Computing, PDGC 2018, pp. 171–175 (2018). https://doi.org/ 10.1109/pdgc.2018.8745995
8. Sarraf, S., De Souza, D.D., Anderson, J., Tofighi, G., Initiativ, A.D.N.: DeepAD: alzheimer's disease classification via deep convolutional neural networks using MRI and fMRI. bioRxiv, no. August 2016, p. 070441 (2017). https://doi.org/10.1101/070441
9. Hoda Badr, T.A.R., Carmack, C.L., Kashy, D.A., Cristofanilli, M.: 基因的改变NIH public access. Bone **23**(1), 1–7 (2011). https://doi.org/10.1161/circulationaha.110.956839
10. Maroco, J., Silva, D., Rodrigues, A., Guerreiro, M., Santana, I., de Mendonça, A.: Data mining methods in the prediction of Dementia: a real-data comparison of the accuracy, sensitivity and specificity of linear discriminant analysis, logistic regression, neural networks, support vector machines, classification trees and random forests. BMC Res. Notes **4**(1), 1–14 (2011)
11. Savio, A.: Supervised classification using deformation-based features for Alzheimer's disease detection on the OASIS cross-sectional database. Front. Artif. Intell. Appl. **243**, 2191–2200 (2012). https://doi.org/10.3233/978-1-61499-105-2-2191
12. Dreiseitl, S., Ohno-Machado, L.: Logistic regression and artificial neural network classification models: a methodology review. J. Biomed. Inf. **35**(5–6), 352–359 (2002). https://doi.org/10.1016/S1532-0464(03)00034-0
13. Solutions. Statistics: "What is Logistic Regression? - Statistics Solutions," Solutions Statistics, p. 1 (2016). https://doi.org/10.1016/j.radonc.2012.09.019
14. Bhol, S.: Comparative analysis for the detection of alzheimer's using multiple machine learning models, pp. 4–6 (2019)
15. Xu, L., Liang, G., Liao, C., Den Chen, G., Chang, C.C.: K-SkIP-N-Gram-RF: arandom forest based method for Alzheimer's disease protein identification. Front. Genet. **10**(FEB), 1–7 (2019). https://doi.org/10.3389/fgene.2019.00033

16. Patil, R.B., Piyush, R., Ramakrishnan, S.: Identification of brain white matter regions for diagnosis of alzheimer using diffusion tensor imaging. In: Proceedings of Annual International Conference of the IEEE Engineering in Medicine and Biology Society, EMBS, pp. 6535–6538 (2013). https://doi.org/10.1109/embc.2013.6611052
17. Anwar, S.M., Majid, M., Qayyum, A., Awais, M., Alnowami, M., Khan, M.K.: Medical image analysis using convolutional neural networks: a review. J. Med. Syst. **42**(11), 1–13 (2018). https://doi.org/10.1007/s10916-018-1088-1
18. Sharma, L., Gupta, G., Jaiswal, V.: Classification and development of tool for heart diseases (MRI images) using machine learning. In: 2016 Fourth International Conference on Parallel, Distributed and Grid Computing, PDGC 2016, no. January, pp. 219–224 (2016). https://doi.org/10.1109/pdgc.2016.7913149

Social Media and Public Health Emergency of International Concern: The COVID-19 Outbreak

Josue Kuika Watat[1]($\boxtimes$) (iD) and Magaly Moukoko Mbonjo[2]

[1] AMBERO Consulting GmbH, 61476 Kronberg Im Taunus, Germany
josuewatat@gmail.com
[2] Queen Mary University of London, London E1 4NS, UK
m.j.e.moukokombonjo@smd19.qmul.ac.uk

Abstract. The coronavirus (COVID-19) epidemic is the cause of several disasters on human health and livelihoods in many countries around the globe. Even though everyone is at risk of infections regardless of ethnicity, income, age, and political affiliation, the consequences of the epidemic will weigh enormously in the global south, at the level of the very fragile sanitary architecture, the economic, social and cultural fabric. This study examines the key determinants of social media adoption and the consequences of their use in managing a public health crisis of International Concern like COVID-19. We propose a theoretical framework resulting from a combination of several approaches, such as the Health Belief Model, the Technology Acceptance Model and the theory of Social Influence. Moreover, we use a mixed research method to carry out various investigations in our study. The findings and recommendations of this research will serve as a research base for government agencies, health organizations and associations in the reflections and strategic actions being implemented to effectively fight against COVID-19 and equip marginalized communities with efficient information through the use of social media.

Keywords: COVID-19 · Sub-Saharan Africa · Public health crisis · Social media · TAM · Health belief model · Social influence

1 Introduction

The coronavirus belongs to a group of viruses responsible for lower respiratory tract infections. Some of its manifestations include symptoms such as cough, shortness of breath and acute respiratory distress [1]. Seven type of coronaviruses are responsible of human infections. In 2003, prior to the SARS-cov-2 (Covid-19) outbreak, SARS-cov emerged in China and affected 8096 people with a 10% mortality rate. In 2012, MERScov was detected in the Middle East and affected 2494 people with a 37% mortality rate [2]. The clinical manifestations of these three viruses may overlap. However phylogenetically, the SARS-cov-2 has a greater similarity with SARS-like coronaviruses derived from bats. Bats are therefore suspected to be the primary host of the novel coronavirus [3].

© IFIP International Federation for Information Processing 2020
Published by Springer Nature Switzerland AG 2020
S. K. Sharma et al. (Eds.): TDIT 2020, IFIP AICT 617, pp. 623–634, 2020.
https://doi.org/10.1007/978-3-030-64849-7_55

The first novel Coronavirus case was discovered in Wuhan (the 7th most populous city in China). The virus is said to have originated from a 'wet market' where wild animals were equally sold since the first four cases discovered in December 2019 were all in contact with that market [1]. Even though the secondary host has not been confirmed, wild animals sold at the market like pangolins have been incriminated. Animal to human transmission was followed by rapid human to human transmission in China and later on all over the world [4]. Epidemiologically, the novel coronavirus has a basic reproduction number R-naught (R0) estimated to range from 2.2–3.6. This implies that, for 1 case in a population, 2–3 other cases could susceptibly be infected in that given population [2, 3].

On January 13th, 2020, Thailand was the first country that reported a case of the novel coronavirus after China [5]. Following the rapid spread of the virus, the WHO declared the coronavirus outbreak as a 'public health emergency of international concern on the 30th January 2020 [1, 6]. The disease was named Covid-19 on the 11th of February 2020 and declared a pandemic on the 11th of March 2020. At that time, more than a hundred thousand cases and thousands of deaths had been confirmed in 118 countries [5, 7]. As of today 10th May 2020, almost 4 million people have been infected in 215 countries, with 272,859 deaths, therefore putting great stress on health systems worldwide [8].

According to WHO, the first case in Africa was confirmed on the 14th February 2020 in Egypt. This raised concerns about the continent's ability to effectively manage the outbreak given the frailty of its health systems [9]. Sub-Saharan Africa in particular has a high burden of disease with half of deaths being attributed to infectious diseases such as HIV/AIDS, Malaria and Tuberculosis [10]. According to WHO regional director for Africa, "the covid-19 pandemic could be devastating socio-economically and cause thousands of deaths". WHO stressed the importance of a contextualized approach including decentralization of resources and expertise, and empowerment of communities as essential in the response towards the fight against Covid-19 in the region [9]. As of today 10th May 2020, 60657 cases have been confirmed with approximately 2115 deaths (<4% mortality rate) [11] (Fig. 1).

Although the African continent has experienced enormous changes in public health crises, it remains an area that is highly vulnerable compared to other continents and faced with the epidemic of coronavirus (Covid-19). According to the vulnerability indicator for so-called infectious diseases, Africa alone counts 22 out of the 25 countries which are particularly vulnerable to several contagious diseases [12]. The high rate of diseases such as tuberculosis, or HIV, as well as several pathogens, contribute to delay the uncertainty of the diagnoses and to worry in the event of a widespread of the Covid19 pandemic. Several speculations have emerged regarding Africans' fragility in the face of the virus. [13] discover that regarding the African population, mostly young, we could witness a drop-in demand for intensive care and hospitalization. It is estimated that deaths in Sub-Saharan Africa can vary from 298,000 when the response strategy has been well conducted with the respect of all measures of social distancing from the first alerts to 2.5 million in an environment where no strategy of response is not implemented [13]. Nevertheless, the estimation did not consider the level of health infrastructure, which is particularly low in Sub-Saharan Africa, but also the co-morbidity variation rate between communities of people.

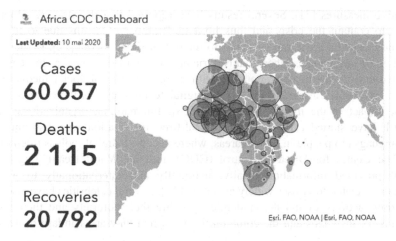

Fig. 1. Distribution of Covid-19 cases in Africa, from CDC Africa [11]

2 Literature Review and Development of Hypotheses

2.1 Multi-country Program on Sexual and Reproductive Health (SRH) for Youth Through Social Media

In sub-Saharan Africa, most of the population is young, making their sexual health vulnerable because they are not informed and equipped with adequate skills and services. The UNICEF global report [14] shows that in sub-Saharan Africa, the birth rate among adolescents is 120, which raises it to the highest rate in the world, against 85 on average in countries in developing. The report says that less than 5% of women between 15 to 19 years old use condoms [15]. In addition, less than 10% of women report using a modern contraceptive method, which draws attention to the need to communicate about health and sexual reproduction for young people [16]. For example, Kenya has set up a dynamic platform (Mobile for Reproductive Health (m4RH) to educate, engage and empower young people on sexual reproductive health and HIV [17]. The organization in charge of planning in Kenya has also created a digital platform to increase the information and knowledge already acquired on sexual health and sexual reproduction [18]. The success of these platforms in raising awareness and information on sexual health has enabled other East African country like Tanzania to use this communication model in order to maximize their communication on HIV AIDS and sexual health [19].

2.2 The Ebola Outbreak in Nigeria

Nigeria was one the most affected country by the Ebola epidemic in 2014. When the disease appeared in the country, fears turned to community contamination towards countries in the West Africa sub-region and across the continent [20]. According to the experience of countries which have managed to contain the crisis, Nigeria has adopted an approach centered on training the general public and health personnel on the various preventive measures [21]. Several results have reported that the strategy adopted by Nigeria to contain the crisis and thus limit the number of deaths due to the Ebola epidemic has had a great impact thanks to the use of social media [22]. In view of the more than 67 million subscribers that Nigeria had at that time, as well as more than 130 million users of smartphones, coupled with a massive use of social media such as Twitter, Facebook, Instagram, the use of digital technology has therefore had a significant impact in the fight against Ebola [23]. International organizations such as UNICEF have started campaigns where real-time information was disseminated in local languages to people in remote areas, where access to digital tools is often difficult [24]. The Center for Diseases control (CDC) and the World Health Organization (WHO) provided information locally, nationally and internationally to make all information related to viruses widely available [25]. Several celebrities have also joined the various actions around the epidemic by using their notoriety and their multiple platforms for their fans and the communities of which they are standard bearers [26].

2.3 Failures Identified in the Existing Literature and Theoretical Transformation

For decades, research has explored several theoretical approaches to explain, improve and even provide answers regarding the acceptance of information systems by users. They have contributed significantly to the literature by producing important information on the affective, cognitive, emotional and behavioural reactions of individuals in contact with technology. These studies have also been shown to be important in explaining the various external factors that gravitate around psychological responses and contribute to their formation. Therefore, this study has made use of several models and theories widely used in the existing literature to explore different options for accepting and using technology.

The present research is based on two specific motivations to explore the adequacy with the arrangement of any model. First, the study is based in sub-Saharan African countries that are at high risk of being seriously affected by the covid-19 outbreak. Indeed, communities in rural Africa have difficulties in having access to reliable and viable information, and communication is often difficult between several stakeholders in view of the particularly difficult economic climate, and the absence of reliable telecommunications infrastructures. Statistics show a low level of digital literacy in rural areas [27]. Doubtlessly, there is a considerable gap between the big cities where the heart of the economic and social activity is concentrated and the rural areas where poor and marginalized communities are not always informed of national and world news. They are therefore ignorant given the barrier measures adopted by governments and the World Health Organization to deal with the pandemic, as well as the daily steps being taken to fight against the disease. Besides, the very conservative aspect, refractory to changes, and beliefs in rites and traditions in several villages and rural areas constitute a colossal obstacle first of all to raising awareness of a possible crisis in view as prevention, but also the penetration of digital tools intended to inform but also raise awareness. This is how the researchers undertook to investigate the possibilities of developing constructs which help to assess and reinforce the use and impact of social media for communication in times of public health crises, such as the coronavirus disease.

Also, the literature reports that there have been few studies on the use of web 2.0 technologies in a public health crisis. This literary vacuum leads to the use of the Health Belief Model (HBM) and the theory of social influence regarding the large volume of information exchanged on social networks in times of health crisis.

2.4 Health Belief Model (HBM)

The Health Belief Model (HBM) was developed to provide answers to the prophylactic approaches of individuals when it comes to their health as well as detecting the elements that justify the failure of the vaccination program [28]. Indeed, the individual should be aware of a certain number of important factors to adopt a prevention approach against the disease: (a) he must realize that his immune system may be vulnerable to a health threat (sensitivity perceived); (b) he should be aware of the severe consequences that the disease could cause in his life; (c) in the event of contamination, the endorsement of individual attitudes could have a severe effect on his life (d) these attitudes would not be obstructed by pain, cost and embarrassment [29]. The IS literature indicates the importance of the HBM in several fields of action related to health. Among these areas, we can list fertility control [30, 31], breast cancer screening [32, 33], HIV-related sex [34, 35].

Perceived Severity of Chronic Disease is one of the key constructs contributing to the formation of the HBM. We adapted it according to [36] and it is defined in this study as the measurement of the incidence leading to repercussions of certain diseases such as covid19 which one can think that an individual suffers from. As for Perceived Susceptibility to chronic diseases, it refers to a subjective feeling of being infected with covid19 or seeing symptoms related to covid19 (fever, dry cough and tiredness, aches and pains, nasal congestion, sore throat or diarrhea) [37, 38]. Perceived Health Risk is therefore the composition of Perceived Severity and Perceived susceptibility. Actions taken to prevent disease or improve health are estimated to be the essential of the health attitude in several theoretical models in the literature [39, 40]. Health Consciousness is therefore a varied but significant concept since it refers to the healthy actions taken by an individual to preserve good health (physical, mental) [41]. Individuals who are concerned about their health tend to adopt behaviours which keep them away from diseases [42] and which reminds them of the consequences of attitudes such as unhealthy environment, poor diet [43]. The use of social media in health has two dimensions: social media for the search for health information, the use of social media to communicate on health problems. According to the adaptations made from the research of [44–46], the use of social media for the search for health information refers in this study to existing information on health which exists on the commonly used social media (Twitter, Facebook, WhatsApp, Snapchat...). They can relate to the evolution of an epidemic in an area, the barrier measures adopted in the face of the disease, information on the treatment of the disease and even the existence of a vaccine to prevent the disease. As for the use of social media to communicate on health problems, it involves communicating to your knowledge network (family friends, professional relationships) on social media, the difficulties/symptoms observed regarding the disease. According to the emerging literature, we propose the following hypotheses:

H1:   Perceived Severity of chronic Diseases is positively related to Perceived Health Risks

H2:   Perceived Susceptibility to Chronic Diseases is positively related to Perceived Health Risk

H3:   Perceived Health Risk is positively related to Perceived Usefulness of Social Media

H4:   Perceived Health Risk is positively related to Health-related Social Media Use

H5:   Health consciousness is positively related to Perceived Usefulness of Social Media

H6:   Health consciousness is positively related to Attitude towards Social Media Use

H7:   Health consciousness is positively related to Health-related Social Media Use

H8:   Social Media Use for Information Seeking is positively related to Health-related Social Media Use

H9:   Social Media Use for Health Communication is positively related to Health-related Social Media Use

2.5   Social Influence Theory

Social influence theory refers to the different external forces that act on an individual so that he can adopt a certain behaviour or perform certain actions. It contains a tripartite differentiation between normative prejudices in order to (1) maintain an honourable bond between the stakeholders with regard to the awards or censorship related thereto, (2) guaranteeing connectedness and a favourable appreciation of self (3) understanding external social domination [47]. The theory of Social Influence registers three dimensions which refer to social influence. The first dimension refers to compliance. These are subjective norms, which refer to "the perceived social pressure to perform or not to perform a behaviour" [48]. It refers to the domination of external expectations over an attitude [49]. Second, social identity(identification) refers to "one's conception of self in terms of the defining features of a self-inclusive social category that renders the self stereotypically interchangeable with other group members, and stereotypically distinct from outsiders" [50]. Third, Group Norm that refers to goals and values adopted by the members of a community and which are conveyed to all members of the community [50]. We Suggest:

H10:   Subjective Norms are positively related to Intention to Use Social Media

H11:   Social Identity is positively related to Intention to Use Social Media

H12:   Group Norm is positively related to Intention to Use Social Media

2.6   Technology Acceptance Model

The Technology Acceptance Model was used in this study to premeditate the use of social media for health communication in a technological aspect [51]. So far, the separate use of the Technology Acceptance Model (TAM) and the Health Beliefs Model (HBM) has not produced concrete results on health-seeking behaviour on social media. TAM was used to explain the different postures adopted by an individual for the use of technology. However, when we want to interpret the behaviour of an individual for the use of technology for health, TAM alone is not enough given its heavy dependence on two of its key constructs, in this case, Perceived Ease of Use (PEOU) and Perceived Usefulness (PU) [52]. Notwithstanding the wide use of the Technology Acceptance model to clarify various attitudes towards the use of a technology [51, 53, 54], its action on the use of social media for health-related purposes can only be complete when it is associates with the dimensions of the model Health Beliefs Model as they exhibit an individual's assent when it comes to health. It is therefore wise to evaluate the use of social media for health purposes in a unifying posture that combines behaviour, attitude, cognition, as well as the artificial examination of an individual's mental conditions regarding the viewpoint of his health status. Regarding the literature on the technology acceptance model, as well as the definition of its constructs, we therefore suggest the following hypotheses:

H13:   Perceived Ease of social Media Use is positively related to Perceived Usefulness of Social Media

H14:   Perceived Ease of social Media Use is positively related to Attitude towards the Use of Social Media

H15:   Perceived Usefulness of social Media is positively related to Attitude towards the Use of Social Media

H16:   Attitude towards Social Media Use is positively related to Intention to Use Social Media.

The research model (Fig. 2) is presented as follows:

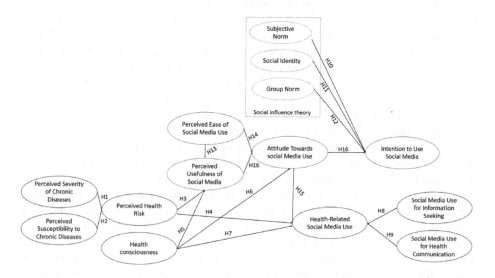

Fig. 2. Research model adapted from [55]

3 Methodology

This research draws its foundations from an inclusive model that reconciles the elements of the Technology Acceptance model, the theory of social influence, as well as research on health beliefs. Works on technology adoption and e-health have historically been managed using surveys [56–59]. The instrument development process is prioritized according to [60]. Items of constructs are collected according to the emerging literature from valid and accessible scales in the literature in order to arrive at an adequate description of each construct resulting from the research model. the terminologies of each construct item are modified and contextualized in research on social media and health. Constructs are evaluated separately in order to reflect the feelings of each individual. For our study, seven-point Likert scales graduated from 1 ("strongly disagree") to 7 ("strongly disagree") was used on each item of the constructs of the research model. As for the data analysis, it will be carried out according to the Partial Least Square to Structural Equation Modeling (PLS-SEM) approach. This approach is contextualized to our study environment because it assesses the existing causal links between the constructs of our research model [61, 62]. For this research, we will use SmartPLS v. 3.2.8.

4 Future Research Directions

In view of the increasingly growing digital evolutions in the world, the use of ICT applications like social media is increasing every day, and their use is becoming more and more diverse and varied, in several areas of life (health, finance, agriculture …). Social media are therefore important applications to large-scale objectives, with the potential to be informed in real-time about what is happening in the world (health crisis, economic and financial crisis, social crisis). In addition, the presence of social media applications in sub-Saharan Africa provides a feeling of satisfaction for many Africans not only because of the fun carcass it contains but the various features it offers in a context marked by an absence of advanced technology and a gloomy socio-economic situation. The success of social media applications in rural Africa is highly dependent on the adoption of this technology by disadvantaged communities living in rural areas. Thus, the objective of this research was to establish a research framework based on the concentration of the Technology Acceptance Model (TAM) with the theory of Social Influence and the Health Belief Model (HBM) which will thus help to detect the key factors impacting the resolution to adopt social media for health communication in rural Africa. The other goal sought in this research was to develop a theoretical model that could increase the use of social media in the field of health in rural Africa. Social media is important in Africa, but so far there has not been a theoretical framework in the existing literature for understanding the factors that can justify the adoption and continuous usage of social media for health communication. Hence, this study, therefore, bridges the existing gap in the literature by merging the TAM, the theory of social influence, as well as the HBM.

The above model can be used for empirical exploration, whether by practitioners or researchers. The empirical acceptance of the proposed research model will allow us to understand the consequences of the independent variables on the dependent variables. It is recommended to conduct an in-depth quantitative study of the proposed model for the purposes of generalization and validation. The continuing quantitative study by using the proposed research model will provide homogeneous responses to universalize the results from a strategic point of view.

References

1. Adhikari, S.P., et al.: Epidemiology, causes, clinical manifestation and diagnosis, prevention and control of coronavirus disease (COVID-19) during the early outbreak period: a scoping review. Infect. Dis. Poverty 9(1), 29 (2020). https://doi.org/10.1186/s40249-020-00646-x
2. Giwa, A., Desai, A.: Novel coronavirus COVID-19: an overview for emergency clinicians. Emerg. Med. Pract. 22(2 Suppl 2), 1–21 (2020)
3. Lai, C.C., Shih, T.P., Ko, W.C., Tang, H.J., Hsueh, P.R.: Severe acute respiratory syndrome coronavirus 2 (SARS-CoV-2) and coronavirus disease-2019 (COVID-19): the epidemic and the challenges. Int. J. Antimicrob. Agents 55(3), 105924 (2020). https://doi.org/10.1016/j.ijantimicag.2020.105924
4. Ciotti, M., et al.: COVID-19 Outbreak: An Overview. Chemotherapy (2020). https://doi.org/10.1159/000507423
5. Di Gennaro, F., Pizzol, D.: Coronavirus diseases (COVID-19) current status and future perspectives: a narrative review. 17(8) (2020). https://doi.org/10.3390/ijerph17082690
6. Sohrabi, C., et al.: World health organization declares global emergency: a review of the 2019 novel coronavirus (COVID-19). Int. J. Surg. (Lond. Engl.) 76, 71–76 (2020). https://doi.org/10.1016/j.ijsu.2020.02.034
7. Cucinotta, D., Vanelli, M.: WHO declares COVID-19 a pandemic. acta bio-medica. Atenei Parmensis 91(1), 157–160 (2020). https://doi.org/10.23750/abm.v91i1.9397
8. WHO: WHO Coronavirus Disease (COVID-19) Dashboard (2020). https://covid19.who.int/. Accessed 10 May 2020
9. WHO: COVID-19 cases top 10000 in Africa (2020). https://www.afro.who.int/news/covid19-cases-top-10–000-africa. Accessed 10 May 2020
10. Fenollar, F., Mediannikov, O.: Emerging infectious diseases in Africa in the 21st century. New Microbes New Infect. 26, S10–S18 (2018). https://doi.org/10.1016/j.nmni.2018.09.004
11. CDC, C.f.D.C.a.P.: Africa CDC Covid-19 dashboard (2020). https://africacdc.org/covid19/. Accessed 10 May 2020
12. Moore, M., Gelfeld, B., Okunogbe, A., Paul, C.: Identifying future disease hot spots: infectious disease vulnerability index. Rand. Health Q. 6, 5 (2017)
13. Walker, P., et al.: Report 12: The global impact of COVID-19 and strategies for mitigation and suppression (2020)
14. Policy, U.J.R.: Generation 2030 Africa: child demographics in Africa. Division of Data (2014)
15. Pettitt, E.D., Greifinger, R.C., Phelps, B.R., Bowsky, S.J.: Improving health services for adolescents living with HIV in sub-Saharan Africa: a multi-country assessment. Afr. J. Reprod. Health 17(4), 17–31 (2013)
16. Pretorius, L., Gibbs, A., Crankshaw, T., Willan, S.: Interventions targeting sexual and reproductive health and rights outcomes of young people living with HIV: a comprehensive review of current interventions from sub-Saharan Africa. Glob. Health Action 8(1), 28454 (2015)

17. Vahdat, H.L., L'Engle, K.L., Plourde, K.F., Magaria, L., Olawo, A.: There are some questions you may not ask in a clinic: providing contraception information to young people in Kenya using SMS. Int. J. Gynecol. Obstet. **123**, e2–e6 (2013)
18. Nyong'o, D.: Strategies for Increasing Visibility and Performance of NonGovernmental Organizations in Kenya: A Case of Family Health Options Kenya (FHOK). United States International University-Africa (2009)
19. Olsen, P.S., Plourde, K.F., Lasway, C., van Praag, E.: Insights from a text messaging-based sexual and reproductive health information program in tanzania (m4RH): retrospective analysis. JMIR mHealth uHealth **6**(11), e10190 (2018)
20. W.H.O: Ebola situation report 20 January 2016. In., pp. 1–13. World Health Organization (2016)
21. Shuaib, F., et al.: Ebola virus disease outbreak—Nigeria. Morb. Mort. Weekly Rep. **63**(39), 867 (2014)
22. Onyeonoro, U.U., Ekpemiro, U.C., Abali, C., Nwokeukwu, H.I.: Ebola epidemic-the Nigerian experience. Pan Afr. Med. J. **22**(Suppl 1), 17 (2015)
23. Odlum, M., Yoon, S.: What can we learn about the Ebola outbreak from tweets? Am. J. Infect. Control **43**(6), 563–571 (2015)
24. O'Donnell, A.: Using Mobile Phones for Polio Prevention in Somalia: An evaluation of the 2013–14 interactive messaging and mobile voucher system deployed in hard to reach areas in Somalia (2015)
25. Bell, B.P.: Overview, control strategies, and lessons learned in the CDC response to the 2014–2016 Ebola epidemic. MMWR Supplements **65** (2016)
26. Vorovchenko, T., Ariana, P., van Loggerenberg, F., Amirian, P.: Ebola and twitter. what insights can global health draw from social media? In: Amirian, P., Lang, T., van Loggerenberg, F. (eds.) Big Data in Healthcare. SPSDD, pp. 85–98. Springer, Cham (2017). https://doi.org/10.1007/978-3-319-62990-2_5
27. Aikins, S.K.: Determinants of digital divide in Africa and policy implications. Int. J. Public Adm. Digital Age (IJPADA) **6**(1), 64–79 (2019)
28. Claar, C.L.: The adoption of computer security: an analysis of home personal computer user behavior using the health belief model. Utah State University (2011)
29. Rosenstock, I.M.: Historical origins of the health belief model. Health Educ. Monogr. **2**(4), 328–335 (1974)
30. Hall, K.S.: The health belief model can guide modern contraceptive behavior research and practice. J. Midwifery Women's Health **57**(1), 74–81 (2012)
31. Eisen, M., Zellman, G.L., McAlister, A.L.: A health belief model approach to adolescents' fertility control: some pilot program findings. Health Educ. Q. **12**(2), 185–210 (1985)
32. Borrayo, E.A., Guarnaccia, C.A., Mahoney, M.J.: Prediction of breast cancer screening behavior among older women of Mexican descent: applicability of theoretical models. Int. J. Clin. Health Psychol. **1**, 73–90 (2001)
33. Rezaeian, M., Sharifirad, G., Mostafavi, F., Moodi, M., Abbasi, M.H.: The effects of breast cancer educational intervention on knowledge and health beliefs of women 40 years and older, Isfahan, Iran. J. Educ. Health Promot. **3**, 43–43 (2014). https://doi.org/10.4103/2277-9531.131929
34. Zhao, J., et al.: Predictors of condom use behaviors based on the Health Belief Model (HBM) among female sex workers: a cross-sectional study in Hubei Province, China. PloS one **7**(11), e49542 (2012)
35. Reback, C.J., Fletcher, J.B., Shoptaw, S., Mansergh, G.: Exposure to theory-driven text messages is associated with HIV risk reduction among methamphetamine-using men who have sex with men. AIDS Behav. **19**(2), 130–141 (2015)

36. Champion, V.L., Skinner, C.S.: The health belief model. Health Behav. Health Educ. Theory Res. Pract. **4**, 45–65 (2008)
37. Deng, Z.: Understanding public users' adoption of mobile health service. Int. J. Mob. Commun. **11**(4), 351–373 (2013)
38. Surveillances, V.: The epidemiological characteristics of an outbreak of 2019 novel coronavirus diseases (COVID-19)—China, 2020. China CDC Weekly **2**(8), 113–122 (2020)
39. Newsom, J.T., McFarland, B.H., Kaplan, M.S., Huguet, N., Zani, B.: The health consciousness myth: implications of the near independence of major health behaviors in the North American population. Soc. Sci. Med. **60**(2), 433–437 (2005)
40. Gould, S.J.: Health consciousness and health behavior: the application of a new health consciousness scale. Am. J. Prev. Med. **6**(4), 228–237 (1990)
41. Jayanti, R.K., Burns, A.C.: The antecedents of preventive health care behavior: an empirical study. J. Acad. Mark. Sci. **26**(1), 6–15 (1998)
42. Kraft, F.B., Goodell, P.W.: Identifying the health conscious consumer. Mark. Health Serv. **13**(3), 18 (1993)
43. Vlontzos, G., Duquenne, M.N.: To eat or not to eat? The case of genetically modified (GM) food. Nutr. Food Sci. (2016)
44. Yoo, E.Y., Robbins, L.S.: Understanding middle-aged women's health information seeking on the web: a theoretical approach. J. Am. Soc. Inf. Sci. Technol. **59**(4), 577–590 (2008)
45. Kim, J., Park, H.-A.: Development of a health information technology acceptance model using consumers' health behavior intention. J. Med. Internet Res. **14**(5), e133 (2012)
46. Hale, T.M., Cotten, S.R., Drentea, P., Goldner, M.: Rural-urban differences in general and health-related internet use. Am. Behav. Sci. **53**(9), 1304–1325 (2010)
47. Wood, W.: Attitude change: persuasion and social influence. Annu. Rev. Psychol. **51**(1), 539–570 (2000)
48. Ajzen, I.: The theory of planned behavior. Organ. Behav. Hum. Decis. Process. **50**(2), 179–211 (1991)
49. Kelman, H.C.: Social influence and linkages between the individual and the social system: further thoughts on the processes of compliance, identification, and internalization. S. 125–171 in: J. Tedeschi. Perspectives on social power. Aldine, Chicago (1974)
50. Varnali, K., Gorgulu, V.: A social influence perspective on expressive political participation in Twitter: the case of# OccupyGezi. Inf. Commun. Soc. **18**(1), 1–16 (2015)
51. Davis, F.D., Bagozzi, R.P., Warshaw, P.R.: User acceptance of computer technology: a comparison of two theoretical models. Manag. Sci. **35**(8), 982–1003 (1989)
52. Davis, F.D.: Perceived usefulness, perceived ease of use, and user acceptance of information technology. MIS Q., 319–340 (1989)
53. Sharif, S.P., Ahadzadeh, A.S., Wei, K.K.: A moderated mediation model of internet use for health information. J. Soc. Sci. (COES&RJ-JSS) **4**(1), 611–625 (2018)
54. Holden, R.J., Karsh, B.T.: The technology acceptance model: its past and its future in health care. J. Biomed. Inf. **43**(1), 159–172 (2010)
55. Ahadzadeh, A.S., Sharif, S.P., Ong, F.S., Khong, K.W.: Integrating health belief model and technology acceptance model: an investigation of health-related internet use. J. Med. Internet Res. **17**(2), e45 (2015)
56. Campbell, J.I., et al.: The technology acceptance model for resource-limited settings (TAM-RLS): a novel framework for mobile health interventions targeted to low-literacy end-users in resource limited settings. AIDS Behav. **21**(11), 3129–3140 (2017)
57. Seth, A., Coffie, A.J., Richard, A., Stephen, S.A.: Hospital administration management technology adoption: a theoretical test of technology acceptance model and theory of planned behavior on HAMT adoption. Am. J. Public Health **7**(1), 21–26 (2019)

58. Beldad, A.D., Hegner, S.M.: Expanding the technology acceptance model with the inclusion of trust, social influence, and health valuation to determine the predictors of German users' willingness to continue using a fitness app: a structural equation modeling approach. Int. J. Hum. Comput. Interact. **34**(9), 882–893 (2018)
59. Watat, J.K., Madina, M.: Towards an integrated theoretical model for assessing mobile banking acceptance among consumers in low income African economies. In: Themistocleous, M., Papadaki, M. (eds.) EMCIS 2019. LNBIP, vol. 381, pp. 165–178. Springer, Cham (2020). https://doi.org/10.1007/978-3-030-44322-1_13
60. Moore, G.C., Benbasat, I.: Development of an instrument to measure the perceptions of adopting an information technology innovation. Inf. Syst. Res. **2**(3), 192–222 (1991)
61. Sarstedt, M., Cheah, J.-H.: Partial least squares structural equation modeling using SmartPLS: a software review. J. Mark. Anal. **7**(3), 196–202 (2019)
62. Sarstedt, M., Ringle, C.M., Hair, J.F.: Partial least squares structural equation modeling. Handbook Mark. Res. **26**, 1–40 (2017)

Factors Influencing AI Implementation Decision in Indian Healthcare Industry: A Qualitative Inquiry

Vranda Jain[1] , Nidhi Singh[1] , Sajeet Pradhan[2] ,
and Prashant Gupta[2(✉)]

[1] Jaipuria Institute of Management, Noida, India
[2] IIM Tiruchirapalli, Tiruchirapalli, Tamil Nadu, India
prashant@iimtrichy.ac.in

Abstract. Recently, Artificial Intelligence has started showing up in the realm of health care innovations with researchers exploring its potential for healthcare organisations. Since healthcare possess industry specific features, the context and challenges of exploring AI adoption in healthcare is different than other industries. This study intends to conduct grounded theory to review the strategic, cultural, environmental and operational factors towards adoption of AI technology in Indian hospitals. The study uses purposive sampling to conduct semi-structured in-depth interviews of the decision makers of various healthcare organizations across the country. The present study would contribute to the existing literature on the impact of disruptive technology on healthcare as it would be a comprehensive study assessing the determinants of adoption in hospitals.

Keywords: Artificial Intelligence · Healthcare · Disruptive technology

1 Introduction

Artificial intelligence (AI), the defining technology of 21st century, with its learning, reasoning and adaptation capabilities, has transformed industries worldwide [1]. Academic literature in AI domain has explored technology adoption across sectors like agriculture [2], architecture, engineering and construction [3], energy [4], smart cities [5], communications [6] and manufacturing [7]. Recently, AI has started capturing attention in the realm of health care innovations [8]. This is supported by an Accenture report, 2017 estimating a CAGR of 40% in AI health market through 2021. Another study by [9] reckon AI health market will grow ten times during 2020–2025.

Since healthcare possess industry specific features [10, 11], the context and challenges of exploring AI adoption in healthcare is markedly different than other industries [12]. While assessing the technology adoption challenges in healthcare sector, [13] found issues pertaining to management, technology, security and legal aspects. Organisational planning and inter departmental integration [14], quality of patients' care [15], management support [15] and an assessment of financial and economic

S. K. Sharma et al. (Eds.): TDIT 2020, IFIP AICT 617, pp. 635–640, 2020.
https://doi.org/10.1007/978-3-030-64849-7_56

benefits [16] have been identified as few of the other challenges in AI adoption in healthcare.

Recent studies have examined the transformational impact of using AI technology in healthcare industry. AI technology has immense potential for healthcare organisations- improving service quality [17], efficiency and productivity [18]; effective resource management [19]; accelerating health responses [20]; automating clinical documentation and upgrading medical records management [21]; improving communication and coordination among users [22]; reducing errors [23] and costs [24]. At the country level, this would improve public health surveillance [25] and encourage targeted research and development. For a developing and world's second most populous country, India, currently undergoing a demographic, economic and epidemiological transition and imposing an increased pressure on existing healthcare infrastructure, such outcomes are much awaited.

Although extant literature highlights the positive impact of AI technology on healthcare, its benefits in Indian context are yet to be capitalized. Existing studies have focused on other segments of healthcare like diagnostics, telemedicine, medical insurance, pharmaceuticals and medical equipment. To the best of our knowledge, there is no systematic study exploring the impact of AI applications on hospitals from an administrator's glance. While studying healthcare centres, though few studies have focused on the existing challenges and barriers to implementation, limited attention has been given to discuss the factors affecting the decision to adopt AI technology. The current study adopts a multi-dimensional approach towards adoption of AI technology in Indian hospitals.

2   Literature Review

Artificial intelligence (AI) is gradually changing business functions in various sectors particularly, healthcare [26]. In line with recent technological innovations, the role of Artificial intelligence (AI) and its incorporation with various applications such as IoT [6], robots [27], data mining [28] are discussed in various studies. According to [29], several empirical studies have been written on the role of AI in the last two decades in sectors such as IT, financial services, healthcare, etc. These studies focused mainly on the drivers for the AI adoption largely economic and technical drivers [30, 31]. According to [32], an increase in productivity and innovation are the potential drivers of AI adoption. Similarly, [33] mentioned about the efficiency of AI enables a system in reducing costs related to human errors, equipment, and taking the decision and making accurate predictions at various points.

Although, these studies confirmed that AI brings revolution, but, many challenges lie ahead too [29, 34]. To this end, few significant studies advanced their work by elaborating on the barriers of AI mainly technical and social aspects of implementation [26, 35]. [36] confirmed that the availability of expertise human assistance and extensive infrastructure support are few main barriers due to the excessive cost associated with it. Another important barrier that is largely discussed is the serious social implications of AI adoption in the healthcare sector [27, 37, 38]. [35] confirmed that lack of knowledge, trust, and ignorance of stakeholders are a few main social barriers to the adoption. Also, increased job insecurity among doctors or nurses is largely discussed in this domain [39].

Another important social barrier is the emotional dependence of patients on hospitals staffs that are missing in non-human caregivers [26, 29, 37]. According to [34], the biggest challenge to the healthcare sector is the social acceptance of AI and robotics models among the staff and patients. Accuracy and effective monitoring of disease assessment by robots and AI models are few other social challenges discussed in previous studies [40]. Also, the privacy of data and health safety issues were stressed in a few significant healthcare studies [28]. Most importantly, behavioral change challenges have been emphasized in most of the studies [41].

There is a lack of reviews outside of the technical and social barriers in the literature [29]. Studies largely focused on technical aspects/barriers of the adoption [26]. But, pieces of evidence are available where the effectiveness of new technologies have been challenged due to cultural biases and environmental issues despite their technical benefits are established [31, 42]. Recently, [38] used discussed various organizational, managerial, operational, strategic aspects for the successful implementation of AI in the healthcare sector.

Based on the findings of a systematic literature review done by [29], there is a need to increase the understanding of strategic, cultural, political, environmental implications and challenges when selecting AI and other disruptive technologies for the healthcare sector. Technical, cost, and social barriers are given high significance in the academic literature [31]. But, a few studies also indicated the impact of AI on management and environment by including variables like job insecurity, safety, errors, trust and dependence [38, 42]. Taking in a clue, the present study is a pioneer in its attempt to suggest a comprehensive model by including strategic, cultural, environmental, and operational challenges to the AI adoption in hospitals.

3   Research Method

In order to have first-hand understanding of the challenges, possibilities and expectations of the various stakeholders regarding the introduction of AI in their organization, we intend to conduct grounded theory by conducting semi-structured in-depth interviews of the decision makers of various healthcare organizations across the country. The interviews will be audio recorded or video recorded. The recorded interviews will be converted into transcripts (textual data). We intend to use NVivo software to analyze the data in order to generate primary codes followed by axial coding which further leads to themes which helps us create a thematic model.

In addition, we also intend to carry out an "external audit" in which a separate coding is done by an external subject matter expert (SME) to verify that findings of the study are impartial and free from the bias and prejudice of the researchers. To achieve that we will conduct inter-rater reliability test and mention the kappa coefficient which offers the degree of commonality between the study scholars' codes and themes and that of the codes and themes of the external SME. The findings of the study are then discussed and elaborated further by the existing literature.

4 Probable Implications

The present study offers few implications. First, the study helps to identify crucial factors for the successful implementation of AI in hospitals. Project managers and administrators in the health domain should review these contexts while using AI for their administrative and medical purpose. Hospital management should understand the role and significant of AI to fulfil the missing of the firm and gain competitive edge in the society. The study is beneficial as it assesses hospital administrators' views about AI technology and their preparation for the adoption in the long run. The study also indicates drivers and barriers of AI adoption in hospitals. Understanding of these variables is crucial from management perspective as AI adoption considered as a capital expenditure which involves huge cost and commitment by the stakeholders.

References

1. Kakkad, V., Patel, M., Shah, M.: Biometric authentication and image encryption for image security in cloud framework. Multiscale Multidiscip. Model. Exp. Des. 2(4), 233–248 (2019). https://doi.org/10.1007/s41939-019-00049-y
2. Talaviya, T., Shah, D., Patel, N., Yagnik, H., Shah, M.: Implementation of artificial intelligence in agriculture for optimisation of irrigation and application of pesticides and herbicides. Artif. Intell. Agric. (2020). https://doi.org/10.1016/j.aiia.2020.04.002
3. Darko, A., Chan, A.P., Adabre, M.A., Edwards, D.J., Hosseini, M.R., Ameyaw, E.E.: Artificial intelligence in the AEC industry: scientometric analysis and visualization of research activities. Autom. Constr. 112, 103081 (2020)
4. Andoni, M., et al.: Blockchain technology in the energy sector: a systematic review of challenges and opportunities. Renew. Sustain. Energy Rev. 100, 143–174 (2019)
5. Singh, S., Sharma, P.K., Yoon, B., Shojafar, M., Cho, G.H., Ra, I.H.: Convergence of blockchain and artificial intelligence in IoT network for the sustainable smart city. Sustain. Cities Soc. 63, 102364 (2020)
6. Alsamhi, S.H., Ma, O., Ansari, M.S.: Survey on artificial intelligence based techniques for emerging robotic communication. Telecommun. Syst. 72(3), 483–503 (2019). https://doi.org/10.1007/s11235-019-00561-z
7. Lee, J., Davari, H., Singh, J., Pandhare, V.: Industrial artificial intelligence for industry 4.0-based manufacturing systems. Manuf. Lett. 18, 20–23 (2018)
8. Academy of Medical Royal College, Artificial Intelligence in Healthcare (2019). http://www.aomrc.org.uk/wpcontent/uploads/2019/01/Artificial_intelligence_in_healthcare_0119.pdf. Accessed 20 Sept 2020
9. Frost and Sullivan.: From $600 M to $6 Billion, Artificial Intelligence Systems Poised for Dramatic Market Expansion in Healthcare (2016). http://ww2.frost.com/news/press-release/600-m-6-billion-artificial-intelligence-systems-poised-dramatic-market-expansion-healthcare. Accessed 24 Sept 2020
10. Gao, F., Thiebes, S., Sunyaev, A.: Rethinking the meaning of cloud computing for health care: a taxonomic perspective and future research directions. J. Med. Internet Res. 20(7), e10041 (2018)
11. Schönberger, D.: Artificial intelligence in healthcare: a critical analysis of the legal and ethical implications. Int. J. Law Inf. Technol. 27(2), 171–203 (2019)

12. Gao, F., Sunyaev, A.: Context matters: a review of the determinant factors in the decision to adopt cloud computing in healthcare. Int. J. Inf. Manage. **48**, 120–138 (2019)
13. Kuo, M.H.: Opportunities and challenges of cloud computing to improve health care services. J. Med. Internet Res. **13**(3), e67 (2011)
14. Wang, Y., Kung, L., Byrd, T.A.: Big data analytics: understanding its capabilities and potential benefits for healthcare organizations. Technol. Forecast. Soc. Chang. **126**, 3–13 (2018)
15. Tsai, J.M., Cheng, M.J., Tsai, H.H., Hung, S.W., Chen, Y.L.: Acceptance and resistance of telehealth: the perspective of dual-factor concepts in technology adoption. Int. J. Inf. Manage. **49**, 34–44 (2019)
16. Varabyova, Y., Blankart, C.R., Greer, A.L., Schreyögg, J.: The determinants of medical technology adoption in different decisional systems: a systematic literature review. Health Policy **121**(3), 230–242 (2017)
17. Martins, S.M., Ferreira, F.A., Ferreira, J.J., Marques, C.S.: An artificial-intelligence-based method for assessing service quality: insights from the prosthodontics sector. J. Serv. Manag. **31**(2), 291–312 (2020)
18. Kelly, C.J., Karthikesalingam, A., Suleyman, M., Corrado, G., King, D.: Key challenges for delivering clinical impact with artificial intelligence. BMC Med. **17**(1), 195 (2019)
19. Dwivedi, Y.K., et al.: Artificial intelligence (AI): multidisciplinary perspectives on emerging challenges, opportunities, and agenda for research, practice and policy. Int. J. Inf. Manag. 101994 (2019)
20. Noorbakhsh-Sabet, N., Zand, R., Zhang, Y., Abedi, V.: Artificial intelligence transforms the future of health care. Am. J. Med. **132**(7), 795–801 (2019)
21. Luh, J.Y., Thompson, R.F., Lin, S.: Clinical documentation and patient care using artificial intelligence in radiation oncology. J. Am. Coll. Radiol. **16**(9), 1343–1346 (2019)
22. Hamet, P., Tremblay, J.: Artificial intelligence in medicine. Metabolism **69**, S36–S40 (2017)
23. Wiljer, D., Hakim, Z.: Developing an artificial intelligence–enabled health care practice: rewiring health care professions for better care. J. Med. Imaging Radiat. Sci. **50**(4), S8–S14 (2019)
24. Bini, S.A.: Artificial intelligence, machine learning, deep learning, and cognitive computing: what do these terms mean and how will they impact health care? J. Arthroplasty **33**(8), 2358–2361 (2018)
25. Bhattacharya, S., Singh, A., Hossain, M.M.: Strengthening public health surveillance through blockchain technology. AIMS Public Health **6**(3), 326 (2019)
26. Yu, K.H., Beam, A.L., Kohane, I.S.: Artificial intelligence in healthcare. Nat. Biomed. Eng. **2**(10), 719–731 (2018)
27. Zengul, F.D., Weech-Maldonado, R., Ozaydin, B., Patrician, P.A., O'Connor, S.J.: Longitudinal analysis of high-technology medical services and hospital financial performance. Health Care Manage. Rev. **43**(1), 2–11 (2018)
28. Ye, T., et al.: Psychosocial factors affecting artificial intelligence adoption in health care in China: Cross-sectional study. J. Med. Internet Res. **21**(10), e14316 (2019)
29. Cubric, M.: Drivers, barriers and social considerations for AI adoption in business and management: a tertiary study. Technol. Soc. **62**, 101257 (2020)
30. Zayyad, M.A., Toycan, M.: Factors affecting sustainable adoption of e-health technology in developing countries: an exploratory survey of Nigerian hospitals from the perspective of healthcare professionals. PeerJ **6**, e4436 (2018)
31. Reddy, S., Fox, J., Purohit, M.P.: Artificial intelligence-enabled healthcare delivery. J. R. Soc. Med. **112**(1), 22–28 (2019)

32. Maita, A.R.C., Martins, L.C., Paz, C.R.L., Peres, S.M., Fantinato, M.: Process mining through artificial neural networks and support vector machines. Bus. Process Manag. J. **21**(6), 1391–1415 (2015)
33. Merkert, J., Mueller, M., Hubl, M.: A survey of the application of machine learning in decision support systems (2015)
34. Jiang, F., et al.: Artificial intelligence in healthcare: past, present and future. Stroke Vasc. Neurol. **2**(4), 230–243 (2017)
35. Rao, A.S., Verweij, G.: Sizing the prize: what's the real value of AI for your business and how can you capitalise. PwC Publication, PwC (2017)
36. Memeti, S., Pllana, S., Binotto, A., Kołodziej, J., Brandic, I.: Using meta-heuristics and machine learning for software optimization of parallel computing systems: a systematic literature review. Computing **101**(8), 893–936 (2018). https://doi.org/10.1007/s00607-018-0614-9
37. Paré, G., Trudel, M.C.: Knowledge barriers to PACS adoption and implementation in hospitals. Int. J. Med. Informatics **76**(1), 22–33 (2007)
38. Alhashmi, S.F., Salloum, S.A., Mhamdi, C.: Implementing artificial intelligence in the United Arab Emirates healthcare sector: an extended technology acceptance model. Int. J. Inf. Technol. Lang. Stud **3**(3), 27–42 (2019)
39. Maalouf, N., Sidaoui, A., Elhajj, I.H., Asmar, D.: Robotics in nursing: a scoping review. J. Nurs. Scholarsh. **50**(6), 590–600 (2018)
40. Malhotra, R., Chug, A.: Software maintainability: systematic literature review and current trends. Int. J. Software Eng. Knowl. Eng. **26**(08), 1221–1253 (2016)
41. Laranjo, L., et al.: Conversational agents in healthcare: a systematic review. J. Am. Med. Inform. Assoc. **25**(9), 1248–1258 (2018)
42. Sun, T.Q., Medaglia, R.: Mapping the challenges of artificial intelligence in the public sector: evidence from public healthcare. Gov. Inf. Q. **36**(2), 368–383 (2019)

Understanding Factors Influencing the Usage Intention of Mobile Pregnancy Applications

Brinda Sampat[1]([⊠]) [iD], Ashu Sharma[2], and Bala Prabhakar[3]

[1] NMIMS – Global Access School for Continuing Education,
NMIMS University, Mumbai, India
brinda.sampat@nmims.edu
[2] School of Business Management, NMIMS University, Mumbai, India
ashu.sharma@sbm.nmims.edu
[3] Shobhaben Pratapbhai Patel School of Pharmacy and Technology
Management, Mumbai, India
bala.prabhakar@nmims.edu

Abstract. Advancement in digital technology and the need to provide alternate healthcare delivery channels to individuals in developing countries has led to the boom in mobile Health (mHealth). A wide range of mHealth applications (apps) and services are available today to combat the maternal and newborn health disparities in India. Yet, there is scant research in understanding the predictors of pregnant women's adoption towards pregnancy apps in developing countries. The objective of this study is to identify the most significant predictors influencing behavioural intention to use pregnancy apps. To meet this objective, a conceptual model was developed and empirically tested by extending UTAUT with relevant constructs namely personal innovativeness in IT and perceived risk. A conceptual model along with the hypothesized causal paths among the constructs are empirically validated with the help of structural equation modeling using Smart PLS 3.0 with a sample of 220 pregnant women. Results showed that intention to use pregnancy apps by women was predicted by six influencing factors: performance expectancy, effort expectancy, facilitating conditions, social influence, personal innovativeness and attitude. Perceived risk had no significant effect on the behavioural intention to use pregnancy apps.

Keywords: mHealth · Mobile pregnancy apps · UTAUT · Developing country · Perceived risk · Personal innovativeness · Health informatics · Pregnancy

1 Introduction

Health 2.0 has enabled to focus more on patient care due to the evolving relations between healthcare providers and patients. Information and Communication Technologies (ICT) usage by hospitals and healthcare professionals has increased tremendously which has enabled new forms of communication between patients and health professionals (Antheunis et al. 2013). There is a shift towards patient empowerment in maternal care, which now accommodates electronic devices into its functioning by incorporating the use of shared maternity care needs. Blogs, wikis, forums, discussion

© IFIP International Federation for Information Processing 2020
Published by Springer Nature Switzerland AG 2020
S. K. Sharma et al. (Eds.): TDIT 2020, IFIP AICT 617, pp. 641–654, 2020.
https://doi.org/10.1007/978-3-030-64849-7_57

groups, social media, mobile health (mHealth) apps have played an important role in eliciting information and gaining support about early motherhood and parenting matters (Doty and Dworkin 2014). Pregnant women consider information obtained through online platforms to be reliable and of good quality (Szwajcer et al. 2008; Huberty et al. 2013). The information found online plays a significant role in women's decision-making during pregnancy (Lagan et al. 2010).

In an increasing digitized world, the introduction of smart phone has revolutionized the way in which healthcare services are provided. Mobile applications (apps) are end user software that are designed to be used on mobile devices like smartphones and tablets. During the first quarter of 2020, there were 43,285 mHealth apps available in the Google Play store, according to the study published in May 2020 by Statista (2019a). According to a report by Statista (2019b), published in May 2020, over 500 million users in India will use mobile phone internet by 2023.

There is a decline in the extended family structure in India. The use of digital media has increased tremendously in supporting the needs of pregnant women. Consultations are limited by time particularly in a busy clinical setting. Women seek information from online media and pregnancy-related apps to search, share personal experiences and information about pregnancy and parenting. The accessibility, pervasiveness and popularity of mobile pregnancy apps make them a cost-effective and easy way for women to monitor their health. However, these apps are fairly new in developing countries, which means that the behavioural intention for women to use them are not completely understood. Thus, the objective of this study is to understand the factors that may directly and indirectly influence user's behavioural intention to use pregnancy apps.

2 Literature Review

Maternal care now accommodates electronic devices into its functioning by incorporating the use of mHealth apps. According to study by Trip et al. (2014), out of the pregnancy apps available in the app distribution platforms, forty per cent of the apps were informative, thirteen per cent interactive, nineteen per cent had medical tools, eleven per cent were social media apps. This study also points that the reliance on healthcare professionals may be reduced with the proliferation of such interactive and personalized apps.

These findings were confirmed by a study in Dublin where women had used an app during pregnancy. Women drew their attention to digital media to get information related to pregnancy, subscribed to the use of online discussion forums, shared their pregnancy photos and status on social media, used micro-blogs and podcasts. Disadvantaged women in Ireland reported high levels of digital media usage during pregnancy to obtain health information (O'Higgins et al. 2014). Similar findings were observed in a focus group study carried out in Australia by Lupton (2017). This study suggested, social media, mobile apps, content-sharing platforms and online platforms were very important to the participants to connect with family and friends, post images about their pregnancy, track their pregnancy, and child's development. Maternal subjects used social media features provided on smartphone apps as a new form of communication, or socialization whilst staying at home. Women view health apps as a means to monitor and improve their pregnancies, health, and their children's development and health (Johnson 2014).

A study on pregnancy and parenting apps usage by 410 Australian women revealed that women found apps useful in providing information, documenting changes in their own bodies, self-monitoring foetal development or child development and providing reassurance. However, while using these media the participants in the focus group had not considered the issues of third-party access and use of personal data. Women were aware of the digital ties these apps had however, they were not fully aware of some of the privacy challenges these apps posed (Lupton and Pedersen 2016).

Convenience, immediacy, ease of access, sharing experiences and easy access to information were the major benefits of pregnancy apps according to the participants in South Korea. Information concerning signs of risk and disease during pregnancy was searched most often followed by physical changes in the body, prenatal education, and breast-feeding (Lee and Moon 2016). Features in pregnancy apps can help pregnant women make informed choices about nutrition, weight gain and development of the baby. According to a study in Australia, parents used online media such as social media platforms, blogs, websites, online discussion forums, apps during pregnancy as they provided immediate, regular, detailed, entertaining, customized, practical, professional, reassuring and unbiased information (Lupton 2016). In another study participants described pregnancy apps being as more significant and beneficial than other forms of health communication in receiving information related to pregnancy (Rodger et al. 2013). Participants in a randomized controlled trial demonstrated higher use of mobile applications as against the use of distributed notebooks to record details about their pregnancy (Ledford et al. 2016).

3   Theoretical Framework

The success of any Information System (IS) depends on the way users accept it (Venkatesh et al. 2003). The most extensively used models to understand technology acceptance are Theory of Reasoned Action (TRA), Theory of Planned Behaviour (TPB), Technology Acceptance Model (TAM) and Unified Theory of Acceptance and Use of Technology (UTAUT).

3.1   UTAUT

UTAUT model focusses on explaining user intentions towards IS usage. The theory has key constructs performance expectancy, effort expectancy, social influence, and facilitating conditions which act as the direct determinants of behaviour intention to use (Venkatesh et al. 2003). Gender, voluntariness of use, experience and age are posited to moderate the impact of the four main constructs on usage intention and behaviour (Venkatesh et al. 2003). Critics believe that attitude leading to behaviour is missing in this model and that intention to use may or may not lead to use behaviour. In this study, the UTAUT model provides the theoretical framework underpinning the research which is extended with personal innovativeness and perceived risk to understand and empirically test the factors that influence user's intention to use mobile pregnancy apps in a developing country's context (Refer Fig. 1).

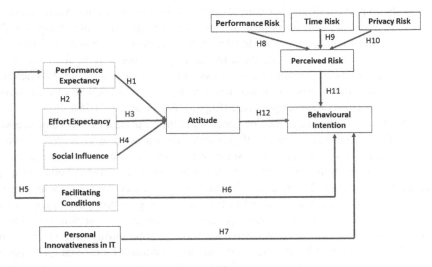

Fig. 1. Proposed Research Model

3.2 Performance Expectancy

Users are inclined to use a technology if they find it useful and advantageous in their day-to-day activities (Alalwan et al. 2016; Davis 1989). Performance expectancy in the context of pregnancy app usage is the degree to which users believe that using pregnancy apps would improve their ability to manage their health. When users perceive pregnancy apps useful in seeking information and managing their health, the perception generates positive attitude towards using them. Thus, it is reasonable to hypothesize that:

H1:   Performce expectancy has a positive and significant effect on attitude to use pregnancy apps

3.3 Effort Expectancy

Effort expectancy is defined as "the degree of ease associated with the use of the system" (Venkatesh et al. 2003, p. 450). Studies related to mHealth applications (Zhang et al.2014) have pointed out that effort expectancy is a major attribute leading to intention to use these systems. Thus, the hypothesis,

H2:   Effort expectancy has a positive and significant effect on performance expectancy to use pregnancy apps

When users perceive using pregnancy apps less complex and requiring less effort to use them, they will use the apps. This leads to the following hypothesis,

H3:   Effort expectancy has a positive and significant effect on attitude to use pregnancy apps

3.4 Social Influence

Social influence is defined as "the degree to which an individual perceives how important others believe he or she should use the new system" (Venkatesh et al. 2003). Social influence helps one understand the fact that though an individual may not have a positive attitude to use a particular technology, how under the influence of family, friends one may use it anyway as it may be expected of one to do so (Venkatesh and Morris 2000). Thus, the following hypothesis is postulated

H4:   Social Influence has a positive and significant effect on attitude to use pregnancy apps

3.5 Facilitating Conditions

Facilitating Conditions (FC) define a users' belief that infrastructure (technical and organizational) are available to support the use of the system (Venkatesh et al. 2003; Dwivedi et al. 2016). In the case of mobile pregnancy apps, not all Indian users have equal access to information, mobile phones, knowledge, internet connectivity and other resources that enable the usage of these apps. Thus, the following hypotheses is proposed,

H5:   Facilitating Conditions has a positive and significant effect on performance expectancy to use pregnancy apps
H6:   Facilitating Conditions has a positive and significant effect on intention to use pregnancy apps

3.6 Personal Innovativeness

Personal Innovativeness in IT describes the tendency of an individual to adopt a product/service relatively before others (Jackson et al. 2013; Lassar et al. 2005; Agarwal and Prasad 1998; Rogers 1983). Agarwal and Prasad (1998) referred to PI as the degree to which a person believes that he/she is positively predisposed towards the use of new technologies. The extent to which a user is open to experimenting, experiencing new technologies indicates their novelty and innovativeness-seeking abilities.

H7:   Personal Innovativeness has a positive and significant effect on intention to use pregnancy apps

3.7 Perceived Risk

Perceived risk refers to the likelihood of certain negative outcomes and consequences from engaging in those behaviours. In the context of pregnancy apps, it is defined as "the degree to which an individual perceives certain negative outcomes and the danger and severity of negative consequences from using pregnancy apps". Performance risk refers to "the possibility of the product malfunctioning and not performing as it was designed and advertised and therefore failing to deliver the desired benefits" (Featherman and Pavlou 2003). It refers to the losses which a user may incur due to incorrect processing of health information.

H8:   Performance Risk is negatively associated with Perceived Risk of using pregnancy apps

In the context of pregnancy apps, some user may be time conscious and guard against the loss of time they may incur in having to learn how to setup, use and maintain the app.

H9:   Time Risk is negatively associated with Perceived Risk of using pregnancy apps

Researchers have studied the effects of privacy risks in the context of online services (Cocosila 2013; Lee 2009; Featherman and Pavlou 2003; Shareef et al. 2014) which affects their intention to use those services. Pregnancy apps may communicate personal information about users with third parties. This uncertainty of how personal information will be used leads to privacy concerns related to the app usage. This leads to the following hypotheses

H10:   Privacy Risk is negatively associated with Perceived Risk of using pregnancy apps

H11:   Perceived Risk is negatively associated with Behavioural Intention of using pregnancy apps

3.8 Attitude

Attitude towards using a system is defined as the extent to which a user positively or negatively evaluates that system to carry out the behaviour in question. In mHealth, a number of studies (Hajiheydari and Ashkani 2018; Canhoto and Arp 2017; Du et al. 2016; Zhao et al. 2018; Deng et al. 2018) have supported the relationship between attitude and behavioural intention. Considering the importance of attitude in IS adoption research, the following hypothesis is proposed:

H12:   Attitude is positively associated with Behavioural Intention to use pregnancy apps

4 Research Methodology

4.1 Instrument Design

Instrument developed for this study borrowed scale items from previously established studies. As the scale items in the study were modified to suit the context of this study, it is essential to test the validity and reliability of the scale. Tests for the construct validity, face validity, content validity, discriminant and convergent validity were performed. Multiple items were used to measure constructs, in order to increase the reliability of the construct. These were measured on a five-point Likert scale with anchors ranging from 1 = "Strongly Disagree" to 5 = "Strongly Agree". The construct validity is met by examining discriminant and convergent validity (Forner and Larcker 1981).

4.2 Data Collection and Sampling

The structured questionnaire was emailed to the participants to collect the primary data for the study. An online link was embedded in an email and sent to the participants. Questionnaires were mailed to 750 participants across the country. 243 completed questionnaires were obtained of which 220 were used for further analysis. 23 responses were eliminated in the process as they were incomplete or had the same value marked for all the questions in the survey. The final response rate was 32.4%.

4.3 Demographic Profile of the Respondents

The sample consisted of 220 females. Table 1 illustrates the respondents' demographic de-tails. 85% of the respondents were less than the age of 35 indicating that the sample comprised of young or middle-aged respondents. 61% of the population was well educated and 47% of the respondents were working professionals.

Table 1. Demographic details of the respondents

Measure	Items	Frequency	Sample percentage
Gender			
	Female	220	100
Age			
	25 or Under	8	3.64
	26–35	179	81.36
	36–45	33	15
Educational background			
	HSC	6	2.72
	Graduate	67	30.45
	Post Graduate	135	61.36
	Other	12	5.45

(continued)

Table 1. (*continued*)

Measure	Items	Frequency	Sample percentage
Occupation			
	Student	6	2.72
	Working Professional	102	46.36
	Self-employed	33	15
	Homemaker	75	34.09
Location			
	Mumbai	184	83.63
	Others	36	16.36
How many Pregnancy apps do you have installed on your phone?			
	1	152	69.09
	2	116	52.72
	3	4	1.81
	More than three	7	3.18

Note: n = 220, Others (Haryana, Kolkata, Nagpur, Jammu)

5 Data Analysis

Tests for missing values and multicollinearity were conducted. The sample did not suffer from any multicollinearity issues as the VIF values were less than 7 (Hair et al. 2011). The data analysis process involves two steps proposed by Hair et al. (2009). The first step aims at evaluating the measurement model followed by the structural model.

5.1 Reliability and Validity Tests

In order to check the reliability of the constructs used in the instrument, the Cronbach alpha values were calculated. Table 2 represents the factor loadings for all constructs were higher than 0.5 (Byrne 2001) and Cronbach's α values ranged from 0.749 to 0.922 establishing reliability of the measure. Convergent and discriminant validity in the study were met as mentioned in Table 3.

Table 2. Reliability and convergent validity of the final measurement model

Constructs	Items	Item Loadings	Cronbach's Alpha	rho_A	Composite Reliability	Average Variance Extracted (AVE)
Performance Expectancy	PE1	0.775	0.749	0.755	0.857	0.666
	PE2	0.84				
	PE3	0.832				
Effort Expectancy	EE1	0.874	0.899	0.9	0.929	0.767
	EE2	0.897				
	EE3	0.881				
	EE4	0.85				
Social Influence	SI1	0.892	0.787	0.795	0.877	0.706
	SI2	0.888				
	SI3	0.731				
Facilitating Conditions	FC1	0.948	0.859	0.879	0.934	0.857
	FC2	0.924				
Personal Innovativeness	PI1	0.872	0.813	0.833	0.88	0.652
	PI2	0.637				
	PI3	0.768				
	PI4	0.922				
Perceived Risk	***	***	0.907	0.919	0.925	0.583
Performance Risk	PERF1	0.839	0.796	0.819	0.877	0.703
	PERF2	0.858				
	PERF3	0.819				
Privacy Risk	PRIV1	0.991	0.901	0.907	0.931	0.772
	PRIV2	0.891				
	PRIV3	0.935				
	PRIV4	0.878				
Time Risk	TRISK1	0.96	0.916	0.916	0.91	0.923
	TRISK2	0.961				
Attitude	ATT1	0.908	0.907	0.909	0.935	0.783
	ATT2	0.867				
	ATT3	0.864				
	ATT4	0.9				
Behavioural Intention	INT1	0.918	0.922	0.929	0.951	0.865
	INT2	0.936				
	INT3	0.936				

Note: *** No loading.

Table 3. Discriminant Validity - Fornell Larker criteria

	Attitude	Behavioural intention	Effort expectancy	Facilitating conditions	Perceived Risk	Performance Risk	Performance Expectancy	Personal Innovativeness	Privacy Risk	Social Influence	Time Risk
Attitude	0.885*										
Behavioural Intention	0.702	0.93*									
Effort Expectancy	0.392	0.36	0.876*								
Facilitating conditions	0.315	0.346	0.592	0.936*							
Perceived Risk	-0.06	0.017	-0.355	-0.241	0.764*						
Performance Risk	-0.023	0.025	-0.187	-0.19	0.806	0.839*					
Performance Expectancy	0.607	0.463	0.671	0.406	-0.246	-0.146	0.816				
Personal Innovativeness	0.413	0.323	0.481	0.33	-0.09	0.01	0.299	0.807			
Privacy Risk	-0.055	0.016	-0.321	-0.174	0.929	0.607	-0.23	-0.081	0.879		
Social Influence	0.516	0.504	0.236	0.105	0.084	0.133	0.351	0.493	0.05	0.84	
Time Risk	-0.079	0.000	-0.418	-0.298	0.83	0.561	-0.257	-0.167	0.666	0.052	0.961

Note: * Square root of AVE

After establishing the reliability and validity of constructs, the hypothesized relations in the model were tested using PLS-SEM. The path coefficients and the corresponding p-values are presented in Table 4.

Table 4. Results

Hypothesis	Path	B values	t-statistics	P values	Result
H1	Performance Expectancy-> Attitude	0.108	4.698	0.00	Supported
H2	Effort Expectancy-> Performance Expectancy	0.115	5.745	0.00	Supported
H3	Effort Expectancy-> Attitude	0.127	0.223	0.82	Not Supported
H4	Social Influence-> Attitude	0.096	3.603	0.00	Supported
H5	Facilitating condition-> Performance Expectancy	0.13	0.101	0.92	Not Supported
H6	Facilitating condition-> Behavioural Intention	0.068	2.334	0.02	Supported
H7	Personal Innovativeness in IT-> Behavioural Intention	0.075	0.119	0.91	Not Supported
H8	Performance Risk-> Perceived Risk	0.033	9.492	0.00	Supported
H9	Time Risk-> Perceived Risk	0.019	15.706	0.00	Supported
H10	Privacy Risk-> Perceived Risk	0.028	19.352	0.00	Supported
H11	Perceived Risk-> Behavioural Intention	0.073	1.298	0.20	Not Supported
H12	Attitude-> Behavioural Intention	0.101	6.482	0.00	Supported

6 Results

This research is concerned with understanding the factors that influence the behavioural intention of women to use mobile pregnancy apps. The model fit indices include SRMR as 0.097, and RMS theta as 0.191. This study aimed at understanding and explaining the significance of these constructs. It also aimed at understanding the driver construct and thus PLS-SEM was used in this study. Smart PLS 3.2.8 (Ringle et al. 2015) was used to analyse the data. The sample size in PLS is considered by the often cited ten times rule Barclay et al. (1995). The sample size in this study meets the recommended rule. The results obtained from the study are presented in Table 4. H1, H2, H4, H6, H8, H9, H10, H12 are supported whereas H3, H5, H7, H11 are not supported.

7 Discussion

In the study on intention to use pregnancy apps, the relationship between performance expectancy and attitude was found to be significant. If women perceive pregnancy apps useful, they develop a positive attitude towards them. Effort expectancy was found to be a significant predictor of performance expectancy. Effort expectancy was not found to be a significant predictor of attitude. This result is not in affirmation with studies that have indicated a strong relationship between the effort expectancy and attitude to use online services (Ruane and Wallace 2013; To et al. 2007; Lee 2009). A reason to this could be as women were educated, belonged to cities and thus, were familiar with the use of mobile applications. Social influence was significantly related to attitude. Women rely on expertise by friends for making information seeking choices during pregnancy (Tiidenberg 2017; Lupton 2017; Lupton and Pedersen 2016). Users did not feel that the access to knowledge and resources would help them improve performance. Facilitating conditions did not have an effect on performance expectancy. The relationship between facilitating conditions and behavioural intention was significant. The relationship between personal innovativeness and behavioural intention was significant. This implies women are wanting to learn new techniques to get more information about their foetus and manage their health well. The relation between perceived risk and behavioural intention was insignificant. Women usually will learn new things for the baby. Most women did not share their photos on these apps and thus did not fear loss of information.

8 Conclusion

From a theoretical perspective, this study adds to the field in two additional ways. First, the study extends UTAUT by adding perceived risk and personal innovativeness in IT to understand user's behavioural intention to use pregnancy apps. Second, the findings extend the existent knowledge on the relationships of UTAUT in the context of mobile pregnancy apps in a developing country.

References

Agarwal, R., Prasad, J.: A conceptual and operational definition of personal innovativeness in the domain of information technology. Inf. Syst. Res. 9(2), 204–215 (1998)

Antheunis, M.L., Tates, K., Nieboer, T.E.: Patients' and health professionals' use of social media in health care: motives, barriers and expectations. Patient Educ. Couns. 92(3), 426–431 (2013)

Alalwan, A. A., Dwivedi, Y. K., Rana, N. P., Williams, M. D.: Consumer adoption of mobile banking in Jordan. J. Enterp. Inf. Manag. (2016)

Barclay, D., Higgins, C., Thompson, R.: The partial least squares (PLS) approach to casual modeling: personal computer adoption and use as an Illustration (1995)

Byrne, B.M.: Structural equation modeling with AMOS, EQS, and LISREL: Comparative approaches to testing for the factorial validity of a measuring instrument. Int. J. Test. 1(1), 55–86 (2001)

Canhoto, A.I., Arp, S.: Exploring the factors that support adoption and sustained use of health and fitness wearables. J. Mark. Manag. 33(1–2), 32–60 (2017)

Cocosila, M.: Role of user a priori attitude in the acceptance of mobile health: an empirical investigation. Electron. Markets 23(1), 15–27 (2013)

Davis, F.D.: Perceived usefulness, perceived ease of use, and user acceptance of information technology. MIS Q. 319–340 (1989)

Deng, Z., Hong, Z., Ren, C., Zhang, W., Xiang, F.: What predicts patients' adoption intention toward mHealth services in China: empirical study. JMIR mHealth uHealth 6(8), e172 (2018)

Doty, J.L., Dworkin, J.: Online social support for parents: a critical review. Marriage Family Rev. 50(2), 174–198 (2014). https://doi.org/10.1080/01494929.2013.834027

Du, H., Venkatakrishnan, A., Youngblood, G.M., Ram, A., Pirolli, P.: A group-based mobile application to increase adherence in exercise and nutrition programs: a factorial design feasibility study. JMIR mHealth Health 4(1), e4 (2016)

Dwivedi, Y.K., Shareef, M.A., Simintiras, A.C., Lal, B., Weerakkody, V.: A generalised adoption model for services: a cross-country comparison of mobile health (m-health). Gov. Inf. Q. **33**(1), 174–187 (2016)

Featherman, M.S., Pavlou, P.A.: Predicting e-services adoption: a perceived risk facets perspective. Inter. J. Hum.-comput. stud. **59**(4), 451–474 (2003)

Fornell, C., Larcker, D.F.: Evaluating structural equation models with unobservable variables and measurement error. J. Market. Res. **18**(1), 39–50 (1981)

Hair, J.F., Black, W.C., Babin, B.J., Anderson, R.E., Tatham, R.L.: Análise multivariada de dados. Bookman Editoral (2009)

Hair, J.F., Ringle, C.M., Sarstedt, M.: PLS-SEM: indeed a silver bullet. J. Market. Theory Pract. **19**(2), 139–152 (2011)

Hajiheydari, N., Ashkani, M.: Mobile application user behavior in the developing countries: a survey in Iran. Inf. Syst. **77**, 22–33 (2018)

Huberty, J., Dinkel, D., Beets, M.W., Coleman, J.: Describing the use of the internet for health, physical activity, and nutrition information in pregnant women. Matern. Child Health J. **17**(8), 1363–1372 (2013)

Jackson, J.D., Mun, Y.Y., Park, J.S.: An empirical test of three mediation models for the relationship between personal innovativeness and user acceptance of technology. Inf. Manag. **50**(4), 154–161 (2013)

Johnson, S.A.: "Maternal devices", social media and the self-management of pregnancy, mothering and child health. Societies **4**(2), 330–350 (2014)

Lagan, B.M., Sinclair, M., George Kernohan, W.: Internet use in pregnancy informs women's decision making: a web-based survey. Birth **37**(2), 106–115 (2010)

Lassar, W. M., Manolis, C., Lassar, S. S.: The relationship between consumer innovativeness, personal characteristics, and online banking adoption. Inte. J. Bank Market. (2005)

Ledford, C.J., Canzona, M.R., Cafferty, L.A., Hodge, J.A.: Mobile application as a prenatal education and engagement tool: a randomized controlled pilot. Patient Educ. Couns. **99**(4), 578–582 (2016)

Lee, M.C.: Factors influencing the adoption of internet banking: an integration of TAM and TPB with perceived risk and perceived benefit. Electron. Commerce Res. Appl. **8**(3), 130–141 (2009)

Lee, Y., Moon, M.: Utilization and content evaluation of mobile applications for pregnancy, birth, and child care. Healthc. Inf. Res. **22**(2), 73–80 (2016)

Lupton, D., Pedersen, S.: An australian survey of women's use of pregnancy and parenting apps. Women Birth **29**(4), 368–375 (2016)

Lupton, D.: It just gives me a bit of peace of mind: Australian women's use of digital media for pregnancy and early mother-hood. Societies **7**(3), 25 (2017)

Lupton, D.: The use and value of digital media for information about pregnancy and early motherhood: a focus group study. BMC Pregnancy Childbirth **16**(1), 1–10 (2016)

O'Higgins, A., Murphy, O.C., Egan, A., Mullaney, L., Sheehan, S., Turner, M.: The use of digital media by women using the maternity services in a developed country. Ir. Med. J. **107**(10), 313–315 (2014)

Ringle, C. M., Wende, S., Becker, J. M.: SmartPLS 3. Boenningstedt: SmartPLS GmbH (2015). http://www.smartpls.com

Rodger, D., et al.: Pregnant women's use of information and communications technologies to access pregnancy-related health information in South Australia. Aust. J. Primary Health **19**(4), 308–312 (2013)

Rogers, E.M.: Diffusion of innovations. The Free Press, New York (1983)

Ruane, L., Wallace, E.: Generation Y females online: insights from brand narratives. Qual. Market Res. Int. J. **16**(3), 315–335 (2013)

Shareef, M.Akhter., Kumar, V., Kumar, U.: Predicting mobile health adoption behaviour: A demand side perspective. J. Customer Behav. **13**(3), 187–205 (2014)

Statista: Number of mHealth apps available at Google Play from 1st quarter 2015 to 3rd quarter 2019 (2019a). https://www.statista.com/statistics/779919/health-apps-available-google-play-worldwide/. Accessed 25 Mar 2020

Statista: Number of smartphone users across India from 2017–2022 (2019b). https://www.statista.com/statistics/938544/mhealth-market-size-forecast-globally/. Accessed 25 Mar 2020

Szwajcer, E.M., Hiddink, G.J., Maas, L., Koelen, M.A., Van Woerkum, C.M.: Nutrition-related information-seeking behaviours of women trying to conceive and pregnant women: evidence for the life course perspective. Fam. Pract. **25**(suppl_1), i99–i104 (2008)

Tripp, N., Hainey, K., Liu, A., Poulton, A., Peek, M., Kim, J., Nanan, R.: An emerging model of maternity care: smartphone, midwife, doctor? Women Birth **27**(1), 64–67 (2014)

Tiidenberg, K., Baym, N.K. : Learn it, buy it, work it: Intensive pregnancy on Instagram. Soc. Media+ Soc. **3**(1) (2017)

Venkatesh, V., Morris, M.G.: Why don't men ever stop to ask for directions? Gender, social influence, and their role in technology acceptance and usage behavior. MIS Q. 115–139 (2000)

Venkatesh, V., Morris, M.G., Davis, G.B., Davis, F.D.: User acceptance of information technology: Toward a unified view. MIS Q. 425–478 (2003)

Zhang, X., Guo, X., Lai, K.H., Guo, F., Li, C.: Understanding gender differences in m-health adoption: a modified theory of reasoned action model. Telemed. e-Health **20**(1), 39–46 (2014)

Zhao, Y., et al.: MHealth approach to promote Oral HIV self-testing among men who have sex with men in China: a qualitative description. BMC Pub. Health **18**(1), 1–8 (2018)

Internet of Things

A Data Driven Approach for Customer Relationship Management for Airlines with Internet of Things & Artificial Intelligence

Rajesh G. Pillai and Poonam Devrakhyani[✉]

Toulouse Business School, Place Alphonse Jourdian,
66810 Toulouse Cedex 7, CS, France
{r.gangadharan.pillai, p.devrakhyani}@tbs-ducation.org

Abstract. Customer Relationship Management is a critical aspect for all service industries and extremely important in aviation industry. With the changing aviation scenario, the travel industry is facing more challenges. Identifying and retaining the profitable customers is very essential for survivability. Customers are well informed about the services that offer them the maximum value proposition and retaining high value customers is very challenging. Airlines currently use many techniques for CRM, but there are drawbacks in the system which can be complimented with emerging technologies. Artificial intelligence & Internet of Things are evolving domains, which have gained lot of importance during the last decade, predominantly due the capacity of systems to gather, store, process & transfer huge amount of data. This paper is indented to improve CRM with the prudent use of AI & IOT and involve airports in implementing smart CRM, ensuring long term profitability and sustained revenues.

Keywords: Smart customer relationship management · Smart airport · Internet of Things · Artificial Intelligence

1 Introduction

Customer relationship management (CRM) is a critical factor across all the service industries. CRM is defined as the approach of managing an organization's interaction with its current and potential customers based on customer data, collected from customer's interactions with the organization. The customer data is analyzed using specialized tools to improve relationships with customers, focusing on customer retention and generating additional revenues. The data required for CRM comes from different communication channels, like official website of firm, call centers, emails, combined loyalty programs with other organizations etc. Recently many organizations have started data mining and use of social media to gather customer information, so that better service can be offered to the customer. Whatever be the CRM implemented by the organization, data and accurate analysis of data is very critical for successful CRM implementation.

Airlines are operating on very narrow margins due to competition and global economic crisis due to pandemic. Many airlines are trying to reduce the operating costs

S. K. Sharma et al. (Eds.): TDIT 2020, IFIP AICT 617, pp. 657–672, 2020.
https://doi.org/10.1007/978-3-030-64849-7_58

by improvements in operation, optimization of fleet and routes and reduction in manpower. However, customer cannot be ignored in the process of regaining operational efficiency. The core service for all airlines is providing basic transportation. All other services like choice of in-flight entertainment, onboard meals, quality of cabin crew, special assistance etc. are supplementary services aiding the core service. Supplementary services help in product differentiation of the core product and create a competitive advantage by facilitating the use of core service and enhancing the value of the core service. To retain customers and improve customer retention, emerging technologies can be used, which can assist airlines in enhancing both the core and supplementary services. An airline's effective CRM program can be a significant factor for sustainable revenues, product differentiation, achieving operational efficiency and long term growth of the organization.

Research towards new paradigm shift for customer relationship management in airlines was carried out by IBM institute of Business Value [1]. The use of data and data mining techniques for customer relationship management [2] has been researched. Studies on behavior of airline customers based on their perception of choice and importance of those factors to develop the appropriate marketing strategies were also carried out [3]. CRM studies at regional level for different airlines at was also done by many researchers [4–6]. Many airlines uses social media for data collection and improvements in CRM [5, 7–9]. However, CRM methods are on the verge of radical changes with emerging technologies [10–13]. This paper tries to propose a smart data driven method for improvement of CRM with prudent use of Artificial Intelligence and Internet of Things and make an airport a key stakeholder of CRM activities.

2   Research Methodology

The research started with interactions with some customers who travel frequently on international airlines, and it was observed that frequent travelers mind each small factor in service of airlines and are not hesitant to switch their loyalty. The existing CRM systems followed by airlines were analyzed and to understand how major airlines try to retain the customers and what are the drawbacks in these systems. Interviews and surveys were carried out among customers to understand the major factors that causes passenger to switch the airlines. The scope of emerging technologies like AI and IoT was further investigated to improve the CRM. The research methodology is briefly described in Fig. 1.

3   Importance of CRM for Airlines

Customers are profitable over a period of time and studies shows that profit can increase by 35 to 85% by retaining just 5% of customers [14]. Getting a customer and retaining him as a loyal customer in long term is an extremely challenging, but highly rewarding activity for airlines. Identifying a potentially profitable customer is a tricky task as customer has lot of options for travel. Airlines use different ways to collect customer information. Most of the airlines use loyalty programs individually or as a

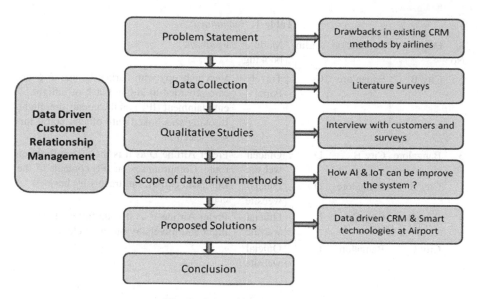

Fig. 1. Research methodology

group of airlines to get customer data and use them for customer relationship management activities. Promotional offers, discounted rates, upgrade of travel class and accessibility to premium facilities are provided to customers based on this data to retain the customer. But there are few drawbacks in the existing method of implementation of CRM based on loyalty programs.

Table 1 shows the behavior of a passenger X, who made 4 international journeys from Bangalore International Airport Limited (BIAL) in a year to different destinations using different airlines all the times. The passenger has also made multiple journeys inside the country which has not been considered for the analysis.

Table 1. Typical passenger travel pattern

Sl No	Origin	Destination	Airline	Mode of booking	Feedback
1	Bangalore	City A	A	Official website	Very disappointed with baggage handling of the airline and decides not to fly with this airline anymore
	City A	Bangalore	A		
2	Bangalore	City B	B	Travel Portal	Prefer Airline B, though it's a connection flight and happy with the experience. Not booking return on this airline as it's a long connection. Booking was not linked with official site as travel portal offered free seat selection

(*continued*)

Table 1. (*continued*)

Si No	Origin	Destination	Airline	Mode of booking	Feedback
	City B	Bangalore	C	Travel Portal	Very unhappy with Airline C, due to poor care provided to kid and lack of inflight entertainment (IFE) on the connection flight. Booking was linked with official portal for seat selection
3	Bangalore	City B	D	Official website	Prefer Airline D as it is the fastest flight on route. Compromises on IFE contents of the European carrier, but travels by business class
	City B	Bangalore	D	Official website	
4	Bangalore	City C	E	Official website	Prefer Airline E as it's the fastest direct flight and travels by business class
	City C	Bangalore	E	Official website	

A few points can be clearly understood from the travel pattern.

- A passenger may use different channels for airline ticket booking. It can be the airline official website or mobile app or third-party travel portals or agents, depending on the convenience and cost. So the data obtained from the official sites alone is not sufficient to understand the travel pattern of a customer.
- Travel history at Si No. 1 shows after travelling, the customer has decided not to travel by the airline anymore. The data indicates that the passenger had used the official app for booking ticket on the airline (Airline A). The booking was done for a higher fare compared to travel portals, but it was done due to convenient procedures for visa approval. But the baggage experience with the airline was very poor, which made the customer decide that he will not prefer this airline anymore. The customer has done lot of travel after that, but never preferred this airline again. Airline keeps sending mails and promotions in the passenger's mail, without any response. In this case, the airline A is not aware of losing the customer and why the customer switched.
- Travel history at Si No. 2 shows booking on third party portal as the inward and outward journey was done on different airlines and customer preferred paying in his local currency. Onward journey shows passenger was extremely happy with Airline B, because of the special attention provided to the kid, quality of food and the choice of in-flight entertainment. He may prefer this airline on future journeys. But as the booking was done on third party site and not linked to any official site, the airline is unaware of a happy and satisfied customer.
- The return journey of this trip is on a different airline (Airline C). The customer linked his booking to the official site for choice of seat and registered to the loyalty program. But as the customer was not satisfied by the cabin crew service offered by the airline, particularly the delay in serving meals to the kids travelling along with,

this airline was never preferred again. The customer was also unhappy with the seating comfort, and the lack of in-flight entertainment provided on the connecting flight. The passenger has made journeys after that, but never preferred this airline. This airline also is unaware that it has lost this customer, but still tries to attract the customer with constant communication, as he has registered in loyalty program.

- Travel history at Si No 3, indicates travel to the same destination, but on a different airline (Airline D). Previous journey also, the customer wanted to book on the same airline, which was the fastest mode of travel on that route. But it could not be done because the journey was planned in a short time and the cost offered by the particular airline was very high compared to fare offered by connection flights. When the customer got sufficient time to plan his next journey, he booked it on the Airline D. The customer was happy with the timings and food, but slightly unhappy with the in-flight entertainment and seating & cabin comfort provided by the airline as this was an old aircraft. But the customer has travelled on business class compared to his previous journeys in economy class.
- Travel history at Si No 4 indicates, the customer has developed his travel choices and is ready to spend more money for travel and his comfort. Again the passenger prefers to fly on business class.

All the airlines mentioned in the case have their own loyalty programs and methods of data collection which act as the base for CRM implementation. The customer here can be considered as a profitable customer based on the travel pattern and willingness to spend. Airline A & C, who still try to attract and retain the customer are clearly losers in this context. Airlines B, D & E haven't lost the customer, but even these airlines have to be careful with CRM to retain this customer and offer the best services.

No CRM methods currently used by airlines can predict this type of customer behavior. The customer mentioned in the case has the potential to become a profitable customer, but drawbacks in the system fail to identify him as s profitable customer due to deficiency in data collection and identifying the reasons for the passenger to switch between airlines. There can be improvements to CRM with use of emerging technologies like Artificial Intelligence & Internet of things, which can be a game changer for airlines in long term.

4   Improved Smart Data Driven CRM for Airlines

The airline market is oligopolic with many airlines providing more or less similar services to the passenger, which make the competition very high and choice abundant for a passenger. An airline with an efficient consumer-centric approach to relationship management will be better positioned to acquire, develop and retain high value customers. An airline's CRM program is the key for product differentiation, achieving operational efficiency and long term business development. To achieve this, the airline has to clearly understand what prompts a customer to switch the airline and who has to be treated as a high value customer.

Decision by a passenger on which airline to travel depends on a lot of factors like cost, convenience & other amenities. The initial choice of an airline by a passenger can be mostly advices from travel agents or friends or based on internet research. Once the passenger uses the airline, he gets a real feel of the services offered by the particular airline. After a journey, a passenger may be fully or partially satisfied by the services offered by the airline or may not be satisfied by the services. Once the passenger is not satisfied, he may decide not to travel by the airline any more or prefer it as the last option.

This paper focuses on two major factors that require attention in CRM and how CRM can be improved by use of emerging technologies ensuring long term revenues.

i. Identification of the factors which results in dissatisfaction to the customer and loss of business and how these can be improved with emerging technology concepts like Internet of Things (IOT) and Artificial Intelligence (AI).
ii. Identification of the high value passengers based on travel history by using advanced technologies at the airport. An airport has to become smart airport using technologies like face recognition and become a centre for data collection.

5 Factors Leading to Customer Dissatisfaction and Loss of Business

There are many factors which make a passenger feel dissatisfied by an airline. Identification of factors leading to passenger rejecting an airline was arrived based on surveys and interactions with passengers. For many passengers, cost of travel was the major factor deciding choice of airline. But there are lots of passengers who are willing to spend little more for comfort and convenience. Airlines have to focus on such passengers for sustained revenues, while not neglecting the cost conscious passengers. Figure 2 shows revenues from a small percentage of high value customers are much higher than the revenues from other passengers.

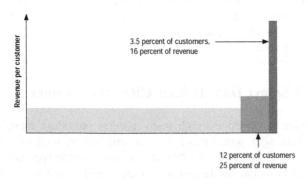

Fig. 2. Airline customer value (IBM analysis)

The core service for airlines is to provide basic transportation. Other services like in-flight entertainment, onboard meals, quality of cabin crew, special assistance etc. are supplementary services aiding the core service. A flower of service model, shown in Fig. 3 was prepared based surveys and interaction with passengers.

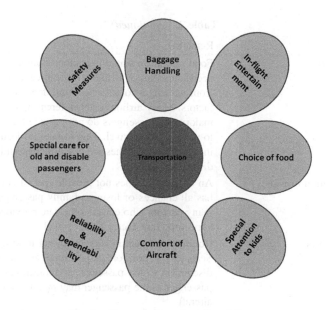

Fig. 3. Flower of services for airlines

The importance of these factors and why these supplementary factors can cause passengers to switch airlines are provided in Table 2.

Table 2. Key reasons for customer switching in Airlines

Factor	Remark
Baggage Handling	Baggage of a passenger is important and requires very careful handling. Loss of baggage, delay in baggage, damages to baggage and theft of items from baggage are few things which create a poor opinion about an airline in customer's mind and can result a customer avoiding an airline. The number of mishandled bags in 2018 was 24.8 million according to SITA [15]. Out of 24.8 million bags mishandled, 18% are damaged and pilfered bags and 5% are stolen. Transfer mishandling is a major reason for delayed bags
In-flight Entertainment	A passenger spending lot of time in aircraft requires entertainment. The choice of in-flight entertainment varies from passenger to passenger and it is dependent on the country of origin, age, personal preferences. Providing good in flight entertainment is an important supplementary factor in passenger retention

(continued)

Table 2. (*continued*)

Factor	Remark
Choice of Food	Food option on board is another complex factor that needs attention of airlines. The choice of food also varies from passenger to passenger and depends on many factors. Many airlines cater different options of food, but majority of passengers do not provide the choice of food to airlines prior travel. This sometimes leads to situation in which some dishes are not sufficient and some of dishes are wasted
Special Attention to Kids	An airline that does not provide special attention to kids has all chances of losing a family passenger. There are many parents who consider the care provided to kids as a very important factor for air travel
Comfort of seats	Comfort of a seat is very important in long haul flights. Seats lose its comfort as the aircraft ages and can result in discomfort to the passenger and rejection of airline by passenger as the passenger may prefer a new comfortable aircraft
Type of aircraft/age of aircraft	There are many passengers who are technically knowledgeable and can select the aircraft based on the seating layout, cabin pressurization, humidity etc. Offering an uncomfortable or old aircraft to a technically educated customer may end up in losing the customer
Reliability & Dependability of the airlines	Issues like delays in journey, trip cancellations also lead to customer dissatisfaction. In many cases, passenger loose connection flights due to delay in one leg of the journey
Special care for old aged/sick and disabled passengers	There are passengers who are old, disabled and suffering from medical conditions who require special assistance for travel. The requirement of these passengers includes wheel chairs and personal attention till the journey is completed. The airlines have to provide preferential treatment to these passengers in coordination with airports
Safety	With emergence of pandemic, safety has become a major concern for most of the passengers. Passengers require clean and sanitized cabin for safer travel, which has become a standard norm for travel. Cleaning and sanitizing the cabins as per standard safety norms adds additional costs to airlines, increase the turnaround time and reduce the operational efficiency of the airlines

6 Use of Emerging Technologies for Enhancing Customer Experience

Many of the existing implementation of CRM fails to get the accurate data for building an efficient CRM. Data and analysis of data is the major building block for any CRM implementation. Some of the attributes that cause passenger switching are intangible. The technologies like Artificial intelligence & Internet of things has gained lot of prominence in the current decade due to their ability to gather and process huge amount of data. With its data handling and data communication capabilities, Artificial Intelligence (AI) and Internet of Things (IOT) are the ideal candidates for improvement in areas where passengers look for satisfaction. Table 3 shows the scope of AI & IOT in retaining the customer for airline along with the suggested improvements in each of the key areas.

Table 3. Brief scope of AI & IOT for CRM

Factor	Enabling technology	Scope of emerging technology
Baggage Handling	IOT	Baggage handling is concern for most of the passengers and most airlines use simple barcodes for baggage handling. Barcodes are cheap, simple and proven technology but require line-of-sight reading by barcode scanners. To reduce the number of lost or delayed baggage, airlines have to comply with IATA Resolution 753, which requires change of technology. Radio Frequency Identification (RFID) tags is an application evolved from the internet of things concept. RFIDs are small electronic chips that can store & transmit the data about the baggage. Handling of baggage can be easily done with low cost RFID tags [16]. The tags can provide real time information of the baggage and it can be easily tracked This information can be provided to the smart mobiles carried by passengers as desired by majority of passengers surveyed. Switching to conventional baggage tagging to RFID baggage tagging can result in customer satisfaction and retention. RFID tagging can also provide information to the airlines to identify and off-load the specific bags in case the passenger is denied boarding or offloaded before flight. In many cases, the delay in off loading bags has resulted in delay to the flight and losses to airlines. This can improve the

(*continued*)

Table 3. (*continued*)

Factor	Enabling technology	Scope of emerging technology
		operating efficiency of the airline. The cost of implementation for airlines is around US\$ 0.1 per passenger, with cost savings of US\$ 0.2 per passenger. The change of technology is beneficial for the airports too with improvement in parameters like time for arrival of bags, number of bags handled and decrease in baggage mishandling rate
In flight Entertainment	IOT	IOT concepts can be very useful in providing appropriate in-flight entertainment to the passengers. Personal choice of the passenger like films, serials etc. can be found from previous history of the passenger. The in-flight view history of a passenger can be collected by small storage devices in IFE which can be mapped to the particular passenger. There can be a central storage of movies and entertainment in the flight, which the cabin crew can load to the IFE of the passenger with connected IFE
Choice of food	AI	Choice of food is highly dependent on person to person, but there can be clues about it food choice from personal information like age, gender and nationality. The typical food usage pattern in a route, the quantity of food wasted etc. can be used as inputs to AI. Artificial intelligence algorithms can be used to predict the food options to be provided based on the details of the travelers, which can reduce the quantity of food wasted and provide each customer the food of his choice. This will allow airlines to reduce the catering expenditure and keep the flyers happy
Special Attention to Kids	IOT	Information about kids travelling has to be handled carefully. The IFE contents in the case have to be interactive games and contents that kids like to watch. This can be done by the connected IFE concept & IOT
Comfort of seats	IOT	Sensors can be fitted on aircraft seats to gather data about the performance of the seats. It can identify occupancy status of seats, the number of times the seat is reclined, the number of times tray table is used and the seatbelt status. An uncomfortable passenger will be moving in

(*continued*)

Table 3. (*continued*)

Factor	Enabling technology	Scope of emerging technology
		the seat and cabin crew can provide special attention to the passenger based on the data from the sensors. The airline can also identify that a seat has lost its comfort and refurbish it based on the sensor data [17]. The cabin crew also will have reduced workload as they do not have to instruct and inspect each passenger about seatbelts
Type of aircraft	AI	AI technologies can be used to find out the type of aircraft that has to be used on the route. Profile of the passengers can be analyzed using AI technologies. A route like Trivandrum-Dubai consists of majority on middle class working people and cost is the most important criteria for these passengers. Providing a slightly older aircraft on the route will not affect the revenues. The passengers on a route like Bangalore-Dubai mostly consist of mostly software professionals who are careful about the aircraft amenities. Providing an old aircraft on the route can result in passenger switching the airline. Passenger profiling can be regularly done using AI technologies for optimal use of the aircrafts in the fleet
Reliability & Dependability of the airlines	AI	Unscheduled maintenance is a major concern for all airlines and these results in delays and trip cancellations. The unscheduled maintenance can be avoided with the use of predictive maintenance. This can be implemented using AI techniques and can predict the failure of a component before actual failure. This can reduce unscheduled maintenance and delays to a large extend and improve the reliability of the airlines
Special care for old aged/sick and disabled passengers	AI & IOT	AI & IOT can play an important role in providing comfortable travel to these classes of passengers. Motorized cars using AI & IOT which can carry two passengers can be used in airport for seamless travel. These vehicles can be parked at designated parking lots at the airports and the passengers can scan their tickets to get boarding pass on the dedicated facility built in on the vehicle without waiting at the normal check in counters. AI techniques can

(*continued*)

Table 3. (*continued*)

Factor	Enabling technology	Scope of emerging technology
		be used to automate the vehicles and move them through the airport with minimum human assistance
Safety Measures	AI	The cleaning and sanitation of the cabin is currently a human intensive process. AI powered ultra violet technology based cleaning robots can be used by airlines for faster and efficient cleaning of the aircraft cabins. This would also reduce the turnaround time for the aircraft and improve the operational efficiency. Additionally AI based thermal body scanners can be used by airlines to check the health status of the passengers before boarding the flight. Machine learning algorithms can be used to predict the symptoms of covid, based on the images from the thermal scanners

With introduction of emerging technologies in data collection and processing, the factors that cause dissatisfaction to the customer can be reduced to a large extent. This can result in better customer pleasure and better customer retention for sustained revenues. Data will be continuously available for the airlines, which can continuously improve its processes. The privacy issues related to data can be a constraint in some of these proposed improvements. The terms and conditions of data collection and sharing of passenger data and its usage for various activities have to be evolved and this can be included in the terms and conditions of travel. Some of these initiatives like baggage handling require co ordination with the airport to attain full efficiency of the system. Some initiatives like in-flight entertainment, choice of food are completely under the control of the airline. Each of these initiatives have efforts required for implementation which has to take care of factors like cost of implementation, technology readiness level of the systems, co ordination with stakeholders like airport, regulatory approvals for use of technology and constraints on the operations. The impact on CRM from of each of initiatives also will be different based on factors like revenues generated, customer satisfaction, efficiency in operations and customer retention. Based on these factors the relative efforts for implementing each of these technologies and their impact on CRM were evaluated. The relative impact on CRM and the effort for implementation for these are provided in Fig. 4.

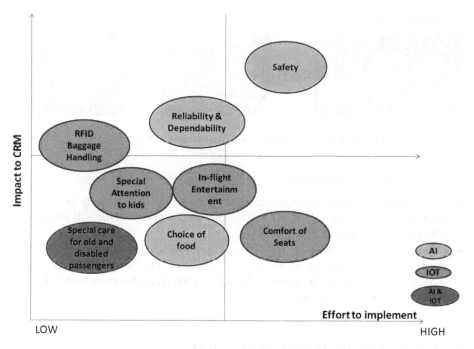

Fig. 4. Impact to CRM& effort in implementation

7 Identification of High Value Customers

Another area in CRM which requires attention is identification of a high value customer. A person who does multiple journeys in a year can be treated as a high value customer. The more number of journeys the person does, the customer becomes more valued and the airlines have to ensure the customer is retained. But as suggested by travel history mentioned in para 2, it is difficult to understand the number of journeys a person does, in case the journeys are performed by multiple airlines and in case the booking is done through different booking channels. An airport enabled with smart technologies can act as a data collection point which can be the baseline for CRM implementation.

An airport traditionally acts the arrival and departure point for the passengers for their air travel. But, an airport can play an important role in analyzing the customer behavior as it is the gateway of a passenger to the system. A passenger will mostly begin the journeys from airport of his home town. Whatever mode a ticket is booked or whichever airline the passenger select, the passenger ultimately travels through the airport and passes through the mandatory check points in the airport. To clearly identify how many times a person travels by air, the best available option is the airport of his home town. Face recognition techniques can be implemented at the airports at security check points. A face recognition system at airport can be useful in identifying a frequent flyer and generating lot of data for CRM activities. The images of the passengers taken from the airport security can be a reliable source of how many times a person travels (Fig. 5).

Face recognition at Airport

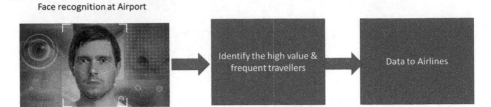

Fig. 5. Face recognition at airport as a data source for CRM

This can serve two purposes:

- Quick identification of passengers using the face recognition techniques and reduce the time in travel procedures like verification of documents. This will improve the efficiency of the airport operations.
- Create a database for travel history of passengers, which can be used for identifying the high value passengers or the frequent travelers. The second point can be the input for many of the CRM activities for airlines which enable them to decide which the passengers to be retained.

8   Benefits of Data Driven Smart CRM

A new smart CRM implementation plan powered by data has been envisaged based on the studies carried out, which can overcome many of the drawbacks in the existing CRM systems. Implementation of the new CRM scheme benefits airlines, airports and passengers. The specific benefits for each of the stakeholders involved are provided in Table 4.

Table 4. Beneficiaries of CRM

Sl No	Beneficiary	Benefits
1.	Airline	Existing CRM has drawbacks cannot capture the entire passenger behavior. Data from the airport can assist airlines in clearly identifying the frequent travelers and IOT & AI can assist in identifying what are the areas of concern for the passengers and offer improvement in these areas. Improvement in Customer Relationship Management can result in increase of revenues by customer retention. The proper use of CRM tools can ensure that the resources are planned and utilized in the optimum way. Providing a more personalized travel experience would make many customers spend little more on air travel which can be very critical in sustainability of the airlines

(continued)

Table 4. (*continued*)

Si No	Beneficiary	Benefits
2.	Airport	Implementation of face recognition techniques in airports offers dual benefits to airports. The techniques can assist in contactless and fast movement of passengers during the check-in & departure process. This can improve the number of passengers travelling through the airport and increase in revenues. Additional revenues can be obtained from providing data to the airlines for their Customer Relationship Management activities. The technologies like RFIDs in baggage handling can improve the efficiency of the airports. The implementation of features for disabled passengers can improve the goodwill factor of the airports along with airlines. Safety features like AI based thermal scanners installed at airports will increase the confidence of many passengers, who are afraid that they are sharing an aircraft with an infected passenger
3.	Passenger	Reduction in time spent for activities like check-in procedures and security checks will be beneficial for the passenger. A personalized experience for the passenger in flight leads to customer satisfaction and customer delight. It can prompt passenger to spent little more money on air travel

9 Conclusion

The aviation industry in the world has seen unforeseen turbulences in the recent times. Many low cost airlines have stopped operations and full service carriers are struggling with huge losses. Retaining the profitable customer is of critical importance in aviation under the current circumstances. Investments have to be made on data and data driven technologies for sustained revenues in the future. Safety of travel is a major concern for all passengers and use of technology to ensure safer cabins is a requirement for all airlines. Full service carriers have to invest in AI & IOT to enhance the customer experience and product differentiation to retain the customers. Investment in AI and IoT is required even for low cost carriers to reduce the losses due to delays and improve the operational efficiency. The new smart CRM implementation is a win-win situation for both airlines and airports.

References

1. Declan, B., Morrison, D., O'Neill, S.: The future of airline CRM. IBM Institute for Business Value (2002)
2. Ngai, E.W.T., et al.: Application of data mining techniques in customer relationship management: a literature review and classification (2008). https://doi.org/10.1016/j.eswa.2008.02.021
3. Liou, J.J.H.: A novel decision rules approach for customer relationship management of the airline market (2008). https://doi.org/10.1016/j.eswa.2008.05.002

4. Eid, R., et al.: CRM in the context of airline industry: a case study of Mexican airline. Int. J. Cust. Relationsh. Mark. Manag. **1**(2), 35–42 (2010)
5. Law, C.: The study of customer relationship management in Thai airline industry: a case of Thai travelers in Thailand. J. Airpt. Airl. Manag. **7**(1), 13–42 (2017)
6. Kabi, B.K., Sajnani, M.: A study of CRM practices in airline industry. 4D Int. J. IT Commer. **3**(3), 101 (2014). ISSN-2319-104X
7. Bygstad, B., Presthus, W.: Social media as CRM? How two Scandinavian airline companies used facebook during the "Ash Crisis" in 2010. Scand. J. Inf. Syst. **25**(1), 51–72 (2013)
8. Gnanprakash, J., et al.: Social CRM in the airline industry: a case study of Indian airline companies. J. Mark. Manag. Consum. Behav. **1**(1), 76–87 (2016)
9. VanAuken, K.: Using social media to improve customer engagement and promote products and services. J. Airpt. Manag. **9**(2), 109–117 (2015)
10. https://www.conztanz.com/landing-page-why-airlines-must-transform-their-call-centers-into-customer-experience-hubs/
11. White paper, The Road to 2025, The Future of Air Travel: Eight Disruptive Waves of Change by Cognizant Business Consulting, June 2017
12. White paper, Internet of Things in commercial Aviation by Wind River Systems, April 2018
13. Khedkar, D.: Whitepaper, Internet of Things and Customer Relationship Management. L& T Infotech, April 2018
14. Shainesh, G., Sheth, J.N.: Customer Relationship Management: A Strategic Perspective. Macmillan, India (2005)
15. Baggage IT Insights, SITA (2019)
16. Koldkjær, K.P.: RFID for Baggage Handling and Tracking, Whitepaper, Lyngsoe Systems (2017)
17. Ciaccia, F.R.D.A.S., et al.: An approach to aircraft seat comfort using interface pressure mapping. Work **41**(Supplement 1), 240–245 (2012)

IoT Based Climate Control Systems Diffusion in Intelligent Buildings - A System Dynamics Model

Arunvel Thangamani[1(✉)], L. S. Ganesh[1], Anand Tanikella[2],
and A. Meher Prasad[1]

[1] Indian Institute of Technology Madras, Chennai 600036, TN, India
arunvel.t@saint-gobain.com
[2] Saint Gobain Research, Northborough, MA 01532, USA

Abstract. The urbanization trend and the prevailing energy crisis in India, makes it important to study the potential of IoT technology in the Indian buildings market. This research work proposes a systems dynamics model of IoT based climate control systems diffusion in Intelligent Buildings. The modeling process leverages the generic Bass model of technology diffusion and augments it with causal loops based on the enablers and barriers to IoT diffusion in buildings identified through literature review. The model encompasses the technological, social, financial, business, regulatory and environmental aspects of the system, and uses stock-flow concepts to represent their dynamic interplay. The model will be useful to value chain players in the construction sector by providing them support for strategic decision-making concerning market entry and new product development. It will also help policy makers to assess industry readiness to tackle the prevailing energy crisis and devise strategies to mitigate it.

Keywords: Internet of Things · Smart buildings · Energy efficient comfort · Technology diffusion · System dynamics

1 Introduction

Modern Buildings consume over 40% of worldwide energy, and a major portion of this is for managing occupant comfort [1]. About 80–85% of the total energy consumption is from the use-phase of the building, where occupancy related loads such as air-conditioning and lighting play a major role [2]. In recent decades, there is a growing attention towards sensors and controls in buildings, contributed by the intelligent building (IB) initiatives across the globe. In the United States of America, 6% energy consumption reduction in commercial buildings is estimated through building control systems [3]. In India, the real estate sector that comprises four sub sectors, viz., housing, retail, hospitality, and commercial construction, is expected to reach a market size of US$ 1 trillion by 2030 and contribute 13% to the country's GDP by 2025 [4]. India's electricity consumption is growing at the rate of 8–10% per year and is about 4% of the world's total consumption. India's total energy shortage is estimated to be 9% and the peak demand is likely to be 323 GW by 2022 and 437 GW by 2027 [5].

© IFIP International Federation for Information Processing 2020
Published by Springer Nature Switzerland AG 2020
S. K. Sharma et al. (Eds.): TDIT 2020, IFIP AICT 617, pp. 673–684, 2020.
https://doi.org/10.1007/978-3-030-64849-7_59

Now, when there is an energy crisis and economy crunch, it is essential to provide a comfortable ambience within buildings, with not only less energy expenditure but also more of intuitiveness to suit occupants' needs.

Currently, the IoT technology for climate control is looked upon to improve energy efficiency in IBs. Despite the promising nature of the technology, the diffusion of information and communication technologies (ICT) is sluggish in construction industry [6]. The IoT industry is showing several positive trends such as sensors price reduction, big data handling ability [7] and higher speed data transfer [8] with the potential to change this situation.

In this direction, system dynamics has been leveraged to understand the time-dependent behavior of this IoT diffusion in the Indian construction industry. System dynamics is a computer aided simulation approach to solve dynamic complex problems involving technological, social, economic, regulatory and business systems [9, 10]. For forecasting technology adoption, system dynamics plays a vital role in assessing uncertainties and gaining insight into various aspects, viz. causal factors and potential diffusion patterns, and thereby supports sound decision making for strategic planning [11]. Most of the ICT/IoT adoption literature in IBs assume a static system, and are deficient in dealing with time-dependent dynamic aspects of adoption. In India, a complex interaction between technology, value chain, policy makers and consumers exist. This is hitherto unexplored to improve technology diffusion. Further, the economic fluctuations, IoT industry growth, booming consumer acceptance of smart phones, etc., contribute to the dynamic aspect of technology diffusion. In this paper, system dynamics is used to model the diffusion of IoT based climate control systems in IBs in India.

1.1 IoT in Intelligent Buildings

According to AlWaer and Clements-Croome (2010) "a sustainable intelligent building can be understood to be a complex system of interrelated three basic issues – People (owners; occupants, users, etc.); Products (materials; fabric; structure; facilities; equipment; automation and controls; services); and Processes (maintenance; performance evaluation; facilities management), and the inter-relationships between these issues [12]." IoT, a technological frontier of ICT, is instrumental to meet the following objectives of IBs.

1. Maximizing the technical performance, investment and operating cost savings, and flexibility [13].
2. Learning capability, self-adjustability, and the relationship between occupants and environment [14].
3. Energy-intelligent concept and satisfying occupants' need with high energy efficiency [14].

Historically, the benefits obtained from relocation flexibility, localized comfort and energy savings have driven wireless sensors' deployment in buildings [15]. Presently, Building Management System (BMS), a computer-based control system, is addressing the needs of comfort and energy management through monitoring and control of sub-systems such as air-conditioning, lighting etc. BMSs consist of the following building blocks: 1. Sensors for collecting indoor environment data, 2. Controllers for climate parameters actuation, 3. Communication hardware and the protocols, and 4. Dashboard. IoT enabled BMS would imply the following advancements to the system stated above [16, 17]: 1) Multi-system integrated functions e.g. energy, camera monitoring etc., 2) IP based wireless communication, 3) Remote access to the building subsystems, 4) Cloud based big data processing, 5) Edge devices for fog computing and data visualization, 6) User (includes occupant) engaging applications, 7) Connectivity to personal mobile devices gathering location data and type of activity promoting people centric sensing, a unique selling proposition.

1.2   System Dynamics (SD) application in Technology Diffusion

Innovation diffusion models suggest that pioneers (innovators) are the first group that adopt the technology and they are followed by imitators, who exist in different levels of the product life cycle. Therefore, the main dynamics are derived from three feedback loops, viz. adoption by innovation, adoption by imitation and adoption by market potential [9]. An overview of the literature on the use of system dynamics for modeling technology adoption/diffusion is presented in Fig. 1 below showing the timeline. The papers on dynamic models of IoT adoption are presented subsequently.

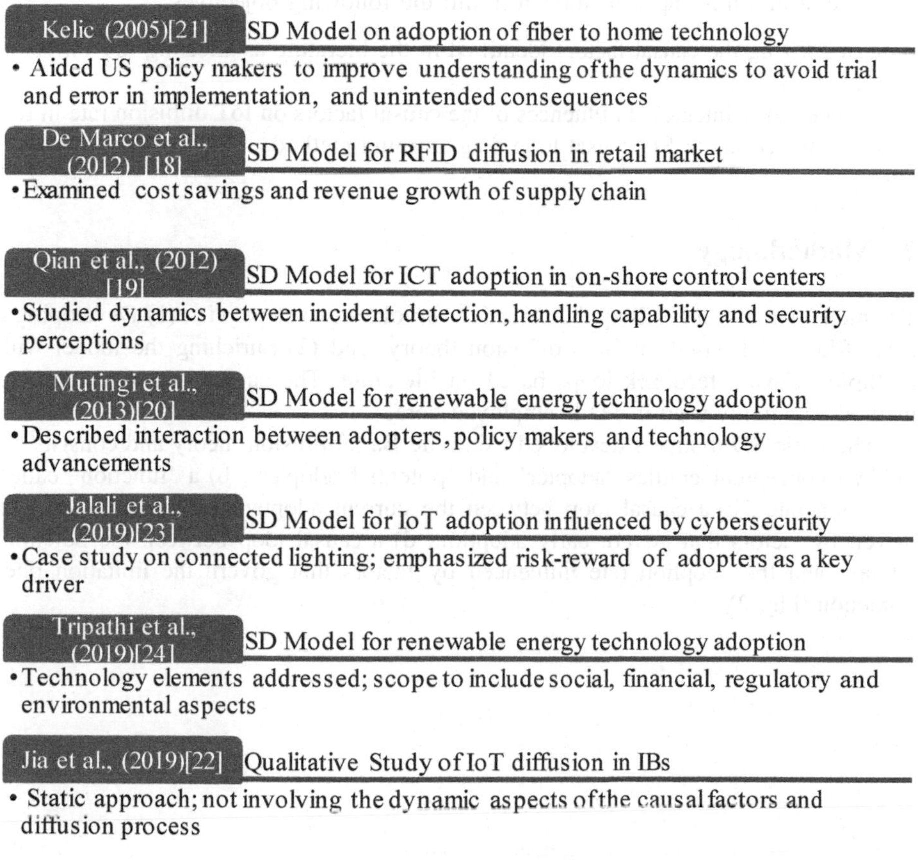

Kelic (2005)[21]   SD Model on adoption of fiber to home technology
- Aided US policy makers to improve understanding of the dynamics to avoid trial and error in implementation, and unintended consequences

De Marco et al., (2012) [18]   SD Model for RFID diffusion in retail market
- Examined cost savings and revenue growth of supply chain

Qian et al., (2012) [19]   SD Model for ICT adoption in on-shore control centers
- Studied dynamics between incident detection, handling capability and security perceptions

Mutingi et al., (2013)[20]   SD Model for renewable energy technology adoption
- Described interaction between adopters, policy makers and technology advancements

Jalali et al., (2019)[23]   SD Model for IoT adoption influenced by cybersecurity
- Case study on connected lighting; emphasized risk-reward of adopters as a key driver

Tripathi et al., (2019)[24]   SD Model for renewable energy technology adoption
- Technology elements addressed; scope to include social, financial, regulatory and environmental aspects

Jia et al., (2019)[22]   Qualitative Study of IoT diffusion in IBs
- Static approach; not involving the dynamic aspects of the causal factors and diffusion process

Fig. 1. SD model applied to technology adoption in relevant areas.

From the literature review, it is evident that the past decade has seen an increase in application of system dynamics model in the technology adoption studies. Adoption of digital technologies such as RFID, IoT, ICT and fiber technology etc. are being addressed in the recent literature. Most of the literature pertaining to adoption of IoT, study the technology related factors and their static nature. Models that concern dynamics are limited in scope and are predominantly case study based, without adequate scope for generalizability.

While it is evident that SD is suitable for studying IoT adoption in IBs, available studies have examined specific aspects, viz., personal, social, technological, regulatory, financial, environmental and business, separately and often without paying attention to the complexities involved due to their interactions, and the consequent dynamics. Hence, there is a clear need to examine IoT adoption in IBs holistically to gain a comprehensive understanding of the phenomenon. The System Dynamics method, being founded on the principles of the Systems Approach, facilitates holistic modeling and analysis. Given (a) the very sharp increase in public and private construction and infrastructure, (b) the corresponding rise in energy consumption coupled with acute energy shortages, and (c) the booming nature of the digital ecosystem in India, SD modeling can benefit stakeholders in the buildings industry and policy makers immensely.

Specifically, this paper attempts to fulfill the following objectives:

a) Categorizing the causal factors identified in the literature as affecting IoT diffusion rate in IBs;
b) Depicting the integrated influences of the causal factors on IoT diffusion rate in IBs using the common SD causal loop diagramming method.

2   Methodology

The methodology for fulfilling the objectives involves two steps, viz., (1) Developing a basic SD model based on Bass diffusion theory, and (2) Enriching the model with multiple, relevant feedback loops based on literature. The causal loop diagramming method commonly used in SD is employed here.

The basic SD model is developed using the Bass diffusion theory and consists of: a) Two conceptual entities 'adopter' and 'potential adopter', b) a 'function' called 'adoption rate', c) a causal loop between the current adopter and the adoption rate driven by factors that govern early adoption, d) a causal loop between the potential adopter and the adoption rate influenced by factors that govern the imitation phenomenon (Fig. 2).

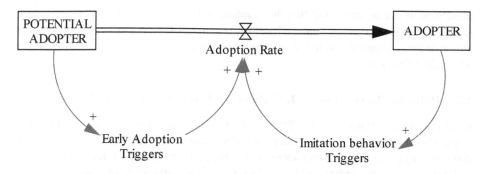

Fig. 2. Basic SD model for technology diffusion

2.1 Early adoption loop - 'Simulations on Building Performance'

During the design stage, simulations are commonly used for driving the adoption of building monitoring and control solutions, and forecasting energy performance of and comfort levels in a building. Most often, these simulations are used to evaluate if a building will meet certain regulatory standards. ASHRAE 90.1 mandated the use of building energy simulation results to rate building energy performance. Other rating systems, such as Leadership in Energy and Environment Design (LEED), follow the same protocols like ASHRAE 90.1 for energy performance rating, and in addition they require comfort simulations such as day lighting and natural ventilation [25]. With a view to promote low energy buildings in order to meet greenhouse gas reduction targets, other government bodies like European Energy Performance of Buildings Directive (EPBD) also require deploying simulation software for building design and operation [26]. Further, to ensure the validity of such simulations, the US department of energy has carried out in-situ studies of certified buildings in the USA. The utility electricity bills collected were compared with the energy ratings issued based on the baseline energy performance predicted by the simulations. The field data showed 1% less consumption than the modeled value, however with a wide variance around the mean [27].

The early adopters in India are found to prefer simulation models during the building concept stage to ascertain if the building design will meet the comfort needs, while minimizing energy expense. Post construction, there is interest to measure the energy savings and comfort conditions with sensors to ensure that the computer models would be actually right. Model driven IoT value prediction is a causal factor that can impress the early adopter in the buildings market. Such early adopters also expect that these models are accurate and that the comfort and energy predictions come close to reality during the operation phase. Therefore, our SD model considers an early adopter loop that incorporates the value from energy, comfort and lifecycle energy simulations and their delivery time.

2.2 Diffusion Barrier Loop - 1. Technology Uncertainties Related

According to Brachman (2013) [28], technical challenges include plurality of devices (from various producers, with different communication modes), scalability (protocols compatibility), wireless communication reliability, power hungry devices, data security and privacy etc. According to Bajer, (2018) [17] uncertainties in this area mainly include the data silos. Each vendor's software platform using their own cloud may lead to duplicating the nodes, increasing expenditure. Further, large IoT Players tend to introduce proprietary protocols, leading to poor interoperability between sub-systems. Therefore, our model considers device plurality (scalability), data silos, reliability, data security, sensing accuracy and energy consumption of sensing devices etc., as factors in the feedback loop.

2.3 Diffusion Barrier Loop - 2. Financial Impact Related

In India ICT/IoT is seen as a high cost addition during the construction phase and customers are afraid of the costs associated with digital platform switch-overs [6]. In addition to sensors for localized comfort, the actuators increase the cost of the system, making it economically unadoptable [29]. Also, IoT system deployment involves increased installation costs along with the unforeseen upgradation costs. Moreover, unknown costs such as BMS licensing fee are also a concern. This has been a discouraging factor in adopting this technology [30]. Therefore, our model considers factors of risk-return ratio from both capital cost and recurring cost fronts in the feedback loop.

2.4 Diffusion Barrier Loop - 3. Personal and Social Impact Related

User Involvement has been seen as a major factor in technology adoption [31]. It is being realized that human perception and understanding is a primary requirement for successful adoption of ICT/IoT in targeted fields. In the context of climate control systems, occupant engagement through smart phones and other such devices pose a good opportunity [32]. However, when plenty of devices are connected to various networks, privacy and security can be a major concern. While there is provision to protect privacy of every individual, there could be a perception risk that affects trust. This has been reported to influence technology adoption and has a role to play in uncertainties surrounding this technology [33]. Also, predicting occupant activities accurately [29], and engaging by sound user experience designs [34] are essential in this context. Therefore, our model considers privacy concerns, data security, predictability of occupant activities and user experience level as factors in the feedback loop.

2.5 Diffusion Barrier Loop - 4. Environmental Impact Related

One of the key factors affecting the environment in relation to IBs is the battery life of electronics, which require frequent replacement. Studies suggest that, on an average, more than 200 million battery changes can happen every day, world-wide [35]. In addition, presence of abundant sensors in low energy buildings can result in higher embodied energy, affecting life cycle energy cost [36]. Therefore, our model considers impact on buildings life cycle energy and battery replacement scale as factors in the feedback loop.

2.6 Diffusion Barrier Loops - 5. Business Proposition and 6. Regulatory Related

IoT startups are struggling with creating grounded business cases in IBs [17]. Lack of win-win business models can result in poor customer acceptance [37]. Further, industry specific challenges include, (a) Plenty of standards, (b) Construction sector not pulling innovations rapidly, (c) Concerns on norm changes, (e) Lack of information flow across the value chain, etc. [38]. To add, the absence of government incentives has also been seen as a major hurdle [39]. Therefore, our model considers industry speed of accepting new technology, business model effectiveness, profitability etc., as factors in the technology diffusion risk feedback loop. Further, from the regulatory angle, concerns on norm changes, standards count, and lack of government incentives have been considered as risks [38] and included in a feedback loop.

3 The Integrated Conceptual Model – A Discussion

By combining individual feedback loops with the basic Bass diffusion model, the integrated SD model results. The model involves an early adoption loop and multiple risk feedback loops in effect. Figure 3 below describes this model.

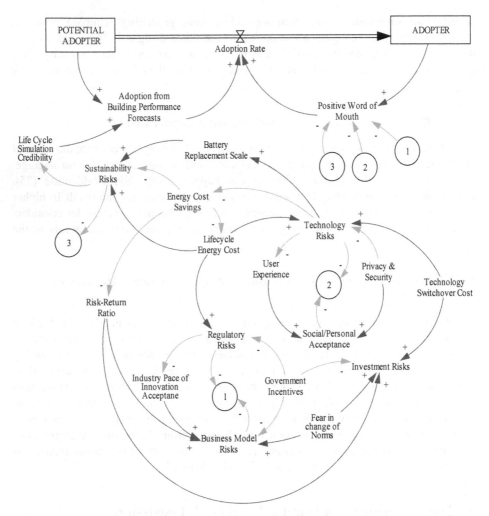

Fig. 3. The integrated conceptual model (only interaction variables and their causal loops are shown)

The early adopter feedback loop is characterized by the value of the building performance simulation. The imitation behavior is characterized by the word of mouth of early adopters, system integrators and consultants who worked with them.

The positive word of mouth is influenced various risk loops such as technology risk, sustainability and regulatory risks etc. It is to be noted that the causal loops could involve interdependence and mutual interactions. For example, the ability of technological factors to influence occupant acceptance might gain momentum in future. In other words, IoT can precisely gather occupant behavior, through the edge devices that are possessed by the occupants. Also, when the financial and regulation loops are examined, government incentives, if issued, may reduce the financial burden on the first cost for building owners. When the sustainability and technology feedback loops are examined, it becomes clear that self-powered IoT devices are the need of the hour, or else the scale of battery replacement could be of immense negative impact to sustainability. When technology and financial loops are examined, elimination of information silos lead to reduction of first costs. Such loop combinations are depicted in the Fig. 3 above.

Out of the multiple loops, generating demand generation potential, by blending technology and user centricity seems to be the first and foremost risk to be retired. This can be made possible through sound business models that do not burden the customer in terms of cost. Revenue sharing type of models, wherein IoT firms receiving margins from the actual energy savings of a building, not only reduces first cost for the building owner, but also gives trust in the value proposition.

There could be potential limitations to this model. As the factors are brought in from multiple international sources, their relevance to Indian conditions may vary. For example, fear of regulation changes in India could be low, and the privacy perception of occupants could be low. On the other hand, the demand for government incentives could be increasingly higher. Also, certain other practices/trends in India deserve critical attention: 1) For example, building performance simulations in India are performed for getting regulatory clearance, but proper comparisons with real building data does not exist. Reforming this behavior in the value chain can bring out the real benefits of monitoring comfort and energy, 2) With the rapid sprouting of IoT startups, application interfaces that handle device heterogeneity can be developed faster and cheaper. Along these lines, there could be more unknown factors that are India-specific and have higher relevance. They have to be dug out for the effectiveness of the forecast.

This paper is an early attempt to integrate, using various literature sources, multiple factors that contribute to the diffusion of IoT in the Indian scenario, and focus on the dynamic aspect of diffusion/adoption, by leveraging SD modeling.

4   Conclusion and future directions

A conceptual model that is essential to predict the dynamic behavior of IoT diffusion in the Indian IB market has been developed. It covers system level aspects from multiple fronts such as technological, social, financial, business, regulatory and environmental, and leverages stock-flow concepts to represent the dynamic behavior. Managerially, this model should aid value chain players in strategic decision making for entering the IB market or to develop new products. It also aids policy makers to assess industry readiness to tackle the prevailing energy crisis and to devise strategies accordingly. Theoretically, this model includes addition of dynamic behavior of IoT diffusion to the current body of IB literature that has focused much more on the static aspects.

In future, the relevance of each causal factor in terms of severity and occurrence will have to be identified through appropriate qualitative and quantitative research techniques such as interviews, group discussions, participative ranking etc. If there are India-specific causal factors that are not identified in this process, they will have to be brought out through expert interactions. Such data collection will form the input and boundary conditions for solving the model. Also, multiple what-if loops that explain the interaction between risk categories can elucidate various resultant scenarios of diffusion/adoption hurdles. Also, interdependence between multiple risk categories will have to be investigated for potential time delays. There could be special scenarios such as technology and regulatory forces relying on each other continuously resulting in a circular causal loop calling for policy interventions.

References

1. Pérez-Lombard, L., Ortiz, J., Pout, C.: A review on buildings energy consumption information. Energy Build. **40**(3), 394–398 (2008)
2. Cabeza, L.F., Rincón, L., Vilariño, V., Pérez, G., Castell, A.: Life cycle assessment (LCA) and life cycle energy analysis (LCEA) of buildings and the building sector: a review. Renew. Sustain. Energy Rev. **29**, 394–416 (2014)
3. Brambley, M.R., et al.: Advanced Sensors and Controls for Building Applications: Market Assessment and Potential R&D Pathways, United States (2005)
4. Indian Real Estate Industry. https://www.ibef.org/industry/real-estate-india.aspx. Accessed 18 July 2020
5. Kumar, A., Hancke, G.P.: An energy-efficient smart comfort sensing system based on the IEEE 1451 standard for green buildings. IEEE Sens. J. **14**(12), 4245–4252 (2014)
6. Ahuja, V., Yang, J., Shankar, R.: Study of ICT adoption for building project management in the Indian construction industry. Auto. Constr. **18**(4), 415–423 (2009)
7. Riggins, F.J., Wamba, S.F.: Research directions on the adoption, usage, and impact of the internet of things through the use of big data analytics. In: 48th Hawaii International Conference on System Sciences, pp. 1531–1540. IEEE (2015)
8. Atzori, L., Iera, A., Morabito, G.: Social internet of things: turning smart objects into social objects to boost the IoT. Newsletter (2014). https://iot.ieee.org/newsletter/november-2014/social-internet-of-things-turning-smart-objects-into-social-objects-to-boost-the-iot.html. Accessed 18 July 2020
9. Sterman, J.: Business Dynamics, System Thinking and Modeling for a Complex World. Irwin/McGraw-Hill, New York (2000)
10. Forrester, J.W.: System dynamics, systems thinking, and soft OR. Syst. Dyn. Rev. **10**(2–3), 245–256 (1994)
11. Fisher, D.K., Norvell, J., Sonka, S., Nelson, M.J.: Understanding technology adoption through system dynamics modeling: implications for agribusiness management. Int. Food Agribusiness Manage. Rev. **3**(3), 281–296 (2000)
12. AlWaer, H., Clements-Croome, D.J.: Key performance indicators (KPIs) and priority settings in using the mutli-attribute approach for assessing sustainable intelligent buildings. Build. Environ. **45**(4), 799–807 (2010)
13. Clements-Croome, T.D.J.: What do we mean by intelligent buildings? Autom. Constr. **6**, 395–399 (1997)
14. Ghaffarianhoseini, A., Berardi, U., AlWaer, H., Chang, S., Halawa, E., Ghaffarianhoseini, A., Clements-Croome, D.: What is an intelligent building? Analysis of recent interpretations from an international perspective. Architectural Sci. Rev. **59**(5), 338–357 (2016)
15. Kintner-Meyer, M.: Opportunities of wireless sensors and controls for building operation. Energy Eng. **102**(5), 27–48 (2005)
16. Minoli, D., Sohraby, K., Occhiogrosso, B.: IoT considerations, requirements, and architectures for smart buildings—energy optimization and next-generation building management systems. IEEE Internet Things J. **4**(1), 269–283 (2017)

17. Bajer, M.: IoT for smart buildings-long awaited revolution or lean evolution. In: IEEE 6th International Conference on Future Internet of Things and Cloud (FiCloud), vol. 154, pp. 149–154. IEEE (2018)
18. De Marco, A., Cagliano, A.C., Nervo, M.L., Rafele, C.: Using system dynamics to assess the impact of RFID technology on retail operations. Int. J. Prod. Econ. 135(1), 333–344 (2012)
19. Qian, Y., Fang, Y., Gonzalez, J.J.: Managing information security risks during new technology adoption. Comput. Secur. 31(8), 859–869 (2012)
20. Mutingi, M.: Understanding the dynamics of the adoption of renewable energy technologies: a system dynamics approach. Dec. Sci. Lett. 2(2), 109–118 (2013)
21. Kelic, A.: Networking technology adoption: system dynamics modeling of fiber-to-the-home. Doctoral dissertation, Massachusetts Institute of Technology (2005)
22. Jia, M., Komeily, A., Wang, Y., Srinivasan, R.S.: Adopting Internet of Things for the development of smart buildings: a review of enabling technologies and applications. Autom. Constr. 101, 111–126 (2019)
23. Jalali, M.S., Kaiser, J.P., Siegel, M., Madnick, S.: The internet of things promises new benefits and risks: a systematic analysis of adoption dynamics of IoT products. IEEE Secur. Priv. 17(2), 39–48 (2019)
24. Tripathi, S.: System dynamics perspective for adoption of internet of things: a conceptual framework. In: 2019 10th International Conference on Computing, Communication and Networking Technologies (ICCCNT), pp. 1–10. IEEE (2019)
25. ASHARE Standard, ANSI/ASHRAE Standard 55. Thermal Environmental Conditions for Human Occupancy. American Society of Heating, Refrigerating and Air-Conditioning Engineers. Inc., Atlanta (1992)
26. Wang, H., Zhai, Z.J.: Advances in building simulation and computational techniques: a review between 1987 and 2014. Energy Build. 128, 319–335 (2016)
27. Schwartz, Y., Raslan, R.: Variations in results of building energy simulation tools, and their impact on BREEAM and LEED ratings: a case study. Energy Build. 62, 350–359 (2013)
28. Brachman, A.: Raport obserwatorium ICT. Internet przedmiotów, Technopark Gliwice (2013)
29. Lilis, G., Conus, G., Asadi, N., Kayal, M.: Towards the next generation of intelligent building: an assessment study of current automation and future IoT based systems with a proposal for transitional design. Sustain. Cities Soc. 28, 473–481 (2017)
30. Rafiq, N.R., Mohammed, S.F., Pandey, J., Singh, A.V.: Classic from the outside, smart from the inside: The era of smart buildings. In: 6th International Conference on Reliability, Infocom Technologies and Optimization (Trends and Future Directions) (ICRITO), Noida, pp. 580–584 (2017)
31. Moreno-Cano, María V., Santa, J., Zamora-Izquierdo, M.A., Skarmeta, A.F.: Future Human-Centric Smart Environments. In: Xhafa, F., Barolli, L., Barolli, A., Papajorgji, P. (eds.) Modeling and Processing for Next-Generation Big-Data Technologies. MOST, vol. 4, pp. 341–365. Springer, Cham (2015). https://doi.org/10.1007/978-3-319-09177-8_14
32. Klein, L., Kwak, J., Kavulya, G., Jazizadeh, F., Becerik-Gerber, B., Varakantham, P., Tambe, M.: Coordinating occupant behavior for building energy and comfort management using multi-agent systems. Autom. Constr. 22, 525–536 (2012)
33. Hsinchun, C., Chiang, R.H.L., Storey, V.C.: Business intelligence and analytics: from big data to big impact. MIS Q. 36(4), 1165–1188 (2012)
34. Knutsen, J.: Uprooting products of the networked city. Int. J. Des. 8(1), 127–142 (2014)
35. Wan, T., Karimi, Y., Stanaćević, M., Salman, E.: Perspective paper–can AC computing be an alternative for wirelessly powered IoT devices? IEEE Embedded Syst. Lett. 9(1), 13–16 (2017)

36. Ramesh, T., Prakash, R., Shukla, K.K.: Life cycle energy analysis of buildings: an overview. Energy Build. **42**(10), 1592–1600 (2010)
37. Zanella, A., Bui, N., Castellani, A., Vangelista, L., Zorzi, M.: Internet of things for smart cities. IEEE Internet Things J. **1**(1), 22–32 (2014)
38. Ma, Z., Badi, A., Jorgensen, B.N.: Market opportunities and barriers for smart buildings. In: 2016 IEEE Green Energy and Systems Conference (IGSEC), pp. 1–6. IEEE (2016)
39. Hsu, C.W., Yeh, C.C.: Understanding the factors affecting the adoption of the internet of things. Technol. Anal. Strateg. Manage. **29**(9), 1089–1102 (2017)

Occupant Adoption of IoT Based Environment Service in Office Spaces: An Empirical Investigation

Arunvel Thangamani[1(✉)], L. S. Ganesh[1], Anand Tanikella[2],
and A. Meher Prasad[1]

[1] Indian Institute of Technology Madras, Chennai 600036, TN, India
arunvel.t@saint-gobain.com
[2] Saint Gobain Research, Northborough, MA 01532, USA

Abstract. Occupant behavior influences energy savings in intelligent buildings over and above the advanced technologies deployed. IoT based interconnected sensors, along with personal devices such as mobile phones, wearables and virtual assistants, can assist building management systems with occupant behavior information paving the way for personalized comfort coupled with energy savings. This work investigates the occupant adoption of such an IoT climate control service in the context of Indian office spaces by examining four theories viz., TRA, TPB, TAM and VAM. The results indicate that TAM and VAM have higher explanatory power among the models considered. Further, TAM's constructs 1. Perceived benefits, viz., improvement in comfort, productivity and wellbeing, and 2. Perceived ease of use, viz., access convenience to climate control in offices are identified as the most significant causal constructs. The results can pave way for IoT players to formulate business and technology strategies for product management and targeting specific customer segments.

Keywords: Internet of Things · Smart building · Energy efficient comfort · Technology adoption · Energy related occupant behavior

1 Background

Out of global energy consumption in 2040, India will account for 11%. During the period of 2017 to 2040, out of the global primary energy demand, India is expected to account for more than 25%. In India, primary grid electricity demand is projected to be between 2040–2857TWh by 2030, out of which about 40% of the energy would be consumed by the building sector, and out of which about 22% would be utilized for air conditioning [1, 2]. In office spaces heating ventilation and air-conditioning (HVAC) and lighting respectively consume up to 40% and 17% of the overall building's energy [3]. The internet of things (IoT) based climate control systems, a recent development in the area of wireless telecommunications, is one of the key technology enablers for energy reduction and comfort control in buildings [4, 5]. Applications such as crowd-sensing wherein large numbers of building occupants through their IoT devices such as

© IFIP International Federation for Information Processing 2020
Published by Springer Nature Switzerland AG 2020
S. K. Sharma et al. (Eds.): TDIT 2020, IFIP AICT 617, pp. 685–693, 2020.
https://doi.org/10.1007/978-3-030-64849-7_60

mobile phones, smart watches and other means providing data to building systems can bring human centric building management [3].

1.1   Occupant Centricity in IoT Climate Control Services

Office workers are known to consume energy in their respective space through the HVAC, lighting and plug loads. Smart comfort control systems aim at reducing energy consumption by enabling interactions between occupants and these systems. Taking both occupant comfort limits and energy expense, these systems can trace occupant schedules, patterns and activities to set the comfort set points such as temperature, relative humidity, LUX, etc. The first-generation smart control systems did not include learning users' individual preferences and adaptive behaviors, and faced hurdles in achieving 'energy efficient comfort'. Emerging works in artificial intelligence that have started to look into this gap are modeling individual comfort preferences. The rising computing power of personalized devices such as mobile phones, aid in the process of gathering and processing large data, not only on a local scale but also in an individual level [6].

In the context of climate control (CC) systems, due to the shortcomings such as fixed value settings, manual intervention necessities, ignored tolerance of occupants, etc., addressing occupant comfort by direct communication, by use of a smartphone has been presented and tested earlier [7, 8]. In office spaces, individual cabins and meeting rooms can be independently controlled and open office desks can be zoned. Further, these zones can also be independently controlled and zones for lighting can be aligned with that of HVAC. However, in most offices, indoor comfort is not within the control of the individual and a generalized setting is used, resulting in loss of energy efficiency and comfort dissatisfaction. In this context, UC Berkeley researchers have developed the 'Building Operation System Services' platform (BOSS) that provides graphic user interfaces, and visualization tools for users, enabling them to request localized (within a zone) and temporary climate control [9].

Similar IoT service platforms available in the market (e.g. Comfy, 75 °F etc.) combine indoor climate monitoring and occupants' comfort feedback. They are socio-technical systems engaging occupants as informers, through a self-reporting web-based mobile app. Combined with zoning, such platforms try to address the needs of various occupants, in addition to considering physical layout of working areas [10]. Such advancements like personalized comfort environments, which involve ventilation in local zones, can ensure thermal comfort improvement with energy consumption reduction up to 45% [11].

1.2   Energy Related Occupant Behavior

Occupant behavior (OB) has a significant impact on comfort and energy performance of buildings. As the technical standards become more stringent, occupant behavioral factors gain higher importance [12]. Studies have confirmed that measured energy use in LEED certified buildings varied from the simulated estimate, which was attributed to the heterogeneous ways of occupants' understanding and using the building control systems [13].

The new paradigm of adaptive comfort questions the validity of 'steady state' theories that recommend a narrow bandwidth of 22 ± 2 °C as in the ASHRAE 55-92 and BS EN ISO 7730 standards [14]. While India is yet to have a custom made adaptive thermal comfort standard, occupant comfort research in Indian office buildings has shown interestingly that comfort temperatures can be as high as 26 °C, despite the geography being hot-humid [15]. Studies recommend 'energy efficient thermal comfort' set points as 26 °C, 24 °C and 22 °C for the respective occupant behavior styles of austere, normal and wasteful [16]. On similar lines, in visual comfort, occupant interaction with artificial lighting and blind systems depend on luminance levels reached with day lighting, length of absence from the room, type of activity, and tendency to avoid direct sunlight/glare etc. [17]. The area of innovative technologies affecting occupants' abilities and approaches to adapt to indoor environments remains less explored [13].

From the literature, it is apparent that IoT has good potential in intelligent buildings (IBs) by leveraging occupant centric approaches to reduce energy consumption while enhancing comfort. But, due to the uncertainties and unknowns in occupant interaction with IoT systems, it is necessary to investigate drivers of occupant adoption of such climate control IoT services. In India, since energy efficient comfort (EEC) is being seen as a necessary condition in buildings [18], a technology adoption study in this area is important for regulatory bodies. In addition, with IoT startups sprouting in India, clarity on demand generation potential of this opportunity will be useful to the industry ecosystem. This paper attempts to explore the parameters that influence the occupant acceptance of IoT comfort and energy management services in intelligent buildings in the Indian office space market.

1.3 Description of the Proposed IoT Climate Control Service

The status-quo in Indian buildings is one prescribed set point (e.g. ASHRAE Class A 22–24 °C) across all floors or zones. It is known that such a single set point is not the best comfort level for all occupants. Facility managers in office buildings are proposing zoned HVAV with EEC set points such as 24–26 °C, with a view to reach an optimal comfort set point, where energy savings are on higher side.

In simple terms, the proposed IoT service collects information on comfort level status, desired comfort level and present zone details from the occupants and tries to place them in the appropriate EEC zone. A communication on potential energy savings would be sent to the occupants, asking them to move to the appropriate zone. If that is denied, a non - EEC zone is assigned by default as per the comfort level demand from the occupant. Also, there can be multiple EEC level zones, prompting occupants to be seated in an appropriate one, as per their personalized comfort preferences. In addition, leveraging machine learning, this service would attempt to personalize a zone for a given type of occupant. This would imply, occupants are grouped across the HVAC zones, offering the facilities team a visibility on the EEC levels and the number of EEC zones. The front end of the service can be a mobile app, operating in the smart device of the occupant.

2   Research Methodology

The study is exploratory in nature aiming at shortlisting a suitable adoption model for this IoT service adoption context.

2.1   Model Development

The Theory of Reasoned Action (TRA), Theory of Planned Behavior (TPB), Technology Acceptance Model (TAM), and Value Adoption Model (VAM) have been used over the years by various researchers to explain the adoption of IoT systems in general [19]. TAM by and large is the most cited model to describe ICT systems adoption in multiple fields including smart homes, construction project management etc. In addition, in ICT individual adoption theme, TAM features as the highly used and cited model [20]. Early exploratory studies on IoT adoption in India have suggested that PU, PEOU as theorized by TAM, and SN and ATT as theorized by TRA, are significantly affecting IoT adoption. However, more context specific variables are needed to explain the phenomenon comprehensively [19]. Studies on user acceptance of smart home services using TPB have recommended to include additional constructs namely mobility, security/privacy risk, and trust in the service provider [21]. Along these lines, for this IoT service in office spaces, the above-mentioned models are fine-tuned, and empirically analyzed.

2.2   Finetuning Constructs of TAM, TRA, TPB and VAM[1]

Further the table below is a list of measured variables for this research, mapped to the standard constructs of the shortlisted models TAM, TRA, TPB, and VAM (Table 1).

Table 1. List of measured variables

Model	Constructs	Measured Variables	References
TAM, VAM	Perceived Usefulness (PU)	Mental and physical well-being, perceived productivity and overall comfort	[22–24]
	Perceived ease of use (PEOU)	1) Ability/mental effort to use the service, 2) Easy to get what occupant wants done (to reach an appropriate EEC zone of optimal comfort), 3) Convenient to access climate control systems using the app	[10, 22, 25]
	Behavioral Intent (BI)	Occupant's volition, planning and expectation to adopt the service	[19, 26]

(continued)

---

[1] **The list of survey questions is available upon request.**

Table 1. (*continued*)

Model	Constructs	Measured Variables	References
TRA & TPB	Attitude (ATT)	Occupant's behavioral beliefs about the outcomes and attributes	[9, 10, 19]
	Subjective Norm (SN)	Beliefs and actions of significant others: 1. Colleagues' usage, 2. Firm's encouragement and 3. Occupants in the near vicinity (e.g. Zone)	
	Perceived Behavioral control (PBC)	Occupant's perceived control over the action of interacting with the app's front end	
VAM	Perceived Enjoyment (FUN)	Positive emotional response of the occupant while using the IoT service	[25, 27]
	Technicality (TEC)	1. Instant connectivity, 2. Faster response time and 3. Simplicity of user interface	
	Perceived Value (PV)	Time and effort the occupant has to invest to use the IoT service against the potential benefits	[25, 28]

2.3 Selection of Suitable Model

Hypotheses as per TAM, VAM, TRA, TPB are framed and the data collection involved a survey with above mentioned constructs and independent measures, in 170 respondents from 6 commercial buildings. This sample size is selected based upon the rule that it is preferred to be ten times the number of observed independent variables [28]. TRA, TAM, TPB and VAM have been tested using multiple regressions. The coefficient of determination (represented by R^2) for the dependent construct, was used to assess the explanatory power of these models.

3 Results and Observations

3.1 Model Checks and Regression Results

Model checks performed in TRA, TPB, TAM and VAM suggested satisfactory levels of construct validity, reliability and discriminant reliability. Cronbach alpha of the constructs PE, PEOU, BI, ATT, SN, PBC, FUN, TEC were above >0.7 indicating good construct reliability. Factor loadings of the measured variables belonging to all constructs were above 0.6 indicating that they are able to represent the hypothesized factors adequately [29, 30]. On similar lines, discriminant validity between constructs are less than 0.4 implying no considerable level of correlation between the independent constructs. In addition, variance inflation factor (VIF) of all the models were less than <5 indicating absence of multicollinearity [31]. R^2 values, the goodness of fit measure of multiple regression, suggested that all the considered models are able to explain the behavioral intention to adopt the proposed IoT service.

The results summary with R^2 and coefficients value is as presented below. Except SN and ATT in TPB, FUN and TEC in VAM, all other constructs had p-values less than 0.05, indicating that they are statistically significant (Table 2).

Table 2. Summary of R^2 and coefficients value

Model	Constructs	Coefficients	Explanatory power R^2
TAM	PU	0.497	37.0%
	PEOU	0.209	
TRA	ATT	0.327	16.7%
	SN	0.199	
TPB	PBC	0.560	35.6%
VAM	PU	0.507	37.3%
	FUN	0.083	
	PEOU	0.210	
	TEC	0.071	

4 Discussion

The objective of this research is to investigate how well existing adoption models are able to quantify the occupant adoption of IoT services in intelligent buildings in the context of comfort and energy savings.

From this exploratory work, TAM is shortlisted as the suitable model. This is because 1) PU of TAM covers productivity, well-being and overall comfort and is statistically significant, 2a) PEOU of TAM covers the aspects of ease of accomplishing EEC zone movement, and the convenience of accessing climate control system and is statistically significant, 2b) TAM has the highest explanatory power among the models considered, 3) VAM did not explain any greater than TAM and additional constructs FUN and TEC were not statistically significant, 4) Explanatory power of TRA and TPB are lesser, when compared with TAM, which by far is the most used and cited model in ICT literature.

From the TAM main effects, it is to be noted that PEOU's influence is found to be lesser than the PU. This is possibly caused by the fact that IoT edge devices (smart watches, virtual assistants and mobile phones with custom software applications) are becoming more and more commonly used by the general public. Their perception that these devices take less mental effort to use, could lead to the lesser significance of PEOU in adoption intent. Nevertheless, it is to be noted that PEOU has been statistically significant, owing to the following reasons: 1) It covers the aspect of ease of getting the objective done, i.e. using the IoT service to pick an EEC zone which offers optimal comfort, 2) Convenience to access, i.e. accessing climate control systems in conventional systems haven't been possible for occupants, but this IoT service makes it possible. The high significance of PU is owing to the fact that it addresses the direct and indirect benefits of the service viz, 1) overall comfort, 2) productivity, and 3) occupant well-being.

Also, the effect of SN is lower than ATT and PBC in TRA and TPB. This can be attributed to the relatively low influence of colleagues, firm and other occupants when compared to an individual's perception of the benefits, importance and interest to use. On similar lines, PBC's higher influence in TPB is attributed to the relative importance given to accessibility and usability by individuals using such IoT services.

It is also to be noted that VAM had little advantage over TAM in the current context. This is owing to, 1) There is no additional fee payable by the occupant to use this IoT service, 2) Occupants in their busy work schedule, probably don't perceive moving between zones as fun, 3) Technicality of using the app is well known to them that they possibly find it insignificant.

These models are limited to only the "Consideration of Technology" aspect in intelligent buildings. Further research is warranted which considers "User Requirements" such as, (a) adaptive occupant behavior, (b) energy-related occupant behavior, (c) occupant privacy, (d) data security, (e) cost consciousness, (f) perceived environment friendliness, (g) perceived impact on occupant productivity and control, etc. With these constructs included, BI can be explained to a significant extent.

5 Conclusions

This exploratory work is based on the four well recognized theories in the area of technology adoption, namely TRA, TAM, VAM and TPB. We have employed a comparative approach to understand the intention of occupants in intelligent buildings to engage with IoT based smart comfort and energy control systems. Our study is perhaps the first in the area of adoption of IoT services in intelligent buildings in India. The results clearly indicate that TAM has the highest explanatory power among the models considered and VAM did not explain any greater than TAM. Further, PU in TAM, ATT in TRA, and PBC in TPB are the most significant predictors of BI to adopt IoT devices in intelligent buildings. The study has also found that PEOU in TAM is a less significant predictor of BI, possibly since occupants of commercial buildings are well-versed in using IoT based smart devices in their day-to-day lives. The other factors including propensity to save energy and reduce consumption costs, propensity to be identified as a champion of energy savings, and environment friendliness, specific to energy- and comfort-related occupant behavior in intelligent buildings, should be identified and evaluated to realize better prediction levels. Further studies should also examine if building location-specific, climate specific, and occupant generation specific factors could help explain technology adoption phenomena better.

References

1. Spencer, T., Awasthy, A.: Analyzing and projecting indian electricity demand to 2030. https://www.teriin.org/sites/default/files/2019-02/Analysing%20and%20Projecting%20Indian%20Electricity%20Demand%20to%202030.pdf. Accessed 17 July 2020

2. BP Energy Outlook–2019 - Insights from the Evolving transition scenario – India. https://www.bp.com/content/dam/bp/business-sites/en/global/corporate/pdfs/energy-economics/energy-outlook/bp-energy-outlook-2019-country-insight-india.pdf. Accessed 17 July 2020

3. Minoli, D., Sohraby, K., Occhiogrosso, B.: IoT considerations, requirements, and architectures for smart buildings–energy optimization and next-generation building management systems. IEEE Internet Things J. **4**(1), 269–283 (2017)

4. Sharples, S., Callaghan, V., Clarke, G.: A multi-agent architecture for intelligent building sensing and control. Sens. Rev. **19**(2), 135–140 (1999)

5. Bajer, M.: IoT for smart buildings-long awaited revolution or lean evolution. In: IEEE 6th International Conference on Future Internet of Things and Cloud (FiCloud), vol. 154, pp. 149–154. IEEE (2018)

6. Auffenberg, F., Stein, S., Rogers, A.: A personalized thermal comfort model using a Bayesian network. In: Twenty-Fourth International Joint Conference on Artificial Intelligence, pp. 2547–2553 (2015)

7. Klein, L., Kwak, J.Y., Kavulya, G., Jazizadeh, F., Becerik-Gerber, B., Varakantham, P., Tambe, M.: Coordinating occupant behavior for building energy and comfort management using multi-agent systems. Autom. Constr. **22**, 525–536 (2012)

8. Jazizadeh, F., Kavulya, G., Klein, L., Becerik-Gerber, B.: Continuous sensing of occupant perception of indoor ambient factors. In: 2011 ASCE International Workshop on Computing in Civil Engineering, pp. 161–168 (2011)

9. Zhao, P., et al.: 2016. Getting into the zone: how the internet of things can improve energy efficiency and demand response in a commercial building. In: Proceedings of ACEEE Summer Study on Energy Efficiency in Buildings. Pacific Grove, CA., vol. 12, pp. 3.1–3.12 (2016)

10. Romero Herrera, N., Doolaard, J., Guerra-Santin, O., Jaskiewicz, T., Keyson, D.: Office occupants as active actors in assessing and informing comfort: a context-embedded comfort assessment in indoor environmental quality investigations. Adv. Build. Energy Res. **14**(1), 41–65 (2020)

11. Metzger, Z.J.Z.I.D.: Taguchi-method-based CFD study and optimisation of personalised ventilation systems. Indoor Built Environ. **21**(5), 690–702 (2012)

12. Turner, C., Frankel, M.: Energy performance of LEED for new construction buildings. New Build. Inst. **4**, 1–42 (2008)

13. Hong, T., Yan, D., D'Oca, S., Chen, C.F.: Ten questions concerning occupant behavior in buildings: the big picture. Build. Environ. **114**, 518–530 (2017)

14. McCartney, K.J., Nicol, J.F.: Developing an adaptive control algorithm for Europe. Energy Build. **34**(6), 623–635 (2002)

15. Indraganti, M., Ooka, R., Rijal, H.B.: Thermal comfort in offices in India: behavioral adaptation and the effect of age and gender. Energy Build. **103**, 284–295 (2015)

16. Sun, K., Hong, T.: A framework for quantifying the impact of occupant behavior on energy savings of energy conservation measures. Energy Build. **146**, 383–396 (2017)

17. Pigg, S., Eilers, M., Reed, J.: Behavioral aspects of lighting and occupancy sensors in private offices: a case study of a university office building. In: ACEEE 1996 Summer Study on Energy Efficiency in Buildings, pp. 161–170 (1996)

18. Explained: Why you should keep the AC at 24 °C. https://www.moneycontrol.com/news/business/economy/explained-why-you-should-keep-the-ac-at-24c-4711541.html. Accessed 17 July 2020

19. Mital, M., Chang, V., Choudhary, P., Papa, A., Pani, A.K.: Adoption of internet of things in india: a test of competing models using a structured equation modeling approach. Technol. Forecast. Soc. Chang. **136**, 339–346 (2018)

20. Korpelainen, E.: Theories of ICT System Implementation and Adoption: A Critical Review. Aalto University, Finland (2011)
21. Yang, H., Lee, H., Zo, H.: User acceptance of smart home services: an extension of the theory of planned behavior. Ind. Manage. Data Syst. **117**(1), 68–89 (2017)
22. Davis, F.D.: Perceived usefulness, perceived ease of use, and user acceptance of information technology. MIS Q. **13**(3), 319–340 (1989)
23. Gou, Z., Prasad, D., Lau, S.S.Y.: Are Green buildings more satisfactory and comfortable?. Habitat Int. 39, 156–161 (2013)
24. Bluyssen, P., Aries, M., Van Dommelen, P.: Comfort of workers in office buildings: the European HOPE project. Build. Environ. **46**, 280–288 (2011)
25. Kim, H.W., Chan, H.C., Gupta, S.: Value-based adoption of mobile internet: an empirical investigation. Decis. Support Syst. **43**, 111–126 (2007)
26. Mathieson, K.: Predicting user intentions: comparing the technology acceptance model with the theory of planned behavior. Inf. Syst. Res. **2**(3), 173–191 (1991)
27. Choi, J.H., Lee, H.J.: Facets of simplicity for the smartphone interface: a structural model. Int. J. Hum. Comput. Stud. **70**(2), 129–142 (2012)
28. Lin, C.H., Sher, P.J., Shih, H.Y.: Past progress and future directions in conceptualizing customer perceived value. Int. J. Serv. Ind. Manage. **16**(4), 318–336 (2005)
29. Comrey, A.L., Lee, H.B.: Interpretation and Application of Factor Analytic Results. In: Comrey, A.L., Lee, H.B. (eds.) A First Course in Factor Analysis 1992, p. 2. Lawrence Eribaum Associates, Hillsdale (1992)
30. Tabachnick, B.G., Fidell, LS., Ullman, J.B.: Using Multivariate Statistics, vol. 5. Pearson, Boston (2007)
31. Sarstedt, M., Ringle, C.M., Hair, J.F.: Partial least squares structural equation modeling. Handb. Market Res. **26**, 1–40 (2017)

Contribution of Trust Factor Towards IOT Diffusion – An Empirical Study Using Acceptance Model

Reuban Gnana Asir[1]([✉]) and Hansa Lysander Manohar[2]

[1] College of Engineering, Cloud Services PLM, Nokia, Guindy, Chennai, India
gnana_asir.reuban@nokia.com
[2] Department of Management Studies, College of Engineering, Guindy, Chennai, India

Abstract. The Internet of Things (IoT) continues to evolve amongst the recent technologies which has a huge growth potential in terms of deployments and usage. The revenues on IoT is already nearing three trillion US dollars by 2020 despite COVID turbulences and the peak scale is expected to be touched by 2022. Literature says there would be 50 billion+ devices consuming 2 Zettabytes of data bandwidth. While more research is ongoing on the technical coverage of IoT and its features, less attention is paid to the behavioral aspects about the perception and usage of the IoT services. This paper makes an empirical study towards the influence of Trust on the acceptance of IoT and the adoption of IoT Services, with an update on UTAUT model. With the survey from 100+ IoT users applied with SEM reveals the significance on the Trust on IoT Provider.

Keywords: IOT · TAM · UTAUT · COVID · SEM · TRUST

1 Introduction

Recent years and the prevailing COVID pandemic witnesses' breakthrough on the usage of IoT enabled devices and services. The roleplay of Trust on IoT services is significant as in the cases like mobile banking services [1]. As per the industry analyst source IDC, the installed base of IoT will increase to 212 billion+devices approximately by this year, that includes up to 30 billion+connected devices. IDC sees the growth is driven by the large amount of intelligent systems that are going to get installed and the data collections across consumer applications, Government Agencies and the Enterprise applications [2]. These types of applications can involve the electric vehicle and the smart house, in which appliances and services that provide notifications, security, energy saving, automation, telecommunications, computers and entertainment will be integrated into a single eco system with a shared user interface. Large investments are made across the globe, including India, towards the IoT research and implementation in various forms as smart projects [3].

While there are plenty of research on the technical evolution of IoT and its Services, very less study is done on the behavioral aspects including perception and usage of IoT Services. Past studies have used TAM model towards assessing the perception

© IFIP International Federation for Information Processing 2020
Published by Springer Nature Switzerland AG 2020
S. K. Sharma et al. (Eds.): TDIT 2020, IFIP AICT 617, pp. 694–706, 2020.
https://doi.org/10.1007/978-3-030-64849-7_61

of users for the acceptance and adoption [4]. The UTAUT model is relatively better than TAM and other theoretical models and not that much deployed effectively [5]. This paper adopts a model based on UTAUT, arrive a prototype, and validate it using survey questionnaire and feedback multiple respondents.

2   Literature Review

Although IoT is relatively new technology in this decade, let's review the literature part of what IoT technology covers, its segments of architecture layers and the prevailing demand on the adoption of IoT. As this paper aims to make a behavioral study, lets use the Acceptance Models that are widely used, TAM and UTAUT.

2.1   IoT Technology

IoT infrastructure is segmented into 4 layers namely, Sensing, Communication, Management and Application layers. The vision of IoT is perceived in 2 ways – 'Thing' centric and 'Internet' centric. Internet services are focus in the Internet centric architecture. The center stage is captured by the smart objects in the object centric architecture [6, 7]. A conceptual framework of integrating the applications and ubiquitous sensing devices are shown in Fig. 1.

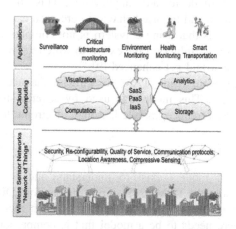

Fig. 1. IoT infrastructure from different layers

In order to get the real computation power of ubiquitous sensing and cloud, its clubbed in this framework to work together and reap the power of both frameworks. The sensor firms were invited to join the networking layer and provide their services towards the tuning of the software to become more effective. The AI part is achieved by the mining techniques available in market, which uses existing tools to manipulate the data which has been collected.

2.2   TAM

There are quite some theoretical models that are proposed to understand the factors that has a potential influence towards the acceptance of information technologies [8, 9]. In these studies, TAM is very key model that gets into the behavior towards the adoption of Information Technology. Goal of TAM is towards discovering the influence caused by external variables on the internal beliefs, attitudes and intentions [10]. The conceptual model of TAM is shown in Fig. 2 [11].

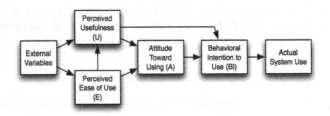

Fig. 2. TAM, version 1, (Davis, Bagozzi & Warshaw 1989)

As per TAM, the primary determinants of the Information Technology adoption in organizations and individuals are based on the ease of use and the usefulness. These acts as the basis for Attitude towards any system. This attitude towards a system identifies the use intention and the use behavior. Perceived ease of use means to what extent the respondent feels that using a system is not complex and will not consume mental efforts. Perceived usefulness is the extent to which the respondent feels that his or her job performance would get enhanced [9].

Lot of researchers were using TAM to validate the acceptance and adoption towards new technology. This mode was used by several studies including cloud computing, electronic governance, mobile learning, electronic learning.

2.3   Unified Theory of Acceptance and Use of Technology (UTAUT)

Plenty of theories and models exist to understand the Information Technology (IT) acceptance behavior, like TAM, Diffusion of Innovation (DOI),Theory of Planned Behavior (TPB), Theory of Reasoned Action (TRA), each focusing various factor of user's acceptance, there needs to be a model that is comprehensive one to facilitate studies on the understanding of user acceptance for any new technology.

UTAUT model proposed by Venkatesh et al. [12] towards the acceptance of adoption of any new technology that integrates the findings of these earlier studies. As per this model, it includes four critical antecedents, which are Facilitating conditions, Effort expectancy, social Influence and Performance expectancy. These variables affect the behavioral intention and the actual behavior.

Gender, experience, age and voluntariness are found to moderate the above relationships. These relationships were validated by various researches including Weerakkody V et al. [13] in the adoption of electronic government, Lian [14] in the adoption of cloud-based e-services and Wang [15] in the interactive decision aids for consumer adoption (Fig. 3).

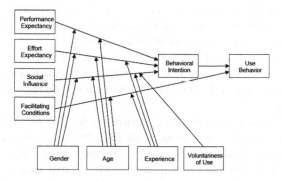

Fig. 3. UTAUT (Venkatesh et al., 2003)

Similarities from other theories and models are accommodated as part of the key variables of UTAUT. For example, the Perceived Usefulness in TAM is like the Performance Expectancy in UTAUT. Table 1 shows the core variables of UTAUT, where we see Venkatesh et al. [12] has combined the previous modes of technology adoption to arrive UTAUT design.

Table 1. The core variables of UTAUT

Variables	Sources
Performance expectancy	Extrinsic motivation (MM); Perceived usefulness (TAM/TAM2/C-TAM-TPV); Relative Advantage (DOI); Job-Fit (MPCU)
Effort expectancy	Complexity (MPCU/DOI); Perceived easy to use (TAM/TAM2)
Social influence	Subjective norm (TRA, TAM2, TPD/DTPB, C-TAM-TPD); Image (DOI); Social factors (MPCU);
Facilitating conditions	Facilitating conditions (MPCU); Perceived behavioural control (TPB/DTPE, C-TAM-TPB); Compatibility (DOI)

Thus, we see UTAUT model is designed specifically to study and investigate the acceptance of users with respect to the new Technology Adoption. It has higher explanatory power than earlier models like TAM and suited for understanding the acceptance of IoT services [16].

3   Critical Review

IoT is a recent evolution and there are limited researches done in this topic, while lot of research are ongoing and expected to get more light in the coming days and months. The research to identify the factors that influences the acceptance and adoption of IoT services by consumers are ongoing in several instances.

According to Gao. L et al. [17], Perceived Ease of Use, Perceived Usefulness, Perceived Behavioral Control and Perceived Enjoyment Social Influence have a significant effect on the use of IoT. This is their finding based on the research done on 368 respondents in China.

As per the research done on 2000 customers in US, by Acquity Group [18] focusing the concerns of customers to adopt IoT, the results indicated that the usefulness, awareness of the technology, security, privacy and price (cost).

With the literature study done by Evans [19] noted that lack of regulations, messaging design, slow technology adoption rate, privacy, issues with interoperability, consumer perception, data collection, cost of implementation and impactful use of big data were the barriers that affects the acceptance of IoT Services. Study done by Abu et al. [20] in Malaysia Small Medium Enterprises reveals that the ease of use, attitude, usefulness are the factors that drives the adoption of technology.

The research done by Kin et al. [21] with 363 students on the acceptance model for smart watches revealed that quality, perceived usefulness, appeal, cost, user attitude and intention to use were the main factors driving wearable technology.

On the study done on the adoption to third party application with 269 students by Han et al. [22] in US revealed that user's trust on the security applications and the technology awareness has a greater role on adoption intention. Significant observation is that, trust plays the mediator role in the security apps.

The research done by Saad T Alharbi on the Trust and Acceptance of Cloud computing [23] trust establishment was noted as one of the main barriers to adopt cloud services and applications. Hence Trust was added as a main construct that directly affects the user's behavior intention to adopt cloud services.

4   Theoretical Framework and Hypothesis Development

The conceptual framework is made on continuation with the study and research findings as discussed in previous sections. As most researchers have applied UTAUT model successfully for the technology adoption topics from smart watches, smart refrigerators till cloud computing, this paper also re-uses the UTAUT model. As per the research on cloud computing [24] where trust has evolved as major construct, this research includes it as a construct on top of UTAUT model. Hence the framework of this model is revised as below (Fig. 4).

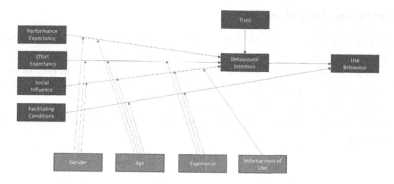

Fig. 4. Research model

4.1 Performance Expectancy

Performance Expectancy refers to the degree to which an individual perceives that using the system will help them to attain gains in job performance [12]. This study has adapted the performance expectancy and defined as the degree to which IOT users find it useful in their lifestyle, enables to accomplish their tasks quickly, increases their chances of better life and productivity.

H1: Performance Expectancy will have a positive and significant impact on Behavioral Intention to use IoT enabled products and services.

4.2 Effort Expectancy

Effort Expectancy refers to the degree associated with the use of the system [12]. This study has adapted effort expectancy and referred it to the easiness of using IoT, learning to operate is easy, interaction with IoT is clear and understandable and it is easy for user to be skillful to use IoT enabled products and services.

H2: Effort Expectancy will have positive and significant impact on Behavioral Intention to use IoT enabled products and services.

4.3 Social Influence

Social Influence refers to the degree to which an individual perceives how others believe that we use the system [12]. This study has adapted the social influence and referred it to the people whom influence my behavior, people I think important feels, I should use IoT. Also, my colleagues, the place of work, work administration is supporting the use of IoT enabled products and services.

H3: Social Influence will have positive and significant impact on Behavioral Intention to use IoT enabled products and services.

4.4 Facilitating Conditions

Facilitating Conditions refers to the degree to which an individual believes that organizational and technical infrastructure exists to support use of the system [12]. This study has adapted the facilitating conditions and referred it the availability of necessary resources, knowledge, availability of alternate technologies for non-compatible cases and the people support to assist in the journey of IoT.

H4:   Facilitating Conditions will have positive and significant impact on Use behavior.

4.5 Trust

Trust refers to the "willingness to be vulnerable to the actions of another party based on the expectation that the other will perform a particular action important to the trustor, irrespective of the ability to monitor or control that other party" [24]. When the IoT concept was still new, researchers are trying to conduct qualitative studies on discovering the factors that influence to adopt this technology.

The factors that contribute to the construct Trust, as per Saad Alharbi [25] were reviewed and re-purposed as following (Table 2):

Table 2. The factors contributing to construct trust

Trust aspects	Related factors
Control (C)	Level of data control
	Physical location
	Location profile
Security (S)	Encryption
	Privacy
	Auditability
Service continuity (SC)	Service legal agreement
	Compensation
	Backup
IoT provider (IP)	Accreditation
	Reputation
	Policy compliance
	Transperancy

Trust is evolved as an important factor in the Cloud Computing Adoption Studies done by multiple researches including Sharma et al. [27]. In this research, the factors contributing to Trust on IoT Provider refers to the security, control, service continuity, reputation, policy compliance, transparency and accreditation of the IoT provider.

H5:   Trust will have a positive and significant impact on Behavioral Intention to use IoT enabled products and services.

5 Research Methodology

5.1 Variable Measurement

The survey items used to measure IoT user's perception is adopted from literature study and expert's opinion. The survey questionnaire was developed and reviewed with 5 experts who contribute to IoT projects within Nokia. The experts feedback helped in enriching the readability of survey questions from the perspective of IoT users, to assess actual usage. The survey questionnaire used the 7-point Likert measurement scale, scaling from 1 = "strongly disagree' to 7 = "strongly agree".

5.2 Data Collection

The survey questionnaire was distributed initially to 10 IoT Software Engineers as a pilot and then the following modes of data collection were used to capture survey feedback. The survey instrument is used with 60 IoT Users in paper (hard copy) format, then the networking sites using Google Forms and Amazon Mech Turk to capture the data across the globe. Due to the limited audience on IoT users, the respondent's numbers did not see a major raise and got limited to 100+ responses.

6 Data Analysis and Results

Let's have a look into the findings and results, we obtain from the survey. PLS regression technique generalizes and combines features from Principle Component Analysis and multiple regressions. PLS readily handles both formative and reflective constructs [28]. PLS regression predicts or analyses a set of dependent variables; from a set of independent variables or predictors. PLS requires a minimum sample size, 10 times greater than the construct or the number of independent constructs directly impacting on dependent construct. Hence the samples size of 80 and above is a balance using PLS study [29].

6.1 Respondents Profile

As IoT is new field of research, the questionnaire was distributed to the people who possess IoT knowledge. The response was captured from 100+ respondents spread across globe. After sorting the feedback with the complete ones, 83 responses were seen complete and used for further analysis (Table 3).

Table 3. Respondents profile

Gender	Frequency	Share (%)	Education	Frequency	Share (%)	Age distribution	Frequency	Share (%)
Men	53	64	UG	52	63	20 to 30 years	77	93
Women	30	36	PG	26	31	30 to 40 years	3	4
Do not prefer to say	0	0	Other	5	6	40 to 50 years	3	4
Total	83	100	Total	83	100	Total	83	100

6.2 Multi Collinearity Test

Multi collinearity is the behavior of predicting a variable using multiple regression techniques. The Variation Influence Factor (VIF) is used as a measure of multi collinearity phenomenon. VIF > 5 indicates the existence of multi collinearity problem. The check on Multi collinearity is done using SmartPLS – Collinearity Statistics and following is the results (Table 4).

Table 4. VIF values.

VIF values																		
PE1	1.921	TIP1	1.047	EE1	1.001	SI1	1.857	SI5	1.217	BI1	2.28	TS2	2.526
PE2	1.966	TIP2	1.652	EE2	1	SI2	1.858	TC1	1.489	BI2	1.043	TS3	1.731
PE3	1.368	TIP3	2.828	EE3	1.491	SI3	1.237	TC2	1.164	BI3	2.328	TSC1	1.809
PE4	1.132	TIP4	2.335	EE4	1.492	SI4	1.077	TC3	1.538	TS1	2.959	TSC2	1.448
												TSC3	1.538

Since the VIF is <3, this data does not suffer multi collinearity problems.

6.3 Measurement Model Result

To see the model fitness, the PLS Algorithm is applied and found the results as below (Fig. 5).

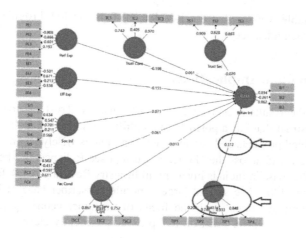

Fig. 5. measurement model result

The early signs indicate that Trust of IoT Provider seems to be a significant predictor of Behavioral Intention towards the adoption of IoT Services.

6.4   Bootstrapping

Bootstrapping is a non-parametric procedure that allows testing the statistical significance of PLS co-efficient. This test of bootstrapping is done on the collected data and following is the result (Table 5).

Table 5. Boot strapping results

BootStrapping output	Original Sample (O)	Sample Mean (M)	Std Dev (STDEV)	T Statistics (|O/STDEV|)	P Values
Eff Exp -> Behav Int	-0.155	0.059	0.207	0.753	0.452
Fac Cond -> Behav Int	-0.061	-0.012	0.122	0.497	0.619
Perf Exp -> Behav Int	-0.198	0.008	0.208	0.954	0.34
Soc Inf -> Behav Int	0.071	0.072	0.129	0.553	0.58
Trust Cont -> Behav Int	0.061	0.09	0.292	0.209	0.834
Trust IoT Prov -> Behav Int	0.312	0.293	0.137	2.28	0.023
Trust Sec -> Behav Int	-0.02	-0.083	0.267	0.076	0.939
Trust Serv Cont -> Behav Int	-0.013	0.006	0.132	0.101	0.919

From this table, we see that the P-Value of Trust on IoT Provider is <0.05 and hence marks its significance.

7 Discussion and Implications

According to the results seen in previous sections, the Trust on IoT Provider is a significant construct that has a positive and significant impact on Behavioral Intention to use IoT enabled products and services. This variable is wisely leveraged by multiple operators in India and across the Globe, as we will see Reliance JIO being the largest mobile subscriber base in India is investing in Industry Revolution 4.0, focusing 'Make in India' strategy [30]. The second largest mobile subscriber base in India, Airtel is focusing on 'zero questions' with the focus of customer centricity [31]. These are significant steps to raise the Trust on IoT provider, evidently clear.

8 Conclusion and Future Study

The research study findings indicate that the Trust on IoT Provider has a significant influence towards the Acceptance of Internet of Things Services. The study will be enhanced further to capture the findings from multiple respondents to achieve significant population. Recent researches including Yogesh Dwivedi et al. [32], Maciel M. Queiroz, Samuel Fosso Wamba et al. [33] evolve in a dimension without the moderators of UTAUT as the influence is not significant in IT evolution. This is also witnessed in the recent technology adoption patterns including the accelerations caused by COVID pandemic, in many facets including, Work From Home, Online Schools, Online Shopping, e-commerce, Digitalization, accelerated 5G [18, 34] deployments across the globe including competitiveness, Government prioritizations.

Acknowledgement. We would like to thank Nokia, College of Engineering Guindy, for giving us such an opportunity to carry out this research work and for providing us the requisite resources and infrastructure for carrying out the research. Special thanks to Mr. Madhu Kumar Krishnan, Mr. Dinesh Birlasekaran, Mr. Wilson Anandaraj from Nokia for being a mentor towards the research on IoT and my friend Mr. Kirubaharan from College of Engineering Guindy, for his valuable review comments.

References

1. Sharma, S.K., Sharma, M.: Examining the role of trust and quality dimensions in the actual usage of mobile banking services: an empirical investigation. Int. J. Inf. Manage. **44**, 65–75 (2019)
2. IDC: Worldwide Internet of Things (IoT) 2013–2020 Forecast, Billions of Things, Trillions of Dollars, Doc # 243661, October 2013
3. Asir, T.R.G., Anandaraj, W., Sivaranjani, K.N.: Internet of things and India's readiness. In: International Conference on Computing Paradigms (ICCP2015), pp. 274–279, 24–25 July 2015

4. Ranasinghe, D.C., Harrison, M., Lopez, T.S., McFarlane, D.: Adding sense to the Internet of Things an architecture framework for smart objective systems. In: Conference on Pervasive Ubiquitous Computing 16, pp. 291–308 (2012)
5. Gao, L., Bai, X.: A unified perspective on the factors influencing consumer acceptance of internet of things technology. Asia Pac. J. Mark. Logistics 26(2), 211–231 (2014). http://doi.org/10.1108/APJML-06-2013-0061
6. Gubbi, J., Buyya, R., Marusic, S., Palaniswami, M.: Internet of Things (IoT): a vision, architectural elements, and future directions. Future Gener. Comput. Syst. 29(7), 1645–1660 (2013)
7. Alharbi, S.T.: Trust and acceptance of cloud computing: revised UTAUT model. In: 2014 International Conference on Computational Science and Computational Intelligence (CSCI), pp. 131–134. IEEE (2014)
8. Venkatesh, V., Davis, F.D.: A theoretical extension of the technology acceptance model:our longitudinal field studies. Manage. Sci. 46(2), 186–204 (2000)
9. Davis, F.D.: Perceived usefulness, perceived ease of use and user acceptance of information technology. MIS Q. 13(3), 319–340 (1989)
10. Marchewka, J.T., Liu, C., Kostiwa, K.: An application of the UTAUT model for understanding student perceptions using course management software. Commun. IIMA 7(2), 93 (2007)
11. Nippie. https://commons.wikimedia.org/w/index.php?curid=14457270
12. Venkatesh, V., Morris, M.G., Davis, G.B., Davis, F.D.: User acceptance of information technology: toward a unified view. MIS Q. 27(3), 425–478 (2003)
13. Weerakkody, V., El-Haddadeh, R., Al-Sobhi, F., Shareef, M.A., Dwivedi, Y.K.: Examining the influence of intermediaries in facilitating e-government adoption: an empirical investigation. Int. J. Inf. Manage. 33(5), 716–725 (2013)
14. Lian, J.W.: Critical factors for cloud based e-invoice service adoption in Taiwan: an empirical study. Int. J. Inf. Manage. 35(1), 98–109 (2015)
15. Wang, W.: Interactive decision aids for consumer decision making in e-commerce: the influence of perceived strategy restrictiveness. MIS Q. 293–320 (2009)
16. Al-Momani, A.M., Mahmoud, M.A., Ahmad, M.S.: Modeling the adoption of internet of things services: a conceptual framework. Int. J. Appl. Res. 2(5), 361–367 (2016)
17. Gao, L., Bai, X.: A unified perspective on the factors influencing consumer acceptance of internet of things technology. Asia Pac. J. Mark. Logistics 26(2), 211–231. http://doi.org/10.1108/APJML-06-2013-0061 (2014)
18. Acquity Group: The Internet of Things: the continuation of the internet, 8–9 (2014)
19. Alolayan, B.: Do i really have to accept smart fridges? an empirical study. In: ACHI 2014: The Seventh International Conference of Advances in Computer-Human Interactions, pp. 186–191 (2014). http://www.iaria.org/conferences2014/ACHI14.html
20. Evans, H.I.: Barriers to successful implementation of the internet of things in marketing strategy. Int. J. Inf. Commun. Technol. Res. 5(9) (2015)
21. Abu, F., Yunus, A.R., Jabar, J.: Modified of UTAUT theory in adoption of technology for Malaysia small medium enterprises (SMEs) in food industry. Aust. J. Basic Appl. Sci. 9(4), 104–109 (2015)
22. Kim, K.J., Shin, D.H.: An acceptance model for smart watches: implications for the adoption of future wearable technology. Internet Res. 25(4), 527–541 (2015)
23. Han, B., Andy, W.Y., Windsor, J.: User's adoption of free third-party security apps. J. Comput. Inf. Syst. 54(3), 77–86 (2014)
24. Mayer, R.C., Davis, J.H., Schoorman, F.D.: An integrative model of organizational trust. Acad. Manage. Rev. 20(3), 709–734 (1995)

25. Alharbi, S.T.: Trust and acceptance of cloud computing: a revised UTAUT model. In: 2014 International Conference on Computational Science and Computational Intelligence (CSCI), vol. 2, pp. 131–134. IEEE (2014)

26. Sharma, S.K., Al-Badi, A.H., Govindaluri, S.M., Al-Kharusi, M.H.: Predicting motivators of cloud computing adoption: a developing country perspective. Comput. Hum. Behav. **62** (2016). https://doi.org/10.1016/j.chb.2016.03.073

27. Hair Jr, J.F., Black, W.C., Babin, B.J., Anderson, R.E.: Multivariate Data Analysis – A Global perspective. 7th ed. (2014)

28. Roca, J., Jose, J.: The Importance of Perceived Trust, Security and Privacy in Online Trading Systems, Information Management and Computer Security, vol. 17, pp 96–113. Emerald Group Publishing Limited, Bingley (2009)

29. https://telecom.economictimes.indiatimes.com/news/reliance-jio-builds-in-house-5g-iottech-to-reduce-dependence-on-foreign-gear-replaces-nokia-oracle-tech-with-owntech/74534777

30. https://www.financialexpress.com/brandwagon/airtel-targets-zero-questions-with-newcampaign/1996084/

31. Dwivedi, Y.K., Rana, N.P., Janssen, M., Lal, B., Williams, M.D., Clement, M.: An empirical validation of a unified model of electronic government adoption (UMEGA). Gov. Inf. Q. **34** (2), 211–230 (2017)

32. Queiroz, M.M., Wamba, S.F., De Bourmont, M., Telles, R.: Blockchain adoption in operations and supply chain management: empirical evidence from an emerging economy. Int. J. Prod. Res. (2020)

33. Asia Video Industry Association, 21 September 2020. https://advanced-television.com/2020/09/21/avia-covid-speeds-up-indias-move-to-digital-tv/

34. TBR Research. https://bit.ly/2USKLMK

Design Space Exploration for Aerospace IoT Products

Thirunavukkarasu Ramalingam[1(✉)], Joel Otto[2],
and Benaroya Christophe[3]

[1] Collins Aerospace, Bangalore, India
thirunavukkarasu.ramalingam@collins.com
[2] Collins Aerospace, Charlotte, USA
joel.otto@collins.com
[3] Toulouse Business School, 31068 Toulouse, France
c.benaroya@tbs-education.fr

Abstract. 'When aviation takes off again, we (industry stakeholders) must ensure it is on a more sustainable flight path, COVID-19 gives us a chance to design an aviation industry fit for the future'– World Economic Forum [14]. IoT in Aerospace & Defense produces more smart and connected products which offers better operation & control, material & energy management, traffic planning, staff & passenger information management, data analytics, and others. The longer life cycle in the A&D sector presents fewer opportunities to introduce capability advancements to stay ahead of the competition. Strong product strategy decisions can make the difference between success and failure in winning business during the available window of opportunity. Developing Product strategy and identifying suitable product in quicker time is more relevant in the current pandemic scenario with reduced spending for research and development initiatives. The investigative research is targeted towards developing a design space exploration methodology to develop IoT products in A&D. This methodology helps in identify the gaps in the existing methods and improvement opportunities to develop the IoT products, quick launch in the market to stay ahead of competition and to stay in the market. This methodology could help A&D players to develop optimized product development strategy by identifying the IoT Values which yields customer benefits with qualitative early decisions in IoT product development cycle.

Keywords: Internet of Things (IoT) · Aerospace systems · Design space · IoT · Value · Aerospace and defense · Product development

1 Introduction

Digital transformation is the heart of business strategies and it begins with the executive mandate. There is a strong sense of urgency among executives as the threat of digitally enabled competitors and disruptive technologies remain high on the list of concerns [12]. Internet of Things (IoT) is becoming more and more important in many industry sectors and domains (see Fig. 1) for the global IoT aerospace and defense market. Digital Technology evolution is happening rapidly and within no time will

© IFIP International Federation for Information Processing 2020
Published by Springer Nature Switzerland AG 2020
S. K. Sharma et al. (Eds.): TDIT 2020, IFIP AICT 617, pp. 707–721, 2020.
https://doi.org/10.1007/978-3-030-64849-7_62

impact every business. However, digital transformation is essentially a commitment by organizations to innovate which would add value to their customers [2].

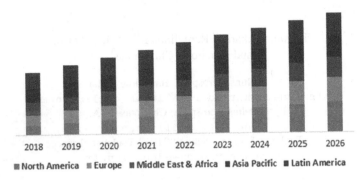

Fig. 1. Global IoT aerospace & defense market [5]

In the two decades since, the concept of IoT–which now encompasses a global ecosystem of sensors, embedded computers and smart devices that communicate with each other and share data–has exploded. Today, approximately 14.2 billion connected devices are currently in use around the world. By 2021, that figure is expected to jump to more than 25 billion due to a combination of cloud computing power, decreasing hardware cost and faster 5G data transfer that will accelerate growth. These devices include smart home appliances and wearable trackers, as well as a large variety of industrial innovations to improve manufacturing and operational efficiency. In the business world, IoT is already having a major impact, from changing the methods of business operations to transforming the way information is collected and exchanged. And every sector is impacted—including aerospace [16].

The Internet of Things is one of the biggest value generation technology in Aerospace and Defense (A&D) industry despite economic downturns. Long term increase in travel demand, development of new technologies and security threat for nations are fueling increase in aircraft production, defense budgets and the need for global supply chain [1]. Aircraft manufacturers and operators are always on the lookout to improve the vehicle performance adopting more connected and smarter systems to achieve the fuel efficiency, zero downtime and route optimization [2].

As there are multifold opportunities opens up due to IoT product, the exploration of design space increases the engineer's understanding of the design problem [4]. The exploration must be done carefully due to a large number of design alternatives. A large system may have millions, if not billions of design alternatives, and it may have infinite alternatives for some design problems [3]. In addition, a larger complex system also has a larger number of design constraints that must be satisfied by every valid design alternative or solution. Furthermore, the analysis of these design alternatives includes higher computational costs.

Design space exploration (DSE) refers to the activity of exploration and investigating design alternatives prior to system implementation. DSE is used for rapid prototyping, optimization and system integration [3]. In rapid prototyping, DSE helps to generate several prototypes before the system implementation. By simulating these prototypes, engineers can increase the understanding of the impact of design decisions. In optimization, DSE can be used to eliminate the lower quality designs and selecting a set of design candidates for further analysis. The elimination is done by comparing one design to another using predefined metrics, for instance, design requirements. In system integration, DSE can be used to find legal assemblies and configurations that satisfy all global design constraints for the integration of multiple components into a working whole system [15].

A SITA air transport study found that 67% of airlines have plans to invest on airline IoT by 2030. One of the drivers is passenger demands for seamless in-flight connectivity. Stimulating this investment is an enabler for IoT, if the passenger demand wasn't there, airlines would not be adding the Internet to the airplane at the rate they are with 50 billion or more IoT devices expected to be in circulation in the world by 2030. In the aviation industry, IoT has the potential for operational improvements in areas including aircraft performance, air traffic control and maintenance schedules – all of which ultimately lead to greater customer satisfaction. Similarly, for supply chain management, IoT has implications for improving product flow and warehouse efficiency, resulting in improved customer experiences and loyalty [17].

1.1 Objective of the Paper

The design of aircraft systems is an extremely complex task involving multidisciplinary studies that address the behavior of the design from mechanical, electrical, aero thermal and producibility aspects. In the early phase of aircraft systems development, engineers rapidly explore the design alternatives or design concepts to achieve design solutions that meet all requirements. This task is called design space exploration. It involves highfidelity physics-based numerical simulations to evaluate each design concept [6, 7]. Due to the time constraints of simulations, it is impossible to explore all these design alternatives. At the same time, exploring very few design concepts result in design issues in later stages. Thus, it is a crucial phase where engineers need support to evaluate design concepts and to prevent product failures.

The concept of IoT bringing new capabilities to interact with products or systems, independent of the core (certified) function of the system. A generator still has to generate, but IoT enables us to do more (predictive maintenance, performance tuning, etc.). Aerospace industries are currently adopting agile way of developing of minimum viable systems/products and are investing heavily to adapt IoT technologies which can yield long term value and benefit to customers. IoT technologies are evolving rapidly, and these have the opportunity to change the product landscape in the aerospace industry as well. However, there is no established approach to identify such systems/products. The objective of this paper to develop methodology that would help in developing minimum viable system/product by A&D industry to focus, while recognizing it must be adapted to fit alongside core certified designs without interference in the core function. There is strong motive in A&D industry to develop IoT products focusing on customer experience and enhanced product capabilities. This exploratory research is targeted towards develop design space exploration methodology for aerospace & defense IoT enabled products.

2 Methodology

A process that facilitates the creation of new functionalities, products, and services thereby making provision for better revenue streams, transform business models, drive measurably better outcomes for customers and every business sector including A&D [18]. The Methodology (see Fig. 2) i). Customer need identification ii). Product selection iii). Minimum Viable Product is developed around these three key steps. All these steps would be iterative till all the stakeholders are satisfied with identified product and its service to customer. First step Customer need identification is the critical one and majority of the time to be spent on this to understand customer interest. As there is no conclusive research findings available to find the best approach to identify the customer need regarding Aerospace IoT products, a survey has been conducted among aerospace and aviation professional group. Remaining two steps would takes less time if the welldefined problem emerges out of customer need identification.

Fig. 2. Design space exploration methodology for aerospace IoT

2.1 Customer Need Identification

Customer Needs Identification is the process of determining what and how a customer wants a product to perform. Customer Needs are non-technical, and they reflect the customers' perception of the product, not the actual design specifications, although frequently they are closely related [13].

There are three ways to identify the customer need Aerospace IoT products (see Fig. 3) Option-1: Customer Feedback, Option-2: Product Improvement opportunities, Option-3: End user level opportunities.

As there is no conclusive research findings available to find the best approach to identify the customer need, a survey has been conducted among aerospace and aviation professional group.

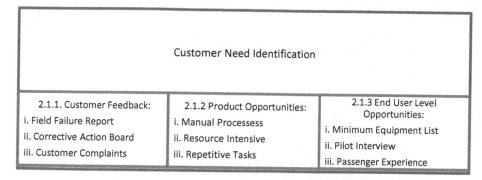

Customer Need Identification		
2.1.1. Customer Feedback: i. Field Failure Report ii. Corrective Action Board iii. Customer Complaints	**2.1.2 Product Opportunities:** i. Manual Processess ii. Resource Intensive iii. Repetitive Tasks	**2.1.3 End User Level Opportunities:** i. Minimum Equipment List ii. Pilot Interview iii. Passenger Experience

Fig. 3. Customer need identification methodology for aerospace IoT

2.1.1 Survey Participants Details

Shown below the (see Fig. 4) survey participants' details with respect to aerospace industry experience, role in the industry and their IoT expertise.

Fig. 4. Survey participant details

2.1.2 Customer Feedback

Customer feedback could be obtained in multiple ways, mentioned below three best possible ways.

i). Field failure report ii). Corrective action board iii). Customer complaints

All the mentioned items shows the unhappy customers and their unsatisfied needs.

Items i & ii are generally received as a document from company nodal point like MRO, Business Development team etc. While analyzing these documents one should pay attention through written language and think like customer to identify their pain areas.

Generally item iii was communicated directly by customer, sometimes they aren't complaints, customer gives ideas that would make a good product to better. Company should effectively apply design thinking techniques and empathies customers untold needs to identify them. Survey results shows (see Fig. 5) that customer complaints is the area to look for potential IoT products.

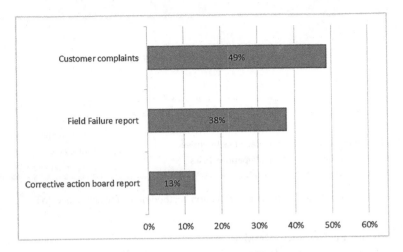

Fig. 5. Survey results on customer feedback parameters

2.1.3   Product Improvement Opportunities

Products/process could be improved when there is a manual, resource intensive and repetitive tasks. Not all the mentioned opportunities could be automated due to compliance, safety and security requirements in A&D. There should be tradeoff between the product improvements and all the mentioned requirement and customer willingness to pay (Value). Shown below (see Fig. 6) survey results for product improvement opportunities. As per the survey results A&D companies could explore repetitive tasks to develop IoT products.

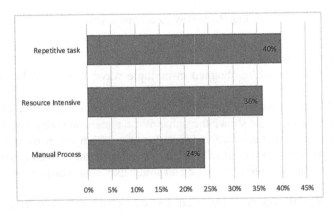

Fig. 6. Survey results on product improvement opportunities

2.1.4   End User Level Opportunities

Aerospace products end users are pilots, cabin crews, maintenance teams and passengers. Minimum equipment list tells flight and maintenance crews if they are able to dispatch an aircraft with a failed piece of equipment. IoT products have the potential to make airline employee tasks more effective or efficient, to engage and empower employees, and to allow the airline to optimize their workforce. Finally, these improvements can also make the passenger experience better, both by providing personnel more time to spend engaging customers, or to empower the passenger to self-serve, helping to retaining the customer for future business. Survey results (see Fig. 7) reveals that passenger experience is the area in which companies could explore and develop IoT products.

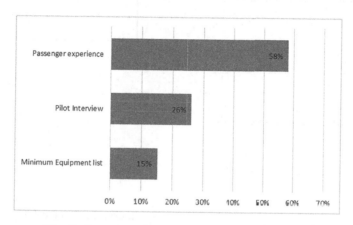

Fig. 7. Survey results on end user level opportunities

2.2   Product Selection

This step introduces the idea of a portfolio of products from a company and the methodology that helps them prioritize the order of products to invest in and what capabilities to introduce. The steps are iterative in nature (see Fig. 8) which would help to pick the most strategic products and determine the associated IoT maturity, Value offering and minimum viable benefits to the customer.

Step-1:   IoT Value Identification
Step-2:   Value Curve Analysis
Step-3:   Benefit Analysis

2.2.1   IoT Value Identification

The value of the Internet of Things increases exponentially on a relatively stable and foreseeable maturity curve. What starts with a "dumb" (non-connected) device should in theory end in a completely cross-ecosystem automated solution [8]. Physical products have been isolated for hundreds of years in aerospace (i.e., not connected or digitally enhanced). Starting in the 1980s, many aerospace devices underwent a digitalization trend. Longevity of the product in A&D sector is the key to decide the

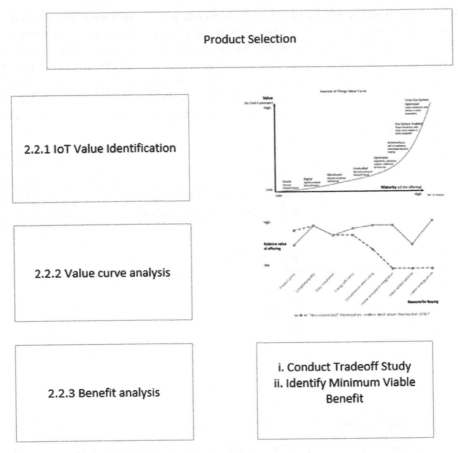

Fig. 8. Proposal of product selection methodology for aerospace IoT

maturity of the offerings as the decision should be made align with company product strategy and along with industry requirements (airworthiness, flight safety etc.).

Once the customer needs are identified, the firms should start with value maturity curve to select their product initial offerings and end user value identification. An IoT value curve (see Fig. 9) can help firms understand their current product offering to compare with competitors and position themselves with their new offerings. This curve also helps to develop product launch strategy while developing a roadmap for long run product success.

Value potential of aerospace IoT varies; not every product will generate benefits by going all the way up the curve. As part of the iterative process, you have to be able to generate incremental value (now or future) as you move up each level of the curve.

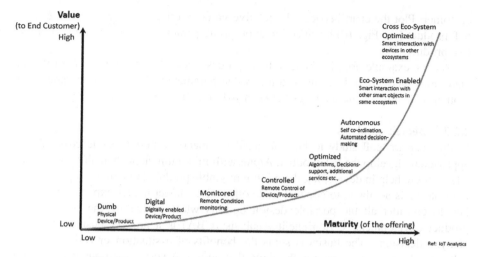

Fig. 9. Generic Internet of Things Value maturity curve [8]

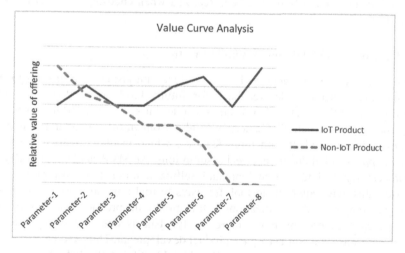

Fig. 10. Generic value curve analysis for IoT & non-IoT product

2.2.2   Value Curve Analysis

Generic value curve analysis (see Fig. 10) establishes the relative value of offerings between IoT and Non-IoT products. From customer stand point the benefits that can be experienced along the value/maturity curve of IoT are numerous and they vary significantly by industry and application [8]. Once the product launch strategy is firmed up the next step is to characterize the customer value Identification for the specific aerospace applications between the IoT and Non-IoT products.

There are generic list of customer values in the Internet of Things given in Appendix 1 which could be good starting point to analyze potential value for the customer. Plot the chart between the relative value offerings between the IoT & Non-IoT product (see Fig. 10) by selecting appropriate parameters (see Appendix-1) in the IoT product.

As an example for the benefit type process (see Appendix-1), category daily operations there are 6 different customer value parameters. These value parameter are plotted as relative value offerings between IoT and Non-IoT products.

2.2.3 Benefit Analysis

In this step tradeoff study to be conducted to select the best possible cost effective approach to develop the IoT product. Along with minimum viable benefit to be selected which could help in developing the minimum viable product in the next step. There are multiple tools available to conduct trade-off study, subject matter experts input is the key to consider all the possible design options while evaluating the cost effective product development. Cost Benefit Analysis (CBA) is a process businesses use to analyze decisions. The business sums the benefits of a situation or action and then subtracts the costs associated with taking that action. A cost-benefit analysis will also factor the opportunity cost into the decision-making process. Opportunity costs are alternative benefits that could have been realized when choosing one alternative over another [19].

2.3 Development of Minimum Viable Product

The Minimum Viable Product (MVP) is a product with just enough features to satisfy early customers that provides feedback for future development [9]. Some experts suggest that in B2B, a MVP also means saleable. "It's not an MVP until you sell it. Viable means you can sell it". Gathering insights from an MVP is often less expensive than developing a product with more features, which increase costs and risk if the product happens to fail due to incorrect assumptions. An MVP can be part of a strategy and process directed toward making and selling a product to customers [10]. In aerospace, this may require us to look for ways to trial a product prior to locking the design and completing the certification/qualification of the product. Once this process is complete, changes become much more costly. This is one of the key differences between aerospace and non-aerospace product development. Things to be considered to develop minimum viable product (see Fig. 11). Identifying the IoT elements and its constraint is the first step to start the product development effort. Then develop MV product with minimum feature identified in step 2.2.3.

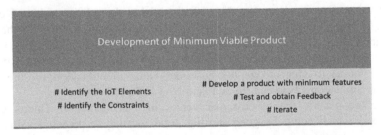

Fig. 11. Methodology for development of minimum viable product

Once the product is developed to satisfy the mentioned conditions it is time to test the product in the field. Customer feedback is an essential asset while maturing an MVP, as their inputs will help in improving the product in the market. Feedback could come in two areas. The first one is on the design of the product and user interface, which could improve the product usability. The second one is about the value realization in terms of its tangible and intangible benefits and cost reduction. Flow chart (see Fig. 12) shows the step by step approach to develop MVP. Logical conclusion for the product is when customer interest turned out to be 'NO'. When we reach this state it is suggested to go back to customer need identification and restart the process of design space exploration methodology.

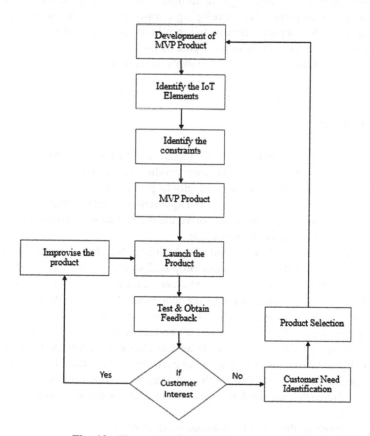

Fig. 12. Flow chart for development of MVP

3 Challenges in Aerospace IoT Design Exploration

The IoT is, in a sense, a hyper-scale System of Systems problem with multiple environments, requirements, governance structures and millions of stakeholders. Metcalfe's Law reminds us that three interconnected components result in a maximum of three interconnections, but with four the maximum number of interconnections rises to six, and with ten components, designers must deal with 45! This law illustrates how so any connected devices will challenge the system design [11]. Design space exploration methodology for aerospace products is having its own challenges some of them listed but not limited to such as criticality of its intended function and IoT capability cannot interfere with that function. Design Constraints such as size and weight of the product which could change the overall system design. Cyber security in the aerospace IoT becomes a critical element when developing connected products for aerospace. Data Ownership is another complication in IoT products as it generates terabytes of data with no defined guidelines on who has rights to use the data. Data access is important aspects in the IoT device if the product controls the function of the system if there is no deterministic/real-time data access.

4 Conclusion

Aerospace and Defense industries are increasing investments in developing IoT products to capture the increased value their product portfolio can deliver to customers and end users. IoT product development should pivot around the customer value as a center point. Systematic methodology and qualitative decision making while identifying the IoT product selection should drive customer adoption while minimizing the iteration in the product development cycle.

The exploratory research developed a methodology based on the both theoretical and industry expertise of authors. This paper proposed step by step approach starting from problem definition based on customer need identification narrowed down using detailed survey conducted among A&D and IoT experienced audience. Then the product selection three step approach IoT value Identification, Value curve analysis and Benefit analysis.

Finally developing the minimum viable product with bare minimum feature could reduce the product launch time and obtain the customer feedback to improvise the product with increased value and benefit the customer with bottom line growth. Survey results indicates that focusing on both end user level opportunities and delivering operational efficiencies are the key areas to consider for the next potential IoT aerospace product.

The limitations of the study is customer need identification as there is lack of robust methodology to identify customer need regarding Aerospace IoT products. Though authors used survey techniques to narrow down the pain points however there are limitation to use the survey results. Another limitations is due to value curve analysis as the graph is plotted using relative value offering which is heavily depend on the

Aerospace and Defense expertise and their knowledge in IoT which would play major role completing the value curve analysis. Future scope of research would be to develop a robust framework for customer need identification and extend the analysis to more international markets.

Appendix-1

Benefit type	Category	Customer value (Parameter)
Product/Machine	Daily operations	• Monitoring • Localization • Control • Safety
	Optimization	• Functionality • Convenience • Cost
	Maintenance/Service	• Availability • Cost
Process	Strategic information	• Choice of machines • Sales optimization
	Daily operations	• Monitoring • Control • Billing • Documentation • Contract management • Usability
	Optimization	• Availability • Quality • Automation • Costs
Emotional	Safety	• Personal security • Employment • Health • Property
	Esteem	• Self-esteem • Confidence • Achievement • Respect
	Self-actualization	• Creativity • Morality • Problem solving

(continued)

(continued)

Benefit type	Category	Customer value (Parameter)
		• Acceptance of facts
Business	Customers	• Customer retention
		• Customer satisfaction
		• Lead generation
		• Offer optimization
		• Sales proposition
	Products	• Requirement management
	New markets	• Data as a product
		• IoT as catalyst
	New business models	• Added-value offering/new services
		• Pay-per use/Product as-a-service
		• Contracting

References

1. Malaval, P., Bénaroya, C., Aflalo, J.: Aerospace Marketing Management. MP. Springer, Cham (2014). https://doi.org/10.1007/978-3-319-01354-1
2. Ramalingam, T., Christophe, B., Samuel, F.W.: Assessing the Potential of IoT in Aerospace. In: Kar, A.K., Ilavarasan, P.V., Gupta, M.P., Dwivedi, Y.K., Mäntymäki, M., Janssen, M., Simintiras, A., Al-Sharhan, S. (eds.) I3E 2017. LNCS, vol. 10595, pp. 107–121. Springer, Cham (2017). https://doi.org/10.1007/978-3-319-68557-1_11
3. Kang, E., Jackson, E., Schulte, W.: An Approach for Effective Design Space Exploration. In: Calinescu, R., Jackson, E. (eds.) Monterey Workshop 2010. LNCS, vol. 6662, pp. 33–54. Springer, Heidelberg (2011). https://doi.org/10.1007/978-3-642-21292-5_3
4. Wang, G.G., Shan, S.: Review of metamodeling techniques in support of engineering design optimization. J. Mech. Des. **129**(4), 370–380 (2007)
5. https://www.maximizemarketresearch.com/market-report/global-iot-in-aerospace-defense/10721/#details
6. Min, A.T.W., Sagarna, R., Gupta, A., Ong, Y.-S., Goh, C.K.: Knowledge transfer through machine learning in aircraft design. IEEE Comput. Intell. Mag. **12**(4), 48–60 (2017)
7. Koch, P.N., Simpson, T.W., Allen, J.K., Mistree, F.: Statistical approximations for multidisciplinary design optimization: the problem of size. J. Aircr. **36**(1), 275–286 (1999)
8. Lueth, K.L.: 2015 whitepaper 'IoT strategy primer: the new sources of value enabled by the Internet of things. Implications of competitive advantage and tools (2015) http://www.iotanalytics.com
9. https://en.wikipedia.org/wiki/Minimum_viable_product
10. Thirunavukkarasu, R., Christophe, B., Samuel, F.: How to find minimum viable product (MVP) in IoTA. In: Conference: The 9th European Congress on Embedded Real-time Software and Systems – 2018, Toulouse, France (2018)
11. Thirunavukkarasu, R., Tweten,D.: Assessing the potential of IoT in systems engineering discipline. In: Conference: The 12th Asia Oceania Systems Engineering conference – 2019, Bangalore, India (2019)
12. Dunbrack, L., Ellis, S., Hand, L., Knickle, K., Turner, V.: 2016 White Paper IoT and Digital Transformation: A Tale of Four Industries Sponsored by SAP (2016)

13. Simpson-Wolf, A.: Electrical and Computer Engineering Handbook – An Introduction to Electrical and Computer Engineering and Product design by TUFT University- Customer Need Identification
14. World Economic forum. https://www.weforum.org/agenda/2020/06/covid-19-sustainable aviation/
15. Wang, G.G., Shan, S.: Review of metamodeling techniques in support of engineering design optimization. J. Mech. Des. **129**(4), 370–380 (2007)
16. Airbus Newsroom Innovation Stories. https://www.airbus.com/newsroom/stories/iot-aerospace-great-new-connector.html
17. https://www.intelligent-aerospace.com/commercial/article/16538797/iot-and-aerospaceimplications-for-improvements-within-supply-chain-management
18. IoT: Setting the pace of progress in aerospace. https://www.quest-global.com/iot-settingpace-progress-aerospace/
19. Cost Benefit Analysis. https://www.investopedia.com/terms/c/cost-benefitanalysis.asp

Author Index

Printed in the United States
by Baker & Taylor Publisher Services